Challenging Behavior
in Elementary
and Middle School

Barbara Kaiser

and

Judy Sklar Rasminsky

Upper Saddle River, New Jersey
Columbus, Ohio

Library of Congress Cataloging-in-Publication Data

Kaiser, Barbara, 1948–
    Challenging behavior in elementary and middle school / Barbara Kaiser,
Judy Sklar Rasminsky.
        p. cm.
    Includes bibliographical references and index.
    ISBN-13: 978-0-205-46099-1 (alk. paper)
    ISBN-10: 0-205-46099-2 (alk. paper)
    1. Behavior modification. 2. School children—Psychology. 3. Middle
school students—Psychology. 4. Classroom management. I. Rasminsky, Judy
Sklar, 1940–   II. Title.

    LB1060.2.K34 2009
    370.15'28—dc22   2008024616

Vice President & Editor in Chief: Jeffery W. Johnston
Publisher: Kevin M. Davis
Series Editorial Assistant: Lauren Reinkober
Director of Marketing: Quinn Perkson
Marketing Manager: Erica Deluca
Production Editor: Paula Carroll
Editorial Production Service/Interior Design: Publishers'
    Design and Production Services, Inc./Lynda Griffiths

Composition Buyer: Linda Cox
Manufacturing Manager: Megan Cochran
Electronic Composition: Publishers' Design and Production
    Services, Inc.
Photo Researcher: Annie Pickert
Cover Administrator: Linda Knowles

This book was set in Berkeley by Publishers' Design and Production Services, Inc.
It was printed and bound by R. R. Donnelley & Sons/Harrisonburg, VA. The cover was printed by Phoenix Color
Corporation/Haggerstown.

Photo credits: pp. 9, 16: Gail Meese/Merrill Education; pp. 12, 20, 41, 57, 59, 90: IndexOpen; pp. 46, 51: Todd Yarrington/Merrill
Education; p. 54: Michael Newman/PhotoEdit; pp. 68, 72, 168, 241, 242, 254: Bob Daemmrich Photography; p. 81: Comstock RF;
pp. 95, 105: Orlando/Hulton Archive/Getty Images; p. 99: Tom Watson/Merrill Education; pp. 122, 145: Mary Kate Denny/PhotoEdit;
pp. 125, 187, 264, 273: Anthony Magnacca/Merrill Education; pp. 150, 153, 177, 180, 221, 235: Lindfors Photography; p. 163:
Frank Siteman;
pp. 198, 211: Ellen B. Senisi; p. 226: David Young-Wolff/PhotoEdit; p. 259: Robert Harbison; pp. 280, 282: Paul Baldesare/Alamy;
p. 296: Corbis RF

Text credit: Material on pages 184–185 from *Teacher Effectiveness Training* by Dr. Thomas Gordon and with Noel Burch,
copyright © 1974–2003 by Gordon–Adams Trust. Used by permission of Three Rivers Press, a division of Random House, Inc.

Some of the material in this book was originally published in *Challenging Behavior in Young Children: Understanding, Preventing, and
Responding Effectively*, 2E, by Barbara Kaiser and Judy Sklar Rasminsky. Published by Allyn & Bacon, Boston, MA. © 2007 by Pearson
Education. Used by permission of the publisher.

This book has been adapted from *Meeting the Challenge: Effective Strategies for Challenging Behaviours in Early Childhood Environments* by
Barbara Kaiser and Judy Sklar Rasminsky © 1999, Canadian Child Care Federation, 201-383 Parkdale Avenue, Ottawa, Ontario, Canada,
K1Y 4T4. The authors wish to express their gratitude to the Canadian Child Care Federation for granting permission for its use.

The name WEVAS™ is a trademark of WEVAS Incorporated.

Pearson® is a registered trademark of Pearson plc
Merrill® is a registered trademark of Pearson Education, Inc.

Pearson Education Ltd.
Pearson Education Singapore Pte. Ltd.
Pearson Education Canada, Ltd.
Pearson Education—Japan

Pearson Education Australia Pty. Ltd.
Pearson Education North Asia Ltd.
Pearson Educación de Mexico, S.A. de C.V.
Pearson Education Malaysia Pte. Ltd.

Merrill
is an imprint of

www.pearsonhighered.com

10 9 8 7 6 5 4 3 2 1

ISBN-13: 978-0-205-46099-1
ISBN-10:   0-205-46099-2

For Jessika and Maita, Sonya and Abigail

Contents

Chapter 6

Opening the Culture Door 95

Chapter 7

Preventing Challenging Behavior: The Social Context   122

Chapter 8

Preventing Challenging Behavior: Physical Space, Classroom Management, and Teaching Strategies   150

Chapter 12

The Inclusive Classroom   241

Chapter 13

Working with Families and Other Experts 264

Chapter 14

Bullying 280

Acknowledgments

Judy's father, a playwright and novelist, used to say that the secret to writing is putting the seat of the pants to the seat of the chair. Like any book, this one has demanded its fair share of solitary sitting. But it has also required Barbara's three decades of work in education and the help of a great many colleagues, friends, and family members.

Our heartfelt thanks go to Neil Butchard and Bob Spencler for their commitment to children and their willingness to share their wonderful WEVAS program; to Larry Wein, Sheila Bruck, Ken Schwartz, Sheila Munro, and Debbie Redden-Cormier for passing along their vast experience and expertise in working with children and their families; to Barbara's fifth-grade teacher, John Darr, who has influenced her thinking, teaching, and writing ever since; and to the extraordinarily gifted teachers in our own families, Joan Rosen Karp and Daniel Sklar, who shared their accumulated wisdom and insight with grace and generosity as well as provided unflagging support.

We also thank our reviewers for their valuable feedback: Nancy Daniels, Helman Elementary School, Ashland, OR; Stacy Duffield, North Dakota State University, Fargo; Laura Feuerborn, University of Washington, Tacoma; Judith M. Geary, University of Michigan, Dearborn; Susan L. Hampton, Virginia Middle School, Bristol, VA; Carol L. Higy, University of North Carolina, Pembroke; Janice Janz, University of New Orleans, LA; Kate Lukaszewicz, Booker T. Washington Middle School, Baltimore, MD; Steven Neill, Emporia State University, KS; Kim Peach, Wilshire Park Elementary School, St. Anthony, MN; Kathy Richards, Lock Haven University, PA; Dan Ryno, Jury Elementary School, Florissant, MO; Emily Tischer, Wilshire Park Elementary School, St. Anthony, MN; and Jolanda Westerhof-Shultz, Grand Valley State University, Allendale, MI.

For their help in understanding the many cultures that make this continent so rich and interesting a place for children to grow up, we are grateful to Amna Al Futaisi, Bibiana Burton, Peggy Clements, Eva Echenberg, Ed Greene, Thao Huynh Thanh, and Dixie Van Raalte.

We very much appreciate the help of our editors, Kevin Davis and Arnis Burvikovs, who admirably supported our efforts to write a more comprehensive text; Paul A. Smith and Anne Whittaker, who held down the fort at Allyn & Bacon; Lauren Reinkober, who picked up the pieces and kept things on track; and the production and design team, who created such a handsome book.

Throughout the writing process, Judy's brother Zachary Sklar and her friend Pat McNees furnished us with wise words and writing tips, while Barbara's friends

Nicole Evans and Bibiana Burton smoothed the bumps by offering chicken soup and chocolates.

Our children have provided infinite inspiration and encouragement. Barbara thanks Jessika for her support, Jessika's husband David for taking such good care of Jessika, and Maita for being so challenging and teaching her so much. Judy thanks Abigail, Sonya, and, by marriage, Oren, for their endless patience as she struggled to meet a deadline, and she sends an enormous hug to her grandson Toby for presenting her with much needed distraction.

We are especially thankful that our husbands, Martin Hallett and Michael Rasminsky, have managed to love and support us, each in his own way, as we labored on. We couldn't have written the brain chapter without Michael's expertise and forbearance. Meals, books, graphs, and journal articles have miraculously appeared, while computer glitches and dirty tea cups miraculously disappeared. Their patience, encouragement, and willingness to roll up their sleeves have made this book possible.

Introduction

Whether a school district is rich or poor, rural, suburban, or urban, it is likely to enroll its fair share of students with challenging behavior. Just one child can turn even the most experienced teacher's classroom upside down—and present an overwhelming challenge to a novice.

A class with a large number of students, legislation such as No Child Left Behind, high-stakes testing, too much material to cover in too short a time—all of these factors play a role in the way teachers react when a child with challenging behavior enters their classroom.

In the primary grades, teachers may feel ill equipped to handle challenging behavior, but they aren't ready to give up. They're committed to the whole child and the belief that if they nurture as they teach, they can help the child succeed. However, as children grow older, we hear more teachers say that it's too late to change students' behavior. Since the shootings at Columbine High School in 1999 and the introduction of zero-tolerance policies, it has become more and more tempting to address disruptive or aggressive behavior by sending students to the principal's office, placing them in detention, or even suspending them. In fact, once these children have departed, the room feels calmer and safer, and both teaching and learning seem almost stress-free, leading teachers to conclude that they've done the right thing.

We, the authors of this book (Barbara is a teacher and consultant with 30 years' experience; Judy is a writer specializing in education), strongly believe that this kind of thinking on the part of teachers betrays children who find it difficult to fit in, who don't have confidence in themselves, and who are heading down a path that no one deserves to tread. For over a decade, we have focused our attention on finding ways to support children with challenging behavior. It is indeed the case that it is harder to guide and assist them as the years pass and their challenging behavior becomes more entrenched, but they are still children, and it remains possible to help them succeed if you have the will, the patience, and the skills the job requires. Students with challenging behavior are dealing with difficult lives in the best way they know how. As a teacher or future teacher, you have two choices. Either you can create an environment that welcomes them and *teaches* them how to become the best people they can possibly be, or you can reinforce their growing suspicion that they will never belong, have nothing to offer, and cannot learn or cope with the demands of school.

Teaching today is highly demanding, and it may seem impossible to find the time to do all that we advocate in this book. However, it is well worth whatever time and effort it takes to build a relationship with every child, teach social and emotional skills, and develop a warm and inclusive classroom environment. Children cannot learn unless they feel safe and valued. In the long run, dedicating a few minutes a day to preventing challenging behavior and creating opportunities for all students to succeed actually *saves* time and enables them to learn not only appropriate behavior but also the content of the curriculum.

By developing the ability to help students with challenging behavior, you are also helping the other children, who in their presence are often frightened or excited and learn to become bystanders, to accept the role of victim, or to join in the aggressive behavior. When you are prepared, all the children will feel safe, and the difficult behavior will be less severe, less frequent, and less contagious. Then it becomes possible to make the commitment that everyone who works with children wants to be able to make: to welcome and help each child in your class.

The students won't be the only winners. You, too, will benefit as you acquire competence and confidence, gain pride and satisfaction in your job, and feel more positive about the children you spend many hours with each day.

What is in this book?

This book is a kind of survival manual. Its aim is to give you the basic facts and skills you need to understand and prevent challenging behavior, to respond to it effectively when it occurs, and to teach appropriate alternatives. It brings together information and research-based techniques drawn from neuroscience, psychology, psychiatry, special education, classroom management, early care and education, child development, cross-cultural research, and proactive social and emotional skills programs. It doesn't provide recipes or formulas, because each child is unique and every situation requires a unique solution. And it certainly doesn't come with a money-back guarantee. But this book does offer ideas and strategies that have been proven to work time and again—and that *will* work if you give them a chance.

The text falls into two major parts. The first four chapters explain the background—some of the theory and research that underlie effective practice. They contain information about aggression, biological and environmental risk factors, protective factors, and the brain's role in challenging behavior. All of this background information provides a context that will enable you to better understand why so many people see adolescence—which can begin as early as age 7—as a risk factor in itself. Once you understand more about why students with challenging behavior act the way they do, it will become easier to care about them and meet their needs.

The ten remaining chapters are more practical. They describe strategies for preventing and managing challenging behavior. Each strategy can be used alone, but they work extremely well together. In Chapter 5 we present the most basic strategy of all: building a relationship with the child—which can make or break any other strategy you use—and explore how your beliefs, expectations, values, and experience influence your teaching style and your ability to tackle challenging behavior. This chapter will also help you keep your cool and not take it personally when a child throws a chair or a four-letter word in your direction. In Chapter 6 we concentrate on culture, which is a vital part of who children are and how they behave.

The next two chapters deal explicitly with the prevention of challenging behavior: Chapter 7 through the social context and Chapter 8 through such traditional methods as physical space, classroom management, and teaching strategies. Chapters 9, 10, and 11 present specific techniques for responding to challenging behavior. Because so many teachers work in inclusive classrooms, Chapter 12 concentrates on the inclusion of children with disabilities. Although this is not a special education text, we present ideas here that will enable you to become more intentional and aware of meeting all students' needs—which is what children with disabilities require. (This chapter will give you a good start, but to teach truly effectively in an inclusive classroom, you will need more knowledge than one chapter can provide, and it's best to do additional reading and coursework.) Chapter 13 is devoted to working with the families of children with challenging behavior. Chapter 14 focuses on bullying, a special variety of challenging behavior, and it comes last because it is a kind of summary. Approaching bullying successfully requires the use of virtually all of the techniques presented in this book.

To help you make this material your own, each chapter ends with a section called "What do you think?" that offers activities to do and questions to ponder. Some chapters have an additional section that presents a short scenario with more information about a student's life and behavior. Some are simply stories, giving you more to think about. Others, entitled "What would you do?" ask how you would respond. We have also suggested readings and resources for further exploration.

Although challenging behavior is more prevalent among boys, it is increasingly common among girls, too. In recognition of this situation—and to avoid the awkwardness of *he or she*—we have called a child *he* in the odd-numbered chapters and *she* in the even-numbered chapters.

We believe that culture is a basic part of who children are, and we have tried very hard to make our text culturally sensitive. However, both of us are European American, and in the end we probably couldn't disguise that fact. It is important for you as readers to be aware of our bias.

Who should read this book?

Sooner or later, every teacher, current and future, will probably encounter a child with challenging behavior. This book is intended for all of you. It can also be useful to administrators, who set the tone in schools and whose backing for teachers as they deal with students with challenging behavior can make an enormous contribution to the success of both teachers and students. In fact, the most successful approach to challenging behavior is what's called a *whole-school policy*, where everyone from the principal to the maintenance staff works together to teach and reinforce appropriate behavior and everyone responds to inappropriate behavior in the same way, using the same rules and vocabulary. But individual teachers can also prevent and manage challenging behavior effectively if they have the knowledge and skills they need.

Many weeks may elapse between the moment you first realize that you need help with a student with challenging behavior and the day that you finally receive support and assistance. This is when you are most liable to burn out—and when the strategies here will be particularly useful. But don't wait until then to try them. They can help every child in your class, not just those with challenging behaviors. And the sooner you begin to use them, the more beneficial they're likely to be.

Here are a few hints to keep in mind:

- Have confidence in your own abilities—you can handle this.
- View inappropriate behavior as an opportunity to teach. That will help with everything you do.
- Take it slowly, one behavior at a time, one child at a time. Build in success by setting realistic goals.
- At the end of the day, reflect on what went wrong and what went right. Make notes in your agenda or on post-its so you can figure out what to do next time.
- Train yourself to look for, measure, and record minute improvements—they are important signs of progress. Remember that you can't eliminate challenging behavior overnight.
- When you try a new approach, things may get worse before they get better. But if you don't see gains within a reasonable time, try another tack.
- If you work with other people, set common goals. Laugh together; support and compliment each other. If you work alone, seek out your peers. Everyone needs someone to talk to.
- Give yourself a reward, not a guilt trip. Eat that brownie, take that walk, rent that video or DVD. Do whatever will keep you going.

Getting to know Andrew and Jazmine

Throughout this book we follow two children, Andrew and Jazmine, who come from very different backgrounds and cultures. Neither has a formal diagnosis, but both experience common academic and behavior problems at school. Their reputations precede them as they move from class to class, and teachers dread finding them on their roster when school opens each fall.

Andrew's story

Nine-year-old Andrew attends the fourth grade of a neighborhood school in a White, middle-class suburb of a large city. He is an only child. His father, who emigrated to the United States from Eastern Europe, is a university professor who travels a great deal and has a reputation with the ladies. His mother, an attractive but overweight woman, teaches elementary school. His mother's large extended family lives nearby and is very willing to pitch in and support his mother in any way.

A large baby, Andrew was delivered by emergency Cesarean section. He was only 10 hours old when a nurse left him with his mother, explaining that he could not stay in the nursery because he was screaming so loudly. At home, he cried incessantly and calmed down only when someone held him.

When Andrew went to preschool, the teacher complained that he bumped into people and pushed, grabbed, and hit his classmates. If she tried to redirect him, he kicked or screamed at her, and he became a regular visitor to the director's office.

Andrew remained large for his age as he grew older, and his father (as well as other members of the family and people in the community) expected him to behave as if he were much older than his actual age. Whenever his father brought him a puzzle or game that Andrew couldn't do immediately, his father quickly lost patience, told Andrew he was stupid, and walked away, making his disappointment very clear.

As a result, Andrew now feels he can't live up to people's expectations and isn't good enough at anything. In his father's presence he is very subdued and compliant, trying desperately to please. His behavior with his mother is very different. When they are alone together, he doesn't listen or do what he is told; instead, he screams at her, calls her names, and throws things.

These days life at home is stressful and chaotic. Andrew's parents frequently argue about him, as they have done since he was born. His father believes in parental authority, strict rules, and firm consequences when rules are broken. Although his father has never physically harmed his mother, Andrew is surrounded by verbal and emotional abuse on a daily basis. It usually ends only when his father leaves the house in a rage. Sometimes he stays away for days. Andrew blames himself for this and has recently started telling his mother that he is sorry he isn't good enough.

Andrew's aggressive behavior has increased. He continues to be rude to his mother, who is so overwhelmed that she lets things slide. But his father hits him, screams at him, or sends him to his room. His father blames his mother for Andrew's problems.

Andrew likes being awake when everyone else is asleep: It gives him a sense of independence and control that he misses during the day. He either watches late-night movies on his TV or plays video games in his room. Because he goes to bed so late, getting him up in the morning turns into a huge battle. On many days, his mother doesn't have the energy for it, and Andrew is late for school. However, when his father is home he pulls Andrew out of bed, shouts and swears at him, stands with him until he is dressed, and yanks him outside to wait for the bus.

When Andrew arrives at school he is usually tired, hungry, and angry. It is not hard to set him off—a look, a comment, too much attention, too little attention, or a change in routine is all it takes.

He has no friends and spends most of his time alone. The other students, who are afraid of him, think he's stupid and mean and that he causes a lot of trouble. He doesn't hesitate to swear at them, or at his teachers, who respond by sending him to the principal and phoning home on a regular basis.

Andrew is of average intelligence and can perform quite well when the circumstances are controlled, the routine is clearly structured, and he receives teacher or parental attention and assistance before he realizes he needs it. He likes to be given responsibility and thrives when he is asked to take a leadership role or help others at the computer, which is the only thing at school he really enjoys. He is also very gentle and patient with younger children, perhaps because he's an only child, perhaps because they aren't threatening. Both his behavior and his academic success appear to be related to his relationship with his teacher.

Andrew is always losing things. He often forgets his books or his lunchbox. His desks, both at home and at school, are totally disorganized. He can rarely locate the pencils, paper, notebook, or textbook he needs, and he makes a great deal of noise looking for them. He feels frustrated and embarrassed about this but lacks the organizational skills to do anything about it. He is not well coordinated, doesn't enjoy sports, and doesn't participate in any after-school activities.

Andrew is easily overstimulated and has trouble listening and concentrating. Reading is difficult for him because he can't remember what he's read. His previous teachers have suspected that he has ADHD, but his mother has never raised the issue with his pediatrician, and there has been no formal diagnosis.

He is convinced that he is stupid, and he's afraid to begin something new unless he's confident that he can do it. The classroom noise and activity confuse him, and in many situations he doesn't understand what he's expected to do. However, he doesn't want anyone to know that he is having difficulty, so he behaves in a way that allows him to save face. He has figured out that if he shouts, swears, or throws furniture, the teacher will usually send him out of the classroom. This happens often enough that his skills are beginning to lag behind those of his classmates, especially in math. Most recently, he was suspended for kicking a teacher when she tried to get him to leave the room.

Jazmine's story

Jazmine, age 13, lives in a housing project in a large eastern city, where she attends grade 8 at the local middle school. Her African American father, who didn't finish high school but had some training in mechanics, was convicted of dealing drugs and incarcerated just after Jazmine was born. She doesn't remember him, but he sends her an occasional letter and birthday card. Her mother, who is Puerto Rican, dropped out of high school when she became pregnant with her first child, Jazmine's older brother, Darryl, born three years before Jazmine. Jazmine's mother also has a younger daughter, now 5, by her live-in boyfriend, Brandon, an African American who's been on disability since he was injured at his factory job several years ago. He also deals drugs, and the family depends on his income because Jazmine's mother earns so little at her cleaning job. Brandon and Jazmine's mother have been together for seven years.

Jazmine was a happy, smiling baby who had no difficulty charming the adults in her world. Even though she didn't get a lot of attention from her mother when she was little, she had an easy temperament and soon learned how to take care of herself. When Brandon joined the household, he took advantage of her easygoing personality, expecting her to wait on him hand and foot and hitting her if she refused. Because her mother feared Brandon would leave them, she never came to Jazmine's defense. However, Darryl, a caring person with whom Jazmine was very close, always protected her when he was around. From Jazmine's point of view, this wasn't often enough: Darryl was usually with his friends, tough kids who drank and smoked dope.

The family has moved five times since Jazmine's birth, and they now live in a neighborhood filled with gangs, drugs, prostitution, and street fighting. Last year Darryl was killed in a gang fight, and Jazmine's mother became severely depressed, drinking and spending most of her time in bed. She lost her job and stopped paying attention to Jazmine and her younger daughter. Eventually Brandon left them. Although she tried to pull herself together, she had a difficult time making ends meet, and she finally decided to look for her boyfriend. Leaving the girls with her sister, who has three small children of her own, she promised to return for them as soon as she was settled, but they haven't heard a word from her in seven months.

Jazmine's aunt holds down two jobs and is always exhausted. Jazmine comes straight home from school to take care of her sister and cousins and prepare supper.

Her bed is the living room couch, which is old and lumpy, and there is so much noise on the street that it's hard to sleep. Jazmine often ends up watching TV much of the night.

Although she wakes up tired and has to help the younger children get ready for the day, Jazmine likes school because she feels safe there and has a lot of friends. She is pretty and cares a great deal about how she looks and what others think. She works hard to fit in and steals in order to acquire the things she wants. She sometimes changes her outfit three or four times before going to school. Most of her clothes are secondhand, but she is very artistic and adept with a needle and thread and she manages to make herself look very attractive.

She has a crush on a ninth-grade boy named Justin. Whenever she sees him at school or in the neighborhood, she tries to get his attention by raising her voice or starting an argument with someone. Justin belongs to a local gang, deals drugs, and cuts school as often as possible. Jazmine's friends have warned her that he only wants her to deal drugs for him, but she perceives his interest in her as genuine.

Jazmine likes the boys to notice her, and she is very preoccupied with her friends. She doesn't have much time for adults because they have always let her down. Although she is smart, she has found it harder to stay focused in class since her brother's death, and the school counselor suspects she's suffering from post-traumatic stress disorder. Her school records show that she has been a difficult student since first grade. Because the family has moved so frequently, she has changed schools several times and begins each year hoping that she can keep up. But as the weeks go by, she is sent out of class on a regular basis for being disruptive—sighing loudly, talking to her friends, making comments out loud to no one in particular, constantly getting out of her seat, passing notes, answering rudely when the teacher calls on her—and she falls further and further behind. Eventually she stops caring and no longer makes any effort to do the classwork, which she generally finds boring and irrelevant.

Jazmine often brings the wrong books to class or forgets her books entirely, and she regularly loses her pens and pencils. Because she can't afford to replace them, she is forced to borrow from her friends or the teacher, which embarrasses her. She manages to escape into another world by doodling. She loves to draw, enjoys art, and eagerly participates in any activity that utilizes her talent. She would love to stay after school and join the art club or paint scenery for the drama productions, but she has to get home to take care of her sister and cousins. She is very curious and observant and never misses a new addition to the bulletin board or a subtle change in someone's appearance, such as a new hairstyle or piece of clothing. Like most girls her age, Jazmine is very self-conscious about her body and will do anything—including cutting gym class—to avoid changing her clothes in the locker room.

Moving on

We hope that you're buckled up and ready to travel on this journey with us. It won't all be easy—you may have to think about things in totally a different way or consider issues you didn't even know existed—but in the end, we're sure that you'll feel the effort was worthwhile.

CHAPTER 1

What Is Challenging Behavior?

Challenging behavior is any behavior that:

- Interferes with a child's cognitive, social, or emotional development
- Is harmful to a child, his peers, or adults
- Puts a child at high risk for later social problems or school failure (Chandler and Dahlquist, 1997; Klass, Guskin, and Thomas, 1995; Ritchie and Pohl, 1995)

This book focuses on behavior that is aggressive, antisocial, or disruptive because its impact is so dramatic and so vast. But many of the ideas and strategies in these chapters will work equally well with students who display other types of challenging behavior—timid and withdrawn, for example.

Aggressive behavior aims to harm or injure others (Parke and Slaby, 1983) and can assume many forms. It can be *physical* or *verbal*, *direct* (hitting, pushing, pinching, spitting, hair-pulling, teasing, name-calling, or bullying) or *indirect* (spreading rumors, excluding others, or betraying a trust). Because indirect aggressive behavior endangers peer relationships, it is sometimes called *social* or *relational aggression* (Crick and Grotpeter, 1995).

Aggressive behavior often overlaps with *antisocial* or *disruptive behavior*, which "inflicts physical or mental harm or property loss or damage on others" (Loeber, 1985, p. 6) and violates social norms and expectations (Walker, Ramsey, and Gresham, 2004). It includes defying rules, instructions, or authority; arguing, swearing, cheating, lying, stealing, bullying, or destroying objects; and acting in ways that are abusive, coercive, or cruel. In adolescence, antisocial behavior may involve vandalism, substance abuse, truancy, and delinquency.

War and Peace

Aggressive or antisocial behavior is not the same as conflict, which occurs when people have opposing goals or interests. Conflict can be resolved in many ways—by negotiating, taking turns, persuading, and so on—and learning to resolve conflict helps children to be assertive about their own needs, regulate their negative feelings, and understand others (Cords and Killen, 1998; Katz, Kramer, and Gottman, 1992). Aggressive behavior is just one tactic for dealing with conflict—in fact, some researchers consider aggressive behavior a mismanagement of conflict (Perry, Perry, and Kennedy, 1992; Shantz and Hartup, 1992). But most conflicts don't involve aggression.

We call this behavior challenging because it is threatening, provocative, and stimulating, all at the same time. To begin with, it is challenging for the student. It puts him in danger by preventing him from learning what he needs to know to succeed in school and get along with his peers. It is also challenging for him because he probably doesn't have much control over it. Even if he knows what to do—and chances are he doesn't—his ability to regulate his feelings and actions just isn't up to the job. Improving matters will be an enormous challenge for him.

Children's challenging behavior is just as challenging for us, their teachers and family. In the face of this behavior, we often find ourselves at a loss, unable to figure out how to turn things around, how to make the situation tenable, how to help the student get back on track, behaving appropriately and feeling good about himself.

A Rose by Any Other Name

Challenging is not the only label that adults have affixed to problem behaviors or the children who use them. Here are some others:

- High maintenance
- Antisocial
- High needs
- Bad
- Out of control
- Hard to manage
- At risk
- Disruptive
- Aggressive
- Violent
- Impulsive
- Spirited
- Oppositional
- Noncompliant
- Mean
- Problematic
- Attention-seeking
- Willful

Labels are extremely powerful, which is why it's wiser not to use them—but if you do, be sure to apply them to the behavior rather than the student. Employing language carefully makes a big difference in the way you see a child and think about what he can and cannot do. Negative labels can all too easily become self-fulfilling prophecies. They prevent you from recognizing the child's positive qualities and may even cause you to lower your expectations of him. A student you've thought of as stubborn could just as easily be tenacious or persistent—important characteristics for success in school.

When you can see a student in a positive light, it helps him to see himself that way, and to act more positively, too.

It is essential for us to rise to this challenge. The child's future can depend on it—to say nothing of our own sanity and the well-being of the other students in the classroom. By its very nature, a challenge is difficult, but once conquered it brings incredible rewards. With the appropriate information and strategies, you can play a pivotal role in the life of this child, helping him avoid serious risk and blossom into the fully functioning person all children deserve to become.

Is challenging behavior ever appropriate?

Any child can exhibit challenging behavior. For a start, it is developmentally appropriate early in life, as children become interested in controlling their own activities and possessions (Coie and Dodge, 1998). In one study, most mothers reported that their toddlers grabbed, pushed, bit, hit, attacked, bullied, or were "cruel" by the time they turned 2 years old. Richard E. Tremblay of the University of Montreal puts it this way: "The question . . . we've been trying to answer for the past 30 years is how do children learn to aggress. But this is the wrong question. The right question is how do they learn not to aggress" (Holden, 2000).

With the aid of families and teachers, most children gradually stop using physical aggression from about the age of 30 months. They learn to regulate their feelings, understand another person's point of view, and employ assertive and prosocial strategies to communicate their needs and achieve their goals. They are also increasingly able to delay gratification and decreasingly tolerant of other children's aggressive acts (Coie and Dodge, 1998). By the time they enter kindergarten, most are relatively pacific (Tremblay, Masse, Pagani, and Vitaro, 1996). All children continue to use challenging behavior once in a while, when they're frustrated, angry, or having a bad day. Some even use it for an extended period when they're confronted with confusing and difficult events, such as a divorce, the arrival of a new sibling, a parent's illness or job loss, or a family move. But with extra support and understanding, they usually manage to cope.

What happens to students with more serious behavior problems?

Some children, however, have much more difficult and persistent problems, and they may come to rely on challenging behavior as the best way to respond to a situation. For this estimated 3 to 7 percent, aggressive and antisocial behavior continues well beyond the age of 3 (Moffitt, Caspi, Dickson, Silva, and Stanton, 1996; Nagin and Tremblay, 1999); and about half are starting down a road that will eventually lead to a delinquent adolescence and a criminal adulthood (Campbell, 2002; Richman, Stevenson, and Graham, 1982). The longer a child continues to use aggressive behavior, the harder it is to change his direction and the more worrisome the fallout becomes. It is therefore important to intervene as early as possible (Broidy et al., 2003; Slaby, Roedell, Arezzo, and Hendrix, 1995).

Children with behavior problems often find themselves rejected by their peers—disliked, ridiculed, and not invited to parties or other children's homes. These experiences wound their self-esteem and self-confidence, leave them isolated and depressed, and deprive them of opportunities to develop and practice the social and emotional skills they desperately need. Instead, they learn to expect rejection and may even discover that the best defense is a strong offense and will strike out preemptively to protect themselves (Moffitt, 1997). Once rejected by a group, a child will probably continue to be rejected and will have a hard time joining a new group (Campbell, 2002).

Behavior problems can lead to scholastic troubles, too. Because their social skills, emotional control, and language development are often below par, many students with challenging behavior are unprepared for the most basic task of their early school years—learning to read (Coie, 1996). It doesn't help that they may also be hyperactive, inattentive, disruptive, and unable to concentrate. As a result, they struggle with virtually everything academic.

Teachers sometimes exacerbate the problem. One study showed that teachers are more likely to punish students with challenging behavior and less likely to encourage them when they behave appropriately (Walker and Buckley, 1973). Teachers also call on children with aggressive behavior less frequently, ask them fewer questions, and provide them with less information (Shonkoff and Phillips, 2000). Not surprisingly, these students soon fall behind, and they're more likely to be held back, placed in a special class, or even expelled (Kazdin, 1987; Pepler and Rubin, 1991; Webster-Stratton and Herbert, 1994). All of this primes them to band together with their like-minded peers, raising their risk for school dropout, delinquency, gang membership, substance abuse, and psychiatric illness. As adults, they find it harder to hold jobs or earn good wages, and they're more likely to commit violent crimes (National Crime Prevention Council, 1996). Their marriages are rockier, the boys may become batterers, and the girls, who are at high risk for early pregnancy and single parenthood, often lack parenting skills and may be mothering the next generation of children with challenging behavior (National Crime Prevention Council, 1996; Serbin, Moskowitz, Schwartzman, and Ledingham, 1991; Tremblay, 1991).

A child who continues to use aggressive behavior is at high risk for school dropout, delinquency, gang membership, substance abuse, psychiatric illness, and a criminal adulthood. It is therefore important to intervene as early as possible.

Does challenging behavior always develop the same way?

Researchers believe that children take different routes to aggressive and antisocial behavior in adolescence and adulthood (Loeber and Farrington, 2001). Because such behavior is three to four times more common in boys (American Psychiatric Association, 1994), most studies have focused on them.

Rolf Loeber and his colleagues at the Pittsburgh Youth Study (Loeber and Farrington, 2001) have found three developmental pathways for boys:

1. Boys on the *overt pathway* use physical aggression, including bullying, which becomes more violent with time.
2. Boys on the *covert pathway* may engage in lying, stealing, and shoplifting, which can escalate into later substance abuse, fire-setting, and vandalism.
3. Boys on the *authority conflict pathway* use stubborn, defiant behavior that can turn into truancy and running away.

A boy can advance on more than one pathway at a time.

Researchers agree that there is a small cluster of boys whose aggression starts when they're very young and carries on as they grow older. Dubbed "early onset" or "life-course persistent," they tend to have neurocognitive deficits and poor emotional control, and they often grow up in families ill equipped to deal with their difficult behavior (Moffitt and Caspi, 2001). Because they're at very high risk for later violent and nonviolent offending, they represent a serious problem for society (Broidy et al., 2003; Loeber and Farrington, 2001; Moffitt, 1993).

Another group—those with so-called "adolescent onset" or "adolescent-limited" disruptive behavior—has divided the research community. Some researchers (Moffitt, 1993) argue that about one-third of boys with no history of antisocial behavior take it up in their teens, perhaps to gain status, privilege, or independence. Unlike the early-onset boys, they behave inconsistently—shoplifting in stores and using drugs with friends but obeying the rules at school—and seem to avail themselves of delinquent behavior only when it serves a purpose. When they reach their 20s and have access to legitimate power, they abandon their antisocial ways; and because they developed competent cognitive, social, and emotional skills in early and middle childhood, they usually return to normal lives. But other experts have found evidence that these late starters don't actually exist, pointing out that even though their aggressive behavior rises during the teen years, it has always been present (Broidy et al., 2003).

The gap between boys' and girls' antisocial behavior seems to close in adolescence (Bierman et al., 2004). However, how this happens remains a puzzle. Some researchers argue that girls follow the late-onset pathway and only begin to display antisocial behavior in their early teens (Silverthorn and Frick, 1999). Others contend that girls start out with disruptive behaviors and relational aggression in elementary and middle school and move on to antisocial behavior later (Bierman et al., 2004).

There is also a small proportion of girls who begin to use physical aggression in preschool and never stop. Like boys who start young, these girls are at high risk for antisocial behavior in adolescence (Moffitt, Caspi, Rutter, and Silva, 2001), as well as depression, anxiety, and substance abuse (Kovacs, Krol, and Voti, 1994; Zoccolillo, 1993).

Relational aggression, which can appear as early as age 3 (Ostrov, Woods, Jansen, Casas, and Crick, 2004), increases dramatically in the transition from childhood to adolescence, especially among girls. But it isn't clear whether it leads to antisocial behavior (Bjorkqvist, Lagerspetz, and Kaukiainen, 1992; Xie, Cairns, and Cairns, 2005). (For more about challenging behavior in girls, see Chapters 2 and 14.)

What do the theorists say about aggression and antisocial behavior?

Because the question goes straight to the heart of who we are as human beings, philosophers have been arguing about the nature of aggression since the time of the Greeks. Some, like Seneca and the Stoics in ancient times and Thomas Hobbes in the seventeenth century, assert that aggression and anger are uncontrollable biological instincts that must be restrained by external force. Others, like the English philosopher John Locke, believe that a child comes into the world as a blank slate—*tabula rasa*—and experience makes him who he is (Dodge, 1991).

Both views still exist today. The *frustration-aggression theory* holds that when people are frustrated—when they can't reach their goals—they become angry and hostile and act aggressively (Dodge, 1991; Reiss and Roth, 1993). *Social learning theory* (Bandura, 1977) takes the Lockean perspective, and it has dominated thinking on the subject of aggression for the last three decades. Based on principles of conditioning and reinforcement, it says that people learn aggressive behavior from the environment and use it to achieve their goals. Of course, these distinctions are difficult to make in practice. When you get right down to it, it's impossible to attribute all aggression to frustration, and the way a person responds to frustration probably depends on what he's learned (Pepler and Slaby, 1994).

The father of social learning theory, psychologist Albert Bandura, contends that children learn aggressive behavior primarily by observing it. Children are great imitators, and they copy the models around them—family, teachers, peers, neighbors, television, and so on. At the same time, they observe and experience the rewards, punishments, and emotional states associated with aggressive and antisocial behavior. When they see that a behavior is reinforced, they're likely to try it for themselves; when they experience the reinforcement directly, they're likely to repeat it (Bandura, 1977). That is, when Andrew pushes Ben and gets to be first in line, he will almost certainly try pushing the next time he wants something.

Social learning theory has spawned several sister theories that place more emphasis on cognition. According to the *cognitive script model*, proposed by L. Rowell Huesmann and Leonard D. Eron, children learn scripts for aggressive behavior—when to expect it, what to do, what it will feel like, what its results will be—and lay them down in their memory banks. The more they rehearse these scripts through observation, fantasy, and behavior, the more readily they spring to mind and govern behavior when the occasion arises (Coie and Dodge, 1998; Pepler and Slaby, 1994; Reiss and Roth, 1993).

Psychologist Kenneth A. Dodge has proposed a *social information processing model* for aggressive and antisocial behavior. In every single social interaction, there is lots of information to be instantly processed and turned into a response. As each social cue comes in, the child must encode it, interpret it, think of possible responses, evaluate them, and choose a response to enact. A child with very challenging behavior often lacks one or more of the skills required to process this information properly, and he tends to see the world with a jaundiced eye. When another child bumps into him in a situation that most children regard as neutral, he thinks the bump was intentional—that the other child wanted to hurt him or be mean to him. Dodge calls this having a *hostile attributional bias*. Furthermore, the child doesn't look for information that might help to solve a problem, and he has trouble thinking of alternative solutions. And because he doesn't anticipate what will happen if he responds aggressively, he often ends up choosing passive or aggressive solutions that don't work (Dodge, 1980; Dodge and Frame, 1982).

This pattern, which becomes stable in middle childhood (Dodge, 2003; Dodge and Pettit, 2003), grows out of their experience. Children who are consistently maltreated at home or rejected by their peers feel angry and alienated, alone in a hostile environment. They learn to defend themselves by becoming extra vigilant and quickly resorting to force (Dodge, 2003). Students who respond to others with relational aggression may also have these hostile attributional biases (Crick, Grotpeter, and Bigbee, 2002).

Like the philosophers, Dodge makes a distinction between two kinds of aggression. Children use *proactive aggression* (also called *instrumental aggression*) as a tool to achieve a goal, such as obtaining a desired object or dominating a peer. Proactive aggression is more common among very young children because they don't yet have the words they need to ask for the ball or the teacher's attention. They aren't angry or emotional; they're just using the means available to get what they want. Interestingly, young children who use proactive aggression don't necessarily earn the rejection of their peers. In fact, they often show leadership qualities. But by the time they reach the primary grades, the other students are no longer willing to tolerate this behavior and will reject a child who uses it (Dodge, 1991).

Reactive aggression (also known as *hostile* or *affective aggression*) appears in the heat of the moment in reaction to some frustration or perceived provocation. Angry, volatile, and not at all controlled, it is often aimed at hurting someone. Children who are prone to reactive aggression are invariably disliked, and they also make errors in

Seeing Straight

Researchers Kenneth Dodge, John E. Bates, and Gregory S. Pettit (1990) wanted to find out if physical abuse affects the way a child processes social information. They showed roughly 300 5-year-olds, some of whom had experienced abuse, a series of cartoon vignettes depicting unpleasant events—a child's blocks get knocked over, a child tries to enter a group and fails, and so on. In some of the stories, the event is an accident, in some it is intentional, and in still others it is hard to tell.

When the researchers asked the children to answer questions about the vignettes, they found that the children who had been physically abused gave answers different from those given by the children who were unharmed. Those who had been maltreated paid less attention to social cues, were more ready to attribute hostile intent to someone in the stories, and were less likely to think up competent solutions to the problems the stories posed. Their teachers also rated their behavior as more aggressive.

The researchers concluded that the experience of being physically abused leads children to see the world as a hostile place and impairs their ability to process social information accurately. These effects held true when the children were retested in grades 8 and 11 (Dodge, 2003).

social information processing, attributing hostile intentions to others in ambiguous or neutral situations (Dodge and Frame, 1982).

Students who behave aggressively show some additional distinctive thought patterns. In their minds, aggression is perfectly acceptable. It can enhance their reputation and make them feel good about themselves, and it doesn't even hurt the guy on the receiving end of it. Moreover, they believe that aggression pays off, and in their experience it often does (Slaby, 1997).

Reactive aggression (also known as *hostile* or *affective aggression*) appears in the heat of the moment in reaction to some frustration or perceived provocation. Angry, volatile, and not at all controlled, it is often aimed at hurting someone.

Teachers sometimes find it hard to distinguish between aggressive behavior and rough-and-tumble play, when children hit, chase, wrestle, and restrain one another for fun. Rough-and-tumble play is a normal activity, more common among boys, that once upon a time probably honed fighting skills and now helps children learn to regulate aggression (Tremblay, 2003) and work out dominance relationships in a group (Berk, 2000). Rough-and-tumble play decreases with physical maturity. British expert Michael Boulton (1994) offers these tips on how to distinguish it from serious combat:

- *Facial and verbal expression.* In rough-and-tumble play, children usually laugh and smile. When they fight for real, they frown, stare, grimace, cry, and get red in the face.
- *Outcome.* Children continue to play together after rough-and-tumble play, but after a real fight they separate.
- *Self-handicapping.* In a play fight, a stronger or older child may let his opponent pin or catch him. This doesn't happen in a serious fight.
- *Restraint.* In playful fighting, the contact between children is relatively gentle. When children are really fighting, they go all out.
- *Role reversals.* In rough-and-tumble play, children alternate roles—for example, they take turns chasing and being chased. This is unusual in a fight.
- *Number of partners.* Lots of children—10 or more—can participate in rough- and-tumble play. Usually just 2 fight when it's serious.
- *Onlookers.* Spectators aren't interested in play fighting, but a real fight or bullying usually draws a crowd.

Children who behave in an aggressive or antisocial manner may also lag behind in moral understanding. They can't see things from another person's perspective, insist on having their own way, blame others when things go wrong (Coie and Dodge, 1998; Perry et al., 1992), and continue to attack even when their target is clearly in pain (Perry et al., 1992). They may also inflate their self-esteem by overestimating their own popularity and social competence (Asher, Parkhurst, Hymel, and Williams, 1990; Hughes, Cavell, and Grossman, 1997). If they're rejected by their peers, students with aggressive behavior experience more stress and record much higher levels of stress hormones than other children in the classroom (Shonkoff and Phillips, 2000).

Aggressive or antisocial behavior is more likely to occur if the environment considers it normal and acceptable and if it is part of a child's usual repertoire of responses (Guerra, 1997). When the environment devalues aggressive behavior and children have competent, effective, nonaggressive responses at their disposal, they have a far better chance of solving their problems amicably.

Does culture play a role in aggressive behavior?

Cultures vary in the way they view aggressive behavior, highlighting the importance of learning. When adults actively discourage aggressive behavior, the outcome is a peaceful society, such as that of the Amish or the Zuni Indian (Delgado, 1979). When they encourage it, an aggressive society is the result. Anthropologist D. P. Fry (1988) studied two neighboring villages in southern Mexico. In La Paz, the

Under the Surface

In 2004, Harvard University sociologist Katherine S. Newman wrote a book that examined school shootings. Her words ring even more true today:

> For the country as a whole, school shootings opened up a searing self-examination as only a total shock can. Have we lost our grip on our children? Do we no longer understand what makes them tick? Are parents too involved in their own lives to pay attention to what their children are doing? Have guns become so ubiquitous that we are hardly even surprised when a postal worker or a disgruntled student fires a few rounds into a terrified crowd of coworkers or classmates? Are we no longer able to judge when a community is safe and when it just looks that way? Or do we need to fear what is bubbling beneath the surface in crime-free suburbs? . . . These explosions are attacks on whole institutions—schools, teenage pecking orders, or communities. Shooters choose schools as the site for a rampage because they are the heart and soul of public life in small towns. (pp. 14–15)

inhabitants frown on aggressive behavior, and there is very little of it. In nearby San Andres, the residents think aggressive behavior is normal, and when children throw rocks at each other, their parents don't intervene. The consequence is a homicide rate five times higher in San Andres than in La Paz.

A study of the behavior of children in six cultures—India, Okinawa, Kenya, Mexico, the Philippines, and the United States—found that, relatively speaking, U.S. parents tolerate a fair amount of aggressive behavior among children (Segall, Dasen, Berry, and Poortinga, 1990). Criminologist Joan McCord called America "the most violent of countries—more violent, in fact, than other industrialized countries" (1997). Just look at the homicide statistics: In the year 2005, the United States averaged 5.6 homicides per 100,000 residents, compared with 2.0 for Canada (Statistics Canada, 2006; U.S. Department of Justice, Federal Bureau of Investigation, 2006). Homicide rates among American youth have been falling since the mid-1990s, but they are still alarmingly high (Child Trends Data Bank, 2003).

In a survey of 10,000 high school students, 13 percent reported that they'd been in at least one physical fight on school grounds in 2003, and 6 percent had brought in a firearm. About 12 percent of boys and 6 percent of girls had been threatened or injured with a weapon on school property (DeVoe, Peter, Noonan, Snyder, and Baum, 2005).

Although there are higher rates of violence among African Americans and Latino Americans than among European Americans (Kaufman, 2005), "ethnicity in and of itself should not be considered a causal or risk factor for violence," reports the American Psychological Association's Commission on Violence and Youth (Eron, Gentry, and Schlegel, 1994, p. 101). In these communities there is much more poverty, which is a significant risk factor for violence. When socioeconomic status is taken into account—along with community disorganization, joblessness, racism, and discrimination—the differences in violence rates are small.

There are no real differences in the rates of aggression between African American and European American elementary school children—or among young people ages 18 to 20 who are employed, married, or living with a partner (Coie and Dodge, 1998). This is an eloquent statement about intervention.

Regardless of their culture, race, or ethnicity, children need to feel safe, respected, and cared for to be able to learn. It's much more difficult to create the conditions that make learning possible when there's a student with challenging behavior in the classroom. The information in the chapters that follow will help you understand challenging behavior as well as the students who use it. It will also enable you to develop the skills you need to prevent and manage challenging behavior effectively so that every child you teach can have the opportunity to learn and reach his potential.

What do you think?

1. What does the following quote by Richard E. Tremblay mean to you? "The question . . . we've been trying to answer for the past 30 years is how do children learn to aggress. But this is the wrong question. The right question is how do they learn not to aggress." How would you explain this question to someone else? Why is it so difficult? Are you surprised by the idea that people are naturally aggressive? If they are, how would that affect their ability to control their aggression?

2. In the text of this chapter, we say, "Negative labels can all too easily become self-fulfilling prophecies. They prevent you from seeing the child's positive qualities and may even cause you to lower your expectations of him." How does labeling affect your attitude? Have you ever been labeled? How did the label affect your behavior and your relationships? Can you think of situations when you have labeled someone else?

3. Why is it hard for children with aggressive behavior to succeed in school? What other problems can aggressive behavior create for them?

4. "There are no real differences in the rates of aggression between African American and European American elementary school children—or among young people ages 18 to 20 who are employed, married, or living with a partner." Why do we say this is an eloquent statement about intervention?

5. Why do you think the United States is so much more violent than other industrialized countries?

Suggested readings

Garbarino, J. (2000). *Lost boys: Why our sons turn violent and how we can save them.* Garden City, NY: Anchor.

Harris, J. R. (1998). *The nurture assumption: Why children turn out the way they do.* New York: Simon & Schuster.

Kagan, J. (1971). *Understanding children: Behavior, motives, and thought.* New York: Harcourt Brace Jovanovich.

Newman, K. S. (2004). *Rampage: The social roots of school shootings.* New York: Basic Books.

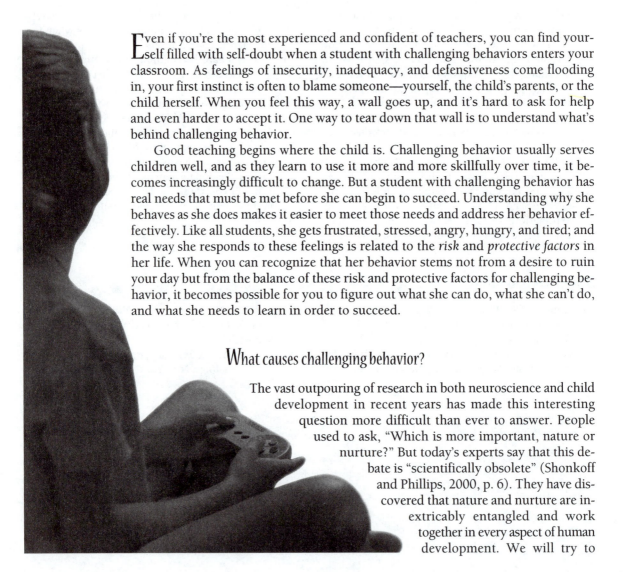

CHAPTER 2

Risk Factors

Even if you're the most experienced and confident of teachers, you can find yourself filled with self-doubt when a student with challenging behaviors enters your classroom. As feelings of insecurity, inadequacy, and defensiveness come flooding in, your first instinct is often to blame someone—yourself, the child's parents, or the child herself. When you feel this way, a wall goes up, and it's hard to ask for help and even harder to accept it. One way to tear down that wall is to understand what's behind challenging behavior.

Good teaching begins where the child is. Challenging behavior usually serves children well, and as they learn to use it more and more skillfully over time, it becomes increasingly difficult to change. But a student with challenging behavior has real needs that must be met before she can begin to succeed. Understanding why she behaves as she does makes it easier to meet those needs and address her behavior effectively. Like all students, she gets frustrated, stressed, angry, hungry, and tired; and the way she responds to these feelings is related to the *risk* and *protective factors* in her life. When you can recognize that her behavior stems not from a desire to ruin your day but from the balance of these risk and protective factors for challenging behavior, it becomes possible for you to figure out what she can do, what she can't do, and what she needs to learn in order to succeed.

What causes challenging behavior?

The vast outpouring of research in both neuroscience and child development in recent years has made this interesting question more difficult than ever to answer. People used to ask, "Which is more important, nature or nurture?" But today's experts say that this debate is "scientifically obsolete" (Shonkoff and Phillips, 2000, p. 6). They have discovered that nature and nurture are inextricably entangled and work together in every aspect of human development. We will try to tease a few threads out of this intricately woven fabric so that we can examine them more closely, but we must warn you that they won't come out neatly. In this chapter, we'll look at the threads that make up the risk factors for challenging behavior; in the next chapter, we'll explore the factors that protect children against it.

The relationship between risk factors and challenging behavior is complicated. Similar risk factors can result in different outcomes, and different risk factors can produce similar outcomes. And risk factors have a cumulative effect. A student who has one risk factor faces no more risk of developing challenging behavior than a student who has none. But a student who has two risk factors faces a risk *four times as great* (Rutter, 2000; Yoshikawa, 1994). Where risk factors are concerned, one plus one equals more than two.

Risk factors are often invisible, and families may not even know they're there. You can ask about risk factors if it seems appropriate, but it's entirely possible that no hard information will ever come to light. At the same time, even though you're not a doctor or a psychologist trained to make diagnoses, you can learn a lot by observing a student with challenging behavior and talking to her family about what's going on. As you do, keep the risk factors in mind. Rarely can you change them, but they will provide you with insight, empathy, and ideas about how to proceed. Understanding risk factors can make a difference in your attitude toward a student and enable you to develop a relationship of trust and caring that can help her feel safe, accepted, and more likely to behave appropriately.

The risk factors for challenging behavior fall into two broad categories, biological and environmental. We've defined *biological* as anything that impinges on the child from conception to birth, and we've organized this section chronologically, beginning with genes. Anything that influences a child after birth we've considered as *environmental*, whether it acts on her directly (such as physical punishment or lead in her drinking water) or indirectly (such as poverty). The environmental section begins with the family—a child's most intimate environment—and gradually moves outward through school and community influences. Although cultural dissonance is an important factor, we won't deal with it here because we've given it a chapter of its own (Chapter 6). Once again, it's important to remember that these factors overlap, and although we present them here as if each is separate, in fact they are constantly interacting and influencing each other.

Juggler

James Garbarino, professor of human development at Cornell University, has been studying violence and its impact on children and youth for 25 years. In *Lost Boys* (1999), he emphasizes the danger of multiple risk factors.

It is the accumulation of threats that does the damage. And trouble really sets in when these threats accumulate without a parallel accumulation of compensatory "opportunity" factors. Once overwhelmed, defenses are weakened. . . . I look at it this way: Give me one tennis ball, and I can toss it up and down with ease. Give me two, and I can still manage easily. Add a third, and it takes special skill to juggle them. Make it four, and I will drop them all. So it is with threats to development. (pp. 75–76)

BIOLOGICAL RISK FACTORS

Genes

Scientists are leaning more and more toward the view that a gene specifically "for" a disorder or condition such as antisocial behavior is very unlikely (Rutter, Moffitt, and Caspi, 2006). Dean Hamer, director of the Gene Structure and Regulation Unit at the National Cancer Institute, writes, "Human behaviors, and the brain circuits that produce them, are undoubtedly the product of intricate networks involving hundreds to thousands of genes working in concert with multiple developmental and environmental events" (2002, p. 72).

Because there are so many elements involved and they interact with one another in such complex ways, it is extremely difficult to disentangle the influence of genes from the influence of the environment. To tease out these different strands and estimate their relative power, behavioral geneticists use twin studies, comparing identical twins (who share all their genes) and fraternal twins (who share about half their genes). The genetic influence on a characteristic such as intelligence, temperament, personality, cognitive style, or psychophysiology is greater when the trait is more similar in identical twins than in fraternal twins. Researchers also study adopted children to see if they are more like their biological parents (with whom they share genes) or their adoptive parents (with whom they share the environment). These studies, which are becoming increasingly analytical and sophisticated, show that antisocial behavior is moderately heritable (Moffitt, 2005), especially antisocial behavior that begins early in life (Arseneault et al., 2003; Rhee and Waldman, 2002).

In addition, scientists have discovered that some genes interact with a particular environment to actually produce a disorder (Rutter et al., 2006); some genes are *expressed* or turned on (or not) because of physical, social, and cultural factors in the environment; and some genes—for example, those that influence difficult temperament, impulsivity, novelty seeking, and lack of empathy—predispose people to be exposed to environmental risks. Genes even help shape the environment. Genes influence how parents bring up their children; genes affect the responses that children evoke from their families and the others around them; and, as children grow older, genes sway their choice of companions and surroundings (Caspi and Silva, 1995; Plomin, Owen, and McGuffin, 1994).

It's important to remember that heredity is not destiny. With the right environmental interventions at the right time, even a trait with a strong genetic foundation (such as antisocial behavior) can be altered.

Double Dose

A study of children adopted in Iowa compared the biological children of parents who were in trouble with alcohol or the law with the biological children of parents who did not have these problems. It turned out that the children who had both the problem genes and a problematic environment in their adopted home were much more prone to aggressive and antisocial behavior than the children who had only the problem genes or only the difficult environment. Their genes made them vulnerable to the environment, or, to view it from another angle, their environment made them vulnerable to their genes (Hamer and Copeland, 1999; Rutter, 2000).

Gender

Almost all experts agree that boys are at greater risk for physical aggression than girls (Underwood, 2003), and several large longitudinal studies bear this out (Broidy et al., 2003). Boys seem more susceptible to many of the risk factors for aggressive behavior—difficult temperament, ADHD, learning disabilities, and nervous system dysfunction, for example (Moffitt and Caspi, 2001; Rutter, Giller, and Hagell, 1998) —and as we saw in Chapter 1, the prevalence rate for aggression in boys is three to four times as high as the rate for girls (American Psychiatric Association, 1994). The social context has a strong influence on how and whether aggressive behavior appears (Maccoby, 2004). Parents treat anger and aggression differently in their sons and daughters and use more physical punishment and power-assertive discipline with their boys (Zahn-Waxler and Polanichka, 2004). Boys hit, push, kick, tease, and insult each other more; spend more time in rough-and-tumble play; and accept aggressive behavior more readily than girls. Physical aggression starts to taper off as boys get older and develop more impulse control (Maccoby, 2004).

Like boys who don't renounce physical aggression before they enter school, girls who continue to act aggressively face the prospect of school failure and rejection by their peers and are also more likely to be depressed (Underwood, 2003). They often join groups of boys, fight with boys, and eventually date—and marry—boys who act aggressively. Without the social and problem-solving skills they need to sustain an intimate relationship, they may find themselves in increasing danger as the boys grow bigger and stronger (Pepler and Craig, 1999). They are also more likely to become teenage mothers (Pepler and Craig, 1999). Although arrest statistics indicate that the rate of physical violence among girls is rising, other studies show that this is a myth: It is not the level of violence that has changed but the labeling of offenses (Chesney-Lind and Belknap, 2004).

As researchers turn their attention to aggressive behavior in girls, they are looking hard at indirect and relational aggression, where the goal is to damage another's self-esteem, social status, or both (Underwood, 2003). Covert tactics—exclusion, back-stabbing, gossiping, belittling, and the like—become more sophisticated and prevalent in middle childhood and are fairly widespread among girls during adolescence. Relational aggression provides a way for them to act on their angry feelings, seek revenge, and assure themselves that they're accepted by the group (Underwood, 2003).

Temperament

In 1956, New York University psychiatrists Alexander Thomas and Stella Chess and their colleagues (Thomas, Chess, and Birch, 1968) began a pioneering longitudinal study of temperament. By collecting data on a sample of 133 children from infancy through young adulthood, they discovered that each child is born with a distinct temperament—an observable, constitutionally based pattern of behavior and emotions, a characteristic way of experiencing and interacting with the world.

Thomas and Chess identified nine traits that appear in different people in different combinations and quantities. These traits emerge early, often become stable by 4 months of age (Shonkoff and Phillips, 2000), and remain into adulthood, although by that time they may look entirely different from the outside (Caspi and

According to Thomas and Chess (Thomas et al., 1968; Thomas and Chess, 1977), children come endowed with a mixture of nine character traits, all of which offer advantages and disadvantages, depending on your point of view.

- *Activity level.* A child's activity level can range from slow and quiet to high energy.
- *Rhythmicity or regularity.* At one end of the scale, a child can be absolutely regular in her sleep, eating, and bowel habits; at the other end, she can appear to have no biological pattern whatsoever.
- *Approach or withdrawal.* This trait has to do with a child's initial response to new people and situations and can extend from categorical rejection to wading right in.
- *Adaptability.* How readily can a child modify her first reaction and settle into a situation? The scale ranges from great willingness to great reluctance to deal with change.
- *Intensity of reaction.* One child may have very mild reactions (you have to pay close attention to know what she's feeling); another may react with great force and power, whether she's ecstatic or furious.
- *Threshold of responsiveness.* Some children don't notice smells, sounds, sights, touch, taste, and pain and need lots of sensory stimulation—loud voices, big bumps—to respond. Others, like the princess and the pea, can't even bear to feel the labels in their shirts.
- *Quality of mood.* Mood can vary from finding pleasure everywhere to seeing the world as a serious place indeed.
- *Distractibility.* Some children can't be derailed no matter what; some pay attention to everything that crosses their paths.
- *Attention span and persistence.* These two characteristics are related. One child tunes in for just a few minutes, then needs a break; another sticks with something that interests her through countless interruptions.

There is no correlation between temperament and intelligence, gender, birth order, or social and economic status (Turecki, 2000; Kurcinka, 1992).

Silva, 1995). This explains why a self-assured young woman who talks easily to strangers at a party may still regard herself as a shy person.

Thomas and Chess (Thomas et al., 1968) made another interesting observation: They found three distinct types of children, whom they classified as easy, slow to warm up, and difficult. The children in the *easy* group had a sunny outlook on life and adapted easily to change. Over the years, a mere 7.5 percent of them developed behavior problems (Chess and Thomas, 1984). The children who were *slow to warm up* took a long time to get used to new things, but with patient care they became interested and involved. About half of them had some problems with behavior (Chess and Thomas, 1984). The *difficult* group of children cried loudly and often, had tantrums, resisted new things and changes in routine, and always seemed to be in a bad mood. Although they made up just 10 percent of the study sample, about 70 percent of them developed problem behaviors (Chess and Thomas, 1984).

In trying to figure out why 30 percent of the children with difficult temperaments managed *not* to develop problems, Thomas and Chess (Thomas et al., 1968) evolved the concept of *goodness of fit.* Serious disturbances are more likely to arise, they found, when the temperament of the child and the expectations of the family or teacher are out of sync. Traits of temperament are neither good nor bad in themselves; what matters is how the environment responds to them.

The theorists who've followed Thomas and Chess—Jerome Kagan, Mary Rothbart, John Bates, and others—have started to pinpoint more precisely the temperamental dimensions associated with problem behavior. Perhaps the most important traits they've identified have to do with the way children experience and regulate their emotions (Frick, 2004).

Some children are easily unsettled and feel their negative emotions, such as anger and frustration, intensely and frequently (Lahey and Waldman, 2003). Untamed, this negative *emotional reactivity* can put them at risk of defiance, tantrums, and other problem behaviors; lead to peer rejection; and impair the development of cognitive skills such as social information processing. However, when negative emotional reactivity is balanced by a good dose of another temperamental quality, *effortful control,* or the ability to inhibit feelings and behavior and focus attention, the risk is attenuated (Rothbart and Jones, 1998).

At the opposite pole of this prickly emotional reactivity is a temperamental trait that also carries a high risk for behavior problems (Frick and Morris, 2004). When their reactions are low key and difficult to arouse, children seem to feel no fear and may actively seek out excitement, novelty, and danger. Those with an extreme version of this trait—variously called *uninhibited* (Kagan, 1998), *daring* (Lahey and Waldman, 2003), *callous-unemotional* (Frick and Morris, 2004), or *low in harm avoidance* (Tremblay, Pihl, Vitaro, and Dobkin, 1994)—aren't deterred by the threat of punishment or moved by others' distress; and they have trouble developing empathy, guilt, and moral reasoning (Frick and Morris, 2004). Their aggressive behavior is likely to be covert and instrumental.

However, like Thomas and Chess before them, the new temperament researchers do not believe that temperament is destiny. Families and teachers who understand and accommodate temperamental traits can gradually extend a child's capacity to cope—to learn to regulate her emotions, maintain relationships, develop empathy and guilt, and follow societal norms (Frick and Morris, 2004). Jerome Kagan (1998), a developmental psychologist who's studied *inhibited* and *uninhibited* temperamental traits in hundreds of babies, has found that only about one-quarter of them still show the same behavioral and biological profile at the age of 11 years (Kagan and Snidman, 2004). Daily experience helped the inhibited children learn to control their fear and irritability and the uninhibited to manage their disobedience, aggressive behavior, and impermeability to adult criticism—or not. Children with more extreme temperamental traits find such learning more difficult, which makes it harder to teach and care for them.

Although the environment can influence temperament, it is important to remember that biology comes first. On average, traits of temperament are about 50 percent heritable (Plomin et al., 1994). Kagan (1994; Kagan and Snidman, 2004) suspects that differences in neurochemical inheritance provide the basis for temperament traits, and he has found several physiological differences between inhibited and uninhibited children. For example, when uninhibited children are stressed, their heart rate is less likely to accelerate—a characteristic that has also been seen in older children with aggressive conduct disorders (Reiss and Roth, 1993).

Influenced by both biology and child-rearing, temperament varies with culture and geography (Kagan and Snidman, 2004). In 1974, medical student Marten deVries

(1989) went to Kenya and Tanzania to collect information about the temperament of the children of the Masai, a semi-nomadic tribe on the Serengeti Plain. Using temperament scales based on Thomas and Chess's criteria, he identified 10 infants with easy temperaments and 10 with difficult temperaments. The area was in the midst of a severe drought, and when deVries returned five months later, most of the Masai's cattle and many of their people had died. Although deVries couldn't locate all of the babies, he found seven with easy temperaments and six with difficult temperaments. Of the seven with easy temperaments, five had died; all but one of those with difficult temperaments had survived.

What accounted for the unexpected survival of the children with difficult temperaments? DeVries credited several factors. First, the Masai admire their warriors and encourage aggressiveness and assertiveness in their children. Second, shared caregiving in the Masai's large extended families makes it easier to deal with children who are difficult. Third, Masai mothers breast-feed on demand, and children who are fussy ask for—and receive—more nourishment. The qualities that European American middle-class families regard as difficult—loud and frequent crying, for instance—are an advantage in an environment of scarcity (Chess and Thomas, 1989; DeVries, 1989).

Complications of pregnancy and birth

To many people it seems intuitively obvious that a woman's state of mind during pregnancy affects the fetus, and now researchers are proving these suspicions correct. New longitudinal studies show that women who experience high stress in early or mid-pregnancy are more likely to have pregnancy complications, early deliveries, and low-birthweight babies (DiPietro, 2002; Van den Bergh and Marcoen, 2004). As toddlers, their children are prone to language and intellectual difficulties (LaPlante et al., 2004); and later they may develop symptoms of ADHD, anxiety, aggression, and other behavioral and emotional problems (O'Connor, Heron, Golding, Beveridge, and Glover, 2002; Van den Bergh and Marcoen, 2004). Boys seem more vulnerable to these effects than girls (DiPietro, 2002).

Researchers believe that improving prenatal care and promoting maternal health can reduce the risk of neuropsychological damage to the baby. In a study in upstate New York (Olds et al., 1998), nurses visited poor, young, or unmarried women at home at least once a month during their pregnancies. Fifteen years later, the children of these women had fewer arrests and ran away from home less often than the children of unvisited mothers. That is, the intervention lowered the risk for these children even though the nurses had never visited after they were born.

Substance abuse during pregnancy

During the prenatal period, the fetus's developing nervous system is extremely vulnerable to assaults from the outside world, as history dramatically shows. Women who took Thalidomide to combat morning sickness during their pregnancies in the 1950s and 1960s gave birth to babies with stunted limbs and defective hearts, intestines, and blood vessels; and pregnant women who catch German measles (also called Rubella) still run a high risk of having children born deaf, blind, or with heart damage.

Alcohol, tobacco, and drugs ingested during pregnancy can do considerable harm. How much harm depends on the fetus's stage of development, as well as how much, how long, and how often exposure takes place. The resilience of the fetus and the mother's health and prenatal care have an impact (Shonkoff and Phillips, 2000), and so does the parents' behavior after the baby's birth. If they continue to abuse drugs or alcohol, their children may face the added danger of neglect, abuse, or chaotic, inconsistent, and unresponsive caregiving (Griffith, 1992; Leslie and DeMarchi, 1996).

Alcohol

Alcohol is responsible for much more damage to unborn babies than any illegal drug. Drinking any amount at any time during pregnancy—especially heavy or binge drinking—causes lifelong damage to the developing brain (U.S. Department of Health and Human Services, Office of the Surgeon General, 2005).

The set of birth defects now known as *fetal alcohol spectrum disorder (FASD)* includes *fetal alcohol syndrome (FAS)*, which is characterized by facial defects, growth deficiency, and brain abnormalities, and *alcohol-related neurodevelopmental disorder (ARND*, also called *fetal alcohol effects*, or *FAE)*, in which cognitive impairments just as serious lie hidden behind perfectly normal faces and bodies. Fetal alcohol spectrum disorder is the leading cause of mental retardation (Friend, 2005), and children with FASD have difficulties with learning, memory, attention, planning, and problem solving, as well as perception and sensory integration. Their motor control and executive functions may be affected, and hyperactivity is a common symptom (Harwood and Kleinfeld, 2002). Easily overwhelmed by stimulation, children with FASD act impulsively and become angry or frustrated quickly. They have difficulty understanding and using language and trouble making friends (Harwood and Kleinfeld, 2002), and they are at increased risk for psychiatric disorders, substance abuse problems, and trouble with the law (Streissguth et al., 2004). They may be eligible for special education under IDEA (see Chapter 12).

Tobacco and nicotine

The warnings on the cigarette packages are there for good reason: Smoking during pregnancy causes babies to be born prematurely and to have low birthweights and low IQs (Fergusson, 2002). Nicotine crosses the placenta and affects the developing nervous system, putting a child at risk for later attention difficulties, impulsiveness, hyperactivity, and problems with language and emotional regulation (Fried, 2002b; Olds, 1997; Olds, Henderson, and Tatelbaum, 1994; Schettler, Stein, Reich, and

Canadian cigarette packages carry health alerts. This one warns of the dangers for the fetus of smoking during pregnancy. Smoking during pregnancy is a risk factor for behavior problems.

Photo courtesy of Health Canada. Licensed under Health Canada copyright.

Valenti, 2000). There is increasing evidence that prenatal exposure to cigarette smoke raises the likelihood of oppositional behavior, conduct disorder, substance abuse, and juvenile crime (Fergusson, 2002).

Illicit drugs

Children who've been exposed to *marijuana* prenatally perform poorly on attention, memory, and verbal tests, and are also more likely to be impulsive and hyperactive (Fried, 2002a; Goldschmidt, Day, and Richardson, 2000). In addition, their executive functions may be impaired, and they may have trouble solving problems that call for integrating, analyzing, and synthesizing information (Fried, 2002a).

The research on children exposed to *cocaine* or *crack* in the womb has yielded mixed results. Some investigators have seen no link with cognitive or academic performance, attention, or language (Chasnoff et al., 1998; Richardson, Conroy, and Day, 1996); others have found an association with behavior problems (Bada et al., 2007; Chasnoff et al., 1998; Shankaran et al., 2007), poorer executive functioning (Shankaran et al., 2007; Warner et al., 2006), and learning disabilities (Morrow et al., 2006). Women who use cocaine during pregnancy probably use other substances as well, raising the risks for their unborn child. The effects of prenatal cocaine exposure seem to increase as children grow, but their living situation has a powerful influence on their outcome (Shankaran et al., 2007).

Injected during pregnancy, *opiates* such as *heroin* cause prematurity and low birthweight in babies and put them at risk for attention and developmental problems. Once again, if they are living with substance-abusing parents, their home environment may hold as many risks as their prenatal drug exposure (Brady, Posner, Lang, and Rosati, 1994; Leslie and DeMarchi, 1996; Shankaran et al., 2007).

Prematurity and complications of delivery

Children who are born prematurely or who experience delivery complications face substantial risk (Brennan, Mednick, and Kandel, 1991). Prematurity predisposes an infant to brain injury and deprives the developing brain of the sustenance it needs (Shonkoff and Phillips, 2000). Premature and low-birthweight babies are more likely to suffer from language and speech disorders and problems with balance, coordination, and perception, all of which are associated with the development of aggression (Reiss and Roth, 1993).

Obstetrical problems may damage the brain mechanisms that inhibit aggressive behavior or cause hyperactivity, impulsivity, and cognitive deficits that can trigger aggressive behavior (Reiss and Roth, 1993). Several studies have linked serious delinquency and criminal offenses to perinatal trauma, and there is even a study connecting children's temper tantrums to a difficult delivery (Raine, 1993).

Problems with brain function

Problems with brain function—with attention, language, and memory in particular—are very common in students with challenging behavior (Reiss and Roth, 1993). Sometimes they take the form of recognizable disabilities, and once a disability has been properly assessed, a student becomes eligible for special education services. But all too often, these problems remain undiagnosed or undiagnosable, and in the meantime a teacher must find her own solutions. (For tips on teaching children with disabilities, see Chapter 12.)

Attention deficit hyperactivity disorder (ADHD)

Challenging behavior very often appears in the company of hyperactivity or inattention (Rutter et al., 1998)—the hallmarks of ADHD (attention deficit hyperactivity disorder, sometimes called attention deficit disorder or ADD). A psychiatric and developmental disorder with a strong genetic base, ADHD has one additional core symptom—impulsivity—that combines with hyperactivity and inattention to create three different forms of the disorder (DuPaul and Stoner, 2003):

1. *Predominantly inattentive type.* Students in this category have memory problems and difficulty focusing their attention. They daydream, make careless mistakes, and forget and lose things.
2. *Predominantly hyperactive-impulsive type.* Quick to anger when they're frustrated or reprimanded, children with this type find it hard to sit still and wait their turn. They leap before they look, and although they know what they should and shouldn't do, they just can't control themselves.
3. *Combination type.* Students with the full-blown disorder exhibit all of its symptoms. Their behavior can be overactive, inattentive, impulsive, noncompliant, and aggressive.

Attention deficit hyperactivity disorder affects 3 to 7 percent of school-age children (American Psychiatric Association, 2000), enough to put one student with ADHD in every classroom in the United States (Agency for Health Care Policy and Research, 1999). It is three times more prevalent in boys than in girls (National Institute of Mental Health [NIMH], 2001) and is frequently accompanied by learning disabilities (American Psychiatric Association, 2000; Schettler et al., 2000). Russell A. Barkley, a leading authority on ADHD, has suggested that the disorder stems from a deficit in the brain's capacity to inhibit behavior, resulting in compromised development of executive functions (discussed next).

In addition to learning problems, children with ADHD have trouble relating to their peers. They start arguments and fights, lose their tempers, struggle to join groups and have conversations, and use aggression to deal with conflict. As a consequence, they often have no friends and are rejected by their classmates (DuPaul and Stoner, 2003).

It is important to know that ADHD is sometimes mistakenly diagnosed when a child has been exposed to violence and is suffering from posttraumatic stress disorder, which we explain on page 39.

Executive functions

Students with challenging behavior often have another subtle brain problem: Their executive functions do not work properly. Any goal-directed or problem-solving activity, from entering a game at recess to studying for a test, requires the use of these interdependent skills, which include:

- Planning and organizing behavior, including anticipating problems and figuring out strategies to cope with them
- Sequencing behavior

- Sustaining attention and concentration
- Being flexible and able to shift from one mindset to another
- Inhibiting responses
- Self-monitoring
- Taking the perspective of others (Moffitt, 1997; Shonkoff and Phillips, 2000)

When their executive functions are out of kilter, students can't consciously regulate their thoughts, actions, and emotions as well as they need to, and they tend to act impulsively, without considering the impact on others (Moffitt, 1997). In adolescence, difficulty with executive function can lead to aggressive behavior, mood swings, thoughts of suicide, problems with attention, and risk-taking behavior such as drug and alcohol use (Zelazo, 2005). Students with ADHD and autistic spectrum disorder often have weak executive functions.

Learning disabilities

Children with learning disabilities have trouble with learning and language-based skills—reading, writing, listening, speaking, reasoning, and computation. As a result, they find academics very tough, despite having IQs that are average or above (National Center for Learning Disabilities, n.d.).

Like students with ADHD, they struggle with cognitive difficulties. It is hard for them to focus; they have problems with auditory and visual-spatial-organizational perception (which may cause clumsiness or communication difficulties); their memory doesn't function properly (Swanson, 2000); and their thinking skills and information processing are impaired—for example, they may need extra help relating new information to old or applying it in different situations (Friend, 2005). Because they often feel responsible for their failures but not their successes, they are prone to *learned helplessness* and may give up on a task before they even begin (Fulk, Brigham, and Lohman, 1998). Students can also have *nonverbal learning disabilities*, which cause difficulties with interpersonal relationships, problem solving, adaptability, planning, and organization (Sands and Schwartz, 2000).

Learning disabilities put children at high risk for challenging behavior. For a start, they encounter frustration more often than most of us (Farmer, 2000). Then their imperfect perception causes problems—if they can't fully hear or understand what's said, they're liable to trip up in social situations (Kavale and Forness, 1996). It is no wonder they often have low self-esteem, are more likely to be rejected by their classmates (Pavri and Luftig, 2000), and become verbally or physically aggressive (Haager and Klingner, 2005).

Although *sensory integration dysfunction* isn't formally designated as a learning disability, many children with learning disabilities (and children with autism spectrum disorder) have trouble sorting out and integrating all the sensory information that comes their way (Emmons and Anderson, n.d.; Sensory Integration International, n.d.). Some hardly seem to notice sensory input; others overreact and develop strong preferences for such items as socks without seams that don't overwhelm their extra-sensitive systems (Greene, 1998). They are liable to be distractible and hyperactive (Ayres, 1979), and they often seem clumsy and uncoordinated, forever tripping and bumping their way through life (Kazdin, 1995; Moffitt, 1997).

Language and verbal skills are utterly essential, and it is easy to see how students without them might turn to challenging behavior. In *The Explosive Child* (1998), child psychologist Ross W. Greene describes some of the barriers that such children encounter.

- *Understanding.* When a child doesn't understand the words of the people around her, she becomes confused and frustrated and finds it hard to respond appropriately.
- *Categorizing, labeling, and storing emotions and previous experiences in language.* If a child can't use language to classify and store her feelings and experience, she doesn't really know how she feels or what she did the last time she felt this way.
- *Thinking things through in language.* When a child can't use words to think things through, she can't figure out what to do, even when she knows what she's feeling.
- *Expressing complicated feelings, thoughts, and ideas.* A child may have trouble going beyond simple language to articulate what's bothering her.

Language and speech disorders

Studies report a 50 percent overlap between language delays and behavior problems (Campbell, 1990). Psychologists often find unsuspected language disorders among the children referred to them with challenging behavior (Campbell, 1990), and language specialists find behavior problems among children referred to them with language delays (Coie and Dodge, 1998). According to psychologist Terrie E. Moffitt, "The link between verbal impairment and antisocial outcomes is one of the largest and most robust effects in the study of antisocial behavior. The verbal deficits of antisocial children are pervasive, affecting their memory for verbal material and their ability to listen and read, to solve problems, and to speak and write" (1997, p. 132).

Besides scholastic problems, students with language or speech impairments have social and self-esteem difficulties. Often teased or isolated, they find it hard to develop social skills and make friends. Children also need language to convert the reassurances and instructions they get from adults into tools for self-control. If they don't really understand the words or principles involved, they may try out many varieties of misbehavior, eliciting punishment instead of positive responses from their parents and teachers. When using language is so difficult, problem behavior can be a much more effective way to get your point across.

Cognitive impairment

Cognitive impairment (which often results from fetal alcohol spectrum disorder) goes by many names, including *cognitive disabilities, developmental disabilities*, and *mental retardation*. It affects all cognitive functions, including thinking, learning, processing and using information, motor skills, complex reasoning, memory, and attention. Like children with ADHD, students with cognitive disabilities can't remember what needs to be done or how much time it takes to do it (Friend, 2005). They learn language more slowly, labor to grasp concepts, and fail to generalize what they've learned. Academics are difficult for them, but they can learn more than people usually anticipate if they work harder and practice more than their peers (Friend, 2005).

Children with cognitive disabilities are also at risk for social problems. Because they are usually immature, often miss social cues, and easily misinterpret others' actions, their classmates tend to reject them and they feel lonely and isolated (Farmer, 2000; Leffert, Siperstein, and Millikan, 2000).

Emotional and behavior disorders

Some experts estimate that up to 20 percent of children have emotional and behavior disorders (Costello et al., 1996), but just a small fraction receive special education services under IDEA's *emotional disturbance* designation (U.S. Department of Education, 2002). Boys are affected six to nine times as often as girls (U.S. Department of Health and Human Services, 1999).

There are two broad classes of emotional and behavior disorders:

1. *Externalizing disorders,* in which the student acts out or directs her feelings outwards. This group includes *oppositional defiant disorder,* where children behave in negative, hostile ways, losing their temper, arguing, defying, and refusing to comply; and *conduct disorder,* where students persistently break rules, bully others, and act aggressively (U.S. Department of Health and Human Services, 2003).
2. *Internalizing disorders,* in which the child withdraws or turns her feelings inward. Included here are *eating disorders; anxiety disorders,* such as *obsessive-compulsive disorder, posttraumatic stress disorder,* and *phobias;* and *mood disorders,* such as *depression, bipolar illness,* and *schizophrenia* (U.S. Department of Health and Human Services, 2003).

Students with emotional and behavior disorders often have ADHD, a learning disability, or difficulty with language as well (Benner, Nelson, and Epstein, 2002; Handwerk and Marshall, 1998). As a result, they have great trouble in the academic realm (Sutherland, Wheby, and Gunter, 2000) and problems with social skills and friendships (Cullinan, Evans, Epstein, and Ryser, 2003).

ENVIRONMENTAL RISK FACTORS

Everything in a child's environment—her family, peers, school, neighborhood, even her exposure to violence, television, and the state of mind of the greater society—presents potential risk factors for challenging behavior. We've arranged these various risk factors as if each could stand alone, starting with the closest to the child and moving to the most distant, but the truth is that these factors continually overlap and interact with one another. Perhaps the best example of this is poverty, which affects virtually all of the others, including the biological risk factors.

Family factors and parenting style

Because parents play so vital a role in their children's development, they are an easy target whenever challenging behavior appears on the scene. Parenting is difficult and complicated work that requires a vast amount of time and energy—which are in short supply in many families. It is important for teachers to understand the parents' role in challenging behavior, but it is equally important not to blame them. It is far better to become their partners.

Any life circumstance that hinders a parent's well-being can put children at risk, including:

- A mother who had her first child when she was very young (Haapasalo and Tremblay, 1994)
- Parents with little education (Coie and Dodge, 1998)
- A parent with mental illness, especially a mother who's depressed (Shonkoff and Phillips, 2000)
- A parent who is abusing alcohol or drugs (Farrington, 1991)
- A parent with antisocial or criminal behavior (Farrington, 1991; Frick et al., 1991)
- Four or more children in the family (Farrington, 1991; Raine, 1993)

Indirectly, all these factors influence the parent–child relationship, the first line of defense against later aggressive behavior. According to *attachment theory*, first described by John Bowlby (1969/1982) and Mary Ainsworth (Ainsworth, Blehar, Waters, and Wall, 1978), a *secure attachment* to a sensitive and responsive primary caregiver provides the foundation for a child's emotional development, enabling her to learn to regulate and express her feelings, cope with stress, and see herself as an effective and lovable person. But when the primary caregiver is unavailable, unpredictable, insensitive, or rejecting, the child forms an *insecure attachment;* and she doesn't trust adults to care for her or help her organize her world, has difficulty regulating her emotions, and feels ineffectual and unworthy of love. Because the parent–child relationship acts as a prototype for the child's future relationships (Bowlby, 1969/1982), children with an insecure attachment have trouble getting along with their peers and teachers at school, and their behavior is often challenging and aggressive (Greenberg, Speltz, and DeKlyen, 1993; Renken, Egeland, Marvinney, Mangelsdorf, and Sroufe, 1989). For more about attachment, see Chapter 5.

Inappropriate parenting practices continue to increase the risk of challenging behavior as children grow older. When parents aren't involved with their children, don't respond warmly to them, don't supervise them properly, and use harsh and inconsistent discipline, the children may react with defiant, aggressive, impulsive behaviors (Coie, 1996; Eron, Huesmann, and Zelli, 1991; Haapasalo and Tremblay, 1994; Raine, 1993; Statistics Canada, 2005).

Gerald R. Patterson of the Oregon Social Learning Center has documented a cycle of interaction between parent and child that he calls "coercive" (1982, 1995). It can begin with a relatively trivial demand, such as a parent asking a child to do, or not do, something. The child ignores the request or refuses to comply. Then the parent responds more aggressively, scolding, nagging, or pleading; the child again refuses, whining, or talking back. The exchanges escalate to yelling and threats, hitting and temper tantrums, until the parent finally gives up and gives in—or explodes into violence—and then the child stops, too.

When the parents give in, which is most of the time, they are rewarding their child's negative behavior and increasing the chances she'll behave the same way again. At the same time, the child is reinforcing the parents by ceasing her own negative behavior (Coie and Dodge, 1998).

E conomists John Donahue and Steven Levitt (2001) have an interesting explanation for the dramatic drop in crime across the United States during the 1990s. They attribute half of it to *Roe v. Wade*, the 1973 Supreme Court decision legalizing abortion.

Donahue and Levitt conclude that children who are wanted are less likely to commit crimes. The peak years for criminal activity are 18 to 24 years, and when the children born in the era of legalized abortion started to turn 18, crime rates began to fall. The rate decreased first in the states that first made abortion legal.

Although the study took into account factors such as rates of imprisonment, number of police, and the state of the economy, the findings have stirred up considerable controversy.

When the parents explode, they are modeling the use of aggression as a way to solve problems. The child may do as they ask, but she is more likely to feel hostile toward them and to become aggressive with both parents and peers in the future, especially if they don't have a warm relationship (Coie and Dodge, 1998). Each time the parents use this method it will be less effective, and they will probably use greater force, which may eventually lead to abuse (American Academy of Pediatrics, 1998).

Whether they give in or resort to violence, the parents become demoralized. To avoid unpleasantness, they interact with their child less and less, missing opportunities to help her gain the emotional, social, and cognitive skills she needs to make friends and succeed at school. They don't keep close track of her activities and whereabouts in elementary school; and as she moves on to middle school, they often don't know her friends, set or enforce a curfew, or pay attention to her academic performance. This abdication of vital parental functions may drive the child toward more deviant peers (Dodge and Pettit, 2003; Tolan, Gorman-Smith, and Henry, 2003).

Children who live in families where this coercive cycle is the norm arrive in school with well-polished antisocial behavior. Because they challenge the teacher and don't follow instructions, it's difficult for them to establish good relationships and learn basic skills, such as reading (Biglan, Brennan, Foster, and Holder, 2004).

It is important to remember, however, that parent–child interaction is a two-way street. The child's temperament strongly influences the way the people in her life react to her, and each parent responds according to his or her own temperament. If the fit between them isn't a good one, poor parenting may be the result.

Peer influences

As children grow older, they spend less time with their parents and more with their peers. During what Erik Erikson (1980) called the *competence versus inferiority* stage of psychosocial development, ages 6 to 12 years, children are learning to work and cooperate with others and beginning to see themselves through the eyes of their peers. Being liked and accepted is a crucial developmental task for this age. During Erikson's next developmental period, which begins at puberty and continues through age 18, children are working on *identity versus role confusion*. As they struggle to figure out who they are, explore relationships with the opposite sex, try to set boundaries, and gain autonomy, their agemates play an increasingly important role.

To find out what boys' friendships are really like, Thomas J. Dishion and his colleagues at the Oregon Social Learning Center (Dishion et al., 1995) interviewed and videotaped 13- and 14-year-old boys and their best friends. They found that boys with antisocial behavior often choose one another as friends, but their friendships satisfy them less and don't last as long as the friendships of boys who are well adjusted.

Why? The researchers learned that the boys acted bossy and coercive to one another, and when their friends treated them badly, they behaved badly right back. Boys with little antisocial behavior didn't rise to the bait of negative behavior.

In later work (Dishion, Spracklen, Andrews, and Patterson, 1996), the researchers discovered that the friendships between two boys with antisocial behavior contained nearly 3 times as much talk about rule breaking and antisocial activity as the friendships involving just one boy with antisocial behavior, and 4.5 times as much as friendships between two boys without aggressive behavior. While the peaceable boys laughed and reacted positively to conversation about ordinary topics, pairs of boys with aggressive behavior laughed and responded positively when talk turned to breaking rules and inappropriate or illegal behavior, thereby reinforcing their antisocial values and behavior.

When they're confused about their identity, their insecurity rises and their self-esteem becomes dependent on the approval of their peers.

According to Abraham Maslow's hierarchy of needs, once a person's basic physiological and safety needs have been met, she will feel the need to have friends and to belong. Children with challenging behavior are often rejected by their peers, and in order to be accepted, they seek out other children who've been rejected or who think and behave the way they do. The result is that they limit their chances to learn social skills from their more competent peers and instead refine their aggressive, coercive behaviors (Snyder, 2002). By banding together, they provide role models for one another; reinforce one another's antisocial values, attitudes, and behavior; pressure one another to take part in antisocial activities; and create opportunities to try out new, more serious delinquent behavior (Dodge and Pettit, 2003; Rutter et al., 1998; Snyder, 2002). In short, a deviant peer group is a training ground for antisocial and delinquent behavior (Snyder, 2002).

Children with challenging and antisocial behavior tend to form friendships with children they meet outside of school in unsupervised settings, but ability tracking in school can also bring them together (Dishion, Andrews, and Crosby, 1995; Kellam, Ling, Merisca, Brown, and Ialongo, 1998).

School

In the 1970s, researchers began to notice that schools vary greatly in their rates of academic performance and emotional and behavioral problems (Rutter and Maughan, 2002). The reasons behind these differences, they found, lie not only in the proportion of disadvantaged and difficult pupils in the student body but also in the schools themselves. Since then, research has uncovered a number of complex factors that contribute to a school's character, including structural features such as resources and size; social organization and climate; the quality of teaching and teacher–pupil interactions; and federal, state, and local education policies.

A school's resources, which depend in large part on the community and school district, play an enormous role in a school's effectiveness. The wealthiest public schools spend at least 10 times as much as the poorest (Darling-Hammond, 2004), so it's no surprise that children in poor neighborhoods attend schools with larger class sizes and fewer books, computers, libraries, materials, supplies, extracurricular activities, counselors, and highly qualified teachers (Beam, 2004; Darling-Hammond, 2004). This shortfall affects students' behavior and their academic performance, which are often related (Gottfredson, n.d.). Sheppard H. Kellam and his colleagues (Kellam et al., 1998) found that boys and girls in poor communities were at greater risk of highly aggressive behavior in middle school, regardless of how they behaved in first grade.

A school's size has a profound influence on social organization and climate—and on behavior as well. In big schools (often defined as more than 400 pupils for elementary schools and more than 800 for middle and secondary schools [Cotton, 1996]), students can more easily become disenfranchised and socially isolated. When they feel they don't belong and nobody at school cares about them, they disengage from school life and cease to care about their own aspirations and performance (Gottfredson, n.d.). This disconnectedness, which by high school affects 40 to 60 percent of students (Klem and Connell, 2004), can have a substantial impact, increasing the risk of bullying, fighting, vandalism, and truancy as well as emotional distress, substance use, and early sexual activity (Blum, 2005).

The way a school is organized and run (including having clear behavioral expectations and rules that are consistently and fairly applied) also shapes school climate (Gottfredson et al., 2004). But it is a challenge for a school to be safe and caring at the same time. Columbine, Virginia Tech, and other school shootings create an environment of fear, especially for students who are already at risk. Schools across the country rely on police, metal detectors, and video cameras to protect their premises from antisocial behavior, drugs, and weapons (Public Agenda, 2004; DeVoe, Peter, Noonan, Snyder, and Baum, 2005), but these strategies can frighten students, destroy trust, and turn the school into a military camp. Rigid, formal discipline and harsh punishment policies such as zero tolerance have a similar effect. Automatic suspensions and expulsions discourage communication and alienate students (Fletcher, 2002). In the face of these inflexible rules, students don't feel comfortable reporting bullying, harassment, violence, or threats (Newman, 2004), making it extremely difficult to address such activity.

What happens inside the classroom matters, too. A chaotic, disruptive atmosphere has long-term effects on children's behavior (Kellam et al., 1998), but over-

Caught in the Middle

Middle and junior high schools provide fertile ground for disorder and crime, studies show (Gottfredson et al., 2004). The transition from elementary school disrupts social networks, making students feel isolated and anonymous. In the bigger new school, competition becomes more intense, teachers seem less friendly and caring, and a smaller proportion of students participate in extracurricular activities (Biglan et al., 2004; Cotton, 1996). As a result, students may turn to cliques and gangs for support (Cotton, 1996; Klonsky, n.d.).

control is not the solution either. Corporal punishment is still allowed in 22 states, and in 2002–2003, more than 300,000 children were subjected to it ("Corporal punishment," 2005), damaging their self-image and academic achievement and stirring up disruptive and violent behavior (American Academy of Pediatrics, Committee on School Health, 2000). Emotional abuse—controlling students through fear and intimidation, bullying, sarcasm, ridicule, or humiliation—is equally harmful and affects every child in the classroom (Hyman and Snook, 1999).

Teachers' expectations have a strong influence on children's behavior (Berk, 2000). In fact, a conflictual relationship with a teacher sets a child up for learning problems (Ladd and Burgess, 2001), poor academic performance (Hamre and Pianta, 2001), misconduct, suspension, and aggressive behavior with peers (Ladd and Burgess, 1999).

The practice of ability tracking, widespread in poor school districts, reinforces feelings of anger, rejection, and disaffection among students (Dahlberg, 1998) and widens both the academic and the behavior gap (Kellam et al., 1998). Because students rarely jump from one track to another, they are stigmatized; and each passing year compounds the problem, creating many classrooms with a persistently aggressive, disruptive atmosphere.

State and local policies and laws such as the federal No Child Left Behind Act of 2002 also have a powerful effect on schools. When the results of a test determine whether a child will move from one grade to the next or whether a school will be taken over by the state, the stakes are very high indeed. To raise their scores on these "high-stakes tests," schools change their priorities and their programs. In the poorest schools in particular (Association for Supervision and Curriculum Development, 2004), teachers are spending more time on reading, writing, math, and science (the subjects tested under No Child Left Behind) and cutting back on subjects not tested—arts, gym, social studies, creative writing, computers, foreign languages, recess, and conflict resolution programs (Mathews, 2005; Perkins-Gough, 2004; Tracey, 2005; Wallis, 2003; Wood, 2004). Test preparation is replacing projects, themes, field trips, and hands-on, experiential learning—the ways that children learn best (Ganesh and Surbeck, 2005; Wood, 2004). One consequence of this narrow focus is enormous stress on everyone from the principal on down; another is an increase in behavior problems (Wallis, 2003).

Poverty and the conditions surrounding it

Because poverty acts on families, peers, schools, and neighborhoods as well as individuals, it has an enormous impact on children's lives and puts them at risk for challenging behavior even before they are born. More than 35 percent of children who live in poor families have seven or more risk factors—versus 7 percent of those who live in wealthy families (Sameroff and Fiese, 2000).

Good prenatal care is often not available to low-income families. In New York City's poorer districts, for example, the infant mortality rate in 2003 rose as high as 12.2 deaths per 1,000 live births, versus a rate of under 3 deaths per 1,000 live births in the city's wealthier sections (New York City Department of Health and Mental Hygiene, 2005). Babies in poor families also confront a higher risk of prematurity, low birthweight, and neurological damage (Sampson, 1997), all players in challenging behavior.

E ven at very low levels, lead in a child's body poisons the developing brain and body. Through its link to hyperactivity, attention deficits, impulsivity, learning disabilities, and lowered IQ (Raine, 1993), lead puts children at high risk of aggressive, delinquent, and criminal behavior (Needleman, Riess, Tobin, Biesecker, and Greenhouse, 1996; Wasserman, Staghezza-Jaramillo, Shrout, Popovac, and Graziano, 1998).

Because it is found in dust, old lead-based paint, water pipes, improperly glazed dishes, and lead-based gasoline embedded in the soil, lead poses an especially potent threat to pregnant women and children living in old housing and poor inner-city neighborhoods (Shonkoff and Phillips, 2000). Although the Centers for Disease Control and Prevention set 10 micrograms of lead per deciliter of blood as an acceptable level, research shows that any amount inflicts serious harm. Each year 400,000 children—a disproportionate number of whom are African American and/or poor—test above the "acceptable" limit (Brody, 2006; Federal Interagency Forum on Child and Family Statistics, 2006).

Malnutrition poses another serious danger. For optimal brain development, a child needs adequate nutrition both before birth and during the first two or three years of life, but some 13 million American children don't get enough to eat (Federal Interagency Forum on Child and Family Statistics, 2005). Malnutrition seems to hit hardest in the social and emotional realms (Shonkoff and Phillips, 2000). One study found that malnourished 3-year-olds are predisposed to neurocognitive deficits, which in turn make them prone to behavior problems throughout childhood and adolescence (Liu, Raine, Venables, and Mednick, 2004). Children who suffer from iron deficiency, which often accompanies malnutrition, score lower on tests of mental and motor development in their elementary school and early teen years. Poor and minority children are at particular risk (Shonkoff and Phillips, 2000).

Poverty brings a high level of stress to families' lives—nonstop anxiety about food, housing, jobs, health care, safety, and more. In high-poverty urban neighborhoods, families often have little or no social support, formal or informal. It is hard to make and keep friends when you're living in a gigantic housing project, when people move all the time and you don't know your neighbors, when one person carries the full responsibility for the family, or when people are afraid to go to church, the local store, even to school. As a result, parenting becomes extremely arduous: There is no one to keep an eye on anyone else's children or property, it's nearly impossible to supervise adolescents, and as children grow, the neighborhood offers them little in the way of access to resources, health and recreational services, and mainstream role models and opportunities. This "social disorganization" (Sampson, 1997), as the sociologists call it, is becoming more and more common in U.S. inner cities (Garbarino, 1999).

About 27 percent of poor African American children and 20 percent of poor Latino American children live in the inner city, compared with 3 percent of poor European American children (Shonkoff and Phillips, 2000). A family who belongs to a minority group faces the additional stress of racial discrimination, which damages self-esteem and provokes feelings of rage and shame (Garbarino, 1999).

It is hard to disentangle the many factors that influence the outcomes of children growing up in poverty, but a natural experiment in North Carolina gave researchers a rare glimpse of the difference money can make (Costello, Compton, Keeler, and Angold, 2003). Right in the middle of the Great Smoky Mountains Study, an eight-year project involving 1,400 school-age children, a casino opened up on the Native American reservation where a quarter of the children in the study lived. By agreement, every six months the families on the reserve received a portion of the profits. Fourteen percent of them were able to climb out of poverty, and their children showed a remarkable 40 percent decrease in serious behavior problems—equal to the rate of children who'd never been poor.

When the scientists tested factors that might account for this dramatic drop, they found just one: Parents who were no longer poor could provide better supervision for their children. Money gave them time—a scarce resource for people in poverty.

Exposure to violence

Violence is endemic in American life and culture. Children run into it everywhere—in the news, in games and sports, in adult conversation, in Saturday morning cartoons, even in their own lives.

In a study in Washington, DC, researchers Esther Jenkins and Carl Bell (1997) found that 31 percent of the fifth- and sixth-graders in their sample had witnessed a shooting, 17 percent had seen a stabbing, and the majority knew either the victim or the perpetrator. When child psychiatrist and public health expert Felton Earls and his colleagues interviewed more than 1,000 12- to 15-year-olds in Chicago (Bingenheimer, Brennan, and Earls, 2005; Holden, 2005), they found that 23 percent had been exposed to gun violence in the last 12 months—and that their exposure doubled the chances these teens would participate in gun violence themselves.

A close encounter with violence makes a deep and powerful impression on children, even when they aren't its victims (Jenkins and Bell, 1997). It changes the way they view the world and "may change the value they place on life itself," according to Betsy Groves and Barry Zuckerman of the Boston Medical Center School of Medicine, who found that it affects children's ability "to learn, to establish relationships with others, and to cope with stress" (1997, p. 183). In addition to feeling unsafe, frightened, vulnerable, anxious, and depressed, some children exhibit symptoms of *posttraumatic stress disorder*. They may become hostile and irritable, and have trouble paying attention, remembering things, and relating to others. They may have flashbacks where they replay the violent incident over and over in their minds, or they may try to avoid thinking about it, experience emotional numbing, or become hyperalert (Jenkins and Bell, 1997; Osofsky, 1997). Many feel more comfortable striking out than they do waiting around for something to happen (Groves, 2002). Parents, who have the most power to help, may also be traumatized and fail to recognize and respond to their children's distress (Osofsky, 1997).

Violence that takes place within the child's family is the most toxic, says Groves (2002). An estimated 3 to 10 million children witness physical assaults between their parents each year (National Resource Center on Domestic Violence, 2002). Even verbal conflict upsets children, and when it's combined with physical conflict it contributes to both emotional problems and challenging behavior (Zeanah and Scheeringa, 1997; Yoshikawa, 1994). In tracking the lives of more than 7,000 young Canadians, the National Longitudinal Survey of Children and Youth (Moss, 2003) found that 43 percent of boys who witness violence at home go on to threaten, attack, or bully others within four years (versus 25 percent of boys who live in more tranquil households).

Abuse and neglect are also shockingly common—approximately 2.9 million cases involving 5.5 million children were reported in the United States in 2003 (U.S. Department of Health and Human Services, Administration on Children, Youth and Families, 2005). Pacific Island, Native American, and African American children are especially at risk. Children who are abused are often insecurely attached to their caregivers (Shonkoff and Phillips, 2000), with whom their behavior is angry, frustrated, and noncompliant. They also act aggressively with their peers, and instead of trying to comfort a friend in distress, they respond with fear, lash out with attacks and anger, or act totally unconcerned.

In addition to their psychological injuries, children who are abused have physical injuries. In infants, abuse accounts for most of the head injuries, which can affect judgment, self-control, empathy, social skills, and problem-solving skills (Raine, 1993). Research connects head injuries firmly to violent and aggressive behavior later on: One study of 15 young murderers on death row found that all of them had had severe head injuries (Raine, 1993).

Violent media

Some experts believe that when it comes to violence, the media exert as much influence as family and peers (Levin, 1998; Slaby, 1997). Eric Harris and Dylan Klebold provide vivid anecdotal evidence for this opinion: The teenagers who killed 13 students and teachers at Columbine High School in Littleton, Colorado, in 1999 played the video game "Doom" obsessively (Bai, 1999).

Almost 70 percent of youngsters aged 8 to 18 years have a television set in their bedroom, and they log an average of 4½ hours a day watching television, videos, DVDs, and movies, as well as an hour playing computer and video games (Rideout, Roberts, and Foehr, 2005). African American children put in the most screen time, European Americans spend the least, and Hispanic Americans fall somewhere between.

In 1972, the Surgeon General's Scientific Advisory Committee on Television and Social Behavior concluded that there is a direct, causal link between seeing violence on television and aggressive behavior. In 2000, six major professional societies—including the American Medical Association, the American Academy of Pediatrics, and the American Psychiatric Association—officially concurred, saying that "the data point overwhelmingly to a causal connection between media violence and aggressive behavior in some children" ("Joint statement," 2000).

Meta-reviews of the most rigorous studies indicate that the effects of television violence are very strong (Coie and Dodge, 1998) and that frequent viewing can shape and reinforce children's cognitive scripts about violence (Rutter et al., 1998). Researchers (Coie and Dodge, 1998; Donnerstein, Slaby, and Eron, 1994; Slaby, 1997) have documented at least four effects:

1. *Aggressor effect.* Children, adolescents, and young adults who watch violent media are more likely to engage in aggressive behavior, especially if they identify with aggressive characters or find the violence realistic and relevant to their own lives. The more they watch, the more aggressive their behavior is likely to

Violence is endemic in American life and culture.

become and the more likely they are to think that aggression is an acceptable way to resolve conflict (Johnson, Cohen, Smailes, Kasen, and Brook, 2002).

2. *Victim effect.* Watching television violence makes some children more fearful. Most vulnerable are those who identify with the victim and perceive the violence as realistic. Heavy viewers of violence can acquire "mean-world syndrome," mistrusting people and seeing the world as more dangerous than it really is.

3. *Bystander effect.* Watching media violence desensitizes children and leads them to think that violence is normal, especially when programs present it as acceptable and without consequences. Instead of responding to real-life pain and suffering with sympathy, child viewers of violence remain indifferent. In one

experiment, children who had watched a violent program were far less likely to intervene or call for help when fighting broke out among the children they were babysitting (Thomas and Drabman, 1975).

4. *Increased appetite effect.* When television violence is fun and exciting, children crave more of it. Children who behave aggressively watch more violent television in order to justify their behavior.

Recent evidence links early television viewing with bullying in school-age children (Zimmerman, Glew, Christakis, and Katon, 2005) and with impulsive behavior and attentional and organizational problems at age 7 (Christakis, Zimmerman, DiGiuseppe, and McCarty, 2004). Prosocial television has prosocial effects, but there is relatively little of it to be seen (Donnerstein et al., 1994; Murray, 1997).

Nearly 80 percent of video games that carry an "E" rating (for everyone) contain violence (Children Now, 2001), and they also have a serious impact: Meta-analyses of research confirm that playing violent video games increases aggressive thoughts, feelings, and behavior and decreases prosocial behavior (Anderson, 2004; Anderson and Bushman, 2001). In one study, eighth- and ninth-graders who played more violent video games fought more with their peers and argued more with their teachers (Gentile, Lynch, Linder, and Walsh, 2004).

Turbulent times

Violence in the lives of children takes on a new meaning during a national crisis. On September 11, 2001, life in the United States changed forever. The extraordinary events of that day shattered everyone's sense of safety and security.

Human-made catastrophes, such as the Oklahoma City bombing in 1995 and the September 11 terrorist attacks on New York and the Pentagon, and natural disasters, such as Hurricane Katrina in 2005 and the California fires in 2007, create a sense of helplessness and make people feel frightened, especially when they happen close to home. Because children depend on the adults around them to make them feel safe, they are particularly vulnerable. Their ability to recover is intimately connected to the ability of their families and teachers to comfort and reassure them.

Several factors influence a child's reaction to a disaster (Hagan and The Committee on Psychosocial Aspects of Child and Family Health, 2005): her age (both chronological and developmental), her temperament, her family's response to the event, the nature of the disaster itself (human-made disasters are psychologically more devastating), and how close she is to the disaster. Children who've lost family or friends or witnessed the event in person will be the hardest hit, but seeing the event on television can also provoke a serious reaction. Boys act more aggressively and take longer to recover; girls express their feelings in words and ask more questions (Hagan and The Committee, 2005).

Each child is different, but in general children respond to a disaster in distinct stages (Hagan and The Committee, 2005). Immediately afterwards, they feel frightened and unsafe; a few days or weeks later, they may feel anxious, fearful, sad, apathetic, hostile, or aggressive. They may become hypervigilant, restless, and unable to concentrate, and they may have headaches, stomachaches, and difficulty sleeping. They're also liable to regress to behaviors they used when they were younger, such as bed-wetting and clinging to their parents. To cope with these feelings, they may talk about the disaster and re-create it in their games and drawings.

Younger school-age children tend to focus on the details of the tragedy; older students, with more cognitive maturity, want to understand why it happened and tend to feel empathy for the families involved. Adolescents struggling to find their own identity are usually depressed and anxious but may also withdraw, hide their reactions, or try risk-taking behaviors, such as using drugs. They are especially vulnerable to lasting behavioral and emotional problems (Hagan and The Committee, 2005).

Extremely sensitive students and those already burdened with stress will have a particularly hard time. Children who've experienced previous loss and trauma (immigrant children, for example), children whose families are too upset and fearful to provide the reassurance they need, and children who were barely coping in the period before the disaster may be overwhelmed. Students whose behavior was already out of control may deteriorate further. Children who are surrounded by angry people looking for revenge may respond with anger that comes to the fore in their interactions with their peers. In all of these cases, challenging behavior is often the result. If these reactions continue and students cannot function, they are at risk of posttraumatic stress disorder and later violent behavior (Hagan and The Committee, 2005).

Understanding risk

After reading this chapter you might feel that it's a miracle if any child manages to behave appropriately. But remember that these risks have a cumulative effect. Each one you can counteract or help a child avoid will make a substantial difference in her ability to cope. The simple fact that you understand more about who she is should increase your empathy and enhance the quality of your relationship—and the strength of your influence.

WHAT DO YOU THINK?

1. In this chapter we've separated biological risk factors and environmental risk factors, but in reality they are inextricably intertwined. Can you think of some examples of how both types of risk factors interact?

2. Temperamental traits are an important influence on the way people relate to one another. How would you describe your own emotional reactivity and your ability to control it? How do these traits affect your response to others' behavior in your own life? How do they affect your response to inappropriate behavior in your students?

3. How would you help students at risk prepare to take high-stakes tests? How would you balance the pressure the school is under with your knowledge of how children learn best?

4. What kinds of stress do families who live in poverty encounter? How does family stress make parenting a more difficult job?

5. Some experts think the media play an extremely important role in increasing aggressive behavior. What do you think? How have the news, films, and television shaped your attitudes toward other people and the world?

After Cho Seung-Hui killed 33 people, including himself, at Virginia Tech on April 16, 2007, investigators discovered that during his short life the 23-year-old senior had presented a number of obvious signs warning of his unstable state of mind. The trouble was that no one knew them all, and the authorities didn't discern a pattern or take any action.

- In his early life in Korea, Cho spoke little, either at home or with other children (Virginia Tech Review Panel, 2007). He continued to be isolated and uncommunicative when the family moved to the United States, although he had some therapy in middle school.
- In high school, Cho was diagnosed with selective mutism, an anxiety disorder, and given special education services. After the Columbine shootings, he had suicidal and homicidal thoughts, which the school handled appropriately, working closely with the family and his outside therapist and psychiatrist (Virginia Tech Review Panel, 2007).
- During Cho's junior year at Virginia Tech, the campus police received several reports about his behavior. One woman complained about his unwelcome attempts to communicate with her, and another asked police to stop his annoying text messaging; but neither woman pressed charges. Later, Cho's roommate informed police that Cho might be suicidal (Virginia Tech Review Panel, 2007). The police referred him to an off-campus mental health agency, where a social worker recommended involuntary commitment. However, an evaluation at a psychiatric hospital concluded he was mentally ill but not an imminent danger to himself or others. He did not obtain the out-patient treatment ordered by the court (Virginia Tech Review Panel, 2007).
- In 2005 and 2006, several members of the English department, where Cho was a major, grew alarmed by both his behavior and his writings (Virginia Tech Review Panel, 2007). He wore reflective sunglasses, introduced himself as "Question Mark," took photos of women from under his desk, and frightened his classmates, some of whom refused to attend class if he was present. His work contained extreme violence and profanity but not explicit threats. Several of his professors reported their concerns to the English department and to university authorities.
- Cho was a loner who had no friends, ate meals alone, played basketball and watched movies by himself, and rarely spoke to his roommates (Virginia Tech Review Panel, 2007). According to sociologist Katherine S. Newman, author of *Rampage: The Social Roots of School Shootings* (2004), such marginalization is a necessary factor in school shootings. Cho's psychological problems magnified his sense of isolation and diminished his ability to cope with everyday life. Even a small slight from a girl might deliver a crushing blow.

Newman (2004) suggests that eliminating even one factor underlying a school shooting will reduce the chances of another rampage. She writes, "First, *academic, counseling, and disciplinary records should be maintained across the bureaucratic boundaries that separate different grades and different schools in the same district.* The commitment to second chances, and the desire to avoid labeling kids in ways that prejudice future teachers is socially worthy, but it exacts too high a cost" (p. 279, italics in original). Newman argues that a more open system would make it possible to spot patterns of behavior and to get help for students who need it.

Privacy laws must balance a person's right to privacy against individual and public health and safety. But they allow officials to disclose information in a potentially dangerous situation. The difficulty is in knowing when a situation is potentially dangerous.

What do you think and what would you do? Is it a good idea for school counselors, administrators, or teachers to have access to a student's records? How complete should these records be? How do you think that knowing a student's previous history of problem behavior would affect your attitude toward him? How would it affect your responses to his behavior and any intervention you might design? How would you balance these conflicting interests?

DuPaul, G. J., & Stoner, G. (2003). *ADHD in the schools: Assessment and intervention strategies* (2nd ed.). New York: Guilford.

Flick, G. L. (1998). *ADD/ADHD behavior-change resource kit: Ready-to-use strategies & activities for helping children with attention deficit disorder.* West Nyack, NJ: Center for Applied Research in Education.

Kleinfeld, J., & Wescott, S. (1993). *Fantastic Antone succeeds! Experiences in educating children with fetal alcohol syndrome.* Fairbanks: University of Alaska Press.

Kranowitz, C. S. (2005). *The out-of-sync child: Recognizing and coping with sensory integrative dysfunction* (Rev. ed.). New York: Perigee.

Kristal, J. (2005). *The temperament perspective: Working with children's behavioral styles.* Baltimore: Brookes.

McCord, J. (Ed.). (1997). *Violence and childhood in the inner city.* New York: Cambridge University Press.

CHAPTER 3

Protective Factors

Challenging behavior is not inevitable, even when a child is at high risk. After decades of trying to figure out why things go wrong, researchers came up with the idea of trying to figure out why things go right, even in adversity. Child-development specialists, pediatricians, psychiatrists, psychologists, and sociologists set to work studying children who were growing up in difficult circumstances—in war, in poverty, in families where there is violence, abuse, or mental illness—to determine why some of them have the ability to develop successfully even when they encounter very high hurdles.

The researchers named this ability *resilience* (Masten and Coatsworth, 1998; Rutter, 2000; Werner, 2000), and found that it is associated with a series of *protective* or *opportunity factors* that counter the impact of the risk factors in a child's life. In general, the more opportunity factors there are and the better they balance the risk factors, the more likely it is that a child will meet the challenges in his life and turn out to be a competent and caring individual (Werner, 2000).

Risk factors have a tendency to pile up, each one bringing others in its wake. A child who can't read in third grade, for example, automatically runs a high risk of school failure, to say nothing of peer rejection and low self-esteem—which in turn raise his risk for aggressive behavior, delinquency, substance abuse, and gang membership. No teacher can change the fact that a family lives in poverty or a child's mother abused drugs when she was pregnant. But teachers can help the child (and maybe even his family) to deal with those risk factors more effectively. If we can bolster some of his protective factors early on, we may be able to minimize or even ward off some of the risks and divert the child onto an entirely different developmental trajectory (Masten and Coatsworth, 1998; Rutter, 1987).

The deeper researchers delve into the subject of resilience, the more complex it reveals itself to be. Resilience is not a static state; it is a dynamic, developmental process that takes place over time and depends heavily on context (Luthar, Cicchetti, and Becker, 2000). Protective factors may protect a child in some domains but not others (Luthar et al., 2000), at some times but not others (Howard, Dryden, and Johnson, 1999), at some levels of risk but not others (Luthar and Goldstein, 2004), for some outcomes but not others (Rutter, Giller, and Hagell,

1998), and in some cultural groups but not others (Cauce, Stewart, Rodriguez, Cochran, and Ginzler, 2003; Richards et al., 2004). Factors that protect children in one context may even render them more vulnerable in others (Luthar, 1999). Each child is an active agent in his own development, and resilience involves constant interactions between him and his environment (Masten, 2004). All of this makes it hard to generalize and next to impossible to say, "This factor is universal and works for everyone" (Fergus and Zimmer, 2005). On the other hand, it has become easier to say that there are many pathways to resilience (Luthar and Zelazo, 2003).

This chapter describes the three distinct waves of resilience research. In the first, investigators identified individual, family, and community factors that protect children from risk. In the second wave, researchers emphasized process, trying to figure out how these factors work. In the third wave, which is ongoing, biology and intervention entered the picture.

The first wave: What qualities help a child bounce back?

Initially, resilience researchers focused on identifying people with natural resilience and created a striking portrait of a child who seemed to emerge unscathed from beneath a stack of risk factors as tall as he was. His family and teachers described him as "very active, affectionate, . . . good-natured, and easy to deal with" (Werner, 2000, p. 120). He was extremely responsive to everyone and everything around him and had a wonderful ability to seek out and relate to other people (Osofsky and Thompson, 2000). As developmental psychologists Emmy E. Werner and Ruth S. Smith put it in *Vulnerable but Invincible* (1982), their pioneering study of resilience on the Hawaiian island of Kauai, "To the extent that children [are] able to elicit predominantly positive responses from their environment, they [are] found to be stress-resistant or 'resilient,' even when growing up in chronic poverty or in a family with a psychotic parent" (p. 158). Because almost anyone who meets such children will happily bend over backwards to help them out, they will probably have little need for challenging behavior.

But what about the children who elicit negative responses from their environment? They are especially vulnerable, and their behavior is far more likely to challenge us. The question is, How can teachers accept the vulnerable children for who they are and at the same time help them to become more resilient? What secrets of success do children with natural resilience hold, and how can we bottle them for everyone's use? The first wave of resilience researchers identified three sets of protective factors: some in the individual child, some in the family, and some in the community (Masten, 2004).

Individual factors

Children who exhibit resilience often have an outgoing, likable temperament and the ability to engage the people around them in a positive way. Because they get lots of practice, they communicate easily with others and they tend to be flexible and empathetic. They also have a good sense of humor (Rutter, 1987). Their intelligence is often above average, which enables them to do well at school (Masten and Coatsworth, 1998) and probably also means that their executive functions are in good working order. Their ability to pay attention, plan, think critically and creatively, and evaluate the consequences of their behavior makes them capable problem solvers (Curtis and Cicchetti, 2003; Rutter, 1987).

In addition, children who are resilient are able to regulate their emotions and behavior effectively and recover quickly from negative events and feelings (Curtis and Cicchetti, 2003). They have good control over their impulses and can do what needs to be done, even in difficult surroundings.

Children who are resilient seem to believe in their own worth and abilities. They have varied talents, interests, activities, and coping strategies that aren't narrowly gender stereotyped and choose or build environments that reinforce their dispositions and reward their competencies. Their outlook is optimistic, filled with hopes, goals, and aspirations for the future (Wyman, 2003). Strongly motivated to persevere and succeed (Masten, 2001), they possess what psychologists term an *internal locus of control*: They ascribe their success to their own efforts and abilities, not sheer luck (Brooks, 1994; Luthar, 1999).

In many cases, children with resilience have a spiritual side that adds meaning to their lives (Masten, 2004). Werner and Smith (1992) found that adults who'd overcome great obstacles often gave credit to their religious faith. A recent study showed that inner-city youth who practice their religion privately—by praying, reading religious literature, watching or listening to religious television or radio programs—have a lower rate of problem behavior (Pearce, Jones, Schwab-Stone, and Ruchkin, 2003).

Even a child with challenging behavior is likely to possess some of these attributes and skills in an embryonic or unconventional form, although it may take extra thought and insight on our part to dig them out. One key to enhancing resilience is to search for these strengths—what psychologist Robert B. Brooks calls "islands of competence" (1994, p. 549)—and use them to build skills and self-esteem. Instead of focusing on what a student does wrong, stop and think about his strengths and likable qualities, what he's good at, what positive contributions he can make, and how you can create opportunities for him to realize whatever he has to offer.

Family factors

There's little doubt that children's individual characteristics weigh heavily in creating resilience, but in the end the environment may carry even more weight (Luthar and Zelazo, 2003). The single most important protective factor for a child is a relationship

Pride and Prejudice

Experiences of discrimination and structural racism pose serious risks to the health and development of African American youth (Spencer, Fegley, and Harpalani, 2003).

In a longitudinal study of almost 600 African American adolescents, Margaret B. Spencer, Suzanne G. Fegley, and Vinay Harpalani (2003) found that Black pride helped boys cope successfully. Those who believed in the importance of African American history and culture had significantly higher scores on emotional well-being, felt more valued by others, had more positive feelings about the future, and perceived themselves as being more popular with their peers than boys who weren't interested in their racial heritage. Surprisingly, this didn't seem to hold true for girls.

There are some indications that ethnic pride may protect children in other cultural groups as well (Szalacha et al., 2003).

with a competent, caring person who is absolutely committed to him, whom he can love and trust in return. Families are on the front line here. Consistent, supportive, and responsive parenting—care that provides warmth, structure, high expectations, and age-appropriate monitoring (Masten et al., 1999)—protects children at various stages of development and with many kinds of risk (Luthar and Zelazo, 2003).

If parents can't provide this crucial bond, someone else can. What matters is that at least one loving and available person—a grandparent, an older sibling, a cousin—supports and accepts the child unconditionally (Rutter, 1987; Werner, 2000; Werner and Smith, 1992). This relationship lays the groundwork for a wide range of skills, including well-regulated emotions, a sense of self-efficacy (Yates, Egeland, and Sroufe, 2003), academic achievement, and sociability with peers (Masten et al., 1999).

For African American children in the inner city, family wields an especially great influence. Research shows that a warm, supportive mother–child relationship, a cohesive family, and a parent's involvement in school all lend a child some protection from risk (Brody, Kim, Murry, and Brown, 2004; Gorman-Smith, Henry, and Tolan, 2004). But unlike children in low-risk neighborhoods, African American children in the inner city clearly benefit from strict parental monitoring (Cauce et al., 2003). When families spend more time with their children, chaperone them closely, and limit the places they go and the time they spend with antisocial peers, children perform better at school (Cauce et al., 2003) and witness less violence, lowering their risk for delinquency as well as for emotional and behavioral problems (Cauce et al., 2003; Richards et al., 2004). In dangerous neighborhoods, this strong control is an adaptive parenting strategy, bringing order, predictability, and safety to children's daily lives (Luthar, 1999).

Community factors

The other people in a child's life and community also play a vital role in fostering resilience, and this support often comes to the child in the form of relationships. Like a parent, caring and competent teachers, neighbors, coaches, or friends can act as positive role models, make a child feel loved and valued, and even help compensate for a difficult family situation (Luthar and Zelazo, 2003). By believing in the child,

Poster Child

You know her as a phenomenally successful talk-show host, actor, and magazine publisher, but Oprah Winfrey is also a model of resilience. She overcame great adversity to become who she is today.

Her parents separated soon after her birth, leaving Oprah in the care of her grandmother on a Mississippi farm ("Oprah Winfrey," n.d.). At the age of 6 she moved to Milwaukee to join her mother. Their stormy relationship—and the sexual abuse she suffered at the hands of a teenage cousin and other male relatives and friends—led her to run away when she was 13.

Oprah ended up in Nashville with her father, and this was perhaps the turning point of her life. A strict disciplinarian, her father had high expectations for his daughter. Each week she had to read and write about a book; each day she had to learn five new vocabulary words or go without dinner. Although her father's parenting techniques may seem extreme to some, in fact this structure and close supervision acted as a protective factor for Oprah. She joined her school's drama club, won a college scholarship, and at age 19—while still a sophomore at Tennessee State University—became the co-anchor of Nashville's evening news program. The rest is history.

I n 1955, Emmy E. Werner and Ruth S. Smith (1982) began a landmark longitudinal study of 698 newborns on the island of Kauai in Hawaii. The fathers of the children were mostly semi-skilled or unskilled laborers, many of their mothers didn't graduate from high school, and about half of the families lived in chronic poverty.

Despite these risk factors, two-thirds of the children became healthy adolescents and adults. Among them were 72 children who faced enormous obstacles—four or more risk factors before the age of 2—who nonetheless turned into "competent, confident, and caring adults" (Werner, 2000, p. 119).

"When asked who helped them succeed against the odds, the resilient children, youth, and adults in the study . . . overwhelmingly and exclusively gave credit to members of their extended family (grandparents, siblings, aunts, or uncles), to neighbors and teachers who were confidantes and role models, and to mentors in voluntary associations, such as 4H, the YMCA or YWCA, and church groups," write Werner and J. L. Johnson (1999, p. 263).

expecting a lot of him, and supporting him as he extends his reach, a caring adult can help him believe in himself, develop competence and confidence, and expand his ability to cope with stress (National Crime Prevention Council Canada, 1995). Over and over again, the children of Kauai pointed to favorite teachers as important influences in their lives (Werner, 2000).

Support from teachers is especially effective for children in poverty (Luthar et al., 2000) and children with learning disabilities (Margalit, 2003). One study found that adolescents who were exposed to violence functioned more adaptively when they had helpful teachers (Ozer and Weinstein, 2004).

A strong bond to school—which may be the only safe haven in the lives of some children—protects them against a wide range of risks, including aggressive behavior and academic failure (Hawkins, Catalano, Kosterman, Abbott, and Hill, 1999). Researchers have identified several factors that increase school bonding—proactive classroom management, interactive teaching, reinforcement of positive social behavior, teaching social and problem-solving skills, and giving students lots of opportunities to participate actively through cooperative learning groups—and have begun to use them in interventions such as the Seattle Social Development Project, where they've had enduring positive effects (Hawkins et al., 1999).

Structured after-school activities such as clubs, sports, music, and religious groups also help students feel connected to the community and its values and lower their risks (Wyman, 2003). The older children get, the more unsupervised time they have on their hands, and when they can use this time productively, learning new skills and making friends who have prosocial values and similar interests, they have less desire—as well as less time—to seek out antisocial activities.

Peers can definitely furnish protection. With a friend, a child can experience intimacy, trust, and support; and being an accepted member of a group diminishes the risk of aggressive behavior posed by poverty, marital conflict in the home, and harsh discipline (Crises, Pettit, Bates, Dodge, and Lapp, 2002). Peers can meet needs and teach skills when a family isn't up to the job, and they may help a student develop more positive views of teachers and school (Criss et al., 2002). Friendship is especially helpful for children who've been maltreated (Bolger and Patterson, 2003) and children with learning disabilities (Miller, 2002).

Teachers, coaches, and friends can act as positive role models and make a child feel loved and valued.

It's important to manage peer groups and partners with care. Because students with challenging behavior tend to band together and encourage one another's anti-social tendencies, teachers and those who supervise after-school activities must ensure that the students who surround a child with problem behavior will model and teach appropriate ways to interact, react, and behave.

The second wave: How do protective factors work?

In the second wave of resilience research, investigators began to study not only protective factors but also the processes and mechanisms behind them (Luthar et al., 2000). Individuals respond to risk in a wide variety of ways, and multiple risk and protective factors are usually involved in any outcome. The child's own history and genetic endowment both play major roles, interacting and influencing one another extensively. During periods of rapid change—for example, when students enter adolescence or start middle school—new strengths and vulnerabilities appear

(Luthar et al., 2000), offering opportunities to redirect the course of development (Masten, 2004). These processes are extremely difficult to untangle, and the work of sorting them out, which involves the collaboration of several disciplines, will doubtless continue for many years to come. Understanding how protection works is crucial to developing interventions.

Protective processes can be *stabilizing* (when they enable children to function even when risk rises), *reactive* (when they work more effectively under low-risk conditions than under conditions of high risk), and *enhancing* (when engaging with risk increases children's competence) (Luthar et al., 2000). British child psychiatrist and resilience expert Michael Rutter (2001; Rutter et al., 1998) has proposed eight possible ways that protective factors may contribute to positive outcomes:

1. *Reduce sensitivity to risk* (e.g., coping successfully with previous adversity makes it easier for a child to meet new challenges).
2. *Reduce the impact of risk* (e.g., parental monitoring and supervision can prevent young adolescents from spending time with antisocial peers).
3. *Reduce the negative chain reactions that follow exposure to risk and perpetuate its effects* (e.g., support and guidance from adults can enable children to cope successfully with the cumulative effects of early stress).
4. *Increase positive chain reactions* (e.g., positive school experiences help adolescents plan for the future—that is, success breeds success).
5. *Promote self-esteem and self-efficacy* (e.g., succeeding in an important task builds self-confidence).
6. *Neutralize or counter the risk directly with compensatory positive experiences* (e.g., having a warm, close relationship with a friend's parents can protect a child from the effects of marital strife in his own home).
7. *Open up opportunities* (e.g., a change of school or neighborhood or trying a new activity gives a child a chance to meet new people and learn new skills).
8. *Support positive cognitive processing of negative experiences* (e.g., focusing on the positive aspects of a difficult experience seems to make adjustment easier).

Some researchers have come up with a radical idea that emphasizes the importance of context and culture. When basic human adaptational systems function normally, children usually manage to find the resources they need to cope, even in adversity (Masten, 2001). But children and youth whose environment doesn't contain the appropriate resources may not turn out so well—at least not in the usual sense. They may have to pay a price in order to achieve some measure of well-being, as these examples show:

- For most children, emotional responsiveness and close relationships promote positive adaptation. But children who experience maltreatment at home seem to fare better when they develop a more restrictive style of emotional self-regulation—when they're less open, less empathetic, less responsive, less connected. Distancing themselves emotionally from their abusive parents enables them to manage their distress (Wyman, 2003).
- Positive expectations for the future help many students engage successfully in school. But for teens with conduct or substance-abuse problems, these same positive expectations may go along with more challenging behavior and less aca-

Abused at home, 11-year-old Allison was transferred from one group home to another every few months. Like many other young people at risk, she took pride in her mouthiness, defiance, bad attitude, sexual promiscuity, emotional dependence, addictions, self-injurious behaviors, and various forms of risk taking.

These behaviors provided a way for her to maintain her mental health and are evidence of her resilience, says Michael Ungar of Dalhousie University in Halifax, Nova Scotia. Although certainly problematic, they reflect Allison's "determination to remain in control of her life when she so evidently had been denied that control" (2004b, p. 172).

demic competence. Researchers believe that wishful thinking about the future may actually get in the way of their ability to function (Wyman, 2003).

Logically extending the notion that children achieve resilience differently in different contexts, some researchers are coming to believe that resilience itself can have different—and sometimes startling—faces (Kaplan, 1999; Wyman, 2003). Psychologist Arnold Sameroff (2005) writes, "It must be noted that resilience is not the same as positive behavior. In stressful circumstances with limited resources, one individual's gain must be at the expense of someone else's loss, a zero-sum game. In such situations, resilience may take the form of antisocial behavior, such as resources gained by criminality in inner-city environments."

The key to this postmodern point of view is to pay close attention to what young people themselves consider successful adaptation (Luthar, 1999), rather than labeling them with our own ideas of adaptation. Sociologist Michael Ungar identifies this approach to resilience as *constructionist* and defines it as "the outcome of negotiations between individuals and their environments to maintain a self-definition as healthy" (2004b, p. 352). He says, "A child chooses to adapt in ways that are most effective, given the available resources. . . . In some instances, the behavior of dangerous, deviant, delinquent, and disordered youth can actually be more effective in nurturing and maintaining their mental health than can conforming to widely accepted, but constraining, social norms" (2004b, p. 69).

Viewed from this angle, it becomes possible to understand a child's behavior as the solution to a problem, not the problem itself. A child who runs away from home in order to escape maltreatment is displaying resilience; likewise (though perhaps more surprisingly), an adolescent who is abusing drugs in order to blunt his overwhelming emotional pain, or a student who uses violence to gain acceptance and status with his peers, can also be regarded as resilient. This behavior helps these students adapt to the difficult circumstances of their lives.

Acknowledging such behavior as adaptive doesn't mean it's appropriate, but validating and accepting it without judgment can help the child, Ungar says. ("It's tough for me to understand but it seems like your behavior is working for you" [2004b, p. 224]). Establishing a close relationship may allow a teacher to see what the child is gaining (or avoiding) with his challenging or antisocial behavior, which in turn helps engage him in thoughtful discussion and find more acceptable, less harmful ways to maintain his mental health (Ungar, 2004b). That is, it's important to understand the function or purpose of the behavior and enable the student to replace it with appro-

Establishing a close relationship may allow a teacher to see what the child is gaining (or avoiding) with his challenging or antisocial behavior, which in turn helps engage him in thoughtful discussion and find more acceptable, less harmful ways to maintain his mental health.

priate behavior that offers the same benefits. This technique is called *functional assessment* (or *positive behavior support*), and Chapter 11 is devoted to it.

It is useful to recognize and support the strengths a child employs to survive his everyday life—strengths that can aid him in identifying areas of competence, control, and power that he can build on (Ungar, 2004b). For example, helping others is a talent that enables many children and teens to nurture their self-image; and having choices and a say about their own world also allows students to feel valued for who they are (Ungar, 2004b).

The third wave: Integrating biology and intervention

The third wave of resilience research, which is now underway, seems to be heading in several directions at once. There is a great deal of interest in integrating the biological perspective—including the study of genes and brain development and their interaction with the environment—with research on behavior and process (Curtis and Cicchetti, 2003); and social scientists are also using intervention as a way to test hypotheses about resilience—and creating it at the same time (Masten, 2004). One example is the Seattle Social Development Project mentioned on page 50 (Hawkins et al., 1999).

The results of these ambitious multidisciplinary efforts are just beginning to emerge. While we wait, we can start to incorporate what we already know about resilience into the classroom by creating strong relationships with students, enhancing their strengths and potential resources, promoting competence and emotional regulation, and paying close attention both to context and to what students tell and show us.

E mmy E. Werner (1984) makes these suggestions for teachers, neighbors, coaches, social workers, community workers, police, and others who spend time with children:

- Accept children's temperamental idiosyncrasies and allow them experiences that challenge, but do not overwhelm, their coping abilities.
- Convey to children a sense of responsibility and caring, and in turn reward them for helpfulness and cooperation.
- Encourage a child to develop a special interest, hobby, or participate in an activity that can serve as a source of gratification and self-esteem.
- Model, by example, a conviction that life makes sense despite the inevitable adversities . . . each of us encounters.
- Encourage children to reach out beyond their nuclear family to a beloved relative or friend.

What do you think?

1. Have you or has anyone else in your family ever had to deal with adversity? Think about your own risk and protective factors. Is there an activity or a person in your life who made a difference—a parent, a friend's parent, a teacher, or a neighbor who helped you recover from a trauma or sustained you through a stressful period? How?

2. Michael Ungar (2004a, p. 360) asks, "Can deviant and disordered behavior be a search for health resources? Can resilience be achieved through pathways thought to indicate vulnerability?" What do you think of this point of view? For example, taking into account factors such as self-esteem, competence, and problem solving, who do you think displays more resilience, the child who's been abused who leaves home and lives on the street, or the child who's been abused who stays at home? Why?

3. After reading this chapter and looking carefully at Andrew's history on pages 4 to 6, what strengths do you see in him, and how can you use these strengths to build his resilience and create opportunities for success?

4. Jazmine, whose story appears on pages 6 to 7, had been hoping her mother would phone her on her birthday, but she called a few days later. When her aunt said her mother was on the line, Jazmine's heart started beating wildly. She took a deep breath and tried not to show her excitement, but she couldn't help saying, "I miss you!"

Her mom began to cry and in a low, subdued voice started telling Jazmine how hard things were. She didn't think she would be coming home soon because she didn't have enough money. "Maybe," she said, "if I find a good job here, you can come and live with us."

Jazmine was horrified. Although life was far from perfect at her aunt's, she knew what her responsibilities were and she was appreciated, fed, and sheltered. She didn't have to worry about her mom's boyfriend, his angry, drunken tirades, his demands, or his reaction if she didn't do what he wanted.

Jazmine tried to tell her mom about her own life and the friends she had made, but her mother kept interrupting her. Finally, the telephone operator said that there was no time left, and her mother didn't have any more change for the pay phone.

Jazmine slowly replaced the receiver and angrily sat down on the couch. Her aunt sat beside her and put her arm around Jazmine's shoulder.

What are Jazmine's protective factors and how will they help her to deal with this situation?

Suggested readings

Luthar, S. S. (Ed.). (2003). *Resilience and vulnerability: Adaptation in the context of childhood adversity*. New York: Cambridge University Press.

Masten, A. S. (2001). Ordinary magic: Resilience processes in development. *American Psychologist, 56*, 227–234.

Ungar, M. (2004). A constructionist discourse on resilience: Multiple contexts, multiple realities among at-risk children and youth. *Youth and Society, 35*, 341–365.

Werner, E. E., & Smith, R. (1992). *Overcoming the odds: High risk children from birth to adulthood*. Ithaca, NY: Cornell University Press.

CHAPTER 4

Behavior and the Brain

Ultimately, all behavior is a result of brain activity, so it is only natural to wonder about the brain's role in challenging behavior.

Every risk and protective factor in a child's life can have an impact on the brain, although we often don't know why or how. The development of the brain is perhaps the most complex phenomenon in all of biology (Nelson and Bloom, 1997); and despite the astonishing progress of the last 20 years, work that uses the techniques of neuroanatomy, molecular biology, molecular genetics, neurochemistry, neurophysiology, brain imaging, and the like does not easily translate into statements about complicated human behavior such as aggression (Kandel, Jessell, and Sanes, 2000; Shonkoff and Phillips, 2000).

Researchers have amassed a great deal of valuable information about behavior and the brain by observing children (DiPietro, 2000; Nelson and Bloom, 1997). But much of what we know so far about the brain's wiring and development comes from studies of animals, particularly from research on the visual system of cats, monkeys, rodents, and even frogs. Those findings can provide extraordinary insights, but we must use caution when we apply them to human beings.

Now neuroscience is bringing some wonderful new tools to the quest to link behavior and the brain, including *magnetic resonance imaging (MRI)*, which provides exquisitely detailed three-dimensional pictures of brain structure without using radiation; *functional MRI (fMRI)*, which can show the brain at work on specific tasks by tracking oxygen in the blood in a particular region; and *positron emission tomography (PET)*, where radioactively labeled compounds can illuminate specific areas of brain activity or track the whereabouts of a particular neurotransmitter in the brain.

The techniques that don't require radiation can be adapted for research with children, and scientists at the National Institute of Mental Health (NIMH) are currently compiling an atlas of normal human brain development by using MRI to look at the brains of more than 500 children aged 3 to 18. As the recently completed map of the human genome supplies new leads to pursue, researchers are also tracing the progress of neurodevelopmental disorders, such as ADHD, autism, schizophrenia, and bipolar disease, as well as the effects on the brain of child maltreatment, prenatal alcohol exposure, maternal depression, prematurity, and even video gaming.

All Roads Lead to Rome

How can we link behavior with brain processes? One hopeful example of convergence comes from psychiatry. Researchers recently demonstrated that two different treatments for obsessive-compulsive disorder—one that used behavior therapy and another that used drug therapy—had identical outcomes. The patients' behavior changed in the same way with both treatments.

PET scans showed that the patients' brains had also changed in the same way, allowing researchers to see how the brain and behavior relate to one another. What's happening on the outside mirrors what's happening on the inside (Baxter et al., 1992; Nelson and Bloom, 1997; Schwartz, Stoessel, Baxter, Martin, and Phelps, 1996).

This chapter will look at some of the connections between behavior and the brain. We begin with early experience and the brain, move on to the adolescent brain, and finish with aggression and the adult brain.

EARLY EXPERIENCE AND THE BRAIN

How does the brain develop?

Not long ago, people believed that genes completely controlled brain development (Shonkoff and Phillips, 2000). Now it's clear that the environment also plays an enormous part, both before and after birth, and is even involved in turning genes on and off (Shonkoff and Phillips, 2000; Nelson, 2000). This is where biology and environment, nature and nurture, merge. Genes may provide the grand plan, but experience is necessary to organize and structure the brain's circuitry (Shonkoff and Phillips, 2000; Nelson and Bloom, 1997).

Between conception and the age of 18 months, babies produce billions of nerve cells, or *neurons*. As they interact with their environment, their nerve cells send and receive signals, making 1,000 trillion connections, or *synapses*, by the time they turn 3 years old.

Until recently, scientists believed that brain development was essentially finished by then. But the new neuroimaging techniques have revealed an unknown world: the rapidly morphing adolescent brain. It turns out that brain development, far from being over, actually undergoes a second major round of activity in the years between early childhood and adulthood. MRI scans of children's brains taken at the NIMH show that from 6 to 12 years the *gray matter*—which is made up of nerve cells—is growing fast, as the neurons sprout dozens of new branches, twigs, and roots and make new connections with one another (Giedd, 2004). When this exuberant growth peaks—at about 11 years for girls and 12 years for boys—it far exceeds adult levels. Then the gray matter gradually thins out, the result, scientists hypothesize, of genetics and the "use-it-or-lose-it" principle. The frequently used connections survive, while those with little or no traffic gradually wither away.

As the gray matter is pruned back, the white matter, which connects areas of the brain to one another, increases in volume, enabling messages to flow more quickly and efficiently. The brain achieves an adult number of connections and finishes its reorganization only when we reach our 20s (De Bellis et al., 1999).

Brain development undergoes a second major round of activity in adolescence.

How does experience affect brain development?

From the very beginning, an individual's experience has a major impact on the way her brain develops and the person she becomes.

William Greenough and his colleagues (Greenough, Black, and Wallace, 1987) have identified two ways that nerve cells use experience to make connections and forge nerve pathways. They call the first *experience-expectant*. Some experiences—such as hearing speech and seeing light and patterns—are readily available in the environment; and as the brain develops, it "expects" to use them to form the connections it needs (Nelson and Bloom, 1997). When experiences occur as expected, brain cells connect and systems organize themselves normally; if the experiences don't occur as expected, neural organization is abnormal.

Nobel Prize winners David Hubel and Torsten Wiesel provided the classical evidence for this pattern in the 1960s. They were intrigued by the observation that children whose cataracts weren't treated promptly remained blind in the obstructed eye even after their cataracts were removed. To explore this phenomenon, Hubel and Wiesel performed experiments where they closed one eyelid of newborn kittens. When they reopened it three months later, the kitten could not see with that eye because its nerve cells hadn't made the proper connections in the brain, despite the fact that the eye itself functioned normally (Bruer, 1999; Shatz, 1992). The brain needed the normal experience of exposure to light and patterns in order to connect with the eye and interpret the information coming from it.

Hubel and Wiesel had discovered a *critical* or *sensitive period* for the visual system. If the nerve cells in the kitten's eye failed to make the appropriate connections in the brain during that sensitive time, the kitten lost sight permanently in that eye

(Hubel and Wiesel, 1970). There is also a critical period for vision in humans, as well as a critical period for sound (Kuhl, Williams, Lacerda, and Stevens, 1992). Other sensory systems may have critical periods, too (Bruer, 1999; Shonkoff and Phillips, 2000).

Critical periods for the development of different brain systems vary and seem to be important only for systems that develop in the same way for all members of a species (Bruer, 1999; Nelson, 2000). For example, all human beings have a visual system, so there is a critical period for developing vision. But not everyone reads, so there is no critical period for reading; one can learn at any time (Bruer, 1999).

Greenough and his colleagues (1987) noticed that experience guides brain development in a second way, which they called *experience-dependent*. Humans need to acquire a great deal of information that is unique to their own environment—how to navigate in their physical surroundings and relate to the individuals around them, for example. Again, experience triggers nerve cells to make connections, but this process isn't subject to critical periods. The brain is constantly restructuring and refining itself to reflect its new experience. In this way, a child actually participates in the development of her own brain (Gopnik, Meltzoff, and Kuhl, 2001). Experience-dependent learning goes on throughout life. Because the brain is so *plastic*—malleable—human beings are incredibly adaptable and attuned to their environment.

Are there any critical periods in the social and emotional realm?

Scientists have known since the 1940s that children brought up under conditions of severe emotional deprivation developed serious behavioral problems (Bruer, 1999; Kandel et al., 2000). Henry and Margaret Harlow (1962) saw similar effects in the 1950s in their landmark work with rhesus monkeys who, when reared with surrogate mothers of wire and terrycloth, were never able to form relationships with other monkeys. These studies led scientists to deduce that there is a critical period for the development of social and emotional traits and behavior (Bruer, 1999).

Investigators are learning more about this critical period by studying children who experienced severe deprivation in Romanian orphanages. Those adopted before the age of 6 months are virtually indistinguishable from peers living with their own parents (Rutter and the English and Romanian Adoptees Study Team, 1998), and many adopted later have made a spectacular recovery in some areas. But researchers have consistently found that children who have lived in orphanages have more behavior problems than other children (Maclean, 2003), and the more time they spent in an institution, the more serious their difficulties.

Even 8 years after being adopted, many of the Romanian orphans have had trouble paying attention, and in a study of Canadian adoptees, 29 percent were diagnosed with ADHD (Maclean, 2003). The adopted children have also found it difficult to get along with their peers, and a substantial minority haven't formed an attachment with their caregivers—instead, they are overly friendly and all too ready to walk off with a stranger (Rutter, O'Connor, and the English and Romanian Adoptees Study Team, 2004).

Researchers speculate that these problems stem from the conditions the children faced in the orphanage, where stimulation and interactions with peers and adults were few and far between (Maclean, 2003). In particular, not having one consistent person to care for them at this early stage put their social development at risk, scientists believe (Rutter et al., 2004). The implication is that at least one close relationship with a caregiver in the first few years is vital for normal brain development.

How does early experience affect the stress system?

There may also be a critical period for the development of the *stress system*, which roars into action when human beings are threatened or frightened. A whole cascade of changes takes place in the brain and body, getting us ready to fight or flee as the steroid hormone *cortisol* floods the brain (Shonkoff and Phillips, 2000). When the threat recedes, cortisol levels return to normal. But if a threat continues over a long period, the stress system may be reset so that it's easier to activate. The result is an animal or human who is quick to experience fear, anxiety, and stress, and may have a hard time turning those feelings off (Gunnar, 2000). A brain in this state is also vulnerable to the toxic effects of cortisol itself, which in large amounts may destroy neurons in areas concerned with memory and emotional regulation (Gunnar, 1998).

Research in rats has shown that effective mothering can increase the cortisol receptors in the brains of rat pups, give them better control over cortisol production, and streamline their stress systems, making them less fearful and less easily unnerved by threat (Meaney, 2001). Megan R. Gunnar, a specialist in cortisol and the stress system, has found similar connections between cortisol and the quality of caregiving in human children that probably reflect changes in brain development (Gunnar, 1998). However, scientists don't yet know how changeable the system is or how early they must intervene to make a difference.

What role do genes play?

Genes and experience are intertwined in such complex ways that it's hard to know where one leaves off and the other begins. The gene for the enzyme monoamine oxidase A, better known as MAOA, is a good example. MAOA is responsible for breaking down some of the *neurotransmitters* in the brain, a process that's essential for the normal use and recycling of these chemicals, which carry messages between nerve cells. When the gene for MAOA is defective, it produces an enzyme that can't do its job properly, and the result is often disturbed neurotransmission, disrupted development, and aggressive behavior that lasts a lifetime.

Researchers (Caspi et al., 2002) noticed that children who suffer from abuse at an early age sometimes develop the same symptoms, including aggressive behavior that persists into adulthood. But maltreatment doesn't always have this effect. The scientists wanted to know why. When they examined their data, they discovered the answer lay in the faulty MAOA gene. Maltreatment almost seemed to activate it. Boys who carried the defective gene and had been abused as children were at extraordinarily high risk: 85 percent developed some form of antisocial behavior, and a disproportionately large number were convicted of violent offenses. On the other hand, boys with the flawed gene who had escaped maltreatment did not behave aggressively; and boys who had been abused but lacked the defective gene ran only a slightly higher risk of behaving aggressively. Either their environment or their genetics protected them.

The same research team (Caspi et al., 2003) found another case where genes and the environment interact to produce behavior, this time in the serotonin-transporter gene. *Serotonin*, a neurotransmitter that's famous for its association with antidepressant drugs, plays a vital role in the regulation of mood. When their lives are free of major stress, people with a short form of the serotonin-transporter gene face no particular risk of depression. But if they endure either child maltreatment or serious stress later, they have a much higher risk of depression than individuals graced with the gene's long form. Once again, the environment makes them vulnerable to their genetics.

Other researchers (Kaufman et al., 2004) added an important twist to the genes–environment story: It is possible to decrease the effects of these co-conspirators. The researchers found that—like adults—children who've been abused and who carry the short form of the serotonin-transporter gene are very prone to depression. But they also discovered that children caught in this double bind are likely to be less depressed when they have strong, frequent social support from an adult— someone to talk to, rely on, and go to for advice. With a little help from its friends, the brain will do its best to develop and function in a healthy way, despite unlucky genes and hostile circumstances.

THE ADOLESCENT BRAIN

One research team that focuses on adolescence defines it as "that awkward period between sexual maturation and the attainment of adult roles and responsibilities" (Dahl, 2004, p. 9). Investigators are beginning to suspect that this "awkward period" may itself be a critical period in brain development (Dahl, 2004). With so much growth and restructuring taking place, the brain is extra sensitive and plastic, making this a time when trajectories into adulthood are set or altered, when potential problems with relationships, careers, smoking, substance abuse, and the like can take root—or not. Adolescence, scientists suggest, offers not only great risks but also great opportunities. Perhaps the most crucial learning occurs in the area of emotional and behavioral regulation, which is associated with aggression (Steinberg, 2005b). Indeed, researchers are asking whether having the right experiences during this period enables children to achieve social and emotional control, and whether it is much more difficult to learn to regulate emotions later in life (Dahl, 2004).

How does puberty affect the brain?

Puberty arrives in all its hormonal splendor while children are attending elementary or middle school. At just 7 years old, 7 percent of European American and 27 percent of African American girls have already developed breast tissue and/or pubic hair (Dahl, 2004). The average age for the onset of puberty is steadily falling (Rutter, 1993), ushering in adolescence earlier and earlier in children's lives.

Puberty hits the brain just as hard as it hits the body (Dahl, 2004). Some of the alterations it brings to the brain take place even before puberty begins and in fact set it off. Other major brain changes—particularly in the areas of arousal and motivation—are actually the result of puberty (Dahl, 2004; Steinberg, 2005b). The emotional intensity of adolescents and their predilection for activities that evoke strong

D uring adolescence, many systems—biological and social—are changing at once, each with its own beginning and end point (Steinberg, 2005a).

Domain	When Adolescence Begins	When Adolescence Ends
Biological	Onset of puberty	Becoming capable of sexual reproduction
Emotional	Beginning of detachment from parents	Attainment of separate sense of identity
Cognitive	Emergence of more advanced reasoning abilities	Consolidation of advanced reasoning abilities
Interpersonal	Beginning of a shift in interest from parental to peer relations	Development of capacity for intimacy with peers
Social	Beginning of training for adult work, family, and citizen roles	Full attainment of adult status and privileges
Educational	Entrance into junior high school	Completion of formal schooling
Legal	Attainment of juvenile status	Attainment of majority status
Chronological	Attainment of designated age of adolescence (e.g., 10 years)	Attainment of designated age of adulthood (e.g., 22 years)
Cultural	Entrance into period of training for a ceremonial rite of passage	Completion of ceremonial rite of passage

Source: From *Adolescence*, 7th ed., by Laurence Steinberg, 2005. New York: McGraw-Hill, p. 6. This material is reproduced with the permission of The McGraw-Hill Companies.

feelings—sex, drugs, music videos, and horror movies, for example—come from changes that puberty causes in the brain. This is also true for adolescents' heightened recklessness, risk taking, novelty seeking, and sensation seeking, as well as their newfound interest in the opposite sex, powerful drives and appetites, and gigantic shifts in sleep needs and patterns (Dahl, 2004). In a study of 11- to 13-year-old boys and girls, researchers found that sensation seeking had nothing to do with age, but it certainly had a great deal to do with puberty. Early-maturing children had significantly higher sensation-seeking scores and were more likely to smoke and drink (Martin et al., 2002).

What about cognitive development?

Although many parts of the brain undergo change during this period, the principal site of ongoing development is the *frontal lobe*, the part that makes us human (Giedd, 2004) and one of the newest parts of the brain from the point of view of evolution. The most extensive modifications take place in the *prefrontal cortex,* a small area of the frontal lobe just behind the forehead. Dubbed the brain's executive or CEO, it controls the brain's most advanced functions that eventually allow us to reason, think abstractly, plan, organize, strategize, set priorities, consider the consequences of our actions, control impulses, and regulate our emotions and behavior (see Figure 4.1).

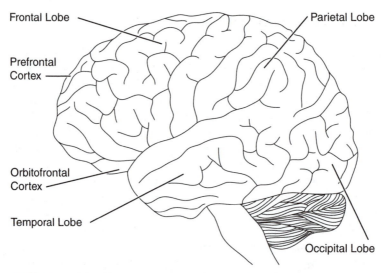

Frontal Lobe

Prefrontal
Cortex

Orbitofrontal
Cortex

Temporal Lobe

Parietal Lobe

Occipital Lobe

FIGURE 4.1 Dubbed the brain's executive or CEO, the *prefrontal cortex,* a small area of the frontal lobe just behind the forehead, controls the brain's most advanced functions that eventually allow us to reason, think abstractly, plan, organize, strategize, set priorities, consider the consequences of our actions, control impulses, and regulate our emotions and behavior.

Unlike the changes triggered by puberty, these changes in cognitive capacity are late bloomers that depend instead on age and experience (Dahl, 2004), developing slowly and continuing long after puberty is over. They are different from earlier changes in that no new abilities come on line; rather, abilities already in place are gradually upgraded and refined (Luna and Sweeney, 2004). Information-processing speed and capacity increase dramatically (Luna and Sweeney, 2004).

In addition to improving the executive functions, changes in the prefrontal cortex influence perception. When children reach puberty, they have more trouble reading emotions in others' faces than they did at an earlier age (McGivern, Andersen, Byrd, Mutter, and Reilly, 2002; Wade, Lawrence, Mandy, and Skuse, 2006). Deborah Yurgelun-Todd and her team (Baird et al., 1999) used functional MRI to investigate this phenomenon and found that when young teens, especially boys, try to identify facial expressions in photos, they use the *amygdala,* an emotional seat of the brain, and often mistake the expression of fear for shock, sadness, or confusion. In contrast, adults activate the prefrontal region and read the feelings in the faces correctly. As teens grow older, their prefrontal cortex becomes more active, and their ability to read expressions improves (Baird et al., 1999; National Institutes of Mental Health, 2006).

If young teens are misperceiving feelings, it helps to explain why miscommunication is so common and why their responses are so often emotional and impulsive. "Our findings suggest that what is coming into the brain, how it's being organized, and then ultimately the response—all three of these may be different in our adolescents," says Yurgelun-Todd ("Interview with Deborah Yurgelun-Todd," 2002). "It's not simply a matter of teenagers feeling . . . that they're just going to give you a hard time."

What happens when emotion and cognition are out of sync?

When the cognitive abilities of school-age children and young adolescents are just beginning to mature, their emotions are already going full blast. The result is an enormous disconnect—and plenty of risk for challenging behavior and serious emotional and behavioral problems. Researchers in the field liken this situation to putting an unskilled driver at the wheel of a car with a turbo-charged engine (Dahl, 2004).

When children and teens take tests under laboratory conditions or in "cool" situations where they have the opportunity to think, they can make rational decisions. But in the real world, where their peers and their own violent feelings often heat things up, thinking and acting rationally present a greater challenge. Psychologists Margo Gardner and Laurence Steinberg (2005) used a video driving game to compare risk taking in adolescents, young adults, and adults. All three groups drove carefully when they played the game alone. But when friends came along to watch and give advice, the teens took much bigger risks.

Children acquire the beginnings of many skills in infancy and polish them up throughout childhood and early adolescence as they practice navigating more and more complex situations. By studying control of eye movements, researchers have watched children develop the skill of *response inhibition*—that is, the ability to choose some ideas and suppress others—which is a key piece of executive control based in the prefrontal cortex. Because selecting one response always means rejecting others, this capacity is present in all voluntary behavior, from paying attention in class to resisting peer pressure (Luna and Sweeney, 2004).

It turns out that younger children can inhibit a response, but they make many more errors than adults. Their performance becomes more and more consistent over time until it stabilizes in mid-adolescence (Luna and Sweeney, 2004).

Acquiring the ability to self-regulate and behave rationally isn't just a matter of waiting until the prefrontal cortex catches up with the emotional circuits of the brain. In fact, the prefrontal cortex needs the collaboration of many widely distributed brain regions and a fully integrated support and communications network in order to function well (Luna and Sweeney, 2004). Adolescents haven't yet established this widely based circuitry—which is why their self-control often breaks down under "hot" conditions (Luna and Sweeney, 2004).

The transition to efficient brain collaboration during adolescence may mark what neuroscientists Beatriz Luna and John A. Sweeney characterize as "the beginning of a new stage in the brain-behavior relationship where newly established distributed brain function, in preference to more regional control, governs behavior" (2004, p. 306).

Juvenile Justice

In 2003, in recognition of the gap that occurs in brain development during adolescence (which doesn't fully close until the third decade of life), the American Bar Association asked the states to abolish the death penalty for juveniles: "For social and biological reasons, teens have increased difficulty making mature decisions and understanding the consequences of their actions" (Wallis and Dell, 2004).

What makes this integration possible? It is probably the individual child's experience, driving the continued pruning of gray matter and thickening of white matter (Kupfer and Woodward, 2004). As youngsters use and refine their skills in their everyday lives, deal with the consequences of their bad decisions, and enjoy the fruits of their good decisions, their brains gradually develop smooth, fast, integrated neural pathways (Paus, 2005) and a full "executive suite" of capabilities (Steinberg, 2005b).

AGGRESSION AND THE ADULT BRAIN

Which parts of the brain are involved in aggressive behavior?

Research on adults reveals that many areas in the brain are involved in aggressive and violent behavior, including the prefrontal cortex. PET studies of adults with impulsive aggression show prefrontal abnormalities, and one study found that impulsive killers (as opposed to murderers who planned their crimes) had less activity in this area (Davidson, Putnam, and Larson, 2000). The prefrontal cortex also has a high density of serotonin receptors, and serotonin helps to inhibit aggression. Some scientists suspect that damage in this area might alter serotonin metabolism and play a role in making aggressive behavior more likely (Davidson et al., 2000).

The *orbitofrontal cortex*, downstairs from the prefrontal cortex, is even more closely associated with antisocial and violent behavior. Through its connections to other brain regions, it regulates negative emotion and helps suppress impulsive outbursts (Davidson et al., 2000). Researchers have found large differences in individuals' ability to suppress their negative emotions—differences that coincide with orbitofrontal activity seen on fMRI scans. Damage to this area produces aggressive behavior, impulsivity, emotional explosions, and a lack of concern, emotion, and guilt (Raine, 1993).

What does all this mean?

As the brain goes through the long process of reorganization and children and teens gradually learn to use their burgeoning regulatory skills more consistently, it is crucial for them to have what adolescent-development specialist Ronald E. Dahl calls "appropriate social scaffolding—the right balance of monitoring and interest from . . . responsible adults" (2004, p. 20). Ideally, this framework of support and

Inhibition Disbarred

The case of Phineas Gage was one of the first to link antisocial behavior with the frontal lobe of the brain. Gage worked as a dynamiter for the Rutland and Burlington Railroad in Vermont. Considered an efficient, reliable, and capable man, he was the foreman of a construction gang and had no history of violent or antisocial behavior.

In 1848, an explosion rammed an iron rod through Gage's head, damaging his left frontal lobe. He survived, but he became an entirely different person—impulsive, irreverent, profane, obstinate, and antisocial (Raine, 1993; "Phineas Gage's Story," n.d.).

protection should stay in place until adolescents can reliably make responsible decisions for themselves.

Teachers play a vital role in erecting and maintaining this scaffolding. Research on both the brain and behavior reveals that nurturing and stable relationships with adults are essential for children. How we respond to students with challenging behavior and difficult temperaments, who need extra help in learning to regulate and cope with their feelings, is especially critical. At the same time, teachers can provide the high-intensity experiences students need at this stage of development by offering them exciting challenges, helping them master skills and achieve goals, and inspiring passion for activities, ideals, and people (Dahl, 2004).

WHAT DO YOU THINK?

1. What is a "critical period"? What is known about critical periods for social and emotional development?
2. Should adolescence be considered a risk factor for challenging behavior or an opportunity to create new pathways? Why?
3. Should the justice system treat teenagers the same way it treats adults? Divide into two teams and debate this question.
4. How does learning about changes in the brain during adolescence affect your thinking about how to approach behavior problems in the classroom?

SUGGESTED READINGS

Bruer, J. T. (1999). *The myth of the first three years: A new understanding of early brain development and lifelong learning.* New York: Free Press.

PBS Frontline: Inside the teenage brain (2002, January 2). www.pbs.org/wgbh/pages/frontline/shows/teenbrain/.

Shonkoff, J. P., & Phillips, D. A. (Eds.). (2000). *From neurons to neighborhoods: The science of early childhood development.* National Research Council and Institute of Medicine, Committee on Integrating the Science of Early Childhood Development, Board on Children, Youth, and Families, Commission on Behavioral and Social Sciences and Education. Washington, DC: National Academy Press.

Strauch, B. (2003). *The primal teen: What the new discoveries about the teenage brain tell us about our kids.* New York: Anchor Books.

CHAPTER 5

Relationship, Relationship, Relationship

Research about the brain and resiliency tells us that consistent, nurturing relationships are a child's best protection against risk—including the risk of challenging behavior. Families have first crack at creating such relationships, but they don't have exclusive rights. Because teachers spend so much time with a child, they, too, have a natural opportunity to forge a strong, positive relationship and thereby boost resilience. This role is particularly important when family relationships are wobbly. In fact, when the National Longitudinal Study of Adolescent Health looked at the factors associated with a healthy outcome for youth, having a supportive relationship with an adult—most often a teacher—topped the list (Resnick et al., 1997).

The caring connection

Your connection with a student is the most powerful tool you have as a teacher. In a safe, caring relationship with an adult, a child feels comfortable exploring the world. He learns to value himself and believe in his own personal power. He discovers that he can influence the people around him and that they will help him fulfill his needs. With a sensitive, responsive adult as a guide and model, the child can learn to understand and control his own feelings and behavior, and he can learn to care about other people, see things from their perspective, and understand their feelings, too (Emde and Robinson, 2000; Greenspan,

This chapter has been adapted from *Partners in Quality, vol. 2/ Relationships* © CCCF 1999, written by Barbara Kaiser and Judy Sklar Rasminsky based on the research papers of the Partners in Quality Project. With permission from the Canadian Child Care Federation, 201-383 Parkdale Avenue, Ottawa, Ontario, K1Y 4R4.

1996). When challenging behavior enters the picture, this crucial relationship may falter. The behavior gets in the way, blocking your view of the child and making it much more difficult to like him and establish a connection with him (Birch and Ladd, 1998). Yet it remains utterly essential to create that bond—because the relationship is the key to success. When you and a student care about each other, he has a desire to learn and a model to emulate, and you have the possibility of real understanding. All of this enormously augments your ability to help him learn to behave appropriately and succeed academically.

This chapter describes four facets of creating a relationship: understanding yourself, understanding the child, establishing a relationship with the child, and establishing a relationship with the family.

UNDERSTANDING YOURSELF

"Who are you?" said the caterpillar

So how do you build a relationship with a student whose behavior challenges you? How can you come to accept him for who he is and care about him no matter how he behaves?

It takes two to have a relationship, and as an adult, you have the responsibility for creating and maintaining that caring connection. You are the mature member of this duo, the one with the ability to size up the situation and adjust your teaching style to enable all the children in the classroom to function and feel comfortable.

Knowing the child well will certainly help, and we will discuss that issue later in the chapter. But to begin with, you have to understand where you are coming from yourself. The reason for this is simple. How you relate to the child depends on what you see when you look at him—and what you see depends on who you are.

Whether you're aware of it or not, everything about your teaching—how you approach and respond to the students, set up your room, choose and present lessons and activities, even your knowledge of child development and theory—filters through the prism of your own beliefs, values, and culture, your own temperament, emotions, education, and experience. A teacher, says William Ayers (1989), is "the perceiver, the selector, and the interpreter of a child's behavior" (p. 137). That is why it's important for you to discover who you are, to know what matters to you, to understand your reasons for doing this work, to figure out your philosophy of education, to know what kind of people you want the students in your classroom to become. Knowing about yourself allows you to see the child much more accurately.

There are more reasons to look inward. When you're with a child with challenging behavior, it's critical to stay cool and collected. If you become defensive and stressed and allow him to push your buttons, you can't think clearly and act rationally. It's also vitally important to show the child that it's possible to accept, control, and express strong and negative feelings in direct and nonaggressive ways. He and the other students need to see that you aren't afraid of his intense emotions and won't punish, threaten, or withdraw from him (Furman, 1986; Gartrell, 1997).

Knowing yourself won't give you magic powers, but it can bring you more control, and it will allow you to accept and talk about your feelings, to be honest with yourself and the children, to see the child and the environment more clearly, and

The Inside View

to empathize and respond more fully and appropriately. As you come to know yourself better, you open the door to new possibilities, new perspectives, and new choices for yourself and for the child.

What influences the way you relate to a child with challenging behavior?

Without question, negative feelings are the most prominent barrier between you and a student with challenging behavior. He evokes plenty of them—fear that someone will get hurt, frustration and anger that you can't do the lesson you'd planned, anxiety that you won't be able to manage his behavior, and a sense of inadequacy that makes you wonder if you've chosen the right profession. He may remind you of qualities you don't particularly admire in yourself, like a tendency to act without thinking, or he may bring back unwelcome memories, like the terror you felt in the presence of that bully in the fourth grade. Although feelings usually intensify reactions, they can also be strong enough to render you numb, unable to respond at all. If you aren't tuned into these feelings, it's hard to control or change them, and they can easily distort your perceptions of a child's behavior and capabilities.

Your early relationship and past experiences with your own family play an important role in what you feel and how you respond to a student (Pianta, 1999). His behavior may open old wounds and activate feelings you had as a child, making it difficult for you to respond in a rational way.

Those long years in school also have a profound influence on how you view teaching, learning, and children's behavior (Bowman, Donovan, and Burns, 2001). If you were a model student, you may have a hard time feeling patience and empathy with a child who misbehaves—you'll remember all too well how frustrated you felt when your classmates acted up ("Oh, no, not again!"). Or you may follow the example of the teacher who sent you to the principal's office for the smallest offense. As Carl Rogers and Jerome Freiberg tell us in *Freedom to Learn* (1994), "We tend to teach the way we've been taught [and] discipline the way we've been disciplined" (p. 241).

When a child with challenging behavior is involved, your temperament often gets into the act, too. If you like to slow down enough to ensure that every student has an opportunity to ask questions and show he understands how to solve the math problems, children with an active temperament who need things to move quickly

W hen a student with challenging behavior comes on the scene, all kinds of feelings, attitudes, and assumptions emerge. Here are some common reactions:

- He shouldn't be in this classroom.
- I'm not trained to work with children like this.
- I can't keep the other students safe.
- The other children aren't getting what they deserve.
- That child is out to get me.
- He never listens to me.
- I can't help him—look at his parents.
- Children have no respect any more.

These feelings provide you with a learning opportunity—they allow you to become aware of what pushes your buttons and do something about it.

---

may respond by creating extra stimulation for themselves. If you're a person with intense moods and reactions, some students may get frightened in your presence and act unpredictably; or if you have an aloof style, you may find that children who need a lot of emotional contact are always in your face (Pianta, 1999).

Values and beliefs also have a powerful effect. Because they're usually part and parcel of the culture you live in and the way you've been brought up, you may not even be aware of them. When a student won't look you in the eye, it's easy to conclude that he's rude if you don't realize that in his culture eye contact with an adult is a sign of disrespect, contempt, or aggression. Or if you've been raised to believe that children should do what adults say, you may be offended by a child who is always questioning your authority.

Left to their own devices, these barriers work full time, influencing the way you see the students, skewing your expectations of them, affecting the way they see themselves—and the way they behave. Fortunately, such obstacles aren't necessarily permanent fixtures. When you take the time to think about who you are and what you believe, it becomes possible to remove or alter them.

What is self-reflection?

In the past few years, you have probably done quite a lot of thinking about what's important to you. You've faced the gigantic question of choosing the work you want to do (perhaps more than once)—which meant figuring out what, where, and how you'd study as well. To make those decisions, you had to scrutinize your interests and talents and weigh them alongside family and financial considerations. In new relationships with friends and partners, you probably also grappled with the beliefs—religious, political, and cultural—you grew up with, and you've had to confront your personal values as you figured out whether to drink or smoke, whether to eat meat, and how to take care of your body and the environment. "We are engaged in a struggle to discover our identity, the person we are and choose to be," Rogers and Freiberg (1994) write. "This is a very pervasive search; it involves our clothes, our

When you think about your feelings, values, and beliefs and how they affect your actions, each task and each interaction with a student becomes more meaningful.

hair, our appearance. At a more significant level it involves our choice of values, our stance in relation to parents and others, the relationship we choose to have to society, our whole philosophy of life" (p. 52). This search continues throughout our lives as we encounter new challenges.

All of this thinking is called *self-reflection*. It is both a method and an attitude—a strategy for increasing your skill and a willingness to dig deep into yourself and your work and to act on what you find. *Why* is at the heart of the matter: Why am I doing what I'm doing the way that I'm doing it?

When you think about your feelings, values, and beliefs and how they affect your actions, each task and each interaction with a student becomes more meaningful. You have more self-respect because you know why you are doing what you do, you have control over it, and you have ownership of it. You are working from a position of strength inside yourself.

How do you reflect?

The process of reflection calls for a mixture of the rational and the intuitive, a melding of knowledge of yourself with knowledge from your training and experience and information gleaned from families, colleagues, and written sources.

In *How We Think* (1933), the philosopher and educator John Dewey, the father of reflective thinking, recommends cultivating three attitudes:

1. *Open-mindedness*, which is the "active desire to hear more than one side; to give heed to facts from whatever source they come; to give full attention to alternative possibilities; to recognize the possibility of error even in the beliefs that are dearest to us" (pp. 30–32)
2. *Whole-heartedness*, which is a willingness to throw yourself totally into the endeavor
3. *Responsibility*, which is a form of integrity; a willingness to consider the consequences of possible changes and to go forward if they're consistent with your beliefs

It is easier to reflect on what's going on between you and the students if you dedicate some time to becoming aware of your own personal history and culture. Where you come from can explain a lot about who you are now, give you insight into your feelings, and help you to regulate your behavior. Think of yourself as an anthropologist setting out to explore that most fascinating person of all: yourself.

How much do you know about your family? Have you ever talked with them about why they or their ancestors came to North America? Where did they come from? What language did they speak? Where did they settle? What was their life like when they were growing up? Did they go to school, and what did they feel about it? How important were politics and religion in their lives? How central was family (Lynch, 1998)?

Think about your childhood. What was your family's child-rearing philosophy? Who took care of you, and how did those caregivers respond when you needed help or comfort? What role did your extended family play? How were you disciplined? Did your parents treat you the same way they treated your brother or sister? Did they encourage you and make you feel special, or did you promise yourself that you'd never use their methods with your own child? If there are things about your upbringing that you don't remember or understand, talk to your parents, siblings, grandparents, aunts, uncles, cousins.

Take a look at your education, too. Which teachers did you like, and which couldn't you stand? Why? What did they say and do, and how did they make you feel?

Can you see the child you used to be in the person you are today? It's likely that he or she is nearby, affecting your perceptions, interpretations, and behavior, while you are interacting with the children in your classroom.

When do you reflect?

Ideally, a teacher in the classroom should always be thinking about what she's doing, why she's doing it, and what she feels. Robert Tremmel (1993) likens the process of listening to your feelings to the practice of Zen Buddhism—paying attention to the here and now and investing the present moment with your full awareness and concentration. This is particularly critical when you're confronted with challenging behavior because your thoughts and feelings affect both your behavior and the behavior of the child.

Who's Got the Button?

M s. Williams had been teaching for years, and she felt confident working with students with difficult behaviors. With her sense of humor and knowledge of kids, she always managed to help them realize they had skills and something special to contribute.

But Ms. Williams was at her wit's end when Joseph entered her class. No matter what she did, his response was always "%\#@% off !!!!" or "%\#@% you!" Although she tried to control herself, whenever Joseph shouted those words she lost her temper. She knew he had found a button to push, a vulnerable spot that grew out of her family upbringing, but she didn't know what to do about it.

One day a friend suggested that she shout the words at herself in a mirror until they lost their meaning. Since nothing else seemed to work, she decided to try. That evening she went into the bathroom, closed the door, and began shouting at herself in the mirror, "%\#@% off, %\#@% you!" A few minutes later her husband knocked frantically on the door, asking, "Are you all right?" She realized she felt better and began to laugh. When she returned to the classroom, she found that she could respond calmly and appropriately to Joseph's outbursts and focus on his feelings instead of her own. After a while the explosions and the bad language both stopped.

Any time a disturbing incident occurs—whether it is major or minor—some reflection is in order. When you're calm (but before you forget what happened) sit down and focus on the event, recollecting what took place, what you felt, and how you reacted. If you can figure out what triggered your emotions and where they came from within you, you can see how they affected your work and how you can begin to improve things. Even if you don't know exactly what caused those feelings, you will have more control over them if you're aware that they exist—and perhaps next time you'll notice them early enough to reframe them.

It takes practice to do this well, but it is definitely possible. Whether or not you've located the source of your unease, you can use an old behavior therapy technique to stop yourself from wallowing in destructive thoughts, put some mental distance between yourself and the situation, and refocus your attention where it belongs. For example, when you find yourself thinking, "Here we go again; he stayed up all night figuring out how to ruin my day," take a deep breath and shout inside your head: "Stop. These thoughts aren't helping me." (Alternately, you can concentrate on the soles of your feet, imagine yourself on a beach in Hawaii, or visualize the trigger thoughts floating away from you—anything that quiets the storm within.) Then replace your negative thoughts with a positive coping one: "He's just testing to see where my limits are. I'm going to stay calm." Once you get past your own knee-jerk reaction, you're ready to take the next step and consider the child's needs: "He's having a rough morning. I bet he could use some attention. I'll go sit beside him and see if I can help" (Strain and Joseph, 2004).

Once in a while, you and a student have a particularly hard time getting along together. You expect him to be nothing but trouble, and of course he obliges. You feel frustrated and out of control, and it becomes increasingly difficult for either of you to have a positive thought about the other. In fact, when you're in a relationship like this, you probably won't even notice the child's positive behavior.

These feelings—which show in your body language and tone of voice despite your efforts to conceal them—warn you that something is desperately wrong between you and the child. In the words of psychologist Robert C. Pianta (1999), your relationship is "stuck" or "locked up," and it's likely to prevent you from teaching effectively.

On the other hand, this situation offers an opportunity for you to take a hard look at yourself and try a fresh approach. The idea, says Pianta (1999), is to identify what you're feeling and to understand how it's connected to what you do (for example, it's difficult to respond positively when you're convinced the student is out to get you). What's most important is to shake up your fixed ideas about the child and open the door to new feelings, perceptions, and interactions. Talking with colleagues can aid in this process. It's also helpful to observe what's going on in the classroom, looking expressly for positive behaviors. Using the technique called *banking time*, which is described on page 86, can also create a different perspective.

Are there any techniques to help you reflect?

There are several tools that can assist you in the process of reflection. One traditional way is to keep a journal. It is both a record and "an instrument for thinking about teaching and children in a critical, sustained way," says Ayers (2001, p. 38). It allows you to return to a situation, to construct a whole out of many bits, and to increase your self-awareness by forcing you to put your thoughts in writing. When you write for yourself, without worrying about what others will say, feelings and ideas have a way of spilling out unbidden, bringing insights in their wake.

You can concentrate on daily events, difficult or memorable incidents, one student or several, one topic or many. If you're using a notebook, try dedicating one side of the page to record-keeping and the other to reflection. Carry it with you or keep it in a handy spot in the classroom. If you set aside a regular time each day to write in it, you're more likely to be faithful to the task. When you have a student with challenging behavior in your class, a journal can help you to identify what's working, what isn't, and why.

Although some people consider reflection a personal matter and believe they can be more honest when they reflect in private, others like to have a sounding board. When you're reflecting, questions inevitably arise, and it's useful to have a safe, supportive environment for sharing your doubts, your feelings, and your experiences. One way to arrange this is to make a regular date to get together—in person, on the phone, via e-mail—with a friend or colleague. Staff meetings, case consultation, and feedback from supervisors also provoke useful reflection, as do occasional talks with the school's counselor or psychologist. Regular, formal meetings where you have the freedom to explore your feelings about the children and your own style and needs are especially useful, because they give reflection and relationships the priority and status they deserve (Pianta, 1999).

We tend to pay attention to problems, but remember to give equal time to your successes. Positive reinforcement works just as well for teachers as it does for children, and your triumphs can tell you as much about your practice as any difficulty.

Be patient with yourself. As you become comfortable with the process, you can expand into more sensitive and difficult arenas. The goal is to turn reflection into a reflex, an instinct that sits quietly at the back of your mind weighing pros and cons and whispering, "Why should I do that?"

You are one essential partner in the relationship equation; the child is the other. And just as you bring your entire history—your temperament, family, education, ethnicity, culture, class, and past experience—into the classroom with you, so does he. The history of a child with challenging behavior is shorter than yours, which means that it's less entrenched, but the baggage he's carting is still very weighty and no doubt includes some of the risk and protective factors we've already mentioned. As you start to build a relationship, part of your job is to have a look at what that suitcase contains.

What is the role of attachment?

One of the most important items that any student carries with him is his relationship with his primary caregiver from the moment he is born. This person is usually his mother but may also be his father, grandmother, or someone else entirely. This very first relationship—a relationship as important in childhood and adolescence as it is in infancy (Marvin and Britner, 1999)—lays the groundwork for his relationship with you.

What we know about early relationships began with the British psychoanalyst John Bowlby, whose ideas are so much a part of society's thinking today that it's hard to imagine how revolutionary they seemed just 50 years ago. Infants are emotional beings who naturally form strong bonds with their parents, Bowlby recognized, and the way those special adults interact with their baby wields a powerful influence on how he turns out (Ainsworth, Blehar, Waters, and Wall, 1978; Bowlby, 1969/1982).

Bowlby (Ainsworth et al., 1978; Bowlby, 1969/1982) realized that human infants, like other animal species, are born with instinctive behaviors that help them survive. Acts such as crying, smiling, vocalizing, and grasping keep babies close to their primary caregivers, who shelter them from danger, feed and soothe them, and teach them about their environment. These *attachment behaviors*, as Bowlby (Ainsworth et al., 1978; Bowlby, 1969/1982) called them, help create *attachment*—children's vital tie to their primary caregiver or *attachment figure* who provides them with protection and emotional support.

In pioneering studies in the 1950s and 1960s, American psychologist Mary Ainsworth (Ainsworth et al., 1978) confirmed Bowlby's theory by documenting for the first time the emotional impact of parents' everyday behavior on their children. In Uganda and then in Baltimore, Ainsworth meticulously observed mothers and babies at home, watching the process of attachment unfold over the first year of life as the babies came to recognize, prefer, seek out, and become attached to their primary caregiver.

These observations enabled Ainsworth to make a critical discovery: A baby's sense of security depends on how his attachment figure cares for him. During his first year, an infant evolves an *attachment strategy*—a way to organize feelings and behavior—that is tailor-made for his own unique caregiving situation, a strategy that will enable him to cope best with his particular stressful circumstances and bring him the most security and comfort (van IJzendoorn, Schuengel, and Bakermans-Kranenburg, 1999; Weinfeld, Sroufe, Egeland, and Carlson, 1999).

When Ainsworth devised the Strange Situation, a laboratory test to assess attachment strategies, she found three basic types: *secure, insecure-resistant* (also called *insecure-ambivalent*), and *insecure-avoidant*. Later, researchers Mary Main and Judith Solomon (1986) identified a fourth type, *disorganized/disoriented* attachment. All attachment strategies are normal, adaptive, and functional; the trouble is that what works best within the child's family may not work outside it (Greenberg, DeKlyen, Speltz, and Endriga, 1997).

How does attachment affect behavior?

According to Bowlby (1969/1982), infants construct *internal working models* of how relationships work based on their experience with their own attachment figure. Although these models aren't conscious, they prepare the foundation for social and emotional development; guide how children see the world, other people, and themselves; and serve as templates for future relationships, including their relationships with teachers and peers.

Building on the work of Bowlby and Ainsworth, researchers have studied the effects of early attachment and these internal working models in both children and adults.

Children who are *securely attached* (Weinfeld et al., 1999) receive consistently warm, sensitive, and responsive care from a primary caregiver who enjoys their company. From this experience, they develop internal working models of other people who are there for them, and they see themselves as capable of eliciting whatever

Infants construct internal working models of how relationships work based on their experience with their own attachment figure.

Photo by Abigail Rasminsky.

they need from their environment. They tend to have a positive view of life, know how to manage and express their feelings (Honig, 2002; Karen 1998), and possess good social skills, many friends, and high self-esteem. Because they are also good problem solvers who can ask for help when they need it, they do well in school (Howes and Ritchie, 2002). About 55 percent of children are securely attached (van IJzendoorn, 1995).

Children who are *resistantly* or *ambivalently attached* experience a different kind of care. Their primary caregiver responds to their signals unpredictably (Ainsworth et al., 1978), and because they can't rely on her to provide comfort and security, they develop internal working models in which others can't be trusted and they're unable to get what they need by themselves. It is no wonder that they become clingy, dependent, and demanding (Weinfeld et al., 1999). In longitudinal studies, L. Alan Sroufe and his colleagues (1983; Weinfeld et al., 1999) found that resistantly attached school-age children were angry, anxious, impulsive, and easily frustrated; and their low self-esteem made them an easy target for bullying. They often focus on the teacher, creating conflict in order to keep her attention (Howes and Ritchie, 2002; Karen, 1998). About 8 percent of children have the resistant/ambivalent attachment pattern (van IJzendoorn, 1995).

The early experience of an *avoidantly attached* child creates yet another set of internal working models. His primary caregiver is rejecting, angry, irritable, and hostile (Weinfeld et al., 1999). Children growing up under these conditions consider themselves unworthy of love and don't believe that other people will be available to them (Karen, 1998; Renken, Egeland, Marvinney, Mangelsdorf, and Sroufe, 1989). To protect themselves from rejection, they turn off their feelings and act as if they don't care, but beneath their tough facade they are hurt, sad, and angry—likely to act aggressively and strike out preemptively (Kobak, 1999). In a study of high-risk elementary school children, Sroufe and colleagues (Renken et al., 1989) found that boys who were avoidantly attached were prone to aggressive, hostile, noncompliant, and disruptive behavior. They lacked empathy, took pleasure in the misery of others, and infuriated their teachers. However, later studies have not found this association between challenging behavior and avoidant attachment among children at low risk (Lyons-Ruth and Jacobvitz, 1999). Approximately 23 percent of children are categorized as avoidant (van IJzendoorn, 1995).

The primary caregiver of a child with *disorganized/disoriented attachment* usually has serious problems of her own—she may be mentally ill, severely depressed, or addicted to drugs or alcohol (Lyons-Ruth and Jacobvitz, 1999). Sometimes she is frightened, unable to manage her life; and sometimes she is frightening—angry, hostile, distant. Very often she abuses her child—48 percent of children who have been maltreated have a disorganized attachment pattern, according to a meta-analysis of nearly 80 studies (van IJzendoorn et al., 1999). At one and the same time she is the source of danger and safety, alarm and comfort (Lyons-Ruth and Jacobvitz, 1999). From this confusing experience, children derive internal working models of people who can't be trusted to care for them or organize their world (Lyons-Ruth, 1996). They are sad and anxious, with poor social skills, self-control, and frustration tolerance. Because they haven't developed an organized strategy for handling stress or strong emotion, they often have serious behavior problems, acting unpredictably and aggressively with their teachers and peers (Lyons-Ruth, 1996; van IJzendoorn et al., 1999).

Although children living with the most difficult conditions—trauma or severe conflict, for example—tend to remain disorganized (Moss, St-Laurent, Dubois-Comtois, and Cyr, 2005), most children with disorganized attachments evolve a new strategy by their early school years. In an attempt to make their relationship with their mother more predictable and less frightening, their behavior becomes *controlling* (Humber and Moss, 2005; Moss et al., 2005), creating problems with peers and teachers, who find them bossy and inflexible (Greenberg, 1999).

Avoidant and disorganized behavior often appear together, and both are associated with peer rejection and poor emotional and school adjustment (Granot and Mayseless, 2001). But it is the children with disorganized attachment (especially those with the controlling variety) who are most likely to behave aggressively (Lyons-Ruth and Jacobvitz, 1999; Moss et al., 2005; van IJzendoorn et al., 1999). About 15 percent of children in middle-class families display disorganized attachment, but in families where there is poverty, maltreatment, or substance abuse the percentage can be two to three times as high (van IJzendoorn et al., 1999).

How does temperament influence attachment?

It would be convenient to believe that children with secure attachments are actually children with easy temperaments and children with insecure attachments have difficult temperaments (see Karen, 1998). Temperament certainly influences how easy or difficult a particular baby is to care for and can make an enormous difference in the way a parent or caregiver responds to the child. But researchers have found clear evidence that attachment doesn't depend on temperament. When mothers learn sensitive ways to parent (van den Boom, 1994, 1995) and when caregivers have solid social support (Crockenberg, 1981; Jacobson and Frye, 1991), babies with a difficult temperament are far more likely to become securely attached. A meta-analysis has even concluded that disorganized attachment is not the consequence of a difficult temperament. However, in the end it seems evident that both temperament and attachment play crucial roles in challenging behavior.

What happens to attachment as children grow older?

As Bowlby saw it, the main function of the attachment system is to protect the child from danger, both physical and psychological (Marvin and Britner, 1999). Because children remain vulnerable throughout childhood and adolescence, they continue to be attached to their primary caregivers. But as their cognitive capacities, skills, and experience increase, their attachment behaviors change in character, becoming more abstract and sophisticated. When they can take more responsibility for themselves and cope more effectively with stress, it's less important for an attachment figure to be physically present. What matters is the child's confidence in the parent's availability and readiness to act as a secure base for exploration and a safe harbor providing comfort, reassurance, and protection in difficult times (Kerns, Tomich, and Kim, 2006; Marvin and Britner, 1999).

In middle childhood and adolescence, children more and more often turn to peers and other adults—including teachers—to meet these needs (Marvin and Britner, 1999). Gradually they transfer their attachment behaviors to their peers (Allen

Culture Bound?

Although most research on attachment has taken place in the European American culture, Bowlby conceived of it as universal, the outcome of an evolutionary process that ensures the survival of the human species (van IJzendoorn and Sagi, 1999). Ainsworth studied mothers and babies in two cultures, Ugandan and North American, and cross-cultural researchers have provided support for Bowlby's ideas by finding the same basic attachment patterns in Israel, Japan, Africa, China, and Colombia. The majority of children are securely attached, even in Israel's kibbutzim, where children live collectively.

There are entire cultures—India and the Islamic world, for example—that researchers haven't yet explored, but it seems likely that attachment occurs everywhere, regardless of race, gender, or social class (Posada et al., 1995; van IJzendoorn and Sagi, 1999).

and Land, 1999), using them first as companions (Kerns, Schlegelmilch, Morgan, and Abraham, 2005) and eventually as intimate partners (Bretherton and Munholland, 1999; Allen and Land, 1999). When children are securely attached to a parent, they're more likely to have close, reciprocal, and responsive friendships with their agemates (Berlin and Cassidy, 1999; Lieberman, Doyle, and Markiewicz, 1999).

It is important to remember that attachment strategies and internal working models are not immutable—they can change along with life circumstances (Weinfeld et al., 1999). When a child's environment remains stable, as it often does for middle-class children, attachment and working models probably remain stable, too (Hamilton, 2000; Moss et al., 2005; Waters, Merrick, Treboux, Crowell, and Albersheim, 2000). But high-risk conditions and difficult experiences can have a powerful impact on parents' ability to parent, and attachment may change as a result (Waters, Weinfeld, and Hamilton, 2000; Weinfeld, Sroufe, and Egeland, 2000). Perhaps more importantly, children can form new relationships with teachers and other adults that modify their view of themselves and the world. It is also useful to bear in mind that attachment is only one factor among many that influences a child's outcome—in itself it is neither necessary nor sufficient to cause later behavior problems (Greenberg et al., 1997).

ESTABLISHING A RELATIONSHIP WITH THE CHILD

Of course, when children go to school, their attachment status doesn't appear in their file—an expert has to assess it and there is little reason to collect this information, apart from research. But whenever a child with challenging behavior appears in your classroom, it is a good idea to remember that attachment issues may be lurking underneath, particularly in children at high risk (Howes and Ritchie, 1999).

How does a close relationship with a teacher protect a child?

A relationship with a supportive adult can play a key role in building children's resilience (Rutter, 1987; Werner, 2000). This special person can provide a child with all the things that a secure attachment entails: the chance to learn that other people can be trusted, to regard himself as a valuable human being who's worthy of love and respect, and to adjust his internal working models to embrace this new, more positive view of the world (Lynch and Cicchetti, 1992; Howes and Ritchie, 1999).

Most children become attached to more than one person (Ainsworth et al., 1978; Bowlby, 1969/1982), and because each attachment relationship is unique and depends on the way the adult responds to the child (van IJzendoorn and DeWolff, 1997), a relationship with you can become an important opportunity, offering an attachment-like experience that provides a secure base for exploration, a safe haven when a child is threatened or afraid, and interactions that help him regulate his emotions (Mayseless, 2005; Pianta, 1999; Zionts, 2005).

A close relationship with a teacher brings a child other "strong and persistent" benefits (Hamre and Pianta, 2001). With the teacher's warm support, children adjust better to school—they like it more (Ladd and Burgess, 2001), participate more actively in the classroom (Hamre and Pianta, 2001; Ladd and Burgess, 2001), and perform better academically (Birch and Ladd, 1998; Ladd, Birch, and Buhs, 1999). Older children have higher self-esteem, feel more competent in school, and are more likely to be intrinsically motivated (Ryan and Grolnick, 1986). At least one study found that among children at high risk for grade retention or referral to special education, those who had a positive relationship with their teacher were less likely to be held back or referred (Pianta, Steinberg, and Rollins, 1995).

When they get along well with their teacher, children get along better with their classmates, are more gregarious and flexible, have better social skills, and can exert more control over their emotions.

Teacher Template

When children are lucky enough to develop a secure attachment to the very first teacher in their lives, other positive relationships are likely to follow. In one longitudinal study, 9-year-olds' relationship with their first teacher predicted what their relationship with their current teacher would be like (Howes, Hamilton, and Phillipsen, 1998). Perhaps children develop internal working models of teachers, too.

When they get along well with their teacher, children get along better with their classmates, are more gregarious and flexible, have better social skills, and can exert more control over their emotions (Howes and Ritchie, 2002; Peisner-Feinberg et al., 2001). Those with disorganized attachments stand a better chance of being accepted by their peers (Zionts, 2005). But above all, their behavior is less challenging and aggressive (Howes, Matheson, and Hamilton, 1994; Peisner-Feinberg et al., 2001). All of this protects them from risk (Pianta, 1999).

On the other hand, a combative relationship with a teacher increases a child's risks. It makes school an unpleasant place (Birch and Ladd, 1997, 1998), and he is more likely to have attention and learning problems (Ladd and Burgess, 2001), low frustration tolerance, and faulty work habits (Pianta, 1994), which, for boys in particular, adds up to a poor academic performance through grade 8 (Hamre and Pianta, 2001). Children who have a rocky relationship with their kindergarten teacher have more misconduct, discipline infractions, and suspensions in elementary and middle school (Hamre and Pianta, 2001; Ladd and Burgess, 2001), and they behave more aggressively with their peers, who often reject or victimize them (Howes and Hamilton, 1993; Ladd and Burgess, 1999).

When conflict with their teachers is chronic, children may have disturbed thinking patterns (and perhaps problems with social information processing), as they obsess about others' motives and see threats everywhere (Ladd and Burgess, 2001). Even children who aren't at risk may develop behavior problems when they have an antagonistic relationship with a teacher (Ladd and Burgess, 2001; Pianta et al., 1995).

For children with challenging behavior, discord with a teacher is especially common (Hughes, Cavell, and Jackson, 1999). Teachers react to them with anger, criticism, and punishment (Coie and Koeppl, 1990; Walker and Buckley, 1973), and their teaching becomes colder, less responsive, and less encouraging (Fry, 1983; Sroufe, 1983). They call on children with aggressive behavior less frequently, ask them fewer questions, and provide them with less information (Shonkoff and Phillips, 2000). The other students take their cue from the teacher's tone and words and also turn against the child with challenging behavior (Hughes, Cavell, and Willson, 2001; White and Kistner, 1992). Feeling dislike and hostility all around him,

Below Par

A surprisingly small proportion of students claim an "adequate" relationship with their teacher—fewer than 40 percent, according to a study of more than 1,200 middle-class students in grades 2 through 8. Middle schoolers felt less engaged than elementary school students (Lynch and Cicchetti, 1997).

the child is likely to respond with more misbehavior and noncompliance (Zionts, 2005).

How can you develop a positive relationship with a child with challenging behavior?

Relationships are actually made up of hundreds, perhaps thousands, of interactions that form a pattern over time (Pianta, 1999). If the teacher responds to a student sensitively, promptly, and consistently, these interactions eventually add up to an emotional investment; a positive, supportive relationship; and an organized way for teacher and child to relate to one another (Howes, 1999).

But constructing such a relationship with children with challenging behavior is often not an easy matter. Their internal working models of adult–child relationships accompany them to school, where the strategies that protect them from rejecting or haphazard caregiving at home may provoke exactly the behavior they are supposed to ward off, alienating them from teachers and classmates (Howes and Ritchie, 2002). As psychologist Robert Karen writes in *Becoming Attached* (1998), "The behavior of the insecurely attached child—whether aggressive or cloying—often tries the patience of peers and adults alike. It elicits reactions that repeatedly reconfirm the child's distorted view of the world" (p. 228). But, Karen concludes, "If adults are sensitive to the anxious child's concerns, they can break through."

Howes and Ritchie (2002) call this process "disconfirming" what the child has learned from previous experience. It depends, they say, on "careful observation and listening to children and on a teacher's reflecting on her or his own practice, examining missteps, and trying again. . . . In order to disconfirm maladaptive interactions, teachers must be able to think about why the patterns of behavior are occurring and consciously work to change them" (pp. 73, 75).

Sensitive, responsive teaching

Where students with challenging behavior are concerned, all too often our interactions are either negative or practically nonexistent. Teachers tend to keep their distance, limiting themselves to the necessary, frequently saying no and feeling annoyed. But if we're going to help a child with challenging behavior learn to act

Troubleshooter

Madison came into grade 5 with a reputation. She hated school, thought little of the rules and those who imposed them, and believed that her classmates liked her because she wasn't afraid of getting into trouble or talking back to adults. But her teacher, Mr. Darr, quickly won her over. He made her feel he cared about her, and as a result she cared about him, too.

He greeted her every morning as though he was sincerely glad to see her and gave assignments that allowed her to utilize—and get credit for—her talent in art. When she brought him the poems she wrote, he took them seriously. After she had surgery on her eyes and wasn't allowed to participate in physical education for two weeks, she spent many hours in his company, never feeling he'd rather be somewhere else. Madison began to gain confidence in herself—maybe she had something to offer others after all.

That year she almost never got into trouble.

appropriately, we have to give top priority to strengthening our relationship with him (Elicker and Fortner-Wood, 1995). We must put these small encounters to work for us by making them the highest quality possible.

So what is a high-quality interaction? The research literature, starting with Bowlby and Ainsworth, returns again and again to two critical characteristics: *sensitivity* and *responsiveness*. As Ainsworth (Ainsworth et al., 1978) saw it, this involves:

- Being aware of the child's signals
- Interpreting them accurately
- Responding to them promptly and appropriately

Being warm, affectionate, and cooperative—guiding without controlling or coercing and synchronizing interactions with the child's cues—is also vital. To this list, Pianta (1999) adds furnishing acceptance and limits and showing that you value the student's point of view.

Building a relationship with a child who has an insecure or disorganized attachment is a long and arduous process requiring many extra doses of sensitive, responsive attention (Howes, 1999). If a child doesn't trust adults to come through for him, the teacher must be, as Sroufe (1983) puts it, "patiently, inevitably, constantly" available (p. 77). If the child expects to be rejected, the teacher must be careful not to exclude him by removing him from the group or sending him out of the class (Karen, 1998). When a teacher always reacts empathically, it becomes possible for the child to believe that people actually do respond to his needs (Weinfeld et al., 1999). In due course, small things—more contact, a calmer tone of voice—accumulate and start to have an effect.

With children who are stressed and children who have a history of difficult relationships, it may be helpful for the teacher to behave as she would with a younger child (Howes and Ritchie, 2002; Pianta, 1999). Although by middle childhood students should be able to use language in order to retain or regain comfort and control, sometimes talking, making choices, and problem solving just overwhelm them. In fact, aggressive or defiant behavior may be a signal that the student needs more assistance (or less challenge) (Pianta, 1999). He may do better when the teacher offers the kind of support that worked for him in the past. Remaining physically nearby and emotionally accessible enables the teacher to act as an organizer for a child's classroom experience (Howes and Ritchie, 2002). By being directive, staying calm, using a warm tone, consistently acknowledging the child's work, and responding positively to his questions, comments, and problems, the teacher is helping the child learn to regulate his own emotions and organize his own behavior.

Instead of waiting for an obvious signal (such as an explosion), sensitive and responsive teachers keep an eye out for subtle signs that appear not only in a student's words but also in his body language or tone of voice—stiff shoulders, gritted teeth, lashing out at peers (Honig, 2002). These are cues to talk with a child about his feelings and show him you care. Chapter 10, the WEVAS strategy, discusses this issue in detail.

Teacher talk

In their observations of children with difficult life circumstances, developmental psychologist Carollee Howes and education specialist Sharon Ritchie (2002) iden-

S tudents of color in urban schools give teachers this advice (Cushman and the students of What Kids Can Do, 2003):

- Don't just look at students for answers, but look at who they *are*, through the way they act. Not "what's going on in our home life"—be perceptive to what's going on in our *classroom*. Who we like, what's hard for us, what's easy for us. If you pay attention you can see it.
- Don't be afraid to talk to us one on one, but don't try too hard to be our friend.
- We don't want something so obvious. We want you to notice the little signals we give in class—the way we answer a question, if we stutter a little or we pause—
- Even the way we look at you! Our body language—
- If there's confusion on my face, I want you to see it. If there's disagreement I want you to say, "You disagree? Why?"
- And without talking to a student for 18 hours, know them well enough to know what their faces mean. (p. 4)

Source: © 2003 by What Kids Can Do, Inc. This piece originally appears in *Fires in the Bathroom: Advice for Teachers From High School Students* by Kathleen Cushman and the students of What Kids Can Do, Inc. Reprinted with the permission of The New Press. www.thenewpress.com.

tified another effective technique for helping students trust the teacher and believe they're worthy of affection: *teacher talk.* Teachers used certain phrases over and over to support the child and explain what they were doing. A teacher would say, "I'm going to help you," "I'm going to stop you," or "I'm going to say no" to remind a child to try to control his own behavior and tell him that she's available to help him help himself: "I'm going to help you organize your desk so that you can join us for small-group time." This repeated phrase assists children in organizing their behavior. As students gained problem-solving skills and needed less direction, teachers began to *ask* children if they wanted help: "Do you want me to help you, or do you want to do it yourself?" (Howes and Ritchie, 2002).

Talk openly about feelings

Open communication about feelings is crucial to building a responsive relationship. For children who've had difficult relationships and children from violent neighborhoods or abusive or stressed families, it is often dangerous to show or express negative feelings at home; as a result they shut down their anger, anxiety, sadness, frustration, and fear and do not learn to control them. But the feelings do not go away and may surge out unexpectedly in stressful situations. When teachers accept and validate these emotions and give the child language to label and talk about his feelings ("I know that makes you mad," "That must be scary"), they tell him that they're listening, help him cope in the classroom, and shore up the teacher–child relationship (Pianta, 1999). With the teacher acting as an emotional coach and modeling self-control, students can develop the ability to soothe themselves and to regulate and express their emotions in appropriate ways (Howes and Ritchie, 2002; Pianta, 1999).

Being positive is another way to improve your relationship with a child with challenging behavior. This may not be easy if your joint history leads you both to expect the unpleasant at every turn, but again it is a matter of giving the relationship priority. If you can notice the child's positive feelings and behaviors and respond positively to his requests, it becomes easier for him to behave positively, too (Elicker and Fortner-Wood, 1995).

Although there are a zillion ways to interact positively with a student, perhaps the most important is simply to spend time with him, one on one. When you keep an eye out for moments to connect, they seem to appear miraculously in the daily routine, whether he's helping you organize a bookshelf, needs help with his reading, or is returning to the classroom after recess (Elicker and Fortner-Wood, 1995). Recess itself often presents excellent opportunities. For more ideas, see "Money in the Bank," page 87.

If the vibes between you and the child always feel negative despite your best efforts, experts recommend a special kind of interaction called *banking time* (Pianta, 1999; Pianta and Hamre, n.d.). This technique is based on the notion that positive experiences with a child protect the relationship against conflict and tension, in the same way that money in the bank provides a buffer against extra expenses, and it introduces new interactions, perceptions, and feelings into a relationship. Pianta (1999; Pianta and Hamre, n.d.) describes its basic rules:

• At least once a week, the teacher sets aside 5 to 15 minutes of special time to spend with the student, one on one. Because this time should not be used to reinforce or punish behavior, it should be arranged regularly and in advance. Although it's hard to schedule, you can usually fit it in during independent work time. (Try to avoid recess or lunch, which give students an opportunity to stretch their legs and build relationships with their peers.) It may be necessary to recruit another adult to assist with the other children.

• During this special time, the student decides what he and the teacher will do together, choosing from a wide range of materials selected by the teacher. The student leads and directs the activity.

• The teacher doesn't teach, direct, reinforce, or focus on the student's performance, but instead remains neutral and objective. In an interested tone of voice, she becomes a kind of sportscaster, describing what the child is doing and labeling his feelings (Barkley, 1987).

• The teacher selects no more than three simple messages to convey. Usually they are ideas such as "You are important," "I will try to be consistent and available," or "I am a helper when you need or ask me," that are chosen to disconfirm the student's negative beliefs and expectations about adults and help him learn to use the teacher as a resource and a source of safety and comfort. The teacher reinforces these messages by communicating them in ordinary situations throughout the day ("I'm happy to help you. Teachers are helpers.").

• When the session is over, the teacher records what happened and what she felt so that she can reflect on it.

Putting the student in charge allows him to behave in new ways and show you different competencies. He can become more interested in you, care more about

Good teaching practices, such as remembering to smile, starting every day with a clean slate, listening carefully whenever children try to communicate, and being available to students before and after school, provide the basis for positive interactions. Researchers and teachers on the frontlines offer these additional tips:

- Address students by their names whenever possible—when you greet them in the morning, when you call on them in class, or when you pass them in the hallway throughout the day.
- Learn about the child's family—who lives with him, the names and ages of siblings and pets—so that you can begin to enter his world ("What did you and Francesca do this weekend?"). For more about relationships with families, see the next section and Chapters 6 and 13.
- Try to discover what the student likes, what's important to him, and what makes him feel good about himself. Create opportunities for him to talk with you and share his memories, experiences, and feelings.
- Tell the child you care about him and think about him when he's not there. For example, call his home if he misses a few days of school, and bring things into the classroom that you know will interest him ("I found a book you're going to like").
- Share your own interests, experiences, and feelings. This lets the child know that the relationship is reciprocal and that you are a person as well as his teacher.
- Catch the student being good. When he's behaving appropriately, give him extra time and attention.
- Perform kind and helpful acts for the child, and find ways to let him help you by giving him reasonable responsibilities. Children feel important when they can help.
- Make comments that give the student the message that you see and hear him ("You seem tired this morning, Ricardo") (Koplow, 2002).
- Create a special signal, exclusive to you and the child. A secret sign, handshake, or password makes it fun to communicate.
- Open your door 15 minutes early each day so that children can come into the classroom and hang out with you (Pianta and Hamre, n.d.).

having your attention and approval, and begin to believe that an adult can be available, responsive, and accepting. You, in turn, may well find him more pleasant, interesting, competent, and amenable to guidance.

Back to the beginning

When you know a child well, you are on firmer ground. You know how to make your interactions more sensitive and responsive, how to incorporate his interests into your activities, how to build on his strengths, and how to teach him the skills he needs. If you pay close attention when you're together, you'll get to know and understand him. Remember that you are a giant player in this game, the adult who has the responsibility and the one who's most capable of reflection and change. It's always useful to examine your own feelings and actions and think about how they're affecting your relationship. When you do, the child benefits, and your own practice becomes more rewarding and meaningful.

Remember that suitcase the child with challenging behavior lugged into your class-room on page 76 of this chapter? Well, one of the most important items it contains is his family—a fact that makes building a good relationship with the family a big part of building a relationship with a child. Where students with challenging be-havior are concerned, teachers need all the help they can get.

Thanks to the ecological theory of Urie Bronfenbrenner (1979) (which urges us to look at the child in the context of family, community, and society) and family-systems theory (which reminds us that family members are all connected to one an-other), we now know that child and family are one big package, an integral whole. By building positive relationships with families, teachers are supporting children's well-being and development.

Here are some of the basic ideas behind this family-centered approach (Chud and Fahlman, 1995):

- Families are central to children's lives—their first and main teachers.
- Each family has its own strengths, competencies, resources, and ways of coping.
- Each family must be respected and accepted on its own terms, without judg-ments or preconceptions.
- Each family's race, culture, ethnicity, religion, language, and socioeconomic sta-tus must be respected.

Three decades of research confirm that when families are involved in their chil-dren's education, children of all ages do better both academically and socially, no matter what the family's income or background (U.S. Department of Education, 2004; Hoover-Dempsey and Sandler, 1997; Weiss, Kreider, Lopez, and Chatman, 2005). In fact, No Child Left Behind mandates parent involvement in the school. When we work together, families, teachers, and students are all much stronger.

What keeps teachers and families apart?

Almost all families care about their children's success at school and want to be good partners (Epstein et al., 2002; Kyle, McIntyre, Miller, and Moore, 2002); almost all teachers and administrators welcome their involvement (Epstein et al., 2002; Lareau, 2000); and these days families can participate in their child's learning in a wide range of ways, both at home and at school.

Nevertheless, collaborating productively is no simple matter. A thousand ob-stacles seem to stand in the way, especially for low-income families and families of different cultures (Trumbull, Rothstein-Fisch, Greenfield, and Quiroz, 2001):

- Time, a precious commodity for all families, is perhaps the most obvious barrier. Few parents can afford not to work, and in low-income families they may hold down two jobs and work odd or irregular shifts just to keep afloat.
- Families may feel uncomfortable or intimidated, perhaps because they grew up outside of the United States and don't speak English well, perhaps because they had little education themselves (Trumbull et al., 2001), perhaps because they carry unpleasant memories of their own school days. They may worry that they won't be able to help their child with his schoolwork and fear they'll be blamed for his poor academic performance or challenging behavior.

- As children grow older and struggle to become autonomous, they may not want their families around (Hoover-Dempsey and Sandler, 1997). This is especially true for children in trouble (Fertman, 2004).
- School policies, programs, activities, and ways of communicating, however well intentioned, may put families off. All too often schools and teachers are unaware that their efforts to involve families grow out of cultural values and knowledge that the families may not share—and find puzzling, alien, or even inappropriate (Trumbull et al., 2001). (Chapter 6 is devoted to this important issue.)
- Many working-class and low-income families, as well as families with different cultural backgrounds, believe that school and family lie in separate realms. They view teachers as professionals with specialized knowledge who are responsible for education (Lareau, 2000); whereas their own role is to send their children to school on time, try to get them to do their homework (Lareau, 2000), and teach them to behave properly and be good people (Trumbull et al., 2001). Because they don't usually socialize with the parents of their children's classmates, they have little of the inside information that middle-class families easily accumulate and utilize in their dealings with the school (Lareau, 2000).

It's important to remember that even when families don't participate in traditional ways, they make a vital contribution by supporting their child's learning at home—by stressing the importance of going to school and studying hard, monitoring homework, and providing high expectations, pride, understanding, and enthusiasm for his school experiences (Nieto, 2003).

Getting to know you

The families who are hardest to connect with may very well turn out to be the ones you most need to get to know—the ones whose children will benefit the most from a relationship. When you know where the child is coming from, you'll understand him better, have more empathy for him, and make a stronger connection. If you can establish some trust with the family, you will have a much better chance of helping one another—and the child—when there's a problem.

How, then, can you break through these formidable barriers and build positive relationships with families?

Research shows that parents are more likely to become involved in a child's education if they believe that they can help him succeed. They are also more likely to get involved if they believe that the teacher's invitation is serious and sincere (Hoover-Dempsey and Sandler, 1997). This is especially important when parents think they won't actually be helpful or that it's not their role to be involved (Hoover-Dempsey and Sandler, 1997).

These findings emphasize the importance of the teacher. Some parents will be involved no matter what you do, and some will never clear the hurdles standing between you. But some may respond if you approach them the right way. What's required is a strong, clear message that their involvement can really help their child and that you truly value and respect their views.

Getting to know families is a process that takes time, so it's vital to start as soon as possible. Each contact helps build trust. One way to begin is to send out a welcome letter before school opens. Introduce yourself by describing your cultural background, the languages you speak, where you grew up, how long you've been

Research shows that parents are more likely to become involved in a child's education if they believe that they can help him succeed.

teaching, whether you're married and have children, how you spent the summer, and one or two of your interests outside of school—whatever information you'd like to share. Telling families who you are will enable them to see you as a person as well as a teacher. Tell them, too, what the children will be learning this year, and let them know they can call you whenever they have questions, concerns, or suggestions. If you're comfortable with the idea, give them your home phone number, or tell them when and how they can reach you at school.

Another tactic for becoming acquainted with the family is to ask your students for help. Early in the term, give them the assignment of interviewing their family. You can brainstorm the questions as a group; for example, ask about other family members, where they come from and where they grew up, what languages they speak, the work they do, and their special interests and activities. Assisting their children with this assignment enables parents to see that you care about the family and gives you a new perspective on the child. It also suggests ideas for creating learning experiences that build on the family's culture and knowledge and for involving the family as experts, resources, and helpers.

Diane W. Kyle and her colleagues (2002) recommend yet another strategy for getting to know the family: Take a walk in the school's neighborhood where the children in your class live. Watch a basketball game; go into the church; buy something at the drugstore; have a snack at a local eatery; talk to people about the school and the community. Draw a map showing the resources that you and the children can utilize, and try to spend a few minutes in the community each week. Make a point of going to street fairs, celebrations, and other activities that families enjoy. If it's a tough neighborhood where you will stick out like a sore thumb, you might ask one of your students to act as a guide.

In a school setting, it is very difficult to meet family members in person. Keep in touch by sending out a newsletter that describes what you're doing in class. (Turn it into a group project by encouraging the children to write in their home language, use the computer, and include drawings and photos.) You can also call or send notes and postcards home when you have good news to relay ("Andrew worked hard on the group mural today. He really helped the other children"). Assignment agendas—with columns for each subject and spaces for both teachers and parents to write in—provide another method for staying in contact. Checked daily at home and at school, they keep everyone connected and up to date, especially in middle school (Kyle et al., 2002). You can even create a website to communicate with parents and students.

What about parent-teacher night?

Parent–teacher night will probably offer the first real opportunity to meet families. This event, held by more than 90 percent of elementary schools, attracts more families than any other (Trumbull et al., 2001). However, many parents, including those you most want to talk with, may be reluctant or unable to attend. You can encourage them by phoning to deliver a personal invitation, letting them know that all family members are welcome, and if necessary setting up an alternative meeting or phone conversation.

In addition to presenting your curriculum to the parents as a group, do your best to help your families feel at home by setting aside some time to socialize, perhaps around coffee and cookies. Make a point of treating each parent as a distinct person in her or his own right, not just as Kevin's mother or Yolanda's father. Parents often want to keep their private lives private (Larner, 1994; Powell, 1989)—but paradoxically they may also want teachers to be interested in them as people (Powell, 1998). Like their children, they have their own temperaments, needs, preferences, and cultures.

When you meet again for individual conferences at report card time, everyone will feel more pressured, with too much to discuss in too short a time. Try to put parents at ease and establish rapport by starting with polite greetings and respectful small talk. With families from the mainstream culture, it's a good idea to say something positive about their child. But with families of diverse cultures, it may be best to deal first with their priorities and talk about the child's contributions to the group (Trumbull et al., 2001). Take careful notes—even about nonacademic matters—so you can ask appropriate questions the next time you meet ("How is your grandmother?") (Trumbull et al., 2001).

A word of caution: In cultures that regard parents or elders as the source of authority and knowledge, it is not proper for a child to act as an interpreter or to lead a parent–teacher conference (Trumbull et al., 2001).

Should teachers visit families at home?

Schools vary enormously in their attitudes toward home visits—some forbid them, others encourage them. Although visiting may seem daunting and time consuming, the experts agree that it is definitely worth the effort, particularly when you're worried about a student or when the family comes from a different culture. Put these families at the top of your list and visit them as soon as possible. You'll get to know one another better as people and gain valuable insights into everything from their daily lives to their values and goals for their children. The child will feel proud to have you in his home, and the family will feel honored to have you as a guest.

To make things easier, you can partner with a colleague, talk about the questions you might want to ask, and role-play to discover possible pitfalls, give yourselves practice, and ward off anxiety. You can also visit in tandem and discuss your impressions afterwards (Ginsberg, 2007).

Be sure to make arrangements in advance, keep your stay to under half an hour, and bear in mind that families who've had negative encounters with social services, immigration, or other authorities may feel uneasy with any kind of visit (York, 1991). If the family doesn't want you to come to their home, offer to get together somewhere else—at the school, a local coffee shop, the community center. Let them know you'd like to meet their other children and family members, too. If they don't respond to your initial invitation, follow up with a phone call; but if the meeting doesn't come off, be careful not to blame the family or to hold it against the child.

As Kyle and her colleagues (2002) put it, the object of a visit is "to learn how I can help your child more" (p. 62), so it presents an opportunity to ask questions and learn about the family's strengths, knowledge, and resources, not to give answers. Once again, begin with polite small talk, say how pleased you are to have their child in your class, and thank them for welcoming you into their home by presenting a small gift of fruit or cookies (Ginsberg, 2007). Let them know up front what you'll be asking, and be sure they understand that they don't have to answer if they don't want to. You might ask about how the child spent the summer, what his talents, interests, and favorite activities are (scholastic and otherwise), how he helps out at

Diplomacy at Home

In *Bridging Cultures between Home and School*, authors Elise Trumbull, Carrie Rothstein-Fisch, Patricia M. Greenfield, and Blanca Quiroz (2001) describe culturally sensitive ways to communicate with parents. They write:

In order to learn through conversation, diplomatic questions must be constructed. Diplomatic questions do not appear invasive, because they are based on background knowledge rather than ignorance; the teacher can use this knowledge to make her information-seeking more indirect. . . .

For example, if a teacher wants to ask an immigrant mother how far she went in school, she can first ask two nonthreatening questions: "Where are you from?" and "How old were you when you came to the United States?" As an example, the mother may answer that she is from rural Mexico and that she was educated there. The teacher can now use her knowledge of Mexican schooling to transform what could be a threatening probe into a welcoming one: "I know that some places in Mexico do not have schools available, or they exist only up to sixth grade. It must have been difficult for you to get an education in Mexico." It is important to notice that this probe is *not* in the form of a question. The statement shows relevant background knowledge, rather than ignorance, making it a socially competent conversational move, not an intrusive probe. (pp. 108–109) home, and who his friends are, both in and out of school. Ask about what upsets him and how they help him to deal with it; and ask about the academic and social skills they'd like him to develop this year (Kyle et al., 2002). You can also ask about what they feel comfortable doing to help their child learn. Although direct questions are considered rude in some cultures, you might ask an immigrant family indirectly about their home country and how they like living in the United States. (See box, page 92.)

As you chat, look around carefully and ask about what you see—pets, photos, artwork, books, musical instruments. They will elicit stories and give you clues about the strengths and interests of the family members and the child himself. Be sure to answer any questions the family may have.

"Without a doubt," Kyle and colleagues (2002) conclude, "we all agree that visiting the family . . . is by far the most valuable experience we have had in teaching. Nothing comes close to doing what visits can do" (p. 75).

The next step

Creating a relationship with children and families who come from a different culture is particularly challenging and important: Research shows that teachers are less likely to reach out to families from diverse cultures (Galinsky and Weissbourd, 1992), and in turn these families are less likely to consider teachers to be a source of information and support (Bowden, 1997; Kontos and Wells, 1986; Trumbull et al., 2001). Fortunately, however, research also shows that families from different cultures have the same high aspirations and strong commitment to their children's education that European American families do, and they're eager to be more involved (Trumbull et al., 2001). Teachers want more communication, too (Epstein et al., 2002; Lareau, 2000).

What is blocking the way? Perhaps the greatest obstacle—and the hardest to see—is the culture difference itself. The next chapter explains how culture influences everyone's values and expectations. It will provide you with a better understanding of how to make both children and families feel recognized and comfortable.

WHAT DO YOU THINK?

1. Have you ever noticed how your own feelings, whether positive or negative, alter what you see or how you act? Can you give an example? Were you able to correct or clarify the situation later?

2. Interview your parents or other family members about your upbringing and about their own past. You can use the questions on page 73 or make up your own, but it might be especially interesting to ask your parents about their own schooling. Did they like school? What was their favorite subject? How far along in school did they go? How did the teachers behave? How did being in school make them feel? As you talk with them, think about questions that your students might comfortably

ask their own parents. Later, take a walk around your family's neighborhood. What does this whole process tell you about you and your family?

3. People have different tolerances and reactions to students' behavior. With a partner in your class, try to figure out which behaviors push your buttons. Why do you think you respond this way? With the rest of the class, discuss how you can go about getting control over your buttons and building a relationship with the child.

4. Even if you don't know a child's attachment status, why is it important to know about attachment and the way it affects children's behavior with their peers, teachers, and others? Think about your own

upbringing. What do you think your own attachment status might be? Do you think it has changed over the years?

5. When you're doing home visits, you may encounter families whose cultures and backgrounds are very different from yours. This could make both you and the family uncomfortable, and if they feel you're judging them, the visit may not go as well as you hope. With other students, role-play how you and the family might feel and act during such a visit, and try to work out a more appropriate approach.

6. Andrew and Jazmine, who appear in the Introduction, come from very different backgrounds. How does knowing that Andrew is from a two-parent, educated, middle-class family and Jazmine has traveled down a much rougher road (incarcerated father, a brother who was murdered, and living with an aunt who isn't very happy about the arrangement) affect your attitude, expectations, and response to their inappropriate behavior?

WHAT WOULD YOU DO?

After a difficult first few weeks of school, Andrew's teachers met to discuss his behavior. Although his grades and inappropriate behaviors (such as calling out, announcing that school was stupid, and saying he wasn't going to do the work) had improved for a brief period, his problems had increased again after the arrival of Jake, a new child in his class. The teachers were spending a lot of time helping Jake to fit in, and Andrew felt abandoned. Jake had easily identified Andrew as a potential co-conspirator, and Andrew, eager to have a friend, was willing to do anything that would make him look cool in Jake's eyes.

His math teacher said that since Jake's appearance, Andrew was impossible in math. His behavior was so disruptive that she couldn't keep him in class and he was falling way behind. Ms. Dalfen, his social studies teacher, added that because reading and concentrat-

ing—staying focused—were hard for Andrew, he seemed convinced that he was stupid. He didn't like to try anything new because he was embarrassed that he wouldn't be able to do it. She also noted that Andrew was always losing things. It took him forever to get started on projects because he had no idea of where to find the materials he needed, and he often forgot his lunch, too.

Then the teachers made an effort to look on the positive side. They had noticed at recess that Andrew was very gentle and patient with the younger children and liked to show them how to do things. Ms. Dalfen mentioned that he was an expert at the computer and liked to help in the classroom as well.

How would building a relationship with Andrew affect his behavior? What are some things that his teachers might do?

SUGGESTED READINGS

Ayers, W. (2001). *To teach: The journey of a teacher* (2nd ed.). New York: Teachers College Press.

Ginsberg, M. B. (2007). Lessons at the kitchen table. *Educational Leadership, 64*(6), 56–61.

Karen, R. (1998). *Becoming attached: First relationships and how they shape our capacity to love.* New York: Oxford University Press.

Kyle, D. W., McIntyre, E., Miller, K. B., & Moore, G. H. (2002). *Reaching out: A K–8 resource for connecting families and schools.* Thousand Oaks, CA: Corwin.

Pianta, R. C. (1999). *Enhancing relationships between children and teachers.* Washington, DC: American Psychological Association.

CHAPTER 6

Opening the Culture Door

Children of color and diverse cultures make up 43 percent of the public school population (Livingston, 2006). Yet the vast majority of teachers are White European American women (Strizek, Pittsonberger, Riordan, Lyter, and Orlofsky, 2006), and even teachers with a different cultural origin usually become acculturated to the mainstream during their education and training (Trumbull, Rothstein-Fisch, Greenfield, and Quiroz, 2001). This culture difference affects our expectations of children and our relationships with them, influences their self-esteem and behavior, and cuts us off from their families—a vital resource when challenging behavior appears.

In *Culturally Responsive Teaching* (2000), Geneva Gay points out that students of color, especially those who are poor and live in urban areas:

- Get less instructional attention
- Are called on less frequently
- Are encouraged to develop intellectual thinking less often
- Are criticized more and praised less
- Receive fewer direct responses to their questions and comments
- Are reprimanded more often and disciplined more severely (p. 63)

Teachers can take a giant step toward bridging this culture gap by getting to know more about their students' culture as well as their own. This chapter will help you to do that by describing what culture is, what happens when home and school culture meet, and some characteristics of specific cultural groups.

This chapter has been adapted from *Partners in Quality, vol. 2/ Relationships* © CCCF 1999, written by Barbara Kaiser and Judy Sklar Rasminsky based on the research papers of the Partners in Quality Project. With permission from the Canadian Child Care Federation, 201-383 Parkdale Avenue, Ottawa, Ontario, K1Y 4R4.

WHAT IS CULTURE?

Everyone has a culture, but most of the time we can't see it. As Eleanor Lynch notes in *Developing Cross-Cultural Competence* (1998a), the book she edited with Marci Hanson, culture is like a "second skin" (p. 24), and it becomes visible only when we brush up against one that's different.

"There is not one aspect of human life that is not touched and altered by culture," says anthropologist Edward T. Hall, one of the foremost authorities on culture. "This means personality, how people express themselves (including shows of emotion), the way they think, how they move, how problems are solved, how their cities are planned and laid out, how transportation systems function and are organized, as well as how economic and government systems are put together and function" (1977, pp. 16–17).

Within each culture there are many variations. Educational level, socioeconomic status, occupation, temperament, and personal experience all influence our values and beliefs (Lynch, 1998a). So do race, language, ethnicity, religion, gender, family, workplace, age, sexual orientation, lifestyle, political orientation, and immigration history—the reason a person came to the United States, her age when she arrived, and how long she has lived here.

What does culture have to do with identity?

Our culture is an integral part of our identity, whether we know it or not. We learn it from our families (who learned it from their families) effortlessly and unconsciously in the course of daily living, and it is reasonably well established by the time we are 5 or 6 years old (Chud and Fahlman, 1985; Lynch, 1998a).

Children naturally develop the characteristics that their own culture values (Lubeck, 1994; New, 1994). Emotional display and affect, communication and learning style, moral development, gender roles, even cognitive abilities depend on what competencies the culture requires of its citizens (New, 1994). Each student brings her own set of culturally based skills and values with her into the classroom.

Teachers have long understood how important it is for children to develop a positive self-concept. We believe that they have the need and the right to feel good about themselves. But we have only recently begun to realize how important a child's culture is to her self-concept—to recognize that students also have the need and the right to be proud of their cultural heritage and the language, abilities, values, attitudes, behaviors, and history that are inseparable from it (York, 1991).

Children start to construct their identity—to understand who they are—from understanding their own culture and by responding to how others see and relate to them. To form a positive self-concept, children need to honor and respect their own culture and to have others honor and respect it, too. When we don't recognize a student's identity—or when we misrecognize it—we can actually harm her by putting her self-concept at risk (LaGrange, Clark, and Munroe, 1994).

Are cultures really so different?

In a word, yes. Mainstream American culture—that is, White European American, middle-class culture, which is based on Western European culture—is different from many other cultures in the world.

Hall (1977) distinguishes between what he calls *low-context* cultures (such as Western European and North American) and *high-context* cultures (such as Asian, South Asian, Southern European, Latino, African American, and Native American). The European American low-context culture is *individualistic*—it values the individual over the group and considers the individual's independence the greatest possible virtue. It sees each person as a unique and separate being who is born with needs, rights, and an identity all his or her own, and it teaches its citizens to assert themselves, take the initiative, make their own choices, explore, compete, and achieve.

Children in individualistic low-context cultures begin to practice independence when they're very small. Their parents put them to sleep alone in cribs in their own rooms; supply them with objects so they can amuse and comfort themselves; transport them in their own strollers and car seats; deposit them on the floor to play alone; give them finger foods and cups so they can feed themselves; and leave them with babysitters when they go out for the evening because they, too, are individuals with separate lives. When children go to school, parents and teachers encourage them to become independent, critical thinkers (Trumbull et al., 2001).

But in about 70 percent of the world's cultures, this notion of the separate, individual self is "a rather peculiar idea," writes anthropologist Clifford Geertz (as cited in Kağıtçıbaşı, 1996, p. 53). Outside of the European American culture, people value *interdependence*—being closely connected—and they are first and foremost members of a group. In these high-context, *collectivist* cultures, children learn that they are part of an extended family and a community and that they are responsible for looking after one another. They value harmony and cooperation and base their self-esteem on their contributions to the good of the whole, not on their individual achievement—which high-context collectivist cultures view as selfish and as a rejection of the family (Lynch, 1998b).

As Lynch puts it, "The majority of people throughout the world have nurtured children for centuries by having them sleep in the parents' bed; following them around in order to feed them; keeping them in close physical proximity through holding, touching, and carrying long after they can walk alone; or taking them wherever the adults go" (1998b, p. 59). When children in high-context cultures go to school, their parents want them to help one another, learn from one another, and cooperate with one another, because cognitive development is inextricably tied to being a good person (Trumbull et al., 2001).

Of course, in the end, every culture needs both group and individual loyalties. The question is, Which takes priority (Gonzalez-Mena, 1997)?

Communication is another area where there are distinct cultural differences. In low-context individualistic cultures, words are primary, and communication is direct, precise, and linear. Speakers focus on the content and include all relevant background information to ensure that their listeners understand them (Delpit, 1995). They consider emotion an illogical force that clouds the argument (Gay, 2000).

But in high-context collectivist cultures, words do not stand alone. Nonverbal cues (such as gestures, facial expression, and movement) and contextual cues (such as shared experience, history, tradition, social status, and the relationship between speaker and listener) play a far greater role in communication. Pauses, silences, and indirect ways of communicating (such as empathy, storytelling, analogies, and talking around a subject) are also critical (Chud and Fahlman, 1995; Gonzalez-Mena,

Apron Strings

C ross-cultural researchers studied childrearing values in nine countries (Kağıtçıbaşı, 1996). When asked to name the most desirable quality in children, 60 percent of Turkish parents chose "obeying their parents" first or second. A mere 18 percent selected "being independent and self-reliant." Thai, Filipino, and Indonesian parents made similar choices. But parents in fast-industrializing Korea and Singapore valued their children's independence even more than U.S. parents.

1997). Meaning is mostly implicit, and it's considered unnecessary, even insulting, to say what everyone already knows (Delpit, 1995).

People in high-context cultures don't focus on objects or information as things in themselves—rather, they derive meaning from the relationships and emotions surrounding them. To a Latina child, for example, an egg isn't a collection of attributes (a shell, a white, a yolk); its meaning is embedded in its history and associations, such as her relationship with her grandmother, whom she often helps when she cooks for the family (Trumbull et al., 2001).

The melting pot and the salad bowl

The United States has always considered itself a *melting pot*, a place where people from all over the world have gathered to become one nation, under God, indivisible. In the past, when newcomers settled into the new land, they gradually assimilated, taking on the characteristics of the dominant, mainstream, middle-class European American culture and giving up their own. But as the world grows smaller and the cultural makeup of the United States becomes more varied, our goals are changing. Members of many cultures are seeking ways to succeed while maintain-

Breaking the Code

E ach culture has its own communication style. Perhaps you've encountered some of these varieties:

- In face-to-face conversation, the European American culture expects eye contact, which conveys honesty, attention, and trustworthiness. But African American, Asian Pacific, Latino, and Native American cultures consider direct eye contact aggressive, disrespectful, or impolite.
- Some cultures, such as the Mediterranean, display emotion openly and spontaneously; others, such as Chinese and Japanese, regard emotional restraint as polite.
- European Americans laugh or smile when they're happy or amused. But in many Asian cultures, people laugh or smile when they're embarrassed, confused, or even sad.
- In Latino, Arabic, and African American cultures, people stand close together to converse; European Americans like to stay an arm's length away. Asian Pacific Islanders also prefer more space.
- Whereas frequent touching is an important part of communication in Mediterranean cultures, the Japanese, Chinese, and Korean cultures avoid physical contact (Chud and Fahlman, 1985; Lynch, 1998b).

ing their cultural identity, and we are increasingly recognizing the rich contributions this diversity brings to our lives. Recently, some people have begun to rethink the metaphor of the melting pot. They would prefer to liken the United States to a cultural mosaic like Canada, or to a *salad bowl*, where the separate pieces mix but retain their own special identity. Perhaps we'll see that vision realized sometime in the future, but until then, the dominant culture—what scholar and educator Lisa Delpit (1995) calls the "culture of power"—will define our thinking and pervade society's institutions.

Anthropologist John U. Ogbu (1994) has developed an influential theory about why different cultural groups have different attitudes about assimilating into the dominant culture. Some are what he calls *voluntary* or *immigrant minorities*, who move to the United States by choice. They believe they will have more freedom, more opportunity, and a better standard of living in this country. Although they would like to retain their own culture, they realize that they will have to learn some aspects of the European American culture in order to succeed in it, and they don't feel that their cultural identity will be threatened if they do. Their children usually do well in school.

Other cultural groups are *involuntary minorities*, Ogbu (1994) says—"those groups (and their descendants) who were initially incorporated into U.S. society against their will by Euro-Americans through slavery, conquest, or colonization. Thereafter, these minorities were relegated to menial positions and denied true assimilation into the mainstream U.S. society" (p. 373). Native Americans, African

Members of diverse cultures are seeking ways to succeed while maintaining their cultural identity, and we are increasingly recognizing the rich contributions they make to our lives.

Americans, and Mexican Americans (because the United States conquered and annexed their territory) make up this group.

Because the United States tried to wipe out the cultures of the involuntary minorities and because they are aware of the racism in U.S. society, the involuntary minorities have defined themselves in opposition to the attitudes, beliefs, and preferences of the dominant culture. As a result, they feel they cannot adopt the dominant culture's ways without losing their own culture. Students with these beliefs and attitudes may not wish to succeed in European American schools. Those who do may be accused of "acting white" and face repudiation from their peers (Ogbu, 1994; Tatum, 1997).

This theory has prompted considerable discussion. Some scholars see the cultivation of a distinct racial or ethnic identity not as a rejection of the dominant culture's standards of achievement but as a source of strength, creating a sense of belonging, connection, and solidarity, as well as providing mechanisms for critiquing and coping with inequality (Carter, 2005).

As part of their Eriksonian search for identity, children of color and diverse cultures become much more aware of their racial and ethnic backgrounds by about grade 6 or 7 (Tatum, 1997). Because other people start to pay more attention to their race as they grow older and bigger—for example, by avoiding them on the street or watching them closely when they enter a store—they perceive themselves

Mirror, Mirror

In an ethnographic study in Yonkers, New York, sociologist Prudence L. Carter (2005) found that low-income African American and Latino young people handled their association with the dominant culture in three distinct ways:

1. *Cultural mainstreamers.* A small number of teens saw Whites' speech, dress, gestures, and music as "regular" and adopted the dominant culture's ideology of assimilation. Often labeled nerds, these students had successful academic careers. Although they were aware of their own cultural heritage, they felt they had to work within the system in order to change it. They risked peer rejection and were frequently accused of "acting white."
2. *Noncompliant believers.* This large group of students believed in education but rejected the dominant culture's rules for achievement. Instead, they embraced their own racial identity and cultural codes and came into conflict with teachers when they talked, acted out, skipped class, and didn't do assignments. Their record reflected this behavior: Their marks ranged from average to failing. They believed that their school experience devalued their culture and academic concerns.
3. *Cultural straddlers.* This group (about one-third of the students) managed to balance the expectations of both peers and teachers. That is, they were able to *codeswitch*—to move comfortably between the two cultures, speaking both Black English and Standard English, doing well in school, and maintaining friendships with their peers.

Why did the noncompliant believers adapt differently from the straddlers, and how can schools respond to their needs and the critique of the mainstream system that is implied? Carter (2005) writes, "One can hardly succeed fully in a place where one's cultural tastes are not welcomed or appreciated. . . . The noncompliant believers in education. . . . compel us to reconsider how we distribute cultural power and to note who chooses and who loses in a democratic society that espouses pluralism" (p. 65).

differently, too. They begin to ask themselves what it means to be African American, Latino, or Asian American and grapple with the notion that they belong to a group that's targeted by racism (Tatum, 1997).

Many children react to this development by spending as much time as possible with their racial and ethnic peers—the only people who really understand what they're going through. As Beverly Tatum (1997) has observed, this is why "all the Black kids are sitting together in the cafeteria." They see themselves as part of a larger group and want to learn more about their own race and culture. By forming a mutual support group, they create a safe place to retreat and regroup. In fact, some researchers have found a link between a strong ethnic identification and high academic achievement (Carter, 2005).

WHEN HOME CULTURE MEETS SCHOOL CULTURE

To teach any child—and a child with challenging behavior in particular—you have to understand where she is coming from. That means you have to understand her culture. But just as your feelings and perceptions create barriers, so does your own culture. Paradoxically, the first step in understanding someone else's culture is to become aware of your own. Then you can see how it influences your behavior and interactions with others—and that it isn't the only valid way to do things.

People who belong to the dominant European American culture often have the mistaken idea that they don't have a culture. That's because they're surrounded by people who think the same way they do and because their way of thinking shapes American society. For the same reason, they know less about other people's cultures. People who are part of a less powerful culture have to learn more about the dominant culture—it's a matter of survival for them (Delpit, 1995; Tatum, 1997).

When you look at your family history, as you do when you're reflecting, you will get some insight into your culture. Another way to bring your culture out of the closet is to pay close attention when you come into contact with different ways of approaching the world—that is, whenever you interact with someone from a different gender, race, ethnic group, religion, nationality, age, even family. If you put up your antennae in these encounters, you can begin to get a glimpse of your own assumptions.

Here are some questions to help you think about your own cultural beliefs and experiences:

- Do you remember the first time you met someone from another culture or ethnic group (Chud and Fahlman, 1985)?
- Do you remember how you first learned about your own ethnic identity (Derman-Sparks and the A.B.C. Task Force, 1989)?
- What is important to you about this aspect of yourself? What makes you proud and what gives you pain (Derman-Sparks et al., 1989)?
- Have you ever experienced prejudice or discrimination for any reason? How did it make you feel? What did you do? Thinking about it now, would you change your response (Derman-Sparks et al., 1989)?
- Can you think of a time when you experienced privilege because of your color, class, or ethnicity? Were you aware of it at the time? How did you feel, then and now?

About being a member of the dominant White culture, culture expert Janet Gonzalez-Mena writes (2003):

> I am white and I see the world from a white perspective. I always thought that I was color-less, normal, regular. I didn't think of myself as having a color, a race, a culture. I understand now that view of myself relates to my having unearned power and privilege. Doors open for me that don't open for people of color. If I go register for a motel room and they tell me there is no vacancy, I don't have to wonder if they are lying. If I'm treated poorly in a restaurant, I put it to rudeness not racism. If my kids come to school tired, dirty, or in worn out clothes, someone may think I'm a neglectful parent, but no one will condemn my whole race. My view is the dominant view and is reinforced on all sides. My culture is the dominant culture and therefore invisible to me.

Source: From "Discovering My Whiteness" by Janet Gonzalez-Mena, 2003. Used with permission of the author.

- Do you and your parents agree about ethnic, cultural, and religious issues? If your beliefs are different, how did they evolve? What will you teach your children (Derman-Sparks et al., 1989)?
- If you've traveled to another country—or even to a different area—how did you feel in those unfamiliar surroundings?

The culture of school

"Schools are more than institutions where teachers impart skills and lessons; they are places where teachers transmit cultural knowledge," says sociologist Prudence L. Carter. "Education is as much about being inculcated with the ways of the 'culture of power' as it is about learning to read, count, and think critically" (2005, p. 47). Our schools naturally teach the European American values of individualism and independence, self-direction, initiative, and competitiveness (among others), using European American methods of communication and learning.

But as we have seen, these values and methods are not universal. Other cultures in the world—including several with deep roots in the United States—bring up their children according to different beliefs and values. And when the children of these cultures enter the European American education system, teachers, children, and families all face new challenges.

The hardest part is that we don't really know how out of touch we are. Locked in our own cultures, we can see only the most obvious differences, such as those in dress, speech, and food. But everything in school reflects the assumptions and values of the dominant culture, whether we're aware of it or not. Here are some examples:

- *Individual learning style.* The European American culture expects students to work independently and compete for rewards (Trumbull et al., 2001). Talking with fellow students is discouraged (Shade, Kelly, and Oberg, 1997). Collectivist cultures, on the other hand, bring up their children to help one another learn (Delpit, 1995; Hale, 2001) and to "fit in, not stand out" (Trumbull et al., 2001, p. 5).

- *Passive-receptive posture.* Interaction in the classroom follows the mainstream model: Students listen quietly while the teacher talks, and when they're called on, they respond one at a time by asking or answering questions. To show they're paying attention, they are supposed to sit still and maintain eye contact (Gay, 2000; Kochman, 1985). But in many interdependent cultures, direct eye contact is considered rude, and children may be reluctant to speak in public—instead, they are expected not to share their views but to watch and listen, because adults are regarded as the source of knowledge (Trumbull et al., 2001). Other cultures have different problems with these mainstream expectations. For example, African American children learn primarily through intense social interaction, which is a collaborative process. In their culture, a speaker is a performer who's making a statement, and while she's speaking, listeners join in and respond with gestures, movement, and words. No one needs permission to enter the conversation, and the discourse is fluid, creative, and emotional (Gay, 2000; Kochman, 1985). In fact, African American families encourage children to assert themselves and display their energy, exuberance, and enthusiasm (Gay, 2000).

- *Dispassionate approach.* In the European American culture, teachers and students strive to be rational and objective. They believe that emotion interferes with open-minded inquiry and accuracy and communicates a dangerous loss of control. Students of color, on the other hand, are used to showing their feelings and depend on close emotional relationships in order to learn. They prefer the teacher to express genuine emotion, even anger, and if she doesn't, they believe she doesn't care about them (Delpit, 1995).

- *Deductive style of inquiry.* European Americans take a deductive approach to problem solving. They emphasize detail and arrange facts in a linear, logical order, then move from the specific to the general, building a whole from the sum of its parts. Collectivist cultures solve problems in a different way: They use inductive means, focusing first on the big picture and moving from the general to the specific. Because the group acts as an anchor or catalyst during this process, its members try to stay connected (Gay, 2000).

- *Decontextualized learning.* In European American schools, teachers focus on abstract ideas and concepts, isolating problems and attributes (such as the shell, white, and yolk of an egg) and seeking technical solutions through the use of books, computers, and other materials. They emphasize words and facts (Delpit, 1995) and expect students to explain their work. But in collectivist cultures, it is the context—the relationship between speaker and listeners, the situation, history, tone of voice, and body language—that matters most. The context is continually shifting, and to understand meaning, children learn to focus on the whole situation, not isolated pieces of it, and connect what's happening to their own experience by telling stories, playing with words, and drawing complex analogies (Heath, 1983).

- *"Known-answer" questions.* In the mainstream classroom, teachers instruct by asking questions—to which they already know the answer ("What are the properties of an egg?"). European American students show their intelligence by supplying the correct answer. But African American students find such questions puzzling. In their culture, adults ask questions to challenge them or to find out new information, and children demonstrate their wit and intellect by responding spontaneously and creatively (Heath, 1983; Meier, 1998).

• *Implicit commands.* A European American teacher uses indirection to tell students what to do ("Talia, would you like to read the first paragraph out loud?"). Children of the dominant middle-class culture understand that this request is actually a command. But children from working-class homes, Black and White, are accustomed to direct, explicit commands ("Talia, read the first paragraph") and may not realize that the teacher isn't asking them a question or offering them a true choice and that there are consequences if they don't comply (Delpit, 1995).

• *Topic-centered narratives.* In the mainstream culture, people tell stories based on one event or topic, arrange the facts and ideas in linear order, and explain the relationship between the ideas and the facts. Sticking to the point is vital (Gay, 2000). In the Latino, African American, and Native American cultures, people tell episodic, anecdotal stories that shift scenes and address more than one issue at a time. Narratives unfold in overlapping loops, not in a straight line; and the relationship between ideas and facts isn't made explicit—it must be inferred (Gay, 2000).

• *Standard English.* Using Standard English signals intelligence in the European American classroom (Carter, 2005), and the dominant culture assumes that its own way is the only correct way to speak and write English. However, linguists have established that there is an equally legitimate English with full-fledged status as a language: African American Vernacular English, also known as Black English or Ebonics (from "ebony" and "phonics"), which is the everyday spoken language of a great many African Americans and is known and used selectively by a great many others (Willis, 1998). Rooted in the Bantu languages of West Africa and the African oral tradition, Black English often sounds like Standard English, but it has different syntax, grammar, meanings, usage, and so on (Smitherman, 1998)—for example, a plural doesn't require an "s" at the end of a word (Meier, 1998). For young African Americans, speaking Black English promotes cultural solidarity, authenticity, and legitimacy (Carter, 2005). But as Delpit (1995) points out, it also puts them at risk in school. Mainstream teachers often view students who speak Ebonics as wrong or ignorant, lower expectations for them, and fail to provide appropriately engaging and challenging instruction (Carter, 2005). In addition, a teacher's suggestion that something is wrong with the student and her family takes a psychological toll and creates resistance to mainstream learning and teachers (Delpit, 2002).

• *Standardized testing, tracking, and ability grouping.* Standardized tests—such as those required by No Child Left Behind—demand a wide range of individualistic skills. The questions are decontextualized, written in Standard English, and based on experiences that are familiar to mainstream children (Hilliard, 2002). Schools and teachers often use the results to create tracks or "ability" groups that reward successful students with higher-level teaching. But interdependent cultures don't necessarily value or teach these skills, and once students are relegated to lower-track classes or groups, they have almost no opportunity to catch up.

How does culture influence behavior?

When the school's values and goals resemble those at home, a child experiences less stress, and home values are reinforced. When school is different from home, there is discontinuity—hence more risk. As soon as they're born, children start to acquire the skills they need to become competent adults in their own culture, and by the time they enter school they're already well on their way. In the new environment, a lot of what they've learned so far in their home culture simply doesn't apply. They must start again from scratch, feeling much less competent.

Students who find themselves in a strange environment may experience feelings of confusion, isolation, alienation, and conflict (Chud and Fahlman, 1995). The curriculum, instruction, and discipline may not recognize or support their culture; and their teachers may not notice or appreciate the talents, skills, and abilities they developed in their own community. As a result, they don't feel accepted, respected, or valued; their self-concept and academic achievement may suffer (Gay, 2000; La-Grange et al., 1994); and they may act out. Experts often blame discontinuity for the high rate of school failure and dropout among children from diverse cultures and poor families (Gay, 2000).

As soon as they're born, children start to acquire the skills they need to become competent adults in their culture.

Given such discontinuity, it is easy to see how a cultural conflict, visible or invisible, can cause or contribute to challenging behavior. What was perfectly acceptable at home may be suddenly and inexplicably inappropriate at school.

If a Latina student who usually does excellent work begins to turn in mediocre papers after you've praised her in front of the class, her behavior may be culturally appropriate, not defiant. She may not wish to perform better than her peers because in her culture it is considered impolite to call attention to yourself. If an African American or Latina child sharpens her pencils, arranges her books, moves around, asks you to repeat the directions, and chats with her friends instead of immediately sitting down to do her writing assignment, she may be warming up—setting the stage and the mood—the way her culture dictates, not trying to avoid the task or disturb the rest of the class (Gay, 2000). If an African American student doesn't answer when you ask her a direct factual question about the social studies lesson you've just taught—or about something else you already know—her behavior may be culturally appropriate. Perhaps she expected you to ask her to analyze or evaluate the material the way her family and friends do (Delpit, 1995).

When faced with culturally unfamiliar behavior, teachers frequently try to control or discipline the student involved (Gay, 2000). A teacher may see an assertive or emotional statement as impulsive, disruptive, or smart-alecky; and she may label fidgeting or moving around as hyperactive, off task, or defiant. She may even regard culturally unfamiliar behavior as a problem that requires intervention or special education (Garcia Coll and Magnuson, 2000; Kağıtçıbaşı, 1996).

It is extremely important to understand the cultural assumptions on both sides—on the one hand why you expect a student to behave in a particular way, and on the other hand why for some students your demand seems unreasonable (or strange). If you are not from the European American culture, you will have cultural expectations of your own, and you'll also encounter behavior that perplexes you. For a teacher from a Latino culture, for example, a child who requires an explanation of why she should do things the way you ask may seem rude and lacking in respect rather than assertive or logical.

The Culture of Poverty

Like students from diverse cultures, students who live in poverty have a culture—they have learned what they need to survive in their world. But many of their competencies, skills, and values don't apply in school. Teachers frequently interpret a student's inappropriate behavior personally, thinking that it is directed at them, but the student may not know any other way to react. For example, a child who laughs when you discipline her is probably saving face; a student who responds with anger may be afraid underneath; and one who gets into fights may believe that this is the appropriate way for a man to behave (Payne, 2005).

In *A Framework for Understanding Poverty* (2005), Ruby K. Payne writes, "An understanding of the culture and values of poverty will lessen the anger and frustration that educators may periodically feel when dealing with [low-income] students" (p. 45).

How can you make your teaching more culturally responsive?

Research shows that learning how to function in more than one language and culture (often called *codeswitching*) can have decided benefits—if it's done in a way that supports the child's home language and culture.

- Children perform better academically and are clear thinkers.
- They are less likely to drop out of school.
- They are able to keep the approval and friendship of their racial and ethnic peers.
- Their risk of emotional or psychiatric illness is lower.
- They can move easily and comfortably from one culture to the other, and they're more likely to adapt well to a new situation (Carter, 2005; Freire and Bernhard, 1997; Gonzalez-Mena, 1997).

In other words, when teachers handle discontinuity in a culturally responsive way, they can make a big difference in children's lives.

Culturally responsive teaching uses the cultural knowledge, prior experience, frames of reference, and performance styles of ethnically diverse students in order to make learning more relevant and effective for them, says Geneva Gay (2000). Compatible with best practice, it does for students of diverse cultures exactly what traditional teaching does for middle-class European Americans: "It filters curriculum content and teaching strategies through their cultural frames of reference to make the content more personally meaningful and easier to master" (Gay, 2000, p. 24).

Here are some of the essential elements of culturally responsive teaching (Howard, 2007).

Form authentic and caring relationships with students

For students of diverse cultures—who learn best through social interactions and are always tuned into context—caring, nurturing relationships with teachers (and with one another) are crucial to learning and behavior (Hale, 2001; Nieto, 2004). Make time to talk with your students inside and outside of class; find out about their lives, families, and interests; show your respect by paying attention and responding to what they say and write, both formally and informally; and offer help with assignments even if they don't ask for it (Neito, 2004). Dedicate some weekly class time to discussing what students think about school, what they're learning, and the world around them (Nicolet, 2006).

Use curriculum that honors each student's culture and life experience

Learning is easier, more fun, and more meaningful when students can make connections between school and home. Studying the literature, history, and achievements of their own culture gives students insights into their identity and pride in their heritage, provides them with role models, expands their horizons, and legitimizes their own experience (Gay, 2000). The Jamie Escalante character summed it up in *Stand and Deliver* with these words to his Latino students in East Los Angeles: "You have to learn math. The Mayans discovered zero. Math is in your blood" (Delpit, 1995). The use of culturally relevant curriculum and text materials improves

Keep It Real

Robert Simmons (2006), an African American teacher in the Detroit public schools, offers this advice about developing relationships with students:

> Too many times I have heard teachers discuss . . . where they got their . . . degrees or whom they know. The fact of the matter is that urban students do not care about that stuff. They want to know if you are "keeping it real." They want to know that when the chips are down you will "have their back.". . . The positive relationship with that tough-to-reach kid could mean the difference between life and death. It could mean the difference between success and failure. How can you establish that relationship? Do not read the student's entire school record file. Reading the file will taint your view. A tainted view of a student does not allow for an honest relationship, but a relationship built on conditions. Eat lunch with students in the cafeteria. There is no more authentic social experience than the school cafeteria. You will begin to see student interests, understand their perspectives on the world, and see their lives at home. Provide students with clear expectations. . . . It is the unspoken rules that often bring about the demise of the teacher/student relationship. . . . Get out into their communities, in the physical sense and the intellectual. Go to the local public library with your students to model research. Visit their places of worship. Attend sporting events. Go to their homes for dinner. Appreciate their culture and heritage by reading about their history (as written by their own authors). (p. 48)

Source: From "The Empty Desk in the Third Row: Experiences of an African American Male Teacher" by Robert W. Simmons III, 2006. In J. Landsman & C. W. Lewis (Eds.), *White Teachers / Diverse Classrooms: A Guide to Building Inclusive Schools, Promoting High Expectations, and Eliminating Racism.* Sterling, VA: Stylus Publishing. Copyright © 2006 by Stylus Publishing, LLC.

motivation, interest, academic skill, and time on task (Gay, 2000). On the other hand, students who don't see their culture reflected in the classroom feel alienated and conclude that their school and teachers aren't interested in them (Garrison-Wade and Lewis, 2006; Ladson-Billings, 1994).

Tap into your students' lives to build your curriculum (for example, for a unit on immigration, encourage them to explore their own family's experience [Villegas and Lucas, 2007], or create a math or science unit based on African American hair and hairstyles [Delpit, 2002]). As well as researching the heroes and accomplishments of your students' cultures, discuss culturally sensitive issues in class, and make a point of getting them to dig into their own lives to discover what they know—about community politics, police brutality, or home remedies, for example (Ladson-Billings, 1994).

Shift instructional strategies to meet the diverse learning needs of students

Different cultures have different learning styles. In the collectivist interdependent cultures, where people value social interaction and collaboration, children become more engaged in learning when they work together as partners or in small groups (Gay, 2000; Ladson-Billings, 1994; Shade et al., 1997). African American students thrive when they have lots of opportunities for hands-on learning, active participation, and emotional expression, in writing and in person—for example in stories, role-plays, drama, and movement (Gay, 2000; Landsman, 2006a). Boys in particular need to move around (Delpit, 1995).

E nglish learners in urban schools have this to say about what they already know and can do (Cushman and the students of What Kids Can Do, 2003, pp. 2, 149):

> Sometimes we know what other people don't know and we can explain it to them. You don't always know what I already know and who I learned it from.
>
> - I know Latin dance, from Peru.
> - I can play the organ.
> - I play guitar. I want to join a band.
> - I have a black belt in judo. I learned in Japan, when I was a little girl.
> - I know how to swim and play piano, but I stopped when I came here from Hong Kong because I don't have time.
> - I can draw the Aztec calendar. And I fix things like lights and chairs. My uncle taught me when I came from Mexico.
> - I write poems. And I like to paint flowers and people. But the brush and paints cost $65!
> - I know soccer. I learned it in Mexico. And I know how to make organic pasta from my restaurant job here.
>
> My first English teacher in middle school saw me and my friend dancing and she made a class after school for us to teach samba to English speaking kids. Teachers can make connections for us if they know what we can do.

Source: © 2003 by What Kids Can Do, Inc. This piece originally appears in *Fires in the Bathroom: Advice for Teachers from High School Students* by Kathleen Cushman and the students of What Kids Can Do, Inc. Reprinted with the permission of The New Press. www.thenewpress.com.

Hold consistent and high expectations for all learners

High standards and expectations are essential: They significantly influence both what teachers teach and what students learn. Students understand all too well—and internalize—what their teachers expect of them, and these expectations affect their self-concept, achievement, motivation, and behavior (Aronson and Steele, 2005; Gay, 2000). Too often, teachers make stereotyped assumptions and believe that their European American and Asian American students will do well (Gay, 2000) and their students from other cultural groups will be loud, troublesome, less intelligent, uninterested in school, or incapable of learning (Garrison-Wade and Lewis, 2006). Teachers who hold this deficit perspective water down the level of curriculum and instruction to their students of color, hence fulfilling their prophecy. When teachers provide appropriate teaching, expect students to try hard and do well—and push them to ensure that they do—students are likely to deliver and reward these teachers with their respect and affection. Such "warm demanders," who combine a loving manner with tough and rigorous expectations, are particularly successful with students from diverse cultures (Kleinfeld, 1975).

Acknowledge and validate children's home languages

Delpit (1995) tells us that it is extremely important for teachers to acknowledge and validate children's home languages, which are "vital to their perception of self and sense of community connectedness. . . . The point must not be to eliminate students' home languages, but rather to add other voices and discourses to their repertoire" (p. 163).

High school social studies teacher Vida Hall was "notorious for 'taking no stuff' and for being 'hard but fair,'" writes Geneva Gay (2000):

> Vida insisted that students in her classes perform to the best of their abilities and consistently conveyed to them that they were capable of doing much more than they imagined. . . . "I can't do" was taboo in her classes.
>
> When this explanation was offered by students, Vida responded with gentle but firm insistence, "Of course you can. Now, tell me what I need to do to help you out. Do I need to review the instructions or go over the content again? Do you and I need to spend some time one-on-one together? Do you need to work with another student in class? Or do I need to let the coach know that you are spending so much time with athletics that it's interfering with you completing your social studies assignments?" These were not threats or intimidations; rather, Vida was proposing different avenues to take to remove obstacles to student achievement. And she stood in readiness to aggressively pursue any or all of them to ensure that her students were successful. . . . Students knew what she expected of them and that she was "in their corner.". . . They worked hard to meet her expectations. (pp. 51–52)

When children come from a different culture and speak a different language at home, it takes time for them to understand what's going on in the classroom. Until they do, they are in what language and literacy expert Patton O. Tabors (1997) calls a double bind: They can't make friends because they can't talk with their peers; and they can't learn to talk with their peers unless they have friends.

While learning a second language, children go through stages (Tabors, 1997):

- *Home language use.* They continue to speak their home language as if everyone understands it.
- *Nonverbal or silent period.* Children watch and listen to others as they gather information about the new language.
- *Telegraphic speech and experimentation.* Children try out the new language using individual words and phrases.
- *Productive use.* Once they've acquired enough vocabulary, children can build sentences, although they may still make mistakes and mix languages together.

In order to master their second language, children must continue to speak their first—whether it's Spanish, Chinese, or Black English, the concepts and skills transfer to and enhance their Standard English (Collier, 1995). In a high-quality bilingual environment, they need five to six years to become proficient in their second language (Thomas and Collier, 2003).

Because learning a new language is stressful and exhausting and because teachers don't understand children's needs and ways of learning, their behavior is sometimes challenging. Initially they may appear shy and remain apart from the group, pointing, gesturing, and making noises to communicate (Hickman-Davis, 2002).

Later they may have trouble following directions, responding to questions, and expressing their ideas and feelings, especially if they're from a collectivist culture where such behavior is not appropriate for a child (Santos and Ostrosky, 2002). Although they may act as if they know what's going on, it's possible that they're pretending. They may understand the words but not the meaning of the words within the cultural context—a meaning that could be quite different in their own culture. Along with the words, students must learn the context—when it's appropriate to speak, to whom, in what manner, and so on—which is every bit as subtle and difficult as the language itself.

Allowing students to use their native language empowers them and helps them develop a strong sense of self. Show them that you and their classmates value their language by encouraging them to speak, read, and write it both in and out of the classroom. Use native-language books, magazines, and movies related to your lessons and permit students to use them for their research (Indiana Department of Education, 2005); sanction reading logs and journals in the home language; partner children with same-language peers; and use bilingual staff to help explain content and check understanding of concepts (Indiana Department of Education, 2005).

To help an English-language learner feel secure, provide consistent routines and explain to the other students that she is learning English and needs their help and understanding. Arrange small groups where first- and second-language speakers mix and there is less pressure; pair her with a buddy who can help at recess and lunch; and keep a watchful eye on her progress yourself. Peer tutoring and homework clubs can also lessen frustration. Building on what the child knows, individualize the curriculum, and scaffold your own interactions with her by using lots of gestures, repetition, cues, and concrete language. Ask her if she understands, and if she doesn't, explain again. Don't require her to speak in front of the class; she'll speak out when she feels confident and comfortable enough to do so. (If she's from a collectivist culture, that day may never come—and that's okay.)

The landmark language studies of ethnographer Shirley Brice Heath (1983, 2002) show that children from working-class families of all cultures benefit greatly from an environment filled with language and talk about language. When children study language, it validates their home language, makes them feel less manipulated and disrespected, renders Standard English less demeaning and threatening, and helps them understand that different contexts call for different forms of English (Baker, 2002).

Students can study the characteristics of their home language and compare it to Standard English (Baker, 2002) by analyzing television characters, taping and listening to speakers from different cultures in various situations, interviewing people about how they use language, creating bilingual dictionaries, memorizing parts in plays, creating puppet shows, and producing a daily or weekly news show where they take on the persona and accent of a famous newscaster (Delpit, 1998). If your students are into hip-hop or rap, ask them to analyze lyrics and discover the rules and patterns of the form. Then you can apply the same method to poetry and Shakespeare and even ask them to translate work back into Ebonics (Delpit, 1995). "By asking students to translate their work," says Julie Landsman (2002b), "you are putting a name to what they do without detracting from their home, how their grandmother . . . speaks" (p. 226).

In the 1970s, in the early days of desegregation, ethnographer Shirley Brice Heath lived and worked in the Carolinas, recording how the children in three neighboring communities learned to use language. The resulting study, *Ways with Words: Language, Life, and Work in Communities and Classrooms* (1983), is recognized as "one of the most important language research projects of all time" (Power, 2002, p. 81).

Although clustered geographically, the three communities had radically different ways of using language, Heath found (1983, 2002). Because cultures evolve extremely slowly, they still apply today.

In the White working-class community of "Roadville," parents believe they must teach their children to speak, and from infancy onwards they talk with them in full sentences. Parents label items in the environment, ask questions such as "Where's your nose?", read to them, and expect them to sit quietly while listening to a story. Roadville children start out doing well in school but run into trouble at about grade 4.

In "Trackton," an African American working-class community, children are immersed from birth "in an ongoing stream of talk from extended family members and a wide circle of friends and neighbors" (2002, p. 76), but adults rarely speak to them directly. As they grow, children learn to tell stories, enter adult conversations, respond to teasing games and questions adults don't know the answer to, and adjust their behavior and speech to their audience. Their method of learning—watching, listening, and trying—doesn't mesh with the school's method of teaching, and their teachers report that they talk too much and work too little. They are often failing by grade 3.

To study the townspeople, both White and Black, Heath enlisted the aid of teacher-researchers and found that these middle-class citizens differ from their working-class neighbors in one very significant respect: The adults talk endlessly to their children about what they're doing. They keep up a running narrative and commentary on surrounding events and items ("Mummy's going to get her purse and then we're going for a ride"), and as soon as children begin to talk, they ask them to construct narratives, too ("What did you do at Zoe's house?"). With their parents' help, children rack up thousands of hours of practice telling and replaying stories with different actors and settings and linking events to past and future.

These children succeed in school because, as the teacher-researchers discovered, school's major activity is producing a narrative ("What did the boy in the story find on his walk?"). Parents' narratives hold the key. Heath writes, "It is as though, in the drama of life, these parents freeze scenes and parts of scenes repeatedly throughout the day. . . . They focus the child's attention, sort out labels to name, and give the child ordered turns for sharing talk about these labels and the properties of the objects or events to which they refer. . . . [Children] are not left on their own to see the relation between two events or to explore ways of integrating something in a new context to its old context" (2002, p. 78).

Much of this talk is about talk—names, ways of retelling information, ways of linking past, present, and future, and the like. The teacher-researchers working with Heath realized that their students from Roadville and Trackton needed "intense and frequent occasions to learn and practice those language uses they had not acquired at home," and they created classrooms focused on talk. Their students "labeled, learned to name the features of everyday items and events, told stories, described their own and others' experiences, and narrated skits, puppet shows, and slide exhibits" (2002, p. 78). They became "language detectives," studying their own language as well as the language of their families and others—how they asked questions, showed politeness, got what they wanted, settled arguments, and told funny stories.

The crash course worked: These students achieved academic success.

Writing workshops, journal writing, writing notes to friends (to be delivered in class), and writing autobiographies all provide opportunities to write drafts in a home language that can be translated later for a more formal presentation in Standard English. Assignments where students write for a real audience with a real purpose (such as letters to the editor about an issue that concerns them) also make writing easier and more interesting and give students the sense that they have a voice in their own learning (Delpit, 1995).

Teachers model Standard English and should read it aloud, but it's important not to teach speech at reading time or correct students' words or pronunciation while they're reading. Instead, concentrate on meaning and understanding (Miner, 1998) so that children get the message that reading is actually about meaning.

SOME CULTURAL CHARACTERISTICS

Does each culture have its own special characteristics?

When a student from a different culture disrupts the class or behaves unexpectedly, it's a good idea to try to figure out if culture is responsible. One way to do this is to learn as much as you can about that particular culture. Find out about its customs and values, study its history, read its literature, and, best of all, get to know the student and her family. As you converse, confer, and collaborate, you will come to understand them and their culture better, and they will shed considerable light on the challenging behavior.

Researchers have identified some cultural traits that can help explain different behavioral expectations and outcomes. The brief cultural profiles that follow are intended to illuminate areas where cultural confusion about challenging behavior may arise. Please note, however, that they are generalizations about characteristics that are often, but not always, found, and we present them as a way to help you think about and understand the behavior that you're observing. Remember, too, that people from different places with similar educational and socioeconomic backgrounds may have more in common with each other than with some members of their own culture. Ultimately, each child is unique.

Latino culture

In 2003, the number of Latinos in the United States surpassed the number of African Americans to become the largest community of color in the country (U.S. Census Bureau, 2006). Latinos, who are also known as Hispanics, come from several different Spanish-speaking areas—most notably Mexico, Puerto Rico, Cuba, the Dominican Republic, and South and Central America (Guzman, 2001). These groups have a lot in common and—depending on the country of origin, education, and socioeconomic status of the family—a lot of differences.

In the collectivist, high-context Latino culture, respect for authority and group harmony are important values (Shade et al., 1997). Children receive directives to follow, and they are expected to respect and obey their elders (including their teachers). It is considered rude to question adults, to argue, or to express negative feelings. There may be real cultural conflict for children with Latino values in a European American school where students are supposed to ask and answer questions and speak up for their rights. They may participate more actively and function better when they work collaboratively with a group of their peers and have a warm, informal relationship with the teacher (Gay, 2000; Greenfield and Suzuki, 1998; Rotheram and Phinney, 1987). It is also extremely important to value their culture and language in the classroom (Gay, 2000).

Family comes first in the Latino culture, and parents want their children to succeed in school so that they can help other members of the extended family both economically and emotionally (Taylor, 2004). At the same time, children's family responsibilities may include caring for younger siblings, making meals, and working after school, even if they sometimes miss class or can't finish their homework as a result.

Courtesy indicates caring, and discipline at home is strict but polite and affectionate (Delgado-Gaitan, 1994; Shade et al., 1997). Children are sensitive to social cues and the nonverbal expression of emotion (Rotheram and Phinney, 1987; Zuniga, 1998). Because direct criticism is a sign of disrespect, it's important for discipline in school to be indirect and polite, too (Shade et al., 1997). (For example, instead of reprimanding a small group of girls who are talking and giggling together while the teacher is talking, she could say to the class as a whole, "It's difficult for me to teach while other people are talking." Because Latino students expect teachers to enforce the rules, it's unlikely that the girls will continue to talk; but if they do, the teacher could approach and politely ask them to talk with her after class.) When a teacher reprimands or corrects them, students may become upset, and although they won't respond, they may lower their eyes as their culture dictates. Because belonging to the group is so vital, being singled out in any way—positive or negative—can be especially disconcerting and humiliating. Humor, jokes, and verbal play are important because they help relieve tension and avoid disagreement (Shade et al., 1997).

In the interdependent Latino culture, it's common for mothers to make sure their children have everything they need. When the teacher expects a student to function independently and do things she's never done before, she may feel unsure of herself, but an offer of assistance will usually reassure her (B. Burton, personal communication, July 2006). Puerto Rican students who don't understand may wrinkle their noses, rather than ask for help (Nieto, 2004).

Because they're often in a large group, Latino children are accustomed to noise and may speak loudly without realizing it (B. Burton, personal communication, July 2006). They may also touch each other and sit and stand close together. When they get too near, children of other cultures may feel uncomfortable and push them away. On the other hand, a teacher who keeps her distance may lead a student to think she isn't sincere, and the child may withdraw or be less likely to cooperate (B. Burton, personal communication, July 2006).

African American culture

For African Americans, family (which may include kin who aren't blood relations but feel they belong to one another) is extremely important and a source of strength and resilience (Willis, 1998). One of the family's primary jobs is to instill a sense of racial identity—to make children proud of their heritage and conscious of being a Black person in a White society (Willis, 1998).

Parents are often strict. They use directives and commands, and they expect obedience and respect (Greenfield and Suzuki, 1998). Discipline may be direct and physical, and it is administered as a way to teach, with love and warmth rather than anger. A recent study found that higher levels of physical punishment led to higher rates of aggressive behavior in European American children—but not in African American children (Deater-Deckard, Bates, Dodge, and Pettit, 1996). Strict discipline is an adaptive response to reality, intended to keep children, especially boys, out of danger and trouble (Willis, 2001). Parents may chaperone their offspring wherever they go, which in turn may limit their opportunities to have friends and practice social skills (Kupersmidt, Griesler, DeRosier, Patterson, and Davis, 1995).

Although perhaps less now than in the past, every responsible adult in the African American community takes part in raising children (Hale, 1986). This provides youngsters with the assurance that an adult will correct their unacceptable behavior, and they feel free to move, explore, and assert themselves as their culture demands. Having this external locus of control can become a problem when teachers expect students to control their behavior from within. Students may interpret the teacher's soft commands, chummy manner, and relatively flat emotional style as a lack of caring, authority, and control in the classroom (Delpit, 1995). As Delpit notes, "Black children expect an authority figure to act with authority" (p. 35).

African American culture places a high value on oral expression, and children (who often speak Black English or Ebonics at home and in their community) learn to express themselves openly, frankly, and freely, playing with words and trading witty insults from an early age. They quickly learn to handle intense feelings without being overwhelmed. This verbal expressiveness—along with expressive clothing, hairstyles, and movement—also helps them establish unique identities, which are vital in a culture that stresses both individuality and interdependence (Peters, 1988; Trumbull et al., 2001). Those who stand on their own two feet can contribute more to those in need (Willis, 1998).

Tough Love

Many African American parents feel that stern discipline is appropriate for teaching their children to function in a society that is full of stereotypes, misconceptions, and racism. One mother explained her views to researchers Ramona Denby and Keith Alford this way:

> I'm real conscious of making sure my cute little black son here doesn't become one of the people [European Americans] are afraid of walking down the street [in] five more years. He's still the same child. He'll be bigger, but he'll become an automatic society threat at age 14. . . . I'm fighting against that already. No matter what . . . he'll be noticed and [people will] be suspicious of him. . . . [I teach him] you go look [at something in a store] but don't pick it up . . . because a person will say that the little black child picked something up. If he were white, they wouldn't even think about watching. (1996, p. 89)

Source: From "Understanding African American Discipline Styles: Suggestions for Effective Social Work Intervention" by Ramona Denby and Keith Alford. *Journal of Multicultural Social Work, 4,* p. 89. Copyright © 1996 by the Haworth Press, Inc. Used with permission.

Code of the Street

S ociologist Elijah Anderson of the University of Pennsylvania carried out an ethnographic
study of a poor inner-city African American community (1997, 1998). He found two value
orientations among the residents.

Most people identify themselves as "decent." They are strong, loving, church-going, and
committed to the middle class values of hard work, self-reliance, and education for their children. Keenly aware of the dangerous environment they live in, they are strict disciplinarians
who supervise their children closely and use physical punishment to teach them to respect
authority and stay out of trouble. They are careful to explain the reasons for it.

Other residents belong to what they call the "street" culture. A response to the failure of
the police and justice systems to protect people in the inner city, it deliberately opposes the
mainstream way of life. "Street" families are usually not as well off as their "decent" neighbors,
and they tend to lead disorganized, isolated lives. Anderson writes, "Frustrations mount over
bills, food, and, at times, drink, cigarettes, and drugs. Some tend toward self-destructive behavior; many street-oriented women are crack-addicted . . . , alcoholic, or repeatedly
involved . . . with men who abuse them" (1997, p. 10). Without resources or support, they
often lash out at their children without explanation. As a result, the children learn to use violence to solve their problems, a lesson that is reinforced on the street, where the winner pre-
vails and earns the respect of the others. The rules that govern respect and the use of
violence are called the "code of the street."

As the "decent" children start to venture out on their own, they must learn the code of
the street in order to survive, and many learn to codeswitch, or shift back and forth between
the two styles of behavior. Because they may look and behave like "street" children, teachers
may have difficulty distinguishing these "decent" children from the real "street" children.

African American children also have a quality that developmental psychologist
A. Wade Boykin (1986) of Howard University calls "verve," a propensity for high levels of stimulation and energetic action and interaction. Although children with verve
sometimes trouble teachers, who may see them as impulsive, overemotional, and out
of control, their behavior is culturally appropriate in homes where there is constant
stimulation and variety—lots of people, music, and activity—and a strong emphasis on emotional expression and sensitivity to emotional cues, which is an important
survival technique (Hale, 2001). Children accustomed to such an environment are
more likely to thrive when teachers use vigorous, variable teaching strategies that
permit plenty of movement and emotion, incorporate many media, and utilize small
groups to nurture interaction with both teacher and peers (Hale, 2001).

Asian Pacific American culture

Asian Pacific Americans are often dubbed the "model minority" because of their extraordinary educational and financial success in North America. But it's important
to know that not all members of this cultural group are doing well, and like other
people of color they often encounter discrimination and racism (Tatum, 1997).
Asian Pacific Americans come from a number of different countries and cultures—
among them Chinese, Filipino, Japanese, Asian Indian, Korean, Vietnamese, and
Pacific Island—and their religious beliefs vary greatly. Whether they embrace Buddhism, Christianity, Hinduism, or another religion, they share certain values (Chao,
1994; Ho, 1994).

The Asian Pacific American cultures are highly interdependent. Family is central, and individuals garner self-esteem by contributing to the success and happiness of the group (Kim and Choi, 1994). Parents are prepared to make great personal sacrifices for their children, whom they see as extensions of themselves, and they expect loyalty, respect, obedience, and high academic achievement in return (Chan, 1998).

Because an individual's behavior and achievement reflect on the honor of the family and its ancestors, parents emphasize good conduct at all times. They are careful to model appropriate behavior, instill an ethic of hard work, help children succeed in school, and teach empathy and concern for others (Chao, 1994). Such parenting may be strict, but it clearly indicates warmth and caring (Chao, 1994; Lebra, 1994).

Social harmony is another key value. It is essential to attend to the needs of others, to pay them proper respect, and to avoid confrontation, criticism, and embarrassment (Chan, 1998; Greenfield and Suzuki, 1998). Communication is indirect—a person does not express his or her own needs but expects others to understand the context, use empathy, and read body language and other signs to formulate a response (Greenfield and Suzuki, 1998). (A student who's struggling with an assignment may start moving around in her seat and become frustrated if you don't read her signals correctly and ask if she needs help.) It is also important to be modest, polite, and self-restrained rather than assertive—qualities that people from an individualistic culture may mistake for lack of interest or drive (Greenfield and Suzuki, 1998).

Children prefer to learn in a group, seeking out one another's opinions and eventually reaching a solution that suits everyone (Gay, 2000). The Asian Pacific American culture has great respect for teachers, who are considered authorities. A student who asks questions is challenging their competence or admitting her own failure to understand, so she may remain silent. Or she may laugh when she's confused (Gay, 2000). This behavior is also easily misunderstood.

Native American culture

There are over 550 Native American tribes, each with its own history, culture, and/or language, but some beliefs are widely shared. In this interdependent, collectivist culture, all living things are related, and property is communal, not personal (Trumbull et al., 2001). Individuals cooperate, share, achieve, and excel for the good of the group (Suina and Smolkin, 1994). Being singled out for either praise or criticism will make a student feel uneasy and may lead to misbehavior or noncompliance, especially at the beginning of the year before she has established a comfortable relationship with the teacher. Group recognition and activities—for example, murals, choral reading, and cooperative learning groups—are far more appropriate.

Traditionally, Native American children learn by careful observation, by listening to respected adults (who are regarded as keepers of knowledge) (Williams, 1994), and by practicing in private (Tharp, 1994). Although someone unskilled in their culture may be unable to read their body language and therefore conclude that they aren't listening or interested, they are actually taking everything in, a fact that will become apparent when they have an opportunity to demonstrate their knowledge in a group setting.

Children are not brought up to "comply." They don't do things simply because you ask or insist but are expected to make their own interpretation of a situation;

they need a reason that stems from respecting the rules or from respecting others. For example, they will put things away in their proper place if told, "We need to put the books back by author so that we can find them the next time."

Direct eye contact, interrupting, and following another's words too closely are considered rude and disrespectful, and it's important to consider issues carefully (Tharp, 1994), which means that conversations may contain long pauses. Native Americans are very comfortable with silences (Shade et al., 1997; Williams, 1994).

Children care for themselves at an early age and exercise a great deal of autonomy, usually deciding what they want to do without asking for adult permission. In fact, it is impolite to tell others what to do; adults provide suggestions and guidance and show that they care by respecting the child's independence (for example, by

A Mother Speaks

In *To Teach* (2001), Ayers published the following letter from an Native American mother. The author is unknown, but the letter has been widely circulated among teachers.

Before you take charge of the classroom that contains my child, please ask yourself why you are going to teach Indian children. What are your expectations? . . . What are the stereotypes and untested assumptions that you bring with you into the classroom?

. . . My child has a culture, probably older than yours; he has meaningful values and a rich and varied experiential background. However strange or incomprehensible it may seem to you, you have no right to do or say anything that implies to him that it is less than satisfactory. . . .

Like most Indian children his age, he is competent. He can dress himself, prepare a meal for himself, clean up afterwards, care for a younger child. He knows his Reserve, all of which is his home, like the back of his hand.

He is not accustomed to having to ask permission to do the ordinary things that are part of normal living. He is seldom forbidden to do anything; more usually the consequences of an action are explained to him, and he is allowed to decide for himself whether or not to act. His entire existence . . . has been an experiential learning situation, arranged to provide him with the opportunity to develop his skills and confidence in his own capacities. Didactic teaching will be an alien experience for him. . . .

He has been taught, by precept, that courtesy is an essential part of human conduct and rudeness is any action that makes another person feel stupid or foolish. Do not mistake his patient courtesy for indifference or passivity.

. . . You will be well advised to remember that our children are skillful interpreters of the silent language. They will know your feelings and attitudes with unerring precision, no matter how carefully you arrange your smile or modulate your voice. . . .

Will [my child] learn that his sense of his own value and dignity is valid, or will he learn that he must forever be apologetic and "trying harder" because he isn't white? Can you help him to acquire the intellectual skills he needs without . . . imposing your values on top of those he already has?

Respect my child. He is a person. He has a right to be himself. (pp. 39–40)

Source: Reprinted by permission of the Publisher. From *To Teach: The Journey of a Teacher*, 2nd edition, by William Ayers. New York: Teachers College Press, © 2001 by Teachers College, Columbia University. All rights reserved.

not restricting visits to the bathroom or water fountain). They also leave children to work out their own conflicts. In addition, children learn to speak for themselves, relating their own opinions, not those of other people (Delpit, 1995). As Chud and Fahlman (1985) point out, a child who's used to this much freedom of choice and action may find the assignments and routines of a school environment very limiting.

Middle Eastern and Arab American culture

The Middle Eastern and Arab American community has its roots not only in the areas in Asia and Africa that we usually consider the Middle East but also in neighboring countries such as Afghanistan and Pakistan that share their religions, languages, and values (Sharifzadeh, 1998). Like the places they or their ancestors come from, Middle Eastern Americans are an enormously diverse group. They can be Christian, Muslim, or Druze, rural or urban, affluent or poor, nineteenth-century settlers or brand-new immigrants. Most are born in the United States and are well educated (Adeed and Smith, 1997).

Middle Eastern Americans have a collectivist, interdependent culture, where the group takes precedence over the individual and the family is paramount. An individual's identity comes from her family's name, honor, reputation, and achievements more than from her own, but at the same time she represents the family in everything she does (Ajrouch, 1999). Family members take responsibility for one another and provide each other with guidance, support, and a social life (Sharifzadeh, 1998).

Children are extremely important, and everyone fusses over them. Although child-rearing is changing among the new generation, in some parents' eyes a child's independence may indicate a failure of parental love and duty (Sharifzadeh, 1998). Children learn to respect and obey their parents more by observing others than by asking questions or listening to explanations (Sharifzadeh, 1998), although this, too, is changing (A. Al Futaisi, personal communication, January 19, 2002). Once children reach 4 or 5 years of age, fathers may take more direct responsibility for discipline (Sharifzadeh, 1998), and boys in particular may have trouble listening to women—like their teachers—in positions of authority (Adeed and Smith, 1997). Education is highly valued and children of both genders are expected to do well at school—although they're occasionally tired from staying up late to spend time with their parents (Sharifzadeh, 1998).

In this high-context, collectivist culture, harmony is important, communication is indirect, and it's essential to pay attention to nonverbal cues. When there's a problem with a student's behavior, be careful to share concerns so that no one loses face (Adeed and Smith, 1997; Schwartz, 1999). Virginia-Shirin Sharifzadeh (1998) points out that it's impolite to say "no" and hurt another's feelings, so a person may reply "maybe" or "yes" instead. It is up to the listener to infer that the speaker means "no." Likewise, the listener must understand that "thank you" or "don't trouble yourself" means "yes."

People of the Middle Eastern American culture are comfortable standing and sitting close to one another, and there is lots of hand-holding and hugging among good friends of the same sex (Adeed and Smith, 1997). It's useful to remember that this close personal space isn't meant to intimidate; discussing this fact will enable the children to respond appropriately. According to Patty Adeed and G. Pritchy Smith (1997), the spoken English of native Arabic speakers may sometimes seem loud, rude, or hostile to ears raised on European American English, but this is nothing personal. Rather it has to do with the intonations inherent in the Arabic language itself.

The Middle Eastern cultures and religions are patriarchal and patrilineal, with sharply defined gender roles. Men have power and status. They earn and control the money, deal with the outside world, make decisions, and act as the moral and disciplinary authority within the family (Abu-Laban and Abu-Laban, 1999; Sharifzadeh, 1998). Women take charge of child-bearing, child-rearing, and homemaking, and girls start to learn these roles very early (Seikaly, 1999). To preserve their modesty, Muslim girls and women wear clothing that covers their heads, and even less devout families may warn girls not to have physical contact with boys starting at about the age of 7 or 8 (A. Al Futaisi, personal communication, January 19, 2002). It's important to be sensitive to their needs and to keep them with other girls as much as possible—for example in same-sex gym classes.

As women join the workforce, these divisions and attitudes begin to break down, and both parents will probably want to take part in any discussion of a problem with their child. However, men in very traditional Muslim families may not allow their wives to talk to strangers; and if they're acting as interpreters they may say or report only what they deem appropriate (Sharifzadeh, 1998). In this case, Sharifzadeh suggests communicating via a trusted friend or relative instead of talking directly with the mother, who is a child's primary caregiver. But, she warns, "never discount the father or his role" (1998, p. 467). If you're using an interpreter, be sure to choose a man to talk with a man and a woman to talk with a woman.

It is difficult for Muslims to find ways to practice their religion in a predominantly Judeo-Christian school. Teachers should take care not to schedule tests on major Islamic holidays, and children who are fasting during Ramadan should be allowed to go to the library instead of the cafeteria (Schwartz, 1999).

Why all this matters

Delpit writes,

> In any discussion of education and culture, it is important to remember that children are individuals and cannot be made to fit into any preconceived mold of how they are "supposed" to act. The question is not necessarily how to create the perfect "culturally matched" learning situation for each ethnic group, but rather how to recognize when there is a problem for a particular child and how to seek its cause in the most broadly conceived fashion. Knowledge about culture is but one tool that educators may make use of when devising solutions for a [teacher's] difficulty in educating diverse children. (1995, p. 167)

All too often, unexamined attitudes and assumptions influence the way we interact with children. When we understand ourselves and our students, we have a far better chance of seeing children clearly, establishing warm and trusting relationships with them, maintaining self-control, and identifying alternate solutions to problems.

WHAT DO YOU THINK?

1. Pages 101 to 102 contain some questions about understanding your own cultural beliefs and experiences that you might like to discuss.
2. Were you brought up in a low-context or high-context culture? How has this affected your attitudes and your interactions with family, peers, teachers, and students?
3. People who belong to the same culture or ethnic group often like to be together. Why do you think this might be? Have you ever tried explaining your family's culture to someone else? How did it feel to you?
4. Divide the class in half and debate this question: Is the United States better off as a "melting pot" or a "salad bowl"? As a teacher, what role do you play in the developing attitudes of your students toward these two different views of American society?
5. From 1870 to 1928, the U.S. government sent Native American children to residential schools in order to eradicate their culture and teach them the knowledge, values, mores, and habits of Christian civilization. Do you think that sending children of diverse cultures to European American schools is the equivalent?
6. Is it possible for children to learn the skills necessary to succeed in the future and at the same time to honor and value their cultural heritage? How will you go about balancing these two goals in your classroom?
7. How has culture influenced the lives and behavior at school of Andrew and Jazmine?

WHAT WOULD YOU DO?

Ms. Evans is concerned because some of her sixth-grade students are having difficulty understanding the basic math concepts she has been teaching. When it is time for math, she distributes a pop quiz. Miguel often finds it hard to stay in his seat and wait to be called on, but he sets to work and soon finishes all the problems. After a while, Luisa, who is clearly struggling, asks Miguel for assistance. Miguel moves his chair closer to her and begins to help. Ms. Evans goes over and tells him to move back to his desk. Miguel reluctantly obeys, but as soon as the teacher looks away, he turns back to Luisa. When Ms. Evans realizes what has happened, she tears up the papers of both students and announces that they will get zeros. Miguel angrily shouts at her and is sent out of the room.

What do you think about the way Ms. Evans handled this situation? In your opinion, what caused her to act the way she did? Could part of the problem have been a cultural misunderstanding? What would you have done?

SUGGESTED READINGS

Carter, P. L. (2005). *Keepin' it real: School success beyond black and white.* New York: Oxford University Press.

Delpit, L. D. (2006). *Other people's children: Cultural conflict in the classroom* (updated ed.). New York: New Press.

Fadiman, A. (1998). *The spirit catches you and you fall down.* New York: Farrar Straus & Giroux.

Heath, S. B. (1983). *Ways with words: Language, life, and work in communities and classrooms.* New York: Cambridge University Press.

Lynch, E., & Hanson, M. J. (Eds.). (1998). *Developing cross-cultural competence: A guide for working with children and their families* (2nd ed.). Baltimore: Brookes.

Sussman, G. L. (2006, Summer). The violence you don't see. *Educational Leadership (online).* http://ascd.typepad.com/blog/publications/index.html.

Tatum, B. D. (1999). *"Why are all the black kids sitting together in the cafeteria?" and other conversations about race.* New York: Basic Books.

Trumbull, E., Rothstein-Fisch, C., Greenfield, P. M., & Quiroz, B. (2001). *Bridging cultures between home and school: A guide for teachers.* Mahwah, NJ: Erlbaum.

CHAPTER 7

Preventing Challenging Behavior

The Social Context

Challenging behavior is troubling and puzzling, and teachers naturally want to know how to respond to it. What do you do when Jazmine keeps shouting out, "This is stupid! I'm not doing it" or when Andrew throws his math book across the room? We will deal with these difficult questions in later chapters. But first consider this: Wouldn't it be wonderful if you never needed that information? Wouldn't you prefer it if challenging behavior never entered your classroom door?

This is a fantasy, of course. It is probably impossible to eliminate challenging behavior entirely. But it isn't a fantasy that a lot of challenging behavior can be prevented. Prevention isn't a sexy topic because it often involves small things, such as reorganizing the room, having the children work in groups, or offering more choices; and it works quietly, without flash or drama. But it can be enormously effective, and for that reason it's very important.

Prevention is also important because it can stop a child from accumulating risk factors. If he continues to behave aggressively, he can easily ride a downward spiral leading to rejection by peers and teachers, school failure, gang membership, substance abuse, or delinquency. Preventing challenging behavior early can head off the development of more serious behaviors later (Guerra, 1997a; Kazdin, 1994; Pepler and Slaby, 1994).

The longer a child uses inappropriate behavior, the harder it is to change. Many children use the same challenging behavior for years because they don't know any other way to behave, and that behavior becomes firmly entrenched. But the more frequently that teachers help children refrain from challenging behavior, the less they're learning to use it—and the less likely it is to embed itself in their brains (Shore, 1997). If you can anticipate when and where a student will have trouble, prevent the situation from occurring, and remind him of what to do instead of waiting for him to make a mistake, you can build a new pattern: The child begins to reap the rewards of appropriate behavior, feels good about himself, and yearns to have that feeling again.

How does prevention work?

Prevention is a way to guide and control behavior. Because it increases a child's chances of success and doesn't tear him down, it helps to build self-esteem, competence, and resilience (Kazdin, 1995). Prevention is more likely to be effective when:

- It starts early (Becker, Barham, Eron, and Chen, 1994; Reiss and Roth, 1993).
- It continues over a long period of time (Kazdin, 1987, 1994; Reiss and Roth, 1993).
- It is developmentally appropriate (Gagnon, 1991).
- It works on several fronts simultaneously—for example, at home as well as school (Reiss and Roth, 1993).
- It takes place in a real-life setting instead of a psychologist's office or a special program (Guerra, 1997b). This last point is critical because it's hard for children to use a new skill outside of the context where they learn it (Mize and Ladd, 1990).

We're all the same, yet we're all different

Students feel competent and are able to learn when the environment meets their physical, cognitive, emotional, and social needs. Then they are less likely to resort to challenging behavior. If you can meet a child's needs before challenging behavior becomes necessary, you will enhance his self-esteem and allow him to begin to think of himself as a person who is capable of success. This is one of the basic ideas behind prevention, and it means that every aspect of the environment—the social context, the physical space, the program, and your teaching style—must take each child's needs into account.

As you come to know your students better, you may find that some of the things you've planned don't work very well. If that happens, it's important to change them. You may even need to change things for just one child. When you enable that child to succeed, it becomes possible for all the children to succeed.

This idea of flexibility—changing your own management style or canceling or altering lessons to suit the needs of one student—shocks many teachers. They think it's unfair. Some say that the child needs to learn to get along in the real world. Others think that if they let one student take untimed tests or work standing up, they're giving him more than they're giving the others.

Lilian G. Katz and Diane E. McClellan turn this argument on its head. "Because children's needs, feelings, dispositions, and behavior vary, it would be unfair to treat them all alike," they write in *Fostering Children's Social Competence* (1997, p. 73). Some students need more individualized support than others in order to learn, and it's only fair to give them the chance. Fair is when every student has the opportunity to participate, learn, and flourish.

Carpe Diem

Ms. Manzur's class was studying World War Two. While they were discussing England's role in the war, Jeremy raised his hand and began to talk about his great-grandmother's experience in Poland. Instead of asking him to wait and tell his story at a more appropriate time, Ms. Manzur encouraged him to share what he knew about the Warsaw Ghetto, the concentration camps, and his great-grandmother's escape.

Jeremy's story shocked the other students, and they began to talk animatedly about the Holocaust and their own families' experiences during the war.

Had Ms. Manzur insisted that Jeremy wait, she would not only have thwarted a wonderful learning opportunity for all the students in the class, but also made Jeremy feel angry, put down, and frustrated. He may have lost interest in history and found inappropriate ways to distract the other students or get Ms. Manzur's attention.

It's easy to confuse being fair with being consistent. The same rules apply to all the students, so any child who hurts another will learn that he is breaking a rule. But every child has different needs, and every child deserves the treatment that is appropriate for him, which means that you may respond one way to Andrew and another to Jazmine. It's a good idea to quietly remind Andrew about the materials he will need for his science experiment before he starts. But it's better for Jazmine to work with a peer who can help her figure out what to do next. Neither student is getting anything extra; they're just getting what they need. That is fair—both for them and for the other students.

If a child with challenging behavior can't function, he will keep other children from functioning by distracting them, frightening them, destroying their work, even hurting them. In addition, he will monopolize your time, deplete your resources, and prevent you from teaching anyone. If you can meet his needs before this happens, you will have more to give to all the students, and the classroom can become a place that's pleasant, relaxed, and conducive to learning.

The students usually understand this. They know that Andrew has trouble organizing his materials, so they don't mind if you help him get started. They know that Jazmine loses control when she's frustrated, so they don't mind if a classmate helps keep her on track. If they don't understand, it's easy to explain. Ross W. Greene, author of *The Explosive Child* (1998), puts it this way: "Everyone in our classroom gets what he or she needs. If someone needs help with something, we all try to help him or her. And everyone in our class needs help with something" (p. 283).

Greene goes further. He suggests that when everyone gets what he or she needs, no one is stigmatized, and the children learn to help one another. They recognize each other's strengths and weaknesses, and they are quick to encourage and reinforce their classmates' positive efforts. Their support can make a real difference. They become part of the solution instead of part of the problem.

In the classroom Greene describes, the social context plays an extremely important role in the way students behave. This chapter will discuss two aspects of the social context: First we'll explore how to create a social context that's positive and supportive, then we'll focus on teaching the social and emotional skills that are so essential to maintaining it.

CREATING THE SOCIAL CONTEXT

Although you can't see or touch it, the social context is everywhere, affecting every-thing you do, whether you're in a football stadium, an elevator, or a school. The so-cial context is a framework that tells us what kinds of attitudes and behaviors are expected, accepted, and valued in a group or setting, and it has amazing power to affect what happens there. The social context creates the social climate—the spirit of the group and the ambience of the classroom.

What kind of social context fosters prosocial behavior and discourages aggressive behavior?

Not surprisingly, the social context influences the appearance of aggressive behav-ior. In an experimental study, 7- and 9-year-old boys playing basketball and other games behaved more aggressively when their group had higher levels of aversive behavior, negative affect, competition, and physical activity (DeRosier, Cillessen, Coie, and Dodge, 1994). When a group was cohesive and friendly—that is, it had a positive social context—its members were less likely to act aggressively.

Researchers have spent a great deal of time looking at the question of social con-text in schools, particularly a phenomenon they variously call "social bonding" (Hawkins and Weis, 1985), "connectedness" (Resnick et al., 1997), "social climate" (Comer and Haynes, 1999) and "a caring community of learners" (Schaps, Battistich, and Solomon, 2004). They have found that students who feel connected to their school benefit in numerous ways. In the academic realm, they like learning and school more and have better attendance, graduation rates, grades, and standardized test scores (Wilson, Gottfredson, and Najaka, 2001). At the same time, their social

When a group is cohesive and friendly—that is, it has a positive social context—its members are less likely to act aggressively.

and emotional skills, relationships with teachers and peers, and prosocial behavior all improve, and their behavior problems diminish (Schaps et al., 2004; Wilson et al., 2001).

What characterizes a caring community? To begin with, it meets children's basic psychological needs, which psychologist Edward L. Deci postulates as *belonging*, *autonomy*, and *competence* (Deci and Ryan, 1985). A caring community provides these essentials:

- Students feel physically and emotionally safe (Blum, 2005).
- Relationships are caring, respectful, and supportive—children, teachers, and parents work at getting along together (Blum, 2005; Schaps et al., 2004).
- Children have many opportunities to participate, help, and collaborate with others (Schaps et al., 2004).
- Students have many chances to make choices and decisions—for example, they have a say in class norms and their own study topics (Schaps et al., 2004).
- Teachers practice proactive classroom management (Hawkins, Guo, Hill, Battin-Pearson, and Abbott, 2001).
- Teachers promote cooperation and cooperative learning (Johnson, Johnson, and Maruyama, 1983; Solomon, Watson, Delucci, Schaps, and Battistich, 1988).
- Teachers actively teach social and emotional skills (Zins, Weissberg, Wang, and Walberg, 2004).
- Teachers set high academic standards and provide the support necessary for students to meet them (Blum, 2005).
- People in the community share common purposes and ideals (Schaps et al., 2004). "When a school community deliberately emphasizes the importance of learning and the importance of behaving humanely and responsibly, students have standards of competence and character to live and learn by," write Eric Schaps, Victor Battistich, and Daniel Solomon of the Developmental Studies Center in Oakland, California (2004, p. 191).

Because children in a caring community feel respected, valued, and cared about, and because they believe that they make a meaningful contribution to the group's activities and plans, they are likely to feel committed to the community's goals and values (Schaps et al., 2004).

What is the teacher's role in the social context?

When it comes to establishing the social context, teachers set the stage and direct the action. They are the primary role models, teaching by everything they say and do, whether they intend to or not. As Daniel Goleman writes in *Emotional Intelligence*, "Whenever a teacher responds to one student, 20 or 30 others learn a lesson" (1997, p. 279). Each child inevitably absorbs information about the power, ability, and worth of everyone in the classroom (San Antonio, 2006).

A teacher's consistent awareness of students' needs and feelings, her caring, helpful behavior, and her high expectations—that the children have, or can develop, the skills to make a friend, understand the math concept, or read the assigned text—set a powerful example and build a positive social climate.

Students also pick up on how their teachers behave with colleagues, administrators, bus drivers, cafeteria workers, and parents. When the adults work as a team,

In classic experiments in the late 1930s, the pioneering social psychologist Kurt Lewin and his colleagues (Lewin, Lippitt, and White, 1939/1999) trained adults in three different leadership styles, then put them in charge of groups of 10-year-old boys. After six weeks, the groups switched leaders. The researchers concluded:

- Under an autocratic leader, the groups became either highly apathetic or highly aggressive—up to 30 times as hostile and 8 times as aggressive as under a democratic leader. Vicious scapegoating also appeared, actually driving members from the group.
- With a laissez-faire leader, hostility declined to a moderate level.
- With a democratic leader, the boys helped one another and made decisions as a group.

The children's behavior reflected the behavior of their adult models and the treatment they received.

share resources, and help each other, the children soak up their cooperative spirit; when there's tension and acrimony, that's contagious, too. Research-based bullying- and violence-prevention programs such as positive behavior support and Second Step advocate a whole-school approach for exactly this reason. The impact of the intervention increases because the students see that the entire community values prosocial, nonviolent, cooperative interaction and problem solving (Olweus, Limber, and Mihalic, 1999; Thornton, Craft, Dahlberg, Lynch, and Baer, 2000).

As the director and role model, the teacher is the group's leader. In *The Nurture Assumption* (1999) Judith Rich Harris describes a leader's power this way:

First, a leader can influence the group's norms—the attitudes its members adopt and the behaviors they consider appropriate. To do this it is not necessary to influence every member of the group directly: influencing a majority of them is enough, or even just a few if they are dominant members. . . .

Second, a leader can define the boundaries of the group: who is us and who is them. . . .

Third, a leader can define the image—the stereotype—a group has of itself.

A truly gifted teacher can exert leadership in all three of these ways. A truly gifted teacher can prevent a classroom of diverse students from falling apart into separate groups and can turn the entire class into an us—an us that sees itself as scholars. An us that sees itself as capable and hard-working. (p. 245)

Us is a caring community, of course. In a class like this, Harris points out, the students cheer on their classmates who have learning and behavior difficulties and encourage one another's efforts to solve problems. Once again, the children can become part of the solution instead of part of the problem.

Why should we include children with challenging behaviors?

Sometimes people think it is pointless to try to help students with challenging behaviors become accepted members of the group—that they are better off in special settings with more expert staff and smaller classes. Of course it depends on the child's needs, but in general if children are going to learn to function in society, they must be in society. A student who interacts everyday with his socially competent peers has many opportunities to learn appropriate ways to behave; and being an accepted member of a caring, nonviolent classroom community where everyone supports his attempts to act appropriately increases the chance that he'll meet those expectations. At the same time, belonging to the community strengthens his bonds to the group's prosocial norms and values (Guerra, 1997a).

Just as it's ethical to include students with disabilities, including students with challenging behavior is the right thing to do. To be equal citizens, they, too, need to participate in regular schools and become part of the community.

How can you create a caring, cooperative, and inclusive community?

Meeting students' need to belong and developing a spirit of community, cooperation, and inclusion in your classroom will reduce the possibility of rejection and exclusion—and at the same time the risk of challenging behavior. The following strategies can help.

Community-building activities

The very beginning of the school year is the best time to start making your classroom into a community, minimizing the opportunity for cliques to develop and allowing individuals to see a place for themselves in the inclusive "us." Psychologist Robert B. Brooks (1999) suggests that students and teachers spend the first few days getting to know one another and helping everyone feel welcome and safe. One approach, Brooks says, is to let the class know it's okay to make mistakes. On the very first day, you might ask, "Who in this class will make mistakes and not understand something this year?" Then quickly raise your own hand and share your memories of your own anxieties. This will evoke a discussion of ways that children and adults can help one another to feel safe when they take risks and make mistakes (p. 71).

Students who come from a different school or classroom need some assistance in getting to know their peers. Games that involve all the members of the group can reduce anxiety, break the ice, and bring people together. For example, you can pair students up and give them each a list of questions (about interests, favorites, family, etc.) to ask one another. When they've completed their interviews, they introduce their partner to the whole class (Leachman and Victor, 2003). You can use similar activities throughout the year, and even integrate them into the curriculum.

The curriculum can help bring the class together, too. Singing is a great way to create unity, and when you read aloud to the whole group every day, students have an important shared interest to connect them (Watson, 2003). (Choose a book that will interest the children but will be a stretch for most of them to read on their own.)

A common history also supports the feeling of community, and to create one for her class, teacher Laura Ecken (Watson, 2003) cultivates class customs and rituals, such as class meetings and lunch with her students in the classroom (rotating small groups so that she spends intimate time with everyone). Eating lunch with your students is a relaxed way to get to know them and build relationships, whether it's every day or once a month, in the classroom or in the cafeteria.

Monkey See, Monkey Do

When food poisoning killed all of the most aggressive males in a troop of savanna ba-
boons in the African grasslands, the social context of the group changed dramatically: It
became more peaceful.

The normally rigid hierarchy loosened, high-ranking males acted less aggressively, and
affiliative behavior increased spectacularly—males and females sat together and groomed
one another far more often.

In order to avoid inbreeding, baboon males migrate to other troops when they reach
puberty. In a conventional baboon troop, the females ignore the newcomers and the males
harass them. But when the new young males arrived in the peaceful troop, they were greeted
by a relaxed atmosphere and generous offers of sex and grooming. They rapidly adopted the
kinder, gentler behavior—the norms and values—of their new social context (Sapolsky, 2006).

For students who come from collectivist cultures, the idea of community will
probably feel very comfortable, even if they've never encountered it in school before.

Affect and language

Students are quick to notice their teacher's affect and body language. When you
smile and show your affection for them and your enthusiasm for the subject you're
teaching, that's catching, and it sets a positive tone for the whole class.

The language you use—what you say and how you say it—also plays a vital part
in establishing the social context. Your tone of voice, the speed and intensity of your
speech, and your choice of vocabulary all set an example. Greeting individuals every
day, addressing them by name, saying "please" and "thank you," expressing your
feelings, being sensitive to others' feelings, offering your help, and accepting the
help of others all show the students that you respect and value them—and demonstrate how they can respect and value each other.

Using inclusive language and pointing out the shared values and characteristics
of the class also build community and a positive social context (Watson, 2003). For
example, you can encourage your students to help one another and remind them of
how they've solved problems in the past.

When you want to talk with an individual student, take the time to walk over
to him so that you can communicate in a normal or quiet tone of voice. Without realizing it, a teacher can easily create an unpleasant and unfriendly environment by
yelling or filling the air with negative imperatives. If you're constantly raising your
voice, the students tune you out and shout more often themselves, and no one can
hear or concentrate.

Choose positive language that tells students what to do, not what not to do.
"Stop running!" is negative, doesn't give the child any instruction, and opens the
door for trouble: Should he hop, skip, jump? "Please walk in the hallway," stated
clearly, calmly, and respectfully, informs him of the expected and desired behavior.
It also deemphasizes the messages hidden in "Don't," "Stop," and "No" sentences,
such as "Don't yell out the answers" and "No looking at your neighbor's paper."

When challenging behavior is involved, it's a good idea to avoid *why* questions.
Andrew may not actually know why he spit at his seatmate, and if you ask, he's

likely to fabricate a reason. He may even come to believe that a good explanation will make the behavior acceptable. But the bottom line is that unacceptable behavior is always unacceptable, whatever the reason for it. *Why* also puts some students on the defensive, making it harder for them to calm down. Although it's difficult, eliminating these little words is worth the effort. Both the social and the learning environment are much more positive without them.

Rules and policies

Rules and policies (sometimes called *behavior standards* or *norms*) set boundaries for behavior and teach students about limits and expectations. At the same time, they make a substantial contribution to the social context.

The children will understand and respect the rules more readily if they create them themselves. Giving students this responsibility shows that you consider them capable and allows them to practice using their reason and judgment (Katz and McClellan, 1997). It also provides them with a sense of ownership and makes the rules seem more fair and relevant, which is a strong incentive to follow them (Brooks, 1994).

It's important for students to realize that rules aren't arbitrary but are actually tools that make it possible for people to treat one another fairly, kindly, and respectfully (Watson, 2003). This is a difficult concept to understand, so plan to work on it over time, using activities and class meetings that raise students' awareness of the way they want their classroom to be (Watson, Solomon, Battistich, Schaps, and Solomon, n.d.) and how they want others to behave toward them (Watson, 2003). Again, it's hard to put specifics into broad categories such as "Be fair," and it may take more than one meeting for students to figure out how to turn their thoughts into general rules.

It's common to begin with the primary need of everyone in the room—to be safe, both physically and emotionally. Students and teachers have proposed:

- Respect yourself.
- Respect others.
- Respect the environment.
- Learn something new each day.

The rules are easier to remember when they aren't too numerous. Help the children to make the final wording clear, explicit, and positive.

When the class is satisfied with the rules they've created, each student should sign the list and take a copy home. To increase understanding, encourage everyone to illustrate the rules, then post artwork and rules in a prominent spot in the classroom.

Throughout the year, use natural opportunities and activities such as storytelling and role-playing to reinforce the rules, reminding students about them whenever they need an extra nudge. Children tend to forget, especially when they're used to acting in a different way, and practice helps them to remember. From time to time, put the rules on the agenda for a class meeting, assess how well they're working, and modify them if necessary. Parents and other adults who come into your classroom should also know and understand them.

You Can't Say You Can't Play

Vivian Paley (1992), a kindergarten teacher at the University of Chicago Laboratory Schools and the recipient of a MacArthur Foundation genius award, was more and more disturbed by exclusion in her classroom. She couldn't accept that some children had the right to limit the social experiences of their classmates. After extensive consultation with the children from kindergarten through grade 5, she brought in a new rule: You can't say you can't play.

"In general," Paley writes, "the approach has been to help the outsiders develop the characteristics that will make them more acceptable to the insiders. I am suggesting something different: the *group* must change its attitudes and expectations toward those who, for whatever reason, are not yet part of the system" (1992, p. 33).

Although it took time to institute, this straightforward assault on the social climate was a resounding success. The most popular girl in the class invited two girls who'd been on her worst-friend list to play, no one was left out, everyone had more turns, the children were nicer to one another, and they were far more willing to try out new roles and new ideas.

Class meetings

Sometimes teachers feel so much pressure to complete the required curriculum that they think they have no time for class meetings. But meetings are a powerful instrument for building community and creating an inclusive social context. They give students a chance to "gather—psychologically and physically—and experience themselves as a group," writes Marilyn Watson in *Learning to Trust* (2003, p. 81). Having a say about what goes on in the classroom helps children meet their need for autonomy, and being able to discuss concerns in a safe and open environment is a key to learning.

Held daily, once, twice, or three times a week for 20 to 30 minutes, class meetings also provide an opportunity to build relationships and foster empathy and responsibility (Leachman and Victor, 2003). As students practice listening to one another, they become more sensitive and responsive, and they hone their problem-solving skills such as brainstorming and sorting through different points of view, options, and outcomes to come up with a solution that works for everyone. Reaching a consensus or a compromise is preferable to voting, which divides the group into winners and losers and leaves some members with little commitment to the solution (Kohn, 1996).

Once you've helped the class establish guidelines (such as respect one another, listen to each other, and everything said in the meeting is confidential) and modeled and taught skills (such as cooperation, active listening, turn-taking, and compromise), the students can run the meetings themselves. They can generate the agenda, decide who'll act as facilitator, select timekeepers to time the speakers, and choose recorders to write down the group's ideas during the meeting and their decisions at the end (keep a special log book for this purpose) (Leachman and Victor, 2003). Everyone should have a chance to speak, but participation should be voluntary. You can make shy or reluctant students feel more comfortable by speaking with them privately and helping them to find thoughts they might share (Watson, 2003), but remember that some cultures disapprove of children's speaking out in public.

What topics should the class tackle? Alfie Kohn (1996) writes that meetings are the place for questions that affect most of the class; sharing (e.g., what you did over the weekend); deciding (e.g., whether to go over the homework as a class or in small groups; how to deal with cheating or teasing); planning (e.g., a field trip); and reflecting (e.g., on values, learning). Other educators believe that a class can also discuss issues involving just a few people (e.g., a student who's angry at someone can put the problem on the agenda). It's a good idea to develop guidelines for these discussions, too—names should not be used, for example. "Simply talking about the problem suggests new ways of behaving," says Elizabeth Campbell Rightmyer (2003). "In fact, *not* naming or punishing wrongdoers seems to make children more willing to accept that their behavior caused a problem and to want to change their behavior" (p. 41).

Experts such as Donna Styles, author of *Class Meetings: Building Leadership, Problem-Solving, and Decision-Making Skills in the Respectful Classroom*, offer these tips for class meetings (Bafile, 2005). Students should:

- Sit in a circle, either on chairs or on the floor.
- Take turns leading the meeting.
- Present a problem that they put on the agenda.
- Discuss both problems and suggestions.
- Encourage and compliment each other.

Teachers should:

- Model respectful behavior.
- Be nonjudgmental.
- Not dominate the meeting but act as a coach, providing information, assistance to the leader, and comments only when necessary to keep the tone positive and helpful.
- Have faith in the problem-solving process and her students' ability to lead, participate, and make decisions that will affect the class.

Hidden Agenda

In the educational approach called the Responsive Classroom, daily morning meetings are a key strategy for building community and validating the importance of relationships. Roxann Kriete (2003) of the Northeast Foundation for Children tells this story about the powerful effects of meetings:

Pete was a 4th grade boy who struggled with anger and bullying tendencies at school. One day, while the principal was talking with Pete about his challenges and progress, the subject of morning meetings came up.

"I hate morning meetings!" Pete blurted out.

This reaction startled the principal. "Most kids really like morning meetings. What do you hate about them?"

Pete had his reasons: "Well, you get to know kids, and you listen to them, and you do stuff together, and sometimes you like them, and then it makes it so you don't want to beat them up on the playground."

When students choose peers to work or study with, the same child often finds himself alone. Children need to feel accepted by their classmates, and when others reject them on a regular basis they may well turn to inappropriate means of getting attention. Although your goal is for students to form friendships and solve problems on their own, it's important to anticipate that some will have a particularly tough time. By selecting partners for the children yourself, you can avoid these opportunities for exclusion and include students who might be rejected. Try to match them with students with similar interests and bring them together in nonthreatening situations. Pairing a more socially skilled child with one who's less skillful can be particularly effective (Hymel, Wagner, and Butler, 1990; Katz and McClellan, 1997). Whether you ask them to read together, check their spelling words together, or carry the books back to the library together, the more expert student is always modeling social skills—and in this one-on-one situation has a chance to discover a more likable side to his awkward peer.

You can also pair up children for more formal learning. In *peer tutoring*, older students can help younger ones, or students the same age can take turns tutoring each other. Besides gaining a deeper understanding of academic content, both children feel needed and empowered and come away with a sense of purpose and a more positive attitude toward themselves and one another (Haager and Klingner, 2005). This technique works best when students meet regularly and receive training in such subjects as problem solving, sensitivity to others' feelings, and giving clear instructions (Walther-Thomas, Korinek, McLaughlin, and Williams, 2000). For example, PALS (Peer Assisted Learning Strategies), a structured peer tutoring program in math and science, is effective with all kinds of students, including those with learning disabilities (Access Center, 2004).

In *partner learning*, a more skilled peer acts as a model, and students work in pairs to practice skills, do academic tasks, follow routines, and participate in social interaction (Walther-Thomas et al., 2000). For example, in Think-Pair-Share, students think about a topic, pair with a partner to discuss it, and share their ideas with the whole group (Slavin, 1995).

Sometimes two classes can team up for a *buddies program* (Schaps, 2003). Each older student becomes the buddy of a younger one for the year, partnering for both academic and recreational activities. They can interview one another, share their classroom portfolios, read or play math or word games together, work together for a cause, do a service activity together, and so on. This arrangement gives a student who's never been looked up to a chance to become important in someone else's eyes.

Group projects and activities

Group projects and routines reduce aggression and strengthen prosocial behavior and acceptance of others (Eisenberg and Fabes, 1998). When students work together toward a common goal, they come to know children they might otherwise avoid or ignore, just as they do when they work in pairs; and in the same way they have a chance to discern previously unknown competencies and talents in one another. Undertakings such as class books, murals, and large construction projects require students to listen to one another's ideas, negotiate, share, and help. Music, dance, and drama lend themselves particularly well to cooperative work, as do co-operative games.

Cooperative learning groups

In *cooperative learning groups*, students working in small, heterogeneous groups are responsible for the learning of every group member. The teacher acts as a facilitator, training children in the skills they need to cooperate successfully, planning the academic content, structuring the group's tasks, selecting its participants, and monitoring progress. Researchers have found that cooperative learning groups decrease challenging behavior (Johnson and Johnson, 2004), improve academic achievement and social skills, and promote perspective-taking and acceptance of diversity (Slavin, 1995). Cooperative learning groups work for any subject and any age (Johnson and Johnson, 2004).

Rachel A. Lotan (2003) of Stanford University outlines five features of "group-worthy tasks" for cooperative learning:

1. The task creates and supports interdependence. Everyone is a valuable member of the group because everyone needs everyone else's contribution to complete the assignment. Each member must also be accountable for his own share of the work.
2. The subject matter is significant, interesting, and relevant to students' lives—a topic they can sink their teeth into.
3. The task is multidimensional, making use of the students' diverse talents, competencies, knowledge, and problem-solving strategies.
4. The task is open ended—that is, it doesn't have a pat answer but contains real-life uncertainties and ambiguities that require analysis, synthesis, and evaluation.
5. The task has clear evaluation criteria.

A student with challenging behavior can enjoy participating in these activities if you assign him a specific role, encourage his attempts to cooperate, and remind him that he has the ability to succeed. It's also wise to place him with at least one supportive peer and to ensure that he has enough personal space so that someone else won't accidentally bump or push him. Making the groups heterogeneous is crucial to their success.

TEACHING SOCIAL AND EMOTIONAL SKILLS

In addition to creating a cooperative, inclusive, prosocial environment, you can tackle the social context head-on: You can teach social and emotional skills, otherwise known as *social competence*. In fact, social and emotional learning and a positive, cooperative social context go together—each enhances the power of the other (Hawkins, Smith, and Catalano, 2004).

There is no doubt that students learn social and emotional skills simply by being part of a group, but they learn much more when you teach these skills proactively. Giving them formal status in the curriculum highlights their value and makes for a more prosocial classroom ambience. More to the point, a social and emotional learn-ing program offers children with challenging behavior a chance to learn skills that they might not learn otherwise.

Social and emotional competence enables students to recognize and manage their emotions, resolve problems more effectively and less aggressively (Fabes and Eisenberg, 1992), initiate and maintain positive relationships with peers and adults (Rubin, Bukowski, and Parker, 1998), gain self-confidence and self-esteem (Michel-son and Mannarino, 1986), avoid peer rejection and victimization (Perry, Kusel, and Perry, 1988), and lower their risk for later delinquency and violence (Nagin and Tremblay, 2001; Tremblay, 1997). Social and emotional learning is also closely linked to better academic performance (Zins et al., 2004), acceptance of differences, and emotional well-being (Hawkins and Weis, 1985; Weissberg and Greenberg, 1998). These skills are especially important in assisting children in low-income fam-ilies to manage the stress in their lives and succeed academically (Raver, 2002).

Because their peers often reject them, students with aggressive behavior may have no friends. As a result, they have few opportunities to learn or practice social skills, and they miss out on chances to build self-confidence. As they become more isolated, their aggressive and disruptive behavior may escalate (Coie and Koeppl, 1990).

Students who behave aggressively may also have difficulty with social informa-tion processing. They don't understand social cues very well, or they tend to assume that others have hostile intentions, even when they don't. It may not occur to them to look around for additional information or think of alternative solutions to prob-lems, and they may not consider what will happen if they respond aggressively (see Chapter 1).

Other students (and teachers) are afraid of students who behave aggressively and often see their behavior in a negative light. Even when children with challenging be-havior begin to learn social and emotional skills, their reputation makes it hard for them to be accepted (Coie and Koeppl, 1990). These are the students who need so-cial skills the most.

How do children learn social and emotional skills?

Adults model, teach, reinforce, and provide feedback about the appropriate behav-ior that children need to practice. But children really learn social skills through lots of observation, repetition, and practice with their peers. With their social equals, children play roles and face dilemmas they don't encounter with adults, so they learn to lead, follow, contribute ideas, communicate, respond assertively to threats and demands, negotiate, compromise, defer, problem-solve, see multiple perspec-tives, work through issues of power, persuade, take turns, reason, cooperate, share, give and accept support, experience intimacy, and learn the rules and subtleties that make interactions run smoothly. The more time they spend interacting with their peers, the better they become at it. Even conflict is useful: It helps them develop all of these skills and understand other people's feelings as well.

Friendship is extremely important for gaining social competence (Katz, Kramer, and Gottman, 1992; Shonkoff and Phillips, 2000). It requires considerable skill to maintain a relationship with a friend. Friends have more disputes because they're to-gether more often. But because the friendship matters to them, their conflicts are less intense and they resolve them more equitably, with more negotiation and compromise. An altercation between nonfriends will bring communication to a halt, but friends will find a way to continue to interact (Rubin et al., 1998). In middle childhood, when conflict occurs more frequently and friendships become more selective, intense, and complex, friends usually manage to overcome their difficulties (Hartup, 1998).

A child can have a friend even after the group has rejected him (Katz and McClellan, 1997), and that friendship will insulate him from some of the pernicious effects of rejection (Andrews and Trawick-Smith, 1996). On the other hand, students who've been rejected because of their aggressive behavior often join up, and this friendship reinforces their antisocial tendencies, particularly in adolescence when they spend more unsupervised time together (Bagwell, 2004).

Peers are extremely important role models: Children tend to imitate those most like themselves (Michelson and Mannarino, 1986). Research shows that when socially skilled peers are involved in an intervention, students with challenging behavior are more likely to become both more accepted and less aggressive (Bierman, 1986; Bierman and Furman, 1984). In a study of children who had been abused and neglected, teachers' reinforcement of desirable behavior worked only 12 percent of the time. But when peers paid attention, the children responded positively 53 percent of the time (Strayhorn and Strain, 1986). Socially competent peers who can model and reinforce appropriate behavior every day are the best possible teachers for students with challenging behavior (Slaby, Roedell, Arezzo, and Hendrix, 1995; Vitaro and Tremblay, 1994).

How do you teach social and emotional skills?

Because students with challenging behavior learn best when they're with their socially skilled peers, it's a good idea to teach social and emotional skills to the whole class—or the whole school. No one is singled out or stigmatized, and students and teachers all learn the same concepts and vocabulary, making it much easier for everyone to model, use, and reinforce the skills throughout the school day. This kind of *universal intervention* works well with approximately 80 to 90 percent of children (Sugai, Horner, and Gresham, 2002). The remaining few may require a more intensive individualized or small-group approach. To learn more about such *targeted interventions*, see Chapters 9, 10, and 11.

Children who don't learn social and emotional skills before they start school are likely to suffer from peer rejection and its consequences (Mize and Ladd, 1990). But later training in social competence is also beneficial and should continue for several years (Mize and Ladd, 1990; Thornton et al., 2000). Learning social skills is a lifelong process.

Successful social and emotional learning programs are often based on Bandura's social cognitive learning theory, and they use a variety of methods, including didactic teaching, modeling, role-playing, feedback, and group discussion. When a child is under stress, it's difficult for him to access a new skill (Elias and Butler, 1999), so regular, plentiful rehearsal and practice in a calm and safe atmosphere are essential. Because it's also hard for students to transfer these skills into their real lives (Guerra, 1997b; Mize and Ladd, 1990), be sure to follow up and reinforce what they've learned in real-life interactions in the classroom and schoolyard.

In fact, it makes sense to integrate social and emotional learning into the curriculum whenever possible. Language arts and social studies in particular provide numerous opportunities—for example, students can practice taking another's perspective by writing or talking about how fictional characters and historical figures feel, discussing the impact of their actions on others, and speculating about what might have happened if they'd made different choices.

Because they have many years' worth of habits to change, and because challenging behavior has worked for them on some level in the past, upper elementary and middle school students may find it hard to learn new skills. But they can master them with clear instruction, continuous practice, and lots of feedback and opportunities to rethink old ideas. Eventually they internalize the new skills, and using them becomes almost automatic (Elias and Butler, 1999).

When you're presenting a social skills activity, remember that you're a role model, and concentrate on being your prosocial best. It is also extremely important to be aware of the needs of individual students. Often, the child who stands to gain the most may be the least interested in taking part. Perhaps the ideas threaten a pattern of behavior he relies on, or he lacks the self-esteem to believe that anything can change his status in the group. If he doesn't want to participate, he can listen from elsewhere in the room. Disguise and recycle real incidents using puppets, photographs, drawings, books, role-playing, and discussion. With this impersonal, externalized approach, no one feels picked on and everyone develops skills for the next time.

Like anything else you teach, a social and emotional learning program should be fun, developmentally appropriate, and culturally sensitive. Here are some ideas to keep things lively:

- Include games and role-plays.
- Videotape what the class is doing and discuss the video afterwards.
- Ask students to share stories about prosocial behavior they see.
- Publicly celebrate accomplishments.
- Connect activities to the students' lives (Thornton et al., 2000).

When students are applying what they've learned in real situations at recess or in the classroom, your job is to stay closely attuned and to coach, prompt, cue, and reinforce them to ensure that they get the desired results. Reinforcing approximations of their intended behavior tells them they're on the right track and encourages them to keep trying. Once a student's skills are firmly established, you can gradually and systematically decrease your reinforcement because the natural rewards—better peer relationships—will be enough.

Researchers have found that a teacher's enthusiasm is key in teaching social and emotional skills successfully (Thornton et al., 2000). To be effective, we have to believe that violence can be prevented and that we can make a difference!

What skills do children need to learn?

The first step in planning a social and emotional learning program is to identify the skills that are likely to promote peer acceptance and the social context you want to create in your classroom. Research-based social and emotional learning programs usually focus on emotional regulation and empathy, impulse control, entering groups, anger management, social problem solving, and responding assertively. (For a list of programs, see page 000.)

Emotional regulation and empathy

Children who manage emotion well have an easier time getting along with their peers (Shonkoff and Phillips, 2000). The process of learning to manage feelings is a complicated one. Infants can't regulate their own internal states and emotions; they

Cause and Effect

Photo by Committee for Children.

The Second Step Violence Prevention Curriculum (Committee for Children, 2002) uses photos and text to teach social and emotional skills. Teachers hold up the large photos, ask the class the questions suggested on the back, and draw on the ideas for integrating the concepts into social studies, language arts, and science. This example from the grade 5 section is intended to teach students that "empathy requires understanding the effects that people have on one another."

This is Donna. Several girls have decided to form a club and make up secret passwords and jokes that only they understand. Other kids in the class, including Donna, have started to have strong feelings about the situation.

1. How do you think the kids who are not members of the club, like Donna, feel about it?
2. How do you think the girls who are members of the club feel about it? When something causes other people to feel or act a certain way, we are talking about an effect. The effect of starting a club in which only some kids are members is that other kids feel bad and left out.
3. What might be the effect if every kid in the class was invited to join the club?
4. Have you ever felt left out? Why did you feel this way? What did you do about it?

Source: From Lesson 3, Grade 5, of *Second Step: A Violence Prevention Curriculum,* 3rd edition, copyright © 2002 by Committee for Children. Reprinted with permission from Committee for Children, Seattle, WA. www.cfchildren.org.

depend on their caregivers to decipher the clues they provide and respond with the help they need (Cicchetti, Ganiban, and Barnett, 1991). The more sensitive and responsive the caregiver is to the baby's signals, the better at regulating his own emotions the child will eventually become. According to attachment theory, if his primary caregiver is unpredictable, unavailable, or rejecting, the child learns ways to manage his feelings that may be inappropriate in the classroom (Greenberg, De-Klyen, Speltz, and Endriga, 1997). His relationship with his primary caregiver also becomes a working model for future relationships and provides the basis for his feelings of self worth (Bowlby, 1969/1982).

During middle childhood, children become much more socially competent. Their thinking is more sophisticated and reflective; they manage their emotional states more successfully; and they have more insight into others' feelings (Raikes and Thompson, 2005). But they continue to need emotional support as they struggle to define their identity and maintain a place in the peer group.

Talking about feelings—acknowledging them, validating them, labeling them, mirroring them, encouraging talk about them—helps students learn to differentiate and label their emotions for themselves (Dunn and Brown, 1991; Joseph, Strain, and Ostrosky, 2005). The ability to recognize and label feelings—especially negative feelings such as anger, fear, sadness, and frustration—is a powerful tool: It permits children to use words to talk through their emotions rather than acting them out (Raver, 2002). Even in middle childhood, many children haven't yet mastered this skill (Hubbard and Dearing, 2004).

Whenever feelings arise in the classroom, it's a good idea to label and discuss them—but try to do this without putting words into students' mouths. Instead, ask how they feel, and if someone is having trouble labeling his feelings, help him with a suggestion or two ("Are you angry because your friends didn't wait for you?"). Don't forget to point out positive feelings, too ("You and Leo look very excited about that book"). You can also help children figure out which situations provoke which feelings ("It's frustrating when you're confused and everyone else looks as though they understand, isn't it?"). It's also useful to talk about how different people can have different feelings about the same situation (Juan may be excited about going to the gym, but Brian dreads it). Students also learn about and control their feelings by observing others, asking questions, being coached through difficult situations, and learning strategies such as self-talk (Dunn and Brown, 1991). In addition, you can use artwork and photos that show people in different emotional states, and as students talk and act in the classroom, point out how their facial expressions, body language, tone of voice, and words match their feelings (Joseph et al., 2005).

When they hit puberty, students who've been highly capable of understanding the feelings and perspectives of others can lose their ability to read social cues (Mc-Givern, Andersen, Byrd, Mutter, and Reilly, 2002; Wade, Lawrence, Mandy, and Skuse, 2006). This is a good reason to teach these skills again, rather than assuming everyone knows them.

But perhaps the best tool you have for helping a child regulate his emotions is your relationship. When you listen and respond empathically, you help him deal with his feelings and at the same time provide the sense that they can be controlled (Karen, 1998). You also convey this message by expressing your own feelings (both positive and negative) directly: He learns it's all right to have and express emotions and that emotions are manageable. If he knows you'll be there when he needs you, he may eventually feel secure and confident enough to handle his own difficult feelings and even have enough energy to think about what others are feeling (Karen, 1998).

Empathy—the ability to understand what others are feeling and to put oneself in their shoes—begins to develop in the second year of life. As children realize that not everyone feels what they feel and that different people can have different feelings, they can learn to anticipate how others might feel and to respond appropriately.

Being able to look at things from another's perspective makes a considerable difference in the way children perceive the world, and it's crucial when it comes to controlling aggressive behavior (Beland, 1996; Cartledge and Milburn, 1995). Students with challenging behaviors find it hard to see things from someone else's point of view, and children who've experienced or witnessed abuse often close down their empathic responses in order to cope (Beland, 1996).

Conversely, children who can imagine another's feelings are less inclined to act aggressively. When they can identify and sympathize with a peer, they're more likely to help him and less likely to become angry or misinterpret events and intentions (Beland, 1996; Eisenberg and Fabes, 1998). They can anticipate the effect of their words and actions and understand that if they push or tease, someone will get hurt. They make better decisions (Greenberg and Kusche, 1998), and they'll probably try to take others' feelings into account when they're solving problems, increasing the chances that the solutions they reach will satisfy everyone (Ianotti, 1985).

You can teach empathy by employing exactly the same tactics you use to help students recognize and label their own emotions. Be sure to explain the connection between a provocative act and an emotional consequence ("It makes Julie feel sad when you leave her out and tell secrets"), encourage and reinforce signs of empathy in the classroom, and regularly assign academic work that requires students to take someone else's perspective. Like other social and emotional skills, becoming empathetic takes practice. In *Teaching Empathy: A Blueprint for Caring, Compassion, and Community* (2005), David Levine suggests using "courageous conversations," asking students to discuss difficult moral situations such as exclusion in the cafeteria.

When it comes to regulating and displaying emotion, different cultures have different beliefs and values. In the individualistic European American culture, children are encouraged to express their feelings. But in some collectivist cultures, such as those of Japan and China, where the harmony of the group takes precedence, people keep their feelings to themselves so that they won't hurt others (Chan, 1998).

Heartache

When Grace L. Sussman (2006), a White teacher, moved to an inner-city school in an impoverished area after years of teaching in the suburbs, she launched a study of the social dynamics of her African American fourth-graders, observing, questioning, listening.

"One episode was particularly illuminating," she writes. "One student approached another who was visibly upset by a previous incident and asked whether she could use her markers. When she didn't get a reply, she decided to take them. In a flash, the two girls were in a fight. Afterward, when they had settled down, I asked them how we can tell that someone is upset. 'Their heart be beepin','' one student told me.

"I asked her whether we could see a beeping heart. 'No,' she said sadly and shook her head."

When children cross from one culture to another to go to school, they may find this different emotional mode disturbing (Shonkoff and Phillips, 2000). It's important for teachers to teach and respond in a culturally sensitive way. For example, when you have students from a collectivist culture, try not to put them into situations where they have to disagree publicly with a classmate. (For more about this issue, see Chapter 6.)

Impulse control

Impulse control has nothing to do with knowing the rules or the consequences of breaking them. Many students with challenging behavior—especially those who interrupt and talk over others, blurt out answers without raising their hands, and have difficulty taking turns—can tell you all about the rules and why their behavior was inappropriate, but this knowledge doesn't help them. In most cases, impulse control is an acquired self-management skill and can be an important deterrent to aggressive behavior. But students with ADHD and FASD, whose problem with impulse control has a biological origin, find it much more difficult to learn.

Daniel Goleman writes, "There is perhaps no psychological skill more fundamental than resisting impulse. It is the root of all emotional self-control, since all emotions, by their very nature, lead to one or another impulse to act" (1997, p. 81). The ability to control impulses gives students the opportunity to notice what they—and others—are feeling.

Besides the ability to delay gratification (if you can wait, you can have two marshmallows), children usually begin to learn self-control skills at about the age of 2 years. These include:

- *Tolerating frustration* (keeping your cool when the person ahead of you in line gets the last chocolate ice cream cone)
- *Inhibiting action*, also called *effortful control* (raising your hand and waiting to be called on when you know you have a good answer)
- *Adapting behavior* to the context (talking quietly in the library)

The Marshmallow Test

Daniel Goleman (1997) describes an extraordinary study begun by psychologist Walter Mischel in the 1960s. In this study, researchers told 4-year-olds that they could have two marshmallows if they could wait about 15 minutes for the researcher to do an errand. If they couldn't wait, they could have a marshmallow right away—but just one.

About two-thirds of the children earned both marshmallows. They covered their eyes, sang, talked to themselves, and played games with their hands and feet to fend off temptation.

The researchers sought these children out again when they were graduating from high school. They discovered that the double-marshmallow children were extremely socially competent—"personally effective, self-assertive, and better able to cope with the frustrations of life" (p. 81). In addition, they were superior students, with SAT scores 210 points higher on average than the single-marshmallow children.

The impulsive children's inability to delay gratification had cost them dearly. As adolescents they were more likely to be seen as stubborn, indecisive, easily upset by frustration, mistrustful, jealous, and prone to fights and arguments.

In the hurly-burly of classroom give-and-take, students often go on automatic pilot and act impulsively. They do what they've always done, and if they've behaved aggressively in the past, then aggressive behavior just reappears. According to Ronald G. Slaby and his colleagues (1995), children act impulsively for several reasons:

- They have trouble regulating their emotions.
- They don't listen carefully.
- If they have verbal skills that could help them to stop and think, they may not use them.
- It doesn't occur to them to consider what else they could do or what will happen if they respond aggressively. To them, passive or aggressive solutions seem perfectly all right.

One of the secrets to impulse control is learning the difference between feelings and actions, Goleman says (1997). When a student learns to recognize that he's feeling angry or frustrated, he can also learn that having that feeling is a signal to stop and think—not a signal to act. Part of learning to identify the feeling is learning that it's all right to feel whatever he's feeling and that he can express those feelings nonviolently.

Remaining calm is also central. The two-marshmallow 4-year-olds employed a strategy that works very well no matter how old you are: *self-speak*, also called *self-talk* or *verbal mediation*. The child thinks out loud (or to himself) to guide his own behavior—to remind himself that he can talk to his friend instead of pushing him, for example. Self-talk enables students to realize they're in charge of their own behavior and gives them a way to pull themselves together and do what they really want to do (Watson, 2003).

Several research-based social skills programs teach children to remind themselves aloud to "Stop, look, and listen" when they realize they're becoming angry or frustrated. Teachers can model this method, making the usually hidden processes of control and reasoning more apparent. Students can also learn to take deep breaths, count to five, or do relaxation exercises.

Practice these techniques with your students when they're composed, and rehearse them in role-plays of potentially provocative situations with puppets, teachers, and classmates before trying them in real life. Provide lots of cues, prompts, and reinforcement when students are using them with their peers in the classroom.

Prevention is extremely important when you're teaching impulse control. As always, knowing the child is crucial: It enables you to predict when and where he's likely to explode. If you monitor closely, remind him of the rules and expected behavior, help him to identify his feelings, and give him a script of what to say or do before he loses control, you are providing information and cues that will eventually enable him to control himself. Give him plenty of encouragement and as much help as he needs to ensure that he'll succeed.

Entering groups

Students must enter groups over and over again each day. But entering a group is no cinch. In studies, even popular elementary school children were rejected or ignored by their peers 26 percent of the time (Putallaz and Wasserman, 1990).

Tralin, one of Laura Ecken's students, worked hard to teach herself to use self-talk as a strategy for self-control. Over the year she became so good at it that she even taught it to others. Ecken (Watson, 2003) writes:

> We were teaching the kids about Kentucky, and we had spent all morning in Shakertown, where they have restored the village and they have people making brooms, doing leatherwork, and weaving and washing and ironing clothes in the old-time way. . . .
> After lunch we went on to Fort Harrod, which was the first settlement in Kentucky.
> When we got to Fort Harrod, Kenny started to whine and cry, "I'm so tired, I don't want to do anything else."
> Tralin said to him, "I'm tired, too, Kenny, but I'm just saying in my mind, 'We're going to see stuff here and let's go do it.'
> I asked Tralin, "Do you really feel like you want to whine and cry right now?"
> She said, "Yes, I'm really tired, but I'm telling myself not to do it."
> I said to Kenny, "What Tralin's doing, that's something you can do when you're really tired but you still know that you've got stuff to do."
> It must have made sense to him. He recovered himself and we had a really nice time.
> (p. 223)

Source: From *Learning to Trust: Transforming Difficult Elementary Classrooms through Developmental Discipline* by Marilyn Watson with Laura Ecken, 2003. San Francisco: Jossey-Bass. Copyright 2003 by John Wiley & Sons, Inc. Reprinted with permission of John Wiley & Sons, Inc.

Impulse control is essential to successful group entry. Students who can wait have more opportunity to figure out what the group is doing and how they can fit in, and when they try again their peers are more receptive. Students who make at least three attempts generally make it, so persistence pays off, too (Putallaz and Wasserman, 1990).

The sequence of tactics also matters. A student's most successful route seems to be:

- Knowing the rules of the game or activity he's trying to enter
- Waiting and hovering on the outskirts of the group without speaking
- When a natural break appears, saying something positive that relates to the group's activity (Putallaz and Wasserman, 1990) or helping others in the group (Walker, Ramsey, and Gresham, 2004)
- Promptly accepting any offer, even for partial involvement (e.g., to become the referee) (Walker et al., 2004)

Asking to join usually works, but students hesitate to try this direct approach, probably because it's harder for them to try again if they're rejected (Putallaz and Wasserman, 1990). What's most important is for the student to focus on the social interaction and the other children's needs and interests and to show that he understands the group's frame of reference (Putallaz and Sheppard, 1992).

Disrupting existing group discussion or activities by bulldozing one's way in, introducing new topics, asking questions that require an answer, directing the conversation to oneself, giving instructions to members of the group, or disagreeing with others will almost certainly lead to failure (Walker et al., 2004). Boys are more likely to adopt these strategies, which enable them to save face after they've been rejected (Putallaz and Wasserman, 1990). Researchers believe that saving face and preserving status in the group are more important to boys than actually entering it.

Teachers can facilitate the process by designing activities for the entire class that are geared to the needs and interests of a specific child. If you know that Luke, who's often left out because of his aggressive behavior, loves trains and knows all about them, create an opportunity to do a project on trains and rail travel in North America. Because of his expertise, Luke will become an attractive member of the group and his peers will look to him for information and resources (Carr, Kikais, Smith, and Littmann, n.d.). Again, teach these skills with discussion, role-playing, rehearsal, prompting, and reinforcement.

Anger management

When Case Western Reserve University psychologist Diane Tice asked 400 people about how they manage their moods, she discovered that they had the most trouble with anger (Goleman, 1997).

Anger in both children and adults comes from a feeling of being in danger—either physical or emotional. When you're insulted, treated unfairly, or thwarted in reaching an important goal, your self-esteem or dignity feels threatened (Goleman, 1997), and the body's first response is to gear up for fight or flight. Then, thanks to the adreno-cortical system, it remains in a state of arousal, ready to convert any new offense into more anger. Even mulling over the original provocative incident—for instance, thinking "That makes me so mad!"—has the effect of escalating anger (Goleman, 1997; Novaco, 1975). This is why venting anger or hitting a pillow doesn't calm people down or teach them to regulate their feelings. On the contrary, it can actually increase aggression (Bandura, 1973; Berkowitz, 1993; Mallick and McCandless, 1966).

To a student with challenging behavior, the world often seems filled with threats and potential sources of anger. Because he can't process social information correctly, he misunderstands others' actions, and he is frequently rejected by his peers, excluded from activities, or frustrated by the task at hand. When he has a math problem that's too difficult, he will probably get angry—angry at his parents for making him go to school, angry at the teacher for giving him such a hard problem, and angry at his classmates for being able to solve it. To keep this anger from blowing up, it's important to intervene early in the anger cycle, while it's still possible to interrupt it. That is precisely what anger-management programs teach students to do.

The best time for them to learn is when they're calm. They aren't listening when they're in the middle of an outburst, and talking may actually add to their frustration and anger. Instead, map out a strategy ahead of time for situations where tempers flare, such as when a child doesn't get what he wants; he's hurt or frustrated; or other children try to provoke him.

The first step is to learn to recognize and label anger, usually by becoming sensitive to body cues: a hot face, clenched fists, a frowning mouth, a wrinkled forehead, crossed arms. Students also need to learn that it's all right to feel angry, that feelings—even feelings that make them uncomfortable—are natural responses to events or actions, and that learning to understand, accept, and label feelings is crucial to managing them and solving problems.

Children must also learn that feelings are signals, and feeling angry is a signal to stop and consider what to do next. Anger-management programs teach direct techniques such as those used for impulse control—self-speak ("stop," "calm down,"

The first step is to learn to recognize and label anger, usually by becoming sensitive to body cues: a hot face, clenched fists, a frowning mouth, a wrinkled forehead, crossed arms.

"I'm getting angry; I'm not going to lose my temper"), slow breathing, relaxation, and counting slowly to five (Coie and Koeppl, 1990; Kreidler and Whittall, 1999; Moore and Blaxall, 1995). Bringing arms and hands toward the body also inhibits physical action (Robin, Schneider, and Dolnick, 1976; Greenberg and Kusche, 1998).

A teacher can also help students reframe their anger by using empathy to look at the situation from a different point of view ("Emma wasn't trying to hurt you; she was trying to help") or by suggesting possible explanations for the event ("Emma banged into you because she was carrying so many things she couldn't see where she was going"). Another way to reframe anger is to externalize it, perhaps with humor (but avoiding sarcasm) ("The computer seems to be in a bad mood today"). Or you can help students understand that when they're provoked into losing their tempers, the other party in the dispute comes out on top (Coie and Koeppl, 1990; Coie, Underwood, and Lochman, 1991).

Once the anger is under control, it's time to apply problem solving to the original problem. At that point, the student can say, "I'm angry because the computer program keeps shutting down, and I just lost half an hour's work," and with the teacher's help he can begin to brainstorm ideas to solve the problem—teaming up with a classmate, using a different program, saving every 5 minutes. Throughout this process it is necessary to ensure that the child understands that it's all right to feel angry but not to scream or throw a chair across the room.

Social problem solving or conflict resolution

Once they have successfully inhibited their impulse to yell, strike out, or otherwise disrupt classroom activity, students can begin to solve their problems nonviolently. Good problem-solving skills enable them to avoid aggression (Richard and Dodge, 1982; Spivack and Shure, 1974), stand up for themselves, build competence and self-esteem (Gonzalez-Mena, 2002), and make and maintain friendships.

The process requires students to be calm and able to listen. Initially they will need your help, and you will need enough time and energy to carry through from beginning to end. There's no point in starting if everyone is exhausted or if you know you'll have to stop in the middle for recess. It's useful to remember that conflicts are normal events that provide excellent teaching and learning opportunities and that students are more likely to honor solutions they've thought up themselves.

Most experts agree about how to proceed. There are five basic steps (Committee for Children, 2002; Johnson and Johnson, 2004; Slaby et al., 1995):

1. *Identify the problem.* A feeling—such as anger—often indicates there's a problem (Elias and Butler, 1999). All participants in the dispute should have a chance to define it as they see it, but in the end the problem must be framed as a shared one where there are competing points of view and a possible solution—a task that isn't always easy. "Cesar pushed me" and "DeShawn won't let me use the computer" are facts, not problems. But DeShawn and Cesar can agree that the problem is "We both want to use the computer." Then they can begin to find solutions.

2. *Brainstorm solutions.* It's good to have a selection to choose from, and it's important to accept every suggestion, no matter how silly or unworkable it seems. To elicit suggestions nonjudgmentally, use a phrase such as, "That's one idea. What's another?" In *The Explosive Child* (1998), Greene recommends reminding children of satisfactory ways they've handled similar problems in the past. It's also helpful for students to think about their goals as they propose (and select) solutions (Elias and Butler, 1999).

3. *Evaluate solutions.* This is the time to examine what might work and why. The Second Step program calls this step "What might happen if . . . ?" to help students learn to think about the possible consequences of a proposed action. The solution should take into account both students' point of view and be agreeable to both.

4. *Choose a solution and try it.* It's a good idea to plan, practice, and anticipate snags before the students put the solution into effect (Elias and Butler, 1999).

5. *Evaluate the outcome.* If the first solution doesn't work, go through the steps once more.

It's especially important for students who have difficulty processing social information to learn and practice these skills. If they believe that their failures are their own fault while their successes are due to luck—as many students with social information processing problems do—they may give up far too easily (Rubin et al., 1998). Learning to problem-solve may empower them at the same time that it boosts their skills. Because they often attribute hostile intentions to the other person in the conflict, they may have trouble coming up with nonaggressive alternative solutions, and they may also believe that aggression will solve the problem satisfactorily (Price and Dodge, 1989). Social and emotional skills programs often help students learn to distinguish accidents from intentional acts. However, it's important to remember that in some environments attributing hostile intent to others is adaptive—and can be a matter of life and death (Guerra, 1997b).

Assertiveness

Whenever a student behaves aggressively, there is also a student on the receiving end of that aggression. He is at risk for more than just physical injury.

A student who's harassed isn't usually chosen at random—he has a kind of "anxious vulnerability" that tells others with aggressive behavior that he's an easy target, according to Michael Troy and L. Alan Sroufe (1987; Crick, Casas, and Ku, 1999). He tends to cry easily; be anxious and withdrawn; lack humor, self-confidence, and self-esteem; and have a hard time finding friends and persuading other children to do what he wants (Hodges, Boivin, Vitaro, and Bukowski, 1999; Olweus, 1991). Most of all, he doesn't defend himself—and by giving in, he reinforces the aggression and ups the odds that he'll be harassed again (Coie and Dodge, 1998; Hodges et al., 1999; Schwartz, Dodge, and Coie, 1993). Other students may even follow the example of the student who attacked him (Patterson, Littman, and Bricker, 1967).

Some students who are victimized are not so passive—in fact, they quickly become angry, provocative, and aggressive. Taking on this dual role makes them even more likely to be rejected than the children who don't fight back (Schwartz, Dodge, Pettit, and Bates, 1997).

When students are targeted over and over again, they may develop a stable tendency to be victimized (Crick et al., 1999; Schwartz et al., 1993). They come to believe that they deserve the attacks, and they may face serious adjustment problems both in school and in their adult lives (Crick et al., 1999).

If teachers solve their problems for them, students who are victimized may learn helplessness and dependency. One way to empower them and help them avoid harassment is to teach them assertiveness skills—how to express their feelings, needs, and opinions and to stick up for themselves without violating the rights of others.

European American Straight Talk

Assertiveness is culture bound. In cultures where modesty and group harmony are important values, it may even be frowned upon (Bedell and Lennox, 1997; Hargie et al., 1994). In European American culture, assertive responses usually involve the following verbal and nonverbal behaviors:

- Facing and looking at the other person without staring
- Speaking loudly, clearly, and directly to the other person in a firm, well modulated voice
- Using "I" statements ("I don't like it when you push me")
- Having a facial expression and body language that match the verbal message
- Standing straight, $1\frac{1}{2}$ to 3 feet from the other person, without invading his personal space
- Replying promptly (Bedell and Lennox, 1997; Rose, 1983; Slaby et al., 1995; Weist and Ollendick, 1991)

Researchers who looked at the assertive responses of popular students noticed that they had a high energy level and gave reasons for their requests and for not complying with unreasonable demands (Weist and Ollendick, 1991).

European American culture associates assertiveness with social competence (Rotheram, 1987). Students who assert themselves are less likely to be targeted and more likely to have friends who protect them (Hodges et al., 1999; Rose, 1983). (For more on this subject, see Chapter 14.)

The European American school day is constantly presenting situations that call for assertive behavior—a student wants to enter a group or have a turn at bat; another child bosses, intrudes, or calls him names (Buell and Snyder, 1981). Knowing how to approach or respond assertively offers students a means to achieve their goals without aggression. An assertive response can protect a child from being victimized, and an assertive overture can enable a child who behaves aggressively to get what he wants without resorting to aggression. When all the students learn these skills, they help one another, reinforce one another's assertive behavior, and avoid blaming or stigmatizing anyone.

Assertive behavior lies on a continuum about halfway between passive behavior (when an individual disregards his own needs in favor of another's) and aggressive behavior (when a person denies other people's rights altogether) (Bedell and Lennox, 1997). Children need a wide range of responses along this continuum so that they can choose the one that best fits a particular situation (Rotheram-Borus, 1988).

Slaby and his colleagues describe two kinds of assertive behavior (1995). *Reactive assertive behavior* is more familiar: It's what a person uses to respond to someone else, to express a different opinion, ask someone to change his behavior, or refuse an unreasonable request. *Proactive assertive behavior* helps a person initiate and maintain interactions, express positive feelings, give and receive compliments, make requests and suggestions, and offer thoughts and ideas in a polite open-ended manner (Hargie, Saunders, and Dickson, 1994). This version of assertiveness comes with a smile and is softer, friendlier, quieter, and more open than the reactive version.

Assertiveness requires several skills. Perhaps the most important is for a student to recognize his own feelings and thoughts, positive and negative. Without this awareness, he can't figure out what he wants to say and do. Because self-esteem also helps a child express disagreement or stand up for his rights, some programs try to bolster confidence by asking students to make positive statements about themselves (Rotheram, 1987). Assertiveness also requires impulse control—the ability to express oneself in an appropriate way and to problem-solve and compromise without losing one's temper.

Like other social skills, assertiveness should be introduced and taught away from the heat of the moment. Coaching and reinforcement are especially important, both in practice sessions and when students are putting their new skills to use in the classroom. Some students may never have heard an effective assertive response and may actually need a script, regardless of how old they are.

Once again we repeat our mantra: Whether you're teaching empathy, impulse control, group entry skills, anger management, problem solving, or assertiveness, it's essential to present, rehearse, and role-play these techniques when the students are calm and collected. When they actually put them into practice in the classroom, they'll need plenty of prompting, coaching, cuing, and reinforcement from you. Although learning social and emotional skills won't solve all the problems that students face, it can go a long way toward creating a positive social climate and helping them feel comfortable and safe.

WHAT DO YOU THINK?

1. Think about what you've learned in this chapter and the previous chapter. Behavior that's adaptive in one context (school, for example) may not be adaptive in another (such as a child's home neighborhood). What do you think about teaching nonaggressive strategies to students who live in dangerous neighborhoods where problems are not solved by mutual agreement?

2. The professor who assigned this text plays a major role in developing and supporting the social context in your classroom. Describe the social context and the methods he or she has used to create it.

3. Cut out a series of photographs from magazines and identify the subjects' emotions. What are the clues (e.g., body language, facial expression) that led you to your conclusions? Be specific.

4. Think about times when you were trying to enter a group. What did you feel? Do you remember what you did? Do you remember what worked and what didn't?

5. How do you know that you are angry? What are your personal cues? How does knowing that you feel angry help you to manage your anger?

WHAT WOULD YOU DO?

The school year has not yet begun. When you receive your class list, you discover that Andrew will be your student. Knowing his story, what can you do to create a social context that will help him feel welcome, make friends, and participate appropriately?

SUGGESTED READINGS AND RESOURCES

Apacki, C. (1991). *Energize! Energizers and other great cooperative activities for all ages.* Newark, OH: Quest Books.

Blum, R. W. (2005). A case for school connectedness. *Educational Leadership, 62*(7), 16–20.

Collaborative for Academic, Social, and Emotional Learning. (2003). *Safe and sound: An education leader's guide to evidence-based social and emotional learning (SEL) programs.* Chicago: Author. www.casel.org/projects_products/safeandsound.php.

Cooperative Learning Center, University of Minnesota. www.co-operation.org/.

Goleman, D. (1997). *Emotional intelligence.* New York: Bantam.

Leachman, G., & Victor, D. (2003). Student-led class meetings. *Educational Leadership, 60*(6), 64–68.

Lotan, R. A. (2003). Group-worthy tasks. *Educational Leadership, 60*(6), 72–75.

Paley, V. (1993). *You can't say you can't play.* Cambridge, MA: Harvard University Press.

Responsive Classroom. www.responsiveclassroom.org/index.html.

In the last few years, a virtual library of user-friendly social and emotional learning programs has appeared on the market. Here are some that are research based and have been proven effective.

PATHS, Promoting Alternative Thinking Strategies, Channing Bete Company, 1 Community Place, South Deerfield, MA 01373-0200; phone 1-800-477-4776; www.channingbete.com.

Peace Builders, Peace Partners Inc., 236 3rd Street, Suite 217, Long Beach, CA 90802-3174; phone 1-877-473-2236; www.peacebuilders.com/.

RCCP, Resolving Conflict Creatively Program, 23 Garden Street, Cambridge, MA 02131; phone 617-492-1764, ext. 31; www.esrnational.org/about-rccp.html.

Second Step: A Violence Prevention Curriculum, Committee for Children, 568 First Avenue South, Suite 600, Seattle, WA 98104-2804; phone 1-800-634-4449; www.cfchildren.org/violence.htm.

CHAPTER 8

Preventing Challenging Behavior

Physical Space, Classroom Management, and Teaching Strategies

Like the previous chapter, this chapter focuses on preventing challenging behavior. Its approach is perhaps more familiar: It describes tried and true methods that every teacher can use to minimize behavior problems in the classroom. We've divided the chapter into four parts. The first section covers the classroom's physical space; the second is about classroom management, including schedules and procedures. The third section describes a variety of teaching strategies, of which homework is one. And the last section, "When circumstances change," deals with methods you might use if you're confronted by an extraordinary event, such as September 11, or a shooting in your neighborhood, and business as usual just isn't an option.

THE PHYSICAL SPACE

"Space speaks to each of us," Jim Greenman writes in *Caring Spaces, Learning Places* (1988, p. 16). Think of a library, a restaurant, even a supermarket—each lets you know exactly what behavior is expected there. So does a classroom.

In Chapter 7 we talked about how the social context delivers much of the message. But the physical environment also provides important clues for the people within the space. Because the immediate surroundings have an enormous impact on all students, the way you set up your classroom can help prevent challenging behavior. The overall plan of the area, the arrangement of the desks—both the students' and your own—and the use of wall space will invite them to be comfortable or uneasy,

151

Preventing Challenging
Behavior: Physical
Space, Classroom
Management, and
Teaching Strategies

inclusive or elitist, orderly or out of control, prosocial or aggressive. It is certainly easier to change a space than to change behavior, but paradoxically, changing the physical space *can* change behavior. This is why cities and property owners rush to scrub off graffiti and repair broken windows: They want people to know that their buildings are cared for and deserve respect.

How can your space help you create a caring, cooperative, and inclusive community that encourages learning and fosters appropriate, prosocial behavior? How can you make it safe and comfortable enough for approximately 30 students to learn and behave appropriately? How can the surroundings help you meet the children's needs for belonging, autonomy, and competence (Deci and Ryan, 1985)?

First impressions are crucial. As you begin to ready your space for the first day of school, take a look at your students' files and talk with their previous teachers to find out more about their lives and interests. When students see themselves reflected in the classroom as individuals and members of a cultural or ethnic group, they are more likely to feel they belong and to become engaged in what's going on. After they've settled in, you can get them involved in rearranging things. Although the responsibility is yours in the end, including them in the decision-making process nourishes their competence and helps them feel at home—which in turn enhances learning and prevents challenging behavior.

Where will they sit?

A classroom's arrangement sends an instant message. You will no doubt reconfigure your space many times over the course of the year (if not the week) as you come to know your students better, shift from subject to subject, teach the whole class, change the size and membership of small groups, hold class meetings, and give children time to work independently. But the basic arrangement—home base—should indicate your top priorities. When you use small tables or push desks together to form clusters of three to six students, it lets everyone know that cooperation and collaboration are the goals of the class. In this position the students are ready for small-group and cooperative learning. Place the tables or desk clusters far enough apart to create well-defined pathways between them. This will allow small groups to work without distracting one another and enable everyone to walk around without bumping into things. As the teacher, you, too, need to walk around, because when the children are working in groups, your job is to facilitate—to move from group to group listening, helping, taking part in discussions.

Although students will collaborate with their classmates much of the time, it's also imperative for them to be able see you from their seats during teacher-directed lessons. Arrange the desks so that even if some students aren't facing you directly, they're not sitting with their backs to you either. Your very visibility will deter challenging behavior, and if you can see everyone, you'll be well-situated to detect early triggers and head off inappropriate behavior before it starts. The gurus of classroom management, Carolyn M. Evertson and Edmund T. Emmer (Evertson, Emmer, and Worsham, 2003), suggest checking for blind spots by standing in different parts of the room.

If you aren't yet comfortable with small-group instruction or if the students have always been in traditional classrooms, you can start off the year with a more traditional arrangement—desks in rows, a horseshoe, a circle. Desks in rows make it

152

Preventing Challenging
Behavior: Physical
Space, Classroom
Management, and
Teaching Strategies

harder for students to talk to one another and show that the classroom is teacher centered. Research has found that teachers who use this formation interact more with the students who sit in the front row and down the middle of the class, as well as with the students who are high achievers (Jones and Jones, 2004). If you choose this arrangement for your room, remember to seat some of the struggling students up front, sprinkle others throughout the class (Jones and Jones, 2004), and make a point of walking around and paying attention to children all over the room. Later in the year you may feel relaxed enough to try other configurations. (For example, a circle is ideal for class meetings or reading a book aloud to the whole class.)

Whatever arrangement you select, assign seats as students enter the room for the first time on the first day of school (Wong and Wong, 2001). Although in many situations it's good practice to let students make their own decisions, this is one time when you absolutely must take charge. If children sit where they please, they're more likely to form and perpetuate cliques, marginalizing or rejecting some of their peers; whereas mixing them up periodically creates new ties, promotes social skills, and enables diverse talents and intelligences to emerge. Tell the students immediately that the seating arrangements will change many times during the year to keep up with the evolving needs of the class (Henley, 2006). Again, reading students' files and talking with colleagues will help you decide who to put where initially. Try to group children so that you foster friendships between students who wouldn't ordinarily sit together.

Students who are easily distracted may need help in focusing. Classroom noise and hubbub affect those with fetal alcohol spectrum disorder (FASD), hearing loss, or sensory integration problems in particular. Cut down on the stimulation around them by seating them near the front of the room and away from windows and high-traffic areas such as doors, your desk, and the pencil sharpener (Yehle and Wambold, 1998). If you place them beside children who find it easy to concentrate, they'll have good role models and partners for collaboration (U.S. Department of Education, 2004).

To be certain the students end up in the right place, project or post a seating chart and label individual placements with the children's names. Place the name cards in full view to help everyone learn which faces and names belong together and facilitate communication between students who don't know each other. Once they're seated, they can fashion cards of their own to replace yours.

Where does the teacher belong?

In conventional classrooms, the teacher's desk stands in the front of the room near the white or chalk board or the screen for the overhead or LCD projector—that is, adjacent to where teachers teach the whole class at once and conveniently placed for storing instructional materials (Emmer, Evertson, and Worsham, 2003; Evertson et al., 2003). But a desk in this position can create a barrier between you and your students, so consider placing it at the back or the side of the room, where you won't have to stand behind it to use the board. If you're feeling brave and you consider the teacher's desk a traditional seat of power and isolation, as some experts do, you could go a step further and do away with it altogether (Yatvin, 2004).

However, if you plan to have a desk and you want to use it to meet with individual students or small groups, be sure to locate it where you won't disturb the other children and where you can see the whole class. Leave enough space around it to prevent traffic jams (Emmer et al., 2003; Evertson et al., 2003). Small touches, such as hanging plants or flowers on your desk, brighten the room and give the students a sense of who you are.

Other spaces

To make the room feel more homey and offer students a choice about how they work, construct a special quiet area where they can study, take a break, meet in a small group, or recover from a meltdown. When you furnish the space with a rug, comfy cushions, an armchair, or a rocking chair, they can relax and learn self-regulation at the same time. For students who prefer to stand up while they work or listen, provide a podium, lectern, or other high surface to make them comfortable. This area might also contain a couple of desk carrels for students who need to limit stimulation (Yehle and Wambold, 1998). If necessary, you or the students could make some portable personal carrels with three pieces of strong cardboard and some tape.

If you're short on space and your school considers it safe, add a quiet annex by appropriating an area in the hallway outside your room (Peterson and Hittie, 2003). Equip it with a white board, some markers and books, an extra desk, or pillows on the floor, and allow students to work there alone or in groups. But beware: A child with autism, or any child with a tendency to wander off, should stay inside the classroom!

To make the room feel more homey and offer students a choice about how they work, construct a special quiet area where they can study, take a break, meet in a small group, or recover from a meltdown.

154

Preventing Challenging
Behavior: Physical
Space, Classroom
Management, and
Teaching Strategies

Each student should have a place of her own to store her belongings. Cubbies, plastic tubs on shelves, or hanging bags will work for children who sit at tables rather than desks (Yatvin, 2004). But as students work independently, move around the room, and interact with their peers, they also need personal space. How much depends on their gender, culture, and temperament. Boys tend to need more space than girls (Gurian and Stevens, 2004), and an environment that seems comfortable, exciting, and warm to a student in an individualistic culture may appear cold and uninteresting to a student in a collectivist culture (Kritchevsky and Prescott, 1977).

Students with challenging behavior often have a definite idea of how much personal space they should have—but at the same time, they can be totally unaware of invading someone else's territory. No matter who's invading whose space, such incursions can easily set off escalating rounds of pushing and shoving. For example, when someone comes too close, Andrew feels threatened and lashes out. Explain to him that his classmate didn't mean to come so near and he can tell her to move back. Such discussions enable him to become aware of his own—and others'—space requirements and extend his tolerance of another person's proximity.

To keep order and make clean-up easier, store frequently used supplies and equipment where they're readily accessible, and mark the spots where they belong with pictures as well as words. You can eliminate clutter by relegating little-used items to storage that's up high or outside of the classroom entirely.

Deck the walls

What you put on the walls also sends a message about what matters to you. Again, this space should show that the classroom belongs to the students. Be sure to put up photos and pictures that reflect their cultural heritage, past and present.

After they've settled in, give the students responsibility for decorating specific wall areas. They can work in teams, bring in items from home, and make their surroundings more user-friendly (Henley, 2006). Displaying student work also nurtures student ownership, especially if you take care to obtain appropriate permission and represent everyone in the class. As H. Jerome Freiberg puts it, "Selecting the work of [only] a few students . . . sends a message that 'only the best need apply'" (1999, p. 167).

Wall of Fame

H. Jerome Freiberg (1999) tells this story about a Chicago mathematics teacher who asked students to choose their best work for display in the classroom.

When three students handed in what amounted to scribble, she placed it on the bulletin board along with the other students' work. During the next class, the three asked her to return their papers: They wanted to re-do them before she posted them on the "wall of fame."

The quality of the students' work improved significantly as they began to assume more responsibility and show pride in their accomplishments. Asking them to pick their own papers for display enabled them to "reflect on their efforts and see other models of student work" (p. 167).

Dedicate some space to the daily assignment and/or schedule, the classroom rules, and a sample heading for written work, as well as lunch menus and emergency escape routes.

Taking responsibility in the classroom

Students can take on a lot of the responsibility for looking after the classroom by doing many of the jobs, large and small, that you might do yourself. They can erase the board, pass out supplies, collect recyclables, bring in the class snack, take messages to the office, water the plants, lead lines, hold doors, and so on (Bovey and Strain, n.d.; Evertson et al., 2003). Ask them what else needs to be done; they'll no doubt come up with plenty of ideas. Students can work in pairs (a good arrangement for children from collectivist cultures) (Trumbull, Rothstein-Fisch, and Greenfield, 2000), each child can have a job of her own, or you can rotate the jobs every week or two. Post the assignments so everyone knows what to do. Giving students the opportunity to maintain the classroom offers them more ownership of the space and involvement in its activities—and furnishes them with legitimate reasons for moving around.

CLASSROOM MANAGEMENT

Classroom management encompasses the many ways a teacher can manage a group of students. Here, we focus specifically on enabling students at risk for challenging behavior to succeed; if you want to read more about classroom management in general, there are many texts devoted to the topic.

Providing a daily schedule

When the environment is orderly, consistent, and predictable, students find it easier to function and behave appropriately. They feel more secure knowing what to do, when and how to do it, and what is coming next, and they have little need for challenging behavior.

There are several key ways to make the classroom more predictable. We discussed one of them in the previous chapter: *Classroom rules* clarify expectations and prevent problem behavior, especially when students understand why they're needed and write the rules themselves (see page 130).

A second way is to develop a *daily schedule*. In general, students enjoy a varied and balanced day of learning activities—quiet and active; individual, small-, and large-group; teacher assigned and self-directed. Consistency is especially important at the beginning of the day. Help your students settle into learning with a regular routine that features a riddle or question of the day, journal writing, a class meeting, or a discussion of last night's news, for example. As part of this routine, you can go over the daily schedule, reminding students of what's coming up when and pointing out anything unusual. Post the schedule so that the children can refer to it later and pace themselves.

156

Preventing Challenging
Behavior: Physical
Space, Classroom
Management, and
Teaching Strategies

Using procedures

Research shows that effective teachers use a third way to create a predictable environment: They develop and teach *procedures*, which specify exactly how to carry out certain activities. These "how-to" measures are the grease that makes the classroom run smoothly, and they can cover virtually everything from entering in the morning to leaving at day's end. Personal needs, transitions, participation in teacher-led activities, working in small groups and centers, getting help, handling materials and equipment, finishing assignments while classmates are still working—all require a procedure. Such routines, taught step by step and practiced assiduously in the early days of the year, contribute substantially to a teacher's effectiveness—and students' success—by helping to meet students' needs, respecting their rights, and creating a positive and relaxed learning environment (Brophy, 1999; Emmer, Evertson, and Anderson, 1980).

Break down the day and think of the times when defined procedures would make things work better in your classroom. Then think about ways to explain and teach them to your students. It's wise to start slowly and introduce just a few procedures at a time. On the opening day of school, begin with those the children need first—putting away their belongings, going to the bathroom, moving around the room, getting help, and asking questions. Over the next few days you can add other essential procedures: transitions at recess, lunch, and dismissal, and that all-important beginning-of-the-day routine. As you begin each new activity, teach the procedures that go with it.

Carefully explain the reasoning behind the procedures, and describe and demonstrate each one. Then rehearse, practice, and review it until the students can do it quickly and automatically. To help them remember what to do, provide them with plenty of prompts and cues, supervise closely, and encourage them with immediate corrective feedback and positive reinforcement (Brophy, 2000; Evertson et al., 2003). Middle schoolers will probably need less instruction and rehearsal, but it's still important to communicate your expectations clearly, monitor closely, and give them feedback right away (Evertson and Emmer, 1982).

Be sure the procedures make sense to the students. Review them regularly, and if they don't seem to be working or are hard to follow, give the students a say in revising them. Their ideas are often innovative and helpful, and when they contribute to developing a procedure, they're more committed to following it. We often create procedures that reflect the classrooms of our childhood, but what really counts is having a clear rationale for each procedure. Although rules and procedures are necessary, they're not ends in themselves. Rather, they're a means for organizing the classroom into an effective learning environment (Brophy, 1999), and they should support the social context as well as instruction.

Some effective procedures require less control and direction than you might imagine. For example, students with challenging behavior often have trouble sitting still. If you furnish them with acceptable reasons to move around, their comfort level, behavior, and learning will probably all improve. One study of seventh-grade students found that about half learned better when their teachers permitted movement in the classroom (Dunn, Beaudry, and Klavas, 1989).

You can legitimize activity (and build trust and a sense of responsibility) by allowing students to sharpen a pencil, hand in an assignment, or throw away their

157

Preventing Challenging
Behavior: Physical
Space, Classroom
Management, and
Teaching Strategies

garbage without asking permission. If you locate the pencil sharpener, the recycling, and the waste basket at the back of the room, with plenty of space between them, they'll offer less temptation and opportunity for students to gather and chat.

You can even allow students to leave the room to get a drink, go to the rest room, or just take a short break from the classroom without asking. To limit confusion and disruption, create a procedure where they leave the room one at a time. For example, hang a hall pass next to the door, and when it's not in its place, a student who wants to leave will know that she must wait for its return. Specify the amount of time she may absent herself—3 to 5 minutes, say—and let her assume responsibility for monitoring the time herself. Of course, if she fails to respect the limit, you will have to discuss the matter when she returns.

Transitions present a special challenge for students with challenging behavior. If Andrew, who has a very persistent and negative temperament, has finally settled down to work on his research project, he is going to find it hard to get into the right frame of mind for math. Children with ADHD or FASD may also have this difficulty.

A procedure for transitions can make a big difference: It is crucial to give a warning. Many teachers teach their students to pay attention when they clap their hands or flash the lights. Tell the class how much time is left, wrap up the lesson by reviewing the important points (Yehle and Wambold, 1998), and remind students of what they need for the next activity ("Please put your history books back on the library shelf, take out your math books, and get into your small group for math").

What's in a Line?

An elementary school teacher talks candidly about her difficulty in getting her students to come in on time after recess (Gordon, 2003):

> Well, this week . . . I told them how tired I was of yelling at them to line up and how afraid I was that the principal was going to give me a poor rating because of all the time we wasted. Then I listened to them.
>
> I couldn't believe my ears. They said they were sick of standing out there in the hot sun waiting for me and asked why they had to line up anyway. They couldn't understand why they couldn't come to the room when the bell rang.
>
> I said that we'd always lined up, and they asked, "Why?" I thought about it for a while and then I said I couldn't think of any reason *why* students had to line up except that it was just the way things were done.
>
> Well, they didn't buy that. We then decided to define our needs. Mine was to have them get from the playground to the classroom in an orderly, disciplined manner in as short a time possible. Theirs was to avoid standing in a line for five or more minutes in the hot sun waiting for me to arrive to escort them to the classroom, and then having to march like soldiers.
>
> We decided on a solution suggested by one of the kids—namely, when the bell rang, they were to walk to the room from the playground. I was to walk from the teacher's lounge, and we'd go in. We've been trying it for three days now, and it's working beautifully. (pp. 245–246)

Source: From *Teacher Effectiveness Training* by Dr. Thomas Gordon with Noel Burch, copyright © 1974–2003 by Gordon-Adams Trust. Used by permission of Three Rivers Press, a division of Random House, Inc.

158

Preventing Challenging
Behavior: Physical
Space, Classroom
Management, and
Teaching Strategies

When you make your instructions specific and detailed, everyone knows what to do. Remember that in some cultures, such signals seem arbitrary; so if you have a diverse classroom, go around to the various groups and centers to deliver your message directly, adding an explanation that gives students a proper reason to finish what they're doing (Delpit, 1995).

Provide some extra help to a student like Andrew who has trouble adapting; don't wait for him to demand it with his behavior. Plan the cues and assistance you'll offer ahead of time—for example, know that while the other children are organizing their materials, you'll go to his side and help him gather what he needs by giving him the instructions one at a time instead of in a series ("Put your history book back on the library shelf"). As he completes each task, move on to the next. If you furnish the support he requires to act appropriately, his self-esteem will remain intact and the whole group can move smoothly from one activity to another. When you've had enough time to establish an inclusive social context, other students will help him, but in the meantime, you can act as a role model so they'll know what to do.

You can also help students make the transition from noisy, active periods (lunch, for example) to quieter learning by reading them a story (Jones and Jones, 2004). Again, it's important to have a plan in mind for the child with challenging behavior. When you help Andrew to calm down and get settled, the rest of the class will follow suit.

Sometimes the transition itself causes the problem. Is a straight line really necessary? If the students are moving from one classroom to another while classes are in session, they'll need to be quiet and keep to the right in an orderly fashion, but worrying about a straight line can cause unnecessary waiting. Students who have to wait tend to find interesting—and not always appropriate—ways to entertain themselves.

Here are some other techniques to ease transitions:

- Give students who are slow to adapt more time to make a change.
- Some children may feel more comfortable when they know all the concrete details about what's coming up next. Tell them where they're going, who will be with them, who will be in charge, how long the activity will last, and so on.
- Some students do better if they have a job to perform during a transition: They can lead the line, hold the door, take a note to the Spanish teacher, or some similar task.
- Some children can use a peer buddy to guide them.

Managing the group

Because the dynamics of the group strongly influence individual behavior, it's essential to pay attention to how the group functions as a whole. The educational psychologist Jacob S. Kounin (1970) dubbed this the *ripple effect* when he noticed that his reprimand of one student changed the attention level of his entire class (Henley, 2006) and decided to undertake the first major studies of *classroom management*. Since then, other researchers have validated his findings many times over (Marzano, 2003). By videotaping and examining the behavior of teachers and students in elementary school classrooms, Kounin discovered that effective classroom management is crucial to effective teaching (Marzano, 2003)—and that proactively preventing challenging behavior is far more important than responding to it afterwards.

To manage the group, effective teachers use a series of techniques that elicit student cooperation and involvement in academic activities, keep the classroom running smoothly, and head off behavior problems before they grow too big to handle (Good and Brophy, 2008; Kounin, 1970):

• *With-it-ness*, or having eyes in the back of your head. Without question, this is the most important strategy that Kounin discovered. In *Looking in Classrooms* (2008), Thomas L. Good and Jere E. Brophy describe teachers who are "with it" in this way:

> Effective managers regularly monitored their classroom. They positioned themselves so that they could see all students and continuously scanned the room, no matter what else they were doing at the time. They let their students know that they were "with it"—aware of what was happening and likely to detect misbehavior early and accurately. This enabled them to nip problems in the bud before they could escalate. If they found it necessary to stop misbehavior, they focused on the students who started the problem or were most responsible for its escalation. If they were uncertain about who was most responsible, they told the entire group involved to resume working on their assignments (to avoid publicly blaming the wrong student). (p. 81)

• *Overlapping*, or the ability to seamlessly do several things at once. It's important to continue an ongoing activity while acknowledging an interruption, such as a late-arriving student, a child who needs help, or a visitor with a note from the office. For example, before she attends to a visitor, the teacher might assign the class some problems appropriate for the math lesson she's been leading (Evertson et al., 2003).

• *Momentum*, or keeping the lesson moving along at a reasonable clip. This requires good organization and preparation as well as unobtrusive, nonverbal strategies (spending time in all sections of the room, making eye contact with all students, moving closer or putting your finger to your lips at the first sign of behavior that might become a problem, for example). Such techniques quickly check potential misbehavior in its earliest stages while allowing lessons or activities to continue uninterrupted.

• *Smoothness*, or keeping the lesson on track. An effective teacher doesn't lose focus, become distracted, or go off on a tangent.

• *Maintaining group focus*, or engaging the attention of the whole class. You can sustain student interest by using suspense, eliciting active participation, holding students responsible for their work, and giving frequent feedback. When you call on them in random order or ask them to write answers, read along, or manipulate materials, they're more likely to stay involved (Evertson et al., 2003).

With relatively little training, teachers can learn these techniques and significantly improve their ability to manage the group, research has shown (Marzano, 2003). They play an especially critical role at the beginning of the school year, when you're setting the tone for everything that follows (Emmer et al., 1980; Evertson and Emmer, 1982).

Classroom Mona Lisa

Robert J. Marzano (2003) describes one teacher's with-it-ness:

"It's cool. She doesn't yell or glare or anything. She just looks." McKinley, an 8th-grader, was describing his math teacher, Ms. Clark, who is known for keeping her students on task and doing so without sending kids to the office or to detention. Whether working with small groups or talking to the entire class, Ms. Clark always notices when kids are beginning to talk or behave inappropriately. No matter what she is doing, she stops, and in an almost frozen position, she makes eye contact with the student or students. Her Mona Lisa-like expression shows no negative emotion, only rapt attention. If the offending students do not notice at first, their peers alert them. When they stop their disruptive behavior, which is almost always in seconds, she continues where she left off. The polite attention and silence both set a positive tone and get the desired results. (p. 70)

In a more recent study, Jere Brophy (1996) found another important difference between effective and ineffective classroom managers: The ineffective managers use the same strategies with all their students, but the effective managers respond to individual needs and approach each student differently. To give themselves as much flexibility as possible, teachers must develop a wide repertoire of skills, Brophy (1996) suggests. Of course, a solid relationship with a child makes it much easier to know what to do. Then you can anticipate situations that may be difficult for her, think through how you will interact with her to minimize problems, remind her of the appropriate behavior in advance, and frame your own thinking so that you expect her to succeed (Marzano, 2003).

TEACHING STRATEGIES

A child with challenging behavior also dares you to examine your teaching strategies—to consider not only the content and skills you want to teach but also the behavior you're trying to encourage. If a task is too difficult, a student will do whatever is necessary to avoid participating and failing. Whether it's a timed history quiz, an oral report that requires a Native American child to stand alone in front of the class, or a physical education activity that demands a lot of coordination, the result will be frustration, and she will probably find a challenging way to escape. Instead of forcing students to fit into the program, you can help them learn by designing and bending the program to meet their needs. If you provide unlimited time and an assortment of ways to answer the questions on a quiz (e.g., using a computer, a scribe, or headphones and a tape recorder to record answers), allow students to speak in a small group rather than to the whole class, and offer a choice of activities in the gym, the child will feel more able to succeed—and challenging behavior probably won't be necessary.

Ultimately, how much the children learn and how much fun they'll have learning will depend on how well your curriculum and teaching strategies reflect the interests, abilities, cultures, temperaments, learning profiles, and readiness of the students in your class. As you plan, it's important to focus on each one as an individual—to think about what each knows and enjoys, what each needs to learn, and how each learns best. This approach is extremely effective in preventing children from feeling frustrated, incompetent, or unsure of themselves—feelings that often lead to challenging behavior.

Differentiated instruction

In *The Differentiated Classroom: Responding to the Needs of All Learners* (1999), Carol Ann Tomlinson writes, "Differentiated instruction isn't an instructional strategy or a teaching mode. It's a way of thinking about teaching and learning that advocates beginning where individuals are rather than with a prescribed plan of action" (p. 106). You don't have to sit down one-on-one with a student for blocks of time to differentiate learning, but you do have to respond to each child's needs. This isn't easy, and it requires careful planning.

Differentiated teaching means that students have a chance to acquire ideas and information in different ways, process what they're absorbing in different ways, and

---

If You Pay Attention You Can See It

In 2002, 40 students of color from urban public high schools wrote about how they act when they don't understand what is said in class (Cushman and the students of What Kids Can Do, 2003):

We cry when we're scared.

We make a face—roll our eyes.

We put our heads down and sleep.

We get angry—we kick the chair; we say bad words.

We interrupt and talk loud.

We cut class.

We daydream in class, don't pay attention, think of other things.

We ask the counselor if we can drop the class, because we're afraid.

We bite our nails.

We listen to music.

We feel hungry.

We fight with other students.

We bother the other students.

We flirt with the other students.

We stay home.

We run away. (p. 156)

Source: © 2003 by What Kids Can Do, Inc. This piece originally appears in *Fires in the Bathroom: Advice for Teachers from High School Students* by Kathleen Cushman and the students of What Kids Can Do, Inc. Reprinted with the permission of The New Press. www.thenewpress.com.

162

Preventing Challenging
Behavior: Physical
Space, Classroom
Management, and
Teaching Strategies

demonstrate what they've learned in different ways (Tomlinson, 2001; Wormeli, 2006). It works best when teachers assume from the outset that their students have diverse needs and proactively plan a variety of routes to learning (Tomlinson, 2001). (Think of the classroom as a huge playground with lots of different equipment suitable for children with a wide range of ages and abilities. With an adult standing by to encourage and help when necessary, the students can choose, explore, and master the various apparatus in their own way, at their own pace.)

Exactly what teachers plan for the classroom depends on what they know about their students, so *ongoing assessment*—which Tomlinson (1999) describes as "today's means of understanding how to modify tomorrow's instruction" (p. 10)—is essential. It begins at the start of a term or unit and continues throughout, looking at three student characteristics (Tomlinson, 2001).

The first is *readiness*. Learning is easier and more natural when students are cognitively and developmentally ready. When the work is too hard, they get frustrated; when it's too easy, they're bored. The tasks and materials for each child should match her knowledge, skills, and understanding and present a moderate challenge as well (Tomlinson, 2005).

The second characteristic is the student's *interests*. When children study what interests them, they're more likely to become engaged in their learning. If you ask them what they'd like to learn and offer them choices, the result is often more satisfaction, creativity, and autonomy (Tomlinson, 2001).

Differentiated teaching means that students have a chance to acquire ideas and information in different ways, process what they're absorbing in different ways, and demonstrate what they've learned in different ways.

The third characteristic to assess is the student's *learning profile*. Each of us has our own particular approach to learning that is a mix of four different components (Tomlinson, 2001):

163

Preventing Challenging
Behavior: Physical
Space, Classroom
Management, and
Teaching Strategies

1. *Learning style* has to do with the environmental and personal factors that help students function at their best—for example, bright or soft light, quiet or noisy surroundings, moving around or sitting still, working alone or in a small group, and using sight, hearing, or touch to understand material. Interestingly, students who underachieve, skip school, or eventually drop out frequently learn better in the afternoon than in the morning, but teachers are often morning people (Dunn et al., 1989). No learning style is any better or worse than any other, but many styles are hard-wired and resistant to change (Dunn et al., 1989).

2. *Intelligence preferences* shape learning, too. According to Howard Gardner (1983), different minds go about processing information in different ways. Some of these cognitive capacities, such as a linguistic or logical-mathematical bent, fit right into conventional methods of teaching and learning; but the others—musical, spatial, bodily-kinesthetic, naturalistic, interpersonal, intrapersonal, and existential—don't often show up in classrooms. It takes thinking outside the box to figure out how to tap into this potential (Moran, Kornhaber, and Gardner, 2006).

3. *Culture* also influences the way students learn. For example, in collectivist cultures, children use inductive reasoning, going from the general to the specific; whereas in individualistic cultures, they take a deductive approach, starting with the specific and moving to the general (Gay, 2000). In individualistic cultures, students understand concepts and facts as things that stand alone, decontextualized; but for children in collectivist cultures, concepts and facts draw their meaning from their context (Trumbull et al., 2000). Do you remember the story of the egg on page 98?

4. Last but not least, *gender* affects how students learn. For instance, research indicates that boys may prefer to compete and girls to collaborate; and that boys' strengths are often in abstract and spatial-mechanical areas, whereas girls' brains tend to devote more space to verbal and emotional matters (Gurian and Stevens, 2006).

Effective differentiation also uses *flexible grouping*, which allows the teacher to help different children explore different skills and subject matter in different ways, at different rates, depending on their needs. In addition, differentiation utilizes *multiple teaching strategies and materials* that encompass a range of reading levels and learning modalities (Good and Brophy, 2008; Tomlinson, 2005). And differentiated instruction *focuses on the big ideas*, concepts, and principles that give meaning to a topic. The teacher bases her lesson on what she believes is essential in a unit—what all children must learn—and figures out different ways for them to go about understanding it and to be evaluated (Scherer, 2006; Tomlinson, 2005). This approach enables teachers to search out and teach to their students' strengths.

Sharing responsibility and providing choice

Just as students can shoulder some responsibility for organizing, decorating, and running the classroom, so they can take on responsibility for their own learning.

164

Preventing Challenging
Behavior: Physical
Space, Classroom
Management, and
Teaching Strategies

Speaking to the Inner You

Carol Ann Tomlinson and Jane Jarvis (2006) relate how a teacher found a wonderful way to integrate the interests of her 12-year-old students into her U.S. history unit on the Civil War.

Mrs. Lupold asked each class to list things that the class members . . . want[ed] to learn more about. . . . The lists included such topics as sports, medicine, music, humor, teenagers, and religion.

"I love learning about the Civil War," Mrs. Lupold shared with her students, "because it speaks to something inside me. Your job is to learn about something that speaks to you, too." She had the students each select a topic from their class list. "The only thing I ask," she added, "is that you study your chosen topic as it relates to the Civil War period."

. . . Each morning in class, hands waved as students added their voices to discussion of the Civil War. "You know that song in the video we just saw?" one student asked his classmates. "It's actually a Civil War song. I heard it last night when I was learning about music from that time period. I can tell everybody the words if you want me to."

"You know how the textbook told about those soldiers dying at Gettysburg?" asked another. "Well, a lot of that is because there were no antibiotics during the Civil War. A lot of those soldiers would have lived if the battle took place today because we could treat their infections."

At the end of the unit, many students commented that studying the Civil War was the highlight of the year. By using students' interests, curiosity, and points of confidence as a starting point for disciplinary inquiry, Mrs. Lupold gave her students a feeling of ownership of the unit. (pp. 19–20)

They can have a say in what they'd like to learn and set learning goals for themselves at the beginning of a unit (Charles and Charles, 2004; Marzano, 2003); help select activities and design their own tasks; and keep a record of their own work, comparing their accomplishments with established goals (Tomlinson, 2001). Along the way, the students can choose their own materials and learning media, select the order in which they'll do things, lead class meetings, act as expert of the day or the resource person for a particular project, monitor the noise level in the class, and help new and absent students.

Learning contracts provide one direct way for students to take charge. Signed agreements between a teacher and a student, they are based on the principle that students are active partners in the teaching–learning process. Together, student and teacher set learning goals; figure out strategies and resources appropriate for the student's interests, academic level, and learning profile; negotiate deadlines; and develop criteria for evaluation.

Once again, making choices and decisions for themselves gives students the opportunity to become more engaged in their learning—which in turn empowers them. Because they don't have to look for inappropriate ways to seek power and assert their independence, they're less likely to need challenging behavior.

A compendium of teaching strategies

165

Preventing Challenging
Behavior: Physical
Space, Classroom
Management, and
Teaching Strategies

Good instruction not only improves learning but also promotes appropriate behavior. Here is a compendium of strategies that can help make your teaching better, whether the children in your classroom have challenging behavior or not.

Expect the best

Having high expectations for your students is imperative. Whether or not you're aware of it, your expectations of each child guide what and how you teach her; and your behavior in the classroom quickly reveals your feelings. Your students internalize your expectations and comply with them. One student puts it this way: "It's okay for your teachers to push you—it just shows they care and they want to see you succeed in life" (Cushman et al., 2003, p. 64).

Some students need your attention more frequently than others. Instead of waiting until they demand it, schedule regular check-in times for them to ask questions, show you what they're doing, or simply touch base. For students who are always seeking the attention of their peers, peer tutoring can work wonders—and teach social skills at the same time (Kern and Clemens, 2007). (See Chapter 7.)

Mix it up

No matter what the activity or lesson, variety will give it some spice. Build changes of pace into the day by scheduling quiet activities, such as reading or language arts, before active ones, such as recess (Evertson et al., 2003). Slow down when you're teaching harder concepts, and speed up when they're easier (Yehle and Wambold, 1998); alternate tedious tasks with more interesting or exciting ones and make a few simple demands before you make a difficult one (Yehle and Wambold, 1998). Highlight important ideas by changing your tone of voice and using colored chalk or ink.

To capture the interest of students with various learning styles and types of intelligence, appeal to different senses by using several media, including videos, audiotapes, computers, live demonstrations, manipulatives, and assistive technology. Children with challenging behavior and children with disabilities may have great strengths in more neglected intelligences—music, art, physical movement, or computers, for example. This approach allows them to develop and showcase their unique abilities. At the same time, mixing up your assessment strategies will enable you to evaluate knowledge and understanding more accurately.

Shake it up

Many students find it hard to sit still, so push your own tolerance for the wiggles as high as you can, stay away from long periods of independent seatwork, and make movement and active participation an integral part of your program. Small-group learning makes movement natural and acceptable without creating a ruckus—with appropriate procedures in place, students can move furniture, walk around to get into and out of their groups, and confer while they're together. Setting up centers in the classroom builds movement into the day, too. When children come to a center to work on a particular topic or activity, they have official approval to use their

166

Preventing Challenging
Behavior: Physical
Space, Classroom
Management, and
Teaching Strategies

High Hopes

Students give these suggestions about how teachers can show they expect their students to try hard and do well (Cushman et al., 2003):

- Remind us often that you expect our best. Be friendly and understanding, but keep pushing us.
- Encourage our efforts even if we are having trouble. Don't disparage or shame us when we don't get things right away.
- Give helpful feedback and expect us to revise.
- Give us plenty of support along the way. Don't leave it to the final presentations to tell us how to improve. Make yourself available for tutoring sessions if we need them.
- Help us set priorities among the different things we do.
- Don't favor the students you think will do the best. Call on students equally in class. Push everyone to improve, and acknowledge signs of improvement right away.
- Don't compare us to other students.
- Stick with us. It's hard for kids to believe we'll succeed if our teachers give up on us. When teachers quit, it sends a message that we aren't worth the trouble, and if a teacher doesn't care enough to stick with it, why should we? (pp. 64–66)

Source: © 2003 by What Kids Can Do, Inc. This piece originally appears in *Fires in the Bathroom: Advice for Teachers from High School Students* by Kathleen Cushman and the students of What Kids Can Do, Inc. Reprinted with the permission of The New Press. www.thenewpress.com.

bodies as well as their heads. Centers will probably also require procedures that include a cleanup routine and a maximum number who can be there at once; and the computer center may also need a time limit. Discuss these questions with the students as you're setting up the procedures, and solicit their feedback about how they're working. Be sure to post the procedures at each center.

In addition to using centers, partners, or small groups regularly, involve the children in acting out stories, historical events, and concepts; turn lessons into games; ask lots of questions and expect lots of answers, alone or in chorus; and let students check each other's work. They retain more and disrupt less when learning is hands-on and physical.

Permit children to work standing up and to use the board as a work area. You can even appoint scribes to write key ideas or words on the board (ADDinSchool .com, n.d.). Teach relaxation, and when the occupational therapist comes into the classroom to help a child with a disability, the whole class can accompany her as she does her therapy exercises. Take regular breaks to enable everyone to stretch, get a drink, or go to the bathroom (Emmer et al., 1980); and allow students to hold objects that they can quietly manipulate to give themselves sensory input (U.S. Department of Education, 2004).

Waiting is hard for everyone, especially for students with ADHD and those who lack impulse control. You can cut down on waiting time by preparing materials in advance and opening classroom centers—the computer area, the reference and reading center—for children to visit when they finish an activity before their classmates (Emmer et al., 2003; Evertson et al., 2003). Students could also tutor their peers or use the time to read material that they keep handy for such an occasion—a book, a magazine, even comic books.

A New Look

167

Preventing Challenging
Behavior: Physical
Space, Classroom
Management, and
Teaching Strategies

Lois Weiner (2006) tells how a young teacher used the technique of *reframing* to change her approach to a student whom she had believed needed medication for hyperactivity and a referral to special education.

> I told April that I understood that she had a lot of energy, and that was great! I let her know that lots of people need to move around in order to learn. It was just another thing that made her special. . . . I asked that April please do her exercises on the carpet or by the classroom library. I let her know that whenever she felt she was ready, she could return to the group. . . . I said that I knew she might forget . . . but that was OK and I would remind her with our special sign—touching the tip of my nose. . . .
>
> The reframing changed my negative, critical attitude toward April's behavior to a positive supportive outlook. As a result, the exercises and movement no longer upset or distracted me. Once I became comfortable with the reframing, April's behavior really improved. Now, [she] automatically moves to the carpet or library to exercise. . . . April is happier and more relaxed during whole-group instruction. (p. 44)

Although it may drive you crazy when a student with ADHD doesn't raise her hand and wait to be called on, remember that although she knows she's supposed to wait, she simply cannot do it. To assist her in gaining control, try to ignore the answer she shouts out, and when her hand goes up, call on her at once. You can help children learn to wait by using a timer that ticks or an egg timer that shows time passing; by teaching deep breathing and self-talk ("I can wait"); and by bookending your activities with clear beginnings and endings (Kostelnik, Onaga, Rohde, and Whiren, 2002).

All the students can benefit from listening to the sound of silence. You don't have to schedule these moments; if you watch the children carefully, you'll know when they're in order. When Andrew is getting too excited, that's a good time to say, "Okay, everyone, stop everything, put your head down on your desk, and think about how you're breathing." Ask them to concentrate on their toes and each individual body part in turn. By the time you've reached the tops of their heads, the atmosphere will be completely altered.

Break it up

Students with memory and information-processing problems can't handle a lot of information at once, but they can succeed when they get their instruction in small, manageable pieces. Analyze the content and skills you're teaching, and break them down into small segments and steps. Provide concrete examples, visual cues, and sequence cards that list or illustrate each step (Cook, Klein, and Tessier, 2004), and teach one step at a time, giving your instructions in clear, direct, positive language. Go forward only when a child has learned the segment. Keep asking for feedback to be sure the student understands, and review the main points at the end (Brophy, 2000). Moving ahead before a child has understood a step will only lead to frustration, low self-esteem, and dislike of school, as well as challenging behavior.

This technique works for long activities as well as for complex ones, and for the whole class as well as for individuals. If your students can't handle a 30-minute meeting time, hold two short meetings instead (DuPaul and Stoner, 2003); and divide the geography lesson into short segments so that they can have a break in

168

Preventing Challenging
Behavior: Physical
Space, Classroom
Management, and
Teaching Strategies

Keep asking for feedback to be sure each student understands, and review the main points at the end. Moving ahead before a child has understood a step will only lead to frustration, low self-esteem, and dislike of school, as well as challenging behavior.

between. Or if you notice that the class is losing interest, move on to something else and plan to return to the topic the next day (Evertson et al., 2003). Even if the students are eagerly awaiting your every word on Wednesday, by Friday they may have lost the ability to stay focused.

Tell it like it is

Communicating clearly is essential. When you begin an activity or lesson, tell the students what you've planned, what they're expected to learn, what materials they'll need, and how they're supposed to behave (for example, they may talk quietly to their neighbors) (U.S. Department of Education, 2004). In addition to giving directions orally, provide a clear written outline of the lesson, including objectives, key concepts, and vocabulary (Yehle and Wambold, 1998).

As you teach, capture and keep your students' attention by calling them by name, using their names and interests in your examples (Yehle and Wambold, 1998), and giving them credit for their ideas (Marzano, 2003) ("Petros said that ads on the front page cost more because more people look at the front page").

Let's Get Organized

169

Preventing Challenging
Behavior: Physical
Space, Classroom
Management, and
Teaching Strategies

Organization and study skills pay off in a big way: They minimize frustration and opportunities to act out.

- Ask students to get color-coded notebooks, folders, and notebook dividers to help organize their work for different subjects (Yehle and Wambold, 1998). Everything should match the color of the textbook (ADDinSchool.com, n.d.).
- Create a regular, weekly time for children to clean out their desks and book bags (ADDinSchool.com, n.d.).
- Make sure each child has an agenda, and establish a routine for using it (Yehle and Wambold, 1998). Students can note timelines for projects and contracts, their responsibilities for their small group, and assignments that they're planning to finish at home. They could also write down one thing they've learned each day to share with their family. If you're assigning homework, either you or a peer buddy can check to see if children have written the assignment correctly (ERIC Clearinghouse, 1998), and both you and the parents should look over assignments and initial the agenda book every day (Yehle and Wambold, 1998). For more about homework, see pages 170 to 172.
- If possible, let students with disabilities keep an extra set of textbooks at home. More than just a useful backup, this strategy helps parents stay up to speed on what their children are doing (Peterson and Hittie, 2003).

Anticipate frustration and offer encouragement: "I know this is going to be tough, but you can do it. I'll go slowly" (Kostelnik et al., 2002). At the same time, you can model cognitive strategies—for example, thinking aloud—that help children verbalize their thought processes.

It's also important to give students plenty of time to think when you're asking them to respond to complex questions. Research shows that waiting at least 3 seconds for a reply will elicit longer answers, more unsolicited and appropriate answers, more questions, and more participation from students who are struggling (Rowe, 1986).

At the end of the lesson, sum up what you've taught, or give the children a chance to say what they've learned.

Out in the open

Because school recess and lunch are often unstructured, boring, and poorly supervised, many children dread their approach. When students use inappropriate ways to let out their classroom frustrations, these periods can spawn aggressive behavior, bullying, and exclusion of those who are different.

Work with the whole class to think up methods for making the playground and cafeteria safer and more pleasant (ADDinSchool.com, n.d.). One possibility is to pair a student who has difficulty with a socially skilled buddy who is willing to help on the playground. Another is to talk with the child about her plans for recess and lunch. With whom will she play or sit? Help her organize a specific activity with a classmate; later ask about what happened and help prepare a strategy for the next day (ADDinSchool.com, n.d.). You could also recruit adult volunteers to stay in the classroom and supervise students who need a peaceful option. Yet another alternative is to invite older children to create some structured noncompetitive games and

170

Preventing Challenging
Behavior: Physical
Space, Classroom
Management, and
Teaching Strategies

activities (or devise some yourself), a tactic that can ward off both isolation and disruption (Litner, 2000).

Sometimes recess is just too long. Enlist the aid of a supervisor, who can help the child divide the period into thirds. She can play for a while, spend some time with the supervisor, and then have a second round of activity (ADDinSchool.com, n.d.).

Jennifer Allen (2006), who organized successful literary lunches for fourth-grade boys in Waterville, Maine, writes, "I asked the boys why they really came to writing group every week. . . . They shared that although they liked writing, they really *didn't* like recess. Some disliked recess because they were bullied; others just believed that there was nothing out there to do. These boys yearned to be heard, and they were begging for a sense of belonging. . . . I now believe that schools need to provide nontraditional offerings during lunch and recess . . . for all students, not just boys" (pp. 69–70).

Homework or not?

The subject of homework for elementary and middle school students continues to spark controversy. Some experts and teachers believe that homework is necessary in order for students to master the content of the mandated curriculum and enable those who work more slowly to complete their assignments. Other experts contend that if students don't have homework in the early years, they won't develop the skills they need to complete it successfully in high school. Still others consider homework a valuable assessment tool that gives teachers information about who needs extra help and which learning objectives to revisit. And some argue that homework provides an important link between school and home.

But homework often precipitates challenging behavior. When a child doesn't—or can't—do an assignment, she enters the classroom filled with anxiety, fear, anger, or frustration; and escape may be foremost in her mind. Challenging behavior will provide it.

Rather than taking homework for granted, think about why you're assigning it. Are you afraid you won't cover all of the material in class or worried about what parents will think? Is it an automatic reflex activated by the fact that you always had homework when you went to school? These questions arise because the utility of homework is far from clear.

Conducting a meta-analysis of the research on the topic led homework expert Harris Cooper of Duke University (2001) to conclude there was little correlation between the amount of homework teachers assigned in elementary school and their students' academic achievement, and just a modest correlation in middle school. Only in high school did homework make a substantial contribution.

It is certain that homework doesn't help students who have trouble following directions, do not listen, or don't understand what they're doing. According to Alfie Kohn, homework may make them feel stupid, accustom them to doing things the wrong way, and subtly teach that "whatever subject they're doing is something people aren't *expected* to understand" (2006, p. 113).

Researchers have also found that homework widens the gap between rich and poor by punishing students from low-income families (Kralovec and Buell, 2001). Middle- and upper-class students can count on home computers and well-educated

171

Preventing Challenging
Behavior: Physical
Space, Classroom
Management, and
Teaching Strategies

parents for assistance. But the parents of children on the bottom of the economic ladder may work at night or speak little English, their home may lack a computer or quiet space to work, or the child may have family responsibilities such as looking after siblings and cooking dinner. About 62 percent of respondents to a recent Canadian survey said that parents didn't have the necessary knowledge to help their children with homework (Mahoney, 2006).

Even if all parents could help with homework, the achievement gap would still exist, says Richard Rothstein of the Economic Policy Institute in Washington, DC: "Middle-class parents—especially those whose own occupational habits require problem solving—are more likely to assist by posing questions that break large problems down into smaller ones and that help children figure out correct answers. Lower-class parents are more likely to guide children with direct instructions. Children from both classes may go to school with completed homework, but middle-class children are more likely to gain in intellectual power from the exercise than lower-class children" (2004, p. 19).

If there has to be homework, many experts recommend waiting until middle school to assign it. They also oppose grading it. Cooper advocates assignments that students can complete successfully and evaluating homework only in order to identify and remediate skill deficits (Bennett and Kalish, 2006). Martin Haberman (1995) believes that homework should not be checked but shared—students should talk about books they're reading and questions they're thinking about. That is, homework should promote learning.

"Assign homework only when you feel it's valuable," advise Sarah Bennett and Nancy Kalish in *The Case against Homework*. "A night off is better than homework that serves no purpose" (2006, p. 228). Here are some suggestions for increasing its value (Bennett and Kalish, 2006; Kohn, 2006a):

- Assign no more than 10 minutes per night per grade.
- Differentiate assignments to meet children's needs and available resources.
- Make weekends, school breaks, and summer vacations homework free, and schedule tests during the week, not following holidays, school breaks, or on Mondays.

Homework that Sings

Educators in innovative urban schools recommend several strategies for engaging students in their homework (Darling-Hammond and Hill-Lynch, 2006):

- *Assign work that is worthy of effort.* When it's authentic and relevant, students have a reason to do it. Project-based work in particular encourages deep involvement.
- *Make the work doable.* Be sure that it relates to the lesson, the directions are clear, and students get the assistance they need to complete the assignment before they leave class.
- *Find out what students need to do the work.* Address problems by meeting with students one-on-one to map out a strategy.
- *Create space and time for homework.* You can do this simply by staying in the classroom during lunch or before or after school. Some schools have advisory periods that can be used for this purpose.

172

Preventing Challenging
Behavior: Physical
Space, Classroom
Management, and
Teaching Strategies

- Reading should be paramount. But, adds Kohn (2006a), don't assign a specific number of pages or a specific number of minutes.
- Allow students to decide whether it makes sense to work on a given project or assignment at home.
- Provide opportunities for children to do their homework at school if they choose.

Get students started in class to be sure they understand the assignment and know what to do (Brophy, 2000). One way to manage this is to form small groups where students help each other to come up with problem-solving strategies (Trumbull et al., 2000). Evertson and colleagues (2003) suggest a similar method for checking homework the next day. In small groups, the children take turns reading and answering the questions and discussing their results, while the teacher circulates from group to group. When she sees which problems the students are struggling with, she knows what to clarify and reteach.

WHEN CIRCUMSTANCES CHANGE

After a catastrophic event such as September 11, Hurricane Katrina, a school shooting, or the untimely death of a student or teacher, what worked in the classroom before may no longer apply. Children cannot learn unless they feel safe. It's hard for them to concentrate, and they may not even see the relevance or importance of the curriculum. Your expectations, schedule, content, classroom procedures, and teaching methods must all adjust if you're going to help them regain a sense of safety and well-being.

Extraordinary events affect everyone. Surrounded by confused and frightened adults, children of all ages feel unsafe and insecure; and your top priority must become providing them with a safe haven. In this situation, your expertise, your experience, and your relationship with your students all come into play. Tuning in to your students' needs as well as your own emotional state will help you to prevent and contain difficult behavior, especially in children at risk.

Providing reassurance

In his book, *What Happened to the World? Helping Children Cope in Turbulent Times* (2001), written after September 11, 2001, Jim Greenman offers useful information for responding to any catastrophic event in a child's life. Greenman says that children want to know three things:

- Will I be okay?
- Will you be okay?
- Will everyone I care about be okay? (p. 12)

Your first job is to reassure them that they are safe and that you and other trustworthy adults (such as the police and firefighters) are in control and will take care of them. You are like the flight attendants on a turbulent flight. If they continue to walk up and down the aisle, calmly serving drinks, everyone feels safe. Their relaxed demeanor tells the passengers the turbulence may be uncomfortable, but it's manageable. When you model calm, self-control, and coping skills in the classroom, the students take their cue from you and feel more secure.

173

Preventing Challenging
Behavior: Physical
Space, Classroom
Management, and
Teaching Strategies

Talking about feelings

It's important for children to have many opportunities to ask questions and express their thoughts and feelings with adults they trust. They may need to be reassured again and again and ask the same questions over and over. Take a deep breath, assess your own feelings, and make sure you're ready to work with your students. If you can't listen, they won't be able to talk, and they will get the message that the disaster is so horrible that you can't deal with it, which intensifies their fear.

Because the event will be foremost in their minds, talk about it with your students the first chance that you have. They will find it helpful to hear that others share their feelings, and as you respond to each child and help her put events into perspective, you'll be helping the whole group. But be prepared for the possibility that what they hear will scare them—some students may strongly communicate their fear; some may share gruesome details or information that others haven't heard.

Students have different concerns and process information in different ways, so it makes sense to talk with them individually as well as in a group. Be careful not to force a child who doesn't want to talk, but watch for a child who seems ready and ask open-ended questions ("What have you heard about what happened in New Orleans?"). Listen carefully and without judging, accept her feelings and worries, and respond calmly in simple, direct language. These conversations will help you clear up misunderstandings and provide her with appropriate support (Gurwitch, Silovsky, Schultz, Kees, and Burlingame, 2005). Finish by reminding her that she's safe and help her to move on to something calming, such as deep breathing, singing, or an art activity. Drawing and writing are extremely useful in helping students to deal with their feelings, and both physical activity and tactile experiences help them to release tension. Under these circumstances, manipulating clay or play-dough can relax even the most sophisticated eighth-grade student.

Let your students know what you're feeling as well (Gurwitch et al., 2005). It's most reassuring when you show them that you're all right even though you feel sad or worried or angry. You can say, "I'm very sad, but I know I'll get through it, and you will, too." When they see that you can cope, it makes it possible for them to do the same.

Routines and activities

When their lives feel unpredictable, children need routine more than ever. Consistency brings comfort and a sense that everyday things are unchanged, so return to normal activities as soon as you can (National Institute of Mental Health, 2006). Because your students will probably be unable to perform at their usual level, choose enjoyable activities that build mastery and self-esteem and forget about giving tests or introducing new or difficult concepts for a while (Gurwitch et al., 2005).

Some students will find it hard to make choices, but others will need choices in order to have more control. Some children will need more structure and others less. Some will have angry outbursts; some will regress into patterns of behavior that are appropriate for younger children (Gurwitch et al., 2005). Be sensitive to what each student needs and adjust the program accordingly.

174

Preventing Challenging
Behavior: Physical
Space, Classroom
Management, and
Teaching Strategies

You may also find that the classroom hustle and bustle has become overstimulating. Slow things down and calm everyone's nerves by playing quiet music, speaking in a calm voice, and moving more slowly.

Children also feel better if they can do something to help (Myers-Walls, 2005). Writing letters to rescue workers, affected families, or public officials; collecting money for victims; or getting involved in an organization that works to prevent such events can direct some of that potentially negative energy in a constructive way and give them a sense that one person can make a difference.

Maintaining the social context

When the media and the politicians talk about nothing but war, terrorism, and violence, when people rush out to buy guns to protect themselves (Baker, 2001), or when thousands lose their homes and belongings and are evacuated from flooded areas, the social context in your classroom is put to the test. Children see adults using violence and power to solve problems, and they hear intolerance and hatred everywhere.

In this situation it's important to continue to model and teach empathy and peaceful problem solving. Discuss current events with the children, listen to what they feel and think, and help them listen to each other. You might even use role-playing to help them put themselves in another's shoes.

It is also critical to watch out for racism and stereotyping and to teach children to respect differences. Provide them with information about other cultures and explain that most people don't believe in hurting others. They find war and terrorist attacks just as upsetting and shocking as we do.

Connecting with colleagues and parents

With your colleagues, figure out how you can best monitor the way that children are handling the situation. But take care not to hold adult discussions of the catastrophic event when students are nearby or you will frighten them all over again (Gurwitch et al., 2005).

It's also essential to communicate with families—children need to know that all the adults in their lives are working together to keep them safe. Different families have different resources for meeting this challenge. Those who manage well will probably have children who manage well, whereas those who are struggling may have difficulty reassuring their children.

You'll have a better chance to connect with parents if you reach out to them in writing and in person. A parent evening, perhaps with a mental health professional as an invited guest, will provide an opportunity for families to share what they're going through. It will also allow you to hear what's on their minds. Some parents will look to you for guidance; others will want to handle things their own way. They will probably also have diverse views about what you're doing in the classroom. Although some families will be eager for you to discuss the events with their children, there will be others who consider the subject taboo. Explain to them why you feel it's important for the children to express themselves, ask questions, and have the opportunity to come to terms with what has happened on their own level. Reassure the parents that you're dealing with the events in a caring, sensitive way.

You can also provide information. Parents may not be aware of what is developmentally appropriate for their child to know or how much she can understand. Although watching television may alleviate their own anxiety, they probably don't realize what impact the news has on their children. Gently help families understand the need to limit what they watch when their child is present. Although older children want to make sense of the events and need information in order to understand, they, too, should be protected from re-exposure to reminders of the trauma (Gurwitch et al., 2005). Parents should watch the news with them and discuss it with them afterwards.

In addition, ask parents to inform you if they notice anything different in their child's behavior. By pooling your observations, you'll know when to get extra help for a child who needs it and may be in danger of developing posttraumatic stress disorder. Students who've been through a previous trauma may be especially vulnerable. There is no definitive period of time that people need to overcome their reaction to a traumatic event. During the remainder of the school year, when you're selecting materials and focusing discussions, remain sensitive to your students' needs.

When you work together, children, families, and teachers all benefit, and a deep sense of community is likely to emerge.

Taking care of yourself

How do you accomplish all of this when you're feeling confused and frightened yourself? Greenman (2001) makes these suggestions:

- Talk about your feelings with adults with whom you feel secure.
- Try to create a daily routine and rituals that support your current needs.
- Try to create a daily routine and rituals that support your family's current needs.
- Live well: eat right, get exercise, sleep.
- Cry when you need to, and seek solitude when you have to.
- Take breaks from the news and headlines.
- Take breaks from others who bring you down.
- Give yourself and those around you some slack for poor behavior under stress.
- Seek help if you feel that life is not becoming more manageable.
- Replenish your spirit with friends, faith, family, music, or nature. (p. 17)

Judith A. Myers-Walls (2005) of Purdue University adds, "Take action and get involved in something. It is not enough to let children take action by themselves. Children who know that their parents [or] teachers . . . are working to make a difference feel hope. They feel safer and more positive about the future. So do something. It will make you feel more hopeful, too. And hope is one of the most valuable gifts we can give children and ourselves."

What do you think?

1. Go to a restaurant, supermarket, library, or if you're teaching or student teaching, look around your classroom. What is the message you get from the physical environment? Why? What are the clues?

2. What do you think about the strategy the teacher used in the box "Wall of Fame" on page 154? Do you think that the end justified the means? How do you think the students felt? How else could the teacher have encouraged the students to improve their work before she posted it?

3. We need classroom procedures at the beginning and end of the day, but when else are they necessary? Consider the needs of Andrew and Jazmine and develop a procedure for a different time or situation when you think one is required. Then gather any materials you may need to implement it, and teach it to the class (or if you're teaching, teach it to your students).

4. Develop a lesson plan implementing differentiated instruction for a hypothetical sixth-grade class. Your 30 students come from diverse cultures and have varying abilities and resources at home. How can you respond to their different needs, interests, cultures, skills, and abilities?

5. Divide the class into two groups and debate the pros and cons of homework.

What would you do?

You are teaching a group of students who have always sat in rows and worked independently. What steps will you take to successfully introduce them to group work and group seating arrangements? Be sure to think about the material in Chapter 7 as well as the material in this chapter.

Suggested readings

Dodge, J. (2006). *Differentiation in action: A complete resource with research-supported strategies to help you plan and organize differentiated instruction.* New York: Scholastic.

Dunn, R., Beaudry, J. S., & Klavas, A. (1989). Survey of research on learning styles. *Educational Leadership, 46,* 50–58.

Greenwood, S. (2003). *On equal terms: How to make the most of learning contracts in grades 4–9.* Portsmouth, NH: Heinemann.

Kohn, A. (2006). *The homework myth: Why kids get too much of a bad thing.* Cambridge, MA: De Capo Press.

Teaching to student strengths. (2006, September, whole issue). *Educational Leadership, 64*(1).

Tomlinson, C. A. (1999). *The differentiated classroom: Responding to the needs of all learners.* Alexandria, VA: Association for Supervision and Curriculum Development.

Tomlinson, C. A. (2001). *How to differentiate instruction in mixed-ability classrooms* (2nd ed.). Alexandria, VA: Association for Supervision and Curriculum Development.

CHAPTER 9

Guidance and Other Discipline Strategies

This chapter and three others that follow describe strategies for working directly with students with challenging behavior.

We offer you several strategies for three reasons. First, people have different styles, values, and life experiences, and what suits the teacher down the hall might not suit you at all. It's important to believe in the strategy you're using; if you don't feel comfortable with it or understand the philosophy behind it, it probably won't work for you. Second, every child is unique, and each requires an approach that fits his state of mind, to say nothing of his temperament, age, stage of development, and culture. When you know how to use several strategies, possibilities open up, and you can choose the one that's most appropriate for the circumstances. As Abraham Maslow once said, "If the only tool you have is a hammer, you tend to see every problem as a nail." Third, if a student's challenging behavior doesn't change over time, what you're doing isn't working, and you will need to try a different tactic—an excellent motive for having many tools in your tool box.

Because they aren't recipes or formulas, you can use these strategies one at a time or mix and match them.

How do strategies differ?

The process of addressing behavior problems and teaching students to behave in socially acceptable ways has several different names. Some people refer to it as *guidance*; others use the word *discipline*; and still others prefer to call it *behavior management*. The name you choose and the method you employ probably depend on your background and philosophy. In this book we use the word *guidance*.

Strategies vary widely in the degree of teacher control they require (Wolfgang, 2001). *Guidance* usually refers to *low-control* methods advocated by Haim Ginott, Thomas Gordon, Alfie Kohn, and Marilyn Watson. Their approach is based on attachment theory, constructivism, and the humanistic psychology of Carl Rogers. These experts believe that children are active participants in their own learning and flourish in a supportive and democratic classroom where they can make their own choices and construct their own values. The teacher's role is to facilitate their development by attending to their feelings, thoughts, and ideas. Children misbehave because their needs aren't being met or because they lack the skills to solve their problems (Burden, 2003; Wolfgang, 2001).

Educators who believe in *medium-control* methods (Rudolf Dreikurs, William Glasser, Richard Curwin and Allen Mendler, Linda Albert, Jane Nelsen, and Forrest Gathercoal) frequently use the term *discipline*. Inspired by the theory of Alfred Adler, they take the position that a combination of internal and external forces governs children's development and a child misbehaves because he has mistaken ideas about how to belong to the group. Teacher and child must work together to help him learn to behave appropriately by understanding the consequences of his decisions. Teachers who take this stance tend to place the needs of the group before the needs of an individual student (Burden, 2003; Wolfgang, 2001).

Teachers who use *high-control* techniques (Lee and Marlene Canter, Fredric Jones, Paul A. Alberto and Ann C. Troutman) usually call their approach *behavior management*. Drawing on the behavior modification theory of B. F. Skinner and the social learning theory of Albert Bandura, they ascribe children's growth and development to external conditions. According to social learning theory, children learn by observing and imitating the people around them. Because they aren't able to monitor and control their own behavior effectively, it is the teacher's responsibility to take charge and assist them by making and enforcing rules, reinforcing appropriate behavior, and applying consequences for inappropriate behavior (Burden, 2003; Wolfgang, 2001).

This chapter takes a look at some specific strategies teachers use to guide students' behavior. It begins with a discussion of what makes any strategy effective, then turns to the strategies themselves. We start with the low-control methods of developmental discipline and active listening (Teacher Effectiveness Training); continue with methods that use more control, such as positive reinforcement (including praise and encouragement) and natural and logical consequences; and move on to the behaviorist-based methods of time-out and punishment (including time-away, a nonpunitive variation of time-out). Finally, we explore the role of culture in guidance.

What makes a strategy work?

Although the experts have their philosophical differences, they agree that several key factors will increase the effectiveness of any strategy.

Since no behavior exists in a vacuum, the first step is to *structure the classroom environment* to prevent challenging behavior. A safe, caring, cooperative, inclusive social context and physical space; clear rules, procedures, and classroom management; and interesting, relevant, differentiated instruction maximize learning, minimize behavior problems, and lay a solid foundation for any guidance strategy.

The essential—and perhaps even more important—partner of a carefully structured environment is a *positive, responsive, trusting teacher–student relationship*. Where children with challenging behavior are concerned, such a relationship may be difficult and time consuming to establish, but it is vital to guiding behavior successfully. (Chapter 5 is devoted to the subject of relationships.)

A crucial part of a positive teacher–student relationship is having *high expectations*. Just as it's important to believe in a student's capacity to learn and consistently demand his best work, so it is critical to believe in his ability to behave appropriately and help him do so.

A willingness to spend time working with students on behavior problems, rather than referring them to the principal or the dean of discipline, is also important. The Classroom Strategy Study (Brophy 1996; Brophy and McCaslin, 1992) found that teachers who didn't rely on quick fixes but directed their efforts at reaching long-term solutions were more effective.

The way you behave during a challenging situation also plays a key role in the effectiveness of a strategy. *Remaining calm*, especially in a crisis, makes it much easier for you to think clearly, stay in control of yourself, solve problems, and prevent the situation from escalating. When you keep your composure and refuse to let a child push your buttons, you are modeling and encouraging emotional control, a vital skill that many students with challenging behavior lack. Keep your *voice low and steady*, your *body language relaxed* (your arms at your sides, for example, not crossed or akimbo) (Kottler, 2002), and your *distance from the student carefully calculated* for his cultural comfort.

Address the behavior, not the person. Make it clear that you still like and value the student; the problem is not with him but with what he did (Kohn, 1996; Kottler, 2002).

A Spoonful of Caring

In *Random Family: Love, Drugs, Trouble, and Coming of Age in the Bronx*, Adrian Nicole LeBlanc (2004) describes with painstaking care several years in the life of a Puerto Rican family. Here, she captures the relationship between Mercedes and her teacher, a bright spot in the child's difficult existence:

> The most important thing was that Mercedes loved her fourth-grade teacher, Mrs. Cormier. Academic performance had never been Mercedes's problem; she passed with little effort; the trouble always had to do with discipline. When confronted, Mercedes became defensive, but her fear was hard to see because she acted so tough. She was opinionated. She also had a slang street style, which some adults found off-putting or intimidating; it was actually her way of testing people's interest and reaching out.
>
> But Mrs. Cormier enjoyed her spiritedness and had deciphered from her meetings with [her mother] that Mercedes's chores at home included parenting; she understood that having such a young mother made Mercedes older than her age. "Mercedes wants to achieve, but she also wants to be in charge," Mrs. Cormier said. So she expanded Mercedes's responsibilities whenever possible and overlooked the small things—the outbursts, Mercedes's "bids for negative attention." Almost always, Mercedes came around. (pp. 354–355)

When there is a problem, talk with the student privately. The presence of an audience heightens embarrassment and often results in grandstanding, which only serves to inflame the situation. It will also make it nearly impossible for either you or the student to disengage without losing face.

When there is a problem, *talk with the student privately*. The presence of an audience heightens embarrassment and often results in grandstanding, which only serves to inflame the situation. It will also make it nearly impossible for either you or the student to disengage without losing face.

Use humor whenever possible. It is a wonderful way to defuse a tense situation and allow everyone to maintain a sense of self-respect (Curwin and Mendler, 2001; Goldstein, Harootunian, and Conoley, 1994). Be sure to avoid sarcasm and put-downs.

Be reflective. At the end of the day, revisit incidents of challenging behavior and try to *figure out the message that the behavior was communicating* (Kottler, 2002). What thoughts, feelings, or needs were behind it (Kohn, 2006b)? Was the child saying he was embarrassed and frustrated because he didn't understand the math concept and needed more teaching? (To learn more about behavior as communication, turn to Chapter 11.)

Be patient and flexible. The child has been using this behavior for a long time, and it's hard to change a habit. A new strategy can take as long as 3 to 4 weeks to work. But once it becomes clear that it isn't having the desired effect, discard it and try another.

Start fresh every day. Whatever happened yesterday, let it go (Curwin and Mendler, 2001).

Above all, remember that you're a teacher and *challenging behavior is an opportunity to teach* (Kohn, 1996). More often than not, when a child engages in challenging behavior, he is telling you that he must learn new skills in order to meet his needs and behave appropriately at the same time.

"Emotional states are contagious, brain to brain," writes Daniel Goleman (2006, p. 77), author of *Emotional Intelligence*. Whenever we interact with someone, the "mirror neurons" in our brain automatically adjust our feelings to synchronize with his (Winkleman and Harmon-Jones, 2006).

The most powerful person in a group—usually the teacher—has the strongest concentration of emotions and is most able to influence others (Barsade, 2002). This state of affairs implies that when you like a child, he will be more likely to like you in return, more likely to listen to you—and to feel better. On the other hand, if a student feels that you dislike him, he'll be less inclined to cooperate, and he'll feel worse.

What is developmental discipline?

Based on attachment theory (see Chapter 5), the low-control classroom management technique known as *developmental discipline* (Watson, 2003) emphasizes the need for teachers to:

- Form warm and supportive relationships with and among their students
- Help their students understand the reasons behind classroom rules and expectations
- Teach any relevant skills the student might be lacking
- Engage students in a collaborative, problem-solving process aimed at stopping misbehavior
- Use nonpunitive ways to externally control student behavior when necessary (p. 4)

This approach takes a great deal of time and effort, and at first a teacher may question whether it's worth it. But when you persevere and you and your students become more proficient at both talking and listening, everything will begin to fall into place. You will succeed in getting your class to care about you, each other, and learning, and you will get your time back.

Developmental discipline assumes that a child's relationship with his caregivers, including his teachers, provides the basis for his development. When those relationships are sensitive and responsive from the start, the child becomes securely attached and learns to regulate his emotions, have confidence in himself, trust other people, and accept support and guidance. In contrast, a child who experiences unresponsive or rejecting caregiving early in life forms an insecure attachment, and with it a mistrust of himself and everyone around him. He is liable to have low self-esteem and difficulty controlling his feelings and behavior; and he doesn't believe that adults will provide the care and support he needs.

For teachers, being able to like students with challenging behavior—to accept them unconditionally—is a key piece of developmental discipline. Because such students don't trust adults and consider themselves unworthy of care, they will test a teacher's caring again and again. Like other children, they need and desire caring, trusting relationships with adults, but they often use inappropriate means to make these connections. In fact, they may regard a teacher's efforts to teach and guide

Unconditional Liking

In *Learning to Trust: Transforming Difficult Elementary Classrooms through Developmental Discipline* (Watson, 2003), teacher Laura Ecken describes one of the ways she used to convince Danny, a student who had disrupted her class for months, that she liked him.

> I just sat down with him, and I said, "You know what, I really, really like you. You can keep doing all this stuff and it's not going to change my mind. It seems to me that you are trying to get me to dislike you, but it's not going to work. I'm not ever going to do that. If you really need to do this stuff all the time, I can deal with it. I'm going to stop you. I'm going to talk to you about it and explain to you why you need to stop it, but it's never going to change the way I feel about you. I'm just letting you know."
>
> It was after that, and I'm not saying immediately, that his disruptive behaviors started to decrease. (pp. 2–3)

Source From *Learning to Trust: Transforming Difficult Elementary Classrooms through Developmental Discipline* by Marilyn Watson with Laura Ecken, 2003. San Francisco: Jossey-Bass. Copyright © 2003 by John Wiley & Sons, Inc. Reprinted with permission of John Wiley & Sons, Inc.

them as a way to control or coerce them (Watson, 2003). A teacher must overcome this opposition and, without diminishing the child's autonomy, establish a caring and trusting relationship in order to help him learn the prosocial and emotional skills he needs. Rewards and punishment won't work—they just confirm the student's view that relationships are about manipulation (Watson, 2003).

So how do you help students who need adult intervention but resist it in any form? Furthermore, how do you provide it respectfully and without punishment? Because developmental discipline sees challenging behavior as the result of mistrust and missing skills, a teacher's first response is to figure out why the student could not do the right thing. As Alfie Kohn (1996) puts it: "Our point of departure should always be this: *How can we work with students to solve this problem? How can we turn this into a chance to help them learn?*" (p. 121). This process involves lots of talking, reasoning, and negotiating, with students fully engaged in both problem solving and planning to prevent the reappearance of challenging behavior. Once the teacher has discovered what the child needs, she knows what and how to provide help—that is, to teach.

Just as you can use *scaffolding*—furnishing assistance that enables students to learn skills and concepts that might otherwise be just slightly out of reach—to teach academic subjects, you can use it to teach social, emotional, and behavior skills. A caring, cooperative social context, where students know what's expected, supplies the foundation for all scaffolding, and teachers can supplement it with support that meets individual needs.

After a student and his teacher have resolved a conflict and created a plan, a teacher often uses *reminders* or *private signals*—a glance, a frown, a few words—that redirect the child to the task at hand or remind him of an agreement they've reached together. These gestures aren't threats; on the contrary, they're given in a helpful spirit and imply that the teacher and the student understand one another. Michael bumps into Andrew as the class is gathering to go to the gym. Andrew raises his hand as if to push Michael back, but the teacher catches his eye and touches her ear, using their special signal to remind him to use words rather than physical force. Andrew puts down his arm and turns to face the door.

But sometimes students with challenging behavior construe a reminder as a menace to their autonomy, and in that case it may be wise to avoid confrontation. Instead, you can make a clear request, ignore the student's defiant attitude, and withdraw, implying that you believe he will choose to do what you've asked. When you give him *time and space*, he may well repay your trust by complying, but if you stand over him, waiting for him to obey, he may see you as a threat, interpret the situation as a win-lose proposition, and act out to save face. You may also literally give students time and space, for example, by sending them to run an errand or get a drink of water, to help them learn to compose themselves and practice self-control.

Developmental discipline also suggests teaching *self-talk* to enable students to take charge of their own behavior. When they can analyze a situation and talk to themselves about it—give themselves instructions in their minds—they can choose what to do, rather than act on impulse (Watson, 2003). (For more about self-talk, see page 142.)

When these methods fail and behavior spirals out of control, you may need to ask a student to *reflect*—to think about the harm he's done and come up with a plan to repair it—or to retire to a quiet spot in the classroom to write a reflection, perhaps from the point of view of a witness to the event or a child who was hurt. The idea here is to help students develop empathy, teach moral values, and "internalize the language and concepts related to self-control and proper school behavior" (Watson, 2003, p. 169). Before you use this option, be sure to discuss it with your students so that they understand the purpose for it and it doesn't seem like punishment. Follow up with a one-on-one conversation about the reflection and other strategies the student can try the next time.

Less Is More

L aura Ecken (Watson, 2003) discovered that Leonard, a student she had initially seen as oppositional, found her requests easier to follow when she didn't hover over him, insisting on obedience. Having a choice empowered him.

> After the class finished performing their role-plays . . . we talked about ways to improve their scripts by tying them more realistically to the story.
>
> Leonard refused. He said, "I'm not doing that. Mine's good enough." And Louise, his partner, agreed.
>
> I said, "You know, Leonard, this is an opportunity to make it better. It is pretty good. But pretty good's not good enough when you've got an opportunity to make it great. And that's what you're getting right now."
>
> He said, "Well, I'm not doing it."
>
> And I said, "You know what? That's your decision."
>
> I left it alone and the next thing I knew, he and Louise were working and getting their role-play all fixed up. (p. 131)

Source: From *Learning to Trust: Transforming Difficult Elementary Classrooms through Developmental Discipline* by Marilyn Watson with Laura Ecken, 2003. San Francisco: Jossey-Bass. Copyright © 2003 by John Wiley & Sons, Inc. Reprinted with permission of John Wiley & Sons, Inc.

Your relationship with a student with problem behavior is tested each time he behaves inappropriately. You can protect this relationship by softening the use of power as much as possible, preserving the child's sense that he is competent, cared for, and autonomous (Watson, Solomon, Battistich, Schaps, and Solomon, 1989). It is also helpful to show empathy for his situation ("I know it makes you angry and it's hard to react calmly when someone insults you, but it's not okay to ruin his work"); to attribute the best possible motives to him when he loses control ("I'm sure you and Patrick were talking about the Civil War, but when you and I are talking at the same time no one can hear"); and to offer the student a choice ("Would you rather take a break at your desk or read a magazine at the back of the room?").

How does teacher effectiveness training work?

Like developmental discipline, Teacher Effectiveness Training (Gordon, 2003) springs from the humanistic psychology of Carl Rogers, who believed that an individual's behavior is primarily determined by his perception of the world around him. Developed by clinical psychologist Thomas Gordon, the low-control approach of Teacher Effectiveness Training also emphasizes the importance of the teacher–student relationship, which Gordon believes has far more power to influence children's learning and behavior than rewards and punishments.

When a problem arises, Gordon (2003) asks teachers to figure out who owns it. When the problem doesn't have any real effect on the teacher but disturbs the student—and the emotions he's experiencing interfere with his ability to learn—the student owns the problem. For example, when Andrew has a fight with his father just before school, it is hard for him to concentrate on his reading because he is feeling anxious and has fewer reserves for dealing with problems. It is important to respond to his anxiety before his behavior escalates and hampers your ability to teach, becoming your problem as well as his. (Chapter 10 describes this state of mind in more detail.)

Teachers can help students resolve their problems. The key lies in listening, which conveys the message that you accept the student just as he is, "troubles and all" (Gordon, 2003, p. 59). First you must find a private moment to show you're available—for example, by saying to Andrew, "You look worried. Would it help to talk?" Then you can listen passively, showing interest with verbal or nonverbal cues, such as "I see," a nod, a smile, a frown. But, depending on your comfort level, *active listening* may be even better. As you listen, try to discover the feelings and message that lie under Andrew's words. Then you can restate the message to confirm that you've understood him ("You're upset because you feel that your father didn't listen to your point of view and may still be angry"). A series of these exchanges encourages Andrew to delve deeper into his problem, helping him to clarify what's bothering him, express his feelings, and start working out a solution.

When the problem belongs to the teacher—hinders your ability to meet your needs or upsets you in some way—Gordon (2003) counsels the use of *I-messages*. A nonjudgmental way of communicating your feelings, I-messages (which begin with "I") allow you to show your human side and are more likely to promote change than messages that blame the child or tell him what to do. I-messages let the student know how his behavior affects you and permit you to take ownership of your feelings instead of hiding them. Whenever you use an I-message, you are modeling how to identify and express feelings and as well as helping the student develop empathy.

Most of all, an I-message places responsibility for changing the behavior squarely on the student, trusting him to respond in a way that takes all parties into account (Ginott, 1956; Gordon, 2000).

Teachers often prefer to seem infallible, and Gordon (2000) points out that using an I-message puts the teacher in a vulnerable position. But he insists that I-messages are worth the risk: "Telling a child how you feel is far less threatening than accusing [him] of causing a bad feeling" (p. 136). Because they require honesty and openness, I-messages foster strong and close relationships. But their effectiveness also depends on these relationships—a student who doesn't care what you feel will probably ignore an I-message.

If you're feeling anger, beware. Gordon (2003) warns that anger isn't a primary emotion; rather, it follows hard on the heels of another feeling, often fear. Receiving an I-message that expresses anger makes a student feel that you're blaming him or putting him down, so before you speak, be sure to search for the emotion lurking underneath. If you can say what's really bothering you, your delivery will probably be calmer, too.

After you've sent an I-message, you'll have to switch to active listening. Even a carefully worded message is bound to leave the student feeling hurt, embarrassed, or some other unpleasant emotion, and the problem will now belong to him.

When I-messages don't work, or when the student's needs come into conflict with yours, the problem belongs to both of you. Solving it requires what Gordon (2003) calls a "no-lose method" of resolving conflicts (p. 220). The steps of the process are similar to those used for problem solving, described on page 146. The idea is to minimize the opportunities for developing harmful, defensive coping mechanisms and to focus instead on increasing cooperation and negotiating skills, allowing you to resolve the issue in a way that satisfies everyone. Again, you will probably need to use both I-messages and active listening.

Gordon (2003) doesn't believe in using power to solve problems. Power creates its own opposition, he says, and it reduces a teacher's influence because it doesn't teach or persuade students to change their behavior but simply forces them to obey temporarily. They will return to their previous behavior as soon as the teacher leaves the room. In addition, the use of power imperils the teacher–student relationship.

Feelings First

I-messages tell students how their behavior affects others and invite them to find solutions to problems (Gordon, 2000). When you're describing unacceptable behavior in an I-message, it is important to avoid labeling and judgmental statements. This is how to construct an I-message:

- *Describe the behavior.* "When you talk while I'm teaching . . ." (Note that this statement doesn't judge or blame.)
- *Describe the tangible effect that the student's behavior has on you.* "I can't make myself heard . . ."
- *Describe your feelings.* "And I get very frustrated."

The three statements can appear in any order. Don't forget that you can use I-messages to convey positive feelings, too.

Occasionally, you have little choice but to use power—for example, in the presence of clear and present danger. But afterwards you can repair the damage to the relationship by explaining why you used power, apologizing, actively listening to the student's feelings, or collaborating on a plan to prevent a recurrence.

How useful is positive reinforcement?

Positive reinforcement is perhaps the most basic of all guidance strategies—so prevalent that we use it almost without noticing. As a formal technique, it draws its inspiration from social learning theory, behaviorism, and operant conditioning. It is, of course, a reward, a pleasant response that follows a behavior and usually increases its frequency or intensity.

Positive reinforcement is actually feedback. It provides information about what behavior you accept and value in your classroom, and it supports students while they're trying it out, making mistakes, and trying again. It can be verbal or physical, social or tangible (such as an encouraging phrase, a pat on the back, a smile, or a sticker).

Although research shows that positive reinforcement can be an effective way to influence behavior (Maag, 1999; Marzano, 2003), its use is extremely controversial. Many in the field (Fields and Boesser, 1998; Gordon, 2003; Kohn, 1996) believe that praise, the traditional positive reinforcer, is "coercive" or "manipulative"—that it motivates students to do things for extrinsic reasons (to please others) and not for intrinsic reasons (to please themselves or because the task is inherently worth doing). In giving praise, a teacher is passing judgment on a student's performance and teaching him to rely on the views of others instead of evaluating his own effort and satisfaction. According to its opponents, praise also hurts relationships, tells students what to feel, and has a dampening effect on their autonomy, creativity, self-control, self-esteem, and pleasure. The critics reserve special scorn for evaluative praise, which expresses the teacher's approval, compares students to one another, or is very general.

The research findings on the subject are inconsistent and confusing (Good and Brophy, 2008). Recent meta-analyses (Deci, Koestner, and Ryan, 1999, 2001) report that tangible rewards undermine intrinsic motivation, but verbal rewards can have a positive effect when they're used primarily to give information, not as a control mechanism. What it boils down to is this: The nature of the reinforcement and how it is presented are what really matter.

As always, your relationship with the student will make a big difference. Alfie Kohn (2001) puts it this way: "Whatever we decide to say has to be offered in the context of genuine affection and love for who kids are rather than for what they've done" (p. 27). When you know a student well, you'll know what kind of support and positive reinforcement will help him to succeed and feel good about himself; when he knows you care about him, he's more likely to be able to accept your guidance. If another teacher has more success with him, watch her, talk to her about what she does, and try it. Ask yourself, "What would Louise do in this situation?"

How can you make positive reinforcement effective?

When you provide a student with *encouragement*, you can avoid the pitfalls of praise. Encouragement is not judgmental, but places the emphasis on behavior and process rather than person and product. By recognizing effort, improvement, and mastery of skills as well as real accomplishment, encouragement expresses trust and confidence in the student (Coloroso, 1995) and nourishes intrinsic motivation, autonomy, and self-esteem. Like Gordon's active listening technique (2003), encouragement reflects back to children what they're doing and helps them feel validated as "potent, competent, and worthwhile human beings" (Grey, 1995).

"All of our students need our authentic interest in their efforts," says Marilyn Watson (2003). "Because we are successful adults, our students look to us to learn the standards for success and to know if they are meeting those standards. We therefore need to pay close attention to their successes and let them know that we admire and appreciate what they have accomplished. Students . . . need expressions of our genuine delight and interest in what they have done and honest feedback about their efforts" (p. 47). Showing "genuine delight and interest" offers a kind of positive reinforcement that probably won't seem coercive to students with challenging behavior. It is also a good way to build a relationship.

It's also useful to *recognize approximations* of desired behavior—effort, progress, and perhaps even pauses in challenging behavior—rather than demanding perfection (Barton, 1986). If Ryan, who has ADHD, raises his hand at the same time that he shouts out an answer, that's progress that deserves recognition, so call on him and look for a private chance to thank him for raising his hand. This positive reinforcement must be unequivocal, with no condescension, sarcasm, implied criticism of past performance, or reminders about the future (Webster-Stratton and Herbert, 1994).

If a student can capture your attention this way and learn to accept your encouragement, he will probably feel less need for challenging behavior. And if you can recognize the strengths in a child who's making your job difficult, chances are you'll

Showing genuine delight and interest offers a kind of positive reinforcement that probably won't seem coercive to students with challenging behavior.

Accentuate the Positive

Any kind of verbal encouragement makes some students with challenging behavior uneasy. To avoid overwhelming them, start out with a little nonverbal encouragement instead, and give them a smile, a high-five, a wink, a nod, or a thumbs-up. To make your verbal encouragement more meaningful, try the following:

- Focus on specific attributes of a student's work rather than on generalities. ("The ending of your story really surprised me.")
- Emphasize the process, and let the student know that mistakes are part of learning. ("You worked on that bar graph for a long time. How did you find so much data?")
- Point out how a child's positive action affects his peers, just as you would point out how a hurtful action impacts them. ("Asking Caitlin to work with you on the social studies project really inspired her to think up lots of ideas for illustrations.")
- Be honest, sincere, and direct. Children can spot a phony a mile away.
- Deliver your encouragement privately.
- Use your natural voice, but be aware that some students prefer enthusiastic, intense interaction. Others, who are easily excited and stimulated, need their positive attention in small, low-key doses.
- Avoid comparisons between children.
- Help children appreciate their own behavior and achievements. ("You must feel proud of the organization you figured out for this paper," rather than "Good job" or "I like the way you organized this paper") (Kohn, 2001).

find yourself feeling more positive, understanding, and empathetic toward him—which may improve your relationship and allow him to behave more appropriately.

What if positive reinforcement provokes challenging behavior?

With some students, positive reinforcement seems to have exactly the opposite effect from what you expect. At the first kind word, they throw books on the floor or kick the nearest person.

Why does a student react this way? The most likely explanation is that positive attention is a rare commodity in his life, and it scares and worries him. In the ordinary course of events, a child with challenging behavior may not receive a lot of positive reinforcement in the academic and social realms. Because he doesn't succeed frequently, he doesn't experience the good feelings and natural reinforcements that come along with success. If his teachers notice that he's acting appropriately, they are so unsure of how to respond and so reluctant to rock the boat that they frequently withdraw from the scene. On the other hand, teachers have eyes in the back of their heads when it comes to inappropriate behavior. The result is that most of their interactions with him are negative and conflictual, and he (and his classmates) learn that the best way to get attention is to make the teacher angry.

A student with challenging behavior knows exactly what to expect if he punches someone—criticism from adults and rejection from his peers. He has become comfortable with this response and believes he deserves it. Convinced that he's unworthy of care and encouragement, he dedicates himself to proving it, following the motto, "If you think I'm bad, why should I be good?" He almost seems to be trying to get you to treat him the way everyone else does—negatively.

When a student has so much trouble with positive reinforcement, it is tempting to conclude that it is the last thing he needs. But such children need *more* encouragement, not less. So what can you do? Combating the student's negative view of himself takes commitment, patience, and perseverance. It requires you to trust, respect, and care for him so that he can learn to trust, respect, and care for himself. It's important to believe in his ability to succeed, to look for what he can do instead of what he can't do. If you expect him to disrupt the class or hurt others, that's what he will do. But if you believe that he can understand the concept, wait his turn, and resolve conflicts with his peers, his potential for success will increase. Your confidence and trust in him can't guarantee it, but they will help.

Every child—even one whose behavior is driving you crazy—does things right some of the time. If you can catch him being good, as the expression goes, and give him proper recognition at those moments, you are emphasizing and enlarging his strengths as well as helping him to replace inappropriate behavior with appropriate behavior and to find ways to feel good about himself. Give him nonverbal positive reinforcement, showing your affection and your belief in him in your body language, tone of voice, and behavior. Watch carefully to see what he likes, what he's good at, what works as a reinforcer for him. Each day offer him activities you know he enjoys, books and materials that interest him, assignments he can complete if he tries. Notice and create positive moments with him, doing something he chooses himself, letting him be in charge, and telling him that you like talking and being with him. Sit beside him or join his activity, share jokes, ask questions about his family, his pet, his culture, and what he likes to do outside of school. Ask him to help you or another student with a task, offer to help him with one, teach him a new skill. Show appreciation for his contributions to the group, his sense of humor, or his sensitivity. Include other students when you can. Gradually you will increase his comfort zone and accustom him to feeling better about himself and less anxious when he is behaving appropriately.

A Penny for Your Thoughts

When Angela wasn't interrupting me, she was talking to her neighbor, getting out of her seat, and taking things from other children's desks. When I tried to talk to her about this behavior, she flipped over her chair or demonstrated her mastery of four-letter words. I became so anxious about having her in the classroom that I could no longer find anything about her to like and I kept hoping she would be absent.

It finally got so bad that I knew I had to do something to break the pattern. A colleague reminded me that teachers are much more effective when their positive interactions with their students far outnumber their negative ones—some experts advise as many as eight positive comments for each criticism (University of Missouri–Columbia, 2007). My colleague suggested a simple strategy. Following her advice, I placed 10 pennies in my right-hand pocket before I went into the classroom in the morning, and every time I found a way to recognize Angela's positive behavior I moved a penny from my right pocket to my left. My goal was to have all the pennies in my left pocket by the end of the day. Sometimes it's so easy to respond to a student's inappropriate behavior that you can't even see when she's doing something right. Using the pennies reminded me to look at Angela in a more positive way, and eventually our relationship improved.

What about natural and logical consequences?

In addition to being a strategy in its own right, positive reinforcement is one-half of another well-known guidance technique: natural and logical consequences. In fact, positive reinforcement *is* a consequence, and as you've just seen, it can be an effective motivating force that also helps children know they're behaving appropriately. When Andrew is working hard on an assignment, a thumbs-up and a smile will make him feel good and tell him that his behavior is acceptable. Often, however, teachers focus on the other kind of consequence, one that's a response to inappropriate behavior.

According to Rudolf Dreikurs (1964), who developed this technique based on the work of Alfred Adler, the most meaningful consequences, positive or negative, flow from the natural or social order of the real world, not from the power or control of adults (Coloroso, 1995; Dreikurs, 1964). The student does something, and something happens as a result of his action. The consequence helps him reflect on the action he's chosen.

Some consequences occur naturally. If a student isn't listening to the teacher's explanation of a science concept, he will have difficulty doing the experiment. But in a situation where natural consequences are too remote or dangerous, teachers can create logical or reasonable consequences instead. For example, if there's a food fight in the cafeteria, the students can clean up the mess and arrange to do some volunteer work in a soup kitchen. Whether they're natural or logical, consequences are a teaching tool, because the child learns from experiencing the consequences of his own behavior (Dreikurs, 1964). The consequences tell him that he has control over his own life and responsibility for what he does (Coloroso, 1995; Dreikurs, 1964). They help him learn to make decisions, profit from his mistakes (Webster-Stratton and Herbert, 1994), express his feelings appropriately, and increase his internal locus of control (Curwin and Mendler, 2001).

To be effective, logical consequences should be related to the student's actions, respectful of his feelings, and reasonable so that he does not interpret them as a threat or a form of punishment. Asking Andrew to mop up the mess he made by spraying water all over the floor at the water fountain is logical; making him stay in for recess is not. In *Discipline with Dignity*, Richard L. Curwin and Allen N. Mendler (2001) advocate having a range of consequences available so that a teacher can choose the most appropriate for the situation.

Because natural and logical consequences are often difficult to distinguish from punishment, they have come in for a fair amount of criticism. Consequences seem

Getting It Right

Consequences can vary with the situation and the teacher's philosophy. Curwin and Mendler (2001) describe four consequences that they believe can be effective when a student breaks a rule:

- A reminder of the rule
- A warning or stern reminder (the warning is the consequence; it is not a threat)
- Developing an action plan for improving behavior
- Practicing appropriate behavior

threatening and punitive when they're arbitrary (such as keeping a student in at recess when he sprayed water on the floor), or when you're feeling angry or vengeful at the time that you're creating them. In fact, your attitude and delivery can make a major difference in whether or not the student perceives your action as a consequence or a punishment. Your respectful, calm, matter-of-fact demeanor, a culturally respectful and comfortable distance between you and the child, a firm but friendly tone of voice, and words free of judgment and criticism will make it possible for the consequences to do their job.

Consequences also have to be enforceable and enforced, because a consequence that isn't enforced doesn't teach what it's supposed to. (Instead, the child and all the other students learn that they can ignore your request because you don't follow through.) This is what Barbara Coloroso (1995) means when she says consequences must be simple and practical, such as asking a student to get ice for an injury he has inflicted. Be careful, too, that the consequences you set up don't unintentionally reinforce inappropriate behavior. When a student who's disrupting a math lesson ends up in the principal's office, you may actually be helping him achieve his goal of avoiding math. (For more information about understanding the purpose of behavior, see Chapter 11.)

If you elect to establish consequences for breaking class rules, it's a good idea for the students to participate in creating them. They will know which consequences are most likely to assist them in controlling their behavior (Curwin and Mendler, 2001), and having their say will help them understand and accept both the rules and the consequences.

Time-out, punishment, and time-away

Like positive reinforcement, time-out—which actually means time-out from positive reinforcement—stems from social learning theory and behaviorism. Although there are many variations, it usually involves requiring a student to leave the group and go to a remote area of the room, the hallway, another classroom, or the principal's office. It reaches its extreme form in suspension and expulsion.

Misused and overused, the practice has been debated in the education community for years. Adherents maintain that time-out tells the student that you care and want to help him keep himself in control. If it's used sensitively and correctly, they say, it assists in maintaining a respectful, trusting relationship. They also believe that time-out interrupts and prevents aggressive behavior, protects the rights and safety of the other students, and keeps them from turning into an admiring and encouraging audience (Rodd, 1996). It allows the child who behaves aggressively, the child who is victimized, and the adult enough time to compose themselves without giving undue attention to the aggressor. According to the yea-sayers, time-out works if it's used consistently and appropriately (American Academy of Pediatrics, 1998).

Opponents argue that time-out is a form of punishment—that is, a penalty for wrongdoing, imposed by someone in power who intends it to be unpleasant in order to decrease inappropriate behavior (Quinn et al., 2000). Punishment also originates with social learning and behavioral theory.

Does punishment work? In the short term, yes. That's why teachers sometimes use it: It provides a quick fix. But its results are fleeting. To remain effective, it has to become stronger and stronger, and because the punishment suppresses the un-

Counterattack

M r. Davis had total control over his sixth-grade class. Everything in his room had a place. The desks were in straight rows, there was no litter or mess, and the papers on his desk were neatly stacked and sorted into piles marked "corrected" or "to be corrected." He made his rules clear, enforced them strictly, and often used a loud voice, embarrassment, or humiliation to keep students in line.

When the bell rang and the students left his room, they exploded and their behavior became a major concern. Children who felt unheard and powerless in his presence were compelled to assert themselves and express their needs. They were constantly fighting, drawing on the walls of the building, and swearing at students and teachers.

desirable behavior only in the punisher's presence, the student may behave the same way when the punisher departs. As B. F. Skinner, the father of behaviorism, once said, "What's wrong with punishments is that they work immediately but give no long-term results. The responses to punishment are either the urge to escape, to counterattack, or a stubborn apathy. These are the bad effects you get in prisons or schools, or wherever punishments are used" (Goleman, 1987, p. B1).

A punishment that requires a student to move to a designated spot creates another problem. Why do teachers expect a child whose behavior is defiant and noncompliant to be agreeable about going to the back of the room or the principal's office? Do you raise your voice? Wait until he changes his mind? Or just give up? If you make a fuss, you may be placing everyone in danger and once again demonstrating that the more challenging his behavior, the more attention you and his classmates will award him. In fact, the other students may be waiting for him to act out and may even egg him on—because this spectacle is much more exciting than your lesson. On the other hand, if you decide not to fight with him and fail to follow through with your original request, the student learns that he is in control. All of this scares the rest of the students, who see that you can't cope and begin to doubt that you can keep them safe.

There are several other powerful arguments against punishment:

- It makes students angry, resentful, and defiant and leads to more aggressive or devious behavior. Some educators suggest that a student in time-out is probably plotting his revenge (Katz and McClellan, 1997).
- It teaches children that it's acceptable to use power to control other people.
- It frightens, embarrasses, and humiliates students in front of their peers.
- It damages their self-esteem and self-concept by saying, in effect, "You are bad, and I don't want you here." For students who belong to cultures where being part of the group is important, time-out has an especially strong impact (Gonzalez-Mena, 2002).
- It doesn't address the causes of challenging behavior and fails to teach appropriate behavior. The proof is that the same students find themselves in time-out again and again. Indeed, time-out may unintentionally increase behaviors you're trying to eliminate. A student sent to the principal's office doesn't have a chance to learn the material you're covering in class, and he will either fall behind or need your help to catch up. This can have a domino effect. He won't be able to do tomorrow's work because he didn't learn today's, and he may spit on the

floor rather than seem stupid in front of his peers—and require another visit to the principal.

- It increases distrust and harms the relationship between adult and child.
- It undermines a child's sense of safety and interferes with learning and the development of initiative and autonomy (Gonzalez-Mena, 2002; Hay, 1994–1995). Kohn (1996) writes, "To help an impulsive, aggressive, or insensitive student become more responsible, we have to gain some insight into why she is acting that way. That, in turn, is most likely to happen when the student feels close enough to us (and safe enough with us) to explain how things look from her point of view. The more students see us as punishers, the less likely it is that we can create the sort of environment where things can change." (p. 27)

Drastic punishment

In 1994, in the aftermath of several school shootings, Congress passed the Gun-Free Schools Act, which requires expulsion for any student who brings a firearm to school (Richart, Brooks, and Soler, 2003). All 50 states soon had laws or policies mandating zero tolerance, some even tougher than the federal legislation.

Although such a response to possession of a gun is understandable, these laws had another effect. In this hypervigilant atmosphere, it became much easier and much more acceptable to suspend and expel students for lesser offenses, even for minor misconduct. For example, according to a recent report (Richart et al., 2003), in Kentucky a "staggering" number of students receive out-of-school suspensions for "board violations" (such as disturbing class, failing to attend detention, profanity, smoking, and "defiance of authority," which are disruptive but not dangerous).

These arbitrary, authoritarian policies, which do not take individual circumstances into account, tell students that the school system doesn't listen to them or value them. Instead of helping them succeed, such a policy interrupts their schooling and puts them onto the streets at a period of their lives when they badly need stability and guidance (Richart et al., 2003). With unsupervised, unstructured time on their hands, they band together, taking lessons in more serious antisocial behavior from their deviant peers (Dishion, McCord, and Poulin, 1999). For some students, getting out of school may even be the goal. When they return to class, they trail farther behind and their attitude is more defiant than ever (Richart et al., 2003). Some experts call suspension the beginning of a "school to prison pipeline" (Richart, 2004, p. 4). The situation for students of color is especially grim. Nationally, the rate of suspension for African American students is far greater than the rate for White students (Richart et al., 2003).

Although in-school suspension is an imperfect solution, at least it keeps students out of trouble and sometimes even provides a supervised learning situation.

What's different about time-away?

Interestingly enough, some of the staunchest foes of punishment and time-out believe in "time-away," "cool-down," "take a break," "private time," or "sit and watch." The two sides agree on these goals:

- To give everyone a chance to regain control in a safe place so that the student is capable of success when he reenters the group

- To teach children to recognize when their emotions are building to a dangerous level and to know when they are ready to function again
- To allow the rest of the group to continue its activities

Advocates for both positions also agree that what a teacher does is actually less important than how she does it: If you ask a student to leave the room when you're angry, frustrated, threatening, or out of control, your motives are suspect and the effect is punitive. To be effective and nonpunitive, your demeanor must be calm and respectful. Kohn (1996) says, "The teacher's tone should be warm and regretful, and she should express confidence that the two of them can eventually solve the problem together" (p. 128).

Time-away is also extremely valuable when you use it preventively. It can offer a kind of redirection, a way to teach impulse control and anger management. When the student feels himself becoming anxious or agitated, he can learn to move away, take some deep breaths, close his eyes, count to 10. This self-directed change in locale, activity, or stimulation level allows him to settle his feelings, just as jogging or having a cup of tea calms and restores us when we're struggling with a problem. He can return to the group whenever he's ready, knowing you'll welcome him warmly. You can suggest he take time away to begin with, but the ultimate goal is for him to figure out when to do this himself.

There may be occasions when time-away inside the classroom doesn't work, and you must try a variation, such as asking the student to leave the room for a prearranged destination—a hiatus with the hall monitor or a colleague who has agreed to take in your students who need some space. The student can bring along a book or a folder of work to do and come back when he's ready (Watson, 2003). However, if the challenging behavior continues after his return, you may have to use your last resort—the principal's office (which may also entail a telephone call to his parents). In case a student refuses to go, a system must be in place—for example, you can send a note informing the principal of the situation, and someone will come to collect him. This move should truly be a last resort, used sparingly. Of course, long before you ever put any of these strategies to use, you must discuss them with your students and be sure that they understand the reasoning behind them.

Time-Away

Working in his small group, Tyrone was starting to raise his voice, drop his pencil, cut the other students off, and look everywhere but at his work.

His teacher realized that Tyrone was getting frustrated and needed some time away. She walked over to his desk and in a quiet, matter-of-fact voice said, "Tyrone, you seem frustrated. Why don't you take a break and look at a magazine in the back of the room or take this book back to the library for me?"

She selected her words, tone of voice, and choices carefully. She wasn't punishing or threatening him; she was offering him an opportunity to regain control. She knew that either option would help him relax.

Tyrone chose to look at a magazine. After about 5 minutes he recovered his composure and returned to the group much better able to communicate his ideas and focus on the task at hand.

How does culture influence guidance?

Although teachers are seldom aware of it, their assumptions about how a classroom should run and how students should behave come straight from their own culture. But students from different cultures bring different assumptions to school with them, and when these divergent cultural views collide, there may be trouble. For example, European American teachers expect children to listen quietly and respond one at a time to the teacher's questions. On the other hand, African American students may show their interest by commenting, reacting, and jumping into the middle of a lecture or a discussion (Gay, 2000). Latino American students, brought up to value group harmony, may respond with challenging behavior when a teacher singles them out or puts them into a competitive situation. Such behavior isn't intended to derail learning or show disrespect to the teacher. Rather, it reflects cultural misunderstanding.

No matter what guidance strategy you use, it is important to be aware of its cultural bias and try to adjust your expectations to the cultural background of your students. Carol Weinstein, Saundra Tomlinson-Clarke, and Mary Curran (2004, p. 27) call this *culturally responsive classroom management*. More a frame of mind than a set of practices, it consists of five essential components:

1. *Recognition of one's own ethnocentrism and biases.* It all begins with knowing yourself. Bringing your own motives, beliefs, values, and assumptions to a conscious level makes you less likely to misinterpret the behavior of children from diverse cultures.

2. *Knowledge of students' cultural backgrounds.* The more you know about where your students are coming from, the better you'll understand their feelings and their actions.

3. *Understanding of the broader social, economic, and political context of our education system,* which reflects the discriminatory practices of the larger society. Tracking and standardized testing, for example, alienate and marginalize students from different cultures, and research shows that disciplinary practices often do the same. Studies in several states have found significant racial disparities in the way schools apply discipline, and a national report showed that African American students—who make up just 17.1 percent of the population—receive 32.7 percent of the suspensions. Latino students were suspended two to three times more often than Whites (Richart et al., 2003).

4. *Ability and willingness to use culturally appropriate classroom management strategies.* Weinstein and her colleagues (2004) counsel us to pay close attention to whether we're being fair with our students ("Are we more patient and encouraging with some? Are we more likely to chastise others?" [p. 32]); to watch out for

Survival Tactics

In an ethnographic study in a middle school, Susan Roberta Katz (1999) found that Latino students emphasized their cultural identity in order to create a sense of belonging in a hostile school environment. Believing that their teachers didn't care about them and actually stereotyped them as gang members, prostitutes, and criminals, the students used nicknames, hairstyles, dress—and even cut class and acted "bad"—as ways to gain some control in an oppressive system.

mismatches between conventional management strategies and students' cultures; and to consider "when to accommodate students' cultural backgrounds and when to expect students to accommodate" (Grossman, 1995, p. 32). Although it is relatively easy to decide to accommodate children from interdependent cultures by introducing cooperative activities, it may be harder to decide whether to use direct commands (Delpit, 1995) in place of the indirect, hidden commands you're accustomed to. When you decide not to accommodate a student's culture, for example by insisting that he arrive on time for class, Weinstein and associates (2004) advise helping the student articulate his own cultural assumptions and making your decision "explicit and visible" (p. 33) by explaining that cultures have different perspectives on time, and punctuality is important to his success at school.

5. *Commitment to building caring classroom communities.* It's important to emphasize once again that a caring relationship with a teacher is an especially powerful factor in the behavior of African American and Latino students (Ferguson, 2002). Weinstein and her colleagues (2004) note that this is not a matter of being warm and fuzzy. Rather, a caring relationship entails expecting a high level of achievement and consistently working with the student to accomplish it (Gay, 2000). In the Students' Multiple Worlds Study (Davidson, 1999), carried out in diverse urban California schools, students facing difficult transitions between their home and school cultures spoke "frequently and ardently" (p. 345) about their desire for a personal relationship with their teachers and preferred teachers who elicited their input, held high expectations of them, and took time to help them understand classroom material. Such teachers were much more likely to earn students' cooperation and even influence whether a student came to class.

Wʜᴀᴛ ᴅᴏ ʏᴏᴜ ᴛʜɪɴᴋ?

1. Now that you've read this chapter, which form of guidance do you feel most comfortable with? Would you consider yourself a low-, medium-, or high-control teacher? Why?

2. How does your relationship with a student affect your choice of strategy? How does the relationship help or hinder you when challenging behavior is involved?

3. With a partner, role-play a situation that includes a student whose behavior is interfering with your ability to teach. Develop a response using an I-message. If the situation calls for it, follow through using active listening and more I-messages. When you're finished, switch roles and repeat the exercise.

4. Annie, who spends a lot of time either annoying her neighbors or staring out the window, is working very hard. How can you let her know that she is on track?

5. What is the difference between a consequence and punishment? Create a scenario and respond using first one and then the other. If you like, you can role-play this to see how it feels to be on the receiving end of both.

6. What cultural assumptions underlie your discipline practices? When you have a child from a different culture in your classroom, how would you feel about adapting your practice to take account of his values?

Wʜᴀᴛ ᴡᴏᴜʟᴅ ʏᴏᴜ ᴅᴏ?

Jazmine arrived at a new school in mid-November, weighed down with a long history of problems at home and school. Her mother had just left to join her

boyfriend, depositing Jazmine and her sister with an aunt who had three small children and no desire to care for her nieces. Believing her mother would return for them, Jazmine had no commitment to her present living situation or school.

Although she had no cognitive disability, Jazmine had missed a lot of class time, and because of her behavior problems and lack of skills, the school assigned a part-time educational assistant to help her get through the grade 8 day. The staff designed a schedule to create as many opportunities for success as possible, and her behavior slowly began to improve. She also began to develop some trust in her teachers and her educational assistant.

After a calm morning, Jazmine ran into trouble one day at recess. When she noticed two girls in close proximity to Justin, a ninth-grade boy she had a crush on, she ran over and tried to join the conversation. Ellen, who also had behavior problems, was jealous of Jazmine and began to shout at her. Fighting broke out almost immediately. A teacher separated the girls and told Jazmine she was taking her to see the principal. Swearing at the top of her lungs, Jazmine refused to budge. The teacher took her by the arm and pulled her into the building. Ellen and her friend resumed their discussion.

If you had been the teacher on duty at recess, what would you have done?

SUGGESTED READINGS

Curwin, R. L., & Mendler, A. N. (2001). *Discipline with dignity*. Upper Saddle River, NJ: Merrill Prentice-Hall.

Gordon, T. (with Burch, N.) (2003). *Teacher effectiveness training*. New York: Three Rivers Press.

Kohn, A. (1996). *Beyond discipline: From compliance to community*. Upper Saddle River, NJ: Merrill Prentice-Hall.

Watson, M. (with Ecken, L.) (2003). *Learning to trust: Transforming difficult elementary classrooms through developmental discipline*. San Francisco: Jossey-Bass.

Weinstein, C., Tomlinson-Clarke, S., & Curran, M. (2004). Toward a conception of culturally responsive classroom management. *Journal of Teacher Education, 55,* 25–38.

CHAPTER 10

The WEVAS Strategy

Even to the most experienced teacher, it sometimes seems as if challenging behavior comes out of nowhere. But according to Canadian psychologists Neil Butchard and Robert Spencler (2000), there are almost always warning signs. If you can recognize them and intervene early enough, you can prevent challenging behavior and help students return to a competent state, where their minds, bodies, and emotions are functioning well and geared up for learning. Butchard and Spencler (2000) have designed a research-based intervention program called WEVAS, Working Effectively with Violent and Aggressive States, based on the work of psychologists Fritz Redl, William C. Morse, and Nicholas J. Long. By using WEVAS's verbal, nonverbal, and physical skills, teachers can keep challenging behavior from escalating and respond safely when it becomes disruptive, assaultive, or out of control. Although WEVAS hasn't yet been formally evaluated, it is used extensively in a number of school districts, and anecdotal evidence from the United States and Canada indicates that it is a very effective method.

The starting point of the WEVAS strategy is the student's state of mind. Its objective is always to help the child reach the *competent state*, where she is ready for learning. But at any time she can slip out of the competent state and into one of four other states:

1. *Anxiety.* This is the first sign that something is amiss. The student's feelings interfere with her ability to concentrate.
2. *Agitation.* Her feelings intensify and her actions start to disrupt the class.
3. *Aggression.* She is driven by emotion and her behavior becomes randomly aggressive, either verbally or physically.
4. *Assaultive.* Her aggression focuses on a specific target, either you or another student.

As the student progressively loses control, she moves from one state to the next, farther and farther away from the competent state, and it becomes increasingly difficult to help

---

A student is centered in the competent state. When she moves out of the center into an anxious, agitated, aggressive, or assaultive state, the role of the teacher is to help the student return to her center. The child usually moves into the anxious state first, and each state that follows is more intense than the one before it. In the diagram, arrows connect the states to one another because a student can move back and forth between them. The outermost circle shows that each state necessitates a different response. Anxiety requires open communication; agitation calls for a teaching or limiting response; aggression demands deescalation; and the assaultive state requires protection for both the teacher and the children. Each response is guided by and responds to a different level of consciousness: the heart, the mind, the body, or the community. The small circles between the competent state and each of the other states represent the open state or the way back. They differ in size because the way back is much more complex when a student is in an assaultive state than when she is in an anxious state.

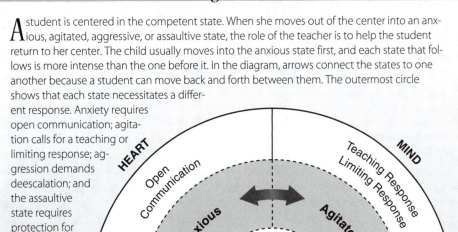

Source: Art © 2000, WEVAS, Inc. Reproduced with the written permission of WEVAS, Inc.

her return. But teachers can stop this slide and restore her to the competent state by using strategies that are appropriate for her current state of mind. This chapter describes these four states of mind as well as the *open state*, which follows the assaultive state, and outlines the strategies that are most effective for each of them.

The WEVAS strategy helps you recognize exactly where the child is, see things from her perspective, understand how your own reactions contribute to her behavior, and match your response to her needs. As psychologist Kevin Leman (1992) points out, there is no way to change anyone else's behavior. You can only change your own, and when you do, the strangest thing happens: Other people make the behavior changes you've been hoping for.

The competent state and calibration

One of the key ideas behind WEVAS is that any student, even a student who's prone to challenging behavior, can be in a *competent state* and open to learning. When you know her well—her temperament, culture, and social and cognitive abilities, what she enjoys, what frustrates her, what makes her sad or mad—you can tell whether she's in or out of a competent state. For example, you know that Jazmine is feeling competent and confident when she's talkative and bright-eyed. If you see her looking at the floor, silently twirling her hair, you can tell that she's not feeling 100 percent. WEVAS calls this act of sizing up a child's mood and state of mind *calibration*. It is crucial to choosing a strategy that's effective for a particular situation—and crucial to letting you know whether that strategy is working. If you smile at Jazmine and she lets go of her hair, sits up straight, and begins to work on her math, you can see that your intervention, subtle as it was, did the trick. Each child has her own characteristic physiological and behavioral signs that can help you figure out how she's feeling.

The anxious state

Anxiety is a kind of early warning system, the first state a student reaches when her world is out of kilter and she is no longer feeling competent. It's hard for a teacher to notice an anxious child in a class of 30 or 40 students with a wide variety of interests and abilities. Anxiety is internal; it doesn't show much and doesn't affect anyone but the student herself. But anxiety interferes with the child's ability to learn and interact with her peers, and it alerts you to trouble ahead. If it goes undetected, it may escalate to agitation, aggressive behavior, or even assaultive behavior. It is therefore extremely important to observe each student closely and learn to read whatever subtle physiological and behavioral clues she gives you as she tries to cope with her anxiety. The way she walks into the classroom and sits down at her desk may be enough to tip you off. It's also useful to have some insight into her thoughts and feelings. Every child has stresses in her life—everything from "Will Rebecca be my friend today?" to "Mom and Dad had a terrible fight last night." These stresses make the child anxious, and as they interact with her thoughts and feelings, her anxiety increases.

Here's how it works. Jazmine's alarm didn't go off this morning, so everything was rush, rush, rush. She didn't have time for breakfast, her favorite jeans were in the wash, her hair looked so horrible she had to wear a hat, and she almost missed

Tell-Tale Signs

You can prevent challenging behavior by catching it in its earliest phase, anxiety. The signs vary with the student, and when you know her well and watch her closely, you can use these indicators to gauge what she's feeling.

- *Physiology.* Tears, clenched teeth, blushing, pallor, rigidity, rapid breathing, sweating, squeaky voice
- *Behavior.* Downcast eyes, withdrawing, hair twirling, sucking hair or clothes, hoarding, biting fingernails or lips, whining, being unusually noisy or quiet, smirking, giggling, grimacing, grumbling, muttering, fidgeting

Psychologist Mary Wood (1986) has identified five central developmental anxieties that often drive the behaviors we see on the surface:

1. *Feeling alone, abandoned, or rejected.* "The other kids don't like me."
2. *Feeling inadequacy or failure.* "I can't understand this chapter. I hope the teacher doesn't call on me."
3. *Feeling guilt or shame.* "It's my fault Mom and Dad are always arguing."
4. *Feeling confused about identity.* "My mom says I'm smart and pretty, so why don't the boys notice me?" Identity becomes more of an issue as children get older and grapple with who they are, how they perceive themselves, and how others see them. They worry about their race, ethnicity, sexuality, and dozens of other questions.
5. *Feeling conflicted.* "I really like Ms. Spencer, but when I fool around in her class everyone seems to like me more." As children struggle to find a balance between doing what they know is right and bending to peer pressure, their anxiety rises.

the bus. These were the external stressors. Then there are internal stressors. Jazmine is hungry, and she needs to go to the bathroom. (That happens when she's stressed.) Her thoughts—irrational because she's anxious—filter the reality and contribute to the stress. "I look so ugly today," she thinks. "Will my friends be nice to me? I hate school." Her feelings add another layer of stress: Jazmine feels inadequate, lonely, and worried.

If you look closely, you'll see the characteristic behavioral and physiological signs of her anxiety as she enters the classroom. She lowers her eyes, doesn't say hello when you greet her, and she's wearing her baseball cap. How you respond to this student will make or break her day.

WEVAS advises us to put away our defenses and open ourselves to the student before us. (Your relationship with her is critical here.) Noticing Jazmine's lowered eyes and baseball cap and remembering that she doesn't talk when she's anxious, try to figure out what she may be feeling and thinking so that you can respond to her honestly and completely. Your concern and empathy will tell her that you care about her, respect her feelings, and are there for her. WEVAS calls this strategy *open communication*: You are open emotionally and respond with your heart. Open communication can be as quick and simple as a smile or a gentle touch on the arm. Two minutes of warm interaction now can spare you hours of trouble later.

The following techniques, drawn from the work of Jack R. Gibb (1961), Robert Carkhuff (1987), and Thomas Gordon (2000, 2003), facilitate open communication and help students return to a competent state:

• *Using door openers.* Gentle comments or questions ("I'm glad you made it to class. Are you okay?" "You look upset. Would you like to talk?" "You seem confused. Can I help?") tell the student you care and are ready to listen. If she decides not to share her feelings or thoughts, respect her wishes. If she is very distraught, make a date to talk again later in the day.

• *Asking open-ended questions.* Genuine requests for information can reduce a student's anxiety by letting her tell her story and giving her a sense of control over events. Showing real interest also facilitates problem solving because, as Gordon says, "People do a better job of thinking a problem through when they can `talk it out'" (2000, p. 67). *Who, what, when, where,* and *how* questions (which aren't judgmental) help a student think about what happened and what she feels. But stay away from *why* questions. Because they undermine your relationship, give the impression you're blaming her, and so often accompany disciplinary interventions, they make a student with challenging behavior clam right up (Quinn et al., 2000).

• *Validating and paraphrasing.* Enter the student's world and let her know that you understand the message and feelings behind her words by restating them in words of your own. It is her perceptions that matter here (Gordon, 2000). When Jazmine says, "My alarm didn't go off, I got here too late to meet Justin before class, and my hair is a mess!" you might answer, "Nothing seems to be going right today."

• *Responding to the need within the message.* Try to hear what the student is really saying. Although her words are "I hate this class!" Jazmine may actually be asking for help. When you offer your assistance, she feels that her needs can be met, and her anxiety will abate.

• *Reframing the student's statements.* Help her see things in a more positive light if you can do this honestly and without judging. "It's hard to start the day off in a rush. Why don't you take a deep breath, and let's begin again."

• *Paying attention to your tone of voice.* Those who study interpersonal communication usually agree that words convey just a small fraction of a message, somewhere between 7 and 15 percent (Mehrabian, 1972). The bulk of what people communicate comes from their voice, facial expressions, and body language. Your tone, cadence, speed, volume, and pattern of speech should match your message. It's helpful to notice the quality of the child's voice as well. When she is anxious, her speech may go to extremes and become fast or slow, high or low, loud or soft. If you match her voice pattern, then slowly make your own more normal, you can lead her into speaking more normally and feeling less anxious.

• *Paying attention to your body language.* Match your facial expression and body language to your message—and to the student's expression and body language as well. This technique, called *mirroring,* often appears when two people are communicating well. To use it effectively, take your cues from the child. If Jazmine is sitting back with her legs crossed, she's letting you know that she's listening but withdrawn. To encourage her to become engaged, try mirroring her position—her facial expressions, her posture, even her mannerisms—to begin with, and then take the lead by moving closer, leaning forward, or placing your arms at your sides. If she mirrors your actions, you'll know she's ready for more personal contact. If she doesn't, or if she withdraws, step back and wait until she's ready.

Calibrate her response. If she seems calmer and ready to listen and learn, you can now ask her to put her hat in her desk.

It's impossible to exaggerate the importance of this early sensitivity. If you respond with *defensive communication* instead, you will find yourself headed in an entirely different direction, away from competence and toward agitation. If, like Jazmine, you are having a bad day or are preoccupied with other matters, you may fail to notice her lowered eyes and withdrawn manner and simply see her cap. In-

Nicholas J. Long (Long, Fecser, and Brendtro, 1998) analyzed 80 school crises where a conflict became explosive and a student attacked a peer or a member of the staff. He concluded:

- Crises usually occurred in the first 40 minutes of the school day, when students were changing classes, or when staff didn't see the precipitating incident but intervened to stop dangerous behavior.
- A minor incident—off-task behavior, walking around the classroom, teasing—often triggered the crisis. Teachers were "quick to speak [and] slow to listen" (p. 9), responded in ways that angered the student, got caught up in a conflict cycle, and made the situation worse.

stead of using the gentle approach of open communication, you might consider the cap a provocation and address her directly. "Jazmine, please take off your hat." Jazmine ignores you, and you walk over to her desk. Standing above her, you repeat your request. When she refuses, you feel indignant, angry, and ready to defend your authority. Unless you can get control of yourself, you and the student are headed for a power struggle no one will win (Long, 1996).

Long and Morse (1996) call this a *conflict cycle*, when you and your student influence one another in turn through your feelings, attitudes, and behavior. Once this cycle begins, it is extremely difficult to halt, and the student will swiftly move into the agitated state or even become aggressive.

Even when you don't feel defensive, you can still create defensive feelings in your student if your tone, posture, or words seem judgmental, manipulative, or uncaring (Gibb, 1961). Disempowerment and defiance may result, transforming anxiety into agitation.

The agitated state

When a teacher doesn't respond to signs of anxiety, or responds defensively, or when open communication doesn't work, a student's behavior can escalate into agitation. Her feelings grow more intense, her actions become larger, she upsets her classmates, and she seems to be losing control. Once she starts to bother others, her problem is no longer her own. The behavior of a student in the agitated state may threaten your authority or interfere with your ability to teach, and it may destroy other students' opportunities to learn or compromise their safety.

There are two levels of agitated behavior. Children at the first level are beginning to lose control. Their strong emotions confuse their thinking, and they don't know how to handle their feelings or their behavior. However, they're still able to listen to you, and they experience real relief when they know what you expect of them. Therefore, at the first level of agitation, the issue is educational, and the response is to teach. At the second level, which we'll discuss on pages 205 to 210, students have lost more control and feel antagonistic and threatened, and the issue is power. It's important to plan and prepare responses to both levels of agitation ahead of time so they'll be ready to go when you need them.

The style of teaching response that you choose depends on both the student's ability to do what you ask and her willingness to do it. Using the Situational Leadership model created by Kenneth Blanchard and Paul Hersey (Hersey et al., 2001), WEVAS suggests how you can match your response to the student's needs. Some situations call for a *directive* response, where you provide more structure, control, and supervision. Others demand a *supportive* response, where you offer more encouragement, listening, and facilitating. Still other situations require both—and some require neither. Most students end up in every category at one time or another.

- *When the student is able and willing to perform a task.* When she has the knowledge and the skills to perform a task, as well as the motivation and confidence, she needs very little supervision or support from you. ("Jazmine, it's time for gym.")
- *When the student is able but unwilling to perform a task.* Although she may have the skills and knowledge to do what you ask, she may lack the motivation. It will require little direction but lots of support to shore up her willingness and bolster her confidence. ("Jazmine, Ms. Carvallo told me you'd be playing your favorite game in gym today, so let's find your gym bag and get ready to go.")
- *When the student is willing but unable to perform a task.* Sometimes a student may be willing to perform a task, but her experience, knowledge, or skills aren't up to the job. In this situation she needs a lot of direction and instruction from you, as well as your full support. ("Jazmine, put your math book away and get your gym bag from your locker. Let's make sure everything you need is in your bag.")
- *When the student is unwilling and unable to perform a task.* There are times when a student has neither the ability nor the willingness to do what you ask. This situation requires you to give clear, firm instructions and supervise closely. ("Jazmine, get your gym clothes and I'll put them in your bag and walk you to gym.")

The student who's able but unwilling is the one most likely to push a teacher's buttons. When this happens, it's important to stay calm and provide extra support so that she becomes willing to work with you.

The first level of agitation

When a student is at the first level of agitation, you want to let her know that her behavior is unacceptable and to teach her acceptable behavior in its place. This is the job of the *teaching response*. Its first principle is to be positive: Tell the child what to do, not what not to do. It should make your expectations absolutely clear. The teaching response should also be polite, respectful, caring, and supportive. It recognizes where the student is coming from and expresses confidence that she can do what you ask, especially if you use empowering language. If Jazmine starts loudly tapping her pencil and gazing out the window when she's supposed to be reading, go over to her and quietly say, "Jazmine, please read your book now. We'll be discussing the chapter in ten minutes and I want to hear what you think."

Using an assertive style like this is likely to influence the student's behavior. It gets her attention, puts your message across, and respects both her needs and yours. It communicates that you have something important to say without putting your relationship in jeopardy. Again, your tone of voice, facial expression, and body language are crucial. Like your words, they must be positive and empowering, not hostile or threatening. When your total message is clear, directive, and supportive, it tells the student what to do in a positive way and gives her the support to actually do it. The key is to offer as much direction and support as each child needs to succeed (Hersey, Blanchard, and Johnson, 2001).

When a student is agitated, it isn't easy to stay on course—that is, to do what's best for the child and the rest of the class. Some students with challenging behavior are experts at turning the tables and making your intervention seem like the problem. By *minimizing* their actions or *denying* that they've done anything, they manage to avoid being held accountable. For example, while you're explaining a new assignment, Jazmine is talking loudly to Carlos. You say, "Jazmine, please face forward and listen so you can hear the directions." Jazmine says, "I was just asking a question. Can't you even ask a question around here?" minimizing the disruption she's caused. Or she says, "I didn't do anything. Why are you always picking on me?" denying involvement altogether. Both these statements suggest that you created the problem, not Jazmine, and leave you trying to justify your actions or ignoring Jazmine's remarks and looking as if you agree with her. A student in an agitated state may also respond to a simple request with questions or statements that divert attention from the task at hand ("Why do we have to do this? It's stupid"). If you answer, you allow the child to take the lead and risk getting lost in the fog—which is why this ploy is called *fogging.*

It is all too easy to feel anger, guilt, or pity and respond emotionally to such tactics. But the best way to influence the student's behavior is to stay rational, clear, kind, and focused. One approach is to help her think about her actions. Rather than telling her what to do, ask her *what* questions: "Jazmine, what are you doing?" After she's told you, you can remind her about what she should be doing: "I understand that you have something you want to tell Carlos. You can talk to him when I'm done explaining the assignment to the class." Once again, avoid asking *why* questions—her answer is likely to lead you even further astray. Remember that your request was reasonable and responsible, listen respectfully to her feelings and opinions, tune in to your own reactions, be kind and caring, but keep your goal at the front of your mind.

If a student is embarrassed or her behavior is meeting an important need, you may have better results if you combine the teaching response with open communication. Then you can maintain your relationship, help her identify the needs that must be considered, and solve the problem together. I-messages can be very useful here. "Jazmine, when you talk while I'm teaching, I lose my train of thought and I feel very frustrated."

Even if the student behaves exactly the same way the next day (and the day after), don't lose heart. Every new situation brings new problems. If she needs your directions again, give them without anger or resentment. It is very important for her to save face.

The second level of agitation

The second level of agitation is a critical stage. The student could either return to a competent state or feel so threatened that she moves into an aggressive state. Your response can determine which way she'll go. Education is no longer the issue; the issue is power, pure and simple. The student doesn't care what you say; she cares only that you're trying to influence or control her. Your job is to create a win-win situation and allow her to change her behavior without losing face or feeling as if she's lost control.

Driven by intense feelings and negative thoughts, a student at this level of agitation is stressed, antagonistic, and irrational. She isn't thinking clearly, she doesn't listen well, and she says and does things she doesn't mean. Her previous life and school experiences filter her perceptions and govern her behavior, whether they relate to the present situation or not (Wood and Long, 1991). She's trapped in a past script, and she's assigning you a role in it. The WEVAS response here is intended to jolt her into rational decision making and help her escape from this old, negative pattern (Wood and Long, 1991).

It's difficult to get a student out of this trap. If you blurt out an angry reaction that confirms her expectations, you become part of her pattern, and the inappropriate behavior scripted by her past will probably escalate (Wood and Long, 1991). It's as if she's stuck on a spinning merry-go-round. If you let her behavior push your emotional buttons and do what she expects ("Jazmine, take off your hat, stop talking to Carlos, and face forward!"), you make the merry-go-round spin even faster. But an unexpected response can stop the merry-go-round. Even if it's just for a minute, that pause may give her enough time to get off. A *limiting response*—a planned response that doesn't fit her expectations—will limit her options in a positive way and help her to slow down and think about what she's doing. The limiting response forces her to become more rational (see Figure 10.1). It may not succeed, but it is the best chance you have to deescalate her behavior.

The key to using the limiting response is to remain in control of your own emotions. If you follow her script, you'll find yourself saying and doing things you never intended to say and do, and you'll confirm all her negative beliefs about authority, teachers, and herself. Instead, remember that a student under stress will naturally

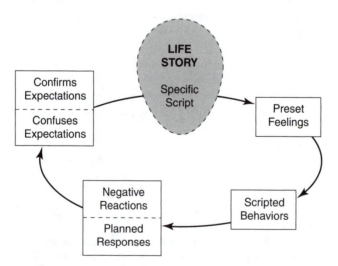

FIGURE 10.1 Your unexpected response to a child's behavior helps her slow down, think about what she's doing, and become more rational.

Source: © 2000, WEVAS, Inc. Reproduced with the written permission of WEVAS, Inc.

Nicholas J. Long and William C. Morse (1996) counsel using self-talk to stay in control of your emotions during a crisis. You can practice self-talk when you're alone at home or any time you want to control your impulses or change the way you look at a situation. (For more about self-talk, see page 142.)

- *Preparing for anger triggers.* . . . This is going to be upsetting, but I can handle it. . . . Stop! . . . Work out a plan. . . . Take a deep breath. . . . Remember to keep your sense of humor. . . .
- *When confronted.* . . . Stop! Stay calm. Think! Don't jump to conclusions. Count to ten. . . . Stick with the plan. You don't need to prove yourself. . . . Look for the positives. . . .
- *Coping when I'm already angry.* . . . My muscles are starting to tense. . . . Slow things down. . . . Lower the tone, lower the volume, speak slower. Getting upset won't help. . . . Take the issue point by point. Try the cooperative approach. Maybe we're both right. . . . Take it easy, don't get pushy! Negotiate. (pp. 342–343)

create angry, aggressive feelings in you, but you don't have to act on those feelings. Take a deep breath, release it slowly, think about what you'll say, and speak calmly. If you can make yourself act calmly, it will help you to feel calm inside (Wright, n.d.). Long (2000) says:

> We have to make a personal choice not to fight or get into power struggles with troubled students. . . . Instead, we are making a decision to see ourselves more like a thermostat than a thermometer. A thermometer reflects the temperature around it. If we are working with a student who gets hot, we also get hot. If we are working with a student who gets cold, we also get cold. If we see ourselves as a thermostat, we will set our emotional temperature at 98.6 degrees. When a student gets hot, we are going to cool him or her down, and when a student withdraws, we are going to heat him or her up. (p. 97)

The interrupt

There are two basic limiting responses: the *interrupt* and the *options statement*. The *interrupt* is a completely unpredictable response that fits neither the student's past experience nor her present expectations. Because it confuses her, it stops her in her tracks. Rather than asking Jazmine to remove her hat (a response that she's expecting), you could say, "Jazmine, that's a great hat! You better put it in your desk before Carlos grabs it!" Such a request relieves the tension and gets her attention without eliciting the usual rebellion, and when she's calm and you have a minute, you can go over to her and explain that you can't see her face when she's wearing her hat. This technique is a form of redirection.

The options statement

The *options statement* provides a student with alternatives. Its intent isn't to teach her how to make good choices but—like the interrupt—to make her stop and think. Because a child in the second level of agitation is usually looking for a challenge, not a choice, options may surprise her. To make a decision, she has to consider the choices, and doing that may be enough to move her out of her cycle and allow her to regain some control.

The student is already feeling picked on and doesn't want any direction from you. It is therefore a significant challenge to turn her feelings around enough to return her to a competent state. The way you structure and deliver your options statement will determine whether you can provoke her into thinking and acting rationally. It is easier to do this well when you recognize that her behavior is related to her past experiences and perceptions of reality, not to a desire to make you miserable. Offering choices makes you seem less threatening, which means you're less likely to push her over the edge. It's most effective to set limits based on values shared by everyone in the class (for example, everyone should be safe).

WEVAS offers these suggestions for creating an options statement:

• *Be aware of your voice and body language.* Your demeanor is contagious. If you can slow down, maintain a relaxed stance, and deliver your message in a calm manner, you'll increase your chances of bringing the student into a rational decision-making process. Bear in mind that an options statement isn't a threat, and your tone of voice must make this absolutely clear. Even a nonpunitive choice, offered in an angry or punitive way, can keep her spinning or send her into the aggressive state. Keeping your message private will also help make the situation less threatening and help slow the merry-go-round.

• *Cue the child.* Your options statement won't have any effect if the student doesn't hear it. Signal her so she knows you're about to speak. The best way to do that is to start with her name, followed by a short pause. "Jazmine . . . it's your decision. . . ." Using pauses makes the child wonder what you're going to say next and helps her move out of her cycle.

• *Pose choices.* Choices empower the student and give her some control over the situation. Starting with "You decide" or "You have a decision to make" hooks her into thinking about her options. The message is, "You have choices in this situation. The decision is yours." Two choices are usually enough.

• *Be clear, concise, and concrete, and present the positive first.* The child thinks this is a control issue, and she won't hear what you're saying if you begin with a negative alternative or lots of words and abstractions. "Jazmine, it's your decision. You can put your hat in your locker and fix your hair in the bathroom, or you can give the hat to me to put on my desk until after class."

• *Make the choices reasonable.* Choices should be fair and related to the problem behavior. She shouldn't have to miss recess because she's wearing a hat in class.

• *Be sure the choices are both enforceable and supportable.* Think through the whole range of appropriate possibilities before you offer a choice. You may not want to offer Jazmine the choice of putting her hat in her locker and going to the bathroom to fix her hair if you're about to begin explaining a new math concept. (On the other hand, if it will defuse the situation, perhaps the math concept can wait a few minutes; if you go ahead without resolving this situation, her behavior may make it impossible to teach the math anyway!)

It helps to keep the outcome you desire squarely in the front of your mind. Above all, the options must give her some control over the situation, make her think about what she'll do, and allow her to save face.

Strategies for dealing with the student's response

Consistently following up a limiting response is just as crucial as framing it well—and requires just as much skill and sensitivity. All too often, even when teachers know it's hard for a student to stop, think, and make a choice, they expect an immediate answer. But because the purpose of a limiting response is to help the child regain control, there is no rush. Let her take her time considering her options. She should feel that this is an opportunity to make a better choice, not a power struggle. You could even move away and proceed with other activities, which may make it easier for her to stow her hat in her desk and get on with her work.

If she does what you ask, it doesn't matter if she complains. Saying "This is stupid!" is her way to save face, be cool, and preserve her reputation and self-esteem. By ignoring her remarks and recognizing her appropriate actions, you give all the students the message that they can comply and still be safe.

If she doesn't act right away, don't repeat the choices. Her actions will tell you what she's decided to do. After a reasonable amount of time, you can assume that she's made a choice. Tell her again what the choice involves: "It appears that you have made a choice, so I will put the hat on my desk and you can have it after class."

Be sure to follow through. If she changes her mind when she sees you walking toward her and tells you she'll put her hat in her locker, respond in a positive way ("That's great") that resolves the situation, rather than in a negative one ("No, you've had your chance") that will escalate it. However, if she continues to wear her hat, you can offer her another choice: "Jazmine, it's your decision. You can take off your hat yourself, or I can take it off for you." If she once again refuses to take off her hat, your response has to be "It appears that you have made a choice, so I will take your hat and put it on my desk." You can soften this by saying, "You can still go to the bathroom and fix your hair."

Once again, knowing the student is crucial. Jazmine may need more empathy, so instead of simply giving her options, it might be a good idea to show her that you understand her feelings and respect her need to express her point of view. An effective way to do this is to use several strategies at once. Combining open communication with a teaching response and an options statement tells her that you care, that she has a choice to make, and that you will follow through. If she continues to wear her hat after you've asked her once to put it away, you can say, "Jazmine, I know that this feels unfair to you, and I'd be happy to talk about it later. Right now the rule is that there are no hats allowed in class, so you have a decision to make. Either you can put the hat in your locker and go to the bathroom to fix your hair, or you can give the hat to me to keep on my desk until the end of class." This combination can be very powerful in enabling a student to return to a competent state.

Another alternative is to use what WEVAS calls *power language*: "Jazmine, if you think you can be quick about it, you can put your hat in your locker and go to the bathroom to fix your hair. But if it will take too long, you can put the hat in your desk." This formulation empowers the student by challenging her to prove she can control her behavior.

Defusion

When a student challenges you in class, it's important to focus on defusing her anger and avoiding a power struggle. Richard L. Curwin and Allen N. Mendler (1997) suggest trying out several possible replies by saying them out loud to an imaginary student, then practicing the ones that feel comfortable to you before you actually use them in class.

- I'm disappointed that you are choosing to use such angry words even though I'm sure there is much to be upset about.
- I know there is a solution to this, but I don't know what it is right now. Let's meet later when we can really figure this out.
- Your words (actions) tell me you are bored. It takes a lot of discipline to hang in there when you are unsure about why we are doing certain things. Thanks for hanging in there.
- You're just not yourself today, and that must feel lousy.
- Throwing books . . . doesn't make problems disappear. It only creates new ones. Let's use our words to say why we feel so mad!
- Wow, you must be feeling awfully mad to use those words in front of everyone. Let's talk later when we can work this out.
- I'm glad you trust me enough to tell me how you feel and I'm concerned. Any suggestions for improvement are appreciated. (p. 69)

You are trying to give her the best possible opportunity to maintain her dignity and save face, but it's important to remember that she has used a very different pattern of behavior over many years and it may take some time for her to learn to respond to your offer in a new way.

The aggressive state

No matter how well you use the WEVAS preventive strategies, there will inevitably be times when a student's behavior becomes aggressive. The aggression can be physical (hitting, pushing, kicking, throwing things, and so on) or verbal (arguing, swearing, putting down others, making threats, being sarcastic, and the like). A child in the aggressive state is irrational and out of control, and she doesn't hear or understand anything you say to her. Reasoning no longer works. She is driven by her emotions and by behavior patterns that worked for her in the past. Her behavior is random—even if she's flinging books or chairs across the room or swearing like a sailor, her actions have no real target. As WEVAS puts it, she has a fire burning inside her. Although the fire isn't meant for any specific person, it will burn anyone who comes too close.

Your goal is to help the student put that fire out or to let it extinguish itself. To do this, you need a plan, and you have to remain calm enough to implement it. Then you can provide the student with the support she needs to return to a competent state. Often you can accomplish this goal in the presence of the whole class. But sometimes the child's anger is so intense or the escalation of her behavior so certain that the best plan is to remove the other students from the classroom. Because this is more likely to be necessary when the student is in the assaultive state, we've discussed this issue on pages 214 to 216.

In the aggressive state, the student is driven by her emotions and by behavior patterns that worked for her in the past. Reasoning no longer works.

Jazmine clearly lost control and crossed over into the aggressive state when you tried to speak to her after she refused to take off her cap. She stood up, started swearing at you, and pushed over her chair. When a student is in this state, words seem to fuel her emotions like gasoline on a fire. Talking is out of the question until she's calm, and you must use your nonverbal skills to communicate with her and deescalate the behavior. She is acutely aware of your physical presence, and your body is your most useful tool. But your instincts can betray you here. If you confront, intimidate, or threaten her by putting your hands on your hips or using your size and body language to exert your power, things will get worse. She will feel smaller and more defensive—and become more likely to lash out at you or at someone smaller when you aren't around. Even if you say nothing, your body language and facial expressions can give you away. Without relinquishing your authority, you must communicate openness, caring, and confidence through your relaxed posture, facial expression, and behavior.

The key to this Houdini act is in your head: You must distance yourself psychologically. Whatever the child says or does, don't take it personally. Your emotions can ensnare you in the struggle, impede your ability to focus on her, and make you ineffective. To keep your cool, imagine yourself by the sea, concentrate on the bottom of your feet, or utilize breathing and self-talk. Repeating a mantra such as "This isn't personal," "This has worked in the past; she's doing the best she can," or "My job is to stay calm and help her learn better ways to behave" can help (Kottler, 2002).

These techniques lend you distance and objectivity and allow you to relax your face even if your stomach is in knots. If mentally you're in Hawaii, you won't feel nearly so angry or terrified.

This doesn't mean that you ignore her or cut off contact. Rather, it means that you aren't getting hooked into an emotional reaction that makes it harder for her to deescalate. You can remain neutrally involved, giving her attention by staying nearby, carefully calibrating her behavior and adjusting your actions. Your message to her is that you're not going to respond to her aggressive behavior, but when she's ready to make other choices, you'll be there.

You must also distance yourself physically to ensure your own safety and allow the child to feel safe. Because she's responding to your physical presence and isn't rational, she may need much more space than usual. Adjust the distance between you until you sense that she feels connected but not threatened.

WEVAS suggests you use a relaxed and flexible standing posture called the *centered L-stance*. In this position you can assume the confident bearing of a person who's in charge of herself and send a message of stability to a student who's out of control and a message of safety to a student who's afraid. In the L-stance you don't face the child directly; instead you stand sideways so that you don't seem so threatening. What's most important is the position of your shoulders. If they're at right angles to the shoulders of the child (forming an L), you appear much less menacing. Your feet are more or less facing in the same direction as your body, although the front one should be turned slightly toward the child at about a 45-degree angle. Keep your feet 12 to 18 inches apart, more if you think there's some danger. Your head is up but not rigidly high, your mouth and eyes are relaxed, your shoulders are dropped but not hunched, your spine is straight, and your knees are slightly bent. For safety's sake, place your weight on the front foot so that you can move out of the way quickly by shifting your weight to your back foot (see Figure 10.2).

When you're standing at right angles to the child in this way, it may give her the feeling that you are uninvolved or don't care. In some cases, it may be important to shift your stance to what WEVAS calls an *acute L-stance*. In this stance you move your shoulders toward the student, balancing the need for safety with her need for involvement and caring.

In the European American culture it's natural to make eye contact, but with a student in the aggressive state, eye contact can sometimes ignite the situation, intensify a power struggle, or reinforce a child whose goal is to get your attention. It is therefore a good idea to avoid eye contact when you first enter the L-stance. If you gaze over her shoulder or at the middle of her body, you remove the eye contact without sending a message of fear. Looking elsewhere also helps to keep your face relaxed and your mind clear; and your averted eyes may well surprise the child, interrupt her cycle, and deescalate her behavior.

Carefully note how your own stance, angle, eye contact, and distance are affecting her, and systematically eliminate any of your behavior that's feeding the fire. Then let her play out the scene that she started.

Even a student in an aggressive state has to breathe from time to time. During these lulls it's important to figure out whether she's actually calming down—moving back into an agitated or anxious state—or simply out of fuel. You can evaluate her state by slowly bringing your eyes to hers to see if she's ready to begin interaction with you again. Try to determine whether eye contact increases or decreases the

FIGURE 10.2 The L-stance sends a message of safety to students who are afraid and a message of stability to students who are out of control.

aggressive behavior. If it increases or maintains it, look away once more. Eventually eye contact becomes a reward reinforcing calmer behavior, and (if it's culturally appropriate) it tells the student that you are there for her. Her response will tell you whether you have judged her state accurately.

If you feel that her behavior has deescalated, you can use nonverbal means to show you've relaxed and to help her relax, too. Move closer, smile, and try a few short, well chosen, empathic words that match her new emotional state. This will help to stabilize her behavior at this level.

Acknowledge the student's feelings. If you can show that you care and understand, she may not feel as much of a need to confront you. At this stage the words that you use are critical, even the small ones. Instead of *but*, use *and* (which doesn't discount the previous statement); in place of *you*, use *we* (which suggests support); and instead of *should*, use *can* (which implies personal choice). Avoid anything that makes her think that you're challenging or devaluing her. "Jazmine, I realize that you're angry and feeling that everyone is against you, and I think we can figure out some ways to deal with the situation."

Mirroring the student's speech helps, too. If you gradually change the tone, volume, speed, and cadence of your voice, you can lead the student to a more effective state. But be careful. If you mirror a student in an aggressive state on all dimensions, she may think you're challenging her and become more aggressive.

Eventually you'll have to debrief (see pages 216 to 219). But at the height of an aggressive outburst your role is to help the student deescalate and stabilize as quickly as possible. A bonus of this approach is that she learns she can calm herself down. And if the rest of the class is present, everyone will see that you aren't afraid of intense emotion.

The L-stance is not a posture that we use on a regular basis, so you should practice it in a relaxed environment. Work with your colleagues, coaching, cuing, and supporting one another.

The assaultive state

Sometimes a student will move from aggressive to assaultive behavior regardless of the strategies you use. Like a child in the aggressive state, a child in the assaultive state has a great deal of negative energy, but it's no longer random. Even if you aren't the cause of her problem, you or another student has become her target. This situation will require all the verbal and nonverbal skills you used to deal with her in the aggressive state. At the same time, you must think of everyone's safety.

If you and the student have a good relationship, it's important for you to stay with her. You are the one who can influence her and calibrate her actions most accurately. Whoever is in her line of vision is her target. When you are the bull's-eye, your principal defenses are to keep a safe distance, stay silent, and use the L-stance. Do not try to move her, talk to her, or make eye contact. Although you need to know what she is doing to order to keep yourself safe, if she senses you're frightened or angry her behavior will escalate, and you'll put yourself in peril. Try to keep track of her movements and actions out of the corner of your eye. Allow this scene to run its full course, making brief eye contact in the lulls and interjecting a few carefully chosen words only when she's ready to listen.

You can also learn specific strategies and releases to protect yourself from grabs, chokes, bites, and hair pulling. We won't describe those here; the best way to learn them is in a course or workshop where you can try them out for yourself and benefit from the expertise of a qualified instructor.

The systems response

You can't focus on the student who's out of control while you're worrying about the other students. To protect them you need a *systems response*—an emergency plan that involves others, such as the teachers down the hall, the school librarian, or even the principal. The most effective way to keep the other children safe is to get them out of harm's way. Taking them out of the room not only protects them but also removes the audience—which may allow the student in the assaultive state to calm down more rapidly.

Just as schools have established procedures for responding to a fire, they have procedures for dealing with a dangerous situation. It is essential to know exactly what your school's procedures are. They will probably include a way to alert the office that you need immediate assistance (for example, a special phone number to call, or a red card with the number of your classroom that a reliable student can carry to the office [Jones and Jones, 2004]); a designated place for your students to go if they must leave the classroom (the gym, the library, the auditorium); a designated

The Center for the Study and Prevention of Violence at the University of Colorado at Boulder (1998) makes the following suggestions for teachers when there's a fight:

- Do not physically get in the middle of a fight or try to restrain fighters.
- Disperse student spectators away from the fight....
- Take time to analyze the fight. You need to know if the fight just began, is winding down, who is the aggressor, etc.
- Obtain additional help from other teachers....
- After any ... incident, there should be immediate documentation of everything that occurred. This documentation should include time, name(s) of the student(s) involved, a brief description of the events that occurred, and any information that pertains to the student(s) or the incident. This report should be submitted to the administration. You should also keep a copy in case of a future conference with parents or school administrators regarding the incident.

person to supervise them if you have no co-teacher, student teacher, or paraprofessional to call on; and even a signal ("Code Red") to put the plan into effect.

In addition, your school is likely to have a protocol to deal with fighting. Because it's dangerous to intervene when students are slugging it out, it's important to have trained, qualified staff you can call for help, as well as another adult witness. Who will be available if a fight breaks out in the classroom, hallway, cafeteria, or schoolyard? How will you reach them? Is training offered to the teachers at your school? Such situations definitely call for a team effort and discussion at a staff meeting at the very beginning of the year.

Even when your school has prepared crisis plans, there are details for you to work out as soon as possible, before you need them. The first priority is always to get help. Which students can you trust to dial the emergency number or bring the red card to the office? If you need the students to exit the room before help arrives, how will they get into the hallway? Will the teacher next door be available and willing to pitch in? When? How long will your students be able to stay in the emergency location, and what will they do there? (Wherever they go, they should be able to stay until you're ready for them to return.) All of these matters must be discussed, decided, and cleared with your principal. Then you must rehearse the plan with your class to ensure it's set to go at a moment's notice. When the students are in a competent state, explain the procedure: "This is like a fire drill, in case we need to leave the room for any reason. We're going to call it 'Code Red.'" Tell them you probably won't need to use it, but you're going to practice it together periodically the same way you practice a fire drill.

What about using restraint?

When a student is dangerously out of control, your instinct may be to restrain her to keep her from hurting herself and others. This is not an acceptable option. Restraint—a physical method of restricting a student's freedom of movement, physical activity, or normal access to her body (International Society of Psychiatric and Mental Health Nurses, 1999)—carries very real risks. It can cause physical and psychological injury (LeBel et al., 2004), violate rights, trample dignity, and inflict further trauma on those who've already been physically or sexually abused. It can even lead to death (LeBel et al., 2004). And the danger isn't limited to the student who's being restrained: The person who's performing the restraint also faces a strong possibility of injury (Peterson, 2002).

Since its introduction in the late eighteenth century, restraint has raised controversy, and there is now a clear national consensus against its use (Families Together, n.d.). Several states have banned or placed strong restrictions on it, and the U.S. Department of Health and Human Services (2005) has implemented a detailed action plan to eliminate it in all publicly funded treatment programs.

According to the president's New Freedom Commission on Mental Health (2003), restraint is not a treatment but a "safety intervention of last resort" that should be employed only when there is an imminent risk of danger to the individual or those around her and no other safe, effective intervention is possible. Medical, psychiatric, and law-enforcement settings have strict guidelines for its use, but most schools do not (Ryan and Peterson, 2004). Anecdotal evidence suggests that it is still commonly used to prevent injury, to protect property, and even to respond to non-compliance, even though no study has shown that it is effective in reducing school violence (Ryan and Peterson, 2004).

Experts recommend that schools fall into line with other institutions and reduce the use of this invasive tactic. In their review of case law, legislation, and recommended procedures from professional organizations and advocacy groups, Joseph B. Ryan and Reece L. Peterson (2004) call for clear standards regarding the use of restraint procedures in schools, as well as for mandatory training of the staff who perform it, improved and standardized record keeping, and prompt notification of administrators and parents of incidents whenever restraint occurs.

The open state

Having just spent many minutes with a student who was out of control, you probably don't feel much like spending more time with her. But before you rejoin the class, you need to understand all you've been through together. This is the moment to cement your relationship, not to let it come unglued, so while the other students return to the classroom and resume work, find a quiet place where the two of you can talk.

As well as posing a danger, a crisis offers an opportunity for growth—a chance for a student to gain new insights and learn new ways to handle difficulties. Some private time with you when she's coming off an aggressive or assaultive state can assist her in becoming more competent and facing her classmates with confidence, self-esteem, and a greater understanding of her behavior (Redl and Wineman, 1957; Wood and Long, 1991).

Based on the work of psychologists Fritz Redl and Nicholas J. Long, this *debriefing*, as WEVAS calls it, is truly a time to learn. Because the student has just lived through an emotional crisis, her defenses are down and she's open to new possibilities, but she also feels extremely vulnerable. Unresolved issues from her past may have resurfaced, and she's exhausted from the ordeal she's just experienced. The more emotional energy she expended, the greater the potential for change. For a few minutes to an hour, there is a window for effective debriefing. The timing is tricky. If you debrief too soon, she feels too exposed, but if you wait too long she'll start to rebuild her defenses.

For learning to take place, the student's energy must be dissipated; she must be composed, and she must feel safe, both physically and emotionally (Wood and Long, 1991). Restoring a child to a competent state without conjuring up her defenses is like a dance. Your words and actions can help her rediscover her personal resources—or send her straight back to her armor. Observe her carefully as you gently search for a way to connect with her positive side. If you connect with her defenses instead, back off and try something else.

The gravity of the incident will tell you how much debriefing is required. Sometimes a word or a gesture will suffice, but a debriefing can take as long as an hour. Be sure to spend as much time as it takes. This can be a slow and emotional procedure, full of long pauses, and there's nothing you can do to speed it up. You want the student to begin the communication process, and she'll talk when she's ready. Take your cues from her. If you start to talk before she's prepared to listen, she may not be ready to reflect on the incident, and the process may fail.

If the student is fidgety and doesn't make eye contact, she's still using these devices to help herself feel comfortable, and it's wise not to draw attention to them. Focus on the incident, request details, and ask questions that lead her to think more objectively about what happened. Don't repeat your questions—if she doesn't answer within a reasonable amount of time, move on. Keep on calibrating her, noting small changes in her gestures, facial expressions, tone of voice, and body language, and mirror her posture, voice, eye contact, and breathing. When she's ready to engage, she'll probably lean toward you with her arms in an open position.

Remember it is the student who is the focus and the student who needs to do the talking. Listen, accept her wherever she is, and use encouraging statements to help her tap into her strengths and identify her feelings and the basic issues. This takes time, trust, honesty, and respect. Let her remain in control so that she feels competent; your role is to help her use that control to solve the problem. This isn't easy, and she'll need your guidance throughout the process. One way to support her is to use language that empowers her (*we* and *us* offer support and acknowledge her feelings); another is to recognize small victories ("I see that you stopped to think about that").

Don't insist on an apology from the student. You will just encourage her to say words she doesn't mean and suggest it's all right to hurt someone if she apologizes afterwards. Instead, talk with her about what might happen when she reenters the classroom, how the other children will receive her, and what she will say and do. It's hard for a student to go back to her peers after an experience in the aggressive or assaultive state. Even if the student is now feeling competent, she's probably also embarrassed and more vulnerable than usual, and she needs your help. Her classmates may be frightened or anxious about having her in their midst again, and they can use your support, too.

Some students may find it easier to return during a teacher-directed activity when tasks and roles are clearly defined. Others may need more space, but not as much as recess or gym would provide. Because you want her reentry attempt to succeed, it's sensible for you to consult with the student about when she should come back and what she should do. As the one who knows her best, you can suggest that she draw (or do another relaxing activity) for awhile to give her enough time to regroup. Be sure she knows you'll stay with her until she's comfortable. If she doesn't have the support she needs, the slightest frustration will set her off again. Your observations and knowledge will help you determine how long to stick around.

What about consequences?

Going through this experience together may actually enhance your relationship with the student. She may learn that an adult who sees her at her worst won't reject her—and will even accept and respect her (Merritt-Petrashek, 1996). She may also be more willing to trust you and turn to you for support before she reaches the crisis point in the future (Long et al., 1998).

Applying consequences now, especially punitive consequences, may well undo all the progress you've made. Consequences will not deter the student from behaving the same way again. (Maintaining a positive relationship and helping her learn new skills are more likely to do that.) And in a supportive, cooperative, caring classroom, not applying consequences will not encourage others in the class to misbehave, even students whose behavior is often challenging. Formative consequences that help a student learn skills and acquire empathy and insight (such as asking her to get ice for an injury she's caused) may be more appropriate.

Of course, if the school's discipline policy sets out specific consequences for specific infractions (if, for example, fighting requires an automatic in-school suspension), then you must follow the rules. You can soften the blow and minimize the damage to your relationship by explaining that this is the school's rule, not your choice. You might even offer to accompany her to the principal's office to share what happened.

Debriefing the class

Any crisis in the classroom will affect the other students. Psychologist Jeffrey A. Kottler (2002) makes these suggestions for activities that encourage them to deal with their own feelings:

- Write a story about someone who becomes very angry and tries to deal with the feelings.
- Act out several scenes in which students have been provoked to the point of anger. Experiment with different ways of responding.
- Talk about the constructive and destructive uses of anger throughout history.
- Have students share in small groups stories about the last time they lost control. . . .
- Use self-disclosure and modeling to talk about a time when you became angry.
- Offer a unit on the psychology of emotions in general and anger in particular.
- With partners, brainstorm a list of the negative side effects that result from anger as well as the possible benefits. . . .
- Assign books or movies in which anger is a major theme. (pp. 22–23)

After a serious altercation, you need debriefing as much as the students do. It doesn't have to take place on the same day, but within a day or two sit down with a good friend, colleague, or the school's counselor or psychologist to discuss what happened. This encounter may have stirred up feelings and filters from your own past, or you may have felt that your personal safety was threatened. Be sure to talk about whatever the incident evoked—frustration, powerlessness, anger, sadness, fear. Acknowledging these feelings in a safe place makes it easier to move on (Education Development Center, 1997). This self-care is essential to survival.

It's also important to evaluate how you handled the event. Was the systems response quick and effective? Did everyone understand her role and do what she was supposed to do? Could you have acted earlier to prevent the crisis? What should you do differently the next time? Talk about what went right as well as what went wrong.

The techniques in the WEVAS strategy ask you to recognize the role you play in the student's behavior. It takes a lot of practice to do them consistently and well. Don't worry if you don't master them immediately, but try to become aware of what you're doing and make the effort to improve. Strategies such as looking for a child's anxiety and stating requests positively will eventually become second nature to you, and you'll find yourself using them in the rest of your life as well!

WHAT DO YOU THINK?

1. You may have been told that if you picked your battles and ignored small things, such as hair-twirling and gazing out the window, a student with challenging behavior would behave appropriately. What does WEVAS tell us about these things?
2. Think of a time when you were feeling anxious and someone helped you feel better. What were you feeling and thinking? What did the person say or do that helped you? How did you know that you were starting to feel better?
3. Describe a situation when a student is feeling agitated and develop a teaching response that will enable her to feel competent. What are the important elements of a teaching response? When is it appropriate to use it?

4. With a partner, do a role-play where one person is the teacher and the other is a student in the second stage of agitation. Using either the interrupt or an options statement, help the child calm down. When you've finished, reverse roles and do the role-play again, using the same type of limiting response to give yourselves more practice.
5. In pairs, do the L-stance. Look at the illustration on page 213 to check your position. Every detail is important. The person playing the student's role should help you stand so that you give a message of safety and stability. Practice in front of a mirror at home.

WHAT WOULD YOU DO?

Because Andrew stays up late playing video games, it's a struggle for him to get up in the morning, especially on weekdays when school is all he has to look forward to. His mother wakes him gently, but he usually ignores her or yells and swears at her. When his father realizes that Andrew isn't getting ready for school, he goes into Andrew's bedroom, screams at him, and pulls him out of bed.

If Andrew hasn't emerged for breakfast within a few minutes, his father demands that his mother make him come downstairs, but when her efforts fail, his father forcefully ushers him to the breakfast table or pushes him out the door toward the bus stop. If Andrew hasn't organized his knapsack the night before, he doesn't have most of what he needs for the day.

More often than not, Andrew has already missed the bus, and he has to return home and ask for a ride to school. After much shouting, one of his parents reluctantly drives him, lecturing him or not speaking a word the whole way.

When Andrew manages to catch the bus, he is so tired, hungry, and angry that he walks to the last row, pushing or kicking anyone who gets in his way. The bus driver has warned him more than once to stop hurting the other children or he won't allow him to ride the bus.

All Andrew can think about is that he doesn't like school, he has no friends, and everyone thinks he's stupid. He didn't study for his Spanish dictation or math quiz.

What would you do when Andrew arrives in your classroom?

SUGGESTED READINGS AND RESOURCES

Curwin, R. L., & Mendler, A. N. (1997). *As tough as necessary: Countering violence, aggression, and hostility in our schools*. Alexandria, VA: Association for Supervision and Curriculum Development.

Gordon, T. (with Burch, N.) (2003). *Teacher effectiveness training*. New York: Three Rivers Press.

Long, N. J., & Morse, W. C. (Eds.). (1996). *Conflict in the classroom: The education of at-risk and troubled students* (5th ed.). Austin, TX: Pro-Ed.

Miller, P. W. (2000). *Nonverbal communication in the classroom*. Munster, IN: Patrick W. Miller & Associates.

WEVAS, Inc., 778 Ibister Street, Winnipeg, Manitoba R2Y 1R4, Canada. Email: neil@WEVAS.net or bob@WEVAS.net

CHAPTER 11

Functional Assessment and Positive Behavior Support

Every challenging behavior can be thought of as a student's solution to a problem and a form of communication. These ideas go back to Plato, who said that a crying baby's behavior serves a function: He is trying to get someone to care for him (Durand, 1990).

This is the underlying principle of *functional assessment* (*FA*, sometimes called *functional behavioral assessment*, or *FBA*) and *positive behavior support* (*PBS*), two linked strategies developed by behavioral psychologists for understanding and remediating a child's challenging behavior. The goal of these techniques is to figure out what is triggering the behavior and what the child is getting from it—and to teach him a more acceptable behavior that can fulfill those needs instead (O'Neill et al., 1997; Repp, Karsh, Munk, and Dahlquist, 1995). Together, they enable you to look at the world through the student's eyes.

Challenging behavior isn't really as random and unpredictable as it seems. By focusing on the student's immediate environment, you can understand where the behavior is coming from, why it's happening at a particular time in a particular place (Durand, 1990), the logic behind it, and the function or purpose it serves for the student (Dunlap and Kern, 1993; Iwata, Dorsey, Slifer, Bauman, and Richman, 1982; O'Neill et al., 1997). Even if the behavior is inappropriate, the function seldom is. Once you understand the function, you can design a *positive behavior support plan*, sometimes called a *behavior intervention plan* or *BIP*, to help the student achieve his purpose in an appropriate way and render the challenging behavior "irrelevant, ineffective, and inefficient" (O'Neill et al., 1997, p. 8).

Of course, all of the causes of challenging behavior aren't in the immediate environment, but viewing it from this angle can be extremely helpful. Functional assessment and positive behavior support are powerful strategies to add to your toolbox, especially when you combine them with other methods and you have a positive relationship with the child. Using functional assessment and positive behavior support takes time and effort, but it's a sound investment. In the end, you'll spend less time addressing behavior problems and more time boosting the learning of all the students in your class, not just the student with challenging behavior.

This chapter is divided into two main sections. The first describes the functional assessment process; the second is about creating a positive behavior support plan. Andrew appears throughout. Because of his consistently inappropriate behavior, his teachers have decided to develop a behavior support plan for him, based on a functional assessment.

PERFORMING A FUNCTIONAL ASSESSMENT

When is it appropriate to use functional assessment and positive behavior support?

Devised in the late 1970s and early 1980s in reaction to the use of punishment with persons with developmental disabilities, functional assessment is usually reserved for serious behavior problems (Gable, Quinn, Rutherford, Howell, and Hoffman, 1998). Positive behavior support extended the use of functional assessment to include preventive strategies and alternative appropriate behaviors that improve a student's social and communication skills and his overall quality of life.

Functional assessment and positive behavior support are particularly effective when you need a fresh approach to a student's very challenging behavior. Most students respond well to the universal strategies we've described in previous chapters, but not all. According to the experts (Curwin and Mendler, 2001; Sugai and Horner, 2002; Walker, Ramsey, and Gresham, 2004), 5 to 10 percent of students will benefit from a specialized, small-group intervention; and approximately 1 to 7 percent—more in some inner-city schools—require individualized intervention (Warren et al., 2003; Clonan, Lopez, Rymarchyk, and Davison, 2004). Behavior that is very dis-

Power Plus

Although functional assessment and positive behavior support were originally intended to help individuals, schools across the country have adapted and adopted PBS as a systemic, whole-school approach for preventing and addressing challenging behavior (Fox, Dunlap, and Cushing, 2002; Sugai et al., 2000). Schoolwide PBS serves as a foundation and support system for both classroom and individual strategies, enhancing their power (Sugai, Horner, and Gresham, 2002).

Because the two techniques are so effective, the Individuals with Disabilities Education Act (IDEA) of 1997 and 2004 counsels their use whenever behavior interferes with learning or requires disciplinary action (Quinn, Gable, Rutherford, Nelson, and Howell, 1998; Mandlawitz, 2005). The National Association of School Psychologists considers them best professional practice (Miller, Tansy, and Hughes, 1998).

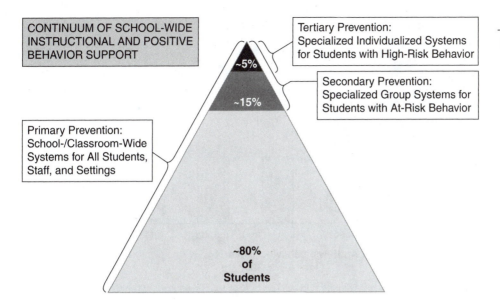

FIGURE 11.1 Most students respond well to universal strategies; 5 to 10 percent benefit from a specialized, small-group intervention; and 1 to 7 percent require individualized intervention.

Source: Technical Assistance Center on Positive Behavioral Interventions and Supports sponsored by the Office of Special Education Programs.

ruptive, destructive, or dangerous clearly qualifies for the use of functional assessment and positive behavior support (see Figure 11.1).

More moderate behaviors—especially those that occur frequently or over a long period and affect learning and social relationships—may be candidates as well (Chandler and Dahlquist, 2005). By the time students with persistent challenging behavior reach fourth grade, they have used this behavior extremely successfully over many years. Because it consistently gets them what they want, creating a new pattern will take hard work and patience.

If you collect some basic preliminary data, you'll have a better idea of whether you need a functional assessment and a positive behavior support plan. An informal observation will help you find out how frequently the challenging behavior actually occurs—how many times a day, how many times a week. You can also note whether the behavior happens at specific times—for example, only during math, or only at the end of the day, when the student is tired.

Record your observations on a simple chart with the days of the week across the top and the times of the day along the side. Write down one or two of the most challenging behaviors (swearing, for example), and put a mark in the appropriate spot each time you see the behavior. Alternately, you could count the frequency by transferring pennies or paper clips from your right pocket to your left, just as you did to remind yourself about positive reinforcement (see page 189). (If you use this system, you'll have to empty your pocket and record the results at regular intervals to know the time of day that the behavior occurs!) If the behavior goes on for a long time, it may be more useful to note its duration. Does the screaming last for 10 minutes or 10 seconds? (A watch with a second hand is helpful here.) Although a behavior's

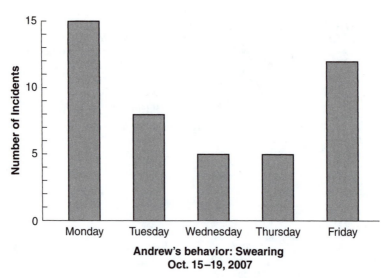

Andrew's behavior: Swearing
Oct. 15–19, 2007

FIGURE 11.2   It's easier to see a pattern in a child's behavior when you make a bar graph with your data.

intensity is difficult to measure, it may also be helpful to use a scale of 1 to 5 to record how serious or destructive it is.

At the end of the day, you'll know how many times the behavior occurred, and after a week or two you can make a bar or line graph that will enable you to visualize exactly what's happening. Put the dates or days of the week along the bottom axis, and the frequencies along the side. You can make a separate graph that shows the times or activities (such as math or recess) when the challenging behavior occurs. For future reference, don't forget to label the graph with the student's name, the behavior you've observed, and the dates.

This information provides you with a reality check: It tells you that you're dealing with real events. In addition, you'll have a much better sense of what provokes the challenging behavior. If your results show that the behavior is truly challenging, the next step is a functional assessment, which will provide the basis for a positive behavior support plan. The frequency of Andrew's swearing, which is making his teachers very uncomfortable, shows up clearly on the bar graph in Figure 11.2.

How do you figure out the function of a behavior?

Enter the teacher as detective. When you perform a functional assessment, you and everyone else who works with the student become a team of sleuths searching together to discover the function of the challenging behavior and solve this case.

The key is to see the situation from the student's point of view (Anderson, Albin, Mesaros, Dunlap, and Morelli-Robbins, 1993). A functional assessment will enable you to figure out the function or purpose of the challenging behavior and to identify events in the environment that trigger and maintain it. With this information in hand, you will be ready to develop an effective positive behavior support plan.

The functional assessment reveals the function by focusing on the context— that is, the environment immediately surrounding the challenging behavior (Carr,

Experts (Center on the Social and Emotional Foundations for Early Learning, 2006; Fox, n.d.) outline these steps for performing a functional assessment and creating an individualized positive behavior support plan for a child with challenging behavior.

- Convene a team and identify the problem behavior and the goals of the intervention.
- Gather information by reviewing records; interviewing the family, teachers, the child, and others; and observing the child in the environment.
- Based on the information, develop a hypothesis and a hypothesis statement.
- Design a behavior support plan.
- Implement and monitor the plan.
- Evaluate the outcomes.

1994). In *Functional Assessment and Program Development for Problem Behavior* (1997), Robert O'Neill and his colleagues put it this way: "Behavior change occurs by changing environments, not [by] trying to change people" (p. 5). The context provides the best clues to understanding why the student is using challenging behavior. Because the ordinary classroom environment is a complex place, filled with social, cognitive, affective, sensory, and biological factors that influence behavior (Gable et al., 1998; Quinn et al., 1998), functional assessment asks teachers to look at it in a special way. An *A-B-C analysis* (Bijou, Peterson, and Ault, 1968) can tease out the essential elements (O'Neill et al., 1997).

A stands for *antecedents*—events that take place right before the challenging behavior and seem to trigger it. The research literature mentions demands, requests, difficult tasks, transitions, interruptions, and being left alone (O'Neill et al., 1997). Peers' actions can be antecedents, too—think of teasing, bullying, showing off, coming too close, and exclusion. Andrew starts talking loudly to his neighbors whenever you introduce a new topic—a new concept in math, a science project, or a research paper—that involves new techniques to master, lots of instructions, or many steps to follow. When you respond by asking him to pay attention so that he'll know what to do, his behavior quickly escalates—he swears at you and pushes over his chair. The introduction of a new topic involving multiple directions is the antecedent for Andrew's challenging behavior.

It is often hard to distinguish between antecedents and their more distant relations—known as *setting events*—that take place before or around the antecedents. Setting events make the student more vulnerable to the antecedents and the challenging behavior more likely to occur (Durand, 1990; Repp et al., 1995). The number of students in the classroom, the setup of the room, the noise level, the lighting, the type of activity, the adults who are present or absent (a substitute teacher often inspires challenging behavior), the sequence of activities (the lunch hour makes some students too hyper to concentrate), and the time of day (some students have a hard time functioning in the morning; others don't function well in the afternoon) can all act as setting events. Conditions in the neighborhood—racial unease, gang warfare—can also be a setting event. So can the student's physical or emotional state—being hungry, tired, or sick; being on medication (or not); spending the weekend with a noncustodial parent; hearing parents fight the night before; and being pushed or bullied on the bus or playground. Even the child's culture can be a setting event—if, for example, behavior that is appropriate or encouraged at home is unacceptable at school (Sheridan, 2000). Setting events are hard to pin down and often depend on information supplied by someone else, such as a conscientious bus driver who informs the principal or a teacher about an incident that occurred on the way to school. Setting events may also be difficult or impossible to change or just plain unknowable (for example, you probably won't know that Andrew had a fight with his father before school). But sometimes they are relatively easy to identify and even amenable to change, so it's important to look for them.

B stands for *behavior*, which you must describe so clearly and specifically that anyone who's observing can recognize and measure it (not "Andrew is disruptive" but "Andrew talks loudly to his neighbors," "Andrew swears," and "Andrew pushes over a chair or desk") (Durand, 1990; Gable et al., 1998). Of course you can't observe or measure thoughts or feelings such as sadness or anger—but you can observe and measure yelling or throwing books (Smith, 1993).

C stands for *consequences*—that is, what happens after the challenging behavior? In this case, you are looking at what you did as well as how Andrew's peers responded. Do you pretend that you didn't hear Andrew talking to his neighbor? Do you reprimand him sternly, take him aside for a private conversation, or change his seat? Do you send him to the back of the room or to the principal's office? What do the other students do? Do they laugh, join in, or tell him to stop? Any of these responses, positive or negative, may have an effect on Andrew's behavior and serve to reinforce and maintain it.

Difficult tasks, demands, requests, transitions, and interruptions often trigger challenging behavior.

What functions can behavior serve?

Taken together, the A-B-Cs and the setting events form a pattern that points you toward the function or purpose of the challenging behavior. Functional assessment postulates three possible functions:

1. *The student avoids or escapes from something* (unwelcome requests, difficult tasks, activities, contacts with particular peers or adults, and the like). When you send Andrew to the back of the room or to the principal's office, he avoids working on the new math or science assignment. Removing him from the situation strengthens his behavior and increases the likelihood it will persist.

2. *The student gets something* (attention from an adult or his peers, access to an object or an activity, and so on). When Ronnie jokes with his peers and asks them questions, they answer, laugh, or tell him to leave them alone. Because he's obtaining their attention, his behavior is being positively reinforced, and it will probably continue.

3. *The student changes the level of stimulation.* All people try to maintain their own comfortable level of stimulation, and when they get too much or too little they act to change it (Karsh, Repp, Dahlquist, and Munk, 1995; Lalli and Goh, 1993; Repp et al., 1995; Repp, Felce, and Barton, 1988). When everyone is working quietly, Jamal meanders around the room, chatting with classmates and writing on their papers, and the world instantly becomes more interesting. Because he is changing the level of stimulation in the environment, his behavior is creating its own reinforcement (Iwata, Vollmer, and Zarcone, 1990).

What about appropriate behavior?

There is also a context for appropriate behavior (Dunlap and Kern, 1993; Iwata et al., 1990; O'Neill et al., 1997), and it, too, has antecedents, setting events, and consequences. Part of developing a positive behavior support plan is knowing how to increase the student's appropriate behaviors; so you'll need to know what engages him, where his talents lie, which peers and teachers he's comfortable with, whether he likes working on his own, with a partner, or with a small group. For example, Andrew is a whiz at the computer. Tuning into his preferences and strengths will enable you to provide him with potent reinforcers for new acceptable behavior.

Working as a team

It takes a team to make functional assessment and positive behavior support work well. Everyone who comes into contact with the student—his family, his teachers, the principal, psychologist, social worker, paraprofessional, bus driver—has something to contribute; and when you pool information and ideas, you are more likely to make connections, see patterns, and come up with an effective plan (Gable et al., 1998; Gable, Quinn, Rutherford, Howell, and Hoffman, 2000). If your school has a *prereferral* or *intervention assistance team* (see page 244), which may include people trained in functional assessment, they should certainly join you. The meetings don't have to be long to help clarify a situation, and if you share your impressions and thoughts frequently, you'll understand one another better, no matter what your discipline or background. You'll also be able to implement the behavior plan more consistently.

When the team comes together for the first time, your tasks are to identify the problem clearly and set goals for your intervention. What do you want to achieve? With Andrew, your overarching long-term goal will probably be to reduce his disruptive behavior so that he can learn and function in class.

You can also begin to think about the purpose of the challenging behavior and the conditions that precipitate it. Brainstorming will prod memories and stimulate thought and ideas. You may be convinced that you already know the behavior's function, but it often turns out to be more complicated than you think. Maybe Andrew wants to get out of doing the math or science assignment as you suspect, but it's also possible that he wants more attention from you or his peers or that being in class makes him hyper and he needs less stimulation. Try to keep all of these possibilities in mind as you gather information. Eventually a hypothesis—a tentative theory or best guess—about the function will emerge.

How do you get the information you need for a functional assessment?

Reviewing records

To create a hypothesis later, you will need current and accurate data, and the more sources you have, the more accurate the information is likely to be (Dunlap and Kern, 1993; Durand, 1990). School records are an obvious starting point. Although schools sometimes have policies about opening their files, they should make information available when the challenging behavior is serious. Grades, medical forms, incident reports, students' personal files, and your own daily logs may be hiding valuable but forgotten nuggets. It's especially important to read carefully through the notes on any previous behavior management plans. Have any strategies worked with this student, even for a little while? Which didn't? You want to be sure you don't repeat them!

Perusing Andrew's file, you see that he has had behavior problems since the first grade—but not in every class. Some of his teachers have managed to engage him and even enjoy him. In addition, one suggested testing for ADHD, but his parents never followed up.

Conducting interviews

Once again, it's tempting to assume that you already know everything you could possibly need to know, but a formal interview helps to put the information into a structured format—and you may come up with some surprises (Durand, 1990).

You can begin by interviewing members of the team, starting with the family, who will have considerable knowledge and insight to share and can add important details and background information. This is a good opportunity to ask about setting events: Sleeping and eating habits, allergies, medical conditions, medications, events in the community, or family problems may all be influencing the student's behavior. Andrew's mother tells you that he stays up late and often comes to school tired.

You also have the impression that his father models a lack of respect for women, which may contribute to Andrew's behavior because all his teachers are women.

As you talk with the family, remember to take your own cultural bias into account. A family from a diverse culture may find the functional assessment process inappropriate, intrusive, or just plain strange (Sheridan, 2000), so be sure to seek their permission to ask questions before you start. Because they may well see both the problem and the solution in quite a different light than you do, it's a good idea to frame issues as a "mismatch" between the school and the child, and emphasize solutions, not problems (Sheridan, 2000). As always, a sensitive and respectful relationship is crucial. Work to gain the family's trust and cooperation by learning as much as you can about their culture, daily lives, and resources; understanding the roles of each family member (Who is the caregiver? Who is the disciplinarian?); and helping them believe that you are on their side. With their goodwill, problem solving will become much easier and much more effective.

You can also interview other members of your team, including Andrew's teachers, past and present (O'Neill et al., 1997). Andrew's computer teacher tells you about his success in class—not a surprise—but you are interested to hear that he gets along well with the social studies teacher. The bus driver mentions that Andrew is frequently in a bad mood when he boards the bus in the morning, and he swaggers down the aisle bugging the other students until he finds a seat alone at the back.

Don't overlook the most obvious source of all: the student himself. Talk with him in a quiet place at a time when he's feeling calm and good about himself. Remember to stay away from *why* questions, which make some students feel defensive, and zero in on his preferences and pleasures as well as his complaints. If your manner, voice, and body language are open, warm, and unthreatening, he'll probably shed some light on what causes his behavior.

You can take questions from existing questionnaires (see the box on page 230 or the suggested readings and resources at the end of this chapter), or make them up yourself. Include some queries about the A-B-Cs. Which circumstances almost always surround this student's challenging behavior and which never do (Dunlap and Kern, 1993; O'Neill et al., 1997)? Why does the interviewee think the child is

Culture Clash

Whenever you're working with a family on a positive behavior support team, forging a trusting relationship is crucial to success (Griggs and Turnbull, n.d.; Sheridan, 2000).

When José's sixth-grade peers made comments that he regarded as disrespectful to both him and his culture, he responded as his Latino upbringing required: He fought back. His teachers disapproved of his tactics, which they considered inappropriate, aggressive, and disruptive, and told him to "Just walk away" or "Think it but don't say it."

José's father sided with his son. In his eyes, José's behavior wasn't a problem; José had done the right thing. If he hadn't responded forcefully, he would have lost respect.

Fortunately, one member of José's behavior support team had earned the family's confidence. Through several discussions, José's family and teachers began to better understand one another's point of view, and they were able to reach a compromise. José would say, "I don't agree with what you told me to do, but I will try it" (Griggs and Turnbull, n.d.).

Collecting Clues

When you're interviewing people who know the student well, experts (Durand, 1990; Gable et al., 1998; Iwata et al., 1990; O'Neill et al., 1997; Quinn et al., 1998) suggest you ask such questions as these:

- Which of the child's behaviors do you consider challenging, and what do they look like?
- When and where does this behavior occur?
- When and where does the child behave appropriately? Which activities does he enjoy?
- Who is present when the challenging behavior occurs? And who is present when the child is behaving appropriately?
- Go over the daily routine in your mind. What activities, events, and interactions take place just before the challenging behavior? How much waiting is there? How much choice does the student have? When the routine changes, is his behavior different?
- What subjects and times of day does the child find difficult?
- What happens after the challenging behavior? How do you react? How do the other students react? Does the child manage to avoid something, such as doing an assignment? Does he get something from the behavior, such as your personal attention or access to the computer? According to Brian Iwata, one of the pioneers of functional assessment, sometimes families and teachers "can describe the functional characteristics of a behavior problem with uncanny accuracy" (1994, p. 414).
- Which approaches work well with the student, and which don't? For example, does he prefer his interaction with you to be loud or soft, fast or slow? How much space does he like to have around him? If a particular family member, teacher, or staff is especially successful with him, what does she do?
- If the child is from a different culture, this behavior may not have the same meaning for the family as it does for you. Is it troubling for them? Why or why not? How would they like you to respond to it?

behaving this way? Interviews also help you fill in particulars about previous interventions, especially if you're talking to someone who participated in developing or implementing them.

Using rating scales

Some experts suggest using a behavior rating scale. There are several that can help you deduce the function of the behavior. The Motivation Assessment Scale, developed by V. Mark Durand and Daniel B. Crimmins (1996–2001), for example, is short, easy to use, and available on the Internet. It asks questions such as "Does this behavior occur following a command to perform a difficult task?" to figure out whether the behavior's function is to obtain attention, escape from something, or change the level of stimulation.

Observing the child and the environment

By far the best way to learn about a student's behavior is to observe and collect data about it (O'Neill et al., 1997). As the great New York Yankee catcher Yogi Berra once said, "You can observe a lot just by watching."

There are three major reasons to observe challenging behavior. The first is that it gives your assessment a scientific base: Collecting data before, during, and after an intervention allows you to find out precisely what you're dealing with and to reliably measure any change that occurs. The second reason is to enable you to see the relationship between the environment and the challenging behavior more directly (Dunlap and Kern, 1993; Repp et al., 1995)—in other words, to pinpoint what triggers the behavior, what consequences are maintaining it, and what the child is avoiding or getting as a result. The third reason is that observation acts as a reality check for both you and the student and may also present some startling revelations. For example, you may discover that Andrew's swearing and his rough treatment of the classroom furniture, which seemed to occur several times a day, happen just two or three times a week. On the other hand, you're equally likely to learn that his challenging behavior is not a figment of your bias or your imagination. Having the facts will certainly help you intervene more effectively.

If your team includes a special education teacher or someone else trained in functional assessment, he or she should certainly be the one to observe the student. The principal or the school psychologist might also lend a hand. But if no one else is available, you and the others who normally spend time with the children—other teachers, student teachers, paraprofessionals—can do an observation yourselves. In fact, you may be able to collect some very good data without outsiders around to make you nervous, distract the students, and change the environment (Durand, 1990; Meyer and Evans, 1993; O'Neill et al., 1997).

Although teachers recognize that observing and recording behavior are crucial to making thoughtful decisions about an individual student, observation isn't always a priority. Other things are more pressing, and when you're teaching a class of 30 or 40, it may seem next to impossible. Teaching and observing at the same time takes will power, a quick and perceptive eye, and a good memory. Fortunately it's like any other skill: As you practice, it will become easier.

Your previous experience with a student or a reputation that precedes him can sometimes make it difficult to observe accurately and objectively. People tend to see what they expect to see—especially if they're expecting challenging behavior. Self-reflection can help here. Try to identify your biases and preconceived notions so that you can observe what's actually happening.

Using the data the team has gathered so far as a guide, select just two or three target behaviors to observe more closely. Plan to observe during a variety of activities, routines, times, and days so that you'll see when and where the behavior occurs—and doesn't. Pay close attention to what happened just before the challenging behavior, who was involved, and what happened afterwards. One of the most daunting aspects of this process is watching yourself. You are not merely observing the student's behavior; you are also observing your own.

There are many ways to record your observations. One is to make a basic *A-B-C chart* with spaces for the A-B-Cs. (Don't forget to write in the student's name, the date, time, subject, and teacher.) Or you can use a special *functional assessment observation form* such as the one developed by O'Neill and his colleagues (1997). (For examples and explanations of how to use both charts, see Appendices A and B, pages 307 to 317.) If you keep the chart on a clipboard stashed in a convenient spot in the classroom, you can write directly onto it. But if you can't get to the chart right away, make notes for yourself and transfer the information later—at lunch, during a free period, or at the end of the day—before it is lost or muddled. Everyone who observes should record and initial her impressions.

Collect data until a clear pattern emerges. This usually takes at least 15 to 20 incidents over several days (O'Neill et al., 1997). Be careful not to jump to conclusions or to interpret the data prematurely. It may be easier to identify a pattern in a student's behavior if you begin with an A-B-C chart and then transfer the information to a functional assessment observation form. If you've made a substantial effort and things still aren't clear, perhaps your description of the target behavior isn't specific enough or your personal biases are getting in the way. You may need to find a different way to observe or bring in additional help.

How do you develop a hypothesis?

When you think you have enough data, call the team together for another brainstorming session. It's time to create a hypothesis and a hypothesis statement. To do this, you must analyze your data and come to a conclusion about what it shows. What triggers the challenging behavior? What are the consequences that maintain it? And what function or purpose does it serve for the student?

Looking at the A-B-C chart and functional assessment observation form on pages 307 to 309 and 313, you can see that Andrew's problem behavior is tied to the introduction of new concepts that require a lot of explanation, especially in math and science. He also has some trouble in English, where he finds it hard to pay attention. But the most interesting information revealed by the data is that Andrew doesn't have this problem with Ms. Dalfen, the social studies teacher. What differences are there between her class and yours, and do they tell you anything about the function of Andrew's challenging behavior?

During the discussion, you discover that when you introduce a new concept or project, you do a whole-class presentation and expect the students to take notes and begin work on the assignment by themselves or in assigned small groups. While you're speaking, Andrew gets fidgety, often talks loudly to himself or his neighbors, and when you ask him to focus, he usually starts to swear and push over his chair. But Ms. Dalfen teaches in a different way. When she introduces a new topic, she gives out a sheet outlining all the main points or steps and goes over them one by one, answering questions and making certain that all the students understand each point before she moves on. She checks in with Andrew before she begins and again as soon as the students start work, ensuring that he knows what to do and helping him with the first step or two. The difference between the two approaches gives a hint about the function of Andrew's behavior.

Your observation of the consequences (which reinforce and maintain the challenging behavior) will help clarify the function. You soon see that when Andrew talks loudly to himself or his seatmates, both his behavior and yours tend to escalate until he is sent out of the room, and he avoids doing the assignment, at least for the moment. Suddenly you realize that Andrew's challenging behavior enables him to avoid showing his classmates how little he actually understands. Now it seems clear that the function of his challenging behavior is to avoid not only the assignment but also the embarrassment of being confused in front of his peers. By removing him from the room you have inadvertently reinforced his loud talk and all the challenging behavior that follows!

Now you can make a hypothesis statement: "When Andrew is confused by new ideas or directions, he talks loudly to himself or a neighbor, and his behavior quickly escalates until he is sent out of the room. This enables him to avoid the assignment and the humiliation of looking stupid in front of his classmates." Be sure your hypothesis statement describes the behavior, the function, the trigger event or antecedent, and the maintaining consequences.

CREATING A POSITIVE BEHAVIOR SUPPORT PLAN

How do you develop a positive behavior support plan?

With a clear hypothesis to guide you, you can create a behavior support plan that teaches the student how to get what he wants through appropriate means and provides the supports necessary to sustain that behavior (Quinn et al., 1998). A positive behavior support plan includes:

- Long- and short-term goals
- Prevention strategies
- Appropriate replacement skills
- Reinforcement for appropriate behavior
- Extinction or planned ignoring (no reinforcement for inappropriate behavior)
- An evaluation framework

At this point you're ready to set long- and short-term goals for Andrew. The positive behavior support team believes that their original long-term goal—to reduce his disruptive behavior so that he can learn and function in class—is still correct. The members decide that a short-term objective should be for him to learn to ask for help when he's confused or doesn't understand the assignment.

The next step is to figure out the strategies that will teach him how to get what he wants through appropriate means (O'Neill et al., 1997). There are three ways to accomplish this, and you should probably use them all: *prevention* (changing the environment so the student won't need the challenging behavior); *teaching replacement skills* (replacing the challenging behavior with appropriate behavior that achieves the same outcome for the child more quickly and with less effort); and *extinction* or *planned ignoring* (stopping reinforcement for inappropriate behavior by ignoring it as much as possible).

Prevention

Begin with the setting events if you can. The data show that Andrew has trouble settling down after recess, which precedes math, so the team asks you to try a calming activity—reading aloud to the class—as soon as the students reenter.

The next step is to change the antecedents. This usually involves changing the physical setup, the task, the materials, your instructional strategies or classroom procedures, and/or your approach to the student himself in order to eliminate opportunities for the challenging behavior to arise. Sometimes this is as simple as reminding the whole class of what behavior is appropriate before the activity begins or reassuring a particular student that you will provide any assistance he needs.

Because you've hypothesized that when Andrew is in a public situation he wants to avoid dealing with anything he finds confusing or hard to understand, you and the rest of the team decide to change your approach to new topics, taking a hint from Ms. Dalfen. You will prepare a written outline for the whole class and preteach any vocabulary or concepts that seem difficult. You will create a more interactive presentation that allows everyone to ask questions, and you will collect some concrete materials and texts on varying levels that students can use on their own. Like the calming activity, these changes will benefit Andrew and the rest of the class at the same time. Finally, you'll be sure to give Andrew extra help, both before and after you introduce the new topic. In the meantime, you will assess his skills to see exactly what you need to teach him. With these changes in place, Andrew will have more assistance, a better chance of understanding the new assignment, and less need to avoid it.

When the members of Ronnie's positive behavior support team examine their data, they see that although he seems to talk incessantly (see page 227), he has no academic problems. But whenever independent work is required he heads straight for his peers, asking them questions or trying to make them laugh. This behavior occurs very frequently, and the teacher often reprimands him. His parents report that he is the youngest of five children, and this is the way he acts at home—even if his siblings find him annoying, they always help him. As is so often the case with students with challenging behavior, Ronnie doesn't care whether the attention he gets is positive or negative, as long as he gets attention. But the team concludes that the function of his challenging behavior is to obtain the attention of his peers, and getting the teacher's attention is a bonus. To cut down on the amount of time that Ronnie spends working alone and to increase his appropriate contact with his classmates, the teacher agrees to shift to more partner and small-group assignments. She is especially eager to try peer tutoring for the whole class, a method where pairs of students take turns tutoring each other, because she believes Ronnie will excel at it.

In the meantime, the positive behavior support team for Jamal, who seems to be bugging his classmates constantly (page 227), discovers that he always manages to complete his work and performs especially well in science and gym, areas that require active physical participation. This observation leads the team members to hypothesize that he needs more stimulation, and they decide to make the class more interactive, with less quiet work time and more small group and partner activities. They also agree to loosen the procedures for getting a drink, sharpening a pencil, and going to the bathroom.

Teaching replacement skills

It is not enough to decide what the student must stop doing; you must also know what you want him to do instead—and what will satisfy him because it enables him to achieve the same results he obtained with his challenging behavior just as efficiently and effectively. If possible, choose a replacement behavior that utilizes skills he already has. You can prompt him to use it at times when the problem behavior usually occurs, and teach and reinforce it throughout the day.

It is difficult to change antecedents and find replacement behaviors for a student who is trying to avoid something. Does he find the task he's trying to escape too easy, too hard, too boring, too stimulating? Does he have to sit still for too long? Does he think no one will want to be his partner? You will probably have to use a variety of tactics and teach new social, cognitive, or physical skills, even if he isn't keen to learn them. "Remember that teaching is among the most powerful behavior management tools at our disposal," O'Neill and his colleagues write (1997, p. 74). Plan to start with skills the student can learn quickly and easily—it's important for him to experience as much success as possible as rapidly as possible so that he begins to build self-esteem. Sometimes we think that if we wait, the student will learn the skill when he's ready, but in fact he often becomes more convinced that he isn't capable of learning or that his classmates don't like him.

As you teach a new skill, give the student plenty of opportunities to use it and give yourself plenty of opportunities to reinforce it with words, body language, and activities he enjoys. Respond immediately to every attempt and approximation, especially in the beginning. To get rid of the old behavior, the new one has to be very successful indeed (Durand, 1990). It's also a good idea to teach these new skills as part of the daily routine—students will learn them more quickly and generalize them more readily if they learn them where they use them (Durand, 1990; Gable et al., 2000).

Andrew's support team decides to teach him an unobtrusive way to ask for assistance when he's confused so that he doesn't have to advertise the fact that he needs help. Together you will arrange a private signal, and whenever he asks for help appropriately, you will provide him with lots of positive reinforcement by promptly giving him the help he needs.

Ronnie's behavior support team has to find an appropriate way for him to get his peers' attention. They decide that a good replacement behavior is to allow him to tutor any student who still needs help after the class peer tutoring session is over. He seems able to explain things clearly, and the other students enjoy his company as much as he enjoys theirs. The team also agrees to urge him to sign up for drama, where his flair for performance and his very social nature will be appreciated.

Jamal needs a replacement behavior that will raise his stimulation level. His behavior support team decides to give him a variety of classroom jobs to do. His teacher will give him responsibility for running the overhead projector and keep a list of other tasks he can do whenever he feels the need to move around—watering the

Teaching new skills is one of the best ways to reduce problem behavior.

Prep Time

Students often use challenging behavior to escape from situations they don't have the skills to handle. They may want to avoid feeling frustrated, stupid, or confused, and they may worry that their peers (or the teacher!) will make fun of them. In *Beyond Functional Assessment* (2000), Joseph S. Kaplan suggests these questions to ponder as you and the rest of the behavior support team decide what to teach and how to teach it:

- Does the student know what's expected of him in this situation? Does he understand it? Are your expectations different from what's required at home?
- Does he know how to do what's expected?
- Does he know when to do what's expected?
- Does he have the self-control to do what's expected?
- Is he aware of his own behavior?
- Seen from the student's point of view, is there more to gain from the challenging behavior or from the appropriate behavior? (It's essential to make the appropriate behavior more rewarding!)
- Are the student's beliefs compatible with the appropriate behavior? For example, does he believe that he's capable of learning and performing the appropriate behavior? Does he believe that he can exert any influence on the situation? Does he believe the new behavior will get him what he wants? Some children may not even try to behave appropriately because they think they have no control over what happens to them.

plants, taking books back to the library, taking notes to the office, and so on. After he finishes his academic assignments, he will be allowed to use the computer, which he enjoys.

Extinction or planned ignoring

Your individualized behavior support plan should work on one additional front: It should help you stop rewarding the problem behavior. The way to do this is to ignore it. Called *extinction* or *planned ignoring*, this action is designed to show the student that the challenging behavior will not serve the function it used to—it will no longer get him what he wants (Durand, 1990; Mace and Roberts, 1993; O'Neill et al., 1997). Any time that you stop reinforcing challenging behavior, there will probably be an "extinction burst" (Durand, 1990, p. 152)—that is, the behavior will get worse. This is a well-known phenomenon, so be prepared, and don't let it discourage you.

Ignoring challenging behavior is not easy, and it is dangerous when someone could get hurt. The students' well-being comes first; therefore extinction must always take a back seat in hazardous situations. To deal with either physical or emotional aggression, try the next best thing—intervene to stop the aggression. But limit the attention you give to the student who attacked by standing with your back to him and cutting off all eye and physical contact (Durand, 1990). Tell him briefly, firmly, and clearly that this behavior is unacceptable—but only after you've attended to the child who's been targeted.

So how can you use extinction? The process is subtle. It doesn't work by itself but depends heavily on your prompt and positive recognition of appropriate replacement behavior that meets the student's needs. Keep your goal in mind and choose a method that's appropriate for the function of the behavior. If the function is for the student to avoid or escape a task or situation, the plan must prevent him from escaping. When Andrew is swearing and pushing over the furniture, remember that he is trying to avoid a task that he finds confusing or hard to understand, and you're trying to keep him in the classroom, on task, so that he can learn. Hang in there and continue what you're doing as if he were sitting and listening. He will get the message, "Your challenging behavior has no effect on me. I'll be happy to give you the help you need if you use appropriate behavior" (Durand, 1990, pp. 148–149). When you see a pause or an action that you can interpret as a tiny effort or an approximation of appropriate behavior on his part, give him some nonverbal positive reinforcement. As he regains control, quietly remind him that you'll help him when he uses your private signal.

Such situations can be tricky, and they require you to think on your feet and use all of the flexibility and ingenuity at your command. The solution may seem silly—he isn't really calm when he takes a breath—but it's close enough, and it works. He stops swearing, he doesn't avoid the task, he doesn't lose face—and neither do you. Needless to say, in order to perform such a maneuver you must stay calm and collected yourself!

On the other hand, if the function of the behavior is to obtain attention, then you must plan not to respond—not to come to his side, speak to him, or look at him when he behaves inappropriately—but provide attention when he is working, involved, raises his hand, or gets your attention in an acceptable manner. It will take time for him to realize that you are serious, so once again it's vital to remember to reinforce appropriate behavior and close approximations. If you are consistent, the student will discover that his challenging behavior isn't working, and as time goes by it will diminish in force and frequency. Because Ronnie is seeking attention from his peers, he may not care if you ignore him as long as his fellow students respond. But you will provide a role model for them, and eventually Ronnie may receive less reinforcement.

With Jamal, the behavior support team urges the teacher to increase her own tolerance of his movement around the classroom—to try to regard it as a physical need rather than a desire to disrupt learning. They advise her to use the impulse control techniques she teaches her students—breathing slowly, counting to 10 backwards—to help her stay calm. If she can resist responding to his perambulations, she can reduce the stimulation she provides and concentrate instead on making the environment more stimulating in legitimate ways.

If you follow your plan and implement your interventions consistently, you should soon see changes. Bear in mind that the student's history will play a role here: The longer he's used his challenging behavior and the more successful it's been for him, the harder it will be to change or eradicate it. Patience is therefore essential (Durand, 1993; O'Neill et al., 1997).

How does the plan look?

When you've figured out the function and carefully considered all three methods for helping the student fulfill his needs appropriately—preventing the behavior by changing the environment (especially the antecedents), replacing the challenging behavior with appropriate behavior, and ignoring challenging behaviors as much as possible—you are well on your way. Now revisit your goals and add some short-term objectives that you can measure (for example, Andrew will ask for help by using a private signal; he will be able to complete a new task), a time frame for reaching them, the methods you've decided to use, and who will be responsible for implementing them. Figure out all the details—what you'll say and do, what materials you'll need, and so on. O'Neill and his colleagues (1997) also recommend including a description of a typical routine and a description of how you'll handle the most difficult situations. Even when you're well prepared, the problem behavior can still occur, and clearly defined procedures ensure that everyone knows what to do and everyone does the same thing. Make sure that the family and all the staff agree and are ready to do their part. To succeed in the long run, a positive behavior support plan has to be acceptable to all of the people who will implement it and live with it: It has to be consistent with your values, skills, and resources. (For a summary of this entire process, see Figure 11.3.)

How do you evaluate the plan?

Decide how you'll measure your progress and set a date to get together to review it. After the behavior plan is in place, it's important to continue observing and recording the student's behavior, using the A-B-C chart, the functional assessment observation form, or the simpler method you used before you began the functional assessment. (Remember that bar graph you made? See page 224.) Depending on the nature of the challenging behavior, you can count the frequency or the duration (both of which should have diminished). You can also note and record increases in positive behavior, such as when the student:

- Copes better with transitions and new ideas
- More often asks appropriately for help or breaks
- Needs the help of the teacher less
- Initiates private time
- Works cooperatively with a partner
- Participates in small groups
- Has a friend
- Doesn't hit or throw furniture when he could have (Meyer and Evans, 1993)

Remember it can take up to six weeks to change a behavior that has worked for a child for many years. Even very small improvements indicate that you're on the right track.

If you notice no progress at all, you may need to go back to your data to look for a new hypothesis, new strategies, or a totally different slant. Dust off and reconsider your earlier hypotheses (perhaps Andrew wanted your attention after all, or perhaps he has too much stimulation). You might try to manipulate the antecedents in another way to see if that changes the student's behavior. Look at how well the team is adhering to the behavior support plan. It probably won't work if you aren't implementing it correctly and consistently. Positive behavior support is an ongoing, cyclical process in which you are constantly trying things out, getting new information, and revising your strategies in order to give the student a better quality of life.

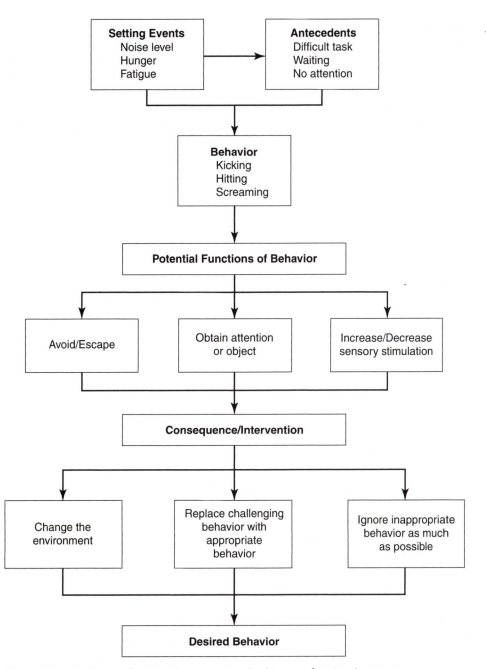

FIGURE 11.3   This diagram illustrates the process involved in using functional assessment to create a positive behavior support plan.

WHAT DO YOU THINK?

1. "Every challenging behavior can be thought of as a student's solution to a problem and a form of communication." What does this mean to you? Can you remember a time when you or someone you know used challenging behavior to communicate or to solve a problem? Why did you use this method? Did you lack the skills required to behave appropriately or did you choose the behavior intentionally? Why is inappropriate behavior sometimes more effective than appropriate behavior?

2. How does understanding that challenging behavior serves a function for the student affect your attitude toward him and his behavior? How does your attitude affect your ability to use an appropriate intervention?

3. What makes functional assessment and positive behavior support so effective?

4. The challenging behaviors of Andrew, Ronnie, and Jamal all have some common elements. How did their behavior support teams figure out the function of their behavior?

5. Look at the running A-B-C chart and the functional assessment observation form for Andrew (pages 307 to 309 and 313). Why was Tuesday a better day for him? Why is it important to look at the reasons for this difference?

WHAT WOULD YOU DO?

In small groups, think of an experience you've had with a child with challenging behavior. Try to figure out the function of the challenging behavior using either the running A-B-C chart (page 307) or the functional assessment observation form (page 313). Fill out the form from your recollection of what you saw in the classroom—bearing in mind that in a real situation accurate observations are essential. Formulate a hypothesis and make a positive behavior support plan. If you have the opportunity to observe a child with challenging behavior, use the information you collect to fill out the form, formulate a hypothesis, and create a positive behavior support plan.

SUGGESTED READINGS AND RESOURCES

Artesani, J. (2000). *Understanding the purpose of challenging behavior: A guide to conducting functional assessments.* Upper Saddle River, NJ: Prentice-Hall.

Chandler, L. K., & Dahlquist, C. M. (2005). *Functional assessment: Strategies to prevent and remediate challenging behavior in school settings* (2nd ed.). Upper Saddle River, NJ: Prentice-Hall.

Fox, L. (n.d.). *What works brief 10: Positive behavior support: An individualized approach for addressing challenging behavior.* Center for the Social Emotional Foundations for Early Learning. www.vanderbilt.edu/csefel/briefs/wwb10.pdf.

Freeman, R. (1990–2005). *Functional behavior assessment.* University of Kansas, Special Connections. www.specialconnections.ku.edu/cgi-bin/cgiwrap/speccon/main.php?cat=behavior&section=main.

Kaplan, J. S. (2000). *Beyond functional assessment: A social-cognitive approach to the evaluation of behavior problems in children and youth.* Austin, TX: Pro-Ed.

O'Neill, R. E., Horner, R. H., Albin, R. W., Sprague, J. R., Storey, K., & Newton, J. S. (1997). *Functional assessment and program development for problem behavior: A practical handbook.* Pacific Grove, CA: Brooks/Cole.

www.1edweb.com/fba%20forms.htm. This website offers a variety of forms that can be easily completed and printed.

CHAPTER 12

The Inclusive Classroom

These days you can take it for granted that you will have at least one student with a disability in your classroom.

The odds are that she'll have a learning disability—because almost half of the children who receive special education services in the United States have learning disabilities (U.S. Department of Education, Office of Special Education Programs, 2006) —but it's also possible that her condition will be a rare one, such as a visual impairment. The disability may be mild or severe, visible or invisible; and the child may spend all, most, or part of the school day with you and the other children. But even if she receives special instruction in a resource room or elsewhere several hours a week, this student is entitled to full membership in your classroom community, with all the rights and opportunities that entails.

Although this book isn't a special education text, we believe it's important to understand the benefits of an inclusive classroom, the philosophy behind it, and some of the issues that may arise. Knowing how to teach all students, including those with disabilities, will only make you a better teacher. This chapter is divided into two major parts. The first presents the philosophy and basic facts of inclusion; the second contains information about preventing and addressing challenging behavior in students with disabilities.

ABOUT INCLUSION

Ever since the early 1970s, when Congress passed the original version of what is now the *Individuals with Disabilities Education Act (IDEA)* and other civil rights legislation, children with disabilities have been taking their places alongside children without disabilities in classrooms across the nation. Reauthorized in 2004, the law views *inclusion* as the norm and gives all children, regardless of abilities, the right to participate actively in regular public and private schools in the community— the *natural environments* that they would attend if they were developing typically. These institutions have the obligation to provide all students with educational opportunities geared to their capabilities and needs, as well as the supports and services necessary for their success (Stainback and Stainback, 1996).

A child with disabilities is entitled to full membership in your classroom community, with all the rights and opportunities that entails.

Why is inclusion important?

Inclusion represents a basic American and human ethical value: equality. It is the same value the Supreme Court upheld in *Brown v. Board of Education* in 1954 when it threw out segregation in the schools and made integration the law of the land. Separate is not equal, the high court said; it is a form of discrimination with noxious effects, including isolation, a sense of inferiority, and slowed educational and mental development (Karagammis, Stainback, and Stainback, 1996).

Inclusion, on the other hand, "is about embracing everyone and making a commitment to provide each student in the community, each citizen in a democracy, with the inalienable right to belong," write Mary A. Falvey and Christine C. Givner (2005). "Inclusion is a belief system, not just a set of strategies; it is about an attitude and a disposition that a school intentionally teaches by example" (p. 5).

Inclusion enables children with disabilities to become part of the fabric of society and promotes appreciation and understanding of diversity among children without disabilities. Both groups acquire better academic and social skills and better preparation for living in the community (Holahan, 2000; Karagammis et al., 1996; Kochhar, West, and Taymans, 2000). Students who are typically developing are less likely to tease or reject their classmates with disabilities and more likely to value differences, develop their capacity for friendship, and accept and include individuals with disabilities as they grow up. Students with disabilities function better in a typical environment and are more likely to succeed in inclusive high schools and later life (Holahan, 2000; Villa and Thousand, 2005).

S pecialists in inclusion describe how one student with an emotional disability made the transition into a general education classroom (Sramek, Brewer, Seger, Huber, and West-pfahl, 2004).

When the time arrived for 10-year-old Corina to enter fourth grade, her special education teachers decided she was ready to move from a self-contained classroom into an inclusive class. With several years of behavioral programming under her belt, Corina usually knew how to handle her own emotional and behavioral needs, although she still sometimes ran into trouble with her peers in the halls and on the playground.

To prepare for the switch, the special and general education teachers sat down together to figure out how to adapt the strategies that had provided Corina with structure and super-vision in the self-contained classroom. They decided to use direct instruction to teach her the classroom rules and expectations, developed plans for proactively preventing situations that triggered problem behavior, and set up a system to facilitate communication between the two sets of teachers.

With ongoing consultation, Corina's inclusion became "a highly successful endeavor" (p. 51).

How does IDEA work?

The Individuals with Disabilities Education Act specifies that all children with disabilities have the right to a *free appropriate public education (FAPE)*, and its 1997 amendments make it clear that children with and without disabilities must be educated together in a regular, general education class—the *least restrictive environment (LRE)*. The school must provide whatever special education supports and related services a student needs to succeed, and it is only when—despite those full supports and services—the student is still unable to succeed that another placement can be considered (Individuals with Disabilities Education Act, 1997).

IDEA describes categories of disability that give children access to special education. These are:

- Learning disabilities
- Speech or language impairments
- Mental retardation (cognitive disabilities)
- Emotional disturbance (emotional and behavior disorders)
- Deafness/blindness (i.e., students who have both)
- Visual impairments
- Hearing impairments
- Orthopedic (physical) impairments
- Other health impairments
- Autism (autistic spectrum disorders or ASD)
- Traumatic brain injury
- Multiple disabilities
- Developmental delays

In 2005, about 6 million school-age children received special education services under IDEA (U.S. Department of Education, Office of Special Education Programs, 2006).

What's happening on the front lines?

Federal legislation mandates inclusion, along with regulations for putting it into effect, and Congress allocates a small percentage of the money to pay for it. But every community implements inclusion differently (Villa and Thousand, 2003). Each state and school district has policies, regulations, and resources of its own, and everything varies—funding, eligibility for services, the proportion of students with and without disabilities in the classroom, the amount of time they spend together, the way children's learning is assessed, the training for teachers, the kinds of support and services students and teachers receive, and so forth. Specialists are in short supply, and some communities have special education services in all schools, some in a few, and some in none (Klass and Costello, 2003). A special education teacher may act as a full-time co-teacher in a general education classroom, as a resource teacher who instructs children with disabilities directly in the classroom or a separate room, or as an itinerant teacher who appears at regular intervals and concentrates on teaching the general education teacher what she needs to know when she's alone in the classroom (Odom, 2000).

How is a child who needs special education identified?

Some children manage at home but can't seem to cope at school. As a teacher knowledgeable about child development, you may be the first to notice that a student requires extra help. In a national random sample of 510 families of children with disabilities, 40 percent credited a teacher with jump-starting their child's evaluation for special education (Johnson and Duffett, 2002). Although most children are identified by grade 3 (Johnson and Duffett, 2002), more than half of the referrals for emotional and behavioral disorders take place in grades 3 to 6. Almost three-quarters of these students are boys (Bauer and Brown, 2001).

Although you are in a prime position to spot problems and suggest a referral or an evaluation, you are not a doctor who is trained to make a medical diagnosis. Be careful not to share your suspicions about what's causing the difficulty (Austin, 2003; Friend, 2005), and remember that you cannot talk to the family's physician without a parent's written permission.

When you have concerns, it's important to observe the child carefully, accurately record what you see, compare her capabilities with those of her peers, and discuss the problem with the family and your colleagues. Think about your student's needs and look hard at what you're doing in class: Would she behave more appropriately if she had a different seat or a different partner? Would she understand the lesson more readily if you broke it down into smaller segments or reviewed the vocabulary before you begin? Would it help if you smiled at her more often or found more opportunities to speak with her privately? As you try out possible solutions, monitor her response carefully.

If your interventions don't seem to work, the next step is to alert the school's principal, psychologist, or *prereferral team* (also called a *screening committee*, a *child study*, *teacher assistance*, *intervention assistance*, or *instructional consultation team*). They will observe in the classroom, review the situation, and generate more ideas. A formal special education assessment under IDEA is in order only when their interventions fail.

M el Levine (2003) gives this example of how important an observant and well informed
teacher can be in spotting—and remediating—learning differences:

> Bruce was disruptive in most of his 7th grade classes. He fashioned himself as an enter-
> tainer and often disengaged from classroom activities. Mr. Jackson, a social studies teacher
> knowledgeable about early adolescent development and learning, made the astute obser-
> vation that Bruce often appeared confused about dates and about the sequences of events
> in the various historical periods that they studied. Mr. Jackson also noted that Bruce often
> looked distressed when given directions. . . .
>   [Bruce's] teacher suspected rightly that this boy was having problems processing se-
> quences—sequential directions, chains of events in history, and multi-step explanations.
> His weak temporal-sequential ordering accounted for his problems in social studies and in
> math. This insight enabled teachers to give Bruce strategies to manage his sequencing
> problems: taking notes, whispering sequences under his breath, and picturing sequences
> in his mind. His behavior and demeanor in class improved dramatically. (p. 18)

An interdisciplinary team (which includes at least one special education teacher, one general education teacher, and a representative of the school district) will carry out the formal evaluation, taking into consideration the student's history, observations by the family and the professionals who've worked with her, and several types of measurements in the language the child knows best (Friend, 2005). This process often includes a functional assessment. To preserve everyone's rights, the evaluation must be culturally appropriate and follow the rules of *due process*. Parents are full partners in this enterprise—they must consent and participate (U.S. Department of Education, Office of Special Education and Rehabilitative Services, 2000). If the parents don't want their child to receive special education services, they can refuse to have her evaluated, but you will continue to have responsibility for helping her to succeed.

If the team concludes that the student is eligible, the evaluation will become the basis for an *individual education program (IEP)* setting out measurable goals for the child for the next year and stipulating all the special education and related services, accommodations, modifications, and supports she must have to accomplish them. The IEP will also indicate how to measure her progress in the general education curriculum and how she will participate in state or district testing. If it's appropriate, the student has the right to take part in the IEP process (U.S. Department of Education, Office of Special Education and Rehabilitative Services, 2000).

The IDEA 1997 amendments called for short-term objectives or benchmarks that spelled out specific steps for reaching the goals in the IEP. Some states continue to provide them, but the 2004 reauthorization of IDEA eliminated them for most students (Council for Exceptional Children, 2004; Mandlawitz, 2005). Even though several states are beginning to try out new multiyear IEPs that can run for up to three years, the IEP team must review the IEP annually in time for the beginning of the school year (U.S. Department of Education, Office of Special Education and Rehabilitative Services, 2005).

Built-In Bias?

A disproportionate number of African American children wind up in special education: 13 percent, versus 9 percent of Whites in 2004 (National Center for Education Statistics, 2007). African American students are 43 percent more likely to receive special education services than their White counterparts. Especially high proportions were identified in the categories of emotional disturbance, cognitive disability, and developmental delay—categories that have the most subjective criteria for eligibility (U.S. Department of Education, Office of Special Education Programs, 2006). In some states, the learning disabilities group also contains a disproportionate number of African American and Latino American students (Donovan and Cross, 2002). In addition, African American children spent less of their school day in regular classrooms than European American children. All too often, the result is negative labeling (National Alliance of Black School Educators, 2002) and lower expectations (Delpit, 1992).

These figures have provoked a great deal of controversy—and soul-searching—in the special education community. Is bias built into the IDEA identification process and the education system itself? Are teachers' attitudes to blame as well?

Higher poverty rates among African Americans certainly contribute to the problem by increasing risk factors for disability, such as tobacco and alcohol exposure during pregnancy, poor nutrition and prenatal care, and lead exposure. But the disproportion remains even when these factors are taken into account (Oswald, Coutinho, and Best, 2002).

To correct the imbalance, experts are looking at alternative prereferral and assessment processes as well as more culturally sensitive curricula and teaching practices (Donovan and Cross, 2002).

Does IDEA include all disabilities?

The Individuals with Disabilities Education Act doesn't cover every disability. A notable exception is attention deficit hyperactivity disorder (ADHD), which may qualify in some states but usually falls under the wider umbrella of civil rights law. *Section 504* of the *Vocational Rehabilitation Act* of 1973 defines disability more broadly than IDEA and offers support and protection from discrimination to students with ADHD or any other physical or mental disability, impairment, or social maladjustment that limits their ability to learn in school (Hayes, n.d.). For instance, students with asthma, allergies, diabetes, or depression may qualify for assistance under Section 504.

The federal government doesn't help fund services for these students, and responsibility for determining eligibility falls on the school district. Teachers often make the initial referral; and a multidisciplinary committee that includes teachers who know the child will draw on a variety of sources to do the evaluation. Parents must give their consent and may participate in decision making. The team then develops a Section 504 or individual accommodation plan (IAP) (Smith, 2006), which, like an IEP under IDEA, must be reviewed periodically and can require a wide range of *accommodations*, including changes in the physical environment, schedule, and instruction. In addition, it can cover after-school and extracurricular activities (Friend and Bursuck, 2002). However, because there are fewer regulations governing a 504 plan, students may receive less assistance and less monitoring than they would under IDEA.

Can an IEP address behavior?

When a child with a disability has serious behavior problems, IDEA 1997 requires the IEP team to create a *behavior intervention plan,* or *BIP,* which immediately becomes part of the IEP. The law places clear limits on the use of punishments such as suspension and expulsion. Instead, the BIP, which is similar to a positive behavior support plan (described in Chapter 11), is intended to prevent behavior problems or catch them at an early stage. It must be based on a functional assessment, which enables the IEP team to identify the purpose or function of the student's challenging behavior; and it outlines individualized positive behavior supports and strategies for replacing inappropriate behavior with appropriate behavior (Bazelon Center for Mental Health Law, 2003). When special and general education teachers and everyone else who works with the child pitches in to develop the BIP and implement it consistently, it is more likely to be effective.

Any student with both a disability and challenging behavior can have a BIP, but children with *emotional and behavior disorders* (called *emotional disturbance* by IDEA) are more likely to need one. Although their behavior probably isn't so different from the behavior of other students, it tends to be more intense, more frequent, and more long lasting (Friend, 2005). The Individuals with Disabilities Education Act specifically excludes students who are *socially maladjusted* from qualifying for special education in this category—a controversial choice (Friend, 2005)—and as a result many children with emotional and behavior disorders aren't eligible. A student may qualify under Section 504 (Friend, 2005), but even if she doesn't, a team can still do a functional assessment and create a positive behavior support plan for her. (For a detailed look at functional assessment and positive behavior support, see Chapter 11.)

Who is responsible for implementing an IEP?

When it comes time to implement a child's IEP, Section 504 plan, or BIP, you (the classroom teacher) are in command. You'll probably have to sit down with your colleagues in special education to figure out any short-term objectives you'll need to reach the child's goals. Rather than mere pieces of paper, these plans are legally binding—but they should also be living documents that you refer to on a daily basis. If they aren't working, you can request a special review (U.S. Department of Education, Office of Special Education and Rehabilitative Services, 2000).

This whole process—from the day you first notice a child needs help until the day you hold her individualized plan in your hand—may take some time. Be prepared to wait.

PREVENTING AND ADDRESSING CHALLENGING BEHAVIOR IN CHILDREN WITH DISABILITIES

Successful inclusion relies on good teaching, and good teaching begins with the understanding that all children are special and every child learns in her own unique fashion. When you spend time thinking about the needs, abilities, interests, preferences, cultures, and learning profiles of each student and then make the program fit the child rather than the child fit the program, you will find ways for all students—with and without disabilities—to participate and succeed.

As you face an inclusive class for the first time, it's natural to feel scared and nervous. You may wonder whether you have the skills and knowledge necessary for this job; and if there haven't been many individuals with a disability in your life, you may feel uneasy about what to say and do. Because your students will take their cue from you, it's important to come to terms with those feelings. The self-reflection strategies in Chapter 5 will help. Talk with your family, close friends, and colleagues; write your thoughts, feelings, concerns, and ideas in a journal; read up on the disabilities of the students in your class; and learn as much as you can from their families. The bottom line is not to let the negative take over. Concentrate on thinking of each child as a child first, search out the many strengths she has within her, and build a relationship. Your direct engagement with her will enable her to succeed (Giangreco, 2003).

As you strive to create an environment that is highly accepting of differences, your attitude is crucial. If you feel that every child belongs in your classroom, that each one has a valuable contribution to make—and your words and actions explicitly foster that acceptance of diversity—you will create a caring community where all children feel connected and all can learn (Haager and Klingner, 2005; Peterson and Hittie, 2003).

Does a student's disability play a role in challenging behavior?

Children with disabilities frequently exhibit more behavior and social problems and are more likely to be rejected by their peers than children without disabilities (Haager and Vaughn, 1995; Odom, Zercher, Marquart, Sandall, and Wolfberg, 2002). And children with common or *high-incidence disabilities*—learning disabilities, speech or language impairments, mild cognitive disabilities, and emotional disturbance, as well as children with ADHD—are at particular risk.

Children's challenging behavior is often their disability talking. For example, a student with sequencing or processing difficulties or a speech impairment who has trouble expressing her needs in words may express them with inappropriate behavior instead. But it is important to remember that virtually all children with challenging behavior—not just those with disabilities—communicate through their behavior. For this reason, when a student with a disability is involved, everything that you know about addressing challenging behavior applies. All the tools at your

Double Disability

High-incidence disorders—which often come with behavior problems attached—tend to overlap, so children may wind up with more than one. You're likely to encounter these combinations:

- Learning disabilities and ADHD (Willicutt and Pennington, 2000)
- Emotional disturbance and ADHD (Handwerk and Marshall, 1998)
- Emotional disturbance and language disorders (Benner, Nelson, and Epstein, 2002)

disposal—a warm relationship with the child and the family; an inclusive social context and physical space; classroom procedures and teaching strategies that prevent challenging behavior; and effective techniques for responding to problem behavior, such as WEVAS, positive behavior support, and functional assessment—become useful, if not downright indispensable. You must make sure that these tools are sharpened, oiled, and in the best possible working order.

Prevention is always the best intervention, and Chapters 7 and 8 are full of ideas that will work for students with and without disabilities. In the pages that follow, we will briefly remind you about some of these methods and present some new ones.

Who can help?

Remember that you have some important allies in this venture. Families are number one, of course. Family plays a central role in the lives of all children, and children with disabilities above all. Perhaps this is because a child with disabilities depends on her family far more than a child without disabilities; and family members, in turn, are asked to give much more of themselves—in time, money, and physical and emotional energy—to help their child succeed. They know that second best won't do, so when it comes to education, the stakes for them and the child are sky high.

If they aren't already experts on their child's disability, they soon will be; and they are certainly experts on the child herself. Families can tell you what works and what doesn't, put you in touch with specialized resources, and raise awareness of disability by sharing information about their child's condition with you and your class (Grigal, 1998).

Most parents of students in special education award high marks to schools and teachers, according to a survey conducted by Public Agenda in 2002 (Johnson and Duffett, 2002). More than two-thirds think their child's school does a good or excellent job of giving their child the help she needs, 84 percent said the teacher really cares about their child as a person, and 77 percent feel treated like part of the team. On the other hand, about 40 percent agree that they have to "stay on top and fight to get the services their child needs" (p. 23).

Researchers Jeannie F. Lake and Bonnie S. Billingsley (2000) have found several causes of conflict between families and schools. They often hold different views of the child and her needs (for example, the family thinks the school focuses on the child's weaknesses rather than seeing her as an individual with unique strengths); and they may disagree about the delivery and quality of inclusion (for instance, the time, money, or personnel available to provide services).

What's most important, the researchers discovered, is trust. When parents and professionals trust one another, they manage to work through their differences. But when trust is broken, there are serious consequences for the child. Lacking confidence in the school's efforts and recommendations, parents ask for new school placements and use the mediation and due process hearings available to them under IDEA.

To establish a trusting relationship with families, it is helpful to keep a positive tone but talk with parents honestly and often; explain how the system works; ask what they need and prefer for their child and what their dreams are; if they're unhappy, ask why; welcome their questions and search out the answers when you don't have them; and listen carefully to what they have to say. If you expect families to value and respect your concerns, you must value and respect theirs. Use your best problem-solving skills, try to match your strategies and resources to what the family desires, and follow through on anything you undertake to do. By supporting the family, you are supporting the child. (For more about working with families, see Chapters 5 and 13.)

Your colleagues will also supply invaluable assistance. In fact, school districts across the country report that collaboration is a key to successful inclusion (Janney and Snell, 1997; Villa and Thousand, 2003). Good collaboration takes effort. Historically, classroom and special education teachers come from different traditions (Friend and Bursuck, 2002; Grigal, 1998). General education teachers usually focus on preparing content and activities for the whole group rather than for individuals (Janney and Snell, 1997), whereas special education teachers begin with objectives and proceed by selecting and organizing step-by-step procedures that will move a particular student closer to those objectives (Janney and Snell, 1997). But these lines between specialties are blurring as all teachers have more opportunities to expand their expertise and share responsibility for students.

Collaboration requires teachers to respect others' beliefs, examine their own, and treat one another as equals who are making a valuable contribution to the success of all students in the classroom (not "yours" and "mine"). It's essential to plan together, clarify how you'll handle procedures and discipline, and talk about problems and disagreements before they get out of hand (Friend and Bursuck, 2002). With time, determination, and conscious planning, you can become a smoothly functioning team who trust and respect each other, share goals and expectations, and communicate and solve problems effectively.

Inclusion experts Richard A. Villa and Jacqueline S. Thousand (2003) describe several ways that general and special education teachers can work together:

- *Consultant.* The special education teacher and the other support personnel (such as the psychologist) help the general education teacher so that she can teach all of the students.

Help Appreciated

Even though Ms. Price had 25 years of teaching experience, she worried about what her fourth-graders were learning this year. Out of 28 children, 7 had been identified with special needs ranging from autism to ADHD, and some had behavior issues. In her inner-city school, where resources were limited, she felt lucky to have the support of a paraprofessional every afternoon and a special education teacher who worked with the whole class three mornings a week. The children looked forward to the days when Ms. Hernandez came. She radiated calm and never got rattled when Ivan screamed or Zoe tried to leave the room.

Although Ms. Price knew that she lacked the skills of the special education teacher, she tried hard to follow Ms. Hernandez's example. Little by little, as she watched her colleague at work and attended professional development workshops on inclusion, she found herself learning what to do and gaining confidence in her ability to do it.

- *Parallel teaching.* The special education teacher, the support personnel, and the classroom teacher rotate among small heterogeneous groups in the classroom.
- *Supportive teaching.* The general education teacher takes the lead role, and the other staff circulate among the students.
- *Complementary teaching.* The support people complement instruction by clarifying, illustrating, paraphrasing, and so on.
- *Co-teaching.* All teachers share responsibility for delivering content, guiding learning, and addressing behavior.

Paraprofessionals are also important members of the classroom team. They go by many names—*paraeducator, paraprofessional, teaching assistant, instructional assistant, educational assistant, one-to-one assistant, therapy assistant, coach.* When an IEP calls for it, you are entitled to have their support. Working under your supervision, paraprofessionals do all kinds of things to make classroom life easier, such as lead small-group instruction, facilitate interaction between children, and assist with personal care and class assignments (French, 1999).

Paraprofessionals may be assigned to one student with a disability, but they should not assume primary responsibility for teaching her—that is your job (Giangreco, 2003). What works best, researchers have found, is when a paraprofessional helps with the whole group. Then students with disabilities interact more with their peers, feel less isolated and stigmatized, and receive more competent instruction (Giangreco, Edelman, Luiselli, and MacFarland, 1997). Ideally, a stranger walking into the classroom shouldn't be able to tell which student is assigned to the teaching assistant.

Here are some tips for working with a paraprofessional (Cook, Klein, and Tessier, 2004; Giangreco, 2003; Lehmann, 2004):

- Carefully decide what you want the paraeducator in your class to do, and give her professional plans to follow. Meet at least once a week to go over these plans and deal with any problems—people work better when they know what's expected of them, as well as why, when, and how.
- Get to know her. Find out about her special skills, talents, training, and what she knows about the children, and use this information to assign her appropriate tasks. Provide training if necessary.
- Supervise her work supportively, giving her specific and timely feedback, asking for her ideas and comments, and letting her know you appreciate her help.
- Share your inclusion and guidance philosophy with her so that you can back each other up in the classroom. Discuss any disagreement outside of the children's hearing, and don't criticize or embarrass her in front of others.
- Develop ways to communicate without speaking.
- Debrief at the end of the day. What worked, what didn't, and why?

The more planning you and your various collaborators can do, the more effective your strategies are likely to be. It's best if your schedule includes a regular time to get together, but if necessary you can squeeze meetings into lunch hours, breaks, or even fit them in before or after school. Solid cooperative relationships with families and colleagues can make a huge difference to your success and your feelings about your work. And when everyone is working toward the same goals and using the same strategies, the student is more likely to thrive.

How can an inclusive social context prevent challenging behavior?

A positive, accepting classroom climate can go a long way toward preventing challenging behavior. Diane Haager and Janette K. Klingner (2005) observe that strong classroom communities have these characteristics:

- There are clear expectations that all children will participate, and there are natural, fluid supports to enable that to happen.
- Students appreciate diversity and understand that they all differ in learning styles and abilities. There is no stigma attached to difference.
- Students help one another learn and feel accountable for both themselves and others.
- Teachers use positive behavior support and emphasize children's strengths and progress.
- Classrooms are child centered. Teachers consider students' interests in their planning and give children the opportunity to make choices and direct their own learning.

Develop sensitivity

Some of your students may never have met a person with a disability. An atmosphere of understanding, cooperation, and support can help all the children feel they belong. Without isolating anyone in the class, explain that a disability doesn't define a person but is only a part of who she is—we are all different in some way. There are several types of disability, some visible (because the child uses a wheelchair, a hearing aid, or sign language, for example) and some invisible (because you can't see a learning disability, an emotional disorder, or ADHD).

With the permission of your students with a disability, ask the members of the class what they know about disability, what they've experienced, and what they think. A student with a disability may want to tell them about her experiences as well. Work together to create guidelines that will help everyone feel at ease and assist one another—for example, focus on each child's strengths (what she can do rather than what she can't do) and allow each child to be the judge of her own capabilities (Karten, 2005).

You can help students understand what the world is like for a person with a disability by scheduling a special day of activities: Ask them to use their nondominant hand to do their written work, complete 10 difficult math problems in an unreasonable amount of time, take a quiz on material they hear in a different language on a tape, and read sentences with reversed and misplaced letters. Leave plenty of time to discuss their feelings and thoughts about this experience (Karten, 2005).

Teach values directly

One way to help the students in your classroom learn to respect and care for one another is to teach them that this behavior matters to you. When you model it yourself, they are more likely to understand what you mean and follow your example. At the same time, teach caring values explicitly by making them part of the curriculum—talk about caring for others and respecting differences as you and the class draw up and follow the class rules; read and discuss books about friendship and books about diversity of all kinds, including disability, culture and ethnicity, social

Louise Derman-Sparks (2006), the mother of antibias education, writes that the underlying intent of antibias education is "to foster the development of children and adults who have the personal strength, critical-thinking ability, and activist skills to work with others to build caring, just, diverse communities and societies for all." She puts forth these goals:

- *Goal 1:* Nurture each child's construction of a knowledgeable, confident self-concept and group identity.
- *Goal 2:* Promote each child's comfortable, empathic interaction with people from diverse backgrounds.
- *Goal 3:* Foster each child's critical thinking about bias.
- *Goal 4:* Cultivate each child's ability to stand up for her/himself and for others in the face of bias. (p. 5)

and economic class, and gender; sing songs such as "That's What Friends Are For" (Salend, 1999); and use an antibias curriculum (Odom et al., 2002). Whatever you're teaching, take every chance to explore, emphasize, and demonstrate inclusive values.

Normalize and include in every possible way

William A. Corsaro (1988), a sociologist who studies children's culture, suggests that children see themselves as members of a group because they are always doing things together. To them, those who don't participate—who ride a different bus, sit on a special chair, leave the room for special instruction—are part of an out-group (Diamond and Stacey, 2002). To minimize this effect, give everyone a special chair; turn therapy into an activity for the whole class; and alter activities to enable every child to take part. *Differentiated instruction* and *activity-based intervention* work very well to make everyone part of the group by expecting each student to choose materials and activities that suit her as an individual and by integrating special teaching seamlessly into lessons, routines, and activities.

Many students with disabilities or challenging behavior do better in a one-on-one situation with an adult (DuPaul and Stoner, 2003), but to avoid singling them out, be sure that special education teachers, therapists, paraprofessionals, and parents who help in the classroom spend their time with many children.

Create opportunities for interaction and friendship

Students with challenging behavior can learn appropriate behavior and social skills—and make friends—by spending time with their more socially accomplished peers. Because it's fun to be with others, this learning is automatically self-reinforcing (Odom et al., 2002). But children with disabilities sometimes need extra help getting together with children who don't usually choose them as partners (Odom et al., 2002).

You can create opportunities for interaction by enhancing *natural supports* and encouraging all the children to assist one another (Bauer and Matuszek, 2001). For example, place students who are more and less skilled together in pairs or small groups for structured or unstructured activities and assignments. Or appoint a child who is socially adept as the special buddy of a child who needs help getting along with others. Teach her how to read the communication cues of her partner and how

Children learn appropriate behavior and social skills—and make friends—by spending time with
more socially accomplished peers.

to engage her in interaction (Cook et al., 2004), then invent opportunities for them
to be together, such as during transitions and doing classroom jobs. Or help students
create a *circle of support,* where a few children volunteer to help one child on a regular basis. For a student with autistic spectrum disorder (ASD) who responds well
to the company of other children, volunteers can learn to relate to her as a friend—
to call her by name, invite her to join them, ask for her help, or offer their own
(Strain and Danko, 1995).

Keep in mind that peer-teaching strategies—cooperative group learning, partner
learning, peer tutoring, group projects, and cooperative activities—serve an important social purpose as well as an academic one, and employ them as often as possible. When students are working with computers or other equipment they could
operate alone, use their shared interests to entice them to collaborate, and create situations where they must share or pass on materials. Be sure to positively reinforce
every student's efforts to help, share, and communicate.

Teach social and emotional skills

When children's social and emotional skills improve, their interactions improve—
and vice versa. We can help students develop the emotional skills that underlie social competence—such as empathy, impulse control, anger management, and
problem solving—by teaching them proactively through direct instruction, role-
play, practice, prompting, and reinforcement (Guetzloe and Johns, 2004). (For more
about teaching social and emotional skills, see pages 135 to 148.)

Classwide peer tutoring can bolster the social standing of students with learning disabilities, researchers have found. Douglas Fuchs and his colleagues (Fuchs, Fuchs, Mathes, and Martinez, 2002) taught teachers and students in grades 2 to 6 in suburban schools to use Peer-Assisted Learning Strategies (PALS), a technique that pairs up struggling readers and higher-achieving peers to read to one another and give each other feedback on a regular basis.

In classrooms that used PALS, students with learning disabilities enjoyed the same social standing as their peers without disabilities. But in classrooms without PALS, their social status was lower. The students who used PALS also made greater strides in their reading.

Share responsibility

Sharing responsibility also strengthens the group's sense of community. Students can take care of the classroom, make decisions about rules and procedures, and participate in class meetings where they organize the agenda and learn to consider everyone's point of view as they resolve problems and conflicts. They can also assume responsibility for their own learning by selecting topics to investigate, setting their own learning goals, and keeping track of their own work.

How can you organize the physical space to prevent challenging behavior?

An inclusive class provides you with an opportunity to look at your space in a new way. Since the message you're trying to convey is acceptance, everything in the room should support that view of the world. Keep the child with a disability in mind as you organize, but don't let the final arrangement put her in the spotlight.

Children with disabilities should be in the thick of things, with full access to the teacher and their peers, not off to the side with a paraprofessional (Giangreco, 2003). It's especially important to seat a child with behavior problems near where you'll be teaching—in the center of the class, in the middle row, at the center of a semicircle (Guetzloe and Johns, 2004).

Keep the aisles wide enough for traffic of all kinds (including a wheelchair) to circulate freely (Bauer and Matuszek, 2001), and remember to create a comfortable, quiet area where a child who has trouble concentrating can work without distraction (Grigal, 1998). If you have space, include several study carrels so that anyone can use them, not just the students with disabilities.

How can classroom routines and teaching strategies prevent challenging behavior?

Predictability, individualization, and good teaching are critical when it comes to preventing challenging behavior.

Make the day predictable

Children with and without disabilities find it easier to behave appropriately when they know what to expect and what is expected of them. Structure and consistency help them feel safe. It is therefore essential to make what happens in your classroom as predictable as possible. Work out a schedule and post it prominently in words and pictures for all to see. For a child with ASD and others who need more help, create a personal picture album of the schedule so they can refer to it throughout the day.

Tactics such as developing class rules, teaching procedures and routines, and utilizing these tools consistently also furnish students with a sense of security that makes challenging behavior less necessary. For a child who finds transitions especially hard, give a personal warning of upcoming changes and use gentle physical support—lead her or show her how to clean up and begin the next activity (Kostelnik, Onaga, Rohde, and Whiren, 2002). Because a child with ASD needs extra assistance with anything new, prepare for schedule changes by rehearsing the activity and going over unfamiliar materials with her ahead of time (Koegel and Koegel, 1995).

Implement the IEP

An IEP is mostly about instruction. It describes (and at the same time prescribes) specific ways to help a particular child learn the core general education curriculum. It provides for the assistance of:

- *Personal supports*, such as a special education teacher, a paraprofessional, peers, and related services staff (e.g., a speech and language therapist or a psychologist)
- *Instructional and assistive technology*, such as computers, ramps, speech output devices, and the like
- *Accommodations and modifications* (Fisher and Kennedy, 2001)

Personal support staff bring their expertise with them into the classroom, and they can probably help you learn about the instructional and assistive technologies your students are entitled to have. (Families may contribute useful information on these topics as well.) Special education teachers are also in the know about accommodations and modifications, but it's important for classroom teachers to understand these techniques, too. The more tools you have in your toolbox, the more flexible, creative, and accessible your lessons can become.

Although IDEA and its regulations don't actually define accommodations and modifications, educators usually agree about their meaning (Families and Advocates Partnership for Education [FAPE], 2001). According to Douglas Fisher and Craig H. Kennedy (2001), an *accommodation* is "a change made to the teaching or testing procedures to provide a student with access to information and to create an equal opportunity to demonstrate knowledge and skills" (p. 54). An accommodation can change the timing, formatting, setting, scheduling, and/or presentation of an assignment or test, but it doesn't alter what it's measuring in any significant way (FAPE, 2001). When a student uses a calculator to do her math or listens to a book on an audiotape while she reads along, that is an accommodation. A *modification* is a change in what the student is supposed to learn and/or demonstrate—for example, when she has fewer math problems to do or when she's responsible for key aspects of the assignment, not for the whole thing (Fisher and Kennedy, 2001).

Every accommodation and modification should maximize the child's chances to succeed and should also be as inclusive and unobtrusive as possible. Each state has its own list of approved accommodations and modifications.

When students with learning disabilities first appeared in her classroom, sixth-grade science teacher Janice Robertson (2002) made some changes in her teaching practices to facilitate their learning. It didn't take long for the rest of her students to clamor for these adaptations, too. Among other items, Robertson created:

- A list of vocabulary terms and definitions for each unit
- A visual form of her oral instruction by writing on the board as she spoke, thereby supporting students with visual strengths
- A master workbook containing all the class's worksheets and a typed version of the notes she wrote on the board. Always available in the classroom, the master workbook helped students figure out how to arrange their own notebooks and fill in material they missed when they were absent

Says Robertson, the changes "have made me a better teacher and benefited *all* my students."

Differentiate instruction and use cooperative learning

As general and special education teachers work together in an inclusive classroom, their thinking and techniques begin to converge. Their styles mesh particularly well in differentiated instruction and cooperative learning—two methods that assume that children come to school with different abilities, outlooks, interests, and skills and make the specialized techniques of special education an integral part of the preparation process. At the same time, both methods offer a variety of ways for students to acquire information and ideas, make sense of what they're learning, and show what they've learned (Tomlinson, 2001; Wormeli, 2006). Differentiated instruction and cooperative learning enable students of all abilities to participate actively in learning without being isolated from the group—and they prevent challenging behavior because children who are fully engaged are less likely to need it.

Both techniques require a lot of planning, the use of multiple teaching strategies and materials, a firm grasp of the content you're teaching, and unwavering attention to the children themselves. They also call for *flexible, mixed-ability grouping*—creating and changing groups to meet children's needs—that doesn't stigmatize low-achieving students, dampen their motivation, or allow them to lag further behind. Haager and Klingner (2005) suggest several ways to group: by type of task or activity, student interest, need to develop a particular skill, complementary work habits, prior knowledge of content (those who already know the material can be together or spread out in different groups to act as experts), prior knowledge of strategies, social skills (more skilled students can help less skilled), or even randomly. Groups can use the same materials, different materials on a similar theme, materials on different topics within a theme, or materials on different themes.

Service learning

When students participate in service programs, which promote learning through active involvement in service experiences and extend it beyond the classroom into the community, both the students and the community win (Muscott, 2004). In fact,

Research shows that many students—especially those with learning disabilities—learn more easily when their teacher uses a technique called *direct instruction* (Friend and Bursuck, 2002, p. 139). Nancy Mather and Sam Goldstein (2001) outline six key elements:

1. Present lessons in a well-organized, sequenced manner.
2. Begin lessons with a short review of previously learned skills necessary to begin the lesson.
3. Begin lessons with a short statement of goals. Provide clear, concise explanations and illustrations of what is to be learned.
4. Present new material in small steps with practice and demonstrations at each step. Provide initial guidance through practice activities.
5. Provide students with frequent opportunities to practice and generalize skills.
6. Ask questions to check students' understanding, and obtain responses from everyone. (p. 146)

service learning—now common in many schools across the country—is an effective way to teach students with emotional and behavioral disorders. By building on their strengths, interests, skills, and knowledge, providing real-life opportunities to take responsibility, and making reflection an integral part of the process, service learning boosts academic achievement, social and personal responsibility, social development, and self-esteem, whether students are coordinating recycling programs, gardening, or reading to a kindergarten class (Muscott, 2004).

Adapt assessment

If a student can't perform at assessment time, the efforts you've made to help her feel valued and capable in day-to-day activities can fall apart in an instant. Her self-esteem will drop, her level of frustration will rise, and she will lose interest in the class, confidence in herself, and trust in you as a teacher. All of this may well lead to challenging behavior. It is therefore essential to accommodate and modify assessment procedures so that every student can experience success.

Because assessment provides information about what and how to teach, try to monitor and assess learning throughout a unit and in many different ways (Onosko and Jorgensen, 1998)—class discussions, oral quizzes, quick reviews at the beginning or end of a lesson, or in-class writing activities, to name a few. When students keep portfolios of their work over time, you can easily observe their progress; and projects or performances at the end of a unit also show what they've learned. In *Inclusion Strategies that Work*, Toby J. Karten (2005) lists these possibilities for assessment:

- Create a play or short video
- Compose a poem
- Make a cartoon
- Create a PowerPoint
- Perform a dance
- Keep a learning log
- Work on a group project
- Teach it to another student
- Do a written report

Inside your own classroom, it's important to accommodate and modify assessment procedures so that every student can experience success. Without these adaptations, the efforts you've made to help every student feel valued and capable in day-to-day activities can fall apart in an instant.

- Give a speech
- Teach a class lesson
- Interview people about the topic
- Write a newspaper article
- Compile a scrapbook
- Create a timeline of important events (p. 277)

Even in a conventional testing situation, there are numerous ways to accommodate a student's needs and test her abilities, not her disabilities. You can give an untimed test or extra time to complete a test, give the test in several sessions or with frequent breaks, or give it at a different time of day; it can take place in a small-group setting, a study carrel, or a quiet room; a student can have the help of a reader or an audiotape to hear the questions instead of reading them herself; the reader can repeat or paraphrase the instructions in simpler language; a student can give answers orally to a scribe or write them with a word processor. Remember what you're measuring. If it's the understanding of a concept and not the student's reading skill, accommodation can be easy.

Measure for Measure

Increasingly, schools are demanding measurement of student progress that's based on evidence, not feelings or impressions. In *curriculum-based assessment (CBA)* and *curriculum-based measurement (CBM)*, teachers use brief, frequent, standard tests to measure how well students are learning the material they've taught in class. The results help them make informed decisions about future instruction (Friend and Bursuck, 2002; Haager and Klingner, 2005).

Schools are also adopting the evidence-based technique called *response to intervention (RTI)*. Used schoolwide to screen students and prevent those who are struggling from falling behind, RTI is also an alternative means of identifying students with learning disabilities (Cortiella, 2006; Friend and Bursuck, 2002). The method uses short, periodic assessments to flag difficulties and monitor progress over time, providing extra, intensive intervention for students who need more help. If they don't respond adequately to supplemental small group or individualized instruction, they may be considered as having a learning disability that makes them eligible for IDEA (Cortiella, 2006; Friend and Bursuck, 2002).

Students with invisible disabilities may be more embarrassed and anxious about taking advantage of such adaptations than students with visible disabilities. A cooperative and caring classroom community will prevent them from feeling isolated and enable each student to use the supports she needs to perform effectively.

Note that even though accommodations and modifications sound a lot alike, there's an important difference between them where state- and districtwide testing is concerned. Under IDEA 2004, modifications are now called *alternative assessments*, and there are new rules governing their use ("Accommodations," 2006; Cortiella, 2005). Before you arrange accommodations or alternate assessments for formal or high-stakes tests, check whether your state department of education will accept the results.

How can you respond effectively to challenging behavior?

Even when teachers use preventive methods consistently, challenging behavior doesn't disappear completely. But if you've done your homework—read the student's file and talked with her family and your colleagues—you can address her behavior effectively. Remember that the basis for all guidance is a caring relationship. When you understand a student's feelings, preferences, and triggers, you can help her learn appropriate behaviors that allow her to do her best. At the same time, when she knows you care about her and support her, she'll come to trust you and respond more positively to whatever you're teaching.

A variety of theoretical perspectives, including humanistic and psychoanalytic thought, social learning theory, and behaviorist theory, underlie the most widely used guidance strategies. If you have several to draw on, you can choose one or a combination that suits the circumstances. *Positive reinforcement,* perhaps the most basic strategy of all, encourages appropriate behavior, and *natural consequences* enable children to learn by experiencing the consequences of their own actions. By and large, educators frown on the use of time-out and other forms of punishment, which undermine the teacher–student relationship. These strategies are discussed in detail in Chapter 9.

WEVAS (*Working Effectively with Violent and Aggressive States*) (Butchard and Spencler, 2000), a research-based intervention program that originated in Canada, emphasizes the importance of the teacher's reactions to a student's emotions and behavior and provides techniques for matching adult responses with children's needs. Chapter 10 is devoted to this method.

Severe or persistent challenging behavior calls for an intervention that is custom made for the child. Recent research and best practice suggest two closely linked strategies, *functional assessment* and *positive behavior support*. The Individuals with Disabilities Education Act counsels their use whenever a student needs a *behavior intervention plan (BIP)* as part of her IEP. Functional assessment (sometimes called *functional behavioral assessment*) provides the means for figuring out the purpose or function of the challenging behavior and guides the IEP team in designing an intervention using positive behavior support. A comprehensive approach, PBS promotes appropriate behavior at the same time that it prevents and minimizes challenging behavior (Fox, Dunlap, Hemmeter, Joseph, and Strain, 2003; Sandall and Schwartz, 2002). For a full description of these techniques, see Chapter 11.

Okay, Michael

The Beach Center on Families and Disabilities (n.d.) at the University of Kansas tells the story of Michael, who joined his peers as a fully included student for the first time in grade 7.

As Michael struggled with the transition—more difficult schoolwork, changing teachers and classes, making new friends—his frustrations ballooned out of control. Concerned about his severe and frequent outbursts, his family, peers, teachers, and other school staff got together to review the situation. A functional assessment revealed that Michael's explosions were precipitated by boredom or confusion about what to do, and Michael usually gave a clear warning that an eruption was on its way: He stretched or yawned.

The team proposed a positive behavior support plan that built on Michael's strengths and allowed him to meet his sensory needs—he could pass out papers in the classroom (which would also allow him to talk with his classmates), help the staff care for sports equipment and set up the cafeteria, and take walks when he needed a break.

The team also developed a handbook to help others give Michael the support he needed. It described his sensory needs, learning style, and classroom strategies that worked for him—having visual schedules, hearing and seeing instructions several times, sitting at the rear of the classroom to minimize distraction. And the handbook emphasized that the word *okay* had special meaning for Michael: It told him that his ideas and requests had been understood and gave him closure on a topic.

Eager to be accepted, Michael often acted inappropriately around his peers, and the positive behavior support plan addressed this problem, too. It created a *circle of friends*, an organized friendship network that provided him with a chance to interact with his peers, a model for appropriate behavior, and friends who offered guidance.

With these supports, Michael seldom got beyond the yawning stage. He learned to calm himself by taking deep breaths or asking for a break; and he made the honor roll, received a citizenship award, and started thinking about college.

Additions to the toolbox

Here are a few more ideas for addressing challenging behavior.

- Know what the student does well and build on her strengths—they offer opportunities for her to succeed.
- Be aware of your buttons, and don't let students push them. Remember that when you get angry, raise your voice, or lose control, you are modeling the very behavior you are trying to eliminate.
- When you want to redirect a child's inappropriate behavior, call her by name to capture her attention.
- Tell students what to do, not what *not* to do—for example, say, "Please walk" rather than "Don't run." This information will help them know what's appropriate.
- Collaborate with a child who loses control easily, and establish simple visual cues to remind her of what she's supposed to do. Before she gets too worked up, move close, make eye contact, and use your prearranged signal—nod, wink, pull on your ear, scratch your head (Cook et al., 2004).
- Children need the opportunity to choose, but you also need to know how many choices each child can handle.
- After an outburst or when students are stressed, they sometimes find it calming to do small motor tasks, such as counting or manipulating worry beads or squeezing a small ball. It's a good idea to give them some time and space before you call on them or draw attention to them in any way.
- Teach students to reward themselves with self-talk (e.g., "You finished writing your story today. How do you feel about that?"). This encourages them to think positively about themselves (ERIC Clearinghouse on Disabilities and Gifted Education, 1998).
- Be patient. Look for small changes—they tell you whether you're on the right track and keep you from getting discouraged.

W HAT DO YOU THINK?

1. What do you think are the benefits of inclusion? How will you help students with and without disabilities take advantage of being together in your class?
2. What steps will you follow when you realize there is a student with a possible learning disability in your class? What is the role of parents as IDEA sees it, and how will you get them involved? What if there is resistance?
3. Imagine you have a child with ADHD in your class. What strategies would you use to prevent

challenging behavior? (Chapter 8 may help you to answer this question.)

4. Knowing that it is important to differentiate instruction when you have a class that includes children with disabilities, how will you fairly evaluate the learning of all the students in your class, including those with disabilities, during both regular classroom activities and high-stakes tests?
5. Should your response to challenging behavior in a student with a disability be different from your response to challenging behavior in a student without a disability? Why or why not?

WHAT WOULD YOU DO?

It was the week before school started, and Ms. Porter was organizing her sixth-grade classroom when the principal called her into his office. Tim, a new student with a disability, had been added to her class list.

After difficult experiences in two other schools, Tim had just moved into the neighborhood. The IDEA assessment team at his previous school had evaluated him as having an *emotional disturbance* (sometimes called an *emotional and behavior disorder*), making him eligible for special education services.

The principal asked Ms. Porter to read Tim's file in the next day or two. He had scheduled a meeting for her with Tim's parents and the paraprofessional who would be working with Tim.

The file was at least 2 inches thick. As Ms. Porter went over it, she discovered that Tim had been having trouble in school since second grade. In third grade,

because he was constantly losing his temper, arguing, going out of his way to annoy his peers, and refusing to comply with his teacher's requests, he had been diagnosed with *oppositional defiant disorder (ODD)*. By grade 5, ADHD had been added to his diagnosis. His grades were very poor, except in gym and art.

Tim's best year was grade 4. He drew illustrations for the class newsletter and played on the basketball team. Noting that he was athletic, his teacher had arranged for him to participate in an after-school sports program.

How will you prepare for the meeting with Tim's parents and the paraprofessional? What changes, if any, will you make in the setup of your room or your teaching strategies to accommodate Tim? What role will the paraprofessional play in the classroom?

SUGGESTED READINGS AND RESOURCES

Karten, T. J. (2005). *Inclusion strategies that work: Research-based methods for the classroom*. Thousand Oaks, CA: Sage.

Kennedy, C. H., & Fisher, D. (2001). *Inclusive middle schools*. Baltimore: Brookes.

Rief, S. F. (2005). *How to reach and teach children with ADD/ADHD: Practical techniques, strategies, and interventions*. New York: Wiley.

Sapon-Shevin, M. (1999). *Because we can change the world: A practical guide to building cooperative, inclusive classroom communities*. Boston: Allyn & Bacon.

U.S. Department of Education, Office for Civil Rights. (2005). *Protecting students with disabilities*. www.ed.gov/about/offices/list/ocr/504faq.html.

CHAPTER 13

Working with Families and Other Experts

Even when you know that the causes of challenging behavior are complex, it's sometimes tempting to put all the blame on a student's family. Perhaps they don't seem interested in their child's school experience, or your encounters with them are critical or combative in tone. But families are not the enemy. On the contrary: They are on your side. Even though it might not appear that way to you, they love their child and want to help him. Creating a partnership with them is definitely the best strategy.

In Chapter 5 we described how to establish a relationship with families. We can't emphasize enough the importance of making this connection promptly—before difficulties arise. When you know that a student has struggled in the past, it's wise to begin connecting with his family as soon as possible. If your first contact with parents is to report a problem, they will probably become defensive.

In this chapter we discuss the process of working with families after challenging behavior has begun to appear. There are three main sections: "Preparing to Meet the Family," "Meeting with the Family," and "Working with Other Experts."

PREPARING TO MEET THE FAMILY

Connecting with a family is important with any child, but it's especially important where challenging behavior is concerned. It's simply too hard to understand and manage behavior problems effectively in a vacuum. Families know their child best, and their insight and collaboration can be invaluable. They can tell you about their lives and their culture—family roles and responsibilities, origin, support network, patterns of authority—and about such stress factors as illness, divorce, gang activity, and money problems. They can tell you about the child's developmental milestones, and they can provide information about the nature, frequency, and severity of the challenging behavior at home and in the past as well as the effect that it's having on them.

Knowing how parents perceive their child's behavior, how they respond to it, and how it affects their lives will help you understand where the child is coming from—and this knowledge will affect your behavior as well. The more aware you are of the child's sense of self and the way he communicates his needs, the better equipped you will be to respond to him appropriately—to notice signs of his anxiety, to identify the function of his behavior.

Besides, it's the family's right to know about any problem as soon as you realize it exists. It's easier to deal with problems sooner rather than later, and by contacting the family before the matter is in the hands of the principal, you're telling them that you care about their child. This early contact also gives you a better chance of enlisting their support and boosts the odds of improving the child's behavior (Walker, Ramsey, and Gresham, 2004).

Although some teachers tend to discount the importance of families as children grow older, in fact family involvement remains vital, and a family-centered approach will be more effective for both the child and the family (Muscott, 2002). This means emphasizing the family's strengths; listening carefully to family members and responding to their concerns in an individualized and flexible manner; and enabling them to choose services and strategies they prefer (Dunst, 2002; Muscott, 2002). If you make the assumption that they are competent, capable people, they're likely to fulfill your expectations, and together you'll come up with a variety of possible solutions.

How do families react to news of challenging behavior?

Families have a strong emotional investment in their children, and they're never really ready to hear about problems, even though they're often acutely aware of them. They may struggle with their child over his friends, curfew, and television viewing, and they may fear that he's cutting classes and taking drugs—but that doesn't mean they're prepared to hear someone else call him difficult. In *Troubled Families—Problem Children* (1994), psychologists Carolyn Webster-Stratton and Martin Herbert write, "It is not easy for parents to admit that they have a child with behavior problems, a child who is different from other children" (p. 201). Even when families

---

Home Remedy

In *To Teach* (2001), William Ayers says, "Parents are a powerful, usually underutilized source of knowledge about youngsters. . . . We too often dismiss their insights as subjective and overly involved. In fact, the insights of the parents—urgent, invested, passionate, immediate—are exactly what we need" (pp. 38–39).

Source: Reprinted by permission of the Publisher. From *To Teach: The Journey of a Teacher*, 2nd edition, by William Ayers. New York: Teachers College Press, © 2001 by Teachers College, Columbia University. All rights reserved.

Special educator Kim Bowie (2005) works with students with ADHD. She writes about how she felt when her son Boyd, who has ADHD, came home from school with "negative reports."

No matter how I tried to encourage him to do better, nothing worked. Then I began looking at the teacher and wondering what was happening in the class. After several talks with her, I realized that she was completely frustrated by my son and didn't see any of his strengths, only his problems. To see my child feel bad about school and worse about himself broke my heart. You don't really understand what a child with ADHD or their parents go through unless you've had the experience. . . .

Before, I was quick to support parents putting their children on medication. Looking back, I'm afraid it had to do more with keeping things peaceful at school than first thinking of students. Now I am completely convinced that we have to remember it is the parents' decision to put their children on medication; my job is to respect their decision. Sometimes as educators, we don't realize how much the medication can change a child and how it can affect the family on a daily basis. When Boyd began taking medication, he became a completely different person. I missed the son that I loved with all my heart, the one who was full of life and laughing. In the end, my husband and I decided to take Boyd off medication and to try alternatives. Boyd's teacher was very upset with our decision, and I think it affected how she treated Boyd. Now I always remember that no matter how tired I am or how tired a classroom teacher is, the parents of students with ADHD are probably ten times more exhausted. The understanding and compassion that the other teachers and I show both the parents and the children determine their future success. (p. 235)

Source: From "The Joys and Challenges of Working with Students Who Are ADHD . . . and Parenting One" by Kim Bowie. In Marilyn Friend, *Special Education: Contemporary Perspectives for School Professionals.* Published by Allyn & Bacon, Boston, MA. Copyright © 2005 by Pearson Education. Reprinted by permission of the publisher.

know that their child is having trouble in school, it's hard to face this fact and even harder to deal with the many feelings and fears that come with it.

Chances are that a family living with a child with challenging behavior is also living with enormous stress (Fox, Vaughn, Wyatte, and Dunlap, 2002; Webster-Stratton and Herbert, 1994). Home is just not a peaceful or pleasant place to be. Depending on the severity of the child's behavior, parents and siblings may be feeling isolated, victimized, insecure, angry, out of control, guilty, depressed, and/or utterly powerless (Webster-Stratton and Herbert, 1994). The child's behavior may cause marital problems because each parent often blames the other. And their inability to cope with the challenging behavior may inadvertently increase it. It is far easier to parent a child who's socially competent!

Many parents judge themselves by their child's behavior and feel that others are judging them, too (Webster-Stratton and Herbert, 1994). In their own minds, having a child with behavior problems is a sign that they aren't good parents, and they feel embarrassed, rejected, and stigmatized by other parents whose children seem perfect. Their own extended family often criticizes the way they discipline the child, making numerous unsupportive suggestions that evoke even more unease and guilt. As you talk with them, you are talking with years of self-blame, disappointment, and defensiveness.

Although this may be the first time you've broached this subject with the family, it probably isn't the first time a teacher has informed them about their child's problems. The previous encounters may have been less than ideal, leaving the parents feeling incompetent, helpless, and alienated. Such an experience makes any discussion seem threatening and paves the way for difficulties. On the other hand, if they're hearing about a problem for the first time, they may be devastated or—because no one has contacted them before—consider you the author of the child's problems. They may even be in a state of denial.

As a result, not all families will be equally willing or able to collaborate with you on a strategy for addressing challenging behavior. Some will want to be involved in every aspect of their child's life and will quickly join you in trying new tactics. Others won't think that's appropriate—for example, many working-class and low-income families believe they can be most helpful by giving the teacher full responsibility for what happens at school (Lareau and Shumar, 1996). Other families distrust or fear teachers and schools because of their own experience or their racial or cultural history with mainstream institutions (Lareau and Shumar, 1996). Yet others may seem disinterested or belligerent because they can't face any more conversations about their child's problems (Martin and Hagan-Burke, 2002). Some would like to get involved but just don't have the resources: the time, the energy, the flexibility, the money. A child with challenging behavior devours a family's reserves. Some parents are so overwhelmed that the issue becomes one of survival, a matter of getting from day to day.

An immigrant family may also be struggling with the language and mores of the dominant culture. Being informed about their cultural background will help you understand the options they have and the choices they're making (Lynch and Hanson, 1998). They may believe it's inappropriate to discuss family dynamics or personal problems with a teacher; they may think it's impolite to disagree with you or even to ask questions when they don't understand; they may seem willing to go along with your suggestions when they really have an entirely different view of the situation and prefer their own methods; or they may see you as the expert, while you are trying to create a partnership. Respecting their beliefs is the first step toward communication, but at the same time it's important to help them become aware of their own expertise where their child is concerned.

Regardless of how the family responds, you cannot allow yourself to become defensive and create a barrier between you. If they resent you or think you don't like their child, they may choose not to share their thoughts or insights with you and shut out anything you say. Without a real exchange of ideas, it will be next to impossible for you to collaborate and support one another's efforts. The bottom line is clear: Responsibility for the success of this venture lies with you, the teacher.

How do you feel?

There may be some anxiety on your side, too. You aren't sure how the family will react to what you have to say, and you may fear they'll hold you responsible for the difficulties the child is having or simply refuse to believe you. If they use very strict—or even physical—discipline at home, and your guidance methods aren't working with their child, the parents may blame you for the trouble because you haven't been strict or direct enough. (They may be correct, depending on the child's culture

Straight Talk

I n *Other People's Children: Cultural Conflict in the Classroom* (1995), Lisa Delpit writes:

A black elementary school principal in Fairbanks, Alaska, reported to me that she has a lot of difficulty with black children who are placed in some white teachers' classrooms. The teachers often send the children to the office for disobeying teacher directives. Their parents are frequently called in for conferences. The parents' response to the teacher is usually the same. "They do what I say; if you just *tell* them what to do, they'll do it. I tell them at home that they have to listen to what you say." (p. 35)

[Delpit, 1995]. For more on this topic, see Chapter 6.) You may also feel angry and upset with the child (Kay, Fitzgerald, and McConaughy, 2002; Friend, 2005). All of these feelings may spill over into your relationship with the family. It's important to use your self-reflection skills to become aware of your emotions and take control of them as you proceed.

You probably bring some biases to the table as well. According to a recent Public Agenda survey (2004), 82 percent of teachers blame parents for not teaching discipline to their children. And researchers have found that teachers often judge marginalized families—those who are outsiders because of their race, class, sexual orientation, disability, or immigrant status—as uninvolved and uncaring, when in fact they are involved in ways that the mainstream culture simply doesn't recognize (Lopez, 2001). It's extremely important to refrain from judging families, to get to know them as people, and to learn something about their culture, particularly about the way they raise their children and communicate with others.

If you don't have any children of your own, it may be hard for you to imagine how the family feels. Nonetheless, you share a commitment to helping the child succeed. When you are open and willing to see the child's behavior and the circumstances surrounding it from the family's point of view, when you can recognize that different settings elicit different behaviors as well as different solutions, you've begun to collaborate.

How can colleagues help?

When you're finding it hard to deal with a student's behavior, you may also be feeling very unsure of yourself. You may even begin to believe that everything is your fault, especially if you're a new teacher. You may be wondering if you should ask for advice.

Part of the job of a principal, vice principal, dean of discipline, special education teacher, school counselor, or school psychologist is to suggest alternative strategies and provide you with information, support, and resources. It makes good sense to reach out to them about any problem you have in the classroom. Although this might be the first time you've encountered a child with challenging behavior, these colleagues have no doubt had many such experiences. Some may have taught your student in previous years and have valuable tips to offer. Others can help you figure out how to approach the family. It is also reasonable to discuss these problems at a grade-level team meeting. In many states, schools have a mandatory *prereferral process* run by a *prereferral* or *teacher assistance team* in order to help teachers tackle problems with their students, understand them more fully, come up with new ideas for solving them, and possibly head off referrals to special education (Buck, Polloway, Smith-Thomas, and Cook, 2003; Friend, 2005).

The problem behavior can be one that's causing trouble for you or the student or simply one that you feel you need to talk about. Any behavior (from refusing to participate to swearing to pushing someone into a locker) is fair game. Any feeling (from frustration to bewilderment to anger) is reason enough to seek out a sympathetic and helpful ear.

If you put off seeking help until you can't face the classroom another day, you've waited too long, and you've made your own job harder and less rewarding. Sometimes people don't ask for assistance because they fear they'll be judged incompetent or because they think it's necessary to fix any problem by themselves. This is a mistake. No one is omnipotent, and no one is an island. Some children are harder to teach, and everyone needs an outlet, peer support, and advice some of the time. Teams are especially important when you're dealing with challenging behavior: People who have different perspectives and skills can help one another come up with creative and effective solutions.

As you discuss a problem, be sure to safeguard the confidentiality of the student and the family. It is your ethical obligation to be discreet in both your professional and private lives. Don't talk in public places or mention last names. You never know who will be sitting behind you in a crowded restaurant or movie theater. This is an important part of being a professional and showing respect for children and families.

MEETING WITH THE FAMILY

How do you arrange a meeting?

Talk to the family before you get to the breaking point—things may escalate out of control if you wait for a regularly scheduled parent–teacher conference. Your first meeting about a child's challenging behavior will establish a new tone and quality for your relationship and classify you as either ally or adversary. That label will influence all your future contacts.

It is important to avoid an expert or authoritarian approach. When you and the parents regard each other as equals, recognize one another's expertise, and acknowledge that differences in opinion are normal, you can use your combined strengths to set goals, make plans, and solve problems.

Even though you may be talking about a student's behavior with a school advisor, it is usually better to meet alone with the family initially. Having other people there makes it look as if you've been discussing their child behind their backs. And with two authority figures present, they're likely to feel intimidated by your collective expertise. Instead, involve the family in the decision to invite another person to a future meeting. Then they'll know why he or she is there and feel comfortable about it.

If the parents are separated or divorced but live in the same city and are both involved in the child's life, ask them both to participate—but tell them ahead of time so they'll be prepared when their former partner walks into the room. This is especially important in cases of joint custody. It is always best if the parents hear what you have to say directly from you and everyone gets the same information at the same time. Invite each concerned person individually. Be sure to find out what names they use and address them (and all families) as Mr. and Ms. on the phone as well as when you meet.

In different cultures, different people are responsible for making decisions about the children. In some cultures, men have the say; in others, it is the oldest family member who is in charge; in still others, mothers are key. Before you call, find out which family member to approach first and who else should be present.

The best way to make the first contact is by telephone. Because calling them at work induces instant panic, phone them at home where you can set a friendlier tone and take the time you need to choose your words carefully. Several family members will probably be around, making it easier to schedule a time that suits everyone. If the family speaks a different language, find someone to interpret.

Whenever you contact a family, it's imperative to begin with a positive statement about the child. If you can't put your finger on any of his strengths, go over the days in your mind and take notes so that you have at least a few positive comments prepared. If you're still drawing a blank, do an observation where you look exclusively for appropriate behavior. When parents know that you notice and appreciate their child's assets, they will feel that you believe in him and his ability to behave appropriately.

Start by introducing yourself, then state the purpose of the call clearly. (It's better not to say vaguely, "I want to talk with you about Andrew," because parents immediately assume the worst.) Tell them that you want to talk with them about what you're doing at school and ask their advice about what works at home. Be careful not to accuse or judge them (Dunst, 2002). ("I'd like to set up a meeting with you because although I really appreciate that Andrew likes to stick with something once he starts it, yesterday he swore at me and threw his chair across the room when it was time to get ready for gym. I had to send him out of class.")

Some parents have been anxiously awaiting this call, and others may be caught totally off guard, but it's unlikely that any family will have a straightforward response. Feelings—of guilt, anger, disappointment, embarrassment—inevitably surge up, coloring their reaction. In their consternation, they may deny, justify, rationalize, minimize, even abdicate responsibility: "He's not like that at home," "Maybe he's bored," "He has lots of friends in the neighborhood," "We've just gone through a divorce," "He never listens to us, even when we ground him." Even parents who sound like partners on the surface may feel helpless and defensive (Losen and Diament, 1978). Show your concern and listen carefully so that you will be able to help them find ways to support their child.

Talk with them long enough to make it obvious that you care about their child and are eager to work with them to help him. Some parents want to stay on the phone indefinitely and then decide there's nothing further to say, hence no reason to meet. Try not to let things reach this stage. Be polite, but point out that it's better to discuss these matters in person. If everyone has time to reflect, the conversation will be more fruitful.

There should be as little delay as possible between the initial call and your first meeting. Family members may not be able to leave their place of employment, so you may have to meet at the end of their work day or in the evening outside of the school in a neutral setting, such as a community center or coffee shop where there are other people around. Schedule a time to end the meeting as well as a time to begin. Knowing when you have to leave helps everyone stay on topic and keeps parents from being insulted when the meeting is over. Be sure to set aside enough time so that you won't be rushed. In some cultures the family will notice that you're in a hurry and defer to your needs. But they may also feel that you aren't showing respect for them and be offended or hurt, which will not help the child.

If you don't speak the same language, ask if they would like an interpreter and decide who will be responsible for finding one. It's better not to press an older sibling into service (Lynch, 1998a). Family members may not want to discuss delicate issues in the sibling's presence, and the child-interpreter may not wish an outsider to know about sensitive family matters. In addition, being placed in this position alters the sibling's relationship to his elders and causes problems for both child and parents. On the other hand, the family may not feel comfortable talking with a stranger, and even a member of the same cultural community may pose problems of privacy and confidentiality (Lynch, 1998a). If you have taken on the task of selecting the interpreter, double-check with the family to be sure they're satisfied with your choice (Joe and Malach, 1998). It's a good idea to use a skillful professional who can interpret cultural cues as well as language and let you know what isn't said as well as what is.

Consider inviting the student to participate as well. As part of the problem, he can also become part of the solution. He will certainly have his own views on the subject, and when he can hear for himself what you and his family have to say, the situation may become clearer and easier to resolve. However, not every family will agree to this arrangement. You can make the suggestion and leave the decision to them.

What should happen in a meeting with the family?

First, like the scouts, be prepared. Decide what you're going to say, and have a plan with the objectives and the main points you want to cover. Gather your reports, notes, observation charts, and grade book together so you don't have to search for things during the meeting.

Choose a private space where no one will interrupt—perhaps the principal will lend you her or his office—and put a sign on the door to deter intruders. If you're meeting in off-hours, arrange for someone else to be in the vicinity in case you need help. Organize adult-sized chairs for everyone, and place them so that there are no physical barriers (such as your desk) between you. Remember, you want to convey partnership, not authority. It's a good idea to have a box of tissues within reach.

You should also give some thought to what you're going to wear. Meeting with a family calls for a more formal style than being in the classroom with the students. Dressing up indicates respect, which is important for any family and especially important for a family from a culture where relationships are formal. But be careful not to overdo it or you may intimidate them. Consider the family you're meeting with and dress accordingly.

In many cultures, communication is indirect and courtesy is very much valued. Lynch and Hanson (1998, p. 505) urge us to use "culturally comfortable" practices such as serving tea or coffee, spending a few minutes in polite general conversation before launching into the subject of the meeting, or conducting the meeting in a

Team Building

When you're about to embark on a partnership, it's a good idea to find out what your new partner values. Researchers (Blue-Banning, Summers, Frankland, Nelson, and Beegle, 2004) asked that question in focus groups and interviews with parents and the professionals who worked with them. Six important themes about the nature of collaborative partnership emerged.

1. *Communication.* Parents want their communication with professionals to be frequent, open, and honest, with no sugar coating or hidden information. At the same time, they like two-way communication and tact—professionals who respect their privacy, don't judge them, and find positive things to say.
2. *Commitment.* Professionals who show dedication to their work—regard it as more than just a job—win parents' approval. Gestures such as meeting outside of regular working hours or remembering a child's birthday demonstrate their devotion.
3. *Equality.* Reciprocity or equality is important in a partnership, parents say. They want professionals to acknowledge the validity of their point of view, and they appreciate a sense of harmony and empowerment in the relationship.
4. *Skills.* Parents admire professionals who can make things happen for their child. They also praise those who admit to not knowing something but are willing to find out.
5. *Trust.* Trust has three different meanings for parents. First, it means *reliability*, a professional doing what she says she will do. Second, it means providing *safety*, assuring that the child is treated with dignity and protected from hurt. Finally, it means *discretion*, keeping personal information confidential.
6. *Respect.* Respect, which is essential to parents, also has several meanings. Professionals show respect by valuing the child as a person and by acting courteously—calling family members by their last names, arriving on time for meetings, and acknowledging parents' efforts and contributions on behalf of their child.

highly formal way, depending on the family's culture (Joe and Malach, 1998). If you're using an interpreter, bear in mind that he or she is a go-between. Talk directly to the family—they are the ones you're actually addressing (Lynch, 1998b).

When you meet with the family, you'll need great sensitivity and your very best listening skills. Take some deep breaths to calm your butterflies, and remember that you have important contributions to make: expertise about children and education, a nonjudgmental ear, and respect for the family's opinions and feelings.

Greet the family with a smile, and before you talk about problems, once again let them know where their child is succeeding: what he does well, who his friends are, what he enjoys. Then you can talk about the challenging behavior you're observing and the things you need their help with, just as you did when you arranged the meeting. Be calm, factual, specific, and objective as you describe the child's behavior, your expectations, and the strategies you've tried—give the family the data you've collected in informal observations rather than telling them what you think. It's always a good idea to talk about what is best for the child and to put his behavior in the context of mastering academic goals (Quinn et al., 2000). (As we saw in the previous chapter, if you're using curriculum-based assessment, you will have objective evidence of the student's scholastic achievement.).

Invite the family to share their thoughts and concerns as well as their past successes with their child and any information they have regarding his behavior or di-

Invite the family to share their thoughts and concerns as well as their past successes with their child and any information they have regarding his behavior or diagnosis (if there is one).

agnosis (if there is one). Do they have any idea about why this might be happening? How does the child behave at home? Have there been any new stresses or changes in routine? Is this behavior new, or has he behaved this way before? What does this behavior mean to them? How have they responded to it in the past? What are they doing now? What works for them? What are their goals for their child? Do these goals suggest any solutions to the problem? Some parents may already be working with specialists and parent groups and know an enormous amount about appropriate methods for managing their child's problems. Do they have any advice to offer? Take the opportunity to learn as much from them as you can, and together brainstorm as many ideas as possible and work out a plan.

If they say their child's behavior is no problem at home, let them know you believe them. They may not perceive the behavior as a problem, and not every child with challenging behavior has problems outside a group setting, especially an only child. But it's important to say politely that his behavior is a problem in your class, where there are few adults, more children, and many more demands.

Even if they acknowledge that there is a problem, any remarks that sound like criticism of their child may cut them deeply. They are doing their best for him, and they may feel upset, defensive, or angry. These are all normal coping mechanisms. Let them vent their feelings, and give them time to come to terms with what you're saying. Again, try to see things from their perspective rather than passing judgment.

Problem solving with families is just like problem solving with students. Experts (Friend and Bursuck, 2003; Gordon, 2003) suggest using these steps:

- *Define the problem.* This is a crucial part of the process and involves gathering information, analyzing it, and reaching agreement about what the problem actually is. Both teacher and family must believe that a problem exists and that they can contribute to solving it. I-messages and active listening are important here.
- *Generate multiple solutions.* Brainstorm as many ideas as you can. In this way, more options and creative suggestions come to the fore. No one's suggestions should be ignored or put down.
- *Evaluate ideas.* Are they acceptable to everyone? Are they feasible? Are they likely to be effective?
- *Come to a consensus.* Everyone should be willing to try the solutions you choose.
- *Discuss how you will Implement the solutions.* What must be done? Who will do it? When?
- *Evaluate the solutions.* Is your approach working? Meet again to go over the evidence and, if necessary, change your strategy.

As you talk, be aware of your body language. Keep your arms open, and mirror the family's message. If they are engaged and leaning forward, you should also be engaged and learning forward. Be conscious of your eye contact as well. Are they comfortable with it, or do they seem more at ease if your eyes don't meet theirs? Remember that this can be a cultural issue, and it is important to communicate respect on their terms. Pay attention to the pace, cadence, and tone of their speech, and decide whether it's better to mirror or lead their actions. Their speech, along with their facial expressions and body gestures, will also give you vital clues about their emotions, which can easily sabotage the proceedings. Nothing will get done if the parents are upset or angry. The open communication skills you learned from WEVAS should help.

Active listening will also enable you to understand what the parents are saying and demonstrate your respect and interest. Listen carefully to both the surface and the underlying message, and comment on the feelings being expressed with phrases such as "That's frustrating, isn't it?" Paraphrase what they have said to clarify the meaning and to verify that you've understood their message.

Sometimes teachers are afraid to discuss the problems they're having with a student because they suspect the family will punish him at home. Families can make a big difference when they reinforce what you're doing in the classroom and use strategies at home that you've developed together. But punishment at home won't help, and neither will unrelated consequences such as grounding a child or forbidding him to watch a favorite television program. It isn't your job to tell families how to parent, and unsolicited advice (no matter how useful) can make families feel their private lives are under attack and convey that you think they're incompetent. Instead, tell the family how you handled the situation, and if they bring up the subject, talk with them about what they feel should happen at home. Perhaps they'll recognize that you've dealt with the matter already or work out a logical and related consequence. You could point out that the most effective consequences are those that follow immediately.

How do you close a meeting?

Once you've generated options together, evaluated them in light of the family's goals for the child, and agreed on a plan, schedule another conference to assess the student's progress. You may have to meet several times to resolve the problem.

Then wrap things up so the family doesn't feel cut off. "Our time is almost up. I just want to be sure that we are all clear about what was said and what we've agreed to do next." Be sure to thank the family for their input and their contributions to the problem-solving process. It's important for them to have a sense of ownership not only of the child and his problems but also of the solutions and the child's potential for success. When they have choices and power, the solutions are more likely to stick.

After the parents leave, record information that will help you understand and respond to the child's behavior. It's also wise to evaluate the meeting so you can improve communication the next time. Did you say what you felt you needed to say? How was the information received by the family? Did the family feel like an equal partner? What commitments did everyone make? Is the follow-up clear? Write a brief note to the family, thanking them again and reiterating the decisions you've made together. If you agreed to send information or call someone, do it as quickly as possible.

What if you and the family disagree?*

You and the family won't always agree, and things won't always run smoothly. When a conflict arises, first pay attention to what you're feeling (which helps defuse those feelings) and then lock the feelings in a drawer, where you can find them later. If you're going to come out of this situation with a solution everyone can live with, you need an open mind, your reason, and your best eyes and ears. This means staying calm and professional. Perhaps your most important goal is to keep the discussion going; resolving differences takes time and communication.

The best thing to do is listen. Even when you don't agree with what the family is saying, it's important to accept what they feel. Accepting their feelings is a way to show respect. Again, active listening will help. If they say, "Andrew says you're always picking on him. You aren't fair," stifle your impulse to say that Andrew has it all wrong. It's normal for them to stand up for their child. Try to hear their feelings and reply, "You're worried because you think I'm not being fair to Andrew."

When you and the family come from different cultures or backgrounds, it's especially easy to misunderstand and to be misunderstood. As people come to know and understand one another and their cultures, the chances of resolution improve. Or at least everyone's ability to handle disagreement gets better.

Some values are nonnegotiable, such as those enshrined in the United Nations Convention on the Rights of the Child (Canadian Heritage, n.d.; United Nations Office of the High Commission on Human Rights, 1989). You would never agree, for

---

*This section has been adapted from *Partners in Quality, vol. 2/ Relationships* © CCCF 1999, written by Barbara Kaiser and Judy Sklar Rasminsky, based on the research papers of the Partners in Quality Project. With permission from Canadian Child Care Federation, 201-383 Parkdale Avenue, Ottawa, Ontario, K1Y 4R4.

example, to hit a child, no matter how passionately and persuasively parents argue their case for you to do so. Nor would you compromise on a matter of racial or gender equality. But other situations aren't quite so clear. You may think initially that you could never change your practice and then come to realize that some changes would make the child much happier. Replacing competition with cooperative group learning might fall into this category.

From there, it's a matter of dialogue, negotiation, problem solving, and compromise, always keeping the best interests of the student in mind. You may reach a solution; you may agree to disagree. Either way is all right if you keep communication open and treat one another with respect. It's better for the student if you and the family are running down the same road in the same direction, but don't despair if that doesn't happen. Work to keep a dialogue going and concentrate on the child. What he learns from you will stay with him.

After meeting alone with a family, you may be worrying that your next meeting will become confrontational. To minimize possible trouble, consider asking a third person to join you. Choose someone with a legitimate reason to come—the assistant teacher, the school psychologist, or the vice principal, for example—and let the family know who will be present.

WORKING WITH OTHER EXPERTS

What about getting additional expert advice?

If you've been working with the school's psychologist, social worker, counselor, or prereferral support team and nothing seems to help, it may be time to call for extra assistance. Remember that asking for help is a sign not of weakness but of wisdom. You are trying to solve your problem by thinking creatively and acquiring new skills. You have to trust your professional judgment—your knowledge of developmental norms, the instinct you've developed by working with children, your awareness of how a particular student is pushing your buttons. The crucial thing is to act *long* before you reach the end of your rope. It may take some time for help to arrive, and a burned-out adult is not capable of dealing objectively with either the student or the challenging behavior. At that point you'll barely hear an expert's advice, let alone follow it.

In this situation, your school's prereferral team or support staff may suggest a formal evaluation for special education under IDEA. You will probably be asked to take part so that the evaluators can benefit from your knowledge of the student and learn about the tactics you've tried in the classroom. The parents must consent to the evaluation, and they have the right to participate in it. A functional assessment and positive behavior support plan may be part of the evaluation. (For more information about special education, see Chapter 12.)

The school's troubleshooters may also recommend bringing in an outside consultant. You may need parental consent to do this, but it shouldn't be a problem if you've been collaborating with the family all along. When you ask for permission, be sure to mention how useful a fresh point of view can be. At the same time, make it clear that the consultant will be watching you and the other students as well as their child. Having this information should make it easier for the parents to agree.

In order to invite a consultant into your classroom, you will have to make a formal request to the principal or dean of discipline, who will then discuss the matter with you, make the necessary arrangements, and remain involved during the consultation process. In order to help you and the child, the consultant must observe you together in the classroom. Before the observation, meet to explain the situation and share what you've observed, the strategies you've tried, and what you know about the family's point of view. After the observation, confer again to go over the consultant's findings and work out a plan. It should include a timeframe and a method for evaluating the effectiveness of your approach.

It's possible that the consultant or your own school support personnel will suggest some kind of therapy for the child or the family. Because a family will be more likely to accept a referral from someone they have a relationship with—someone who really knows their child (Koplow, 2002)—it's a good idea for you to participate in the meeting where this is discussed, even if the principal is in charge. When the referral comes from a stranger, the family may not believe that extra help is necessary, and they probably won't follow through. If they fear that a social services agency will get involved, they may look for another school where the teachers "care more" about the students, or even move.

If the consultant recommends therapy, the best option is no doubt the school psychologist, counselor, or social worker. Their services are easily accessible and free of charge, which increases the probability the student will be able and willing to attend. But these workers are usually swamped with cases and other responsibilities, so the family may have to make their own appointments and decisions about where to go. It's important to tell them as much as you can about how the system works and the resources that are available in their community. The principal or the school's professional support personnel can help you to compile a list.

Information from you will probably help an outside professional make an accurate diagnosis or assessment. Request the parents' permission to send a letter, and be sure to supply them with a copy. If you would like feedback from the specialist in return, ask the family to authorize him or her to speak with you, although the parents may prefer to tell you about the findings themselves—or to keep them confidential.

Raising such a subject with the family will require extraordinary delicacy. Even though you've already had several difficult talks, this will probably be the hardest. Don't try to impose your values, and be sure to separate the child from the behavior. Be specific about why you still have strong concerns. Tell the parents again about the strategies you've tried, and explain that you believe it's important for the child's long-term success to get help for him. If they're starting to focus too much on the negative, remind them of their child's strengths, and repeat that you appreciate their collaboration.

All of this is serious stuff, and it's much harder to accept than merely "having trouble" in school. The family may not even hear what you have to say, so be sure to impress on them that they can call you later with their questions. Reassurance is definitely required. Some families may find the idea of special education or a specialist totally alien and see it as a rejection or a form of stigmatization. They may feel angry that the problem has been ignored for such a long time; they may have fears about what this step might mean for their child and themselves; and they may need emotional support. If therapy is involved, they may also be worrying about the cost and length of the treatment (Losen and Diament, 1978) and wondering how they can possibly fit it into their already overburdened lives. If they've had a negative experience, they may be reluctant to try again. In addition, their culture may consider it inappropriate to discuss family problems with a stranger.

It is possible that the family will reject the idea of outside intervention. This is their right, and their decision doesn't imply that they don't love their child—only that circumstances make it impossible, that they aren't ready, or that their view of the situation is different from yours. Remind them again of how important it is for the child to get the assistance he requires, emphasizing that the idea of inclusion is not to send him away but to bring whatever help he needs directly into the classroom (Friend and Bursuck, 2002).

Whether the family accepts the expert's recommendations or not, cooperates with you or not, don't give up. Both the child and the family are entitled to your full respect and support. Try to believe the best about them and begin each day fresh and new.

W HAT DO YOU THINK?

1. Examine your own attitude. Do you feel that families are responsible for how their child behaves at school? How? What other factors may be involved?
2. Talk to a teacher who has a child with challenging behavior in her class about working with the parents. What are some of her attitudes? Has she been successful in creating a positive relationship? How? If she hasn't managed to develop a sense of teamwork, what has she done, or not done, that might have played a part in the family's position?

3. With a classmate, prepare and role-play a parent–teacher meeting with one person acting as the teacher and the other the parent of a child with challenging behavior. Evaluate the meeting. What were some of the difficulties for the teacher? For the parent? What would you do differently? Conduct a follow-up meeting to iron out some of the problems that arose.
4. Reverse roles and do the previous exercise again.

W HAT WOULD YOU DO?

Andrew's report card arrived, and his grades weren't as good as I thought they could be—he always has difficulty applying himself. But he hadn't said much about school, and I hadn't heard a word from his teacher, so a reasonable report card and the absence of that dreaded phone call were a relief. Maybe this year's parent–teacher conference would be better.

Andrew's father wanted to attend the meeting as well, so we met at the school. Outside the classroom, I watched other parents exit with a smile and started to feel hopeful. Finally it was our turn. The teacher seemed warm and friendly, but I could see her expression change as soon as we introduced ourselves.

She sat down at her desk and indicated that we should sit on the chairs beside it. She began by saying, "I'm really glad you're here. Usually only the parents of children who are doing well come to this first meeting." Oh my God, I thought, what is she going to say

and how is my husband going to respond? She pulled out several pieces of paper and showed us incomplete assignments and tests. She told us that Andrew often came to class without books, paper, or pencils. She listed the times she had had to send him out of the room because he was disturbing the other students, becoming physically aggressive with his classmates, and even verbally abusing her.

I was on the verge of tears and felt like walking out the door. "Why didn't you contact us before?" I asked. She said she was hoping Andrew would settle down, and she didn't want us to punish him at home as a result of his behavior at school. However, she added, "Now that he's missed so much class time, he's fallen behind, and I'm concerned that things are only going to get worse." She said that she had tried to partner him with another student, but there were no volunteers.

Andrew's father was clenching his fists, and I could feel him trying to stay in control. When the teacher finished speaking, he asked if there was anything else she wanted to say. She suggested that we help Andrew to organize his belongings and consider testing him for possible learning problems, maybe even ADHD. She didn't ask us a single question.

When we left the room, my artificial smile vanished. The minute we reached a quiet corner, I burst into tears. Andrew's dad was furious and anxious to talk to Andrew. We drove home in silence. I knew if I spoke we'd argue about what to do.

If you were Andrew's teacher, how would you have handled this parent–teacher conference?

SUGGESTED READINGS

Blue-Banning, M., Summers, J. A., Frankland, H. C., Nelson, L. L., & Beegle, G. (2004). Dimensions of family and professional partnerships: Constructive guidelines for collaboration. *Exceptional Children*, 70, 167–184.

Fox, L., Vaughn, B. J., Wyatte, M. L., & Dunlap, G. (2002). "We can't expect other people to understand": Family perspectives on problem behavior. *Exceptional Children*, 68, 437–450.

Lareau, A., & Shumar, W. (1996). The problem of individualism in family-school policies. *Sociology of Education*, special issue, 24–39.

Trumbull, E., Rothstein-Fisch, C., Greenfield, P. M., & Quiroz, B. (2001). *Bridging cultures between home and school: A guide for teachers*. Mahwah, NJ: Erlbaum.

CHAPTER 14

Bullying

Bullying has probably existed forever, but few researchers took it seriously until 1982, when newspapers in Norway reported that three boys, ages 10 to 14, had committed suicide after being bullied by their peers. The news shocked the country, and in 1983 Norway's Ministry of Education launched a nationwide program against bullying in primary and junior schools (Olweus, 1991, 1993). Since then, interest in the subject has spread around the world (Smith et al., 1999).

Because bullying is such a complex topic, we have left it for last. To address it, you will need to use all the knowledge and strategies you learned in the previous chapters. In the three parts of this chapter, you'll learn what bullying is, how teachers can reduce and prevent it, and how to respond to it.

WHAT IS BULLYING?

Bullying is a special form of aggressive behavior. The world's leading authority on bullying, Dan Olweus, who designed the Norwegian intervention program, defines it this way: "A person is being bullied when he or she is exposed, repeatedly and over time, to negative actions on the part of one or more other persons" (Olweus, 1991, 1993). What differentiates bullying from other aggressive acts is that the student who bullies intends to harm, there is more than one incident, and an imbalance of power makes it hard for the child who's being bullied to defend herself. This difference in power can be physical—the child who bullies can be older, bigger, stronger; or several children can gang up on a single child. It can also be psychological, which is harder to see but just as potent—the student who bullies can have more social status or a sharper tongue, for instance. And for the child who is victimized, oppression is always the result, according to the English criminologist David Farrington (Rigby, 2001b).

There are several kinds of bullying:

- *Physical* bullying, which is the easiest to identify, includes a variety of behaviors such as hitting, kicking, shoving, and taking or destroying property. Physical bullying is more widespread among boys (Nansel et al., 2001).

- *Verbal* bullying includes name-calling, insulting, intimidating, mocking, threatening, taunting, teasing, and making racist, sexist, or sexual comments. When does teasing cross the line and turn into bullying? Not everyone agrees, but some researchers (Froschl, Sprung, and Mullin-Rindler, 1998) see both teasing and bullying as points on a continuum of intentionally hurtful behavior, different only in degree. In a study of bullying in the Midwest, Ronald Oliver, John H. Hoover, and R. J. Hazler (1994) found that students are confused about teasing: They said it was done in fun, but they also ranked it as the most frequent bullying behavior. Verbal abuse is the most common form of bullying for both sexes (Kochenderfer and Ladd, 1996; Nansel et al., 2001).

- *Relational or psychological* bullying uses relationships to control or harm another person (Crick, Casas, and Ku, 1999; Crick et al., 2001)—excluding her from the group or events, talking behind her back, spreading rumors, telling lies about her, giving her the silent treatment, and so on. According to Nicki Crick and her colleagues (Crick et al., 2001), relational bullying deprives children of the opportunity to be close to and accepted by their peers—needs that are important for their well-being and development. Girls are more likely to use, and to become the targets of, relational bullying (Crick et al., 1999; Crick and Grotpeter, 1995), but both boys and girls consider it the most hurtful type of bullying (Rigby, 2002).

Although they're hard to classify, making faces and gesturing can be bullying, too.

In recent years, two more forms of bullying have stepped into the limelight:

- *Sexual harassment* reached national consciousness when Anita Hill testified in the hearings leading up to Clarence Thomas's appointment to the Supreme Court in 1991. Sexual harassment—unwanted or unwelcome sexual behavior that interferes with a student's life—is about power, not sex (Craig, Pepler, and Connolly, 2003; Schwartz, 2000). It includes being the target of sexual comments, jokes, gestures, or looks; being called gay or lesbian; being touched, grabbed, pinched, or brushed up against in a sexual way; being flashed or mooned; being the object of sexual rumors or graffiti; being spied on while undressing or showering; having clothing pulled down or off; and being forced to kiss or do something sexual (American Association of University Women, 2001). Both boys and girls are harassed and harass others (Craig et al., 2003). Among preteens and young teens, homophobic insults to boys are the most common kind of sexual harassment (Craig et al., 2003). Gay, lesbian, bisexual, and transsexual students face an especially high risk of harassment—90 percent of those in one survey had been verbally or physically harassed in the previous year (Harris Interactive and Gay, Lesbian and Straight Education Network, 2005).

The difference in power can be physical—the student who bullies can be older, bigger, or stronger; or several children can gang up on a single child. It can also be psychological, which is harder to see but just as potent.

- *Cyberbullying* usually takes place off school grounds, but it affects the way students feel and behave at school. Cyberbullying utilizes all of the paraphernalia of modern life—cell phones, instant messaging, videos, e-mail, chatrooms, blogging, social networking sites such as Facebook, and so on—to threaten, insult, harass, spread rumors, and impersonate others. Because it can continue 24 hours a day, 7 days a week, and because perpetrators remain anonymous, invisible, unpunished, and distant from the impact of their actions, cyberbullying can be even more vicious than ordinary bullying ("What are the forms," n.d.; Willard, 2006).

The experts also categorize bullying as *direct,* which is when a student bullies openly, allowing the child under attack to identify her assailant (Olweus, 1993), or *indirect,* which is when the student doing the bullying tries to inflict harm without revealing her intention (Sullivan, Cleary, and Sullivan, 2004). Physical bullying is usually direct, but verbal and relational bullying, sexual harassment, and cyberbullying can be either direct or indirect. As children get older, they tend to use more subtle and indirect methods, such as never finding space at the lunch table for Aisha (Craig et al., 2003).

By and large, bullying is a clandestine activity. The favorite venues for harassment—playgrounds, hallways, cafeterias, locker rooms, and bathrooms (Glover, Gough, Johnson, and Cartwright, 2000)—feature few or no adults. Children who've been victimized may find ways to stay in the classroom during recess and willingly endure great physical discomfort to avoid using school bathrooms.

Ten-year-old Vicky waited for all her friends to get their lunches and sit at the table. Then she asked them to raise their hands if they liked chocolate. She raised her hand, and everyone followed. Next she said, "Raise your hand if you like spaghetti." She lifted her hand, and once again so did everyone else. Finally she said, "Raise your hand if you like Carmen." She didn't put up her hand, and neither did any of the other girls. Carmen, who was seated near the end of the table, quickly left the cafeteria.

How common is bullying?

Bullying appears in all racial and ethnic groups and all socioeconomic classes (Orpinas and Horne, 2006), whether schools are large or small, urban or rural (Olweus, 1993). Although most children experience a minor and fleeting form of it at some point during their school careers (Juvonen and Graham, 2001; Pepler and Craig, n.d.), for a surprising number bullying is a frequent and serious occurrence.

The first large-scale study of bullying in the United States—a representative sample of more than 15,000 students in grades 6 to 10 in public and private schools throughout the country—revealed that almost 30 percent of children are involved in bullying either moderately ("sometimes") or frequently (once a week or more). Thirteen percent bully others, 10.6 percent are targeted, and 6.3 percent both bully others and are targeted themselves (Nansel et al., 2001). Canadian and U.S. statistics are similar, and when Wendy Craig and Debra J. Pepler (1997) videotaped and recorded bullying on Toronto playgrounds, they saw a bullying act every seven minutes. More than half of students experience verbal sexual harassment at school occasionally or often, and a third encounter physical sexual harassment just as frequently (American Association of University Women, 2001). According to a study of students in grades 4 to 8, about 40 percent have been bullied online (iSAFE, n.d.).

Bullying peaks in early adolescence—during grades 6 to 8 (Nansel et al., 2001)—when students move from small, personal elementary schools to larger, less supportive middle schools, junior highs, or secondary schools. Boys in particular find that bullying is an effective way to establish their status within their new peer group (Pellegrini and Long, 2002). Bullying tapers off in the older grades, but some children never give it up. We call their handiwork by different names in adult life—spousal abuse, child abuse, racism, and sexual harassment (Pepler and Craig, n.d.; Smith, Cowie, and Sharp, 1994).

Because of the secret nature of bullying, teachers often underestimate its prevalence. Craig and Pepler's (1997) videos captured teachers intervening in only 4 percent of bullying incidents, although 75 percent said they always responded. This low rate probably means that the teachers didn't actually see or recognize the harassment.

Who are the students who bully others?

By definition, children who use bullying behavior are strong individuals who choose to dominate their weak peers. They may have an impulsive temperament and a tendency to hotheadedness; and more importantly, they have a positive attitude toward violence. Boys who bully may be physically strong and good at sports and fighting (Olweus, 1993). In elementary school their marks are average, but they have trouble following rules and often behave aggressively and defiantly toward adults. In middle school they usually receive lower marks and dislike school (Olweus, 1993).

Children who target others probably acquire their view of violence at home, where they see up close how effective it can be. They may have observed parents or siblings bullying others or may have been bullied themselves (Sharp and Smith, 1994). Olweus (1993) found that the families of children who bully often use power-assertive child-rearing methods, such as physical punishment and violent emotional outbursts. They don't set clear limits or outlaw aggressive behavior, and they are usually cold and indifferent toward their child, which leads to an avoidant attachment relationship and increases the risk of aggressive behavior. A child in such a family grows up with a strong need to dominate others, to get her own way, and to be in control, and she isn't interested in negotiating, cooperating, or accepting anyone else's ideas (Hoover and Hazler, 1991; Olweus, 1993; Rigby, 1998). Pepler and Craig (n.d.) point out that she has learned some important lessons—that having power allows people to be aggressive, and that power and aggression can bring dominance and status.

Unlike children who use aggressive behavior indiscriminately, students who bully are generally well liked and surrounded by friends and supporters, although their popularity decreases in their midteens (Olweus, 1993; Rigby, 1998). They may try out their tactics on several targets before settling on one who doesn't resist (Perry, Perry, and Kennedy, 1992). Because they choose carefully and use power swiftly and unemotionally to get what they want (Perry et al., 1992), their behavior elicits little negative reaction from their peers and seems to be an acceptable way to achieve social success (Hoover and Hazler, 1991).

It is a myth that students who use bullying behavior lack social skills and self-esteem (Olweus, 1991, 1993). They actually tend to be outgoing and self-confident and feel little anxiety or insecurity. Some researchers (Sutton, Smith, and Sweetenham, 1999) have suggested that they have a superior *theory of mind* or *social cognition*—that is, an advanced ability to understand and manipulate the minds of others. This is especially important in indirect bullying, where the student who's doing the bullying must know which of her peers will join in her efforts to exclude another child and what sort of justification the group will find acceptable. Even direct bul-

Leading the Pack

Liz had the same name as me, and because she was funny looking, I wanted to be sure that no one would think we were at all alike. From first grade on, I would tease her and pick on her. The strange thing was that the other kids started to do it too, and that made me feel powerful, like a leader—it was my idea to make her life miserable. Liz just took it. She never told anyone, and it continued for years. Even in seventh grade she wanted to be part of my crowd, the popular crowd, and would try to hang out with us at recess and after school. It didn't seem to matter what we said to her; she was always there. As we got older, we got crueler. We would tell her that she was ugly and stupid; we believed we had the right to say anything we wanted to. We thought it was fun to watch her react to our insults and come back for more.

lying takes sharp social insight: The student who's bullying must avoid detection and choose a method that leaves her unscathed while hurting the target.

Although children who are adept at bullying understand others' emotions, they don't seem able to share them. In other words, they have little empathy and don't worry about the pain or discomfort they cause (Olweus, 1993). On the contrary, they may even enjoy it (Rigby, 2001b).

But this description doesn't fit all students who victimize others (Craig and Pepler, 2003; Sutton et al., 1999). Some may lack social skills and impulse control and have more anxiety and insecurity, particularly "bully-victims" (see pages 287 to 288) and the followers who assist the leader of the bullying (Olweus, 1993).

As they grow older, children who bully are at risk for a whole host of problems (Olweus, 1991; Pepler and Craig, 2000):

- Aggressive behavior
- Alcohol and drug abuse
- Delinquency, gang involvement, and vandalism
- Sexual harassment and dating aggression
- Academic problems and school dropout
- Peer rejection

Students who bully might also suffer from mental health problems such as conduct disorder, depression, and anxiety (Olweus, 1991; Pepler and Craig, 2000). Olweus (1993) found that by the age of 24 about 60 percent of the boys who had bullied others in grades 6 to 9 had been convicted of a criminal offense, and 35 to 40 percent had three or more convictions. Students who use relational bullying also face risks: They struggle with behavior problems and self-esteem and are likely to be lonely, depressed, and rejected (Crick, Casas, and Mosher, 1997; Wolke, Woods, Bloomfield, and Karstadt, 2000).

Who are the targets of bullying?

It is no fun to be on the receiving end of bullying. The immediate effects—physical injury, humiliation, helplessness, rejection, unhappiness—are painful enough, but the knowledge that all this will soon be repeated multiplies the distress. Children who are harassed experience fear, anxiety, insecurity, oppression, depression, inability to concentrate in class, low marks, headaches, stomachaches, and nightmares. It is not surprising that they want to avoid school (Kochenderfer and Ladd, 1996). Being bullied has a devastating effect on self-esteem. It's hard for a child to stop thinking that she deserves whatever she gets (Boivin, Hymel, and Hodges, 2001; Rigby, 2001b; Wilczenski et al., 1994), and the worse she feels about herself, the more susceptible she becomes (Swearer, Song, Cary, Eagle, and Mickelson, 2001). Because perpetrators often deny they've done anything wrong, students who've been targeted by relational bullying even learn to mistrust the evidence of their own senses (Simmons, 2002).

How does a student become the target of bullying? What makes her vulnerable? Part of the explanation is temperament. Olweus (1993) has found that most children who are harassed are what he terms "passive victims": "cautious, sensitive, quiet, withdrawn, passive, submissive and shy, . . . anxious, insecure, unhappy, and distressed" (p. 57). They may also be physically weak (Perry, Hodges, and Egan, 2001) and have what Olweus (1993) calls "body anxiety": They're clumsy, afraid of being hurt, and weak at sports and fights. They are always the last ones chosen for the team.

Students who are bullied often have a history of insecure attachment, trouble separating from their parents, and a fear of exploring their surroundings. Their families tend to overprotect them, manipulate their thoughts and feelings, or use coercive and power-assertive discipline. These tactics threaten the development of the child's sense of self, undermine her confidence, and batter her self-esteem (Perry et al., 2001).

Sensing a child's vulnerability, a more powerful student or group may decide to tease or ridicule her (Rigby, 2002), and instead of standing up for herself, she feels threatened and scared, cries, or runs away, signaling that she's an easy mark. Because a child who's targeted usually has poor social skills and few or no friends, the student doing the bullying knows that no one will come to her defense (Egan and Perry, 1998; Hodges, Boivin, Vitaro, and Bukowski, 1999; Perry et al., 2001). Other students join in the attack, escalating the abuse and dampening concern and sympathy for the targeted child. Indeed, her peers will probably blame her for being bullied and isolate her even further (Oliver et al., 1994). Some students are so eager to belong to a group that they'll put up with any kind of abuse (Roberts, 2006).

Research suggests children get locked into the role of victim at 8 or 9 years of age (Pepler, Smith, and Rigby, 2004). Even when they enter a new classroom or school, they communicate their insecurity and fear to their classmates, setting themselves up for more victimization (Salmivalli, Kaukiainen, and Lagerspetz, 1998).

Are children bullied because they're different? Psychologists David G. Perry, Ernest V. E. Hodges, and Susan K. Egan (2001) point out that physical differences seem to incite teasing, which can cause distress and a loss of self-esteem—and may put a child at risk of harassment. Among boys and girls bullied at least once a week, about 20 percent were victimized because of their looks or speech, according to a

Not Too Bad

Carl is a fourth-grader. His mother wrote the following (Boivin et al., 2001):

I asked Carl after school how his day had gone. Reluctant to tell me because he was embarrassed, he replied, "It wasn't too bad today," and proceeded to list the following: One classmate stuffed their garbage into his backpack, M. [the bully] yelled at him in front of the rest of the class that Carl's art project was "dumb," M. imitated his voice throughout the day whenever Carl spoke and quietly sang jeering songs about him, Carl's seating partner harassed him throughout the day with such things as songs about Carl "being dead" and another boy drew a number of pictures of Carl and proceeded to rip the heads off each one. In addition, a classmate of Carl's said that the kids are also in the habit of making comments to each other about "how he smells". . . . This was a *pretty good day* for Carl. (p. 266)

Source: From "Toward a Process View of Peer Rejection and Harassment," by M. Boivin, S. Hymel, and E. V. E. Hodges, 2001. In J. Juvonen & S. Graham (Eds.), *Peer Harassment in School: The Plight of the Vulnerable and Victimized*. New York: Guilford. Reprinted by permission of the publisher.

survey of 15,000 U.S. students (Nansel et al., 2001), and researchers in the Midwest found that the top reason for being bullied was "just didn't fit in" (Hoover and Oliver, 1996). Other studies show that children with disabilities (Whitney, Smith, and Thompson, 1994) and children who are obese (Janssen, Craig, Boyce, and Pickett, 2004) face a higher risk of harassment. As Keith Sullivan, Mark Cleary, and Ginny Sullivan (2004) note in *Bullying in Secondary Schools*, "Once a bullying culture is operating, those who are somehow different . . . are likely to be singled out, but the random and indiscriminate nature of bullying means that no one is immune" (p. 13).

Ethnicity or culture sometimes makes a child a target. In the large U.S. study (Nansel et al., 2001), about 8 percent of students who were bullied once a week or more reported being harassed because of their race or religion. But other studies have found much higher rates. In surveys in middle schools in New York and New Jersey, 40 to 45 percent of African American, Latino, and European American students and 60 to 65 percent of Asian American students reported that their peers had harassed or discriminated against them because of their race or ethnicity (Way and Hughes, 2007).

Because racial harassment has profound educational, emotional, and physical consequences for the students who are targeted, it is a federal offense (U.S. Department of Education, 2005a). Racial harassment can damage self-esteem, self-efficacy, and control, and lead to feelings of helplessness, frustration, and depression, as well as challenging behavior and lower academic performance (Fisher, Wallace, and Fenton, 2000; Greene, Way, and Pahl, 2006; Wong, Eccles, and Sameroff, 2003).

Not all students who are harassed are passive. Perhaps 10 to 20 percent fight back and even egg on their abusers. Dubbed "provocative victims" by Olweus (1993), they are also called "aggressive victims" or "bully-victims." Like children who bully, they have trouble concentrating, and they're likely to be impulsive and hyperactive. They try to dominate others, and their behavior is often aggressive and antisocial (Olweus, 1993). Like children who are targeted but don't retaliate, they are anxious, depressed, rejected, and lonely. Lacking social skills, they have few friends (Perry et al., 2001; Perry et al., 1992; Schwartz, Proctor, and Chen, 2001). They are also physically weak and have the same body anxiety as children who respond passively to harassment (Olweus, 1993).

Targeting Difference

To show their respect for God, followers of the Sikh faith never cut their hair and wear it tucked inside a religious turban.

But many Sikh boys who attend school in the New York City borough of Queens are regularly harassed and intimidated by their peers, who hit them on the head or on their turbans and call them "terrorists" or "diaperheads," according to a recent survey (Singh and Aung, 2007). After an argument, an older student attacked a younger one in the school bathroom and cut off all his hair.

Although in this case the assailant was charged with a hate crime, such a response is rare: Students who are harassed seldom complain to school authorities because they don't expect action. In fact, the survey found that administrators failed to respond about one-third of the time (Singh and Aung, 2007).

But perhaps their most prominent quality is their volatility. Because they can't regulate their emotions, they lose their tempers, overreact, argue, and fight about all kinds of things, and they almost invariably lose. For this reason, some researchers (Perry et al., 1992) call them "ineffectual aggressors" (p. 320, 323). Their lack of self-control also means they have trouble in school (Schwartz et al., 2001). With this irritating, provocative behavior, they manage to elicit negative reactions from just about everyone (Olweus, 1993).

It is no surprise that students who combine aggressive behavior with victimization usually come from a harsh environment where the parenting is hostile and punitive and there is lots of conflict and violence. In a prospective study, 38 percent of the boys who emerged as "aggressive victims" had been physically abused and many had witnessed domestic violence (Schwartz, Dodge, Pettit, and Bates, 1997).

In the long run, there is risk for any child who is bullied. When Olweus (1993, 2001) followed up on boys who'd been bullied in grades 6 through 9, he found that at the age of 23 they were more depressed and had lower self-esteem than their non-victimized peers. The Australian bullying expert Ken Rigby (2001a) reported that students who'd been victimized were more likely to be anxious, depressed, socially dysfunctional, and physically unwell three years later; many thought about killing themselves. And a Dutch study of children dealing with harassment revealed that some as young as 9 years of age had suicidal thoughts (van der Wal, de Wit, and Hirasing, 2003). In later life, students who've been the targets of relational bullying face risks above and beyond those encountered by the targets of physical bullying. They are even more depressed, lonely, anxious, and rejected (Crick et al., 1999; Crick et al., 2001). "Bully-victims" are the most disturbed of all, with the most serious behavior problems and difficulties at school (Juvenon, Graham, and Schuster, 2003; Kumpulainen, Rasanen, and Henttonen, 1999; Wolke et al., 2000).

Who are the bystanders?

Bullying is a group activity, situated in a social context that influences both the emergence of bullying and the response to it. The hard evidence of Craig and Pepler's

The Bitter Fruit of Bullying

Children who are the targets of bullying may retaliate or strike preemptively (Slaby, 1997). An analysis of 37 school shootings disclosed that 70 percent of the shooters had been bullied by their peers (Vossekuil, Fein, Reddy, Borum, and Modzeleski, 2002). The words of one Columbine High School athlete give some sense of what Dylan Klebold and Eric Harris were facing before they killed 12 students and one teacher:

> Columbine is a clean, good place except for those rejects. Most kids didn't want them here. They were into witchcraft. They were into voodoo dolls. Sure, we teased them. But what do you expect with kids who come to school with weird hairdos and horns on their hats? It's not just the jocks; the whole school's disgusted with them. They're a bunch of homos, grabbing each other's private parts. If you want to get rid of someone, usually you tease 'em. So the whole school would call them homos, and when they did something sick, we'd tell them, "You're sick and that's wrong." (Gibbs and Roche, 1999)

cameras (1997) showed that peers were involved in 85 percent of bullying incidents, and even though the bullying usually stopped right away when students stood up for the child being bullied, they did so in just 19 percent of the incidents (Hawkins, Pepler, and Craig, 2001). Bullying lasts longer when more peers are present (O'Connell, Pepler, and Craig, 1999), and when they don't intervene—sending the unmistakable message that they condone the behavior—bullying becomes increasingly acceptable. The result is a harsher, less empathetic social climate that fosters more bullying.

An audience is the lifeblood of a student who bullies. The bystanders' reactions—their active assistance, comments, and laughter—reinforce and incite her behavior (Slaby, 1997), spread word of her power, and raise her status with her schoolmates (Sutton et al., 1999). Psychologist Christina Salmivalli and her colleagues in Finland (1999, 2001) have shown that during bullying episodes students take on different roles, depending on their individual dispositions and the group's expectations. In addition to bullying and being victimized, they play the following parts:

- *Assistants* help and join the child who is doing the bullying. Salmivalli (1999) found that about 7 percent of sixth-grade students acted as assistants.
- *Reinforcers* come to see what's going on and encourage bullying behavior by laughing and commenting on the action. According to Salmivalli (1999), 19.5 percent of sixth-grade students took on this role.
- *Outsiders* stay away and don't take sides, but their silence permits bullying. Almost 24 percent of sixth-graders fit this description (Salmivalli, 1999).
- *Defenders* side with the targeted child, comfort her, and try to stop the bullying. In Salmivalli's study (1999), 17.3 percent of students in sixth grade came to the defense of the child under attack. Defenders are more likely to be self-confident, popular, and well liked by their peers.

Enablers

British bullying experts Helen Cowie and Sonia Sharp (1994) describe two powerful ways that children support bullying:

> First, pupils can passively support the bullying behaviour by ignoring it or by remaining silent. These pupils can maintain the victim's role by avoiding the bullied pupil(s) or by not inviting them to join their social group. They can socially reinforce the pupils who are doing the bullying by co-operating with them, being friendly towards them or by not saying anything to them about the bullying behaviour. They can even help to enhance the reputation of the bullying pupil by gossiping about bullying incidents.
>
> Second, pupils can support bullying behaviour in a much more active way. They can do this by: verbally encouraging the behaviour; preventing the pupil being bullied from escaping the situation; shielding the situation from adult view; acting as "look out" or warning the pupils who are bullying that an adult is approaching; generally assisting the pupil to bully by holding the pupil being bullied, or holding coats or bags; directing the bullying behaviour, e.g., "Go on, put her bag down the toilet!"; acting as a messenger for the pupils who are bullying; laughing or smiling at the bullying behaviour; writing graffiti confirming the role of the pupil as victim or bully; refusing to give information about the situation even when asked. (p. 89)

Between Angel and Devil

SuEllen Fried (Fried and Fried, 2003) received the following letter from a student in a bullying workshop:

> There is this girl in my grade who is a target for verbal bullying. People say things behind her back, but act caring and concerned when she's around. I have tried to be respectful to her, but sometimes that's hard to do. I feel like I'll become a target if I be her friend. She is really quiet, and usually doesn't catch on to what people are saying about her. Because I'm a witness, I feel trapped in the middle of things. The angel on one shoulder is telling me to do what is right and just. The devil on the other says, "Just go with the flow, or you might be next."
>
> Normally, I listen to neither of the two and do nothing. I pretend I don't know what's going on and tell myself, "What could I do about it anyway?" (pp. 276–277)

Source: From *Bullies, Targets, and Witnesses: Helping Children Break the Pain Chain* by SuEllen Fried and Paula Fried, 2003. New York: M. Evans and Company, Inc. Copyright © SuEllen Fried and Paula Fried, 2003. Reprinted by permission of the Publisher.

In other words, about 58 percent of the children, including those who were doing the bullying, took a pro-bullying stance. Among older children these numbers are higher (Salmivalli, 2001).

Paradoxically, 83 percent of the students in a large Canadian survey reported that bullying made them feel uncomfortable (O'Connell et al., 1999), and many felt they should step in to help a person who's being bullied (Hawkins et al., 2001). Witnessing an attack can even traumatize some children (Garbarino and deLara, 2002). Clearly, there is a gap between students' attitudes and their behavior.

Why do bystanders behave the way they do?

• *Attraction to aggression.* As Pepler and Craig (2000) put it, "Peers are the audience for the theater of bullying" (p. 9), which excites and arouses them. They may also fear the student who bullies and realize that if they try to defend the child who's been targeted, they will put their own safety at risk (O'Connell et al., 1999).

• *Social contagion.* When they see someone acting aggressively, students tend to act more aggressively themselves. This effect increases when the observers think highly of the aggressor. The student who bullies is a model of aggressive behavior, and the admiring assistants and reinforcers follow her lead. Olweus (1993) says these followers are likely to be anxious, insecure, and dependent, and siding with the child who's doing the bullying boosts their social status and protects them from future harassment.

• *Weakening of the controls against aggressive behavior.* Children's inhibitions against aggressive behavior become loosened when they realize that it has no negative consequences and is even rewarded. Seeing that aggressive behavior pays off may also desensitize children to violence. This phenomenon is well established for television violence.

• *Diffusion of individual responsibility.* When several people are involved, each individual feels less empathy, less guilt, and less responsibility (Thompson and Grace, 2001).

Just Deserts?

Jada, an attractive and popular eighth-grade student, stood by and watched as a group of girls teased and pushed Isabel. Later she explained her behavior by saying, "I don't hang out with her. Besides, look at how she dresses. She was asking for it."

- *Changes in perception of the students involved in bullying.* The student who bullies gains a reputation as a protector; but the more harassment a child endures, the more her peers regard her as weird, worthless, and deserving of abuse (Olweus, 1993). Oliver, Hoover, and Hazler (1994) found that many students thought bullying "teaches about behavior unacceptable to the group" (p. 15). Two-thirds of those in another study (Graham and Juvonen, 2001) believed the child being victimized could control her own behavior and was therefore responsible for her own harassment. Just 25 percent thought the bullying was due to factors beyond her control, such as being younger or weaker. In general, people who blame uncontrollable circumstances are more sympathetic and willing to help. Students may also blame the targeted child because it's difficult to function in life if one believes that things are random and unfair. It's far less threatening to take the view that the world is a just place and people get what they deserve (Wilczenski et al., 1994).

- *Role stabilization.* Once a child assumes a role in a group, it's hard to change it. The other group members expect her to behave in a way that's appropriate for her role, and she begins to define herself this way as well (Salmivalli, 1999).

- *Scapegoating.* When there is bullying, everyone in the group is placed in an "unavoidably active" role. According to psychiatrists Stuart W. Twemlow, Peter Fonagy, and Frank C. Sacco (2004), all members of the group contribute to the proceedings and the outcome by their action or inaction. A student who bullies operates with the support of the group members and on their behalf. To feel better about themselves, they project their worst fears and impulses onto the child who assumes the role of victim. This child becomes a scapegoat, ostracized from the school community. When she is targeted, many children don't consider it bullying—they think the treatment is deserved (Thompson and Grace, 2001).

- *Lack of understanding.* Last but not least, students don't intervene to help a peer who's being harassed because they don't understand the process of bullying and don't know how to counteract it (O'Connell et al., 1999).

HOW CAN TEACHERS REDUCE AND PREVENT BULLYING?

It isn't easy to eliminate bullying, but finding ways to cut down on its frequency or duration can make an important difference in a child's ability to cope (Ladd and Ladd, 2001).

The whole-school approach

To reduce and prevent bullying, Olweus and other researchers advocate a *whole-school approach*, where all the people in the environment—teachers, students,

administrators, parents, paraprofessionals, bus drivers, lunch supervisors, counselors, nurses, clerical staff—become attuned to bullying and undertake to fight it.
This is the method the Norwegian government used so successfully in its national
bullying intervention from 1983 to 1985. According to an evaluation of 2,500 elementary and junior high school students in Bergen, Norway, bullying of all kinds decreased by half or more (Olweus, 1993, 2001). There was also substantial
improvement in the schools' social climate: Students had more positive social relationships and more positive attitudes toward school and schoolwork, and vandalism,
fighting, theft, and truancy declined. The effects were cumulative, better after the
second year than the first.

Replications of the intervention in the United States and elsewhere have pro-
duced some small reductions in bullying (Smith, Schneider, Smith, and Ananiadou,
2004), but it has become apparent that the Norwegian model is not the ultimate answer to the problem. As bullying experts Ken Rigby, Peter K. Smith, and Debra J. Pepler (2004) put it, "The task of describing best practice remains" (p. 2). Nonetheless,
researchers agree that a systemic approach is essential (Rigby, 1998; Rigby et al.,
2004; Sharp and Thompson, 1994). The level of bullying varies greatly from school
to school, and it is related to students' attitudes toward harassment (Rigby, 2002).
When everyone is on the same page, the antibullying message comes through loud
and clear (Sharp and Thompson, 1994).

The goal of the whole-school approach is to restructure the environment so
there are fewer opportunities and rewards for bullying and more reinforcement for
positive behavior (Olweus, 1993, 2001; Sharp and Thompson, 1994). This change
in the social context lets students know that bullying is not acceptable and adults will
intervene consistently to protect them. A school must take one additional step: Once
it has adopted an antibullying policy, it must commit itself to the values and beliefs
that underlie the policy and implement it fully. Otherwise it will provide little protection and even put students at risk (Sullivan et al., 2004).

Working in your own classroom

If your school doesn't have an antibullying policy, you can introduce one in your
own classroom. Much of what we suggest here has been discussed in previous chapters, so you have already made a good start. Be aware that it takes time to create an
antibullying culture. As your students become more aware of bullying, things may
get worse before they get better (Pepler and Craig, 2000).

Because of the power imbalance inherent in bullying, children cannot fight it
alone, and adult inaction equals tacit approval: Experts have known for decades that
the presence of passive adults—bystanders—increases children's aggressive behavior (Siegel and Kohn, 1959). In classrooms where teachers don't intervene to stop
bullying incidents, children don't step in either (Slee, 1993). As the teacher and
leader of the class, you hold the key to the success of your antibullying project. Your
commitment and enthusiasm, along with the belief that you can actually change
things, will influence how effective you can be (Rigby, 1998).

First and foremost, you are a role model. If you insult, bully, or put your students down, you will give them "a first-hand lesson in the effectiveness of the use
of power and aggression," Pepler and Craig write (2007, p. 9). Instead, you can
demonstrate the positive use of power on a daily basis and role-model respectful

behavior toward all students, especially those who are rejected or treated badly (Sullivan et al., 2004).

Teachers bring some other valuable tools to the antibullying enterprise: an ability to develop warm, sensitive, and responsive relationships with students; a capacity to build an inclusive, cooperative classroom climate; and a willingness to place firm limits on unacceptable behavior (Olweus, 1993; Pepler et al., 2004; Roland and Galloway, 2002). If you're going to have any effect on a student who bullies, you will need all of these strategies because you must create an environment where bullying doesn't work. Attempting to change bullying behavior without altering the surrounding environment will merely drive bullying underground.

The best way to establish limits is to involve the whole class in creating clear rules against bullying. You can incorporate them into the classroom rules your students developed at the beginning of the year (see page 130) or draw up a whole new set to deal with bullying. As you begin, engage your students in a discussion about what bullying is, how it differs from other forms of conflict and aggression, and how it affects everyone in the group. You may also want to talk about what rules can do to make the environment safer. Olweus (1993, p. 82) suggests three rules:

1. We shall not bully other children.
2. We shall try to help children who are bullied.
3. We shall make a point of including children who are easily left out.

When you combine classroom rules with regular class meetings on the subject of bullying, you can reduce harassment even further (Olweus, 1993). Power, empathy, peer pressure, courage, prosocial behavior, the difference between accidental and on purpose, the line between teasing and bullying, and how it feels to be unwelcome—all of these topics kindle interesting debate, and you can expand and reinforce the antibullying message with age-appropriate books, drawings, puppet plays, role-playing responses to bullying, and writing assignments. For example, students can write about how a particular word—such as *stupid* or *fat*—or a racial slur affected them (Bott, 2004). In other words, bullying issues (along with nonsexist, nonracist, and nonviolent ideas and values) should also be an ongoing, integral part of the curriculum—in English, history, and anywhere else an opportunity arises.

Be sure to use your class meeting time to sensitize the students to the role of the bystander. Explain that they probably don't realize it, but their presence during a bullying incident, even if they're only watching, actually supports the child who's doing the harassing. Discuss and role-play what they can do instead—walk away, tell the student who's bullying to stop, tell the teacher, include the child who's left out, and so on. When students act collectively, they can change the balance of power, so give them scripts of what to say and do and coach them to step in together (Pepler and Craig, 2007). If they suggest an aggressive response, help them understand that although force may work in the short run, in the long run it escalates aggression, endangers the child who's intervening, and reinforces the idea that it's an acceptable way to resolve problems (Hawkins et al., 2001).

Emphasize that secrecy enables bullying to continue. You can encourage students to tell you or another adult when they encounter bullying by carefully clarifying the difference between tattling to get someone into trouble and telling to get someone out of trouble. Invite the school's principal, nurse, counselor, and

Solid Pink

When a ninth-grade newcomer wore a pink shirt on the first day of high school, the local bullies turned out in force. Six to 10 older students mocked him, called him a homosexual, and threatened to beat him up (Fairclough, 2007).

But two senior boys, who had themselves been targets of bullying when they were younger, came to his defense in a colorful way: They created Pink Day. Using the Internet, telephone, and text messages, they contacted as many students as they could, bought 75 men's pink tank tops, and handed them out before class the next day. About half of the school wore pink ("Pretty in Pink," 2007).

A week later, on the International Day of Peace, students at about 30 area schools showed their solidarity by joining in the pink protest against bullying (Jones, 2007).

psychologist to speak to your class so that students will feel more inclined to trust them as confidants (Wright, 2004). You will also need a system that allows students to report bullying anonymously—one possibility is to install boxes for comments and suggestions in various places around the school. In the end, students will report only if they feel certain that you will believe them and act discreetly and effectively to stop the bullying.

To increase awareness of bullying, help your class identify bullying hot-spots such as bathrooms and secluded areas on the playground and discuss how students can protect themselves—avoid this territory, go with a friend, or stay within a reasonable distance of a teacher's watchful eye. Of course, it's best if the school can eliminate these hot-spots, but it's also helpful to increase supervision (for example by making unannounced appearances in bathrooms), stock the playground with lots of age-appropriate equipment (Swearer and Doll, 2001), and organize non-competitive games and activities, which can significantly decrease both playground and classroom bullying (Froschl et al., 1998). A safe room—one that's always staffed by adults—can serve as a refuge for students in need (Wright, 2004). To convey that someone is watching over a public space (e.g., the hallway outside your classroom), have your class adopt it—decorating it and keeping it clean will make it a less alluring site for harassment (Wright, 2004).

Because teachers and families need to work together to protect children, tell your students that you will call their parents any time bullying is suspected. Bring parents into the picture as early as possible. The more they know about bullying and the class rules, the more support they can provide. One way to involve them is to invite them to see a video about bullying. (See page 306 for suggestions.) After the showing, present your policy and the important facts about bullying, and encourage them to discuss the topic. To help them talk with their children at home, be sure to explain the bystanders' role, the difference between tattling and telling to protect someone, and how their children can assist a child who's being harassed or excluded (Olweus, 1993).

You can also pique parental interest by using drama. If the whole class participates in writing and putting on a play about bullying, the students can stage an evening performance, and most families will probably attend. The students learn a great deal about bullying during the play's creation process, which requires lots of thinking and role-playing. But be careful not to cast a student who bullies in a bullying role or a student who is victimized in a role where she's harassed. It's probably also wise not to let a child who bullies take the part of a targeted child, since this may provide her with yet more insight into how to harass.

What helps students cope with bullying?

Researchers have singled out some protective factors and strategies that enable students to avoid bullying, to respond in ways that deter future attacks, and to cope without becoming overwhelmed. We mentioned a few in the previous section, but students who are targeted need a range of responses. Although some protective factors are the result of natural endowment (such as physical strength and intelligence) (Smith, Shu, and Madsen, 2001), there are other qualities and techniques that teachers can help students to acquire.

- *Self-esteem.* Students who feel good about themselves refuse to tolerate bullying and defend themselves assertively and effectively (Egan and Perry, 1998). To build self-esteem, encourage and reinforce children's strengths—pay attention to their potential, help them develop it, and give them lots of opportunities to feel proud of their accomplishments. It is especially important to encourage and reinforce positive interactions with peers.

- *Assertiveness skills.* When children respond assertively, the perpetrators of bullying will stop or move on. Assertiveness training (which includes role-playing, lots of practice, and drawing a clear distinction between assertiveness and aggression) helps children gain self-control, confidence, and self-esteem (Sharp and Cowie, 1994). Assertiveness training isn't just for those who are harassed. It can also assist students who take the role of assistants or reinforcers to resist peer pressure and refrain from bullying, and it can encourage the outsiders to act as defenders (Salmivalli, 1999). Changing the attitudes and behavior of her associates may help to change the behavior of the student who bullies.

- *Social and emotional skills.* The ability to share, take turns, be a friend, enter a group, regulate emotion, empathize, manage anger, have a sense of humor, and other social and emotional skills aid a student to become a valued member of a group and provide her with some immunity to bullying (Egan and Perry, 1998; Perry et al., 2001). Training in social and emotional skills can be helpful for bystanders and students who are victimized, but it is not a panacea. For example, researchers have found that problem solving can deescalate a bullying situation when it's used well, but children who are bullied seldom possess the social competence and supportive peer group necessary to make this strategy work (Kochenderfer-Ladd and Skinner, 2002; Wilton, Craig, and Pepler, 2000). In fact, neither conflict resolution nor mediation is an appropriate way to deal with bullying (U.S. Department of Health and Human Services, 2004). There is also little evidence that training in social competence will help students who bully (Rigby et al., 2004). Although they often cannot imagine what others are feeling, it is probably ill advised to teach them empathy, which may heighten their already acute social perception and inadvertently boost their bullying skills. Several researchers (Sutton et al., 1999) instead suggest trying

Having a best friend can be a powerful buffer against harassment.

to change their positive attitudes toward aggression and focusing on moral issues (Thompson and Grace, 2001).

• *Cooperation skills.* Students who bully and students who are victimized both tend to be less cooperative—the former because they have little empathy and the latter because they're often introverted and less accepted by their peers (Rigby, 1998). Children who cooperate with others are happier and more popular, so this is a valuable skill to teach. A cooperative, inclusive social context and techniques such as cooperative learning groups and peer tutoring can foster cooperation, build friendships, and prevent bullying.

• *A friend.* Having a best friend can be a powerful buffer against harassment, reducing the likelihood of victimization (Boivin et al., 2001) and cushioning a child who's been bullied from later emotional and behavioral problems (Hodges et al., 1999). But researchers have also observed that a weak friend who can't protect a child may actually increase the risk of harassment (Hodges et al., 1999). Teachers can help students learn about friendship through literature, modeling, and discussion, and they can play an important role in decreasing the isolation that makes students vulnerable (Hazler and Carney, 2006). By using cooperative learning groups, organizing a buddy system or a circle of friends for a solitary student, and selecting teams, groups, and seating so that she's always included, teachers can increase a child's social support, help her to make friends, and surround her with peers who will stand up for her (Pepler and Craig, 2007).

- *An internal locus of control.* When a student feels that something immutable in her character makes her a target, she is likely to feel helpless or depressed and ready to give up. But when she believes that she has some control over her life, she is more likely to look for ways to change and cope—to seek help or use positive self-talk, for example (Graham and Juvonen, 2001; Ladd and Ladd, 2001). You can nurture self-efficacy by giving students responsibility and opportunities to succeed and encouraging them to reflect on their own competence (Doll, Song, and Siemers, 2004).

- *Telling a teacher.* A large Australian study (Rigby, 2002) found that when students told someone they'd been victimized, the bullying situation improved about 50 percent of the time. This finding held true for both boys and girls, but reporting worked better for younger children than for older ones, for whom it is more effective to ignore bullying and give less feedback to the students who harass (Smith et al., 2001). Disclosure made matters worse in about 10 percent of the Australian cases (Rigby, 2002) and in about 16 percent of the cases in an English study (Smith and Shu, 2000). A school's social climate and the attitudes and skills of the teacher who responds to a bullying report will probably influence how the child feels and what happens as a result (Rigby, 2002; Smith et al., 2001; Unnever and Cornell, 2003).

Many of these strategies are described in more detail in Chapter 7. Role-playing and rehearsal are essential for learning them all.

RESPONDING TO BULLYING

Despite your best efforts to prevent it, bullying may still arise. Before it does, take some time to understand your own feelings on the subject. If you bullied, or were bullied, as a child, your emotions may be surprisingly strong, and it's important to understand them and separate them from what your students are experiencing. In a bullying situation, where a clear head and a nonthreatening tone of voice and body language are essential, you absolutely must keep your cool.

What does the law say?

Federal law prohibits sexual harassment, as well as harassment on the basis of race, ethnicity, religion, or disability (American Association of University Women, 2004; U.S. Department of Education, 2005a, 2005b). In addition, most states and school districts have antibullying legislation and/or policies and procedures (McGrath, 2007) that require schools to provide a safe educational environment and oblige school staff to take immediate appropriate steps to stop bullying behavior and prevent it from happening again (McGrath, 2007; U.S. Department of Education, 2005a, 2005b). It is essential for you to know exactly what your local laws and policies compel you to do.

In many bullying situations and when harassment involves sex, race, ethnicity, sexual orientation, or disability, teachers have an obligation to report the incident (or rumor) to a designated school official. This person is often the *Title IX coordinator*, who is responsible for ensuring that the school complies with Title IX, the federal law that prohibits discrimination in education. The school will probably also have a procedure for dealing with complaints. If so, the Title IX coordinator or someone else may take over the case.

How do you respond to bullying?

Acting to stop harassment is more than a legal obligation; it is a necessity. A teacher's response to bullying sends a message: Every student in the school learns either that bullying will be tolerated (which gives students a license to bully and makes everyone feel unsafe), or that bullying won't be tolerated (which may give bystanders the courage to show disapproval or tell an adult) (Sullivan et al., 2004). Even small incidents demand a response, and handling them effectively will help prevent an escalation in harassment (Sullivan et al., 2004). This doesn't imply that zero tolerance is in order; rather, the response must make it clear that bullying is unacceptable and at the same time teach prosocial ways to relate to others.

When you see bullying, you must intervene at once. Whether the attack is verbal or physical, inside or outside of the classroom, the best plan is to do what you'd do with any other act of aggression. Separate the students if necessary, protect the student who's being harassed, let her know you support her, and help her respond assertively (Sharp and Cowie, 1994). When you leave the scene, you may have to take her with you to secure her safety. Your response to the student who's teasing or harassing should be explicitly educational and public: "That is bullying," or "What you said is harassment on the basis of race [sex, disability, etc.]," and "Here at our school we treat all students with respect" (Sapon-Shevin, 2003).

Bully Radar

In *Bullying in Secondary Schools* (2004), Sullivan and colleagues warn that the following signs may indicate the presence of bullying:

- Members of a class titter, snigger, or nudge each other when a particular student comes in, answers a question, or draws attention to him or herself.
- A student appears despondent, listless, or unhappy.
- A student is mostly alone, and/or is actively left out of activities.
- A student who is working well and getting good grades seems to work less well and gets worse grades.
- A student is frequently absent. (p. 13)

School psychologist Jim Wright (2004) suggests another way to detect bullying: Make a point of watching your class during recess or lunch when they're not expecting you. In this less supervised, unstructured environment, you may witness bullying that is invisible inside the classroom, and this glimpse will help you monitor your students' activity more effectively.

A teacher quoted in Rachel Simmons's *Odd Girl Out* (2002) adds this clue for identifying those targeted by relational bullying: "[Girls become] very withdrawn. Their personalities change. Their facial expressions change. It's almost like a sadness, an intimidation. . . . Even their posture [changes]. . . . They just withdraw—from the teachers, their group of friends. . . . I like for a child to smile. Lots of times I say, 'Give me a smile,' and if they really cannot smile, you know something is wrong" (pp. 229–230).

What if you don't see the bullying?

It is more likely that a student will tell you about bullying that you haven't witnessed yourself.

In addition to concealing bullying from view, children are reluctant to tell anyone about it. In one study, 30 percent of targeted students told neither their parents nor their teachers (Smith and Shu, 2000). Boys tend to tell less often than girls (Rigby and Slee, 1999), and older students less often than younger ones (Smith et al., 2001). Only about 20 percent of students who've been sexually harassed disclose this information to an adult at school (American Association of University Women, 2001). Cyberbullying also remains secret, probably because students fear they'll lose their cell phone or their Internet privileges ("What are the forms," n.d.; iSAFE, n.d.). The children who are the most likely to report are the ones who are the most frequently victimized (Smith et al., 1999; Unnever and Cornell, 2004)—and the bullying has probably gone on for a long time before they finally reveal it (Smith et al., 2001). Furthermore, students do not make up tales about being harassed (Pepler and Craig, 2000), and telling a teacher can be difficult and risky, even for a student who isn't the target. If word gets out about who told, the bullying may escalate and spread to the defender.

It is therefore essential to believe your informant. Thank her for having the courage to come to you, and tell her that she made the right decision. If she wants to stay anonymous, let her know that you will do your best to keep your source of information confidential, but this will limit your ability to deal with the situation and may not be possible if other students are at risk. Reassure her that you will divulge her name only on a need-to-know basis (McGrath, 2007; U.S. Department of Education and National Association of Attorneys General, 1999).

You may never know exactly what happened, but that isn't really important. What matters is knowing that bullying has occurred and who was involved—the student or students who bullied, the student who was targeted, and the bystanders. If you know where and when the harassment is taking place, you can move to prevent it and help the student who was harassed protect herself. To begin with, you can figure out how to supervise more closely and step up your work with the whole group.

What do you say to students involved in bullying?

Once you know about bullying, what do you do next? Here, the experts disagree. Pepler and her colleagues (2004) point out that the decision rests in part on your perception of the problem. If you believe bullying is a matter of one student's aggressive behavior, you'll probably want to speak with that student one-on-one and arrange consequences. But if you think that bullying depends on group dynamics, you'll favor a group solution. Olweus (1993) leans toward the first view. He recommends "serious talks" with both the student who's been harassed and the student who did the bullying, and he imposes sanctions if talks don't work. Other researchers prefer *formative consequences*, and still others champion a *no-blame* approach, where the group is the object of the intervention and no penalties are attached.

Guiding Principles

Peter K. Smith, Helen Cowie, and Sonia Sharp (1994), who directed a successful bullying intervention in Sheffield, England, recommend four principles when working with students involved in bullying:

- Focus on solving the problem.
- Encourage the pupils themselves to propose solutions to the problem.
- Employ assertive styles of communication rather than aggression or passivity.
- Ensure that other steps are taken to deal with the problem on a long term basis. (p. 212)

Talking with the student who's been targeted

No matter what your philosophical perspective, you will need to talk with the student who's been victimized. Because she'll be upset, you'll probably want to sit down with her as soon as possible—and before you give your attention to the child who bullied her. Tell her that she has the right to feel safe, and make it clear that you will protect and support her (Pepler and Craig, 2000). Active listening and the WEVAS open communication strategies may be the most appropriate way to proceed (see pages 201 to 202). Use open-ended questions to discuss what happened, taking care not to suggest that the bullying is her fault or in any way deserved. Together explore ideas for improving the situation. Remind her of assertive responses, suggest that she avoid areas where bullying is likely to occur, and help her find a buddy—or a mentor in a higher grade—to coach her in needed social skills and enable her to feel safer and less alone (Pepler and Craig, 2000). Reassure the student that you'll assist her in putting these plans into action. If she appears to be a "bully-victim," whose impulsive, argumentative behavior and inability to regulate her emotions seem to provoke bullying, try to understand the reasons behind her behavior, and use your relationship to work with her on improving her self-esteem, sense of belonging, and social and emotional regulation skills. You might also organize a mini-support group for students who've been victimized. Getting them together will help them realize they're not alone (Committee for Children, 2001). (Such a group would be counterproductive for students who bully because they quickly learn new tactics from one another.)

It's also important to tell a student who's been targeted that you're going to speak to her parents. Explain that they will want to help and it is safer if they know what's going on. If the student protests, encourage her to accept the idea, but eventually you will have to go ahead anyway—with her knowledge but without her permission.

Talking with the student who bullies

Next, you want to speak with the student who bullied. This may not be easy, because she is likely to deny any wrongdoing and push your emotional buttons (Roberts, 2006). But if you're going to make any headway, it's essential to treat her with respect and dignity and listen to what she has to say without judging her.

The discussion needn't be long, and it needn't be an interrogation, because it's not necessary to find out exactly what happened. The goal is to convey that bullying is unacceptable and must stop, not to intimidate or disempower the student.

Accorging to the bullying prevention program *Steps to Respect* (Committee for Children, 2001), the following questions can help you assess whether a student who was bullied needs further help:

- Does the child have any friends? Is the child always alone?
- Has the child been bullied (1) by multiple children; (2) on several occasions; (3) across school years?
- Has the child's school performance deteriorated?
- Does the child have difficulty concentrating on school work?
- Has the child refused to attend school?
- Is the child afraid to ride the bus or walk to school?
- Does the child try to avoid recess or unsupervised contact with peers?
- Has the child experienced a recent loss or trauma?
- Has the child talked about suicide or expressed the feeling that he or she would be better off dead? (If so, immediately refer the child to a qualified mental health professional for evaluation.)
- Has the child threatened violence toward others? (If so, immediately refer the child to a qualified mental health professional for evaluation.)

Source: From "Identifying and Referring Children with Additional Needs," from *Steps to Respect: A Bullying Prevention Program* © 2001 Committee for Children. Reprinted with permission from Committee for Children, Seattle, WA. www.cfchildren.org.

Stay away from power-assertive language and methods such as hostility, aggression, sarcasm, threats, and humiliation. They are sure to backfire, providing a justification for more bullying and inspiring the invention of more covert ways to bully (Sharp and Cowie, 1994; Sharp, Cowie, and Smith, 1994).

Instead, sit down with the student who bullied in a quiet, private spot and remind her of the rules. (Even if you have no antibullying rules, you should have rules about respecting, taking care of, or not hurting others.) Talk with her about how her behavior is affecting her peers, and tell her that you'll be contacting her parents.

Although it may be hard to get to know a student who bullies, spending one-on-one time with her is extremely important. A positive relationship can help you understand some of the reasons behind her bullying, focus on her strengths, recognize and redirect her leadership abilities, and think up positive replacement behaviors that can meet her needs.

If several students participated in the bullying activity, plan to speak with them individually, one right after the other, so they won't have a chance to cook up a common response or use the group as a power source.

Should there be consequences for students who bully?

Olweus (1993) regards a serious talk with a student who's bullying as a consequence. Some schools use behavior contracts where, without actually admitting to bullying, the student promises not to bully in the future and understands the consequences of breaking the contract (O'Moore and Minton, 2004). Pepler and Craig (2000, p. 19) favor "formative" consequences, which teach empathy, awareness, and social skills at the same time that they hold children responsible for their behavior and

In *Bullying Prevention*, psychologists Pamela Orpinas and Arthur M. Horne (2006) emphasize the importance of connecting with students who bully. They make these suggestions:

- *Establish an invitational approach.* Present this conversation as an opportunity for open dialogue, rather than mandatory counseling. "I'd like to talk with you about what's going on, to get your sense of what's behind the problems" (p. 193).
- *Show respect and dignity.* Students who bully are used to being in trouble and expect to be treated ignominiously. It is therefore doubly important to treat them with respect.
- *Be honest and direct.* Without blaming the student, identify the problem and state what's necessary to resolve it.
- *Be understanding but not approving.* Make an effort to understand the point of view of the student who harasses, but avoid giving the impression that you approve of inappropriate behavior. "We need to find a different way for you to manage your anger and a way for you to tolerate other students, even if you don't like them" (p. 194).
- *Accept that the child doing the bullying and her parents are doing the best they can* under the circumstances. "I think that you are doing the best you can right now to deal with Gene, but what you've been doing isn't working. . . . My goal is to spend some time helping you to identify new ways of getting along with Gene and other people, ways you haven't been able to use because you didn't know about them" (p. 195).

emphasize that bullying is unacceptable. Formative consequences are logical—they help a student who acts in a cruel way to learn to treat others with more kindness and make amends for her behavior, for example by asking her to figure out how she can repair the damage she's done, whether emotional or physical. This approach enables children who bully to "turn their negative power and dominance into positive leadership" (p. 19). In *The Bully, the Bullied, and the Bystander* (2002), Barbara Coloroso also endorses giving children who bully the opportunity to have responsibility, make a contribution, and experience their own ability to "do good" (p. 113).

Although their views have created controversy, many experts on bullying believe that penalties don't deter students with serious bullying problems, particularly as they grow older (Stevens, deBourdeaudhuij, and VanOoost, 2000). Punishment leads not to lasting change but to resentment and more serious, and often covert, attacks. The student who bullies may blame her punishment on the child she targeted, and she may seek vengeance and issue new threats (Robinson and Maines, 2000). Punishment also bolsters the idea that bullying is acceptable if you have power.

Instead, Rigby (1998) and others come down on the side of a respectful, humanistic approach based on the desire to understand, not blame, all of the students involved. They propose listening carefully, establishing two-way communication, and using a technique like the No Blame Approach developed by George Robinson and Barbara Maines in England (1994, 2000) or the Method of Shared Concern created by Anatol Pikas in Sweden (1989, 2002). As the names imply, these procedures don't blame anyone or require any agreement about what happened. But they don't let anyone off the hook either—rather, they deescalate denial and defensiveness, focus on the impact of the bullying, and redirect the strengths of the students who

Pepler and Craig (2000) believe that consequences should help students who bully to learn skills and acquire insight. Here are some suggestions:

- Read a book or watch a movie about bullying and talk or write about how bullying makes people feel.
- Observe and report on acts of kindness around the school and in the community.
- Under the teacher's supervision, help out in a kindergarten or first-grade classroom or teach a skill to younger children.

Pepler and Craig suggest encouraging the student who bullies "to identify the link between power (or strength) and kindness. It is important for [her] to view prosocial behaviour as worthwhile, valid, and consistent with positive leadership" (p. 20).

are bullying to more positive ends. The goal is to arouse the empathic concern of the students who bully, help them break away from a bullying group, and reflect on how to resolve the problem (Smith et al., 1994). The process subtly changes the group's power structure and prods the leader to find more prosocial ways to lead and retain her status in the group (Sullivan et al., 2004). Like all antibullying interventions, both methods tend to be more successful in an inclusive social context.

Working with the parents of students involved in bullying

When there's bullying among the students in your classroom, it's imperative to tell the parents (Pepler and Craig, 2000). Olweus's Bergen study (1993) showed that parents wanted to know about bullying problems when their child was involved, even if the teacher "merely suspected bullying was taking place" (p. 95). When they aren't informed, they can easily become mistrustful and suspicious, which doesn't help you deal with the situation. It's always best for the child when teachers and families share information and work together, so as soon as you have spoken with the students involved, arrange to meet separately with each set of parents. You might ask a colleague or your principal to join you. She can furnish moral support and take notes, leaving you free to focus on the discussion (Suckling and Temple, 2002). At the end of the meeting, ask her to read back her notes; you can all sign them to remind you of what you agreed and protect you in case of future problems.

Whether their child is being harassed or doing the bullying, parents may know nothing about it. One study showed that just 48 percent of students who bully and 62 percent of students who are targeted tell a parent (Pepler and Craig, 2000). It's humiliating to tell, and this step is often a last resort for a child who's being bullied and is worried that her parents will interfere and make the problem worse. Learning about the bullying may bring the parents a surprising sense of relief and explain why their child doesn't want to take the school bus, stay at school for lunch, or go to school at all. But once they've processed this news, they're likely to feel angry, embarrassed, and helpless, blaming you and the school for failing to protect their child. They'll want action right away, and they may also want retribution (Pepler and Craig, 2000).

No Blame

The No Blame Approach, created by George Robinson and Barbara Maines (2000), works with the group, not individuals, and focuses on solving problems, not meting out blame or punishment. It starts with the student who was targeted, because Robinson and Maines believe that bringing her feelings to the group is the best way to evoke empathy and change.

- *Step 1.* In a private meeting, reassure the student who was victimized that she is not in danger because the students who bullied her will not be punished. Then concentrate on what she's feeling about being harassed, and invite her to produce a piece of artwork or writing that illustrates those feelings. Secure her permission to relay her feelings and present her work to those involved in the bullying, and ask her to suggest others who could contribute to a discussion of the situation—observers, friends, and peers she'd like to befriend. Include one or two students you can count on to act responsibly and who can influence the group.
- *Step 2.* Without the child who was harassed, meet with the students you've selected, including those directly or indirectly involved in the bullying (6 to 8 students in all). Reassure them that they're not in trouble but were chosen to help solve a problem.
- *Step 3.* To raise empathy in the members of the group, explain that you're worried about the student who's being harassed. Share her feelings and the artwork or written piece she's offered, and ask whether any of them has ever been bullied. Listen to their responses.
- *Step 4.* Give the group responsibility for helping the student who's been victimized to feel safe at school, assuring them that they can solve this problem.
- *Step 5.* The group is usually moved by the student's distress, and power shifts from the leader to the group as a whole. Don't ask for promises, but encourage each student to say what he or she can do to support the targeted student ("I'll ask her to sit with us at lunch").
- *Step 6.* Thank the group and express confidence in the students' ability to implement their plans.
- *Step 7.* A week later, interview the students one at a time, starting with the student who was harassed. If the bullying has stopped, thank the others for their good work. According to Robinson and Maines, two follow-up interviews are usually sufficient, but continue to watch the situation and if necessary convene a different group of students and start the process again.

On the other hand, it is equally conceivable that you will learn about the bullying from irate, stressed, and worried parents. The fact that you're just hearing about the situation will make it difficult to offer useful feedback—and once again, they will be angry and construe your ignorance as incompetence. They may also take their child's version of events as gospel, down to the last detail.

Under these circumstances, your primary job is to listen and to be empathetic and supportive. It's essential not to become defensive. Let the parents know that you take the matter seriously and will make it a priority. Tell them you will need some time to investigate, and you want to work with them to make school a safe place for their child (Suckling and Temple, 2002). Get back to them quickly with information about what you found out and what you're doing about the situation, and arrange another meeting to talk about what you can do together.

If you haven't seen the bullying yourself, tell the parents that it's the policy to talk with them whenever bullying is suspected. Let them know that students rarely fabricate stories about being bullied and that it's your job to follow through for the sake of all the children. Tell them that their cooperation and support will make any intervention much more effective.

Although you'll meet separately with the parents of the students involved, with both families it's important to keep three strategies firmly in mind:

1. Let the parents know that you care about their child and are trying hard to help her.
2. Avoid blame and arguments—nothing will sabotage your efforts more quickly. Listen to the parents' concerns and try to see things from their perspective, but don't get hooked, even if they attack you.
3. Remember that you are presenting a problem to be solved, and the best way to solve it is with their collaboration. Parents who play an active role will feel less angry, anxious, and helpless. Be sure they realize that they can support their child, help you identify the child's strengths, and figure out strategies to reinforce your efforts at home.

In other ways your conversations with these two sets of parents may be quite different. The parents of the student who's bullying may deny there's a problem or see bullying as a normal part of growing up. Be understanding but firm. The issue is not whether bullying is acceptable; the purpose of the meeting is to find common ground and develop a strategy to stop it. Describe the school's policy (and yours!) of creating a safe and caring environment for all students (Pepler and Craig, 2000). Tell them briefly what their child has done, but be sure to emphasize that it is her behavior that is unacceptable, not the child herself. Remember to talk about her positive side as well. At the same time tell them about your expectations and the actions you've taken so far, and try to establish a shared concern for the child who was targeted. Listen to their ideas, and work together to develop a plan. Try to project a sense of optimism—all parents ultimately want their child to succeed (Beane, 1999).

The parents of the student who's been harassed may feel guilty or embarrassed that their child doesn't stand up for herself, and they may think you're accusing them of overprotecting her. If they were bullied when they were young, their feelings will be magnified. And they will probably still be angry that you've let their child be hurt (Pepler and Craig, 2000). Listen to their concerns empathetically, explain your antibullying policy, and let them know what you're doing to protect their child and educate all the students about bullying. Discuss what you can do together to keep the child from becoming a target in the future, and encourage them to continue advocating for her. Remember to inform the child about any plan that you develop. Let both sets of parents know that you will stay in touch by phone and they are welcome to call you at any time.

It's important to remember that even though bullying has probably gone on for centuries, researchers have only recently started to examine it closely. They are making good progress, but definitive answers to its thorny problems are still a long way off. We've presented a rundown of knowledge and best practice to date, but the field is evolving quickly, and it would be a good idea to consult the latest research literature whenever you're dealing with a bullying problem.

What do you think?

1. How has your past experience influenced your attitudes about students who bully, students who are victimized, and bystanders?
2. When you're teaching English, you can reinforce learning about bullying through your choice of books. In other subjects, such as history or social studies, you will have to look at events through a different lens of awareness. Choose a subject and develop a lesson plan that enables you to integrate the topic of bullying.
3. How does what you learned in the prevention chapters (Chapters 7 and 8) relate to what you now know about bullying?
4. Which behavior do you think is the hardest to change—behavior of children who bully, behavior of children who are victimized, or bystanders? Why?
5. What do you think about using consequences for students who bully? Or do you prefer the "no-blame" approach? Why?
6. Is it a good idea to involve parents when a bullying incident occurs? Why or why not?
7. Do you think you should have the consent of the child who was victimized before you implement a plan to deal with the child who bullies? Why or why not?

What would you do?

Maybe the problems started because Luke was short and hyperactive. Called names and beaten up by his peers for years, by eighth grade he felt as if he didn't want to live any more, and he refused to go to school. He stayed home for a month. When he finally returned to classes, his middle school administration protected him by scheduling a short school day for him and keeping him under adult supervision at all times. He didn't eat lunch with the other students, couldn't go out for any sports, and went to the bathroom during class time when it was less likely to pose a danger.

What do you think of this school's solution to a bullying problem? How would you handle this situation?

Suggested readings and resources

Bongs, M., & Stoker, S. (2000). *Bully-proofing your middle school*. Longmont, CO: Sopris West.

Bott, C. J. (2004). *The bully in the book and the classroom*. Lanham, MD: Scarecrow.

Committee for Children. (2001). *Steps to respect: A bullying prevention program*. Seattle: Author.

Olweus, D. (1994). *Bullying at school: What we know and what we can do*. Malden, MA: Blackwell.

Operation Respect (n.d.). *Don't laugh at me* [Video]. http://operationrespect.org/curricula/index.php.

Page, M. (Producer), & Perlman, J. (Writer/Director/Animator). (2000). *Bully dance* [Video]. National Film Board of Canada. (Available from National Film Board of Canada, 1123 Broadway, Suite 307, New York, NY 10010; 1-800-542-2164; Fax 1-866-299-9928. www.nfb.ca/collection/films/fiche/?lg=en&id=33918.)

Pepler, D. J., & Craig, W. (2000). *Making a difference in bullying*. Toronto: LaMarsh Centre for Research on Violence and Conflict Resolution, York University, Report No. 60. www.arts.yorku.ca/lamarsh/pdf/Making_a_Difference_in_Bullying.pdf.

Rigby, K. (2002). *New perspectives on bullying*. London, UK: Jessica Kingsley.

Suckling, A., & Temple, C. (2002). *Bullying: A whole school approach*. London, UK: Jessica Kingsley.

Simmons, R. (2002). *Odd girl out: The hidden culture of aggression in girls*. New York: Harcourt.

U.S. Department of Education, Office for Civil Rights. (2005). *Sexual harassment: It's not academic*. www.ed.gov/about/offices/list/ocr/docs/ocrshpam.html.

The A-B-C Chart

Andrew's A-B-C Chart

Date	Subject/ Teacher	Antecedent	Behavior	Consequence	Possible Function
Monday 11/19/07	English/SL	Andrew is the last student to enter the class	Sits at desk with head lowered and arms folded across his chest	Ignored	Obtain attention
		Teacher begins whole-group grammar lesson	Sighs loudly, puts his head down on the desk	Reprimand—told to sit up straight	Avoid difficult task
		Reprimand	Does nothing	Teacher ignores and continues lesson	Avoid difficult task
		Teacher instructs students to take out materials required to construct proper sentences—scissors, glue—and hands out garbled sentences that need to be cut and pasted in the proper order	Fumbles in desk, takes everything out, puts it on the floor, crumples paper, and slams desk shut	Teacher ignores and continues lesson	Obtain attention
		Can't find required materials	Goes to pencil sharpener and hits Nancy lightly on the head	Reprimand—teacher tells Andrew to sit down and get to work	Avoid activity
		Reprimand	Swears and throws his book against the wall	Teacher tells Andrew to leave classroom; he leaves	Obtain attention
	Spanish/ CR	Teacher, speaking Spanish, reviews text and begins a dictation	Andrew talks loudly to neighbor	Reprimand—teacher tells Andrew to listen so that he can do his work	Avoid difficult task
		Reprimand	Swears at teacher	Reprimand—teacher tells Andrew to work at the back of the room	Avoid difficult task
		Reprimand	Andrew pushes his desk and laughs	Andrew told to leave classroom; Andrew leaves	Avoid difficult task

(continues)

Date	Subject/ Teacher	Antecedent	Behavior	Consequence	Possible Function
Monday 11/19/07 (cont.)	Math/SL	Teacher tells students to take their seats	Andrew swears	Ignored	Obtain attention
		Teacher introduces a new concept	Andrew drops his math book	Ignored	Avoid activity
		Teacher continues explaining new concept	Andrew goes to sharpen his pencil	Reprimand—teacher tells Andrew to sit down and pick up his book	Avoid activity
		Reprimand	Andrew picks up his book and slams it on the desk	Ignored	Obtain attention
		Teacher asks students to complete a worksheet	Andrew talks to his neighbor	Reprimand—teacher tells Andrew to do his work	Avoid activity
		Reprimand	Andrew says, "I wouldn't be asking Julie if you were a better teacher"	Teacher tells Andrew to leave classroom; he leaves	Avoid activity
	Social Studies/ KD	Teacher greets Andrew as he enters the room	Andrew smiles and sits at his desk	Teacher waits until Andrew is seated, catches his eye, and gives him a thumbs up	
		Teacher divides class into small groups	Andrew joins his group	Teacher smiles at Andrew	
		Teacher goes over to Andrew and explains what materials will be required	Andrew finds and takes out materials	Andrew participates in lesson	
	Science/ SL	Teacher tells students to pick a partner and find a place at a microscope	Andrew stands still waiting to be chosen	No one chooses Andrew	
		No one chooses Andrew	He goes over to a microscope and pushes the slides and related materials off the table	Teacher sends Andrew to the office; he leaves	Obtain attention
Tuesday 11/20/07	English/SL	Andrew enters the class with a smile and goes to his desk	Sitting at desk	Ignored	
		Teacher returns spelling test from last week	Makes noise opening and closing his desk	Ignored	Avoid activity
		Teacher returns Andrew's test	Andrew crumples the paper, gets up, and throws it in the garbage	Teacher tells Andrew to take the paper out of the garbage and return to his seat	Avoid activity

Date	Subject/Teacher	Antecedent	Behavior	Consequence	Possible Function
Tuesday 11/20/07 (cont.)	English/SL	Teacher begins to go over the spelling	Andrew is still standing by the garbage	Teacher repeats request	Avoid request
		Teacher request	Andrew kicks over the garbage	Teacher tells Andrew to leave the class	Avoid request
	Computer Science/RC	Teacher distributes assignment, assigns groups, and makes Andrew a group leader	Andrew goes to the computer	Group works on assignment	
	Math/SL	Andrew enters room with one of his computer partners	They stand and talk	Teacher tells students to take their seats	
		Teacher distributes a short quiz and says students can use their books	Andrew takes out his book and starts the quiz	Teacher ignores Andrew	
		Working on quiz	Andrew throws his book on the floor and screams, "This is stupid!"	Teacher picks up Andrew's book, hands it to him, and tells him to leave the room	Avoid task
	Social Studies/KD	Students working in groups. Andrew arrives late	Walks to his seat with his head down	Teacher walks over to Andrew and asks if he's okay	
		Students have been working on project in groups for 10 minutes	Andrew asks teacher if he can have a break	Andrew goes to the computer and plays a game	
		Teacher goes to Andrew and asks him to return to group	Andrew returns to group	Teacher talks to Andrew's group about what they are doing and makes sure they are on track	
	Physical Education/VF	Group enters gym	Andrew pushes Sam	Sam pushes back; teacher tells Andrew to keep his hands to himself	Avoid activity
		Sam pushes Andrew	Andrew swears at Sam and sits on bench	Teacher tells Andrew he must participate in activity	Avoid activity
		Teacher tells Andrew he must participate	Andrew swears at the teacher	Teacher sends Andrew to the principal	Avoid activity

A-B-C Chart

Date	Subject/ Teacher	Antecedent	Behavior	Consequence	Possible Function

The Functional Assessment Observation Form*

Understanding the Functional Assessment Observation Form

Robert O'Neill and his colleagues have developed a chart for recording observations for a functional assessment. The functional assessment observation form is organized around what the authors call "problem behavior events." An event could be one challenging behavior that lasts for mere seconds (Andrew swears) or an incident that includes several challenging behaviors (kicking, screaming, shouting) and continues for some time. The event starts when the first problem behavior begins and ends when three minutes have passed without any problem behaviors.

The functional assessment observation form indicates:

- The number of events of problem behavior
- The problem behaviors that occur together
- The times when the problem behaviors are most and least likely to occur
- The antecedent events
- Your perception of the function of the behavior
- The actual consequences

You'll find two copies of this form following this explanation. There is one form filled out for an observation of Andrew's behavior (discussed in Chapter 11) and there is a blank one for you to use later. The form's eight sections are as follows:

A. At the top, write the child's name and the dates of the observation. You can use this form to record observations over one day or several.
B. In the column on the extreme left, indicate the time of day and/or the subject being taught ("10:00–10:45 Math").
C. List the behaviors you want to observe (those you identified in your team's discussions and interviews) in the section labeled "Behaviors." Note each behavior separately so that you can figure out which ones occur together.
D. Just under the date, there is a space to put the antecedents that immediately precede the challenging behaviors. Again, your interviews will tell you what

---

*Explanation and chart (pages 311 and 314) adapted from *Functional Assessment and Program Development for Problem Behavior: A Practical Handbook*, 2nd edition, by R. E. O'Neill, R. H. Horner, R. W. Albin, J. R. Sprague, K. Storey, and J. S. Newton. © 1997. Reprinted with permission of Wadsworth, a division of Thomson Learning. www.thomsonrights.com. Fax 800-730-2215.

these are likely to be. The most common—demands/requests, difficult tasks, transitions, interruptions, and lack of attention—are already listed. If you suspect other antecedents are involved, write them into the empty slots. Some likely possibilities are a particular activity, task, or setting event (such as noise) or a peer or an adult whose presence seems related to the behavior.

E. The next group of columns is for your perception of the behavior's function. What purpose does it serve for the child? Does he get something, avoid or escape something, or change the level of stimulation? Why do you think he behaved this way? Again, the functions most often found in the literature are already listed, and there is space for you to add functions that you identified in interviews and discussions.

F. The next section is for consequences. What follows the behavior? When you're setting up the chart, fill in the diagonal blanks with the consequences that actually seem to occur most often. Do you ignore the behavior, reprimand the child, or send him out of the room? How do the other children react? Observing the consequences will help you see exactly what the student is getting from his behavior and provide more evidence of its function. For example, if you're sending a child out of the room when he wants to avoid an activity, the consequence is actually reinforcing the problem behavior.

G. The last column on the right is for comments or initials. Be sure to initial the form so you'll know that you were observing during this time period even if there were no behaviors to record.

H. Finally, the bottom rows, "Events" and "Date," enable you to keep track of the number of events and the days on which you observed them. We'll explain how in the next section.

Using the functional assessment observation form

The first time a problem behavior occurs, write *1* in the appropriate box in the "Behavior" column at the right time of day. As you continue to observe that behavior, continue across the form writing *1* in the appropriate boxes for the antecedents, functions, and consequences. Finally cross off the number *1* in the "Events" row at the bottom. When the second behavior occurs, write *2* in the appropriate boxes across the form, then cross off *2* in the Events row, and so on.

At the end of the day, draw a line after the last number you crossed off in the "Events" row and write the date beneath it. This will show you how many incidents occurred that day and allow you to compare the frequency of events over time.

You can also use this form to observe and record appropriate behaviors. But it probably makes more sense to do that on a chart dedicated to that purpose. Spending several days observing only appropriate behaviors could provide some very interesting ideas for your intervention plan.

You should always assist a child who needs your help, even when you're observing.

Andrew's Functional Assessment Observation Form

A — Name: Andrew

B — **Starting Date:** Nov. 19 **Ending Date:** Nov. 20

Time/Subject (B)	Hits, pushes	Loud talking	Pushes or throws objects	Rude, swears	Makes noise	Demand/Request	Difficult Task	Transition	Interruption	No Attention	Attention	Desired Item/Activity More/Less Stimulation	Demand/Request (Escape)	Activity (Escape)	Person	Sent to back of class	Reprimand	Ignored	Sent out of class	Comments/Initials (G)
	Behaviors (C)					**Antecedents (D)**					**Obtain (E)**		**Escape/Avoid**			**Consequences (F)**				
7:15 – 9:00 English	3	4, 15	4	1, 2, 14			1, 2			3, 14	2		1, 15	3, 14			1, 3	2, 14	4, 15	SL
9:00 – 9:45 Spanish	5	7	6	6	6, 7	5, 6, 7	5						5, 6, 7			5, 6		7		CR
10:05 – 10:50 Math	11	16	8, 12, 16	9, 10	8, 10, 12	8, 10	9, 11, 16				8, 10		9, 11, 12, 16				11	8, 9, 10	12, 16	SL
10:50 – 11:35 Social Studies																				KD
12:20 – 1:05 Science	13								13		13								13	SL
1:05 – 1:50 Computers																				JP
1:50 – 2:35 Phys ed	17	18, 19	18, 19		19	17, 18	17, 18						17, 18, 19				17, 18		19	VF
Totals (H)	5	6	7	6	6	7	8		1	2	4		11	2			5	6	7	

E — Possible Functions

Events: ̶1̶ ̶2̶ ̶3̶ ̶4̶ ̶5̶ ̶6̶ ̶7̶ 8 9 10 11 12 13 14 15 16 17 18 19 20 21 22 23 24 25

Date: Mon., Nov. 19 | Tues, Nov. 20

Source: Adapted from *Functional Assessment and Program Development for Problem Behavior: A Practical Handbook,* 2nd edition, by R. E. O'Neill, R. H. Horner, R. W. Albin, J. R. Sprague, K. Storey, and J. S. Newton. © 1997. Reprinted with permission of Wadsworth, a division of Thomson Learning: www.thomsonrights.com. Fax 800-730-2215.

Functional Assessment Observation Form

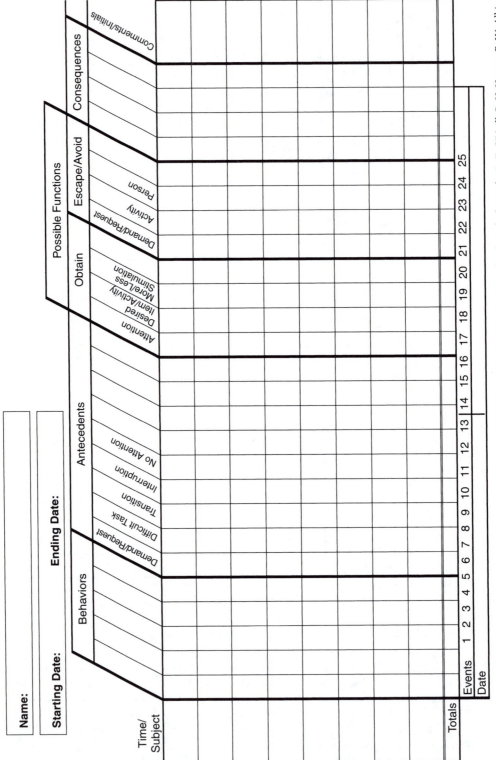

Source: Chart adapted from *Functional Assessment and Program Development for Problem Behavior: A Practical Handbook*, 2nd edition, by R. E. O'Neill, R. H. Homer, R. W. Albin, J. R. Sprague, K. Storey, and J. S. Newton. © 1997. Reprinted with permission of Wadsworth, a division of Thomson Learning: www.thomsonrights.com. Fax 800-730-2215.

Converting an A-B-C Chart into a Functional Assessment Observation Form

The A-B-C running chart is a way to record observations. The chart on pages 307 to 309 describes Andrew's behavior as seen by observer/recorders, who could be his teachers, the school counselor, or someone else. The Functional Assessment Observation Form on pages 313 to 314 is another way to record observations that, in addition, helps you detect patterns in the function of the behavior. It can be used either by itself or with the A-B-C chart. This section explains how to take the information that you've gathered on the A-B-C chart and put it onto the observation form. On page 311 there is a separate explanation of how to use the observation form.

You should use your knowledge of the child to help you figure out the antecedent and the possible function of each behavior. There are 13 events recorded on the observation form for Monday and 6 events for Tuesday. Note that some items on the A-B-C chart aren't recorded on the observation form because the team has not selected those behaviors for observation. We've put these behaviors in brackets to set them off from the incidents that belong on the observation form.

Monday, November 19, 2007

English. [Although the first observation on the A-B-C chart is important, it is not a behavior that the team is looking at with the functional assessment. It is therefore not included on the observation form.]

When the teacher begins the grammar lesson, Andrew sighs and puts his head down. Because his actions make a noise that disturbs the class, we mark the behavior on the observation form (1). This behavior (as well as its antecedent, its possible function, and its consequence) continues to be called (1) all the way across the form. The antecedent, seen from Andrew's perspective, is a difficult task, and the possible function is to avoid it. The consequence is that the teacher reprimands him by telling him to sit up. [Although Andrew ignores the teacher's request to sit up, this is not a behavior we are observing so we don't mark it on the observation form.]

When the teacher directs the students to take out their materials for the lesson, Andrew again makes disturbing noises (2), fumbling with his things and slamming his desk shut. The teacher believes that the function of this behavior is to get his classmates' attention, and she ignores him.

In incident (3), Andrew gets up from his desk and bothers a classmate by hitting her lightly on the head (3). The antecedent is that the teacher ignored him (that is, she didn't help him find the materials he needed); and the possible purpose of his behavior is to avoid the assignment. The consequence is that the teacher tells Andrew to sit down and get to work. This reprimand is the antecedent for incident (4)—Andrew swears and throws his book against the wall. Once again, the teacher believes the function of the behavior is to get the attention of his peers. The consequence is that she asks him to leave the class.

Spanish. In his next class, the teacher speaks only Spanish. When she begins to give a dictation, a difficult task for Andrew, he talks loudly to his neighbor (5), presumably to avoid the activity. The teacher reprimands him by telling him to listen, a response that turns into the antecedent for the next behavior—Andrew swears at the teacher (6). The teacher then asks Andrew to move to the back of the room, but he just pushes his desk away and laughs (7), leading the teacher to send him out of the room. Again, the possible function for all 3 events (5, 6, and 7) is to avoid the dictation, a difficult task.

Math. After recess, Andrew rejoins his class for math with the same teacher he has for English. When she tells the students to take their seats, Andrew begins to swear. (8). The teacher ignores him. She believes that the purpose of this behavior is to get attention from his peers.

As the teacher introduces a new concept, Andrew drops his math book to the floor, making a noise (9); the teacher again pays no attention, presuming that he is trying to avoid the new work. [While the teacher is explaining the concept to the class, Andrew gets up to sharpen his pencil, but we don't include this behavior on the form because it wasn't selected for study in the functional assessment.] When the teacher reprimands Andrew, telling him to return to his desk and pick up his book, he slams the book down on his desk (10). The teacher ignores this action, which she believes is intended to get her attention. The next antecedent is that she distributes a worksheet to help the students practice the new concept, at which point Andrew talks loudly to his neighbor (11). The teacher thinks that the function of this behavior is to enable him to avoid the work. The consequence is a reprimand, telling him get to work, which acts as an antecedent for yet another behavior, a rude remark (12). At last, the teacher asks him to leave the class.

Social Studies. After lunch, Andrew goes to Social Studies. There are no incidents!

Science. Seeking attention but ignored by his peers when it's time to find a partner, Andrew pushes the materials off the table (13). Because safety is so important in the science lab, the teacher sends him out of the room.

Tuesday, November 20, 2007

English. [Although the A-B-C chart indicates that the teacher ignores Andrew when he enters class in a good mood, this information is not part of the functional assessment and isn't included on the observation form.] Andrew begins to make noise (14) as the teacher returns the spelling test from the day before. The teacher guesses that Andrew wants to avoid the activity because he knows he failed the test. She ignores his behavior and eventually returns his test paper to him. [Andrew crumples his paper and throws it in the garbage. This behavior isn't noted on the functional assessment chart; nor is the fact that he doesn't move when the teacher tells him to take the paper out of the garbage and return to his seat.] When the teacher repeats her demand, Andrew kicks over the garbage can (15) in order to avoid complying, and once again the consequence is that he's sent from the room.

Computer Science. There are no incidents.

Math. [We do not note Andrew's initial behavior on the observation form.] Because he missed part of yesterday's class, the quiz is probably too difficult, and he throws his book on the floor, screaming, "This is stupid!" (16) so he won't have to finish the quiz. The teacher sends him out of the class.

Social Studies. No incidents.

Physical Education. Andrew pushes Sam as soon as he enters the gym (17), probably anticipating a difficult task that he wants to avoid. Both Sam and the teacher react—Sam pushes back, and the teacher reprimands Andrew by telling him to keep his hands to himself. Andrew swears at Sam (18), again to avoid the gym activity. When the teacher tells him that he has to participate, he swears at the teacher (19), a behavior he knows is not tolerated at school, and he is removed from class.

References

Abu-Laban, S. M., & Abu-Laban, B. (1999). Teens between: The public and private spheres of Arab-Canadian adolescents. In M. W. Suleiman (Ed.), *Arabs in America: Building a new future* (pp. 113–128). Philadelphia: Temple University Press.

Access Center. (2004). Using peer tutoring to facilitate access. Retrieved July 27, 2007, from www.k8accesscenter.org/training_resources/documents/PeerTutoringFinal.pdf.

Accommodations, modifications, and alternate assessments: How they affect instruction and assessment. (2006). Retrieved October 3, 2007, from www.schwablearning.org/articles.aspx?r=306.

ADDinSchool.com. (n.d.). *ADDinSchool.com presents resources for parents*. Retrieved February 2, 2005, from http://addinschool.com/elementary.

Adeed, P., & Smith, G. P. (1997). Arab Americans: Concepts and materials. In J. A. Banks (Ed.), *Teaching strategies for ethnic studies* (6th ed., pp. 489–510). Boston: Allyn & Bacon.

Agency for Health Care Policy and Research. (1999, August). *Diagnosis of attention-deficit/hyperactivity disorder, Summary, Technical review no. 3*. Rockville, MD: Author. Retrieved March 29, 2005, from www.ahrq.gov/clinic/epcsums/adhdsutr.htm.

Ainsworth, M. D. S., Blehar, M., Waters, E., & Wall, S. (1978). *Patterns of attachment: A psychological study of the strange situation*. Hillsdale, NJ: Erlbaum.

Ajrouch, K. (1999). Family and ethnic identity in an Arab-American community. In M. W. Suleiman (Ed.), *Arabs in America: Building a new future* (pp. 129–139). Philadelphia: Temple University Press.

Allen, J. (2006). My literary lunches with boys. *Educational Leadership, 64*(1), 67–70.

Allen, J. P., & Land, D. (1999). Attachment in adolescence. In J. Cassidy & P. R. Shaver (Eds.), *Handbook of attachment theory and research* (pp. 319–335). New York: Guilford.

American Academy of Pediatrics. (1998). Guidance for effective discipline (RE 9740). *Pediatrics, 101,* 723–728.

American Academy of Pediatrics, Committee on School Health. (2000). Policy statement: Corporal punishment in schools. *Pediatrics, 106,* 343.

American Association of University Women. (2001). *Hostile hallways: Bullying, teasing, and sexual harassment in school*. Washington, DC: American Association of University Women Educational Foundation.

American Association of University Women. (2004). *Harassment-free hallways: How to stop sexual harassment in school: A guide for students, parents, and schools*. Washington, DC: American Association of University Women Educational Foundation.

American Psychiatric Association. (1994). *Diagnostic and statistical manual of mental disorders* (4th ed.). Washington, DC: Author.

American Psychiatric Association. (2000). *Diagnostic and statistical manual of mental disorders* (4th ed., Text revision). Washington, DC: Author.

Anderson, C. A. (2004). An update on the effects of playing violent video games. *Journal of Adolescence, 27,* 113–122.

Anderson, C. A., & Bushman, B. J. (2001). Effects of violent games on aggressive behavior, aggressive cognition, aggressive affect, physiological arousal, and prosocial behavior: A meta-analytic review of the scientific literature. *Psychological Science, 12,* 353–359.

Anderson, E. (1997). Violence and the inner-city street code. In J. McCord (Ed.), *Violence and childhood in the inner city.* New York: Cambridge University Press.

Anderson, E. (1998). *Code of the street: Decency, violence, and the moral life of the inner city.* New York: Norton.

Anderson, J. L., Albin, R. W., Mesaros, R. A., Dunlap, G., & Morelli-Robbins, M. (1993). Issues in providing training to achieve comprehensive behavior support. In J. Reichle & D. P. Wacker (Eds.), *Communicative alternatives to challenging behavior: Integrating assessment and intervention strategies* (pp. 363–406). Baltimore: Brookes.

Andrews, L., & Trawick-Smith, J. (1996). An ecological model for early childhood violence prevention. In R. L. Hampton, P. Jenkins, & T. P. Gullotta (Eds.), *Preventing violence in America* (pp. 233–261). Thousand Oaks, CA: Sage.

Aronson, J., & Steele, C. M. (2005). Stereotypes and the fragility of human competence, motivation, and self-concept. In C. Dweck & E. Elliot (Eds.), *Handbook of competence and motivation* (pp. 436–456). New York: Guilford.

Arseneault, L., Moffitt, T. E., Caspi, A., Taylor, A., Rijadijk, F. V., Jaffee, S. R., et al. (2003). Strong genetic effects on cross-situational antisocial behaviour among 5-year-old children according to mothers, teachers, examiner-observers, and twins' self reports. *Journal of Child Psychology and Psychiatry, 44,* 832–848.

Asher, S. R., Parkhurst, J. T., Hymel, S., & Williams, G. A. (1990). Peer rejection and loneliness in childhood. In S. R. Asher & J. D. Coie (Eds.), *Peer rejection in childhood* (pp. 253–273). New York: Cambridge University Press.

Association for Supervision and Curriculum Development. (2004, September 28). The effect of state testing on instruction in high-poverty elementary schools. *ASCD Research Brief, 4*(20). Retrieved December 14, 2005, from www.ascd.org.

Austin, V. L. (2003). Pharmacological interventions for students with ADD. *Intervention in School and Clinic, 38*(5), 288–296.

Ayers, W. (1989). *The good preschool teacher: Six teachers reflect on their lives.* New York: Teachers College Press.

Ayers, W. (2001). *To teach: The journey of a teacher.* New York: Teachers College Press.

Ayres, A. J. (1979). *Sensory integration and the child.* Los Angeles: Western Psychological Services.

Bada, H. S., Das, A., Bauer, C. R., Shankaran, S., Lester, B., LaGasse, L., et al. (2007). Impact of prenatal cocaine exposure on child behavior problems through school age. *Pediatrics, 119,* 348–359.

Bafile, C. (2005). Class meetings: A democratic approach to classroom management. *Education World.* Retrieved July 18, 2007, from www.educationworld.com/a_curr/profdev/profdev012.shtml.

Bagwell, C. L. (2004). Friendships, peer networking, and antisocial behavior. In A. H. N. Cillessen & L. Mayeux (Eds.), *Children's peer relations: From development to intervention* (pp. 37–57). Washington, DC: American Psychological Association.

Bai, M. (1999, May 3). Anatomy of a massacre. *Newsweek, 133,* 24–31.

Baird, A. A., Gruber, S. A., Fein, D. A., Maas, L. C., Steingard, R. J., Renshaw, P. F., et al. (1999). Functional magnetic resonance imaging of facial affect recognition in children and adolescents. *Journal of the American Academy of Child and Adolescent Psychiatry, 38,* 195–199.

Baker, A. (2001, December 16). Steep rise in gun sales reflects post-attack fears. *New York Times,* pp. A1, B10.

Baker, J. (2002). Trilingualism. In L. Delpit & J. K. Dowdy (Eds.), *The skin that we speak: Thoughts on language and culture in the classroom* (pp. 49–61). New York: New Press.

Bandura, A. (1973). *Aggression: A social learning analysis.* Englewood Cliffs, NJ: Prentice-Hall.

Bandura, A. (1977). *Social learning theory.* Englewood Cliffs, NJ: Prentice-Hall.

Barkley, R. (1987). *Defiant children: A clinician's manual for parent training.* New York: Guilford.

Barsade, S. (2002). The ripple effect: Emotional contagion and its influence on group behavior. *Administrative Science Quarterly, 47,* 644–675.

Barton, E. J. (1986). Modification of children's prosocial behavior. In P. S. Strain, M. J. Guralnick, & H. M. Walker (Eds.), *Children's social behavior: Development, assessment, and modification* (pp. 331–372). Orlando: Academic.

Bauer, A. M., & Brown, G. M. (2001). Who are the students in an inclusive high school? In A. M. Bauer & G. M. Brown (Eds.), *Adolescents and inclusion: Transforming secondary schools* (pp. 43–66). Baltimore: Brookes.

Bauer, A. M., & Matuszek, K. (2001). Designing and evaluating accommodations and adaptations. In A. M. Bauer & G. M. Brown (Eds.), *Adolescents and inclusion: Transforming secondary schools* (pp. 139–166). Baltimore: Brookes.

Baxter, L. R., Schwartz, M. M., Bergman, K. S., Szuba, M. P., Guze, B. H., Mazziotta, J. C., et al. (1992). Caudate glucose metabolic rate changes with both drug and behavior therapy for obsessive-compulsive disorder. *Archives of General Psychiatry, 49,* 681–689.

Bazelon Center for Mental Health Law. (2003, May). *Suspending disbelief: Moving beyond punishment to promote effective interventions for children with mental or emotional disorders.* Washington, DC: Author. Retrieved November 21, 2006, from www.bazelon.org/issues/children/publications/suspending/suspendingdisbelief.pdf.

Beach Center on Disabilities. (2007). Positive behavior support: Classroom and group support. Retrieved August 7, 2007, from www.beachcenter.org/pbs/pbs_at_school/classroom_and_group_support.aspx.

Beach Center on Families and Disabilities. (n.d.). *Success stories.* OSEP Technical Assistance Center on Positive Behavioral Interventions and Supports. Retrieved November 21, 2006, from www.pbis.org/english/Success_Stories.htm.

Beam, J. M. (2004, January 20). The blackboard jungle: Tamer than you think. *New York Times,* p. A19.

Beane, A. L. (1999). *The bully free classroom: Over 100 tips and strategies for teachers K–8.* Minneapolis: Free Spirit.

Becker, J. V., Barham, J., Eron, L. D., & Chen, S. A. (1994). The present status and future directions for psychological research on youth violence. In L. D. Eron, J. H. Gentry, & P. Schlegel (Eds.), *Reason to hope: A psychosocial perspective on violence & youth* (pp. 435–446). Washington, DC: American Psychological Association.

Bedell, J. R., & Lennox, S. S. (1997). *Handbook for communication and problem-solving skills training: A cognitive-behavioral approach.* New York: Wiley.

Beland, K. R. (1996). A schoolwide approach to violence prevention. In R. L. Hampton, P. Jenkins, & T. P. Gullotta (Eds.), *Preventing violence in America* (pp. 209–231). Thousand Oaks, CA: Sage.

Benner, G. J., Nelson, J. R., & Epstein, M. H. (2002). Language skills of children with EBD: A literature review. *Journal of Emotional and Behavioral Disorders, 10,* 43–59.

Bennett, S., & Kalish, N. (2006). *The case against homework: How homework is hurting our children and what we can do about it.* New York: Crown.

Berk, L. E. (2000). *Child development* (5th ed.). Boston: Allyn & Bacon.

Berkowitz, L. (1993). *Aggression: Its causes, consequences, and control.* New York: McGraw-Hill.

Berlin, L. J., & Cassidy, J. (1999). Relations among relationships: Contributions from attachment theory. In J. Cassidy & P. R. Shaver (Eds.), *Handbook of attachment theory and research* (pp. 688–712). New York: Guilford.

Bierman, K. L. (1986). Process of change during social skills training with preadolescents and its relation to treatment outcomes. *Child Development, 57,* 230–240.

Bierman, K. L., Bruschi, C., Domitrovich, C., Fang, G. Y., Miller-Johnson, S., & the Conduct Problems Prevention Research Group. (2004). Early disruptive behaviors associated with emerging antisocial behavior among girls. In M. Putallaz & K. L. Bierman (Eds.), *Aggression, antisocial behavior, and violence among girls: A developmental perspective* (pp. 137–161). New York: Guilford.

Bierman, K. L., & Furman, W. (1984). The effects of social skills training and peer involvement on the social adjustment of preadolescents. *Child Development, 55,* 151–162.

Biglan, A., Brennan, P. A., Foster, S. L., & Holder, H. D. (with Miller, T. R., Cunningham, P., Derzon, J. H., Embry, D. D., Fishbein, D.

H., Flay, B. R., et al.) (2004). *Helping adolescents at risk: Prevention of multiple problem behaviors*. New York: Guilford.

Bijou, S. W., Peterson, R. F., & Ault, M. H. (1968). A method to integrate descriptive and experimental field studies at the level of data and empirical concepts. *Journal of Applied Behavior Analysis, 1,* 175–191.

Bingenheimer, J. B., Brennan, R. T., & Earls, F. J. (2005). Firearm violence exposure and serious violent behavior. *Science, 308,* 1323–1326.

Birch, S. H., & Ladd, G. W. (1997). The teacher-child relationship and children's early school adjustment. *Journal of School Psychology, 35,* 61–79.

Birch, S. H., & Ladd, G. W. (1998). Children's interpersonal behaviors and the teacher–child relationship. *Developmental Psychology, 34*(5), 934–946.

Bjorkqvist, K., Lagerspetz, K. M. J., & Kaukiainen, A. (1992). Do girls manipulate and boys fight? *Aggressive Behavior, 18,* 117–127.

Blue-Banning, M., Summers, J. A., Frankland, H. C., Nelson, L. L., & Beegle, G. (2004). Dimensions of family and professional partnerships: Constructive guidelines for collaboration. *Exceptional Children, 70,* 167–184.

Blum, R. W. (2005). A case for school connectedness. *Educational Leadership, 62*(7), 16–20.

Boivin, M., Hymel, S., & Hodges, E. V. E. (2001). Toward a process view of peer rejection and harassment. In J. Juvonen & S. Graham (Eds.), *Peer harassment in school: The plight of the vulnerable and victimized* (pp. 265–289). New York: Guilford.

Bolger, K. E., & Patterson, C. J. (2003). Sequelae of maltreatment: Vulnerability and resilience. In S. S. Luthar (Ed.), *Resilience and vulnerability: Adaptation in the context of childhood adversity* (pp. 156–181). New York: Cambridge University Press.

Bott, C. J. (2004). *The bully in the book and the classroom*. Lanham, MD: Scarecrow.

Boulton, M. (1994). How to prevent and respond to bullying behaviour in the junior/middle school playground. In S. Sharp & P. K. Smith (Eds.), *Tackling bullying in your school: A practical handbook for teachers* (pp. 103–132). New York: Routledge.

Bovey, T., & Strain, P. (n.d.). *What works briefs 5: Using classroom activities and routines as opportunities to support peer interaction.* Center on the Social and Emotional Foundations for Early Learning. Retrieved July 31, 2007, from www.vanderbilt.edu/csefel/briefs/wwb5.pdf.

Bowden, F. (1997). *Supported child care: Enhancing accessibility.* Victoria: British Columbia Ministry for Children and Families and Human Resources Development Canada.

Bowie, K. (2005). The joys and challenges of working with students who are ADHD . . . and parenting one. In M. Friend, *Special education: Contemporary perspectives for school professionals.* Boston: Allyn & Bacon.

Bowlby, J. (1969/1982). *Attachment and loss: Vol. 1. Attachment.* New York: Basic Books.

Bowman, B. T., Donovan, M. S., & Burns, M. S. (Eds.). (2001). *Eager to learn: Educating our preschoolers.* National Research Council Committee on Early Childhood Pedagogy. Commission on Behavioral and Social Sciences and Education. Washington, DC: National Academy Press.

Boykin, A. W. (1986). The triple quandary and the schooling of Afro-American children. In U. Neisser (Ed.), *The school achievement of minority children.* Hillsdale, NJ: Erlbaum.

Brady, J. P., Posner, M., Lang, C., & Rosati, M. J. (1994). *Risk and reality: The implications of prenatal exposure to alcohol and other drugs.* Washington, DC: U.S. Department of Health and Human Services and U.S. Department of Education. Retrieved October 14, 2007, from http://aspe.hhs.gov/hsp/cyp/drugkids.htm.

Brennan, P., Mednick, S., & Kandel, E. (1991). Congenital determinants of violent and property offending. In D. J. Pepler & K. H. Rubin (Eds.), *The development and treatment of childhood aggression* (pp. 81–92). Hillsdale, NJ: Erlbaum.

Bretherton, I., & Munholland, K. A. (1999). Internal working models in attachment relationships: A construct revisited. In J. Cassidy & P. R. Shaver (Eds.), *Handbook of attachment theory and research* (pp. 89–111). New York: Guilford.

Brody, G. H., Kim, S., Murry, V. M., & Brown, A. C. (2004). Protective longitudinal paths linking child competence to behavioral problems among African American siblings. *Child Development, 75,* 455–467.

Brody, J. E. (2006, January 17). Dally no longer: Get the lead out. *New York Times.* Retrieved January 23, 2006, from http://select.nytimes.com/mem/tnt.html?tntget+2006/01/17/health/.

Broidy, L. M., Tremblay, R. E., Brame, B., Fergusson, D., Horwood, J. L., Laird, R., et al. (2003). Developmental trajectories of childhood disruptive behaviors and adolescent delinquency: A six-site, cross-national study. *Developmental Psychology, 39,* 222–245.

Bronfenbrenner, U. (1979). *The ecology of human development: Experiments by nature and design.* Cambridge, MA: Harvard University Press.

Brooks, R. B. (1994). Children at risk: Fostering resilience and hope. *American Journal of Orthopsychiatry, 64,* 545–553.

Brooks, R. B. (1999). Creating a positive school climate: Strategies for fostering self-esteem, motivation, and resilience. In J. Cohen (Ed.), *Educating minds and hearts: Social emotional learning and the passage into adolescence* (pp. 24–39). New York: Teachers College Press.

Brophy, J. (1996). *Teaching problem students.* New York: Guilford.

Brophy, J. (1999). Perspectives of classroom management: Yesterday, today, and tomorrow. In H. J. Freiberg (Ed.), *Beyond behaviorism: Changing the classroom management paradigm* (pp. 43–56). Boston: Allyn & Bacon.

Brophy, J. (2000). *Teaching.* Geneva: International Bureau of Education. (ERIC Document No. ED440066)

Brophy, J., & McCaslin, M. (1992). Teachers' reports of how they perceive and cope with problem students. *Elementary School Journal, 93,* 3–68.

Brophy, J. E. (1996). *Teaching problem students.* New York: Guilford.

Bruer, J. T. (1999). *The myth of the first three years: A new understanding of early brain development and lifelong learning.* New York: Free Press.

Buck, G. H., Polloway, E. A., Smith-Thomas, A., & Cook, K. W. (2003). Prereferral intervention processes: A survey of state practices. *Exceptional Children, 69,* 329–360.

Buell, G., & Snyder, J. (1981). Assertiveness training with children. *Psychological Reports, 49,* 71–80.

Burden, P. R. (2003). *Classroom management: Creating a successful learning environment* (2nd ed.). Hoboken, NJ: Wiley.

Butchard, N., & Spencler, N. (2000). *Working effectively with violent and aggressive states (WEVAS).* Winnipeg, MB: Authors.

Butchard, N., & Spencler, R. (2000). *Working with older children.* Winnipeg, MB: WEVAS, Inc.

Campbell, S. B. (1990). *Behavior problems in preschool children.* New York: Guilford.

Campbell, S. B. (2002). *Behavior problems in preschool children: Clinical and developmental issues* (2nd ed.). New York: Guilford.

Canadian Heritage. (n.d.). *UN convention on the rights of the child in child friendly language.* Retrieved October 2, 2007, from www.rcmp-grc.gc.ca/pdfs/NCD-poster_e.pdf.

Carkhuff, R. (1987). *The art of helping.* Amherst, MA: Human Resource Development Press.

Carr, A., Kikais, T., Smith, C., & Littmann, E. (n.d.). *Making friends: A guide to using the assessment of peer relations and planning interventions.* Vancouver, BC: Making Friends.

Carr, E. G. (1994). Emerging themes in the functional analysis of problem behavior. *Journal of Applied Behavior Analysis, 27,* 393–399.

Carter, P. L. (2005). *Keepin' it real: School success beyond black and white.* New York: Oxford University Press.

Cartledge, G., & Milburn, J. F. (1995). *Teaching social skills to children: Innovative approaches* (3rd ed.). Boston: Allyn & Bacon.

Caspi, A., McClay, J., Moffitt, T. E., Mill, J., Martin, J., Craig, I. W., et al. (2002). Role of genotype in the cycle of violence in maltreated children. *Science, 297,* 851–854.

Caspi, A., & Silva, P. A. (1995). Temperamental qualities at age three predict personality traits in young adulthood: Longitudinal evidence from a birth cohort. *Child Development, 66,* 486–498.

Caspi, A., Sugden, K., Moffitt, T. E., Taylor, A., Craig, I. W., Harrington, H. L., et al., (2003). Influence of life stress on depression: Moderation by a polymorphism in the 5-HTT gene. *Science, 301,* 386–389.

Cauce, A. M., Stewart, A., Rodriguez, M. D., Cochran, B., & Ginzler, J. (2003). Overcoming the odds? Adolescent development in the context of urban poverty. In S. S. Luthar (Ed.), *Resilience and vulnerability: Adaptation in the context of childhood adversity* (pp. 343–363). New York: Cambridge University Press.

Center for the Study and Prevention of Violence. (1998). Responding to violence in the schools. Institute of Behavioral Science, University of Colorado at Boulder. Retrieved March 2, 2007, from www.colorado.edu/cspv/publications/factsheets/safeschools/FS-SC14.pdf.

Center on the Social and Emotional Foundations for Early Learning (2006). *Promoting social and emotional competence*. Retrieved March 3, 2008, from www.vanderbilt.edu/csefel/preschool.html.

Chan, S. (1998). Families with Asian roots. In E. W. Lynch & M. J. Hanson (Eds.), *Developing cross-cultural competence: A guide for working with children and their families* (pp. 251–344). Baltimore: Brookes.

Chandler, L. K., & Dahlquist, C. M. (1997, April). Confronting the challenge: Using team-based functional assessment and effective intervention strategies to reduce and prevent challenging behavior in young children. Workshop presented at SpeciaLink Institute on Children's Challenging Behaviours in Child Care, Sydney, NS.

Chandler, L. K., & Dahlquist, C. M. (2005). *Functional assessment: Strategies to prevent and remediate challenging behavior in school settings* (2nd ed.). Upper Saddle River, NJ: Prentice-Hall.

Chao, R. K. (1994). Beyond parental control and authoritarian parenting style: Understanding Chinese parenting through the cultural notion of training. *Child Development, 65,* 1111–1119.

Charles, C. M., & Charles, M. G. (2004). *Classroom management for middle-grades teachers*. Boston: Allyn & Bacon.

Chasnoff, I. J., Anson, A., Hatcher, R., Stenson, H., Laukea, K., & Randolph, L. A. (1998). Prenatal exposure to cocaine and other drugs: Outcome at four to six years. *Annals of the New York Academy of Sciences, 846,* 314–328.

Chesney-Lind, M., & Belknap, J. (2004). Trends in delinquent girls' aggression and violent behavior: A review of the evidence. In M. Putallaz & K. L. Bierman (Eds.), *Aggression, antisocial behavior, and violence among girls: A developmental perspective* (pp. 203–220). New York: Guilford.

Chess, S., & Thomas, A. (1984). *Origins and evolution of behavior disorders from infancy to early adult life*. New York: Brunner/Mazel.

Chess, S., & Thomas, A. (1989). Temperament and its functional significance. In S. I. Greenspan & G. H. Pollock (Eds.), *The course of life: Vol. 2, Early childhood* (pp. 163–228). Madison, CT: International Universities Press.

Child Trends Data Bank. (2003). *Teen homicide, suicide, and firearm death*. Retrieved May 2, 2007, from www.childtrendsdatabank.org/indicators/70ViolentDeath.cfm.

Children Now. (2001, December). *Fair play: Violence, race and gender in video games*. Los Angeles: Author. Retrieved January 30, 2006, from www.childrennow.org/assets/pdf/issues_media_fcccomments_Sept04.pdf.

Christakis, D. A., Zimmerman, F. J., DiGiuseppe, D. L., & McCarty, C. A. (2004). Early television exposure and subsequent attentional problems in children. *Pediatrics, 113,* 708–713.

Chud, G., & Fahlman, R. (1985). *Early childhood education for a multicultural society*. Vancouver: Faculty of Education, University of British Columbia.

Chud, G., & Fahlman, R. (1995). *Honouring diversity within child care and early education: An instructor's guide*. Victoria: British Columbia Ministry of Skills, Training, and Labour and the Centre for Curriculum and Professional Development.

Cicchetti, D., Ganiban, J., & Barnett, D. (1991). Contributions from the study of high risk populations to understanding the development of emotional regulation. In J. Garber & K. A. Dodge (Eds.), *The development of emotional regulation and dysregulation* (pp. 15–48). New York: Cambridge University Press.

Clonan, S. M., Lopez, G., Rymarchyk, G., & Davison, S. (2004). School-wide positive behavior support: Implementation and evaluation at two urban elementary schools. *Persistently Safe Schools: The National Con-*

ference of the Hamilton Fish Institute on School and Community Violence. Retrieved August 15, 2007, from http://gwired.gwu.edu/hamfish/merlin-cgi/p/downloadFile/d/16824/n/off/other/1/name/08Clonanpdf/.

Coie, J. D. (1996). Prevention of violence and antisocial behavior. In R. DeV. Peters & R. J. McMahon (Eds.), *Preventing childhood disorders, substance abuse, and delinquency* (pp. 1–18). Thousand Oaks, CA: Sage.

Coie, J. D., & Dodge, K. A. (1998). Aggression and antisocial behavior. In N. Eisenberg (Ed.), *Handbook of child psychology: Vol. 3, Social, emotional, and personality development* (5th ed., pp. 779–862). New York: Wiley.

Coie, J. D., & Koeppl, G. K. (1990). Adapting intervention to the problems of aggressive and disruptive children. In S. R. Asher & J. D. Coie (Eds.), *Peer rejection in childhood* (pp. 309–337). New York: Cambridge University Press.

Coie, J. D., Underwood, M., & Lochman, J. E. (1991). Programmatic intervention with aggressive children in the school setting. In D. J. Pepler & K. H. Rubin (Eds.), *The development and treatment of childhood aggression* (pp. 389–410). Hillsdale, NJ: Erlbaum.

Collier, V. P. (1995). Acquiring a second language for school. *Directions in Language and Education, 1*(4). Retrieved July 7, 2005, from http://ncela.gwu.edu/pubs/directions/04.htm.

Coloroso, B. (1995). *Kids are worth it! Giving your child the gift of inner discipline.* Toronto, ON: Somerville House.

Coloroso, B. (2002). *The bully, the bullied, and the bystander.* Toronto, ON: HarperCollins.

Comer, J. P., & Haynes, N. M. (1999). The dynamics of school change: Response to the article, "Comer's School Development Program in Prince Georges County, Maryland: A theory-based evaluation," by T. D. Cook et al. *American Educational Research Journal, 36,* 599–607.

Committee for Children (2002). *Second step: A violence-prevention curriculum.* Seattle: Author.

Committee for Children. (2001). *Steps to respect: A bullying prevention program.* Seattle: Author.

Cook, R. E., Klein, M. D., & Tessier, A. (with Daley, S. E.) (2004). *Adapting early childhood curricula for children in inclusive set-tings* (6th ed.). Upper Saddle River, NJ: Merrill Prentice-Hall.

Cooper, H. (2001). Homework for all—In moderation. *Educational Leadership, 58*(7), 34–38.

Cords, M., & Killen, M. (1998). Conflict resolution in human and nonhuman primates. In J. Langer & M. Killen (Eds.), *Piaget, evolution, and development* (pp. 193–218). Mahwah, NJ: Erlbaum.

Corporal punishment in U.S. public schools. (2005, November). U.S. Department of Education, Office for Civil Rights. Retrieved July 31, 2006, from www.stophitting.com/disatschool/statesBranning.php.

Corsaro, W. (1988). Peer culture in the preschool. *Theory into Practice, 27*(1), 19–24.

Cortiella, C. (2005). *No Child Left Behind: Understanding assessment options for IDEA-eligible students.* National Center for Learning Disabilities. Retrieved October 3, 2007, from www.schwablearning.org/articles.aspx?r=995.

Cortiella, C. (2006). *A parent's guide to Response-to-Intervention.* National Center for Learning Disabilities. Retrieved October 1, 2007, from www.ncld.org/images/stories/downloads/parent_center/rti_final.pdf.

Costello, E. J., Angold, A., Burns, B. J., Erkanli, A., Stangl, D. K., & Tweed, D. L. (1996). The Great Smoky Mountains study of youth: Functional impairment and serious emotional disturbance. *Archives of General Psychiatry, 53*(12), 1137–1143.

Costello, E. J., Compton, S. N., Keeler, G., & Angold, A. (2003). Relationships between poverty and psychopathology: A natural experiment. *Journal of the American Medical Association, 290,* 2023–2029.

Cotton, K. (1996, May). *School size, school climate, and student performance, Close-up #20.* Northwest Regional Educational Laboratory. Retrieved July 31, 2006, from www.nwrel.org/scpd/sirs/10/c020.html.

Council for Exceptional Children. (2004). *The new IDEA: CEC's summary of significant issues.* Arlington, VA: Author. Retrieved March 28, 2005, from www.cec.sped.org/pp/IDEA_120204.pdf.

Cowie, H., & Sharp, S. (1994). Tackling bullying through the curriculum. In P. K. Smith & S. Sharp (Eds.), *School bullying: Insights and perspectives* (pp. 84–107). New York: Routledge.

Craig, W. M., & Pepler, D. J. (1997). Observations of bullying and victimization in the school yard. *Canadian Journal of School Psychology, 13,* 41–60.

Craig, W. M., & Pepler, D. J. (2003). Identifying and targeting risk for involvement in bullying and victimization. *Canadian Journal of Psychiatry, 48,* 577–582.

Craig, W. M., Pepler, D. J., & Connolly, J. (2003). What we've learned about victimization. Toronto, ON: LaMarsh Centre for Research. Retrieved April 10, 2007, from www.arts.yorku.ca/lamarsh/projects/trp/trp_wwl03.html.

Crick, N. R., Casas, J. F., & Ku, H.-C. (1999). Relational and physical forms of peer victimization in preschool. *Developmental Psychology, 35,* 376–385.

Crick, N. R., Casas, J. F., & Mosher, M. (1997). Relational and overt aggression in preschool. *Developmental Psychology, 33,* 579–588.

Crick, N. R., & Grotpeter, J. K. (1995). Relational aggression, gender, and social-psychological adjustment. *Child Development, 66,* 710–722.

Crick, N. R., Grotpeter, J. K., & Bigbee, M. S. (2002). Relationally and physically aggressive children's intent attributions and feelings of distress for relational and instrumental peer provocations. *Child Development, 73,* 1134–1142.

Crick, N. R., Nelson, D. A., Morales, J. R., Cullerton, C., Casas, J. F., & Hickman, S. E. (2001). Relational victimization in childhood and adolescence: I hurt you through the grapevine. In J. Juvonen & S. Graham (Eds.), *Peer harassment in school: The plight of the vulnerable and victimized* (pp. 196–214). New York: Guilford.

Criss, M. M., Pettit, G. S., Bates, J. E., Dodge, K. A., & Lapp, A. L. (2002). Family adversity, positive peer relations, and children's externalizing behavior: A longitudinal perspective on risk and resilience. *Child Development, 73,* 1220–1237.

Crockenberg, S. (1981). Infant irritability, mother responsiveness, and social suppor influences on the security of infant-mother attachment. *Child Development, 7,* 169–176.

Cullinan, D., Evans, C., Epstein, M. H., & Ryser, G. (2003). Characteristics of emotional disturbance of elementary school students. *Behavioral Disorders, 28,* 94–110.

Curtis, W. J., & Cicchetti, D. (2003). Moving research on resilience into the 21st century: Theoretical and methodological considerations in examining the biological contributors to resilience. *Development and Psychopathology, 15,* 773–810.

Curwin, R. L., & Mendler, A. N. (1997). *As tough as necessary: Countering violence, aggression, and hostility in our schools.* Alexandria, VA: Association for Supervision and Curriculum Development.

Curwin, R. L., & Mendler, A. N. (2001). *Discipline with dignity.* Upper Saddle River, NJ: Merrill Prentice-Hall.

Cushman, K., & the students of What Kids Can Do. (2003). *Fires in the bathroom: Advice for teachers from high school students.* New York: New Press.

Dahl, R. E. (2004). Adolescent brain development: A period of vulnerabilities and opportunities: Keynote address. *Annals of the New York Academy of Sciences, 1021,* 1–20.

Dahlberg, L. L. (1998). Youth violence in the United States: Major trends, risk factors, and prevention approaches. *American Journal of Preventive Medicine, 14,* 259–272.

Darling-Hammond, L. (2004). From "separate but equal" to "No Child Left Behind": The collision of new standards and old inequalities. In D. Meier & G. Wood (Eds.), *Many children left behind: How the No Child Left Behind Act is damaging our children and our schools* (pp. 3–32). Boston: Beacon.

Darling-Hammond, L., & Hill-Lynch, O. (2006). If they'd only do their work! *Educational Leadership, 63*(5), 8–13.

Davidson, A. L. (1999). Negotiating social differences: Youths' assessments of educators' strategies. *Urban Education, 34,* 338–369.

Davidson, R. J., Putnam, K. M., & Larson, C. L. (2000). Dysfunction in the neural circuitry of emotion regulation—A possible prelude to violence. *Science, 289,* 591–594.

Deater-Deckard, K., Bates, J. E., Dodge, K. A., & Pettit, G. S. (1996). Physical discipline among African American and European American mothers: Links to children's externalizing behaviors. *Developmental Psychology, 32,* 1065–1072.

De Bellis, M. D., Keshavan, M. S., Clark, D. B., Casey, B. J., Giedd, J. N., et al. (1999). Developmental traumatology part II: Brain development. *Biological Psychiatry, 45,* 1271–1284.

Deci, E. L., & Ryan, R. M. (1985). *Intrinsic motivation and self-determination in human behavior.* New York: Plenum.

Deci, E., Koestner, R., & Ryan, R. (1999). A meta-analytic review of experiments examining the effects of extrinsic rewards on intrinsic motivation. *Psychological Bulletin, 125,* 627–668.

Deci, E., Koestner, R., & Ryan, R. (2001). Extrinsic rewards and intrinsic motivation in education: Reconsidered once again. *Review of Educational Research, 71,* 1–27.

Delgado, J. M. R. (1979). Neurophysiological mechanisms of aggressive behavior. In S. Feshbach & A. Fraczek (Eds.), *Aggression and behavior change: Biological and social processes* (pp. 54–65). New York: Praeger.

Delgado-Gaitan, C. (1994). Socializing young children in Mexican-American families: An intergenerational perspective. In P. M. Greenfield & R. R. Cocking (Eds.), *Cross-cultural roots of minority child development* (pp. 55–86). Hillsdale, NJ: Erlbaum.

Delpit, L. (1995). *Other people's children: Cultural conflict in the classroom.* New York: New Press.

Delpit, L. (1998). What should teachers do? Ebonics and culturally responsive instruction. In T. Perry & L. Delpit (Eds.), *The real Ebonics debate: Power, language, and the education of African-American children* (pp. 17–26). Boston: Beacon.

Delpit, L. (2002). No kinda sense. In L. Delpit & J. K. Dowdy (Eds.), *The skin that we speak: Thoughts on language and culture in the* classroom (pp. 31–48). New York: New Press.

Delpit, L. D. (1992). Education in a multicultural society: Our future's greatest challenge. *Journal of Negro Education, 61,* 237–239.

Denby, R., & Alford, K. (1996). Understanding African American discipline styles: Suggestions for effective social work intervention. *Journal of Multicultural Social Work, 4,* 81–98.

Derman-Sparks, L. (2006). Anti-bias education goals. In L. Derman-Sparks & P. G. Ramsey (with J. O. Edwards) (Eds.), *What if all the kids are white? Anti-bias multicultural edu-cation with young children and families* (p. 5). New York: Teachers College Press.

Derman-Sparks, L., & the A.B.C. Task Force (1989). *Anti-bias curriculum: Tools for empowering young children.* Washington, DC: National Association for the Education of Young Children.

DeRosier, M. E., Cillessen, A. H. N., Coie, J. D., & Dodge, K. A. (1994). Group social context and children's aggressive behavior. *Child Development, 65,* 1068–1079.

DeVoe, J. F., Peter, K., Noonan, M., Snyder, T. D., & Baum, K. (2005, November). *Indicators of school crime and safety: 2005* (NCES 2006-001/NCJ 210697). Washington, DC: U.S. Departments of Education and Justice. Retrieved July 28, 2006, from http://nces .ed.gov/pubs2006/2006001.pdf.

deVries, M. W. (1989). Temperament and infant mortality among the Masai of East Africa. *American Journal of Psychiatry, 141,* 1189–1194.

Dewey, J. (1933). *How we think.* Boston: Heath.

Diamond, K. E., & Stacey, S. (2002). The other children at preschool: Experiences of typically developing children in inclusive programs. In S. Sandall & M. Ostrosky (Eds.), *Natural environments and inclusion* (pp. 59–68). Denver and Longmont, CO: Division for Early Childhood of the Council for Exceptional Children.

DiPietro, J. (2002). Prenatal/perinatal stress and its impact on psychosocial child development. In R. E. Tremblay, R. G. Barr, & R. DeV. Peters (Eds.), *Encyclopedia on early childhood development.* Montreal, QC: Centre of Excellence for Early Childhood Development. Retrieved June 25, 2005, from www.excellence-jeunesenfants.ca/documents/ DiPietroANGxp.pdf.

DiPietro, J. A. (2000). Baby and the brain: Advances in child development. *Annual Review of Public Health, 21,* 455–271.

Dishion, T. J., Andrews, D. W., & Crosby, L. (1995). Antisocial boys and their friends in adolescence: Relationship characteristics, quality, and interactional processes. *Child Development, 66,* 139–151.

Dishion, T. J., McCord, J., & Poulin, F. (1999). When interventions harm: Peer groups and problem behavior. *American Psychologist, 54,* 755–764.

Dishion, T. J., Spracklen, K. M., Andrews, D. W., & Patterson, G. R. (1996). Deviancy training in male adolescent friendships. *Behavior Therapy, 27,* 373–390.

Dodge, K. A. (1980). Social cognition and children's aggressive behavior. *Child Development, 51,* 162–170.

Dodge, K. A. (1991). The structure and function of reactive and proactive aggression. In D. J. Pepler & K. H. Rubin (Eds.), *The development and treatment of childhood aggression* (pp. 201–218). Hillsdale, NJ: Erlbaum.

Dodge, K. A. (2003). Do social information-processing patterns mediate behavior? In B. B. Lahey, T. E. Moffitt, & A. Caspi (Eds.), *Causes of conduct disorder and juvenile delinquency* (pp. 254–274). New York: Guilford.

Dodge, K. A., Bates, J. E., & Pettit, G. S. (1990). Mechanisms in the cycle of violence. *Science, 250,* 1678–1683.

Dodge, K. A., & Frame, C. L. (1982). Social cognition biases and deficits in aggressive boys. *Child Development, 53,* 620–635.

Dodge, K. A., & Pettit, G. S. (2003). A biopsychosocial model of the development of chronic conduct problems in adolescence. *Developmental Psychology, 39,* 349–371.

Doll, B., Song, S., & Siemers, E. (2004). Classroom ecologies that support or discourage bullying. In D. L. Espelage & S. M. Swearer (Eds.), *Bullying in American schools: A socio-ecological perspective on prevention and intervention* (pp. 161–183). Mahwah, NJ: Erlbaum.

Donahue, J. J., & Levitt, S. D. (2001, May). The impact of legalized abortion on crime. *The Quarterly Journal of Economics, 116,* 379–420.

Donnerstein, E., Slaby, R. G., & Eron, L. D. (1994). The mass media and youth aggression. In L. D. Eron, J. H. Gentry, & P. Schlegel (Eds.), *Reason to hope: A psychosocial perspective on violence & youth* (pp. 219–250). Washington, DC: American Psychological Association.

Donovan, M. S., & Cross, C. T. (Eds.). (2002). *Minority students in special and gifted education.* Washington, DC: National Academies Press.

Dreikurs, R. (with Soltz, V.) (1964). *Children: The challenge.* New York: Hawthorn.

Dunlap, G., & Kern, L. (1993). Assessment and intervention for children within the instructional curriculum. In J. Reichle & D. P. Wacker (Eds.), *Communicative alternatives to challenging behavior: Integrating assessment and intervention strategies* (pp. 177–204). Baltimore: Brookes.

Dunn, J., & Brown, J. (1991). Relationships, talk about feelings, and the development of affect regulation in early childhood. In J. Garber & K. A. Dodge (Eds.), *The development of emotional regulation and dysregulation* (pp. 89–108). New York: Cambridge University Press.

Dunn, R., Beaudry, J. S., & Klavas, A. (1989). Survey of research on learning styles. *Educational Leadership, 46,* 50–58.

Dunst, C. J. (2002). Family-centered practices: Birth through high school. *Journal of Special Education, 36,* 139–147.

DuPaul, G. J., & Stoner, G. (2003). *ADHD in the schools: Assessment and intervention strategies* (2nd ed.). New York: Guilford.

Durand, V. M. (1990). *Severe behavior problems: A functional communication training approach.* New York: Guilford.

Durand, V. M. (1993). Functional assessment and functional analysis. In M. D. Smith (Ed.), *Behavior modification for exceptional children and youth* (pp. 38–60). Boston: Andover Medical Publishers.

Durand, V. M., & Crimmins, D. B. (1996–2001). Motivation assessment scale. Retrieved January 15, 2007, from www.monacoassociates.com/mas/aboutmas.html.

Education Development Center. (1997). *Supporting children with challenging behaviors: Training guides for the Head Start learning community.* Washington, DC: U.S. Department of Health and Human Services, Head Start Bureau.

Egan, S. K., & Perry, P. G. (1998). Does low self-regard invite victimization? *Developmental Psychology, 34,* 299–309.

Eisenberg, N., & Fabes, R. A. (1998). Prosocial development. In N. Eisenberg (Ed.), *Handbook of child psychology. Vol. 3, Social, emotional, and personality development* (5th ed., pp. 701–778). New York: Wiley.

Elias, M., & Butler, L. B. (1999). Social decision making and problem solving: Essential skills for interpersonal and academic success. In J. Cohen (Ed.), *Educating minds and hearts: Social emotional learning and the passage into adolescence* (pp. 74–94). New York: Teachers College Press.

Elicker, J., & Fortner-Wood, C. (1995). Adult-child relationships in early childhood programs. *Young Children, 51*(1), 69–78.

Emde, R. N., & Robinson, J. (2000). Guiding principles for a theory of early intervention: A developmental-psychoanalytic perspective. In J. P. Shonkoff & S. J. Meisels (Eds.), *Handbook of early childhood intervention* (2nd ed., pp. 160–178). New York: Cambridge University Press.

Emmer, E. T., Evertson, C. M., & Anderson, L. M. (1980). Effective classroom management at the beginning of the school year. *Elementary School Journal, 80,* 219–231.

Emmer, E. T., Evertson, C. M., & Worsham, M. E. (2003). *Classroom management for secondary teachers* (6th ed.). Boston: Allyn & Bacon.

Emmons, P. G., & Anderson, L. M. (n.d.). Sensory integration dysfunction—Becoming a sensory detective. Retrieved May 18, 2007, from www.comeunity.com/disability/sensory_integration/sensoryintegrationdysfunction.html.

Epstein, J. L., Sanders, M. G., Simon, B. S., Salinas, K. C., Jansorn, N. R., & Van Voorhis, F. L. (2002). *School, family, and community partnerships: Your handbook for action* (2nd ed.). Thousand Oaks, CA: Corwin.

ERIC Clearinghouse on Disabilities and Gifted Education. (1998). *Teaching children with attention deficit/hyperactivity disorder.* Reston, VA: Author. (ERIC Digest E569).

Erikson, E. (1980). *Identity and the life cycle.* New York: Norton.

Eron, L. D., Gentry, J. H., & Schlegel, P. (Eds.). Introduction: Experience of violence: Ethnic groups. In *Reason to hope: A psychosocial perspective on violence & youth* (pp. 101–103). Washington, DC: American Psychological Association.

Eron, L. D., Huesmann, L. R., & Zelli, A. (1991). The role of parental variables in the learning of aggression. In D. J. Pepler & K. H. Rubin (Eds.), *The development and treatment of childhood aggression* (pp. 169–188). Hillsdale, NJ: Erlbaum.

Evertson, C. M., & Emmer, E. T. (1982). Effective management at the beginning of the school year in junior high classes. *Journal of Educational Psychology, 74,* 485–498.

Evertson, C. M., Emmer, E. T., & Worsham, M. E. (2003). *Classroom management for elementary teachers* (6th ed.). Boston: Allyn & Bacon.

Fabes, R. A., & Eisenberg, N. (1992). Young children's coping with interpersonal anger. *Child Development, 63,* 116–128.

Fairclough, I. (2007, September 13). "I've stood around too long." *Halifax, NS Chronicle Herald.* Retrieved September 22, 2007, from www.thechronicleherald.ca/print_article.html?story=858884.

Falvey, M. A., & Givner, C. C. (2005). What is an inclusive school? In R. A. Villa & J. S. Thousand (Eds.), *Creating an inclusive school* (2nd ed., pp. 1–11). Alexandria, VA: Association for Supervision and Curriculum Development.

Families and Advocates Partnership for Education (FAPE). (2001). School accommodations and modifications. FAPE 27. Minneapolis: PACER Center. Retrieved November 21, 2006, from www.fape.org/pubs/FAPE-27.pdf.

Families Together. (n.d.). Growing national consensus to limit the use of seclusion and restraint. Wichita, KS: Author. Retrieved February 27, 2007, from www.familiestogetherinc.com/Attachment_Growing_National_Consensus_to_Limit_the_Use_of_Seclusion_and_Restraint%5B1%5D.pdf.

Farmer, T. W. (2000). Misconceptions of peer rejection and problem behavior: Understanding aggression in students with mild disabilities. *Remedial and Special Education, 21,* 194–208.

Farrington, D. P. (1991). Childhood aggression and adult violence: Early precursors and later life outcomes. In D. J. Pepler & K. H. Rubin (Eds.), *The development and treatment of childhood aggression* (pp. 5–30). Hillsdale, NJ: Erlbaum.

Federal Interagency Forum on Child and Family Statistics. (2005). Food security and diet quality. In *America's children in brief: Key national indicators of well-being 2005*. Retrieved May 20, 2007, from www.childstats.gov/amchildren05/eco.asp.

Federal Interagency Forum on Child and Family Statistics. (2006). Lead in the blood of children. In *America's children in brief: Key national indicators of well-being, 2006*. Retrieved May 20, 2007, from www.childstats.gov/americaschildren05/spe.asp.

Fergus, S., & Zimmerman, M. A. (2005). Adolescent resilience: A framework for understanding healthy development in the face of risk. *Annual Review of Public Health, 26,* 399–419.

Ferguson, R. F. (2002, October). *What doesn't meet the eye: Understanding and addressing racial disparities in high-achieving suburban schools*. Retrieved January 5, 2007, from www.hks.harvard.edu/inequality/Seminar/Papers/Ferguson.pdf

Fergusson, D. (2002). Tobacco consumption during pregnancy and its impact on child development. In R. E. Tremblay, R. G. Barr, & R. DeV. Peters (Eds.), *Encyclopedia on early childhood development*. Montreal, QC: Centre of Excellence for Early Childhood Development. Retrieved June 25, 2005, from www.excellence-jeunesenfants.ca/documents/FergussonANGxp.pdf.

Fertman, C. I. (2004). Schools and families of students with an emotional disturbance: Allies and partners. In D. B. Hiatt-Michael (Ed.), *Promising practices connecting schools to families of children with special needs* (pp. 79–99). Greenwich, CT: Information Age Publishing.

Fields, M., & Boesser, C. (1998). *Constructive guidance and discipline: Preschool and primary education* (2nd ed.). Upper Saddle River, NJ: Prentice-Hall.

Fisher, C. B., Wallace, S. A., & Fenton, R. E. (2000). Discrimination distress during adolescence. *Journal of Youth and Adolescence, 29,* 679–695.

Fisher, E., & Kennedy, C. H. (2001). Access to the middle school core curriculum. In C. H. Kennedy & D. Fisher (Eds.), *Inclusive middle schools* (pp. 43–59). Baltimore: Brookes.

Fletcher, M. A. (2002, April 12). Connectedness called key to student behavior. *Washington Post*, p. A03. Retrieved February 8, 2006, from www.washingtonpost.com/ac2/wp-dyn/A34686-2002Apr11?1.

Fox, L. (n.d.). *What works briefs 10: Positive behavior support: An individualized approach for addressing challenging behavior*. Center on the Social Emotional Foundations for Early Learning. Retrieved January 15, 2007, from www.vanderbilt.edu/csefel/briefs/wwwb10.pdf.

Fox, L., Dunlap, G., & Cushing, L. (2002). Early intervention, positive behavior support, and transition to school. *Journal of Emotional and Behavioral Disorders, 10,* 149–157.

Fox, L., Dunlap, G., Hemmeter, M. L., Joseph, G. E., & Strain, P. S. (2003, July). The teaching pyramid: A model for supporting social competence and preventing challenging behavior in young children. *Young Children, 58*(4), 48–52.

Fox, L., Vaughn, B. J., Wyatte, M. L., & Dunlap, G. (2002). "We can't expect other people to understand": Family perspectives on problem behavior. *Exceptional Children, 68,* 437–450.

Freiberg, H. J. (1999). Sustaining the paradigm. In H. J. Freiberg (Ed.), *Beyond behaviorism: Changing the classroom management paradigm* (pp. 164–173). Boston: Allyn & Bacon.

Freire, M., & Bernhard, J. K. (1997). Caring for and teaching children who speak other languages. In K. M. Kilbride (Ed.), *Include me too! Human diversity in early childhood* (pp. 160–176). Toronto, ON: Harcourt Brace & Company Canada.

French, N. K. (1999). Paraeducators and teachers: Shifting roles. *Teaching Exceptional Children, 32*(2), 69–73.

Frick, P. J. (2004). Integrating research on temperament and childhood psychopathology: Its pitfalls and promises. *Journal of Clinical Child and Adolescent Psychology, 33,* 2–7.

Frick, P. J., Lahey, B. B., Kamphaus, R. W., Loeber, R., Christ, M. G., Hart, E. I., et al. (1991). Academic underachievement and the disruptive behavior disorders. *Journal of Consulting and Clinical Psychology, 59,* 301–315.

Frick, P. J., & Morris, A. S. (2004). Temperament and developmental pathways to conduct problems. *Journal of Clinical Child and Adolescent Psychology, 33,* 54–68.

Fried, P. A. (2002a). Adolescents prenatally exposed to marijuana: Examination of facets of complex behaviors and comparisons with the influence of in utero cigarettes. *Journal of Clinical Pharmacology, 42,* 97S–102S.

Fried, P. A. (2002b). Tobacco consumption during pregnancy and its impact on child development. In R. E. Tremblay, R. G. Barr, & R. DeV. Peters (Eds.), *Encyclopedia on early childhood development.* Montreal, QC: Centre of Excellence for Early Childhood Development. Retrieved June 25, 2005, from www.excellence-jeunesenfants.ca/documents/FriedANGxp.pdf.

Fried, S., & Fried, P. (2003). *Bullies, targets, and witnesses: Helping children break the pain chain.* New York: Evans.

Friend, M. (2005). *Special education: Contemporary perspectives for school professionals.* Boston: Allyn & Bacon.

Friend, M., & Bursuck, W. D. (2002). *Including children with special needs: A practical guide for classroom teachers* (3rd ed.). Boston: Allyn & Bacon.

Froschl, M., Sprung, B., & Mullin-Rindler, N., (with Stein, N., & Gropper, N.) (1998). *Quit it! A teacher's guide on teasing and bullying for use with students in grades K–3.* Washington, DC: NEA Professional Library.

Fry, D. P. (1988). Intercommunity differences in aggression among Zapotec children. *Child Development, 59,* 1008–1019.

Fry, P. S. (1983). Process measures of problem and non-problem children's classroom behaviour: The influence of teacher behaviour variables. *British Journal of Educational Psychology, 53,* 79–88.

Fuchs, D., Fuchs, L. S., Mathes, P. G., & Martinez, E. A. (2002). Preliminary evidence on the social standing of students with learning disabilities in PALS and no-PALS classrooms. *Learning Disabilities Research and Practice, 17,* 205–215.

Fulk, B. M., Brigham, F. J., & Lohman, D. A. (1998). Motivation and self-regulation: A comparison of students with learning and behavior problems. *Remedial and Special Education, 19,* 300–309.

Furman, E. (1986). Stress in the nursery school. In E. Furman (Ed.), *What nursery school teachers ask us about: Psychoanalytic consultations in preschools.* Madison, CT: International Universities Press.

Gable, R. A., Quinn, M. M., Rutherford, R. B., Jr., Howell, K. W., & Hoffman, C. C. (1998). *Addressing student problem behavior: Part II—Conducting a functional behavioral assessment* (3rd ed.). Washington, DC: Center for Effective Collaboration and Practice. Retrieved January 16, 2007, from http://cecp.air.org/fba/problembehavior2/main2.htm.

Gable, R. A., Quinn, M. M., Rutherford, R. B., Jr., Howell, K. W., & Hoffman, C. C. (2000). *Addressing student problem behavior: Part III—Creating positive behavioral intervention plans and supports.* Washington, DC: Center for Effective Collaboration and Practice. Retrieved January 17, 2007, from http://cecp.air.org/fba/problembehavior3/main3.htm.

Gagnon, C. (1991). Commentary: School-based interventions for aggressive children: Possibilities, limitations, and future directions. In D. J. Pepler & K. H. Rubin (Eds.), *The development and treatment of childhood aggression* (pp. 449–455). Hillsdale, NJ: Erlbaum.

Galinsky, E., & Weissbourd, B. (1992). Family-centered child care. In B. Spodek & O. Saracho (Eds.), *Issues in child care: Yearbook in early childhood education, Vol. 3* (pp. 47–65). New York: Teachers College Press.

Ganesh, A., & Surbeck, D. (2005, December 8). An investigation of the impact of standardized testing in second grade. Presentation at National Association for the Education of Young Children conference, Washington, DC.

Garbarino, J. (1999). *Lost boys: Why our sons turn violent and how we can save them.* New York: Free Press.

Garbarino, J., & deLara, E. (2002). *And words can hurt forever: How to protect adolescents from bullying, harassment, and emotional violence.* New York: Free Press.

Garcia Coll, C., & Magnuson, K. (2000). Cultural differences as sources of developmental vulnerabilities and resources. In J. P. Shonkoff & S. J. Meisels (Eds.), *Handbook of early childhood intervention* (2nd ed., pp. 94–114). New York: Cambridge University Press.

Gardner, H. (1983). *Multiple intelligences: The theory in practice*. New York: Basic Books.

Gardner, M., & Steinberg, L. (2005). Peer influence on risk taking, risk preference, and risky decision making in adolescence and adulthood: An experimental study. *Developmental Psychology, 41*, 625–635.

Garrison-Wade, D. R., & Lewis, C. W. (2006). Tips for school principals and teachers: Helping Black students achieve. In J. Landsman & C. W. Lewis (Eds.), *White teachers/diverse classrooms: A guide to building inclusive schools, promoting high expectations, and eliminating racism* (pp. 150–161). Sterling, VA: Stylus.

Gartrell, D. (1997). Beyond discipline to guidance. *Young Children, 52*, 34–42.

Gay, G. (2000). *Culturally responsive teaching: Theory, research, and practice*. New York: Teachers College Press.

Gentile, D. A., Lynch, P. J., Linder, J. R., & Walsh, D. A. (2004). The effects of violent video game habits on adolescent hostility, aggressive behaviors, and school performance. *Journal of Adolescence, 27*, 5–22.

Giangreco, M. F. (2003). Working with paraprofessionals. *Educational Leadership, 61*(2), 50–53.

Giangreco, M. F., Edelman, S. W., Luiselli, T. E., & MacFarland, S. Z. C. (1997). Helping or hovering? Effects of instructional assistant proximity on students with disabilities. *Exceptional Children, 64*, 7–18.

Gibb, J. R. (1961). Defensive communication. *The Journal of Communication, 11*, 141–148.

Gibbs, N., & Roche, T. (1999, December 20). The Columbine tapes. *Time, 154*(25), 40–51.

Giedd, J. N. (2004). Structural magnetic resonance imaging of the adolescent brain. *Annals of the New York Academy of Sciences, 1021*, 77–85.

Ginott, H. G. (1956). *Between parent and child*. New York: Avon.

Ginsberg, M. B. (2007). Lessons at the kitchen table. *Educational Leadership, 64*(6), 56–61.

Glover, D., Gough, G., Johnson, M., & Cartwright, N. (2000). Bullying in 25 secondary schools: Incidence, impact, and intervention. *Educational Research, 42*, 141–156.

Goldschmidt, L., Day, N. L., & Richardson, G. A. (2000). Effects of prenatal marijuana exposure on child behavior problems at age 10. *Neurotoxicology and Teratology, 22*, 325–336.

Goldstein, A. P., Harootunian, B., & Conoley, J. C. (1994). *Student aggression: Prevention, management, and replacement training*. New York: Guilford.

Goleman, D. (1987, August 25). Embattled giant of psychology speaks his mind. *New York Times*, pp. B1, B3.

Goleman, D. (1997). *Emotional intelligence*. New York: Bantam.

Goleman, D. (2006). The socially intelligent leader. *Educational Leadership, 64*(10), 76–81.

Gonzalez-Mena, J. (2002). *The child in the family and the community* (3rd ed.). Upper Saddle River, NJ: Merrill Prentice-Hall.

Gonzalez-Mena, J. (1997). *Multicultural issues in child care*. Mountain View, CA: Mayfield.

Gonzalez-Mena, J. (2003). Discovering my whiteness. Presentation at the National Association for the Education of Young Children conference, Chicago.

Good, T. L., & Brophy, J. E. (2008). *Looking in classrooms* (10th ed.). Boston: Allyn & Bacon.

Gopnik, A., Meltzoff, A. N., & Kuhl, P. K. (2001). *The scientist in the crib: What early learning tells us about the mind*. New York: Perennial.

Gordon, T. (2000). *Parent effectiveness training: The proven program for raising responsible children*. New York: Three Rivers Press.

Gordon, T. (with Burch, N.) (2003). *Teacher effectiveness training*. New York: Three Rivers Press.

Gorman-Smith, D., Henry, D. B., & Tolan, P. H. (2004). Exposure to community violence and violent perpetration: The protective effects of family functioning. *Journal of Clinical Child and Adolescent Psychology, 33*, 439–449.

Gottfredson, D. (n.d.). School-based crime prevention. In L. W. Sherman, D. Gottfredson, D. MacKenzie, J. Eck, P. Reuter, & S. Bushway, *Preventing crime: What works, what doesn't, what's promising*. Washington,

DC: U.S. National Institute of Justice. Retrieved July 28, 2006, from www.ncjrs.gov/works/.

Gottfredson, G. D., Gottfredson, D. C., Czeh, E. R., Cantor, D., Crosse, S. B., & Hantman, I. (2004, November). *Toward safe and orderly schools—The national study of delinquency prevention in schools.* Washington, DC: National Institute of Justice. Retrieved July 29, 2006, from www.ncjrs.gov/pdffiles1/nij/205005.pdf.

Graham, S., & Juvonen, J. (2001). An attributional approach to peer victimization. In J. Juvonen & S. Graham (Eds.), *Peer harassment in school: The plight of the vulnerable and victimized* (pp. 49–72). New York: Guilford.

Granot, D., & Mayseless, O. (2001). Attachment security and adjustment to school in middle childhood. *International Journal of Behavioral Development, 25,* 530–541.

Greenberg, M. T. (1999). Attachment and psychopathology in childhood. In J. Cassidy & P. R. Shaver (Eds.), *Handbook of attachment theory and research* (pp. 469–496). New York: Guilford.

Greenberg, M. T., DeKlyen, M., Speltz, M. L., & Endriga, M. C. (1997). The role of attachment processes in externalizing psychopathology in young children. In L. Atkinson & K. Zucker (Eds.), *Attachment and psychopathy* (pp. 196–222). New York: Guilford.

Greenberg, M. T., & Kusche, C. (1998). *Blueprints for violence prevention: Book 10, Promoting Alternative Thinking Strategies (PATHS).* Boulder: Institute of Behavioral Science, University of Colorado.

Greenberg, M. T., Speltz, M. L., & DeKlyen, M. (1993). The role of attachment in the early development of disruptive behavior problems. *Development and Psychopathology, 5,* 191–213.

Greene, M. L., Way, N., & Pahl, K. (2006). Trajectories of perceived adult and peer discrimination among black, Latino, and Asian American adolescents: Patterns and psychological correlates. *Developmental Psychology, 42,* 218–238.

Greene, R. W. (1998). *The explosive child: A new approach for understanding and parenting easily frustrated, "chronically inflexible" children.* New York: HarperCollins.

Greenfield, P. M., & Suzuki, L. K. (1998). Culture and human development: Implications for parenting, education, pediatrics, and mental health. In I. E. Sigel & K. A. Renninger (Eds.), *Handbook of child psychology: Vol. 4, Child psychology in practice* (5th ed., pp. 1059–1109). New York: Wiley.

Greenman, J. (1988). *Caring spaces, learning places: Children's environments that work.* Redmond, WA: Exchange Press.

Greenman, J. (2001). *What happened to the world? Helping children cope in turbulent times.* Retrieved July 31, 2007, from www.brighthorizons.com/talktochildren/docs/whathapp.pdf.

Greenough, W. T., Black, J. E., & Wallace, C. S. (1987). Experience and brain development. *Child Development, 58,* 539–559.

Greenspan, S. I. (1996). *The challenging child: Understanding, raising, and enjoying the five "difficult" types of children.* Reading, MA: Addison-Wesley.

Grey, K. (1995). *Not in praise of praise.* Redmond, WA: Child Care Exchange.

Griffith, D. R. (1992). Prenatal exposure to cocaine and other drugs: Developmental and educational prognoses. *Phi Delta Kappan, 74,* 30–34.

Grigal, M. (1998). The time-space continuum: Using natural supports in inclusive classrooms. *Teaching Exceptional Children, 30*(6), 44–51.

Griggs, P., & Turnbull, A. (n.d.). Addressing cultural and economic diversity in PBS. Rehabilitation Research and Training Center. Retrieved August 15, 2007, from www.apbs.org/files/PBSprac.div.pdf.

Grossman, H. (1995). *Classroom behavior management in a diverse society* (2nd ed.). Mountain View, CA: Mayfield.

Groves, B. M. (2002). *Children who see too much: Lessons from the Child Witness to Violence Project.* Boston: Beacon.

Groves, B. M., & Zuckerman, B. (1997). Intervention with parents and caregivers of children who are exposed to violence. In J. D. Osofsky (Ed.), *Children in a violent society* (pp. 183–201). New York: Guilford.

Guerra, N. G. (1997a). Intervening to prevent childhood aggression in the inner city. In J. McCord (Ed.), *Violence and childhood in the inner city* (pp. 256–312). New York: Cambridge University Press.

Guerra, N. G. (1997b, May). Violence in schools: Interventions to reduce school-based violence. Presentation at the Centre for Studies of Children at Risk conference, Hamilton, ON.

Guetzloe, E. C., & Johns, B. H. (2004). Instructional strategies for students with emotional and behavioral disorders in inclusive settings. In B. H. Johns & E. C. Guetzloe (Eds.), *Inclusive education for children and youths with emotional and behavioral disorders: Enduring challenges and emerging practices* (pp. 11–17). Arlington, VA: Council for Children with Behavioral Disorders.

Gunnar, M. R. (1998). Quality of early care and buffering of neuroendocrine stress reactions: Potential effects on the developing human brain. *Preventive Medicine, 27,* 208–211.

Gunnar, M. R. (2000, July). Brain-behavior interface: Studies of early experience and the physiology of stress. Presentation at the World Association for Infant Mental Health meeting, Montreal, QC.

Gurian, M., & Stevens, K. (2004). With boys and girls in mind. *Educational Leadership, 62*(3), 21–26.

Gurwitch, R. H., Silovsky, J. F., Schultz, S., Kees, M., & Burlingame, S. (2005). *Reactions and guidelines for children following trauma/disaster.* American Psychological Association. Retrieved May 4, 2005, from www.apa.org/practice/ptguidelines.html.

Guzman, B. (2001, May). *The Hispanic population: Census 2000 brief.* Washington, DC: U.S. Census Bureau. Retrieved July 25, 2006, from www.census.gov/prod/2001pubs/c2kbr01-3.pdf.

Haager, D., & Klingner, J. K. (2005). *Differentiating instruction in inclusive classrooms: The special educator's guide.* Boston: Allyn & Bacon.

Haager, D., & Vaughn, S. (1995). Parent, teacher, peer, and self reports of social competence of students with learning disabilities. *Journal of Learning Disabilities, 28,* 205–215, 231.

Haapasalo, J., & Tremblay, R. E. (1994). Physically aggressive boys from ages 6 to 12: Family background, parenting behavior, and prediction of delinquency. *Journal of*

Consulting and Clinical Psychology, 62, 1044–1052.

Haberman, M. (1995). Star teachers of children in poverty. West Lafayette, IN: Kappa Delta Pi.

Hagan J. F., Jr., & The Committee on Psychosocial Aspects of Child and Family Health, & The Task Force on Terrorism of the American Academy of Pediatrics. (2005). Psychosocial implications of disaster or terrorism on children: A guide for the pediatrician. *Pediatrics, 116,* 787–795.

Hale, J. E. (1986). *Black children: Their roots, culture, and learning styles.* Baltimore: Johns Hopkins Press.

Hale, J. E. (2001). *Learning while black: Creating educational excellence for African American children.* Baltimore: Johns Hopkins Press.

Hall, E. T. (1977). *Beyond culture.* Garden City, NY: Anchor Press/Doubleday.

Hamer, D. (2002). Rethinking behavior genetics. *Science, 298,* 71–72.

Hamer, D., & Copeland, P. (1999). *Living with our genes: Why they matter more than you think.* New York: Anchor Books.

Hamilton, C. E. (2000). Continuity and discontinuity of attachment from infancy through adolescence. *Child Development, 71,* 690–694.

Hamre, B. K., & Pianta, R. C. (2001). Early teacher–child relationships and the trajectory of children's school outcomes through eighth grade. *Child Development, 72,* 625–638.

Handwerk, M. L., & Marshall, R. M. (1998). Behavioral and emotional problems of students with learning disabilities, serious emotional disturbance, or both conditions. *Journal of Learning Disabilities, 31,* 327–338.

Hargie, O., Saunders, C., & Dickson, D. (1994). *Social skills in interpersonal communication* (3rd ed.). New York: Routledge.

Harlow, H., & Harlow, M. (1962). Social deprivation in monkeys. *Scientific American, 207,* 137–146.

Harris Interactive & Gay, Lesbian and Straight Education Network. (2005). *From teasing to torment: School climate in America, a survey of students and teachers.* New York: GLSEN.

Harris, J. R. (1999). *The nurture assumption: Why children turn out the way they do.* New York: Touchstone.

Hartup, W. W. (1998). The company they keep: Friends and their developmental significance. In A. Campbell & S. Muncer (Eds.), *The social child* (pp. 143–163). Hove, East Sussex: Psychology Press.

Harwood, M., & Kleinfeld, J. S. (2002). Up front, in hope: The value of early intervention for children with fetal alcohol syndrome. *Young Children, 57*(4), 86–90.

Hawkins, D. L., Pepler, D. J., & Craig, W. M. (2001). Naturalistic observations of peer interventions in bullying. *Social Development, 10,* 512–527.

Hawkins, J. D., Catalano, R. F., Kosterman, R., Abbott, R., & Hill, K. G. (1999). Preventing adolescent health-risk behaviors by strengthening protection during childhood. *Archives of Pediatric and Adolescent Medicine, 153,* 226–234.

Hawkins, J. D., Guo, J., Hill, K. G., Battin-Pearson, S., & Abbott, R. D. (2001). Long-term effects of the Seattle Social Development Project on school bonding trajectories. *Applied Developmental Sciences, 5,* 225–236.

Hawkins, J. D., Smith, B. H., & Catalano, R. F. (2004). Social development and social and emotional learning. In J. E. Zins, R. P. Weissberg, W. C. Wang, & H. J. Walberg (Eds.), *Building academic success on social and emotional learning: What does the research say?* (pp. 135–150). New York: Teachers College Press.

Hawkins, J. D., & Weis, J. G. (1985). The social development model: An integrated approach to delinquency prevention. *Journal of Primary Prevention, 6,* 73–79.

Hay, T. (1994–1995, Winter). The case against punishment. *IMPrint, 11,* 10–11.

Hayes, N. (n.d.). Section 504: It is not "unfunded" special education. New Horizons for Learning. Retrieved November 21, 2006, from www.newhorizons/org/spneeds/inclusion/law/hayes4.htm.

Hazler, R. J., & Carney, J. V. (2006). Critical characteristics of effective bullying prevention programs. In S. R. Jimerson & M. J. Furlong (Eds.), *The handbook of school violence and school safety: From research to practice* (pp. 275–291). Mahwah, NJ: Erlbaum.

Heath, S. B. (1983). *Ways with words: Language, life, and work in communities and classrooms.* New York: Cambridge University Press.

Heath, S. B. (2002). A lot of talk about nothing. In B. M. Power & R. S. Hubbard (Eds.), *Language development: A reader for teachers* (2nd ed., pp. 74–79). Upper Saddle River, NJ: Merrill Prentice-Hall.

Henley, M. (2006). *Classroom management: A proactive approach.* Upper Saddle River, NJ: Merrill Prentice-Hall.

Hersey, P., Blanchard, K. H., & Johnson, D. E. (2001). *Management of organizational behavior: Leading human resources* (8th ed.). Englewood Cliffs, NJ: Prentice-Hall.

Hickman-Davis, P. (2002, Spring). "Cuando no hablan Inglés": Helping young children learn English as a second language. *Dimensions of Early Childhood,* 3–10.

Hilliard, A. G., III. (2002). Language, culture, and the assessment of African American children. In L. Delpit & J. K. Dowdy (Eds.), *The skin that we speak: Thoughts on language and culture in the* classroom (pp. 87–105). New York: New Press.

Ho, D. Y. F. (1994). Cognitive socialization in Confucian heritage cultures. In P. M. Greenfield & R. R. Cocking (Eds.), *Cross-cultural roots of minority child development* (pp. 285–314). Hillsdale, NJ: Erlbaum.

Hodges, E. V. E., Boivin, M., Vitaro, F., & Bukowski, W. M. (1999). The power of friendship: Protection against an escalating cycle of peer victimization. *Developmental Psychology, 35,* 94–101.

Holahan, A. (2000). A comparison of developmental gains for preschool children with disabilities in inclusive and self-contained classrooms. *Topics in Early Childhood Special Education, 19*(4), 224–235.

Holden, C. (2000). The violence of the lambs. *Science, 289,* 580–581.

Holden, C. (2005). Controversial study suggests seeing gun violence promotes it. *Science, 308,* 1239–1240.

Honig, A. S. (2002). *Secure relationships: Nurturing infant/toddler attachment in early care settings.* Washington, DC: National Association for the Education of Young Children.

Hoover, J., & Hazler, R. J. (1991). Bullies and victims. *Elementary School Guidance and Counseling, 25,* 212–219.

Hoover, J. H., & Oliver, R. (1996). *The bullying prevention handbook: A guide for principals, teachers, and counselors.* Bloomington, IN: National Educational Service.

Hoover-Dempsey, K. V., & Sandler, H. M. (1997). Why do parents become involved in their children's education? *Review of Educational Research, 67,* 3–42.

Howard, G. R. (2007). As diversity grows, so must we. *Educational Leadership, 64*(6), 16–22.

Howard, S., Dryden, J., & Johnson, B. (1999). Childhood resilience: Review and critique of literature. *Oxford Review of Education, 25,* 307–323.

Howes, C. (1999). Attachment relationships in the context of multiple caregivers. In J. Cassidy & P. R. Shaver (Eds.), *Handbook of attachment theory and research* (pp. 671–687). New York: Guilford.

Howes, C., & Hamilton, C. E. (1993). The changing experience of child care: Changes in teachers and in teacher-child relationships and children's social competence with peers. *Early Childhood Research Quarterly, 8,* 15–32.

Howes, C., Hamilton, C. E., & Phillipsen, L. C. (1998). Stability and continuity of child-caregiver and child-peer relationships. *Child Development, 69,* 418–426.

Howes, C., Matheson, C. C., & Hamilton, C. E. (1994). Maternal teacher and child care history correlates of children's relationships with peers. *Child Development, 65,* 264.

Howes, C., & Ritchie, S. (1999). Attachment organizations in children with difficult life circumstances. *Development and Psychopathology, 11,* 251–268.

Howes, C., & Ritchie, S. (2002). *A matter of trust: Connecting teachers and learners in the early childhood classroom.* New York: Teachers College Press.

Hubbard, J. A., & Dearing, K. F. (2004). Children's understanding and regulation of emotion in the context of their peer relations. In A. H. N. Cillessen & L. Mayeux (Eds.), *Children's peer relations: From development to intervention* (pp. 81–99). Washington, DC: American Psychological Association.

Hubel, D. H., & Wiesel, T. N. (1970). The period of susceptibility to the physiological effects of unilateral eye closure in kittens. *Journal of Physiology, 206,* 419–436.

Hughes, J. N., Cavell, T. A., & Grossman, P. B. (1997). A positive view of self: Risk or protection for aggressive children? *Development and Psychopathology, 9,* 75–94.

Hughes, J. N., Cavell, T. A., & Jackson, T. (1999). Influence of the teacher–student relationship on childhood conduct problems: A prospective study. *Journal of Clinical Child Psychology, 28,* 173–184.

Hughes, J. N., Cavell, T. A., & Willson, V. (2001). Further support for the developmental significance of the quality of the teacher–student relationship. *Journal of School Psychology, 39,* 289–301.

Humber, N., & Moss, E. (2005). The relationship of school and early school-age attachment to mother–child interaction. *American Journal of Orthopsychiatry, 75,* 128–141.

Hyman, I., & Snook, P. A. (1999). *Dangerous schools: What we can do about the physical and emotional abuse of our children.* San Francisco: Jossey-Bass.

Hymel, S., Wagner, E., & Butler, L. J. (1990). Reputational bias: View from the peer group. In S. R. Asher & J. D. Coie (Eds.), *Peer rejection in childhood* (pp. 156–186). New York: Cambridge University Press.

Ianotti, R. J. (1985). Naturalistic and structured assessments of prosocial behavior in preschool children: The influence of empathy and perspective taking. *Developmental Psychology, 21,* 46–55.

Indiana Department of Education, Language Minority and Migrant Programs. (2005, March 8). *Best practices: The use of native language during instructional and non-instructional time.* Retrieved July 20, 2006, from www.doe.state.in.us./lmmp.

Individuals with Disabilities Education Act Amendments of 1997, P.L. 105–17.

International Society of Psychiatric and Mental Health Nurses. (1999). ISPN position statement on the use of restraint and seclusion. *Journal of Child and Adolescent Nursing, 14,* 100–102.

Interview with Deborah Yurgelun-Todd. (2002, January 2). *PBS Frontline: Inside the teenage brain: Interviews.* Retrieved February 16, 2006, from www.pbs.org/wgbh/pages/frontline/shows/teenbrain/interviews/todd.html.

iSAFE. (n.d.). Beware of the cyber bully. Carlsbad, CA: Author. Retrieved April 9, 2007, from www.isafe.org/imgs/pdf/education/CyberBullying.pdf.

Iwata, B. A. (1994). Functional analysis methodology: Some closing comments. *Journal of Applied Behavior Analysis, 27,* 413–418.

Iwata, B. A., Dorsey, M. F., Slifer, K. J., Bauman, K. E., & Richman, G. S. (1982). Toward a functional analysis of self-injury. *Analysis and Intervention in Developmental Disabilities, 2,* 3–20.

Iwata, B. A., Vollmer, T. R., & Zarcone, J. R. (1990). The experimental (functional) analysis of behavior disorders: Methodology, applications, and limitations. In A. C. Repp & N. N. Singh (Eds.), *Perspectives on the use of nonaversive and aversive interventions for persons with developmental disabilities* (pp. 301–330). Sycamore, IL: Sycamore.

Jacobson, S. W., & Frye, K. F. (1991). Effect of maternal social support on attachment: Experimental evidence. *Child Development, 62,* 572–582.

Janney, R. E., & Snell, M. E. (1997). How teachers include students with moderate and severe disabilities in elementary classes: The means and meaning of inclusion. *Journal of the Association for Persons with Severe Handicaps, 22,* 159–169.

Janssen, I., Craig, W. M., Boyce, W. F., & Pickett, W. (2004). Associations between overweight and obesity with bullying behaviors in school-aged children. *Pediatrics, 113,* 1187–1194.

Jenkins, E. J., & Bell, C. C. (1997). Exposure and response to community violence among children and adolescents. In J. D. Osofsky (Ed.), *Children in a violent society* (pp. 9–31). New York: Guilford.

Joe, J. R., & Malach, R. S. (1998). Families with Native American roots. In E. W. Lynch & M. J. Hanson (Eds.), *Developing cross-cultural competence: A guide for working with children and their families* (pp. 127–164). Baltimore: Brookes.

Johnson, D. W., & Johnson, R. T. (2004). The three Cs of promoting social and emotional learning. In J. E. Zins, R. P. Weissberg, W. C. Wang, & H. J. Walberg (Eds.), *Building academic success on social and emotional learning: What does the research say?* (pp. 40–58). New York: Teachers College Press.

Johnson, D. W., Johnson, R. T., & Maruyama, G. (1983). Interdependence and interpersonal attraction among heterogeneous and homogeneous individuals: A theoretical formulation and a meta-analysis of the research. *Review of Educational Research, 53,* 5–54.

Johnson, J., & Duffett, A. (with Farkas, S., & Wilson, L.) (2002). *When it's your own child: A report on special education from the families who use it.* New York: Public Agenda. Retrieved November 24, 2004, from www.publicagenda.org/research/pdfs/when_its_your_own_child.pdf.

Johnson, J. G., Cohen, P., Smailes, E. M., Kasen, S., & Brook, J. S. (2002). Television viewing and aggressive behavior during adolescence and adulthood. *Science, 295,* 2468–2471.

Joint statement on the impact of entertainment violence on children: Congressional Public Health Summit. (2000, July 26). Retrieved June 30, 2005, from www.aap.org/advocacy/releases/jstmtevc.htm.

Jones, L. (2007, September 21). Pink hot in anti-bullying campaign. *Halifax, NS Daily News.* Retrieved September 22, 2007, from www.hfxnews.ca/index.cfm?sod=64252&sc=89.

Jones, V., & Jones, L. (2004). *Comprehensive classroom management: Creating communities of support and solving problems* (7th ed.). Boston: Allyn & Bacon.

Joseph, G., Strain, P., & Ostrosky, M. M. (2005). *What works briefs 21: Fostering emotional literacy in young children: Labeling emotions.* Center for the Social Emotional Foundations for Early Learning. Retrieved August 24, 2006, from www.vanderbilt.edu/csefel/briefs/wwb10.pdf.

Juvonen, J., & Graham, S. (2001). Preface. In J. Juvonen & S. Graham (Eds.), *Peer harassment in school: The plight of the vulnerable and victimized* (pp. xiii–xvi). New York: Guilford.

Juvenon, J., Graham, S., & Schuster, M. A. (2003). Bullying among young adolescents: The strong, the weak, and the troubled. *Pediatrics, 112,* 1231–1237.

Kagan, J. (1994). *Galen's prophecy: Temperament in human nature.* New York: Basic Books.

Kagan, J. (1998). Biology and the child. In N. Eisenberg (Ed.), *Handbook of child psychology: Vol. 3, Social, emotional, and personality development* (5th ed., pp. 177–235). New York: Wiley.

Kagan, J., & Snidman, N. (2004). *The long shadow of temperament.* Cambridge, MA: Belknap.

Kağitçibaşi, C. (1996). *Family and human development across cultures: A view from the other side.* Mahwah, NJ: Erlbaum.

Kandel, E. R., Jessell, T. M., & Sanes, J. R. (2000). Sensory experience and the fine-tuning of synaptic connections. In E. R. Kandel, J. H. Schwartz, & T. M. Jessell (Eds.), *Principles of neural science* (4th ed., pp. 1115–1130). New York: McGraw-Hill.

Kaplan, H. B. (1999). Toward an understanding of resilience: A critical review of definitions and models. In M. D. Glantz & J. L. Johnson (Eds.), *Resilience and development: Positive life adaptations* (pp. 17–83). New York: Kluwer Academic/Plenum.

Kaplan, J. S. (2000). *Beyond functional assessment: A social-cognitive approach to the evaluation of behavior problems in children and youth.* Austin, TX: Pro-Ed.

Karagammis, A., Stainback, W., & Stainback, S. (1996). Rationale for inclusive schooling. In S. Stainback & W. Stainback (Eds.), *Inclusion: A guide for educators* (pp. 3–16). Baltimore: Brookes.

Karen, R. (1998). *Becoming attached: First relationships and how they shape our capacity to love.* New York: Oxford University Press.

Karsh, K. G., Repp, A. C., Dahlquist, C. M., & Munk, D. (1995). In vivo functional assessment and multi-element interventions for problem behavior of students with disabilities in classroom settings. *Journal of Behavioral Education, 5,* 189–210.

Karten, T. J. (2005). *Inclusion strategies that work: Research-based methods for the classroom.* Thousand Oaks, CA: Corwin.

Katz, L. F., Kramer, L., & Gottman, J. M. (1992). Conflict and emotions in marital, sibling, and peer relationships. In C. U. Shantz & W. W. Hartup (Eds.), *Conflict in child and adolescent development* (pp. 122–149). New York: Cambridge University Press.

Katz, L. G., & McClellan, D. E. (1997). *Fostering children's social competence: The teacher's role.* Washington, DC: National Association for the Education of Young Children.

Katz, S. R. (1999). Teaching in tensions: Latino immigrant youth, their teachers, and the structures of schooling. *Teachers College Record, 100,* 809–840.

Kaufman, J., Yang, B.-Z., Douglas-Palumberi, H., Houshyar, S., Lipschitz, D., Krystal, J. H., et al. (2004). Social supports and serotonin transporter gene moderate depression in maltreated children. *Proceedings of the National Academy of Sciences, 101,* 17316–17321.

Kaufman, J. M. (2005). Explaining the race/ethnicity violence relationship: Neighborhood context and social psychological processes. *Justice Quarterly, 22,* 224–251.

Kavale, K. A., & Forness, S. R. (1996). Social skill deficits and learning disabilities: A meta-analysis. *Journal of Learning Disabilities, 29,* 226–237.

Kay, P., Fitzgerald, M., & McConaughy, S. H. (2002). Building effective parent–teacher relationships. In B. Algonzzine & P. Kay (Eds.), *Preventing problem behaviors: A handbook of successful intervention strategies* (pp. 104–125). Thousand Oaks, CA: Council for Exceptional Children and Corwin Press.

Kazdin, A. E. (1987). Treatment of antisocial behavior in children: Current status and future directions. *Psychological Bulletin, 102,* 187–203.

Kazdin, A. E. (1994). Interventions for aggressive and antisocial children. In L. D. Eron, J. H. Gentry, & P. Schlegel (Eds.), *Reason to hope: A psychosocial perspective on violence & youth* (pp. 341–382). Washington, DC: American Psychological Association.

Kazdin, A. E. (1995). *Conduct disorders in childhood and adolescence* (2nd ed.). Thousand Oaks, CA: Sage.

Kellam, S. G., Ling, X., Merisca, R., Brown, C. H., & Ialongo, N. (1998). The effect of the level of aggression in the first grade classroom on the cause and malleability of aggressive behavior into middle school. *Development and Psychopathology, 10,* 165–185.

Kern, L., & Clemens, N. H. (2007). Antecedent strategies to promote appropriate classroom behavior. *Psychology in the Schools, 44,* 65–75.

Kerns, K. A., Schlegelmilch, A., Morgan, T. A., & Abraham, M. M. (2005). Assessing attachment in middle childhood. In K. A. Kerns & R. A. Richardson (Eds.), *Attachment in middle childhood* (pp. 46–70). New York: Guilford.

Kerns, K. A., Tomich, P. L., & Kim, P. (2006). Normative trends in children's perceptions of availability and utilization of attachment figures in middle childhood. *Social Development, 15,* 1–22.

Kim, U., & Choi, S.-H. (1994). Individualism, collectivism, and child development: A Korean perspective. In P. M. Greenfield & R. R. Cocking (Eds.), *Cross-cultural roots of minority child development* (pp. 227–258). Hillsdale, NJ: Erlbaum.

Klass, C. S., Guskin, K. A., & Thomas, M. (1995). The early childhood program: Promoting children's development through and within relationships. *Zero to Three, 16,* 9–17.

Klass, P., & Costello, E. (2003). *Quirky kids: Understanding and helping your child who doesn't fit in—When to worry and when not to worry.* New York: Ballantine.

Kleinfeld, J. (1975). Effective teachers of Eskimo and Indian students. *School Review, 83*(2), 301–344.

Klem, A. M., & Connell, J. P. (2004). Relationships matter: Linking teacher support to student engagement and achievement. *Journal of School Health, 74,* 262–273.

Klonsky, M. (n.d.). Small schools: The numbers tell a story. Retrieved July 31, 2006, from www.smallschoolsworkshop.org/klonsky .html.

Kobak, R. (1999). The emotional dynamics of attachment relationships: Implications for theory, research, and clinical intervention. In J. Cassidy & P. R. Shaver (Eds.), *Handbook of attachment theory and research* (pp. 21–43). New York: Guilford.

Kochenderfer, B. J., & Ladd, G. W. (1996). Peer victimization: Manifestations and relations to school adjustment in kindergarten. *Journal of School Psychology, 34,* 267–283.

Kochenderfer-Ladd, B., & Skinner, K. (2002). Children's coping strategies: Moderators of the effects of peer victimization? *Developmental Psychology, 38,* 267–278.

Kochhar, C. A., West, L. L., & Taymans, J. M. (2000). *Successful inclusion: Practical strategies for a shared responsibility.* Upper Saddle River, NJ: Merrill Prentice-Hall.

Kochman, T. (1985). Black American speech events and a language program for the classroom. In C. B. Casden, V. P. John, & D. Hymes (Eds.), *Functions of language in the classroom* (pp. 211–261). Prospect Heights, IL: Waveland.

Koegel, R. L., & Koegel, L. K. (1995). *Teaching children with autism: Strategies for initiating positive interactions and improving learning opportunities.* Baltimore: Brookes.

Kohn, A. (1996). *Beyond discipline: From compliance to community.* Upper Saddle River, NJ: Merrill Prentice-Hall.

Kohn, A. (2001). Five reasons to stop saying "Good job!" *Young Children, 56,* 24–28.

Kohn, A. (2006a). *The homework myth: Why kids get too much of a bad thing.* Cambridge, MA: De Capo Press.

Kohn, A. (2006b). *Unconditional parenting: Moving from rewards and punishments to love and reason.* New York: Atria.

Kontos, S., & Wells, W. (1986). Attitudes of caregivers and the day care experiences of families. *Early Childhood Research Quarterly, 1,* 47–67.

Koplow, L. (2002). *Creating schools that heal: Real-life solutions.* New York: Teachers College Press.

Kostelnik, M. J., Onaga, E., Rohde, B., & Whiren, A. (2002). *Children with special needs: Lessons for early childhood professionals.* New York: Teachers College Press.

Kottler, J. A. (2002). *Students who drive you crazy: Succeeding with resistant, unmotivated, and otherwise difficult young people.* Thousand Oaks, CA: Corwin.

Kounin, J. S. (1970). *Discipline and group management in classrooms.* New York: Holt, Rinehart & Winston.

Kovacs, M., Krol, R., & Voti, L. (1994). Early onset psychopathology and the risk for teenage pregnancy among clinically referred girls. *Journal of the American Academy of Child Adolescent Psychiatry, 33,* 106–113.

Kralovec, E., & Buell, J. (2001). End homework now. *Educational Leadership, 58*(7), 39–42.

Kreidler, W. J., & Whittall, S. T. (with Doty, N., Johns, R., Logan, C., Roerden, L. P., Raner, C., & Wintle, C.) (1999). *Early childhood adventures in peacemaking.* Cambridge, MA: Educators for Social Responsibility.

Kriete, R. (2003). Start the day with community. *Educational Leadership, 61*(1), 68–70.

Kritchevsky, S., & Prescott, E. (with Walling, L.) (1977). *Planning environments for young children: Physical space.* Washington, DC: National Association for the Education of Young Children.

Kuhl, P. K., Williams, K. A., Lacerda, F., & Stevens, K. N. (1992). Linguistic experience alters phonetic perception in infants by 6 months of age. *Science, 255,* 606–608.

Kumpulainen, K., Rasanen, E., & Henttonen, I. (1999). Children involved in bullying: Psychological disturbance and the persistence of the involvement. *Child Abuse & Neglect, 23,* 1253–1262.

Kupersmidt, J. B., Griesler, P. C., DeRosier, M. E., Patterson, C. J., & Davis, P. W. (1995). Childhood aggression and peer relations in the context of family and neighborhood factors. *Child Development, 66,* 360–375.

Kupfer, D. J., & Woodward, H. R. (2004). Adolescent development and the regulation of behavior and emotion: Comments on part VIII. *Annals of the New York Academy of Sciences, 1021,* 320–322.

Kurcinka, M. S. (1992). *Raising your spirited child: A guide for parents whose child is more intense, sensitive, perceptive, persistent, energetic.* New York: Harper Perennial.

Kyle, D. W., McIntyre, E., Miller, K. B., & Moore, G. H. (2002). *Reaching out: A K–8 resource for connecting families and schools.* Thousand Oaks, CA: Corwin.

Ladd, B. K., & Ladd, G. W. (2001). Variations in peer victimization: Relations to children's maladjustment. In J. Juvonen & S. Graham (Eds.), *Peer harassment in school: The plight of the vulnerable and victimized* (pp. 25–48). New York: Guilford.

Ladd, G. W., Birch, S. H., & Buhs, E. S. (1999). Children's social and scholastic lives in kindergarten: Related spheres of influence. *Child Development, 70,* 1373–1400.

Ladd, G. W., & Burgess, K. B. (1999). Charting the relationship trajectories of aggressive, withdrawn, and aggressive/withdrawn children during early grade school. *Child Development, 70,* 910–929.

Ladd, G. W., & Burgess, K. B. (2001). Do relational risks and protective factors moderate the linkages between childhood aggression and early psychological and school adjustment? *Child Development, 72,* 1579–1601.

Ladson-Billings, G. (1994). *The dreamkeepers: Successful teachers of African American children.* San Francisco: Jossey-Bass.

LaGrange, A., Clark, D., & Munroe, E. (1994). *Culturally sensitive child care: The Alberta study.* Edmonton: Alberta Association for Young Children and Government of Alberta Citizenship and Heritage Secretariat.

Lahey, B. B., & Waldman, I. D. (2003). A developmental propensity model of the origins of conduct problems during childhood and adolescence. In B. B. Lahey, T. E. Moffitt, & A. Caspi (Eds.), *Causes of conduct disorder and juvenile delinquency* (pp. 76–117). New York: Guilford.

Lake, J. F., & Billingsley, B. S. (2000). An analysis of factors that contribute to parent–school conflict in special education. *Remedial and Special Education, 21,* 240–251.

Lalli, J. S., & Goh, H.-L. (1993). Naturalistic observations in community settings. In J. Reichle & D. P. Wacker (Eds.), *Communicative alternatives to challenging behavior: Integrating assessment and intervention strategies* (pp. 11–40). Baltimore: Brookes.

Landsman, J. (2002a). Educating Black males: Interview with Professor Joseph White, Ph.D. In J. Landsman & C. W. Lewis (Eds.), *White teachers/diverse classrooms: A guide to building inclusive schools, promoting high expectations, and eliminating racism* (pp. 52–60). Sterling, VA: Stylus.

Landsman, J. (2006b). When truth and joy are at stake: Challenging the status quo in the high school English class. In J. Landsman & C. W. Lewis (Eds.), *White teachers/diverse classrooms: A guide to building inclusive schools, promoting high expectations, and eliminating racism* (pp. 221–233). Sterling, VA: Stylus.

LaPlante, D. P., Barr, R. G., Brunet, A., du Fort, G. G., Meaney, M., Saucier, J.-F., et al. (2004). Stress during pregnancy affects general intellectual and language functioning in human toddlers. *Pediatric Research, 56,* 1–11.

Lareau, A. (2000). *Home advantage: Social class and parental intervention in elementary school* (2nd ed.). Lanham, MD: Rowman and Littlefield.

Lareau, A., & Shumar, W. (1996). The problem of individualism in family-school policies. *Sociology of Education,* special issue, 24–39.

Larner, M. (1994). *Parent perspectives on child care quality.* New Haven, CT: Quality 2000.

Leachman, G., & Victor, D. (2003). Student-led class meetings. *Educational Leadership, 60*(6), 64–68.

LeBel, J., Stromberg, N., Duckworth, K., Kerzner, J., Goldstein, R., Weeks, M., et al. (2004). Child and adolescent inpatient restraint reduction: A state initiative to promote strength-based care. *Journal of the American Academy of Child and Adolescent Psychiatry, 43,* 37–45.

LeBlanc, A. N. (2004). *Random family: Love, drugs, trouble, and coming of age in the Bronx.* New York: Scribner.

Lebra, T. S. (1994). Mother and child in Japanese socialization: A Japan-U.S. comparison. In P. M. Greenfield & R. R. Cocking (Eds.), *Cross-cultural roots of minority child development* (pp. 259–274). Hillsdale, NJ: Erlbaum.

Leffert, J. S., Siperstein, G. N., & Millikan, E. (2000). Understanding social adaptation in children with mental retardation: A social-cognitive perspective. *Exceptional Children, 66,* 530–545.

Lehmann, K. J. (2004). *Surviving inclusion.* Lanham, MD: Scarecrow.

Leman, K. (1992). *The birth order book: Why you are the way you are.* New York: Bantam-Dell.

Leslie, M., & DeMarchi, G. (1996). Understanding the needs of substance-involved families and children in a child care setting. *Ideas, 3*(2), 12–16.

Levin, D. E. (1998). *Remote control childhood? Combating the hazards of media culture.* Washington, DC: National Association for the Education of Young Children.

Levine, D. (2005). *Teaching empathy: A blueprint for caring, compassion, and community.* Bloomington, IN: Solution Tree.

Levine, M. (2003). Celebrating diverse minds. *Educational Leadership, 61*(2), 12–18.

Lewin, K., Lippitt, R., & White, R. K. (1999). Patterns of aggressive behavior in experimentally created "social climates." In M. Gold (Ed.), *The complete social scientist: A Kurt Lewin reader* (pp. 227–250). Washington, DC: American Psychological Association. (Reprinted from *Journal of Social Psychology, S.P.S.S.I. Bulletin, 1939, 10,* 271–299.)

Lieberman, M., Doyle, A.-B., & Markiewicz, D. (1999). Developmental patterns in security of attachment to mother and father in late childhood and early adolescence: Associations with peer relations. *Child Development, 70,* 202–213.

Litner, B. (2000). Teaching children with ADHD. In J. Andrews & J. Lupart, *The inclusive classroom: Educating exceptional children.* Scarborough, ON: Nelson Canada.

Liu, J., Raine, A., Venables, P. H., & Mednick, S. A. (2004). Malnutrition at age 3 years and externalizing behavior problems at ages 8, 11, and 17 years. *American Journal of Psychiatry, 161,* 2005–2013.

Livingston, A. (2006, June). *The condition of education 2006 in brief* (NCES 2006-072). Washington, DC: U.S. Department of Education, National Center for Education Statistics. Retrieved July 26, 2006, from http://nces.ed.gov/pubs2006/2006072.pdf.

Loeber, R. (1985). Patterns and development of antisocial and delinquent child behavior. *Annals of Child Development, 2,* 77–116.

Loeber, R., & Farrington, D. (2001). The significance of child delinquency. In R. Loeber & D. Farrington (Eds.), *Child delinquents: Development, intervention, and service needs* (pp. 1–22). Thousand Oaks, CA: Sage.

Long, N. J. (1996). The conflict cycle paradigm on how troubled students get teachers out of control. In N. J. Long & W. C. Morse (Eds.), *Conflict in the classroom: The education of at-risk and troubled students* (5th ed., pp. 244–265). Austin, TX: Pro-Ed.

Long, N. J. (2000). Personal studies in reclaiming troubled students. *Reclaiming Children and Youth, 9*(2), 95–98.

Long, N. J., Fecser, F. A., & Brendtro, L. R. (1998). Life Space Crisis Intervention: New skills for reclaiming students showing patterns of self-defeating behavior. *Healing Magazine, 3*(2). Retrieved February 27, 2007, from www.kidspeace.org/documents/LSCI_Reprint05.pdf.

Long, N. J., & Morse, W. C. (Eds.). (1996). *Conflict in the classroom: The education of at-risk and troubled students* (5th ed.). Austin, TX: Pro-Ed.

Lopez, G. R. (2001). The value of hard work: Lessons on parent involvement from an (im)migrant household. *Harvard Educational Review, 71,* 416–437.

Losen, S., & Diament, B. (1978). *Parent conferences in the schools: Procedures for developing effective partnership.* Boston: Allyn & Bacon.

Lotan, R. A. (2003). Group-worthy tasks. *Educational Leadership, 60*(6), 72–75.

Lubeck, S. (1994). The politics of developmentally appropriate practice: Exploring issues of culture, class, and curriculum. In B. L. Mallory & R. S. New (Eds.), *Diversity and developmentally appropriate practice: Challenges for early childhood education* (pp. 17–43). New York: Teachers College Press.

Luna, B., & Sweeney, J. A. (2004). The emergence of collaborative brain function: fMRI studies of the development of response inhibition. *Annals of the New York Academy of Sciences, 1021,* 296–309.

Luthar, S. S. (1999). *Poverty and children's adjustment.* Thousand Oaks, CA: Sage.

Luthar, S. S., Cicchetti, D., & Becker, B. (2000). The construction of resilience: A critical evaluation and guidelines for future work. *Child Development, 71,* 543–562.

Luthar, S. S., & Goldstein, A. (2004). Children's exposure to community violence: Implications for understanding risk and resilience. *Journal of Child and Adolescent Psychology, 33,* 499–505.

Luthar, S. S., & Zelazo, L. B. (2003). Research on resilience: An integrative review. In S. S. Luthar (Ed.), *Resilience and vulnerability: Adaptation in the context of childhood adversity* (pp. 510–549). New York: Cambridge University Press.

Lynch, E. W. (1998a). Conceptual framework: From culture shock to cultural learning. In E. W. Lynch & M. J. Hanson (Eds.), *Developing cross-cultural competence: A guide for working with children and their families* (pp. 23–45). Baltimore: Brookes.

Lynch, E. W. (1998b). Developing cross-cultural competence. In E. W. Lynch & M. J. Hanson (Eds.), *Developing cross-cultural competence: A guide for working with children and their families* (pp. 47–86). Baltimore: Brookes.

Lynch, E. W., & Hanson, M. J. (1998). Steps in the right direction: Implications for interventionists. In E. W. Lynch & M. J. Hanson (Eds.), *Developing cross-cultural competence: A guide for working with children and their families* (pp. 491–512). Baltimore: Brookes.

Lynch, M., & Cicchetti, D. (1992). Maltreated children's reports of relatedness to their teachers. In R. Pianta (Ed.), *Beyond the parent: The role of other adults in children's lives* (pp. 81–107). San Francisco: Jossey-Bass.

Lynch, M., & Cicchetti, D. (1997). Children's relationships with adults and peers: An examination of elementary and junior high students. *Journal of School Psychology, 35,* 81–99.

Lyons-Ruth, K. (1996). Attachment relationships among children with aggressive behavior problems: The role of disorganized early attachment patterns. *Journal of Consulting and Clinical Psychology, 64,* 64–73.

Lyons-Ruth, K., & Jacobvitz, D. (1999). Attachment disorganization: Unresolved loss, relational violence, and lapses in behavioral and attentional strategies. In J. Cassidy & P. R. Shaver (Eds.), *Handbook of attachment theory and research* (pp. 520–554). New York: Guilford.

Maag, J. W. (1999). *Behavior management: From theoretical implications to practical applications.* San Diego, CA: Singular.

Maccoby, E. E. (2004). Aggression in the context of gender development. In M. Putallaz & K. L. Bierman (Eds.), *Aggression, antisocial behavior, and violence among girls: A developmental perspective* (pp. 3–22). New York: Guilford.

Mace, F. C., & Roberts, M. L. (1993). Factors affecting selection of behavior interventions. In J. Reichle & D. P. Wacker (Eds.), *Communicative alternatives to challenging behavior: Integrating assessment and intervention strategies* (pp. 113–134). Baltimore: Brookes.

Maclean, K. (2003). The impact of institutionalization on child development. *Development and Psychopathology, 15,* 853–884.

Mahoney, J. (2006, October 11). Not up to homework help, parents say. *Toronto Globe and Mail*, p. A8.

Main, M., & Solomon, J. (1986). Discovery of an insecure-disorganized/disoriented attachment pattern. In T. B. Brazelton & M. W. Yongman (Eds.), *Affective development in infancy* (pp. 95–124). Norwood, NJ: Ablex.

Mallick, S. K., & McCandless, B. R. (1966). A study of catharsis aggression. *Journal of Personality and Social Psychology, 4,* 591–596.

Mandlawitz, M. (2005). *What every teacher should know about IDEA 2004*. Boston: Allyn & Bacon.

Margalit, M. (2003). Resilience model among individuals with learning disabilities: Proximal and distal influences. *Learning Disabilities Research and Practice, 18,* 82–86.

Martin, C. A., Kelly, T. H., Rayens, M. K., Brogli, B. R., Brenzel, A., Smith, W. J., et al. (2002). Sensation seeking, puberty, and nicotine, alcohol, and marijuana use in adolescence. *Journal of the American Academy of Child and Adolescent Psychiatry, 41,* 1495–1502.

Martin, E. J., & Hagan-Burke, S. (2002). Establishing a home-school connection: Strengthening the partnership between families and schools. *Preventing School Failure, 46*(2), 62–65.

Marvin, R. S., & Britner, P. A. (1999). Normative development: The ontogeny of attachment. In J. Cassidy & P. R. Shaver (Eds.), *Handbook of attachment theory and research* (pp. 44–67). New York: Guilford.

Marzano, R. J. (with Marzano, J. S., & Pickering, D. J.) (2003). *Classroom management that works: Research-based strategies for every teacher*. Alexandria, VA: Association for Supervision and Curriculum Development.

Masten, A. S. (2001). Ordinary magic: Resilience processes in development. *American Psychologist, 56,* 227–234.

Masten, A. S. (2004). Regulatory processes, risk, and resilience in adolescent development. *Annals of the New York Academy of Sciences, 1021,* 310–319.

Masten, A. S., & Coatsworth, J. D. (1998). The development of competence in favorable and unfavorable environments: Lessons from research on successful children. *American Psychologist, 53,* 205–220.

Masten, A. S., Hubbard, J. J., Gest, S. D., Telegen, A., Garmezy, N., & Ramirez, M. (1999). Competence in the context of adversity: Pathways to resilience and maladaptation from childhood to late adolescence. *Development and Psychopathology, 11,* 143–169.

Mather, N., & Goldstein, S. (2001). *Learning disabilities and challenging behaviors: A guide to intervention and classroom management*. Baltimore: Brookes.

Mathews, J. (2005, September 20). Teachers stir science, history into core classes. *Washington Post*, p. A16.

Mayseless, O. (2005). Ontogeny of attachment in middle childhood: Conceptualization of normative changes. In K. A. Kerns & R. A. Richardson (Eds.), *Attachment in middle childhood* (pp. 1–23). New York: Guilford.

McCord, J. (1997). Placing American urban violence in context. In J. McCord (Ed.), *Violence and childhood in the inner city* (pp. 78–115). New York: Cambridge University Press.

McGivern, R. F., Andersen, J., Byrd, D., Mutter, K. L., & Reilly, J. (2002). Cognitive efficiency on a match to sample task decreases at the onset of puberty in children. *Brain and Cognition, 50,* 73–89.

McGrath, M. J. (2007). *School bullying: Tools for avoiding harm and liability*. Thousand Oaks, CA: Corwin.

Meaney, M. J. (2001). Maternal care, gene expression, and the transmission of individual differences in stress reactivity across generations. *Annual Review of Neuroscience, 24,* 1161–1192.

Mehrabian, A. (1972). *Nonverbal communication*. Chicago: Aldine Atherton.

Meier, T. (1998). Teaching teachers about Black communications. In T. Perry & L. Delpit (Eds.), *The real Ebonics debate: Power, language, and the education of African-American children* (pp. 117–125). Boston: Beacon.

Merritt-Petrashek, C. A. (1996). Emotional first aid: Bandaids for the bumps. In N. J. Long & W. C. Morse (Eds.), *Conflict in the classroom: The education of at-risk and troubled students* (5th ed., pp. 429–435). Austin, TX: Pro-Ed.

Meyer, L. H., & Evans, I. M. (1993). Meaningful outcomes in behavioral intervention:

Evaluating positive approaches to the remediation of challenging behavior. In J. Reichle & D. P. Wacker (Eds.), *Communicative alternatives to challenging behavior: Integrating assessment and intervention strategies* (pp. 407–428). Baltimore: Brookes.

Michelson, L., & Mannarino, A. (1986). Social skills training with children: Research and clinical applications. In P. S. Strain, M. J. Guralnick, & H. M. Walker (Eds.), *Children's social behavior: Development, assessment, and modification* (pp. 373–406). Orlando: Academic.

Miller, J. A., Tansy, M., & Hughes, T. L. (1998). Functional behavioral assessment: The link between problem behavior and effective intervention in schools. *Current Issues in Education, 1*(5) Retrieved May 2, 2008, from http:/cie.asu.edu/volume1/number 5/index.html.

Miller, M. (2002). Resilience elements in students with learning disabilities. *Journal of Clinical Psychology, 58,* 291–298.

Miner, B. (1998). Embracing Ebonics and teaching Standard English: An interview with Oakland teacher Carrie Secret. In T. Perry & L. Delpit (Eds.), *The real Ebonics debate: Power, language, and the education of African-American children* (pp. 79–88). Boston: Beacon.

Mize, J., & Ladd, G. W. (1990). Toward the development of successful social skills training for preschool children. In S. R. Asher & J. D. Coie (Eds.), *Peer rejection in childhood* (pp. 338–361). New York: Cambridge University Press.

Moffitt, T. E. (1993). Adolescent-limited and life-course-persistent antisocial behavior: A developmental taxonomy. *Psychological Review, 100,* 674–701.

Moffitt, T. E. (1997). Neuropsychology, antisocial behavior, and neighborhood context. In J. McCord (Ed.), *Violence and childhood in the inner city* (pp. 116–170). New York: Cambridge University Press.

Moffitt, T. E. (2005). The new look of behavioral genetics in developmental psychology: Gene-environment interplay in antisocial behaviors. *Psychological Bulletin, 131,* 533–554.

Moffitt, T. E., & Caspi, A. (2001). Childhood predictors differentiate life-course persistent and adolescence-limited antisocial pathways among males and females. *Development and Psychopathology, 13,* 355–375.

Moffitt, T. E., Caspi, A., Dickson, N., Silva, P., & Stanton, W. (1996). Childhood-onset versus adolescent-onset antisocial conduct problems in males: Natural history from ages 3 to 18 years. *Development and Psychopathology, 8,* 399–424.

Moffitt, T. E., Caspi, A., Rutter, M., & Silva, P. (2001). *Sex differences in antisocial behavior.* Cambridge, UK: Cambridge University Press.

Moore, K., & Blaxall, J. (1995, October). Developing empathy and building social skills. *Ideas, 2*(2), 16–21.

Moran, S., Kornhaber, M., & Gardner, H. (2006). Orchestrating multiple intelligences. *Educational Leadership, 64*(1), 22–27.

Morrow, C. E., Culbertson, J. L., Accornero, V. H., Xue, L., Anthony, J. C., & Bandstra, E. S. (2006). Learning disabilities and intellectual functioning in school-age children with prenatal cocaine exposure. *Developmental Neuropsychology, 30,* 905–931.

Moss, E., St-Laurent, D., Dubois-Comtois, K., & Cyr, C. (2005). Quality of attachment at school age: Relations between child attachment behavior, psychosocial functioning, and school performance. In K. A. Kerns & R. A. Richardson (Eds.), *Attachment in middle childhood* (pp. 189–211). New York: Guilford.

Moss, K. (2003). *Witnessing violence: Aggression and anxiety in young children.* Statistics Canada 82-003. Retrieved July 29, 2006, from www.statcan.ca/english/freepub/82-003-SIE/2003000/pdf/82-003-SIE2003006.pdf.

Murray, J. P. (1997). Media violence and youth. In J. D. Osofsky (Ed.), *Children in a violent society* (pp. 72–96). New York: Guilford.

Muscott, H. S. (2002). Exceptional partnerships: Listening to the voices of families. *Preventing School Failure, 46*(2), 66–69.

Muscott, H. S. (2004). I can be of help too! Service learning as a tool for enhancing the education of students with emotional and behavioral disorders. In B. H. Johns & E. C. Guetzloe (Eds.), *Inclusive education for children and youths with emotional and behavioral disorders: Enduring challenges and emerging practices* (pp. 19–31). Arlington, VA: Council for Children with Behavioral Disorders.

Myers-Walls, J. A. (2005). *Talking with children when the talking gets tough.* West Lafayette, IN: Purdue Extension, Consumer and Family Sciences. Retrieved October 16, 2006, from www.ces.purdue.edu/cfs/topics/HD/TalkChildrenTalkGetsTough.pdf.

Nagin, D., & Tremblay, R. (1999). Trajectories of physical aggression, opposition, and hyperactivity on the path to physically violent and non-violent juvenile delinquency. *Child Development, 70,* 1181–1196.

Nagin, D. S., & Tremblay, R. E. (2001). Parental and early childhood predictors of persistent physical aggression in boys from kindergarten to high school. *Archives of General Psychiatry, 58,* 389–394.

Nansel, T. R., Overpeck, M., Pilla, R. S., Ruan, J., Simons-Morton, B., & Scheidt, P. (2001). Bullying behaviors among U.S. youth: Prevalence and association with psychosocial adjustment. *Journal of the American Medical Association, 285,* 2094–2100.

National Alliance of Black School Educators. (2002). *Addressing over-representation of African American students in special education: The prereferral intervention process.* Arlington, VA: Council for Exceptional Education.

National Center for Education Statistics. (2007). *Table 8.1a. Percentage of children ages 3 to 5 and 6 to 21 served under the Individuals with Disabilities Education Act (IDEA) by race/ethnicity: 1998–2004.* Retrieved October 3, 2007, from http://nces.ed.gov/pubs2007/minoritytrends/tables/table_8_1a.asp?referrer=report.

National Center for Learning Disabilities. (n.d.). *LD at a glance. Fact sheet.* New York: Author. Retrieved March 29, 2005, from www.ld.org/LDInfoZone/InfoZone_FactSheetLD_.cfm.

National Crime Prevention Council Canada. (1995, November). *Resiliency in young children.* Ottawa: Author.

National Crime Prevention Council Canada. (1996). *Preventing crime by investing in families.* Ottawa: Author.

National Institute of Mental Health. (2001). *Attention deficit hyperactivity disorder (overview).* Washington, DC: Author. Retrieved March 29, 2005, from www.nimh.nih.gov/publicat/helpchild.cfm.

National Institute of Mental Health. (2006). Helping children and adolescents cope with violence and disasters (NIH publication No. 01-3518). Bethesda, MD: Author. Retrieved October 16, 2006, from www.nimh.nih.gov/publicat/violence.cfm.

National Institutes of Mental Health. (2006, February 17). Teenage brain: A work in progress. Retrieved February 20, 2006, from www.nimh.nih.gov/publicat/teenbrain.cfm.

National Resource Center on Domestic Violence. (2002, March). *Children exposed to intimate partner violence.* Harrisburg, PA: Author. Retrieved July 31, 2006, from www.vawnet.org/NRCDVPublications/TAPE/Packets/NCR_Children.pdf.

Needleman, H. L., Riess, J. A., Tobin, M. J., Biesecker, G. E., & Greenhouse, J. B. (1996). Bone lead levels and delinquent behavior. *Journal of the American Medical Association, 275,* 363–369.

Nelson, C. A. (2000). The neurobiological bases of early intervention. In J. P. Shonkoff & S. J. Meisels (Eds.), *Handbook of early childhood intervention* (2nd ed., pp. 204–227). New York: Cambridge University Press.

Nelson, C. A., & Bloom, F. E. (1997). Child development and neuroscience. *Child Development, 68,* 970–987.

New Freedom Commission on Mental Health. (2003). *Achieving the promise: Transforming mental health care in America. Final report.* Rockville, MD: U.S. Department of Health and Human Services. Retrieved February 27, 2007, from www.mentalheathcommission.gov/reports/FinalReport/downloads/FinalReport.pdf.

New, R. S. (1994). Culture, child development, and developmentally appropriate practice: Teachers as collaborative researchers. In B. L. Mallory & R. S. New (Eds.), *Diversity and developmentally appropriate practice: Challenges for early childhood education* (pp. 65–83). New York: Teachers College Press.

Newman, K. S. (2004). *Rampage: The social roots of school shootings.* New York: Basic Books.

New York City Department of Health and Mental Hygiene. (2005, September 8). Citywide infant mortality rate was 6.1 in 2004, a decline of 6% from 2003. Retrieved January 29, 2006, from www.nyc.gov/html/doh/html/pr/pr095-05.shtml.

Nicolet, J. (2006). Conversation—A necessary step in understanding diversity: A new teacher plans for competency. In J. Landsman & C. W. Lewis (Eds.), *White teachers/diverse classrooms: A guide to building inclusive schools, promoting high expectations, and eliminating racism* (pp. 203–218). Sterling, VA: Stylus.

Nieto, S. (2004). *Affirming diversity: The sociopolitical context of multicultural education* (4th ed.). Boston: Allyn & Bacon.

Norland, M. (2003). *Differentiated instruction: Meeting the needs of all students in your classroom.* Lanham, MD: Scarecrow.

Novaco, R. W. (1975). *Anger control: The development and evaluation of an experimental treatment.* Lexington, MA: D. C. Heath.

O'Connell, P., Pepler, D., & Craig, W. (1999). Peer involvement in bullying: Insights and challenges for intervention. *Journal of Adolescence, 22,* 437–452.

O'Connor, T. G., Heron, J., Golding, J., Beveridge, M., & Glover, V. (2002). Maternal antenatal anxiety and children's behavioural/emotional problems at 4 years. *British Journal of Psychiatry, 180,* 502–508.

Odom, S. L. (2000). Preschool inclusion: What we know and where we go from here. *Topics in Early Childhood Special Education, 20*(1), 20–27.

Odom, S. L., Zercher, C., Marquart, J., Li, S., Sandall, S. R., & Wolfberg, P. (2002). Social relationships of children with disabilities and their peers in inclusive preschool classrooms. In S. L. Odom (Ed.) (with Beckman, P. J., Hanson, M. J., Horn, E., Lieber, J., Sandall, S. R., Schwartz, I. L., et al.), *Widening the circle: Including children with disabilities in preschool programs* (pp. 61–80). New York: Teachers College Press.

O'Moore, M., & Minton, S. J. (2004). *Dealing with bullying in schools: A training manual for teachers, parents, and other professionals.* London, UK: Paul Chapman.

O'Neill, R. E., Horner, R. H., Albin, R. W., Sprague, J. R., Storey, K., & Newton, J. S. (1997). *Functional assessment and program development for problem behavior: A practical handbook* (2nd ed.). Pacific Grove, CA: Brooks/Cole.

Ogbu, J. U. (1994). From cultural differences to differences in cultural frame of reference. In P. M. Greenfield & R. R. Cocking (Eds.), *Cross-cultural roots of minority child development* (pp. 365–395). Hillsdale, NJ: Erlbaum.

Olds, D. (1997). Tobacco exposure and impaired development: A review of the evidence. *Mental Retardation and Developmental Disabilities Research Review, 3,* 257–269.

Olds, D., Henderson, C. R., Jr., Cole, R., Eckenrode, J., Kitzman, H., Luckey, D., et al. (1998). Long-term effects of nurse home visitation on children's criminal and antisocial behavior: 15-year follow-up of a randomized controlled trial. *Journal of the American Medical Association, 280,* 1238–1244.

Olds, D., Henderson, C. R., Jr., & Tatelbaum, R. (1994). Intellectual impairment in children of women who smoke cigarettes during pregnancy. *Pediatrics, 93,* 221–227.

Oliver, R. O., Hoover, J. H., & Hazler, R. J. (1994). The perceived roles of bullying in small-town midwestern schools. *Journal of Counseling and Development, 72,* 416–420.

Olweus, D. (1991). Bully/victim problems among schoolchildren: Basic facts and effects of a school-based intervention program. In D. J. Pepler & K. H. Rubin (Eds.), *The development and treatment of childhood aggression* (pp. 411–448). Hillsdale, NJ: Erlbaum.

Olweus, D. (1993). *Bullying at school: What we know and what we can do.* Malden, MA: Blackwell.

Olweus, D. (2001). Peer harassment: A critical analysis and some important issues. In J. Juvonen & S. Graham (Eds.), *Peer harassment in school: The plight of the vulnerable and victimized* (pp. 3–20). New York: Guilford.

Olweus, D., Limber, S., & Mihalic, S. F. (1999). History and description of the Bullying Prevention Program. Excerpted from *Blueprints for violence prevention: Book 9, Bullying Prevention Program.* Boulder, CO: Center for the Study and Prevention of Violence. Retrieved November 3, 2001, from www.colorado.edu/cspv/blueprints/model/chapt/BullyExec.htm.

Onosko, J. J., &. Jorgensen, C. M. (1998). Unit and lesson planning in the inclusive classroom: Maximizing learning opportunities for all students. In C. M. Jorgensen (Ed.), *Restructuring high schools for all students: Taking inclusion to the next level* (pp. 71–105). Baltimore: Brookes.

Oprah Winfrey. (n.d.). In *Black history*. Gale. Retrieved May 28, 2007, from www.gale.com/free_resources/bhm/bio/winfrey_o.htm.

Orpinas, P., & Horne, A. M. (2006). *Bullying prevention: Creating a positive school climate and developing social competence*. Washington, DC: American Psychological Association.

Osofsky, J. D. (1997). Children and youth violence: An overview of the issues. In J. D. Osofsky (Ed.), *Children in a violent society* (pp. 3–8). New York: Guilford.

Osofsky, J. D., & Thompson, M. D. (2000). Adaptive and maladaptive parenting: Perspectives on risk and protective factors. In J. P. Shonkoff & S. J. Meisels (Eds.), *Handbook of early childhood intervention* (2nd ed., pp. 54–75). New York: Cambridge University Press.

Ostrov, J. M., Woods, K. E., Jansen, E. A., Casas, J. F., & Crick, N. R. (2004). An observational study of delivered and received aggression, gender, and social-psychological adjustment in preschool: "This white crayon doesn't work ..." *Early Childhood Research Quarterly, 19,* 355–371.

Oswald, D. P., Coutinho, M. J., & Best, A. M. (2002). Community and school predictors of overrepresentation of minority children in special education. In D. Losen & G. Orfield (Eds.), *Racial inequity in special education* (pp. 1–13). Cambridge, MA: Harvard Education Publishing.

Ozer, E. J., & Weinstein, R. S. (2004). Urban adolescents' exposure to community violence: The role of support, school safety, and social constraints in a school-based sample of boys and girls. *Journal of Child and Adolescent Psychology, 33,* 463–476.

Paley, V. G. (1992). *You can't say you can't play*. Cambridge, MA: Harvard University Press.

Parke, R. D., & Slaby, R. G. (1983). The development of aggression. In P. Mussen & E. M. Hetherington (Eds.), *Handbook of child psychology: Vol. 4, Socialization, personality, and social development* (pp. 547–641). New York: Wiley.

Patterson, G. R. (1982). *Coercive family process*. Eugene, OR: Castalia.

Patterson, G. R. (1995). Coercion—A basis for early age of onset for arrest. In J. McCord (Ed.), *Coercion and punishment in long-term perspective* (pp. 81–105). New York: Cambridge University Press.

Patterson, G. R., Littman, R. A., & Bricker, W. (1967). Assertive behavior in children: A step toward a theory of aggression. *Monographs of the Society for Research in Child Development, 32* (5, Serial No. 113).

Paus, T. (2005). Mapping brain maturation and cognitive development during adolescence. *Trends in Cognitive Sciences, 9,* 60–68.

Pavri, S., & Luftig, R. (2000). The social face of inclusive education: Are students with learning disabilities really included in the classroom? *Preventing School Failure, 45*(1), 8–14.

Payne, R. (2005). *A framework for understanding poverty* (4th ed.). Highlands, TX: aha! Process.

Pearce, M. J., Jones, S. M., Schwab-Stone, M. E., & Ruchkin, V. (2003). The protective effects of religiousness and parent involvement on the development of conduct problems among youth exposed to violence. *Child Development, 74,* 1682–1696.

Peisner-Feinberg, E. S., Burchinal, M. R., Clifford, R. M., Culkin, M. L., Howes, C., Kagan, S. L., et al. (2001). The relation of preschool child care quality to children's cognitive and social developmental trajectories through second grade. *Child Development, 72,* 1534–1553.

Pellegrini, A. D., & Long, J. D. (2002). A longitudinal study of bullying, dominance, and victimization during the transition from primary school through secondary school. *British Journal of Developmental Psychology, 20,* 259–280.

Pepler, D. J., & Craig, W. (1999). *Aggressive girls: Development of disorder and outcomes* (Report No. 57). Toronto, ON: LaMarsh

Research Centre for Violence and Conflict Resolution, York University.

Pepler, D. J., & Craig, W. (2000). *Making a difference in bullying*. Toronto, ON: LaMarsh Centre for Research on Violence and Conflict Resolution, York University, Report No. 60. Retrieved April 10, 2007, from www.arts.yorku.ca/lamarsh/pdf/Making_a_Difference_in_Bullying.pdf.

Pepler, D. J., & Craig, W. (2007, February). *Binoculars on bullying: A new solution to protect and connect children*. Voices for Children. Retrieved April 9, 2007, from www.voicesforchildren.ca/documents/Voices_Report-Bullying.pdf.

Pepler, D. J., & Craig, W. (n.d.). *Making a difference in bullying: Understanding and strategies for practitioners*. Toronto, ON: LaMarsh Centre for Research on Violence and Conflict Resolution, York University. Retrieved April 10, 2007, from www.arts.yorku.ca/lamarsh/pdf/pedia.pdf.

Pepler, D. J., & Rubin, K. H. (1991). Introduction: Current challenges in the development and treatment of childhood aggression. In D. J. Pepler & K. H. Rubin (Eds.), *The development and treatment of childhood aggression* (pp. xiii–xvii). Hillsdale, NJ: Erlbaum.

Pepler, D. J., & Slaby, R. G. (1994). Theoretical and developmental perspectives on youth and violence. In L. D. Eron, J. H. Gentry, & P. Schlegel (Eds.), *Reason to hope: A psychosocial perspective on violence & youth* (pp. 27–58). Washington, DC: American Psychological Association.

Pepler, D., Smith, P. K., & Rigby, K. (2004). Looking back and looking forward: Implications for making interventions work effectively. In P. K. Smith, D. Pepler, & K. Rigby (Eds.), *Bullying in schools: How successful can interventions be?* (pp. 307–324). Cambridge, UK: Cambridge University Press.

Perkins-Gough, D. (2004). The eroding curriculum. *Educational Leadership, 62*(1), 84–85.

Perry, D. G., Hodges, E. V. E., & Egan, S. K. (2001). Determinants of chronic victimization by peers: A review and new model of family influence. In J. Juvonen & S. Graham (Eds.), *Peer harassment in school: The plight of the vulnerable and victimized* (pp. 73–104). New York: Guilford.

Perry, D. G., Kusel, S. L., & Perry, L. C. (1988). Victims of peer aggression. *Developmental Psychology, 24,* 807–814.

Perry, D. G., Perry, L. C., & Kennedy, E. (1992). Conflict and the development of antisocial behavior. In C. U. Shantz & W. W. Hartup (Eds.), *Conflict in child and adolescent development.* (pp. 301–329). New York: Cambridge University Press.

Peters, M. F. (1988). Parenting in Black families with young children: A historical perspective. In H. Pipes McAdoo (Ed.), *Black families* (2nd ed., pp. 228–241). Newbury Park, CA: Sage.

Peterson, J. M., & Hittie, M. M. (2003). *Inclusive teaching: Creating effective schools for all learners.* Boston: Allyn & Bacon.

Peterson, R. L. (2002, June). Physical restraint. Safe and Responsive Schools. Retrieved February 27, 2007, from www.unl.edu/srs/pdfs/physrest.pdf.

Phineas Gage's Story (n.d.). Retrieved October 14, 2007, from www.deakin.edu.au/hmnbs/psychology/gagepage/Pgstory.php.

Pianta, R. C. (1994). Patterns of relationships between children and kindergarten teachers. *Journal of School Psychology, 32,* 15–31.

Pianta, R. C. (1999). *Enhancing relationships between children and teachers.* Washington, DC: American Psychological Association.

Pianta, R. C., & Hamre, B. K. (n.d.). *Banking time: Investing in relationships between children and teachers.* Retrieved December 16, 2004, from www.people.virginia.edu/~pnm3r/banking/materials/index.htm#TopOfPage.

Pianta, R. C., Steinberg, M. S., & Rollins, K. B. (1995). The first two years of school: Teacher–child relationships and deflections in children's classroom adjustment. *Development and Psychopathology, 17,* 295–312.

Pikas, A. (1989). The common concern method for the treatment of mobbing. In E. Roland & E. Munthe (Eds.), *Bullying: An international perspective.* London, UK: Fulton.

Pikas, A. (2002). New developments of the Shared Concern Method. *School Psychology International, 23,* 307–326.

Plomin, R., Owen, M. J., & McGuffin, P. (1994). The genetic basis of complex human behaviors. *Science, 264,* 1733–1739.

Posada, G., Gao, Y., Wu, F., Posada, R., Tascon, M., Schoelmerich, A., et al. (1995).

The secure-base phenomenon across cultures: Children's behavior, mothers' preferences, and experts' concepts. In E. Waters, B. E. Vaughn, G. Posada, & K. Kondo-Ikemura (Eds.), Caregiving, culture, and cognitive perspectives on secure-base behavior and working models: New growing points for attachment theory and research. *Monographs of the Society for Research in Child Development, 60*(2-3, Serial No. 244), 27–48.

Powell, D. R. (1989). *Families and early childhood programs*. Washington, DC: National Association for the Education of Young Children.

Powell, D. R. (1998). Reweaving parents into the fabric of early childhood programs. *Young Children, 53,* 60–66.

Power, B. M. (2002). Crawling on the bones of what we know: An interview with Shirley Brice Heath. In B. M. Power & R. S. Hubbard (Eds.), *Language development: A reader for teachers* (2nd ed., pp. 81–88). Upper Saddle River, NJ: Merrill Prentice-Hall.

Pretty in pink. (2007, October 1). *Macleans, 120*(38), 12.

Price, J. M., & Dodge, K. A. (1989). Peers' contributions to children's social maladjustment. In T. J. Berndt & G. W. Ladd (Eds.), *Peer relationships in child development* (pp. 341–370). New York: Wiley.

Public Agenda. (2004, May). *Teaching interrupted: Do discipline policies in today's public schools foster the common good?* New York: Author. Retrieved February 8, 2007, from www.publicagenda.org/research/pdfs/teaching_interrupted.pdf.

Putallaz, M., & Sheppard, B. H. (1992). Conflict management and social competence. In C. U. Shantz & W. W. Hartup (Eds.), *Conflict in child and adolescent development* (pp. 330–355). New York: Cambridge University Press.

Putallaz, M., & Wasserman, A. (1990). Children's entry behavior. In S. R. Asher & J. D. Coie (Eds.), *Peer rejection in childhood* (pp. 60–89). New York: Cambridge University Press.

Quinn, M. M., Gable, R. A., Rutherford, R. B., Nelson, C. M., & Howell, K. W. (1998). *Addressing student problem behavior: Part I—An IEP team's introduction to functional behavior assessment and behavior interven-tion plans.* Washington, DC: Center for Effective Collaboration and Practice. Retrieved January 15, 2007, from http://cecp.air.org/fba/problembehavior/main.htm.

Quinn, M. M., Osher, D., Warger, C. L., Hanley, T. V., Bader, B. D., & Hoffman, C. C. (2000). *Teaching and working with children who have emotional and behavioral challenges.* Longmont, CO: Sopris West.

Raikes, H. A., & Thompson, R. A. (2005). Relationships past, present, and future: Reflections on attachment in middle childhood. In K. A. Kerns & R. A. Richardson (Eds.), *Attachment in middle childhood* (pp. 255–282). New York: Guilford.

Raine, A. (1993). *The psychopathology of crime: Criminal behavior as a clinical disorder.* San Diego: Academic.

Raver, C. C. (2002). Emotions matter: Making the case for the role of young children's emotional development for early school readiness. *Social Policy Report, 16,* 3–18.

Redl, F., & Wineman, D. (1957). *The aggressive child.* Glencoe, IL: Free Press.

Reiss, A. J., Jr., & Roth, J. A. (Eds.). (1993). *Understanding and preventing violence.* Washington, DC: National Academy Press.

Renken, B., Egeland, B., Marvinney, D., Mangelsdorf, S., & Sroufe, L. A. (1989). Early childhood antecedents of aggression and passive-withdrawal in early elementary school. *Journal of Personality, 57*(2), 257–281.

Repp, A. C., Felce, D., & Barton, L. E. (1988). Basing the treatment of stereotypic and self-injurious behaviors on hypotheses of their causes. *Journal of Applied Behavior Analysis, 21,* 281–289.

Repp, A. C., Karsh, K. G., Munk, D., & Dahlquist, C. M. (1995). Hypothesis-based interventions: A theory of clinical decision-making. In W. T. O'Donohue & L. Krasner (Eds.), *Theories of behavior therapy: Exploring behavior change* (pp. 585–608). Washington, DC: American Psychological Association.

Resnick, M. D., Bearman, P. S., Blum, R. W., Bauman, K. E., Harris, K. M., Jones, J., et al. (1997). Protecting adolescents from harm: Findings from the National Longitudinal Study on Adolescent Health. *Journal of the American Medical Association, 278,* 823–832.

Rhee, S. H., & Waldman, E. D. (2002). Genetic and environmental influences on antisocial behavior: A meta-analysis of twin and adoption studies. *Psychological Bulletin, 128,* 490–529.

Richard, B. A., & Dodge, K. A. (1982). Social maladjustment and problem-solving in school aged children. *Journal of Consulting and Clinical Psychology, 50,* 226–233.

Richards, M. H., Larson, R., Miller, B. V., Luo, Z., Sims, B., Parrella, D. P., et al. (2004). Risk and protective contexts and exposure to violence in urban African American young adolescents. *Journal of Child and Adolescent Psychology, 33,* 138–148.

Richardson, G. A., Conroy, M. L., & Day, N. L. (1996). Prenatal cocaine exposure: Effects on the development of school-age children. *Toxicology and Teratology, 18,* 627–634.

Richart, D. (with Soler, M., Spurlock, S., Scantlebury, J., & Tandy, K. B.) (2004, April). *Northern lights: Success in student achievement and school discipline at Northern Elementary School.* Washington, DC: Building Blocks for Youth. Retrieved January 5, 2007, from http://buildingblocksforyouth.org/kentucky/kentucky2.pdf.

Richart, D., Brooks, K., & Soler, M. (2003, February). *Unintended consequences: The impact of "zero tolerance" and other exclusionary policies on Kentucky students.* Washington, DC: Building Blocks for Youth. Retrieved January 5, 2007, from http://buildingblocksforyouth.org/kentucky/kentucky.pdf.

Richman, N., Stevenson, J., & Graham, P. J. (1982). *Preschool to school: A behavioural study.* London: Academic.

Rideout, V., Roberts, D. F., & Foehr, U. G. (2005, March). *Generation M: Media in the lives of 8- to 18-year-olds.* Menlo Park, CA: Kaiser Family Foundation. Retrieved January 31, 2006, from http://kff.org/entmedia/upload/Executive-Summary-Generation-M-Media-in-the-lives-of-8-to-18-year-olds.pdf.

Rigby, K. (1998). *Bullying in schools and what to do about it.* Markham, ON: Pembroke.

Rigby, K. (2001a). Health consequences of bullying and its prevention in schools. In J. Juvonen & S. Graham (Eds.), *Peer harassment in school: The plight of the vulnerable and victimized* (pp. 310–331). New York: Guilford.

Rigby, K. (2001b). What is bullying? Defining bullying: A new look at an old concept. Retrieved April 10, 2007, from www.education.unisa.edu.au/bullying/define.html.

Rigby, K. (2002). *New perspectives on bullying.* London, UK: Jessica Kingsley.

Rigby, K., & Slee, P. T. (1999). Australia. In P. K. Smith, Y. Morita, J. Junger-Tas, D. Olweus, R. Catalano, & P. Slee (Eds.), *The nature of school bullying: A cross-national perspective* (pp. 324–339). New York: Routledge.

Rigby, K., Smith, P. K., & Pepler, D. (2004). Working to prevent school bullying: Key issues. In P. K. Smith, D. Pepler, & K. Rigby (Eds.), *Bullying in schools: How successful can interventions be?* (pp. 1–12). Cambridge, UK: Cambridge University Press.

Rightmyer, E. C. (2003). Democratic discipline: Children creating solutions. *Young Children, 58*(4), 38–45.

Ritchie, J., & Pohl, C. (1995). Rules of thumb workshop. *The Early Childhood Educator, 10,* 11–12.

Roberts, W. B., Jr. (2006). *Bullying from both sides: Strategic interventions for working with bullies and victims.* Thousand Oaks, CA: Corwin.

Robertson, J. (2002). Inclusion can work—Without too much work! *Education World.* Retrieved November 21, 2006, from www.educationworld.com/a_curr/profdev007.shtml.

Robin, A. L., Schneider, M., & Dolnick, M. (1976). The turtle technique: An extended case study of self control in the classroom. *Psychology in the Schools, 13,* 449–453.

Robinson, G., & Maines, B. (1994). The No Blame Approach to bullying. Summary of a presentation at a meeting of the British Association for the Advancement of Science. (ED414028) Retrieved April 10, 2007, from http://eric.ed.gov/ERICDocs/data/ericdocs2/content_storage_01/0000000b/80/23/64/14.pdf.

Robinson, G., & Maines, B. (2000). *Crying for help: The No Blame Approach to bullying.* Bristol, UK: Lucky Duck Publishing.

Rodd, J. (1996). *Understanding young children's behavior: A guide for early childhood professionals*. New York: Teachers College Press.

Rogers, C., & Freiberg, J. (1994). *Freedom to learn* (3rd ed.). New York: Merrill.

Roland, E., & Galloway, D. (2002). Classroom influences on bullying. *Educational Research, 44,* 299–312.

Rose, S. R. (1983). Promoting social competence in children: A classroom approach to social and cognitive skill training. In C. W. LeCroy (Ed.), *Social skills training for children and youth.* New York: Haworth.

Rothbart, M. K., & Jones, L. B. (1998). Temperament, self-regulation, and education. *School Psychology Review, 27,* 479–491.

Rotheram, M. J. (1987). Children's social and academic competence. *Journal of Educational Research, 80,* 206–211.

Rotheram, M. J., & Phinney, J. S. (1987). Ethnic behavior patterns as an aspect of identity. In J. S. Phinney & M. J. Rotheram (Eds.), *Children's ethnic socialization: Pluralism and development* (pp. 201–218). Newbury Park, CA: Sage.

Rotheram-Borus, M. J. (1988). Assertiveness training with children. In R. H. Price, E. L. Cowen, R. P. Lorion, & J. Ramos-McKay (Eds.), *Fourteen ounces of prevention: A casebook for practitioners.* Washington, DC: American Psychological Association.

Rothstein, R. (2004). Class and the classroom. *American School Board Journal, 191*(10), 16–21.

Rowe, M. (1986). Wait time: Slowing down may be a way of speeding up! *Journal of Teacher Education, 37,* 43–50.

Rubin, K. H., Bukowski, W., & Parker, J. G. (1998). Peer interactions, relationships, and groups. In N. Eisenberg (Ed.), *Handbook of child psychology: Vol. 3, Social, emotional, and personality development* (5th ed., pp. 619–699). New York: Wiley.

Rutter, M. (1987). Psychosocial resilience and protective mechanisms. *American Journal of Orthopsychiatry, 57,* 316–331.

Rutter, M. (1993). *Developing minds: Challenge and community across the lifespan.* New York: HarperCollins.

Rutter, M. (2000). Resilience reconsidered: Conceptual considerations. In J. P. Shonkoff & S. J. Meisels (Eds.), *Handbook of early childhood intervention* (2nd ed., pp. 651–682). New York: Cambridge University Press.

Rutter, M. (2001). Psychosocial adversity: Risk, resilience, and recovery. In J. M. Richman & M. W. Fraser (Eds.), *The context of youth violence: Resilience, risk, and protection* (pp. 13–45). Westport, CT: Praeger.

Rutter, M., & Maughan, B. (2002). School effectiveness findings 1979–2002. *Journal of School Psychology, 40,* 451–475.

Rutter, M., & the English and Romanian Adoptees Study Team. (1998). Developmental catch-up, and deficit, following adoption after severe global early privation. *Child Psychology and Psychiatry, 39,* 465–476.

Rutter, M., Giller, H., & Hagell, A. (1998). *Antisocial behavior by young people.* New York: Cambridge University Press.

Rutter, M., Moffitt, T. E., & Caspi, A. (2006). Gene-environment interplay and psychopathology: Multiple varieties but real effects. *Journal of Child Psychology and Psychiatry, 47,* 226–261.

Rutter, M., O'Connor, T. G., & the English and Romanian Adoptees Study Team. (2004). Are there biological programming effects for psychological development? Findings from a study of Romanian adoptees. *Developmental Psychology, 40,* 81–94.

Ryan, J. B., & Peterson, R. L. (2004). Physical restraint in school. *Behavioral Disorders, 29,* 154–168. Retrieved February 27, 2007, from www.bridges4kids.org/PBS/articles/RyanPeterson2004.htm.

Ryan, R. M., & Grolnick, W. S. (1986). Origins and pawns in the classroom: Self-report and projective assessments of individual differences in children's perceptions. *Journal of Personality and Social Psychology, 50,* 550–558.

Salend, S. J. (1999). Facilitating friendships among diverse students. *Intervention in School and Clinic, 35*(1), 9–15.

Salmivalli, C. (1999). Participant role approach to school bullying: Implications for interventions. *Journal of Adolescence, 22,* 453–459.

Salmivalli, C. (2001). Group view on victimization: Empirical findings and their implications. In J. Juvonen & S. Graham (Eds.), *Peer harassment in school: The plight of the vulnerable and victimized* (pp. 398–419). New York: Guilford.

Salmivalli, C., Kaukiainen, A., & Lagerspetz, K. (1998). Aggression in the social relations of school-aged girls and boys. In P. T. Slee & K. Rigby (Eds.), *Children's peer relations* (pp. 60–75). New York: Routledge.

Sameroff, A. (2005). Early resilience and its developmental consequences. In R. E. Tremblay, R. G. Barr, & R. DeV. Peters (Eds.), *Encyclopedia on early childhood development*. Montreal, QC: Centre of Excellence for Early Childhood Development. Retrieved May 30, 2007, from www.excellence-earlychildhood.ca/documents/SameroffANGxp.pdf.

Sameroff, A. J., & Fiese, B. H. (2000). Transactional regulation: The developmental ecology of early intervention. In J. P. Shonkoff & S. J. Meisels (Eds.), *Handbook of early childhood intervention* (2nd ed., pp. 135–159). New York: Cambridge University Press.

Sampson, R. J. (1997). The embeddedness of child and adolescent development: A community-level perspective on urban violence. In J. McCord (Ed.), *Violence and childhood in the inner city* (pp. 31–77). New York: Cambridge University Press.

San Antonio, D. M. (2006). Broadening the world of early adolescents. *Educational Leadership, 63*(7), 8–13.

Sandall, S. R., & Schwartz, I. S. (with Joseph, G. E., Chou, H.-Y., Horn, E. M., Lieber, J., Odom, S. L., & Wolery, R.) (2002). *Building blocks for preschoolers with special needs.* Baltimore: Brookes.

Sands, A. S., & Schwartz, S. J. (2000, May-June). Nonverbal learning disabilities. *Child Study Center, 4*(5), 1–4. Retrieved May 18, 2007, from www.aboutourkids.org/aboutour/letter/2000/may_jun.pdf.

Santos, R. M., & Ostrosky, M. M. (2002). *What works briefs 2: Understanding the impact of language differences on classroom behavior.* Center on the Social and Emotional Foundations for Early Learning. Retrieved July 16, 2007, from www.vanderbilt.edu/csefel/briefs/wwb2.pdf.

Sapolsky, R. (2006, April). A natural history of peace. *Harper's,* 15–22.

Sapon-Shevin, M. (2003). Inclusion: A matter of social justice. *Educational Leadership, 61*(2), 25–28.

Schaps, E. (2003). Creating a school community. *Educational Leadership, 60*(6), 31–33.

Schaps, E., Battistich, V., & Solomon, D. (2004). Community in school as key to student growth: Findings from the Child Development Project. In J. E. Zins, R. P. Weissberg, W. C. Wang, & H. J. Walberg (Eds.), *Building academic success on social and emotional learning: What does the research say?* (pp. 189–205). New York: Teachers College Press.

Scherer, M. (2006). Celebrate strengths, nurture affinities: A conversation with Mel Levine. *Educational Leadership, 64*(1), 8–15.

Schettler, T., Stein, J., Reich, R., & Valenti, M. (2000). *In harm's way: Toxic threats to child development.* Boston: Greater Boston Physicians for Social Responsibility. Retrieved October 14, 2007, from www.psr.org/site/DocServer/In_Harm_s_Way_complete.pdf?docID=661.

Schwartz, D., Dodge, K. A., & Coie, J. D. (1993). The emergence of chronic peer victimization in boys' play groups. *Child Development, 64,* 1755–1772.

Schwartz, D., Dodge, K. A., Pettit, G. S., & Bates, J. E. (1997). The early socialization of aggressive victims of bullying. *Child Development, 68,* 665–675.

Schwartz, D., Proctor, L. J., & Chen, D. H. (2001). The aggressive victim of bullying: Emotional and behavioral dysregulation as a pathway to victimization by peers. In J. Juvonen & S. Graham (Eds.), *Peer harassment in school: The plight of the vulnerable and victimized* (pp. 147–174). New York: Guilford.

Schwartz, J. M., Stoessel, P. W., Baxter, L. R., Martin, K. M., & Phelps, M. E. (1996). Systematic changes in cerebral glucose metabolic rate after successful behavior modification treatment of obsessive-compulsive disorder. *Archives of General Psychiatry, 53,* 109–113.

Schwartz, W. (1999, March). Arab American students in public schools. New York: ERIC Clearinghouse on Urban Education. Digest No. 142. (ED429144). Retrieved July 20, 2006, from www.ericdigests.org/1999-4arab.htm.

Schwartz, W. (2000). Preventing student sexual harassment. New York: ERIC Clearinghouse on Urban Education. Digest No. 160.

(ED448248). Retrieved March 18, 2007, from www.ericdigests.org/2001-3/preventing.htm.

Segall, M. H., Dasen, P. R., Berry, J. W., & Poortinga, Y. H. (1990). *Human behavior in global perspective: An introduction to cross-cultural psychology.* New York: Pergamon.

Seikaly, M. (1999). Attachment and identity: The Palestinian community of Detroit. In M. W. Suleiman (Ed.), *Arabs in America: Building a new future* (pp. 25–38). Philadelphia: Temple University Press.

Sensory Integration International. (n.d.). Answers to frequently asked questions. Retrieved May 18, 2007, from www.sensoryint.com/faq/html.

Serbin, L. A., Moskowitz, D. S., Schwartzman, A. E., & Ledingham, J. E. (1991). Aggressive, withdrawn, and aggressive/withdrawn children in adolescence: Into the next generation. In D. J. Pepler & K. H. Rubin (Eds.), *The development and treatment of childhood aggression* (pp. 55–70). Hillsdale, NJ: Erlbaum.

Shade, B. J., Kelly, C., & Oberg, M. (1997). *Creating culturally responsive classrooms.* Washington, DC: American Psychological Association.

Shankaran, S., Lester, B. M., Das, A., Bauer, C. R., Bada, H. S., Lagasse, L., et al. (2007). Impact of maternal substance use during pregnancy on childhood outcome. *Seminars in Fetal and Neonatal Medicine, 12,* 143–150.

Shantz, C. U., & Hartup, W. W. (1992). Conflict and development: An introduction. In C. U. Shantz & W. W. Hartup (Eds.), *Conflict in child and adolescent development* (pp. 1–11). New York: Cambridge University Press.

Sharifzadeh, V.-S. (1998). Families with Middle Eastern roots. In E. W. Lynch & M. J. Hanson (Eds.), *Developing cross-cultural competence: A guide for working with children and their families* (pp. 441–482). Baltimore: Brookes.

Sharp, S., & Cowie, H. (1994). Empowering pupils to take positive action against bullying. In P. K. Smith & S. Sharp (Eds.), *School bullying: Insights and perspectives* (pp. 57–83). New York: Routledge.

Sharp, S., Cowie, H., & Smith, P. K. (1994). How to respond to bullying behaviour. In S. Sharp & P. K. Smith (Eds.), *Tackling bullying in your school: A practical handbook for teachers* (pp. 79–101). New York: Routledge.

Sharp, S., & Smith, P. K. (1994). Understanding bullying. In S. Sharp & P. K. Smith (Eds.), *Tackling bullying in your school: A practical handbook for teachers* (pp. 1–6). New York: Routledge.

Sharp, S., & Thompson, D. (1994). The role of whole-school policies in tackling bullying behaviour in schools. In P. K. Smith & S. Sharp (Eds.), *School bullying: Insights and perspectives* (pp. 57–83). New York: Routledge.

Shatz, C. J. (1992). The developing brain. *Scientific American, 267,* 60–67.

Sheridan, S. M. (2000). Considerations of multiculturalism and diversity in behavioral consultation with parents and teachers. *School Psychology Review, 29,* 344–353.

Shonkoff, J. P., & Phillips, D. A. (Eds.). (2000). *From neurons to neighborhoods: The science of early childhood development.* National Research Council and Institute of Medicine, Committee on Integrating the Science of Early Childhood Development, Board on Children, Youth, and Families, Commission on Behavioral and Social Sciences and Education. Washington, DC: National Academy Press.

Shore, R. (1997). *Rethinking the brain: New insights into early development.* New York: Families and Work Institute.

Siegel, A. E., & Kohn, L. G. (1959). Permissiveness, permission, and aggression: The effects of adult presence or absence on aggression in children's play. *Child Development, 36,* 131–141.

Silverthorn, P., & Frick, P. J. (1999). Developmental pathways to antisocial behavior: The delayed-onset pathway in girls. *Development and Psychopathology, 11,* 101–126.

Simmons, R. (2002). *Odd girl out: The hidden culture of aggression in girls.* New York: Harcourt.

Simmons, R. W., III. (2006). The empty desk in the third row: Experiences of an African American male teacher. In J. Landsman & C. W. Lewis (Eds.), *White teachers/diverse classrooms: A guide to building inclusive schools, promoting high expectations, and eliminating racism* (pp. 43–51). Sterling, VA: Stylus.

Singh, N., & Aung, K. M. (2007, September 23). A free ride for bullies. *New York Times*.

Slaby, R. G. (1997). Psychological mediators of violence in urban youth. In J. McCord (Ed.), *Violence and childhood in the inner city* (pp. 171–206). New York: Cambridge University Press.

Slaby, R. G., Roedell, W. C., Arezzo, D., & Hendrix, K. (1995). *Early violence prevention: Tools for teachers of young children*. Washington, DC: National Association for the Education of Young Children.

Slavin, R. E. (1995). *Cooperative learning: Theory, research, and practice* (2nd ed.). Boston: Allyn & Bacon.

Slee, P. (1993). Bullying: A preliminary investigation of its nature and the effects of social cognition. *Early Child Development and Care, 87*, 47–57.

Smith, J. D., Schneider, B. H., Smith, P. K., & Ananiadou, K. (2004). The effectiveness of whole-school anti-bullying programs: A synthesis of evaluation research. *School Psychology Review, 33*, 547–560.

Smith, M. D. (1993). *Behavior modification for exceptional children and youth*. Boston: Andover Medical Publishers.

Smith, P. K., Cowie, H., & Sharp, S. (1994). Working directly with pupils involved in bullying situations. In P. K. Smith & S. Sharp (Eds.), *School bullying: Insights and perspectives* (pp. 193–212). New York: Routledge.

Smith, P. K., Morita, Y., Junger-Tas, J., Olweus, D., Catalano, R., & Slee, P. (Eds.). (1999). *The nature of school bullying: A cross-national perspective*. New York: Routledge.

Smith, P. K., & Shu, S. (2000). What good schools can do about bullying: Findings from a survey in English schools after a decade of research and action. *Childhood, 7*(2), 193–212.

Smith, P. K., Shu, S., & Madsen, K. (2001). Characteristics of victims of school bullying: Developmental changes in coping strategies and skills. In J. Juvonen & S. Graham (Eds.), *Peer harassment in school: The plight of the vulnerable and victimized* (pp. 332–351). New York: Guilford.

Smith, T. E. C. (2006). Section 504, the ADA, and public schools. LD OnLine. Retrieved November 21, 2006, from www.ldonline.org/article/6108?theme=print.

Smitherman, G. (1998). Black English/Ebonics: What it be like? In T. Perry & L. Delpit (Eds.), *The real Ebonics debate: Power, language, and the education of African-American children* (pp. 29–37). Boston: Beacon.

Snyder, J. (2002). Reinforcement and coercion mechanisms in the development of antisocial behavior: Peer relationship mechanisms. In J. B. Reid, G. R. Patterson, & J. Snyder (Eds.), *Antisocial behavior in children and adolescents: A developmental analysis and model for intervention* (pp. 101–122). Washington, DC: American Psychological Association.

Solomon, D., Watson, M. S., Delucci, K. L., Schaps, E., & Battistich, V. (1988). Enhancing children's prosocial behavior in the classroom. *American Educational Research Journal, 25*, 527–555.

Spencer, M. B., Fegley, S. G., & Harpalani, V. (2003). Theoretical and empirical examination of identity as coping: Linking coping resources to the self processes of African American youth. *Applied Developmental Science, 7*, 181–188.

Spivack, G., & Shure, M. B. (1974). *Social adjustment of young children. A cognitive approach to solving real-life problems*. San Francisco: Jossey-Bass.

Sramek, B., Brewer, R., Seger, V., Huber, S., & Westpfahl, L. (2004). Inclusion—What works. Case studies. In B. H. Johns & E. C. Guetzloe (Eds.), *Inclusive education for children and youths with emotional and behavioral disorders: Enduring challenges and emerging practices* (pp. 49–57). Arlington, VA: Council for Children with Behavioral Disorders.

Sroufe, L. A. (1983). Infant-caregiving attachment and patterns of maladaption in preschool: The roots of maladaption and competence. In M. Perlmutter (Ed.), *Minnesota Symposium on Child Psychology* (Vol. 16, pp. 41–81). Hillsdale, NJ: Erlbaum.

Stainback, S., & Stainback, W. (1996). *Inclusion: A guide for educators*. Baltimore: Brookes.

Statistics Canada. (2005, February 21). National Longitudinal Survey of Children and Youth: Home environment, income and child behaviour. *The Daily*. Retrieved July

29, 2006, from www.statcan.can/Daily/English/050221/d0502211b.htm.

Statistics Canada. (2006, July 20). Crime statistics. *The Daily*. Retrieved April 30, 2007, from www.statcan.ca/Daily/English/060720/d060720b.htm.

Steinberg, L. (2005a), *Adolescence* (7th ed.). New York: McGraw-Hill.

Steinberg, L. (2005b). Cognitive and affective development in adolescence. *Trends in Cognitive Sciences, 9*, 69–74.

Stevens, V., deBourdeaudhuij, I., & VanOoost, P. (2000). Bullying in Flemish schools: An evaluation of anti-bullying interventions in primary and secondary schools. *British Journal of Educational Psychology, 70*, 195–210.

Strain, P. S., & Joseph, G. E. (2004). Engaged supervision to support recommended practices for young children with challenging behavior. *Topics in Early Childhood Special Education, 24*(1), 39–50.

Strain, P.S., & Danko, C. D. (1995). Caregivers' encouragement of positive interaction between preschoolers with autism and their siblings. *Journal of Emotional and Behavioral Disorders, 3*(1), 2–12.

Strayhorn, J. M., & Strain, P. S. (1986). Social and language skills for preventive mental health: What, how, who, and when. In P. S. Strain, M. J. Guralnick, & H. M. Walker (Eds.), *Children's social behavior: Development, assessment, and modification* (pp. 287–330). Orlando: Academic.

Streissguth, A. P., Bookstein, F. L., Barr, H. M., Sampson, P. D., O'Malley, K., & Young, J. K. (2004). Risk factors for adverse life outcomes in fetal alcohol syndrome and fetal alcohol effects. *Developmental and Behavioral Pediatrics, 25*, 228–236.

Strizek, G. A., Pittsonberger, J. L., Riordan, K. E., Lyter, D. M., & Orlofsky, G. F. (2006, April). *Characteristics of schools, districts, teachers, principals, and school libraries in the United States 2003–04. Schools and staffing survey* (NCES 2006-313 revised). Washington, DC: U.S. Department of Education, National Center for Education Statistics. Retrieved July 26, 2006, from http://nces.ed.gov/pubs2006/2006313-1.pdf.

Suckling, A., & Temple, C. (2002). *Bullying: A whole school approach.* London, UK: Jessica Kingsley.

Sugai, G., & Horner, R. H. (2002). Introduction to the special series on positive behavior support in schools. *Journal of Emotional and Behavioral Disorders, 10*, 130–135.

Sugai, G., Horner, R. H., Dunlap, G., Hieneman, M., Lewis, T. J., Nelson, C. M., et al. (2000). Applying positive behavior support and functional behavioral assessment in schools. *Journal of Positive Behavior Interventions, 2,* 131–143.

Sugai, G., Horner, R. H., & Gresham, F. M. (2002). Behaviorally effective school environments. In M. R. Shinn, H. M. Walker, & G. Stoner (Eds.), *Interventions for academic and behavior problems II: Preventive and remedial approaches* (pp. 315–350). Bethesda, MD: National Association of School Psychologists.

Suina, J. H., & Smolkin, L. B. (1994). From natal culture to school culture to dominant society culture: Supporting transitions for Pueblo Indians. In P. M. Greenfield & R. R. Cocking (Eds.), *Cross-cultural roots of minority child development* (pp. 115–131). Hillsdale, NJ: Erlbaum.

Sullivan, K., Cleary, M., & Sullivan, G. (2004). *Bullying in secondary schools: What it looks like and how to manage it.* Thousand Oaks, CA: Corwin.

Surgeon General's Scientific Advisory Committee on Television and Social Behavior. (1972). *Television and growing up: The impact of televised violence.* Washington, DC: U.S. Government Printing Office.

Sussman, G. L. (2006, Summer). The violence you don't see. *Educational Leadership (online)*. Retrieved July 26, 2006, from http://ascd.typepad.com/blog/publications/index.html.

Sutherland, K. S., Wheby, J. H., & Gunter, P. L. (2000). The effectiveness of cooperative learning with students with emotional and behavioral disorders: A literature review. *Behavioral Disorders, 25*, 225–238.

Sutton, J., Smith, P. K., & Sweetenham, J. (1999). Bullying and "theory of mind": A critique of the "social skills deficit" view of anti-social behaviour. *Social Development, 8*, 117–127.

Swanson, H. L. (2000). Are working memory deficits in readers with learning disabilities hard to change? *Journal of Learning Disabilities, 33,* 504–532.

Swearer, S. M., & Doll, B. (2001). Bullying in schools: An ecological framework. In R. A. Geffner, T. Loring, & C. Young (Eds.), *Bullying behavior: Current issues, research, and interventions* (pp. 7–47). New York: Haworth.

Swearer, S. M., Song, S. Y., Cary, P. T., Eagle, J. W., & Mickelson, W. T. (2001). Psychosocial correlates in bullying and victimization: The relationship between depression, anxiety, and bully/victim status. In R. A. Geffner, T. Loring, & C. Young (Eds.), *Bullying behavior: Current issues, research, and interventions* (pp. 95–121). New York: Haworth.

Szalacha, L. A., Erkut, S., García Coll, C., Fields, J. P., Alarcón, O., & Ceder, I. (2003). Perceived discrimination and resilience. In S. S. Luthar (Ed.), *Resilience and vulnerability: Adaptation in the context of childhood adversity* (pp. 414–435). New York: Cambridge University Press.

Tabors, P. O. (1997). *One child, two languages: A guide for preschool educators of children learning English as a second language.* Baltimore: Brookes.

Tatum, B. D. (1997). *"Why are all the Black kids sitting together in the cafeteria?" and other conversations about race.* New York: Basic Books.

Taylor, A. (2004, September). Journey to thinking multiculturally: A cultural exploration of the Latino community. *NASP Communiqué, 33*(1). Retrieved July 24, 2006, from www.nasponline.org/publications/cq331latino.html.

Tharp, R. G. (1994). Intergroup differences among Native Americans in socialization and child cognition: An ethnogenetic analysis. In P. M. Greenfield & R. R. Cocking (Eds.), *Cross-cultural roots of minority child development* (pp. 87–106). Hillsdale, NJ: Erlbaum.

Thomas, A., & Chess, S. (1977). *Temperament and development.* New York: Brunner/Mazel.

Thomas, A., Chess, S., & Birch, H. G. (1968). *Temperament and behavior disorders in children.* New York: New York University Press.

Thomas, M. H., & Drabman, R. S. (1975). Toleration of real-life aggression as a function of exposure to television violence. *Merrill-Palmer Quarterly, 21,* 227–232.

Thomas, W. P., & Collier, V. P. (2003). The multiple benefits of dual language. *Educational Leadership, 61*(2), 61–64.

Thompson, M., & Grace, C. O. (with Cohen, L. J.) (2001). *Best friends, worst enemies: Understanding the social lives of children.* New York: Ballantine.

Thornton, T. N., Craft, C. A., Dahlberg, L. L., Lynch, B. S., & Baer, K. (2000). *Best practices of youth violence prevention: A sourcebook for community action.* Atlanta: Centers for Disease Control and Prevention, National Center for Injury Prevention and Control. Retrieved October 18, 2007, from www.cdc.gov/ncipc/dvp/bestpractices.htm.

Tolan, P. H., Gorman-Smith, D., & Henry, D. B. (2003). The developmental ecology of urban males' youth violence. *Developmental Psychology, 39,* 274–291.

Tomlinson, C. A. (1999). *The differentiated classroom: Responding to the needs of all learners.* Alexandria, VA: Association for Supervision and Curriculum Development.

Tomlinson, C. A. (2001). *How to differentiate instruction in mixed-ability classrooms* (2nd ed.). Alexandria, VA: Association for Supervision and Curriculum Development.

Tomlinson, C. A. (2005). Traveling the road to differentiation in staff development. *Journal of Staff Development, 26*(4). Retrieved September 21, 2006, from www.nsdc.org/library/publications/jsd/tomlinson264.cfm.

Tomlinson, C. A., & Jarvis, J. (2006). Teaching beyond the book. *Educational Leadership, 64*(1), 16–21.

Tracey, C. (2005). Listening to teachers: Classroom realities and No Child Left Behind. In G. L. Sunderman, J. S. Kim, & G. Orfield (Eds.), *No Child Left Behind meets school realities: Lessons from the field* (pp. 81–103). Thousand Oaks, CA: Corwin.

Tremblay, R. E. (1991). Aggression, prosocial behavior, and gender. In D. J. Pepler & K. H. Rubin (Eds.), *The development and treatment of childhood aggression* (pp. 71–78). Hillsdale, NJ: Erlbaum.

Tremblay, R. E. (1997, May). Early identification and intervention. Presentation at the

Centre for Studies of Children at Risk conference, Hamilton, ON.

Tremblay, R. E. (2003). Why socialization fails: The case of chronic physical aggression. In B. B. Lahey, T. E. Moffitt, & A. Caspi (Eds.), *Causes of conduct disorder and juvenile delinquency* (pp. 182–224). New York: Guilford.

Tremblay, R. E., Masse, L. C., Pagani, L., & Vitaro, F., (1996). From childhood physical aggression to adolescent maladjustment. In R. DeV. Peters & R. J. McMahon (Eds.), *Preventing childhood disorders, substance abuse, and delinquency* (pp. 268–298). Thousand Oaks, CA: Sage.

Tremblay, R. E., Pihl, R. O., Vitaro, F., & Dobkin, P. L. (1994). Predicting early onset of male antisocial behavior from preschool behavior. *Archives of General Psychiatry, 51*, 732–739.

Tremmel, R. (1993). Zen and the art of reflective practice in teacher education. *Harvard Educational Review, 63*, 434–458.

Troy, M., & Sroufe, L. A. (1987). Victimization among preschooolers. *Journal of the American Academy of Child and Adolescent Psychiatry, 26*, 166–172.

Trumbull, E., Rothstein-Fisch, C., & Greenfield, P. M. (2000). *Bridging cultures in our schools: New approaches that work.* Retrieved October 16, 2006, from www.wested.org/online_pubs/bridging/welcome.shtml.

Trumbull, E., Rothstein-Fisch, C., Greenfield, P. M., & Quiroz, B. (with Altchech, M., Daley, C., Eyler, K., Hernandez, E., Mercado, G., Pérez, A. I., & Saitzyk, P.) (2001). *Bridging cultures between home and school: A guide for teachers with a special focus on immigrant Latino families.* Mahwah, NJ: Erlbaum.

Turecki, S. (with Tonner, L.). (2000). *The difficult child* (2nd revised ed.). New York: Bantam.

Twemlow, S. W., Fonagy, P., & Sacco, F. C. (2004). The role of the bystander in the social architecture of bullying and violence in schools and communities. *Annals of the New York Academy of Science, 1036*, 215–232.

Underwood, M. K. (2003). *Social aggression among girls.* New York: Guilford.

Ungar, M. (2004a). A constructionist discourse on resilience: Multiple contexts, multiple realities among at-risk children and youth. *Youth and Society, 35*, 341–365.

Ungar, M. (2004b). *Nurturing hidden resilience in troubled youth.* Toronto, ON: University of Toronto Press.

United Nations Office of the High Commission on Human Rights. (1989). *Convention on the rights of the child.* Retrieved October 2, 2007, from www.unhchr.ch/html/menu3/b/k2crc.htm.

U.S. Census Bureau. (2006, January). Race and Hispanic origin in 2004. *Population profile of the United States: Dynamic version.* Retrieved July 26, 2006, from www.census.gov/population/pop-profile/dynamic/RACEHO.pdf.

U.S. Department of Education. (2002). *Twenty-fourth annual report to Congress on the implementation of the Individuals with Disabilities Education Act.* Retrieved March 28, 2005, from www.ed.gov/about/reports/annual/isep/2002/section-ii.pdf.

U.S. Department of Education (2004, April 23). *Parental involvement: Title I, Part A: Non-regulatory guidance.* Author: Washington, DC. Retrieved June 28, 2006, from www.ed.gov/programs/titleiparta/parentinvguid.doc.

U.S. Department of Education, Office for Civil Rights. (2005a). Frequently asked questions about racial harassment. Retrieved April 8, 2007, from www.ed.gov/about/offices/list/ocr/qa-raceharass.html.

U.S. Department of Education, Office for Civil Rights. (2005b). *Sexual harassment: It's not academic.* Retrieved April 9, 2007, from www.ed.gov/about/offices/list/ocr/docs/ocrshpam.html.

U.S. Department of Education, Office for Civil Rights, and National Association of Attorneys General. (1999, January). *Protecting students from harassment and hate crime: A guide for schools.* Retrieved April 9, 2007, from www.ed.gov/offices/OCR/archives/Harassment/harassment.pdf.

U.S. Department of Education, Office of Special Education and Rehabilitative Services. (2000, July). *A guide to the individualized education program.* Retrieved November 20, 2006, from www.ed.gov/parents/needs/speced/iepguide/index.html.

U.S. Department of Education, Office of Special Education and Rehabilitation Services, Office of Special Education Programs. (2004). *Teaching children with ADHD: Instructional strategies and practices.* Retrieved March 28, 2005, from www.ed.gov/teachers/needs/speced/adhd/adhd-resource-pt2.pdf.

U.S. Department of Education, Office of Special Education and Rehabilitative Services. (2005, December 19). *Individuals with Disabilities Education Act multi-year individualized education program demonstration program.* Retrieved November 20, 2006, from www.ed.gov/legislation/FedRegister/proprule/2005-4/121905a.html.

U.S. Department of Education, Office of Special Education Programs, Data Analysis System. (2006). *Children with disabilities receiving special education under Part B of the Individuals with Disabilities Education Act, 2005. Table 1-3. Students ages 6 through 21 served under IDEA, Part B, by disability category and state: Fall 2005.* Retrieved November 21, 2006, from www.ideadata.org/tables29th%5Car_1-3.htm.

U.S. Department of Health and Human Services. (1999). Children and mental health. In *Mental health: A report of the surgeon general.* Rockville, MD: Author.

U.S. Department of Health and Human Services. (2003). *Children's mental health facts: Children and adolescents with mental, emotional, and behavioral disorders.* Washington, DC: SAMHSA's Mental Health Information Center. Retrieved March 30, 2005, from www.mentalhealth.org/publications/allpubs/CA-0006/default.asp.

U.S. Department of Health and Human Services. (2004). *Stop bullying now resource kit.* Washington, DC: Author. Retrieved April 9, 2007, from www.stopbullyingnow.hrsa.gov.

U.S. Department of Health and Human Services. (2005). *Roadmap to seclusion and restraint-free mental health services.* Rockville MD: Center for Mental Health Services, Substance Abuse and Mental Health Services Administration. Retrieved March 3, 2007, from http://mentalhealth.samhsa.gov/publications/allpubs/sma064055/.

U.S. Department of Health and Human Services, Administration on Children, Youth and Families. (2005). *Child maltreatment 2003.* Washington, DC: U.S. Printing Office. Retrieved February 1, 2006, from www.acf.hhs.gov/programs/cb/pubs/cm03/summary.htm.

U.S. Department of Health and Human Services, Office of the Surgeon General. (2005, February 21). *U.S. Surgeon General releases advisory on alcohol use in pregnancy.* Retrieved April 6, 2005, from www.hhs.gov/surgeongeneral/pressreleases/sg02222005.html.

U.S. Department of Justice, Federal Bureau of Investigation. (2006). Crime in the United States by volume and rate per 100,000 inhabitants, 1986–2005, Table 1. Retrieved May 2, 2007, from www.fbi.gov/ucr/05cius/data/table_01.html.

University of Missouri–Columbia. (2007). Positive behavior support coach competencies, competency 5. Retrieved August 7, 2007, from http://metamissouri.edu/MUPBIS/comp5.htm.

Unnever, J. D., & Cornell, D. (2003). The culture of bullying. *Journal of School Violence, 2,* 5–27.

Unnever, J. D., & Cornell, D. (2004). Middle school victims of bullying: Who reports being bullied? *Aggressive Behavior, 30,* 373–388.

Van den Bergh, B. R. H., & Marcoen, A. (2004). High antenatal maternal anxiety is related to ADHD symptoms, externalizing problems, and anxiety in 8- and 9-year-olds. *Child Development, 75,* 1085–1097.

van den Boom, D. C. (1994). The influence of temperament and mothering on attachment and exploration: An experimental manipulation of sensitive responsiveness among lower-class mothers with irritable infants. *Child Development, 65,* 1457–1477.

van den Boom, D. C. (1995). Do first-year intervention effects endure? Follow-up during toddlerhood of a sample of Dutch irritable infants. *Child Development, 66,* 1798–1816.

van der Wal, M. F., de Wit, C. A. M., & Hirasing, R. A. (2003). Psychosocial health among young victims and offenders of direct and indirect bullying. *Pediatrics, 111,* 1312–1317.

van IJzendoorn, M. H. (1995). Adult attachment representations, parental responsiveness, and infant attachment: A meta-analysis on the predictive validity of the Adult Attachment Interview. *Psychological Bulletin, 117,* 387–403.

van IJzendoorn, M. H., & DeWolff, M. S. (1997). In search of the absent father: Meta-analysis of infant-father attachment. *Child Development, 68,* 604–609.

van IJzendoorn, M. H., & Sagi, A. (1999). Cross-cultural patterns of attachment: Universal and contextual dimensions. In J. Cassidy & P. R. Shaver (Eds.), *Handbook of attachment theory and research* (pp. 713–734). New York: Guilford.

van IJzendoorn, M. H., Schuengel, C., & Bakermans-Kranenburg, M. J. (1999). Disorganized attachment in early childhood: Meta-analysis of precursors, concomitants, and sequelae. *Development and Psychopathology, 11,* 225–249.

Villa, R. A., & Thousand, J. S. (2003). Making inclusive education work. *Educational Leadership, 61*(2), 19–23.

Villa, R. A., & Thousand, J. S. (2005). The rationales for creating and maintaining inclusive schools. In R. A. Villa & J. S. Thousand (Eds.), *Creating an inclusive school* (2nd ed., pp. 41–56). Alexandria, VA: Association for Supervision and Curriculum Development.

Villegas, A. M., & Lucas, T. (2007). The culturally responsive teacher. *Educational Leadership, 64*(6), 28–33.

Virginia Tech Review Panel. (2007, August). *Mass shootings at Virginia Tech, April 16, 2007.* Retrieved October 7, 2007, from www.governor.virginia.gov/TempContent/techPanelReport.cfm.

Vitaro, F., & Tremblay, R. E. (1994). Impact of a prevention program on aggressive children's friendships and social adjustment. *Journal of Abnormal Child Psychology, 22,* 457–475.

Vossekuil, B., Fein, R. A., Reddy, M., Borum, R., & Modzeleski, W. (2002). *Final report and findings of the Safe School Initiative: Implications for the prevention of school attacks in the United States.* Washington, DC: U.S. Department of Education, Office of Elementary and Secondary Education, Safe and Drug-Free Schools Program, and U.S. Secret Service. Retrieved April 10, 2007, from www.ed.gov/admins/lead/safety/preventingattacksreport.pdf.

Wade, A. M., Lawrence, K., Mandy, W., & Skuse, D. (2006). Charting the development of emotional recognition from 6 years of age. *Journal of Applied Statistics, 33,* 297–315.

Walker, H. M., & Buckley, N. K. (1973). Teacher attention to appropriate and inappropriate classroom behavior. *Focus on Exceptional Children, 5,* 5–11.

Walker, H. M., Ramsey, E., & Gresham, F. M. (2004). *Antisocial behavior in school: Evidence-based practices* (2nd ed.). Belmont, CA: Wadsworth.

Wallis, C. (2003, December 15). Does kindergarten need cops? *Time.* Retrieved July 31, 2006, from www.time.com/time/archive/preview/0,10987,1006435,00.html.

Wallis, C., & Dell, K. (2004, May 10). What makes teens tick. *Time.* Retrieved July 28, 2006, from www.time.com/time/archive/preview/0,10987,994126,00.html.

Walther-Thomas, C., Korinek, L., McLaughlin, V. L., & Williams, B. T. (2000). *Collaboration for inclusive education.* Boston: Allyn & Bacon.

Warner, T. D., Behnke, M., Eyler, F. D., Padgett, K., Leonard, C., Hou, W., et al. (2006). Diffusion tensor imaging of frontal white matter and executive functioning in cocaine-exposed children. *Pediatrics, 118,* 2014–2024.

Warren, J. S., Bohanon-Edmonson, H. M., Turnbull, A. P., Sailor, W., Wickham, D., Griggs, P., et al. (2003). School-wide positive behavior support: Addressing behavior problems that impede student learning. *Educational Psychology Review, 18,* 187–198.

Wasserman, G. A., Staghezza-Jaramillo, B., Shrout, P., Popovac, D., & Graziano, J. H. (1998). The effect of lead exposure on behavior problems in preschool children. *American Journal of Public Health, 88,* 481–486.

Waters, E., Merrick, S., Treboux, D., Crowell, J., & Albersheim, L. (2000). Attachment security in infancy and early adulthood: A twenty-year longitudinal study. *Child Development, 71,* 684–689.

Waters, E., Weinfeld, N. S., & Hamilton, C. E. (2000). The stability of attachment security from infancy to adolescence and early adulthood: General discussion. *Child Development, 71,* 703–706.

Watson, M. (with Ecken, L.) (2003). *Learning to trust: Transforming difficult elementary classrooms through developmental discipline.* San Francisco: Jossey-Bass.

Watson, M., Solomon, D., Battistich, V., Schaps, E., & Solomon, J. (n.d.). Developmental discipline. Retrieved August 23, 2006, from http://tigger.uic.edu/~Inucci/MoralEd/practices/practice2watson.html.

Watson, M., Solomon, D., Battistich, V., Schaps, E., & Solomon, J. (1989). The Child Development project: Combining traditional and developmental approaches to education. In L. Nucci (Ed.), *Moral development and character education: A dialogue.* Berkeley, CA: McCutchan, 1989. Retrieved January 5, 2007, from http://tigger.uic.edu/~Inucci/MoralEd/practices/practice2watson.html.

Way, N., & Hughes, D. (2007, March 25). The middle ages. *New York Times.*

Webster-Stratton, C., & Herbert, M. (1994). *Troubled families—Problem children: Working with parents: A collaborative process.* Chichester, UK: Wiley.

Weiner, L. (2006). Challenging deficit thinking. *Educational Leadership, 64*(1), 42–45.

Weinfeld, N. S., Sroufe, L. A., & Egeland, B. (2000). Attachment from infancy to early adulthood in a high-risk sample: Continuity, discontinuity, and their correlates. *Child Development, 71,* 695–702.

Weinfeld, N. S., Sroufe, L. A., Egeland, B., & Carlson, E. A. (1999). The nature of individual differences in infant–caregiver attachment. In J. Cassidy & P. R. Shaver (Eds.), *Handbook of attachment theory and research* (pp. 68–88). New York: Guilford.

Weinstein, C., Tomlinson-Clarke, S., & Curran, M. (2004). Toward a conception of culturally responsive classroom management. *Journal of Teacher Education, 55,* 25–38.

Weiss, H. B., Kreider, H., Lopez, M. E., & Chatman, C. C. (Eds.). (2005). *Preparing educators to involve families: From theory to practice.* Thousand Oaks, CA: Sage.

Weissberg, R. P., & Greenberg, M.T. (1998). School and community competence-enhancement and prevention programs. In W. Damon, I. E. Siegel, & K. A. Renninger (Eds.), *Handbook of child psychology: Vol. 4, Child psychology in practice* (5th ed., pp. 877–954). New York: Wiley.

Weist, M. D., & Ollendick, T. H. (1991). Toward empirically valid target selection: The case of assertiveness in children. *Behavior Modification, 15,* 213–227.

Werner, E. E. (1984). Resilient children. *Young Children, 40,* 68–72.

Werner, E. E. (2000). Protective factors and individual resilience. In J. P. Shonkoff & S. J. Meisels (Eds.), *Handbook of early childhood intervention* (2nd ed., pp. 115–132). New York: Cambridge University Press.

Werner, E. E., & Johnson, J. L. (1999). Can we apply resilience? In M. D. Glantz & J. L. Johnson (Eds.), *Resilience and development: Positive life adaptations* (pp. 259–268). New York: Kluwer Academic/Plenum.

Werner, E. E., & Smith, R. S. (1982). *Vulnerable but invincible: A longitudinal study of resilient children and youth.* New York: McGraw-Hill.

Werner, E. E., & Smith, R. S. (1992). *Overcoming the odds: High risk children from birth to adulthood.* New York: Cornell University Press.

What are the forms that cyberbullying might take? (n.d.). Retrieved April 9, 2007, from http://cyberbullying.ca/.

White, K. J., & Kistner, J. (1992). The influence of teacher feedback on young children's peer preferences and perceptions. *Developmental Psychology, 28,* 933–975.

Whitney, I., Smith, P. K., & Thompson, D. (1994). Bullying and children with special educational needs. In P. K. Smith & S. Sharp (Eds.), *School bullying: Insights and perspectives* (pp. 213–240). New York: Routledge.

Wilczenski, F. L., Steegmann, R., Braun, M., Feeley, F., Griffin, J., Horowitz, T., et al. (1994). Promoting "fair play": Interventions for children as victims and victimizers. Presentation at the meeting of the National Association of School Psychologists, Seattle. (ERIC document No. ED380744).

Willard, N. (2006, December). *An educator's guide to cyberbullying and cyberthreats: Responding to the challenge of online social aggression, threats, and distress.* Center for Safe and Responsible Use of the Internet. Retrieved April 9, 2007, from www.cyberbully.org/docs/cbcteducator.pdf.

Williams, L. R. (1994). Developmentally appropriate practice and cultural values: A case in point. In B. L. Mallory & R. S. New (Eds.), *Diversity and developmentally appropriate practice: Challenges for early childhood education* (pp. 155–165). New York: Teachers College Press.

Willicutt, E. G., & Pennington, B. F. (2000). Co-morbidity of reading disability and attention-deficit/hyperactivity disorder: Differences by gender and subtype. *Journal of Learning Disabilities, 33,* 179–191.

Willis, W. (1998). Families with African American roots. In E. W. Lynch & M. J. Hanson (Eds.), *Developing cross-cultural competence: A guide for working with children and their families* (pp. 165–207). Baltimore: Brookes.

Wilson, D. B., Gottfredson, D. C., & Najaka, S. S. (2001). School-based prevention of problem behaviors: A meta-analysis. *Journal of Quantitative Criminology, 17,* 247–272.

Wilton, M. M. M., Craig, W. M., & Pepler, D. J. (2000). Emotional regulation and display in classroom victims of bullying: Characteristic expressions of affect, coping styles and relevant contextual factors. *Social Development, 9,* 226–245.

Winkleman, P., & Harmon-Jones, E. (2006). *Social neuroscience.* New York: Oxford University Press.

Wolfgang, C. H. (2001). *Solving discipline and classroom management problems: Methods and models for today's teachers* (5th ed.). New York: Wiley.

Wolke, D., Woods, S., Bloomfield, L., & Karstadt, L. (2000). The association between direct and relational bullying and behaviour problems among primary school children. *Journal of Child Psychology and Psychiatry, 41,* 989–1002.

Wong, C. A., Eccles, J. S., & Sameroff, A. (2003). The influence of ethnic discrimination and ethnic identification on African American adolescents' school and socioeconomical adjustment. *Journal of Personality, 71,* 1197–1232.

Wong, H. K., & Wong, R. T. (2001). *The first days of school: How to be an effective teacher.* Mountain View, CA: Harry K. Wong Publications.

Wood, G. (2004). A view from the field: No Child Left Behind's effects on classrooms and schools. In D. Meier & G. Wood (Eds.), *Many children left behind: How the No Child Left Behind Act is damaging our children and our schools* (pp. 33–50). Boston: Beacon.

Wood, M. M. (1986). *Developmental therapy in the classroom: Methods for teaching students with emotional or behavioral handicaps.* Austin, TX: Pro-Ed.

Wood, M. M., & Long, N. (1991). *Life Space Intervention: Talking with children and youth in crisis.* Austin, TX: Pro-Ed.

Wormeli, R. (2006). Differentiating for tweens. *Educational Leadership, 63*(7), 14–19.

Wright, J. (2004). *Preventing classroom bullying: What teachers can do.* Intervention Central. Retrieved April 9, 2007, from www.jimwrightonline.com/pdfdocs/bully/bullyBooklet.pdf.

Wright, J. (n.d.). Dodging the power-struggle trap: Ideas for teachers. Retrieved February 27, 2007, from www.jimwrightonline.com/pdfdocs/behtrap.pdf.

Wyman, P. A. (2003). Emerging perspectives on context specificity of children's adaptation and resilience: Evidence from a decade of research with urban children in adversity. In S. S. Luthar (Ed.), *Resilience and vulnerability: Adaptation in the context of childhood adversity* (pp. 293–317). New York: Cambridge University Press.

Xie, H., Cairns, B. D., & Cairns, R. B. (2005). The development of aggressive behaviors among girls: Measurement issues, social functions, and differential trajectories. In D. J. Pepler, K. C. Madsen, C. Webster, & K. S. Levene (Eds.), *The development and treatment of girlhood aggression* (pp. 105–136). Mahwah, NJ: Erlbaum.

Yates, T. M., Egeland, B., & Sroufe, L. A. (2003). Rethinking resilience: A developmental process perspective. In S. S. Luthar (Ed.), *Resilience and vulnerability: Adaptation in the context of childhood adversity* (pp. 243–266). New York: Cambridge University Press.

Yatvin, J. (2004). *A room with a differentiated view: How to serve all children as individual learners.* Portsmouth, NH: Heinemann.

Yehle, A. K., & Wambold, C. (1998, July/August). An ADHD success story: Strategies for teachers and students. *Teaching Exceptional Children, 30*(6), 8–13.

York, S. (1991). *Roots & wings: Affirming culture in early childhood programs*. St. Paul, MN: Redleaf.

Yoshikawa, H. (1994). Prevention as cumulative protection: Effects of early family support and education on chronic delinquency and its risks. *Psychological Bulletin, 115*, 28–54.

Zahn-Waxler, C., & Polanichka, N. (2004). All things interpersonal: Socialization and female aggression. In M. Putallaz & K. L. Bierman (Eds.), *Aggression, antisocial behavior, and violence among girls: A developmental perspective* (pp. 48–68). New York: Guilford.

Zeanah, C. H., & Scheeringa, M. S. (1997). The experience and effects of violence in infancy. In J. D. Osofsky (Ed.), *Children in a violent society* (pp. 97–123). New York: Guilford.

Zelazo, P. D. (2005, June 24). The development of executive function across the lifespan. Retrieved February 13, 2006, from www.aboutkidshealth.ca/ofhc.

Zimmerman, F. J., Glew, G. M., Christakis, D. A., & Katon, W. (2005). Early cognitive stimulation, emotional support, and TV watching as predictors of subsequent bullying among grade-school children. *Archives of Pediatric and Adolescent Medicine, 159*, 384–388.

Zins, J. E., Weissberg, R. P., Wang, W. C., & Walberg, H. J. (Eds.). (2004). *Building academic success on social and emotional learning: What does the research say?* New York: Teachers College Press.

Zionts, L. T. (2005). Examining relations between students and teachers: A potential extension of attachment theory? In K. A. Kerns & R. A. Richardson (Eds.), *Attachment in middle childhood* (pp. 231–254). New York: Guilford.

Zoccolillo, M. (1993). Gender and the development of conduct disorder. *Development and Psychopathology, 5*, 65–78.

Zuniga, M. E. (1998). Families with Latino roots. In E. W. Lynch & M. J. Hanson (Eds.), *Developing cross-cultural competence: A guide for working with children and their families* (pp. 209–250). Baltimore: Brookes.

Index